SWING HACKS™

Other Java™ resources from O'Reilly

Related titles

Java™ Swing
Java™ Threads
JavaServer™ Faces
Java™ in a Nutshell
Java™ Foundation Classes
   in a Nutshell

QuickTime for Java™: A
   Developer's
   Notebook™
Head First Java™
Head First Design
   Patterns

Hacks Series Home

hacks.oreilly.com is a community site for developers and power users of all stripes. Readers learn from each other as they share their favorite tips and tools for Mac OS X, Linux, Google, Windows XP, and more.

**Java Books
Resource Center**

java.oreilly.com is a complete catalog of O'Reilly's books on Java and related technologies, including sample chapters and code examples.

OnJava.com is a one-stop resource for enterprise Java developers, featuring news, code recipes, interviews, weblogs, and more.

Conferences

O'Reilly brings diverse innovators together to nurture the ideas that spark revolutionary industries. We specialize in documenting the latest tools and systems, translating the innovator's knowledge into useful skills for those in the trenches. Visit *conferences.oreilly.com* for our upcoming events.

Safari Bookshelf (*safari.oreilly.com*) is the premier online reference library for programmers and IT professionals. Conduct searches across more than 1,000 books. Subscribers can zero in on answers to time-critical questions in a matter of seconds. Read the books on your Bookshelf from cover to cover or simply flip to the page you need. Try it today.

SWING HACKS™

Joshua Marinacci and Chris Adamson

O'REILLY®

Beijing · Cambridge · Farnham · Köln · Paris · Sebastopol · Taipei · Tokyo

Swing Hacks™

by Joshua Marinacci and Chris Adamson

Copyright © 2005 O'Reilly Media, Inc. All rights reserved.
Printed in the United States of America.

Published by O'Reilly Media, Inc., 1005 Gravenstein Highway North, Sebastopol, CA 95472.

O'Reilly books may be purchased for educational, business, or sales promotional use. Online editions are also available for most titles (*safari.oreilly.com*). For more information, contact our corporate/institutional sales department: (800) 998-9938 or *corporate@oreilly.com*.

Editor:	Brett McLaughlin	**Production Editor:**	Marlowe Shaeffer
Series Editor:	Rael Dornfest	**Cover Designer:**	Ellie Volckhausen
Executive Editor:	Dale Dougherty	**Interior Designer:**	David Futato

Printing History:

June 2005:	First Edition.

RepKover™ This book uses RepKover™, a durable and flexible lay-flat binding.

ISBN: 0-596-00907-0
[M]

Contents

Credits ix

Preface xiii

Chapter 1. Basic JComponents 1

   1. Create Image-Themed Components   1
   2. Don't Settle for Boring Text Labels   8
   3. Fill Your Borders with Pretty Pictures   14
   4. Display Dates in a Custom Calendar   19
   5. Add a Watermark to a Text Component   23
   6. Watermark Your Scroll Panes   26
   7. Put a NASA Photo into the Background of a Text Area   29
   8. Animate Transitions Between Tabs   32
   9. Blur Disabled Components   39
   10. Building a Drop-Down Menu Button   43
   11. Create Menus with Drop Shadows   49
   12. Add Translucence to Menus   52

Chapter 2. Lists and Combos 58

   13. Filter JLists   58
   14. Add a Filter History   63
   15. Make JLists Checkable   66
   16. Make Different List Items Look Different   70
   17. Reorder a JList with Drag-and-Drop   80
   18. Animate Your JList Selections   87

19. Turn Methods into List Renderers   92

20. Create a Collections-Aware JComboBox   95

Chapter 3. Tables and Trees **102**

21. Size Your Columns to Suit Your JTable's Contents   102

22. Add Column Selection to JTables   107

23. Let Your JTables Do the Sorting   110

24. Create a JDBC Table Model   122

25. Export Table Data to an Excel Spreadsheet   130

26. Search Through JTables Easily   133

27. Animate JTree Drops   139

Chapter 4. File Choosers **149**

28. Add a Right-Click Context Menu to the JFileChooser   149

29. Display Shortcuts in the JFileChooser   154

30. Real Windows Shortcut Support   158

31. Add Image Preview to File Choosers   164

32. Preview ZIP and JAR Files   167

Chapter 5. Windows, Dialogs, and Frames **175**

33. Window Snapping   175

34. Make a Draggable Window   178

35. Add Windows Resize Icons   181

36. Add Status Bars to Windows   187

37. Save Window Settings   193

38. Earthquake Dialog   197

39. Spin Open a Detail Pane   202

40. Minimize to a Mini-Frame   207

Chapter 6. Transparent and Animated Windows **213**

41. Transparent Windows   213

42. Make Your Frame Dissolve   219

43. Create Custom Tool Tips   225

44. Turn Dialogs into Frame-Anchored Sheets   228

45. Animating a Sheet Dialog   233

46. Slide Notes Out from the Taskbar   240

47. Indefinite Progress Indicator   247

Chapter 7. Text **257**

48. Make Text Components Searchable   257

49. Force Text Input into Specific Formats   261

50. Auto-Completing Text Fields   265

51. Write Backward Text   272

52. Use HTML and CSS in Text Components   275

53. Use Global Anti-Aliased Fonts   278

54. Anti-Aliased Text Without Code   283

55. Anti-Aliased Text with a Custom Look and Feel   285

Chapter 8. Rendering **287**

56. Create a Magnifying Glass Component   287

57. Create a Global Right-Click   293

58. Block a Window Without a Modal Dialog   296

59. Create a Color Eyedropper   300

60. Changing Fonts Throughout Your Application   304

61. Load New Fonts at Runtime   307

62. Build a Colorful Vector-Based Button   309

63. Add a Third Dimension to Swing   316

64. Turn the Spotlight on Swing   321

Chapter 9. Drag-and-Drop **330**

65. Drag-and-Drop with Files   330

66. Handle Dropped URLs   336

67. Handle Dropped Images   340

68. Handling Dropped Picts on Mac OS X   345

69. Translucent Drag-and-Drop   350

Chapter 10. Audio **358**

70. Play a Sound in an Applet   359

71. Play a Sound with JavaSound   364

72. Play a Sound with Java Media Framework   368

73. Play a Sound with QuickTime for Java   371

74. Add MP3 Support to JMF   376

75. Build an Audio Waveform Display   378

76. Play Non-Trivial Audio   386

77. Show Audio Information While Playing Sound   392
78. Provide Audio Controls During Playback   401

Chapter 11. Native Integration and Packaging **408**

79. Launch External Programs on Windows   408
80. Open Files, Directories, and URLs on Mac OS X   411
81. Make Mac Applications Behave Normally   413
82. Control iTunes on Mac OS X   418
83. Control iTunes Under Windows   421
84. Construct Single-Launch Applications   424
85. Stuff Stuff in JARs   428
86. Make Quick Look and Feel Changes   434
87. Create an Inverse Black-and-White Theme   439

Chapter 12. Miscellany **443**

88. Display a Busy Cursor   443
89. Fun with Keyboard Lights   446
90. Create Demonstrations with the Robot Class   450
91. Check Your Mail with Swing   454
92. Don't Block the GUI   459
93. Code Models That Don't Block   465
94. Fire Events and Stay Bug Free   472
95. Debug Your GUI   478
96. Debug Components with a Custom Glass Pane   481
97. Mirror an Application   486
98. Add Velocity for Dynamic HTML   492
99. Get Large File Icons   499
100. Make Frames Resize Dynamically   500

Index **503**

Credits

About the Authors

Joshua Marinacci started playing with Java in the summer of '95 at the request of his favorite TA and has never looked back. Since then he has built all manner of Java software for clients ranging from large Fortune 500 companies to small Internet startups. He quickly discovered his passion for user interfaces and client software, building a reputation in the desktop Java world and finally joining the Swing Team at Sun in the spring of 2005. In his spare time, Joshua writes articles and weblogs for Java.net while contributing to the JDIC, JDNC, and WinLAF open source projects. He also heads up Flying Saucer, an open source, all-Java XHTML renderer. This is his first book, but hopefully not his last. He lives in historic East Atlanta with his girlfriend Kim and their yellow labrador Eliza.

Chris Adamson is the Editor of O'Reilly's ONJava site and the Associate Online Editor for Java.net, a collaboration of O'Reilly, Sun Microsystems, and CollabNet. He also writes about Java and Mac topics online and speaks at conferences such as ADHOC/MacHack and the O'Reilly Mac OS X Conference. He develops media applications under the guise of his consulting company, Subsequently & Furthermore, Inc. He has an M.A. in Telecommunications from Michigan State University and a B.A. in English and B.S. in Symbolic Systems from Stanford University. He lives in Atlanta with his wife, Kelly, and their children, Keagan and Quinn, and he has thus far managed to own seven and a half Macs.

Contributors

Swing is big enough that surely everyone who works with it takes away some new ideas for how to hack it. Our contributors helped flesh this book out with hacks that blew us away and that we're sure you'll like, too.

- Romain Guy is a French student currently working as an intern with the Swing Team at Sun Microsystems in California. He discovered Java in 1998 and contributed to the Open Source/Free Software community with Jext, a Java source code editor he developed over five years. He is also a freelance journalist for *Login:*, a French computing magazine. Never short for ideas, he also wrote for *Javalobby*, the Java developer's journal, and a couple of French magazines. Romain seeks for other experiences whenever he can: he works as a translator for O'Reilly France, he taught Java in a French university, he fulfilled several missions as a freelance Java developer, and he even worked as a video game programmer. Today, Romain focuses on UI design and humane interaction. He shares his work on his weblog: *www.jroller.com/page/gfx*.

- Jonathan Simon is a comprehensive client-side expert, designing and developing mission-critical financial trading clients for Wall Street investment banks. This requires a fluid combination of business and task analysis and interaction design with the intricacies of Java rich-client development to create content rich, ergonomic trading applications. He has written extensively about his experiences for Java.net, IBM DeveloperWorks, JavaWorld, and Addison Wesley. An avid percussionist, composer, and electronic musician, Jonathan also develops music software in Java. He is especially interested in interaction design and data visualization.

Acknowledgments

Joshua

This book has gone faster that I ever imagined, from original concept to final draft in less than a year. Writing *Swing Hacks* was harder than I ever thought, giving me great respect for those who write complete novels. I have had the utmost fun, however, and wouldn't trade the experience for the world.

I would first like to thank Kimi, my loving partner who convinced me to pursue writing as a serious endeavor. She has always believed that I could be more than just a contract coder. I couldn't have done it without you, Sweetie.

Many thanks to my family and friends who always said that I was never living up to my potential. Thank you for raising, loving, and teaching me. I promise to live up to my potential now, starting next week.

Thanks to the great team at O'Reilly, especially Brett, who tirelessly read through my drafts, dotted the *t*s, crossed the *i*s, and made my prose readable.

Thanks go out to the readers of Java.net and Daniel Steinberg, my Java.net editor, who have always provided encouragement, feedback, and constructive criticism. Without the Java community's ecology of code and fresh ideas, this book wouldn't have been possible.

Special thanks to Jonathan and Romain who gave us the boost we needed to get the book finished. They've put in some great stuff. *I've* even learned a few things.

Extra special thanks to Chris who believed from the start that this was a great idea for a book. He guided me through the proposal process, shaped our draft, and always kept the book on track. Maybe we can finally get that Okama GameSphere.

And, finally, my unending thanks to all of the Swing Team developers who put in 10 years of blood and sweat, making Swing the powerful toolkit it is today. I hope we can keep pushing it forward.

Chris

Credit for this book needs to begin with Joshua—I'm still tempted to type "Joshy" because that's his username everywhere—who started this book as an informal series on his popular Java.net weblog and had the wherewithal to push through a book proposal.

Also, all the really cool hacks are his. But I think that's what everyone involved with this book has been saying when they read what the others have contributed.

And speaking of them, thanks also to our contributors, Romain and Jonathan, who came in at just the right time to get this book over the hump and make it real. Their inventiveness and responsiveness helped us pull through.

Thanks to Brett McLaughlin, who was on the receiving end of a pretty wild brain-dump, with two authors and two contributors going on wildly different tangents. He helped shape this book into something readable and fun.

Lots of other people in O'Reilly production will handle this book after I finish writing this acknowledgment, and I thank them in advance for everything they do.

And, of course, thanks to Kelly and Keagan for holding down the fort at home while daddy was in the office working on this book. Quinn also contributed, sleeping on my lap while I banged out parts of Chapters 10 and 11.

Obligatory O'Reilly tune check: this time it was Delgados, The Tubes, Green Day, L'Arc~en~Ciel, David Bowie, Frank Zappa, Puffy AmiYumi, Little Feat, the *Gundam Wing Endless Waltz* soundtrack and the *Armitage's Dimension* stream.

Preface

Hi, welcome to *Swing Hacks*! This book is a reference, but not a complete reference of the Swing API. We already have that. It's called *Java Swing*, is published by O'Reilly, and weighs in at over 1,200 pages. It's available for purchase at fine bookstores and Russian black market web sites everywhere. We're not saying that it isn't a great book. It's fantastic! We've owned many weathered copies over the years. The problem is...it's huge! This isn't really the book's fault: Swing *itself* is huge. I once saw an API diagram that took an entire 30-inch poster. Swing is powerful, but it takes a long time to explore fully, simply because it *is* so big. That's not what this book is about.

This book is a reference to the cool stuff. It's about the interesting things you learn over the years. The weird hacks that make you say, "I didn't know you could even *do* that!" After years of working with Swing, you start to learn what the API is good at and what it lacks. Some days you learn something that makes your life as a developer easier, a way to do something quicker than the standard route. That's what we put into this book. Some days you learn a workaround for a long-standing bug or a missing feature that you've been dying to have. We put that stuff in the book, too. Sometimes it's something fun—an interesting API that makes us think, "Well, if we were *evil* what could we do with it?" This is usually followed by the pinkie up to the mouth and cackling that can be heard outside our underground lair. After much consultation with lawyers and gods, we slipped some of these into the book, too.

Why Swing Hacks?

The term *hacking* has a bad reputation in the press. They use it to refer to people who break into systems or wreak havoc with computers as their weapon. Among people who write code, though, the term *hack* refers to a quick-and-dirty solution to a problem, or a clever way to get something done. And the term *hacker* is taken very much as a compliment, referring to someone as being *creative*, having the technical chops to get things done. The Hacks series is an attempt to reclaim the word, document the good ways people are hacking, and pass the hacker ethic of creative participation on to the uninitiated. Seeing how others approach systems and problems is often the quickest way to learn about a new technology.

In the short term, we hope this book will show you how to do fun things that will enhance your own applications directly. Some are visual enhancements to make your software look better. Some are functional improvements to make your software do something it couldn't do before. Some are even just plain silly, in print only to prove it could be done. Whatever your interest, we hope you will find both better ways of doing old things and learn something new about techniques you never even thought of.

In the long term, we hope this book will give you a small glimpse of the applications coming in the future. This year (2005) we hope will be a watershed year for Java on the desktop. Users are demanding more advanced user interfaces than the Web can provide, and Java is poised to provide them. New technology is streaming into the Java community at a blistering rate, and it gives application developers a whole new set of blocks to play with. This is important because we are going to need these new technologies.

New desktop software promises greater integration between the Web, external devices, and software sitting right on your desktop. RSS readers and iPods. iTunes and photo collaboration. Gaming on desktops, servers, and cell phones; *all at the same time*. This is the future of desktop software. Swing is just a small part of desktop Java, but we feel it is the focal point—the place where desktop technology (AWT, Java2D, JavaSound), network technology (web services, XML, JXTA), and device technology (iPods, cell phones, TVs) all converge upon Java. Many of the hacks in this book are not strictly about Swing, but about using Swing to do cool things with the rest of the world. And it's more than just "cool"—animation is a powerful way to show a change in content or context, and sound can get the user's attention when he or she is away from the keyboard. These features are important parts of delivering user-centric, quality desktop applications.

How to Use This Book

You can read this book from cover to cover if you like, but each hack stands on its own, so feel free to browse and jump to the different sections that interest you most. If there's a prerequisite you need to know about, a cross-reference will guide you to the right hack. The code all works (we tried it) but in case you can't get a hack to work, let us know at the book's web site: *http://www.oreilly.com/catalog/swinghks*. You can also download the book's code online, or contribute your own tips and tricks. If we collect enough new material, and this book sells more than 10 copies, then the publishers might let us make *Swing Hacks 2: The Endless Repaint*.

With few exceptions, the hacks in this book were written for Java 2 Standard Edition (J2SE), version 1.4, which you can get from *http://java.sun.com/j2se/*. A few hacks depend on open source packages, which are freely downloadable from their home pages, as described in the hack itself. The only exceptions are two hacks that use QuickTime for Java—this is freely available from Apple (and installed by default on Mac OS X), but it is proprietary and available for Mac and Windows only.

Because this is a book about Swing, the program listings will be using the classes from the Swing and AWT packages, so we've skipped `import javax.swing.*` and `import java.awt.*` statements for space. You can also assume that any listing involving event handling will `import java.awt.event.*` and probably `import javax.swing.event.*` as well. Java2D hacks implicitly `import java.awt.image.*`. In short, we'll include import statements only when a hack involves non-core, and/or non-obvious imports, like the hacks that use JDBC, Lucene, Velocity, QuickTime for Java, etc.

How This Book Is Organized

The book is divided into several chapters, organized by subject:

Chapter 1, *Basic JComponents*
> Here you'll find simple hacks for the basic components like labels, buttons, and text fields. This chapter contains a lot of bang for the buck, and it illustrates some of the techniques that we will explore more fully later on. From fancy JLabels to translucent menus, this is a great place to start.

Chapter 2, *Lists and Combos*
> This chapter features complicated Swing components that are used everywhere. Bend them to your will! Make them look good with polymorphic renderers and animated selections. Make them perform well with filtering and Collections support.

Chapter 3, *Tables and Trees*

This chapter revelas the secrets of these mystic components—from Excel exporting to proper JTree drop targets. Make the JTree and JTable dance.

Chapter 4, *File Choosers*

One of Swing's most maligned components, the JFileChooser, actually has a lot of power hiding inside some murky APIs. This chapter will let you use custom icons, detect Windows shortcuts, and even navigate ZIP files.

Chapter 5, *Windows, Dialogs, and Frames*

This is where the fun begins. Every application needs a container, so why not make it pretty and powerful? Make your windows drag and snap. Build custom windows like the earthquake login and spin open dialog. You can even save your window settings automatically with almost no code changes.

Chapter 6, *Transparent and Animated Windows*

If you went through the previous chapter and still want more, then this chapter is for you. We push windows to the limit with transparency, animations, slide-in OS X stylesheets, and some of the coolest special effects you've ever seen.

Chapter 7, *Text*

Text components seem boring, but there's a lot of power hiding in there. This chapter will show you how to do regular expression searching, dot completion, backward text, and even three different ways to give your application the bright sheen of anti-aliasing.

Chapter 8, *Rendering*

This chapter has the meat of the graphics hacks. Custom fonts, a magnifying glass, vector buttons, and even some work with Java3D. We've got some great things to make your application pop.

Chapter 9, *Drag-and-Drop*

When your users want two pieces of software to work together the first thing they want to do is drag-and-drop data from their other programs to yours. This chapter covers how to do robust and attractive drag-and-drop entirely within Java.

Chapter 10, *Audio*

What would be a cool modern application without some media support? This chapter covers four different ways to play sound, how to display waveforms, and how to embed MP3 support in your own programs.

Chapter 11, *Native Integration and Packaging*

The best software works well with the native operating system. Here you'll learn how to launch web browsers, hack the Windows registry, customize your program for specific platforms, and even control iTunes.

Chapter 12, *Miscellany*

This chapter offers a grab bag of things that didn't fit anywhere else, but were too cool not to include. Animated cursors, better threading, flashing the keyboard lights, and a bunch of quick one-liners to let you make the most of your busy day.

Conventions Used in This Book

The following is a list of the typographical conventions used in this book:

Italics

Used to indicate URLs, filenames, filename extensions, and directory/folder names. A path in the filesystem will appear as */Developer/Applications*, for example.

`Constant width`

Used to show code examples, the contents of files, and console output, as well as the names of variables, commands, and other code excerpts.

`Constant width bold`

Used to highlight portions of code, typically new additions to old code.

`Constant width italic`

Used in code examples and tables to show sample text to be replaced with your own values.

Color

The second color is used to indicate a cross-reference within the text.

You should pay special attention to notes set apart from the text with the following icons:

This is a tip, suggestion, or general note. It contains useful supplementary information about the topic at hand.

This is a warning or note of caution, often indicating that your money or your privacy might be at risk.

The thermometer icons, found next to each hack, indicate the relative complexity of the hack:

 beginner    moderate    expert

Using Code Examples

This book is here to help you get your job done. In general, you may use the code in this book in your programs and documentation. You do not need to contact us for permission unless you're reproducing a significant portion of the code. For example, writing a program that uses several chunks of code from this book does not require permission. Selling or distributing a CD-ROM of examples from O'Reilly books *does* require permission. Answering a question by citing this book and quoting example code does not require permission. Incorporating a significant amount of example code from this book into your product's documentation *does* require permission.

We appreciate, but do not require, attribution. An attribution usually includes the title, author, publisher, and ISBN. For example: "*Swing Hacks* by Joshua Marinacci and Chris Adamson. Copyright 2005 O'Reilly Media, Inc., 0-596-00907-0."

If you feel your use of code examples falls outside fair use or the permission given above, feel free to contact us at *permissions@oreilly.com*.

How to Contact Us

We have tested and verified the information in this book to the best of our ability, but you may find that features have changed (or even that we have made mistakes!). As a reader of this book, you can help us to improve future editions by sending us your feedback. Please let us know about any errors, inaccuracies, bugs, misleading or confusing statements, and typos that you find anywhere in this book.

Please also let us know what we can do to make this book more useful to you. We take your comments seriously and will try to incorporate reasonable suggestions into future editions. You can write to us at:

O'Reilly Media, Inc.
1005 Gravenstein Highway North
Sebastopol, CA 95472
(800) 998-9938 (in the U.S. or Canada)
(707) 829-0515 (international/local)
(707) 829-0104 (fax)

To ask technical questions or to comment on the book, send email to:

bookquestions@oreilly.com

The web site for *Swing Hacks* lists examples, errata, and plans for future editions. You can find this page at:

http://www.oreilly.com/catalog/swinghks

For more information about this book and others, see the O'Reilly web site:

http://www.oreilly.com

Got a Hack?

To explore Hacks books online or to contribute a hack for future titles, visit:

http://hacks.oreilly.com

Safari Enabled

 When you see a Safari® Enabled icon on the cover of your favorite technology book, that means the book is available online through the O'Reilly Network Safari Bookshelf.

Safari offers a solution that's better than e-books. It's a virtual library that lets you easily search thousands of top tech books, cut and paste code samples, download chapters, and find quick answers when you need the most accurate, current information. Try it for free at *http://safari.oreilly.com*.

CHAPTER ONE

Basic JComponents

Hacks 1–12

Swing is a powerful toolkit, filled to the brim with complicated components, extension APIs, and large Model-View-Controller (MVC) systems. It can be quite daunting. The current edition of O'Reilly's *Java Swing* book now stretches over 1,200 pages! Swing now extends from the simplest JButton to the full Look and Feel API. I am still amazed at the power and flexibility of Swing, and quite aware of its complexity. Some of the more esoteric parts can take years to master. However, you don't need to go straight into the JTree or Look and Feel APIs just to do something cool. There are still a lot of fun things waiting in the standard components we don't always think about.

This chapter covers some of the basic components that every Swing developer uses: buttons, labels, menus, and the occasional scroll pane. From this base you will learn how to create image buttons, put watermarks into your text areas, and even build a new component or two. These are the components that seem boring, but with a little imagination, they can do a whole lot, and the techniques here lay the foundation for even more exciting hacks later in the book.

HACK #1

Create Image-Themed Components

This hack shows how to use Swing's built-in image support to create a completely custom image-based user interface.

Most Swing applications get their look from a Look and Feel (L&F)—either a standard one provided by the VM or a custom one. L&Fs are a whole lot of work to build and still aren't completely custom. You can redefine a button to look like red stoplights, but then all buttons throughout your application will look like red stoplights. Sometimes all you really want is a look built entirely out of images, much like image-based web navigation.

To give you an idea of where this hack is going, Figure 1-1 shows our target: a frame with a panel containing a label, a button, and a checkbox. The panel, label, and button will be completely drawn with images, using none of the standard L&F. The checkbox will be a standard checkbox, but it should be transparent to fit in with the image background.

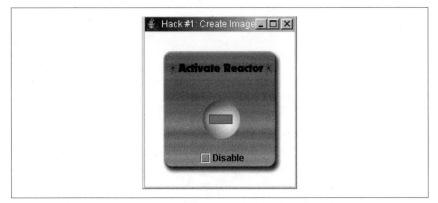

Figure 1-1. A component rendered with images

The first step toward image nirvana is the background. Because this type of component is quite reusable, I built a subclass of JPanel called ImagePanel, shown in Example 1-1.

Example 1-1. A Custom subclass of JPanel

```
public class ImagePanel extends JPanel {

    private Image img;

    public ImagePanel(Image img) {
        this.img = img;
        Dimension size = new Dimension(img.getWidth(null),
                                       img.getHeight(null));
        setSize(size);
        setPreferredSize(size);
        setMinimumSize(size);
        setMaximumSize(size);
        setLayout(null);
    }

}
```

The constructor takes the image to draw and saves it for later use in the img variable. Then it calls setSize( ) and setPreferredSize( ) with the size of the image. This ensures that the panel will be the size of the image exactly. I had to set the preferred, maximum, and minimum sizes as well—this is because the panel's parent and children may not be using absolute layouts.

> *Absolute layout* means that there is no layout manager to position the components appropriately (which can be set by calling setLayout(null)).

In this case, the explicit size and position will be used (via setSize( ) and setLocation( )). When a layout manager *is* set, the preferred, minimum, and maximum sizes may be used. To cover all of the bases, simply set all four values to the image size.

Now that the panel is sized appropriately, you can paint the image by overriding paintComponent( ):

```java
public void paintComponent(Graphics g) {
    g.drawImage(img,0,0,null);
}
```

> It's important to override paintComponent( ) instead of paint( ), or else the child components won't get drawn.

To test it, Example 1-2 uses an ImagePanel and the usual JFrame.

Example 1-2. Testing out image-based panels

```java
public class ImageTest {

    public static void main(String[] args) {
        ImagePanel panel = new ImagePanel(new
            ImageIcon("images/background.png").getImage( ));

        JFrame frame = new JFrame("Hack #1: Create Image-Themed Components");
        frame.getContentPane( ).add(panel);
        frame.pack( );
        frame.setVisible(true);
    }
}
```

When run, the ImageTest program looks like Figure 1-2.

Now that the background is done, it's time to focus on the label, Activate Reactor. This is just a static image that sits at a certain position on the background. You could use another ImagePanel, but since the Activate Reactor text is logically a JLabel, you can just create an ImageLabel subclass, as shown in Example 1-3.

Figure 1-2. Background only

Example 1-3. An image-based label

```
public class ImageLabel extends JLabel {

    public ImageLabel(ImageIcon icon) {
        setSize(icon.getImage( ).getWidth(null),
                icon.getImage( ).getHeight(null));
        setIcon(icon);
        setIconTextGap(0);
        setBorder(null);
        setText(null);
        setOpaque(false);
    }

}
```

As with the `ImagePanel`, set the size of the label to match the size of the image. The rest of the sizing isn't needed because the `JLabel` will take care of that itself. Next, set the icon to your image, which lets the `JLabel` take care of the image drawing. Setting the icon text gap to zero and the border and text to `null` will remove any extra space around my image, resulting in a perfect mesh with the background. The final `setOpaque(false)` tells the label not to draw its own background. If your image fills the label then this won't matter, but if the image has transparent areas (as PNG files often do), then this will let the background shine through the transparent parts.

Add this code to `ImageTest`'s `main( )` method:

```
ImageLabel label = new ImageLabel(new ImageIcon("images/reactor.png"));
label.setLocation(29,37);
panel.add(label);
```

The result is shown in Figure 1-3.

Figure 1-3. A custom JLabel

Next comes the button. Because buttons have rollovers and states, they are a bit trickier. Again, start with a JButton subclass, as in Example 1-4.

Example 1-4. Creating an image-based button

```
public class ImageButton extends JButton {

    public ImageButton(ImageIcon icon) {
        setSize(icon.getImage( ).getWidth(null),
                icon.getImage( ).getHeight(null));
        setIcon(icon);
        setMargin(new Insets(0,0,0,0));
        setIconTextGap(0);
        setBorderPainted(false);
        setBorder(null);
        setText(null);
    }

}
```

The code is almost the same as JLabel. The only difference is the addition of the setMargin( ) and setBorder( ) calls. Most Look and Feels use a border and margin to indicate when the button has been selected. Labels aren't selectable so they don't have those methods. In any case, these are two more properties you can simply turn off.

Add this code to ImageTest's main( ) method:

```
final ImageButton button = new ImageButton("images/button.png");
button.setLocation(60,74);
panel.add(button);
```

The result is shown in Figure 1-4.

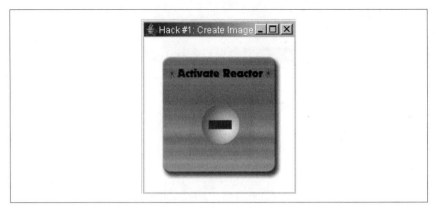

Figure 1-4. Image button

Now that the button is visible, you only have to add the rollovers and other states. Fortunately, this doesn't require any new coding in the subclass—JButton already provides support for images representing the rollover, pressed, selected, disabled, and disabled selected states. You can add various states by using normal set methods:

```
button.setPressedIcon(new ImageIcon("images/button-down.png"));
button.setRolloverIcon(new ImageIcon("images/button-over.png"));
button.setSelectedIcon(new ImageIcon("images/button-sel.png"));
button.setRolloverSelectedIcon(new ImageIcon("images/button-sel-over.png"));
button.setDisabledIcon(new ImageIcon("images/button-disabled.png"));
button.setDisabledSelectedIcon(
    new ImageIcon("images/button-disabled-selected.png"));
```

Figures 1-5 and 1-6 are the images I used to represent each state. The rollover effect is done with an outer glow, and I used a blur for the disabled state. The red rectangle in the middle represents the selected state, and it includes its own color change and red glow mimicking a real glowing lightbulb.

Figure 1-5. Unselected button with rollover

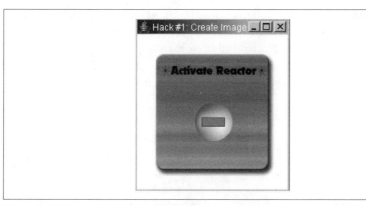

Figure 1-6. Selected button

On Image Creation

I created these images by drawing everything in a separate layer in Photoshop. Keeping it all separate means I could save any section of the image as it's own file, with or without effects and backgrounds. Photoshop has a great feature called *slices* that lets you divide the image up into malleable sections. Photoshop's companion program, ImageReady, takes slices a step further by managing slice states for you. This lets you create rollovers, in and out images, and disabled states. When you Save Optimized, ImageReady automatically saves each slice state to a different file with the appropriate name (e.g., *button-disabled-selected.png*). Slices were originally created for web design, but they can be put to great use in Swing applications as well.

To fully demonstrate all of the states, I have added a standard JCheckBox. Normally, it would draw a gray background (or striped on the Mac) but a simple setOpaque(false) fixes that. The call to checkbox.setSize(checkbox. getPreferredSize( )) is needed to make the checkbox size itself properly when there is no layout manager in the parent, which is the case for this panel:

```
final JCheckBox checkbox = new JCheckBox("Disable");
checkbox.setLocation(70,150);
checkbox.setOpaque(false);
checkbox.setSize(checkbox.getPreferredSize( ));
panel.add(checkbox);
checkbox.addActionListener(new ActionListener( ) {
    public void actionPerformed(ActionEvent evt) {
        button.setEnabled(!checkbox.isSelected( ));
    }
});
```

With the addition of this code to ImageTest's main( ) method, the image-based showcase program is complete. Figure 1-7 shows what the running program looks like in the selected but disabled state.

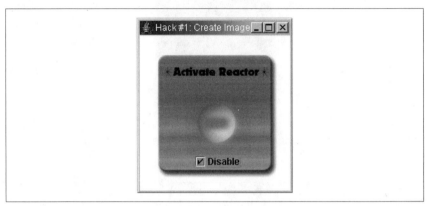

Figure 1-7. Selected and disabled

H A C K   Don't Settle for Boring Text Labels
#2

JLabel is a Swing staple; but it's easy to spruce up boring labels with drop shadows, outlines, and even 3D text.

When you want to draw non-editable text, Swing provides only the JLabel. You can change the font, size, color, and even add an icon. By using HTML in your components **[Hack #52]**, you can even add things like underline and bullets. This is fine for most jobs, but sometimes you need more. What if you want a drop shadow or an embossed effect? The JLabel is simply inadequate for richer interfaces. Fortunately, the Swing Team made it very easy to extend the JLabel and add these features yourself.

A great many text effects can be achieved with two simple features. First, you can draw text multiple times, with each iteration slightly offset or in a different color, to create effects like drop shadows and embossing. Second, you can adjust the spacing between letters in a word (a feature known as *tracking* in text-processing circles). Tracking is always specified *in addition* to the default tracking specified by a font. Thus, a tracking of +1 would be drawn as one extra pixel between each letter. A tracking of 0 would have the same spacing as no extra tracking at all.

To implement all of this, you must override both the sizing and the painting code in JLabel, which of course calls for a subclass; see Example 1-5 for details.

Example 1-5. Defining a richer JLabel

```
public class RichJLabel extends JLabel {

    private int tracking;
    public RichJLabel(String text, int tracking) {
        super(text);
        this.tracking = tracking;
    }

    private int left_x, left_y, right_x, right_y;
    private Color left_color, right_color;
    public void setLeftShadow(int x, int y, Color color) {
        left_x = x;
        left_y = y;
        left_color = color;
    }

    public void setRightShadow(int x, int y, Color color) {
        right_x = x;
        right_y = y;
        right_color = color;
    }
```

RichJLabel extends the standard javax.swing.JLabel and adds a tracking argument to the constructor. Next, it adds two methods for the right and left shadow. These are called shadows because they will be drawn below the main text, but whether they actually look like shadows depends on the color, as well as the x- and y-offsets passed into each method.

With the boilerplate out of the way, you need to handle sizing issues. The JLabel automatically tells layout managers its preferred size based on the font size. When you add custom tracking, this sizing would be incorrect, resulting in labels too small for the text they contain. For small font sizes it won't be noticeable, but with large fancy text and cool effects—and we all want cool effects—it could chop off half of a letter or more.

Every Swing component returns its desired size using the getPreferredSize( ) method. By adjusting the returned size to be a bit bigger, layout controls using this component will give the label the extra room it needs:

```
public Dimension getPreferredSize( ) {
    String text = getText( );
    FontMetrics fm = this.getFontMetrics(getFont( ));

    int w = fm.stringWidth(text);
    w += (text.length( )-1)*tracking;
    w += left_x + right_x;
```

```
      int h = fm.getHeight();
      h += left_y + right_y;

      return new Dimension(w,h);
  }
```

This implementation of getPreferredSize( ) calculates the size based on the font metrics of the currently set text. The FontMetrics object contains methods to get the width and height of the font for the current text. Because the tracking variable adds to the existing tracking of the font, you can expand the width by adding a tracking width between each letter—one per letter, except the last letter. The line w += (text.length( )-1)*tracking does just that. The shadows will be drawn the same size as the base text, but they will be offset by the left_x and right_x values, so you need to add those in as well. Tracking only affects the horizontal space between letters, so height can be calculated normally via the fontmetrics.getHeight( ) method.

Don't forget to account for those shadow offsets!

With the sizing handled, the only thing left is actually drawing the text on screen. As with all Swing components, override the paintComponent( ) method (and not paint( )) so that the child components will be handled properly.

Here's the first bit of the paintComponent( ) method:

```
public void paintComponent(Graphics g) {
    ((Graphics2D)g).setRenderingHint(
        RenderingHints.KEY_TEXT_ANTIALIASING,
        RenderingHints.VALUE_TEXT_ANTIALIAS_ON);

    char[] chars = getText().toCharArray();

    FontMetrics fm = this.getFontMetrics(getFont());

    int h = fm.getAscent();
    int x = 0;
```

First, paintComponent( ) turns on the graphics object's anti-aliasing hint. Because the RichJLabel class will typically be used for large font sizes that need to be attractive, it's probably a safe bet that the developer wants smooth text.

Next, the method grabs the font and line metrics for the current text in the current font. The graphics object always draws text from the bottom of the letter, rather than from the top, as you would expect with a rectangle or line.

To account for this, you need to know how far down a letter goes (its *ascent*), which is retrieved from fm.getAscent( ).

 A font's ascent is *not* the same as the height of the font. The height includes the part of letters that extend below the baseline. Most letters stop at the baseline but some, like lowercase *y*s and *g*s extend further down. The ascent only includes the part of the letters above the baseline, which is what you want.

After setting up the variables, you can start drawing each letter (this code is still in the paintComponent( ) method):

```
for(int i=0; i<chars.length; i++) {
    char ch = chars[i];
    int w = fm.charWidth(ch) + tracking;

    g.setColor(left_color);
    g.drawString(""+chars[i],x-left_x,h-left_y);

    g.setColor(right_color);
    g.drawString(""+chars[i],x+right_x,h+right_y);

    g.setColor(getForeground());
    g.drawString(""+chars[i],x,h);

    x+=w;
}

((Graphics2D)g).setRenderingHint(
    RenderingHints.KEY_TEXT_ANTIALIASING,
    RenderingHints.VALUE_TEXT_ANTIALIAS_DEFAULT);

} // end paintComponent()
```

This is a simple loop that calculates the width of each character, plus the tracking, then draws it three times: first with the left offsets, next with the right offsets, and finally in the normal position. At the end of the loop, you just increase x to move on to the next letter. The rendering hint line at the bottom returns the graphics object to its original anti-aliasing state.

With the class completed, it's time to try some effects. This code will draw large (140 pt) text in gray with a black drop shadow and a slight, white highlight:

```
public static void main(String[] args) {
    RichJLabel label = new RichJLabel("76", -40);
    // drop shadow w/ highlight
    label.setLeftShadow(1,1,Color.white);
    label.setRightShadow(2,3,Color.black);
```

```
label.setForeground(Color.gray);
label.setFont(label.getFont( ).deriveFont(140f));

JFrame frame = new JFrame("RichJLabel hack");
frame.getContentPane( ).add(label);
frame.pack( );
frame.setVisible(true);
}
```

Figure 1-8 shows what the code looks like running.

Figure 1-8. Drop shadow text

If you change the shadows to be only one pixel offset from their normal position and to share the same color, then you can create a subtle outline effect. Setting the tracking to -30 pulls the letters close enough to overlap for a nice logo effect (as seen in Figure 1-9):

```
RichJLabel label = new RichJLabel("76", -30);

// subtle outline
label.setLeftShadow(1,1,Color.white);
label.setRightShadow(1,1,Color.white);
label.setForeground(Color.blue);
label.setFont(label.getFont( ).deriveFont(140f));
```

Figure 1-9. Outlined text

The shadow offsets let you effectively rearrange the letters to create a faded 3D effect (shown in Figure 1-10):

```
// 3d letters
label.setLeftShadow(5,5,Color.white);
label.setRightShadow(-3,-3, new Color(0xccccff));
label.setForeground(new Color(0x8888ff));
label.setFont(label.getFont().deriveFont(140f));
```

Figure 1-10. 3D faded letters

You could expand on this hack by combining it with images and nice gradients like the Christmas Countdown counter in Figure 1-11. Simple graphical effects like the ones shown in the RichJLabel are easy to create with Swing thanks to the power of Java2D, and they can really make your interfaces pop.

Figure 1-11. Mild emboss effect

Fill Your Borders with Pretty Pictures

Swing comes with a set of customizable borders, but sometimes you want more than they provide. This hack shows how to create a completely image-based border that can be resized.

Swing has a prefabricated border, called the MatteBorder, which can accept an image in its constructor. For simple tiled backgrounds, such as a checker-board pattern, this works fine. However, if you want to have particular images in each corner, creating a fully resizable image border, then you'll need something more powerful. Fortunately, Swing makes it very easy to create custom border classes. The image border in this hack will produce a border that looks like Figure 1-12.

Figure 1-12. An image-based border

The first step to any custom border is to subclass AbstractBorder and imple-ment the paintBorder( ) method. The class will take eight images in the con-structor, one for each corner and each side; all the code is shown in Example 1-6.

Example 1-6. Building an image-based border

```
public class ImageBorder extends AbstractBorder {

    Image top_center, top_left, top_right;
    Image left_center, right_center;
    Image bottom_center, bottom_left, bottom_right;
    Insets insets;

    public ImageBorder(Image top_left, Image top_center, Image top_right,
        Image left_center, Image right_center,
        Image bottom_left, Image bottom_center, Image bottom_right) {

        this.top_left = top_left;
        this.top_center = top_center;
        this.top_right = top_right;
        this.left_center = left_center;
        this.right_center = right_center;
        this.bottom_left = bottom_left;
        this.bottom_center = bottom_center;
        this.bottom_right = bottom_right;
    }
```

Example 1-6. Building an image-based border (continued)

```
public void setInsets(Insets insets) {
    this.insets = insets;
}

public Insets getBorderInsets(Component c) {
    if(insets != null) {
        return insets;
    } else {
        return new Insets(top_center.getHeight(null),
            left_center.getWidth(null),
            bottom_center.getHeight(null), right_center.getWidth(null));
    }
}
```

The two methods after the constructor control the border insets. These are the gaps between the panel's outer edge (and its parent) and the inner edge of the panel where the panel's children are drawn. setInsets( ) lets you set any size insets, but most of the time you want the insets to be based on the actual images that make up the border. The implementation of getBorderInsets( ) returns the insets variable if it's not null. However, if the developer didn't set the insets, then they will be derived from the widths and heights of the images that make up each side of the border (top, bottom, left, and right).

To actually draw the border, align the corner images to the appropriate corners and then tile the side images along each border side. Doing this will require using the TexturePaint class, which is an implementation of the Paint interface. Unfortunately, TexturePaint takes only BufferedImages, not regular ones, so you've got to convert your images before use.

BufferedImages are a special form of image that the Java2D framework can read and write at a pixel level. The standard Image is controlled by the operating system and is very difficult to access at the pixel level. Java doesn't let you do a straight conversion between the two kinds of images, but you can just draw one image on top of another, which is what this method in the ImageBorder class does:

```
public BufferedImage createBufferedImage(Image img) {
    BufferedImage buff = new BufferedImage(img.getWidth(null),
            img.getHeight(null), BufferedImage.TYPE_INT_ARGB);
    Graphics gfx = buff.createGraphics( );
    gfx.drawImage(img, 0, 0, null);
    gfx.dispose( );
    return buff;
}
```

createBufferedImage( ) first creates an empty buffered image with the same size as the original image. The image type is TYPE_INT_ARGB, which makes the image have full 24-bit color with an alpha channel (transparency). Next, it draws the original image on top of the buffered image. The dispose( ) call releases any extra resources so that the code won't waste any memory, and then it returns the newly minted BufferedImage.

With buffered images in hand, the stage is set for actually filling areas of the border with images. The next ImageBorder method, fillTexture( ), creates a TexturePaint using the appropriate image and then fills in the requested area:

```
public void fillTexture(Graphics2D g2, Image img, int x, int y, int w, int
h) {
    BufferedImage buff = createBufferedImage(img);
    Rectangle anchor = new Rectangle(x,y,img.getWidth(null),img.
getHeight(null));
    TexturePaint paint = new TexturePaint(buff,anchor);
    g2.setPaint(paint);
    g2.fillRect(x,y,w,h);
}
```

The second line of this code creates an anchor rectangle. The image will be tiled to fill the entire border area, but the anchor rectangle is needed to specify where the image will be anchored. We normally think of images being anchored to (0,0), which works fine for the upper-left corner of the border but wouldn't work for the other sides. The right corners would need to be right aligned instead of left aligned, as would happen with (0,0). By setting the anchor to be the location and dimensions of the image itself, you take care of anchoring altogether. The tiling will start wherever the single image would have been drawn.

Now that you can fill an area with a properly aligned texture, you are ready for the paintBorder( ) method, shown in Example 1-7.

Example 1-7. Painting the border

```
public void paintBorder(Component c, Graphics g, int x, int y,
                        int width, int height) {
    g.setColor(Color.white);
    g.fillRect(x,y,width,height);

    Graphics2D g2 = (Graphics2D)g;

    int tlw = top_left.getWidth(null);
    int tlh = top_left.getHeight(null);
    int tcw = top_center.getWidth(null);
    int tch = top_center.getHeight(null);
    int trw = top_right.getWidth(null);
    int trh = top_right.getHeight(null);
```

Example 1-7. Painting the border (continued)

```
        int lcw = left_center.getWidth(null);
        int lch = left_center.getHeight(null);
        int rcw = right_center.getWidth(null);
        int rch = right_center.getHeight(null);
        int blw = bottom_left.getWidth(null);
        int blh = bottom_left.getHeight(null);
        int bcw = bottom_center.getWidth(null);
        int bch = bottom_center.getHeight(null);
        int brw = bottom_right.getWidth(null);
        int brh = bottom_right.getHeight(null);

        fillTexture(g2,top_left,x,y,tlw,tlh);
        fillTexture(g2,top_center,x+tlw,y,width-tlw-trw,tch);
        fillTexture(g2,top_right,x+width-trw,y,trw,trh);
        fillTexture(g2,left_center,x,y+tlh,lcw,height-tlh-blh);
        fillTexture(g2,right_center,x+width-rcw,y+trh,rcw,height-trh-brh);
        fillTexture(g2,bottom_left,x,y+height-blh,blw,blh);
        fillTexture(g2,bottom_center,x+blw,y+height-bch,width-blw-brw,bch);
        fillTexture(g2,bottom_right,x+width-brw,y+height-brh,brw,brh);
}
```

The first two lines fill the entire border area with white. Then you have to cast the Graphics to a Graphics2D object because you will be doing some advanced painting later on. Next, save a reference to the width and height of each image (the top left, top center, top right, etc.). Finally, call fillTexture( ) on each section of the border to fill it in.

The test program shown in Example 1-8 creates a panel that uses the ImageBorder. It creates a nested frame, panel, and button, and then it creates an ImageBorder for the panel using eight images.

Example 1-8. Testing out an image-based border

```
public class ImageBorderHack {

    public static void main(String[] args) {
        JFrame frame = new JFrame("Hack #3: Fill Your Borders with Pretty
                                    Pictures");
        frame.setDefaultCloseOperation(JFrame.EXIT_ON_CLOSE);
        JPanel panel = new JPanel();
        JButton button = new JButton("Image Border Test");
        panel.add(button);

        ImageBorder image_border = new ImageBorder(
            new ImageIcon("images/upper_left.png").getImage( ),
            new ImageIcon("images/upper.png").getImage( ),
            new ImageIcon("images/upper_right.png").getImage( ),

            new ImageIcon("images/left_center.png").getImage( ),
            new ImageIcon("images/right_center.png").getImage( ),
```

Example 1-8. Testing out an image-based border (continued)

```
            new ImageIcon("images/bottom_left.png").getImage( ),
            new ImageIcon("images/bottom_center.png").getImage( ),
            new ImageIcon("images/bottom_right.png").getImage( )
            );
    panel.setBorder(image_border);

    frame.getContentPane( ).add(panel);
    frame.pack( );
    frame.setVisible(true);
    }

}
```

The sample border is made out of a single image sliced into eight pieces using Photoshop (the center image is discarded). You can see these slices in Figure 1-13.

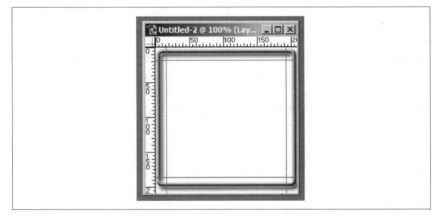

Figure 1-13. Source image in Photoshop with slices

The completed `ImageBorder` class will take the Photoshop slices and tile them to create the finished border, as seen in Figure 1-14.

Figure 1-14. Completed image border

The best thing about these image-based borders is that you can completely change their look by just dropping in new images, which is easy to do with the slice tool in Photoshop. When you create your own image borders, I recommend starting with a rectangular shape layer and then using filters and effects to create drop shadows, bevels, and stroked borders. ·

Display Dates in a Custom Calendar

You can download calendar components from third parties, but real hackers can use Swing to build a custom calendar widget on their own.

When you design an application, you'll often want to use standard widgets to display information. Swing doesn't always give you what you need, though. Consider the calendar component: Swing doesn't come with one, so most users have to download widgets to integrate into their application. However, why not go with a cool and hip teen-friendly application with an attractive, image-based component, as shown in Figure 1-15?

Figure 1-15. Custom calendar component

That would be a bit more fun, wouldn't it? This hack will show you how to build a completely custom calendar component using `java.util.Calendar` and a few images.

First, consider what you'll need. You've got to have pretty images, a component to paint them on, and then some logic to handle the different parts of the date, including what day of the week starts off the current month. You should also provide a `setDate( )` method, so that MVC frameworks can play well with your calendar. Let's get started.

Create the Images

I created three images in Photoshop: one for the background, one for each day, and one for the current day. These are shown in Figures 1-16, 1-17, and 1-18.

Figure 1-16. calendar.png for the general background

Figure 1-17. day.png for the day backgrounds

Figure 1-18. highlight.png for the current day

> I could have separated the day names and the title, but since they don't change, it was simpler to make them part of the image.

A Component to Paint

The easiest way to create a custom component with fancy drawing is to start off with a JPanel and override the paintComponent( ) method, as shown in Example 1-9.

Example 1-9. A Calendar base component

```
public class CalendarHack extends JPanel {
    protected Image background, highlight, day_img;
    protected SimpleDateFormat month = new SimpleDateFormat("MMMM");
```

Example 1-9. A Calendar base component (continued)

```java
    protected SimpleDateFormat year = new SimpleDateFormat("yyyy");
    protected SimpleDateFormat day = new SimpleDateFormat("d");
    protected Date date = new Date();

    public void setDate(Date date) {
        this.date = date;
    }

    public CalendarHack() {
        background = new ImageIcon("calendar.png").getImage();
        highlight = new ImageIcon("highlight.png").getImage();
        day_img = new ImageIcon("day.png").getImage();
        this.setPreferredSize(new Dimension(300,280));
    }

    public void paintComponent(Graphics g) {

        ((Graphics2D)g).setRenderingHint(RenderingHints.KEY_ANTIALIASING,
            RenderingHints.VALUE_ANTIALIAS_ON);
        g.drawImage(background,0,0,null);
        g.setColor(Color.black);
        g.setFont(new Font("SansSerif",Font.PLAIN,18));
        g.drawString(month.format(date),34,36);
        g.setColor(Color.white);
        g.drawString(year.format(date),235,36);
    }
}
```

This loads the images in the constructor and sets up date formatters for the month, year, and day. Override the paintComponent() method to turn on anti-aliasing, draw the background, and then draw the month and year for the current date.

You'll notice that there is a default date in case the developer doesn't set one (always a good practice).

Draw the Days of the Month

The java.util.Calendar object handles all date calculations, so let's start there. You'll need two calendars: one to represent the current date (today) and one that you update as you loop through the grid of dates (cal). Here's what that looks like in code:

```java
    Calendar today = Calendar.getInstance();
    today.setTime(date);
    Calendar cal = Calendar.getInstance();
    cal.setTime(date);
```

```
cal.set(Calendar.DATE,1);
cal.add(Calendar.DATE,-cal.get(Calendar.DAY_OF_WEEK)+1);
for(int week = 0; week < 6; week++) {
    for(int d = 0; d < 7; d++) {
        Image img = day_img;
        Color col = Color.black;
        // only draw if it's actually in this month
        if(cal.get(Calendar.MONTH) == today.get(Calendar.MONTH)) {
            if(cal.equals(today)) {
                img = highlight;
                col = Color.white;
            }
            g.drawImage(img,d*30+46,week*29+81,null);
            g.drawString(day.format(cal.getTime()),
                d*30+46+4,week*29+81+20);
        }
        cal.add(Calendar.DATE,+1);
    }
}
```

You'll notice that both calendars are initialized to date, but then the code resets cal's date to the first of the month and subtracts the current day of the week. This has the effect of setting cal to the last Sunday before (or equal to) the real current date. You have to perform this calculation because you need to start drawing in the upper-lefthand corner of the calendar grid, which will almost always include a few days from the previous month. Once all of that is done, the code loops through each week and draws each day.

Now, here's the tricky part: cal goes back seven days, which is almost certainly going to run back into the previous month. Because the calendar is month-based, those days in the previous month shouldn't be drawn. That's why there is a check to see if cal's month is equal to today's month. If they are equal, then you can draw the day safely; if not, skip drawing and just increment the date.

The last thing to check is if the current day in cal is equal to the real current date. If it is, you want to use a different color and background image (highlight). Finally, the image and day numbers are drawn, with the position determined by the current day of the week and week number. You can adjust the multipliers and offsets (30, 46, 29, 81) to suit your taste. The drawString() method has a few extra pixels of padding to make the day number appear more centered in the day image.

And now you have a completely custom calendar, suitable for placement within the zaniest of interfaces.

Add a Watermark to a Text Component

HACK #5

This hack will show how to create a custom image background for the JTextField, a complex Swing component that does not already support backgrounds or icons by default.

One of Swing's most underused features is the ability to partially override drawing code. Most programs enhance widgets by using renderers or completely overriding the paint code. By only *partially* overriding the drawing, however, you can create some very interesting effects that blend both new and existing drawing commands.

Some components, like JList and JTable, use renderers to customize their look. To put a background in a JTextField, however, requires more. The plan is to subclass JTextField, prepare the resources for drawing a background (loading the image, etc.), and then draw a new background while preserving the normal JTextField drawing code for the text and cursor.

The actual drawing will be done with a TexturePaint. Java2D allows you to fill any area with instances of the Paint interface. Typically you use a color, which is an implementation of Paint, but it is possible to use something else, such as a texture or gradient. This class will use a TexturePaint to tile an image across the component's background.

The first step is to create a JTextField subclass (shown in Example 1-10).

Example 1-10. Preparing a field for watermarking

```
public class WatermarkTextField extends JTextField {
    BufferedImage img;
    TexturePaint texture;

    public WatermarkTextField(File file) throws IOException {
        super();
        img = ImageIO.read(file);
        Rectangle rect = new Rectangle(0,0,
                img.getWidth(null),img.getHeight(null));
        texture = new TexturePaint(img, rect);
        setOpaque(false);
    }
}
```

Example 1-10 creates a class called WatermarkTextField. It is a subclass of JTextField with a custom constructor that accepts a File object containing an image. It also defines two member variables: img and texture. After the obligatory call to super( ), the constructor reads the file into the BufferedImage variable, img. If the file isn't a valid image—or can't be read for some other reason—the method will throw an exception (hence the throws IOException clause on the constructor definition).

After the image is loaded successfully, the constructor creates a TexturePaint. TexturePaints must be created with a source image and a rectangle. The rectangle defines the portion of the source to be tiled. In this case, you want the entire image to be used, so the rectangle is the same size as the image.

> If you wanted to use just a portion of the image, you could make the rectangle smaller. This would also give you the ability to store all of your textures in a single large image, which could save loading time and memory.

The last thing the WatermarkTextField constructor does before returning is call setOpaque(false). As you have seen earlier in this chapter (and will see again), the setOpaque( ) method is one of the core tools for hacking Swing. In this case, it is used to turn off the default background of the TextField, allowing you to substitute your own.

With the subclass created, you can add a method to do the actual drawing:

```
public void paintComponent(Graphics g) {
    Graphics2D g2 = (Graphics2D)g;
    g2.setPaint(texture);
    g.fillRect(0,0,getWidth(),getHeight( ));
    super.paintComponent(g);
}
```

WatermarkTextField overrides the parent class's paintComponent( ) method with its own version. The actual drawing is pretty simple: cast to a Graphics2D object (which understands how to work with Paint classes), then fill in the background with the texture paint and call super( ).

Earlier, I said that you will override the parent class *partially* rather than completely. This is because the code still calls the parent class's paintComponent( ) method, but it does it after painting the new background. Because the opaque property is set to false, the parent class will not draw its own background, allowing your custom one to show through. The component will draw the text, selections, and cursors as normal on top of the custom background.

With the class ready, it's time to pull together an example—Example 1-11.

Example 1-11. Trying out the watermarked text field

```
public static void main(String[] args) throws Exception {
    JFrame frame = new JFrame("Watermark JTextField Hack");

    JTextField textfield = new WatermarkTextField(new File("red.png"));
    textfield.setText("A Text Field");
```

Example 1-11. Trying out the watermarked text field (continued)

```
    frame.getContentPane( ).add(textfield);
    frame.pack( );
    frame.show( );
}
```

The main( ) method creates a JFrame with one child: the custom text field. It creates a new WatermarkTextField with an image file in the constructor, then it packs and shows the frame. The text field is every bit a normal JTextField except for the constructor, so you can use a variable of type JTextField with no problem.

The image, red.png, looks like Figure 1-19.

Figure 1-19. red.png, the background image

Once tiled across the background of the component, it looks like Figure 1-20.

Figure 1-20. The running program

Going Further

Overriding a component's background with custom drawing code is a simple technique that can be used in some surprising ways. The next hack will reuse the watermark code to create a JTextPane with light clouds in the background and a small image badge in the upper-righthand corner. With custom backgrounds you could also add animation, status reports, or even rotating space images (see "Put a NASA Photo into the Background of a Text Area" **[Hack #7]**).

Watermark Your Scroll Panes

HACK
#6

This hack creates a text area with a tiled background image that is fixed, even when the text area scrolls, and also a fixed foreground image that appears above the text, much like the station badges now affixed to the lower-righthand corner of most TV broadcasts.

The Swing framework was designed to let developers override portions of every component, both the visual appearance (the view) and the behavior (the model and controller). This design gives developers great flexibility. One of my favorites is the JScrollPane. Its nested composite design allows developers to create some stunning effects.

Once again, the idea is to override the drawing code of a standard component to create the visual effects **[Hack #5]**. The difference here is that you must deal with a composite object, the JScrollPane. A JScrollPane is not a single Swing component—it's actually a wrapper around two scrollbars and the component that does the real scrolling is a JViewport. This viewport is the actual target component; you will subclass it to draw both above and below the View component (as seen in Example 1-12). The View is the Swing widget being scrolled; in this case, it is a JTextArea.

Example 1-12. Modifying the viewport for watermarking

```
public class ScrollPaneWatermark extends JViewport {
    BufferedImage fgimage, bgimage;
    TexturePaint texture;

    public void setBackgroundTexture(URL url) throws IOException {
        bgimage = ImageIO.read(url);
        Rectangle rect = new Rectangle(0,0,
                bgimage.getWidth(null),bgimage.getHeight(null));
        texture = new TexturePaint(bgimage, rect);
    }

    public void setForegroundBadge(URL url) throws IOException {
        fgimage = ImageIO.read(url);
    }
}
```

The ScrollPaneWatermark class inherits from JViewport, adding two methods: setBackgroundTexture( ) and setForegroundBadge( ). Each takes a URL instead of a File to allow for images loaded from places other than the local disk, such as a web server or JAR file.

setBackgroundTexture( ) does the same thing that the WatermarkTextField did in the previous hack. It loads the image, creates a same-size rectangle, then initializes a TexturePaint for later use. setForegroundBadge( ) is even simpler, only loading the image and storing it in the fgimage variable.

With the class set up, it's time to draw. The code below calls super. paintComponent( ) first, and then draws the texture on top of the component. This is because the existing background might need to show through in case the texture has translucent sections. This would be especially important if the standard view background isn't just a solid color. Under Mac OS X, for example, the background is often a striped, light blue pattern. Here's the code to handle texturing:

```
public void paintComponent(Graphics g) {
    // do the superclass behavior first
    super.paintComponent(g);

    // paint the texture
    if(texture != null) {
        Graphics2D g2 = (Graphics2D)g;
        g2.setPaint(texture);
        g.fillRect(0,0,getWidth(),getHeight());
    }
}
```

ScrollPaneWatermark draws the foreground image badge by overriding the paintChildren( ) method, calling the superclass, and then drawing the image. This ensures that the badge is always on top of the children or view:

```
public void paintChildren(Graphics g) {
    super.paintChildren(g);
    if(fgimage != null) {
        g.drawImage(fgimage,
            getWidth( )-fgimage.getWidth(null), 0,
            null);
    }
}
```

The view (a text area in this example) will usually draw its own background. Because, by definition, the view is as big as the viewport (if not bigger), its background will cover up the viewport's nice texture completely. To stop that, you need to call setOpaque( ) on the view:

```
public void setView(JComponent view) {
    view.setOpaque(false);
    super.setView(view);
}
```

The setView( ) method overrides the existing version (from JViewport) to call setOpaque(false) on the view before calling the super( ) method. By putting this call here, instead of calling setOpaque( ) from the normal setup routines, it frees the developer using the ScrollPaneWatermark class from having to call setOpaque( ) manually, making the class more reusable.

With all of the pieces in place, you can now create a text area inside the custom scroll pane. The main( ) method in Example 1-13 tests it out.

Example 1-13. Testing the scroll pane watermark

```
public static void main(String[] args) throws Exception {
    JFrame frame = new JFrame("Scroll Pane Watermark Hack");

    JTextArea ta = new JTextArea( );
    ta.setText(fileToString(new File("alice.txt")));
    ta.setLineWrap(true);
    ta.setWrapStyleWord(true);

    ScrollPaneWatermark watermark = new ScrollPaneWatermark( );
    watermark.setBackgroundTexture(new File("clouds.jpg").toURL( ));
    watermark.setForegroundBadge(new File("flyingsaucer.png").toURL( ));
    watermark.setView(ta);

    JScrollPane scroll = new JScrollPane( );
    scroll.setViewport(watermark);

    frame.getContentPane( ).add(scroll);
    frame.pack( );
    frame.setSize(600,600);
    frame.show( );
}
```

The main( ) method in Example 1-13 creates a frame containing a scroll pane that contains a text area. fileToString( ) is a utility function that loads a text file into the text area.

> For brevity, the code for fileToString( ) is not printed here, but you can see it in the full source on the book's web site: *http://www.oreilly.com/catalog/swinghks*.

After setting up a standard JTextArea, the code creates a new ScrollPaneWatermark viewport and loads up the images (*clouds.jpg* is a tileable image of pale, fluffy clouds, and *flyingsaucer.jpg* is a small image of a flying saucer with a translucent drop shadow that will blend nicely over the text). Finally, the main( ) method sets the text area as the viewport's view, creates a new scroll pane, and then sets the watermark as the scroll pane's viewport.

Figure 1-21 shows what it looks like when it's all put together.

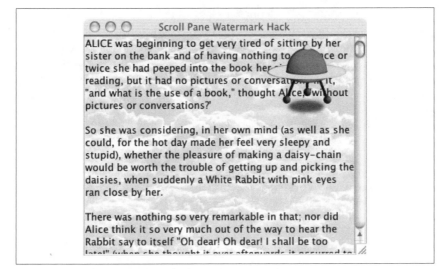

Figure 1-21. Finished ScrollPane hack

HACK #7 Put a NASA Photo into the Background of a Text Area

This hack will repurpose an existing web page, one of NASA's photo sites, by pulling their "Astronomy Picture of the Day" into the background of a text area.

You've already learned how to draw a watermark image in the background of a text area **[Hack #6]** using a `ScrollPaneWatermark`. This hack will pull a photo down from the Web and reuse that class to put the photo in the background. The photo itself comes from NASA's "Astronomy Picture of the Day" page: *http://antwrp.gsfc.nasa.gov/apod/*. The URL to the image changes each day, but the page itself does not. To pull the image down you will load the page, find the image URL, then load the image itself and put it into the `ScrollPaneWatermark`. Depending on the day, it may look something like Figure 1-22.

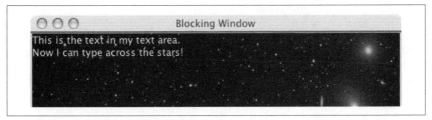

Figure 1-22. Text area with a background image

The code in Example 1-14 defines a class called BackgroundLoader, which implements Runnable so it can be placed on its own thread. The constructor takes as an argument the ScrollPaneWatermark, which the loader will put the image into. The run( ) method contains a loop that will run every two hours, loading the page, finding the SRC URL, then loading the image into the watermark.

Example 1-14. A thread to load a background image

```java
public class BackgroundLoader implements Runnable {

    private ScrollPaneWatermark watermark;
    public BackgroundLoader(ScrollPaneWatermark watermark) {
        this.watermark = watermark;
    }

    public void run( ) {

        while(true) {
            try {
                String base_url = "http://antwrp.gsfc.nasa.gov/apod/";
                URL url = new URL(base_url);

                Reader input = new InputStreamReader(url.openStream( ));
                char buf[] = new char[1024];
                StringBuffer page_buffer = new StringBuffer( );
                while(true) {
                    int n = input.read(buf);
                    if(n < 0) { break; }
                    page_buffer.append(buf,0,n);
                }

                // Locate the Image URL (see next section)

            } catch (Exception ex) {
                System.out.println("exception: " + ex);
                ex.printStackTrace( );
            }
        }
    }
}
```

First, you open the web page and load it into a page_buffer by looping through an InputStreamReader, copying the page data into a string buffer.

The Reader will take care of encoding issues so you don't need to worry about reading HTTP headers or converting to Unicode.

Page in hand, now you need to find the URL for the image itself. If you load the page into a web browser and view the page source, you will see that there is only a single IMG tag in the entire page. This makes the image very easy to find:

```
Pattern pattern = Pattern.compile("<IMG SRC=\"(.*)\"");
Matcher matcher = pattern.matcher(page_buffer);
matcher.find( );
String img_url = base_url + matcher.group(1);

watermark.setBackgroundTexture(new URL(img_url));
watermark.repaint( );

Thread.currentThread( ).sleep(1000*60*60*2);
```

First, you must create a Pattern object with a *regex* (regular expression) that matches the URL. You will notice in the previous code that there are parentheses around the .*. This is called a *grouping*. The matcher will store anything that matches the parentheses in a series of groups that you can query later. This lets you define exactly which part of the pattern you want to pull out. After creating a Matcher and calling find( ), you can pull out the image URL with the line matcher.group(1), prepending it with the base URL for the page.

With the final image URL ready, just set the background texture for the watermark, refresh the screen, and then sleep for two hours. The calculation in the code (1000*60*60*2) evaluates to the number of milliseconds in a two-hour block of time. The page only changes once a day, but this way the change will be picked up sooner if the program is running overnight.

With all of the parts assembled, you can now create a main method, shown in Example 1-15, that builds a simple text editor with the ScrollPaneWatermark to show the space image in the background.

Example 1-15. Testing the space image background

```
public static void main(String[] args) throws IOException {
    JFrame frame = new JFrame("Blocking Window");
    JTextArea jta = new JTextArea(10,40);
    jta.setForeground(Color.white);

    ScrollPaneWatermark viewport = new ScrollPaneWatermark( );
    viewport.setView(jta);
    viewport.setOpaque(false);

    JScrollPane scroll = new JScrollPane( );
    scroll.setViewport(viewport);

    Container comp = frame.getContentPane( );
    comp.add("Center",scroll);
```

Example 1-15. Testing the space image background (continued)

```
        frame.pack( );
        frame.show( );

        new Thread(new BackgroundLoader(viewport)).start( );
}
```

The last line of the main( ) method starts a new thread to manage the background image.

> Because the code is completely encapsulated in the BackgroundLoader class, you could add space images to a component that uses a scroll pane, not just a JTextArea.

Animate Transitions Between Tabs

HACK #8

This hack shows how to create animated transitions that play whenever the user switches tabs on a JTabbedPane.

One of Swing's great strengths is that you can hack into virtually anything. In particular, I love making changes to a component's painting code. The ability to do this is one of the reasons I prefer Swing over SWT. Swing gives me the freedom to create completely new UI concepts, such as transitions.

With the standard paint methods, Swing provides most of what you will need to build the transitions. You will have to put together three additional things, however. First, you need to find out when the user actually clicked on a tab to start a transition. Next, you need a thread to control the animation. Finally, since some animations might fade between the old and new tabs, you need a way to provide images of both tabs at the same time. With those three things, you can build any animation you desire.

Building a Basic Tabbed Pane

To keep things tidy, I have implemented this hack as a subclass of JTabbedPane, except for the actual animation drawing, which will be delegated to a further subclass. By putting all of the heavy lifting into the parent class, you will be able to create new animations easily.

Example 1-16 is the basic skeleton of the parent class.

Example 1-16. A skeleton for the transition manager

```
public class TransitionTabbedPane extends JTabbedPane
    implements ChangeListener, Runnable {

    protected int animation_length = 20;
```

Example 1-16. A skeleton for the transition manager (continued)

```
public TransitionTabbedPane( ) {
    super( );
    this.addChangeListener(this);
}

public int getAnimationLength( ) {
    return this.animation_length;
}

public void setAnimationLength(int length) {
    this.animation_length = length;
}
```

TransitionTabbedPane extends the standard JTabbedPane and also implements ChangeListener and Runnable. ChangeListener allows you to learn when the user has switched between tabs. Since the event is propagated *before* the new tab is painted, inserting the animation is very easy. Runnable is used for the animation thread itself.

 You could have split the thread into a separate class, but I think that keeping all of the code together makes the system more encapsulated and easier to maintain.

TransitionTabbedPane adds one new property, the animation length. This defines the number of steps used for the transition, and it can be set by the subclass or external code.

Scheduling the Animation

Since the pane was added as a ChangeListener to itself, the stateChanged( ) method will be called whenever the user switches tabs. This is the best place to start the animation thread. Once started, the thread will capture the previous tab into a buffer, loop through the animation, and control the repaint speed:

```
// threading code
public void stateChanged(ChangeEvent evt) {
    new Thread(this).start( );
}

protected int step;
protected BufferedImage buf = null;
protected int previous_tab = -1;

public void run( ) {
    step = 0;
```

```
    // save the previous tab
    if(previous_tab != -1) {
        Component comp = this.getComponentAt(previous_tab);
        buf = new BufferedImage(comp.getWidth( ),
            comp.getHeight( ),
            BufferedImage.TYPE_4BYTE_ABGR);
        comp.paint(buf.getGraphics( ));
    }
```

Notice that the run( ) method grabs the previous tab component only when the previous_tab index isn't -1. The component will always have a valid value, except for the first time the pane is shown on screen, but that's OK because the user won't have really switched from anything anyway. If there is a previous tab, then the code grabs the component and paints it into a buffer image.

It's important to note that this is *not* thread-safe because the code is being executed on a custom thread, not the Swing thread. However, since the tab is about to be hidden anyway—and, in fact, the next real paint( ) call will only draw the new tab—you shouldn't have any problems. Any changes introduced by this extra paint( ) call won't show up on screen.

With the previous component safely saved away, you can now loop through the animation:

```
    for(int i=0; i<animation_length; i++) {
        step = i;
        repaint( );
        try {
            Thread.currentThread( ).sleep(100);
        } catch (Exception ex) {
            p("ex: " + ex);
        }
    }

    step = -1;
    previous_tab = this.getSelectedIndex( );
    repaint( );
```

This code shows a basic animation loop from 1 to *N*, with a 100-millisecond duration for each frame.

A more sophisticated version of the code could have dynamic frame rates to adjust for system speed.

Once the transition finishes, the animation step is set back to -1, the previous tab is stored, and the screen is repainted one last time, without the transition effects.

Drawing the Animation

The TransitionTabbedPane is now set up with the proper resources and repaints, but it still isn't drawing the animation. Because the animation is going to partially or completely obscure the tabs underneath, the best place to draw is right after the children are painted:

```
public void paintChildren(Graphics g) {
    super.paintChildren(g);

    if(step != -1) {
        Rectangle size = this.getComponentAt(0).getBounds( );
        Graphics2D g2 = (Graphics2D)g;
        paintTransition(g2, step, size, buf);
    }
}

public void paintTransition(Graphics2D g2, int step,
    Rectangle size, Image prev) {
}
```

This code puts all of the custom drawing into the paintTransition( ) method, currently empty. It will only be called if step isn't -1, meaning during a transition animation. The paintTransition( ) method provides the drawing canvas, the current animation step, the size and position of the content area (excluding the tabs themselves), and the image buffer that stores the previous tab's content. By putting all of this in a single method, subclasses can build their own animations very easily. Example 1-17 is a simple transition with a white rectangle that grows out of the center, filling the screen, then shrinking again to reveal the new tab content.

Example 1-17. Setting up an animated transition

```
public class InOutPane extends TransitionTabbedPane {

    public void paintTransition(Graphics2D g2, int state,
            Rectangle size, Image prev) {

        int length = getAnimationLength( );
        int half = length/2;

        double scale = size.getHeight( )/length;
        int offset = 0;
        // calculate the fade out part
        if(state >= 0 && state < half) {
```

Example 1-17. Setting up an animated transition (continued)

```
            // draw the saved version of the old tab component
            if(prev != null) {
                g2.drawImage(prev,(int)size.getX(),(int)size.getY( ),null);
            }
            offset = (int)((10-state)*scale);
        }

        // calculate the fade in part
        if(state >= half && state < length) {
            g2.setColor(Color.white);
            offset = (int)((state-10)*scale);
        }

        // do the drawing
        g2.setColor(Color.white);
        Rectangle area = new Rectangle((int)(size.getX( )+offset),
            (int)(size.getY( )+offset),
            (int)(size.getWidth( )-offset*2),
            (int)(size.getHeight( )-offset*2));
        g2.fill(area);
    }
}
```

InOutPane implements only the paintTransition( ) method, leaving all of the harder tasks to the parent class. First, it determines how long the animation will be, and then it calculates an offset to grow and shrink the white rectangle. If the drawing process is currently in the first half of the animation (step < half), then it draws the previous tab below the rectangle, creating the illusion that old tab content is still really on screen with the rectangle growing above it. For the second half of the animation, it just draws the rectangle, letting the real tab (the new one) shine through as the rectangle shrinks.

Putting It All Together

Because TransitionTabbedPane is just a JTabbedPane subclass, it can be used wherever the original would be. Example 1-18 creates a frame with two tabs, each containing a button. The running program looks like Figure 1-23. As you switch between the tabs, you will see an animation like that shown in Figure 1-24.

Example 1-18. Testing out tabbed animation transitions

```
public class TabFadeTest {

    public static void main(String[] args) {

        JFrame frame = new JFrame("Fade Tabs");
```

Example 1-18. Testing out tabbed animation transitions (continued)

```
    JTabbedPane tab = new InOutPane( );
    tab.addTab("t1",new JButton("Test Button 1"));
    tab.addTab("t2",new JButton("Test Button 2"));

    frame.getContentPane( ).add(tab);
    frame.pack( );
    frame.show( );
}

}
```

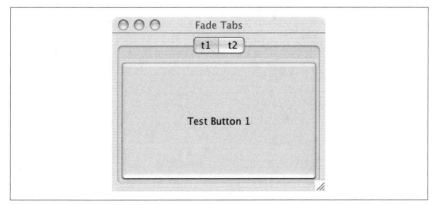

Figure 1-23. Two tabs, before transition effect begins

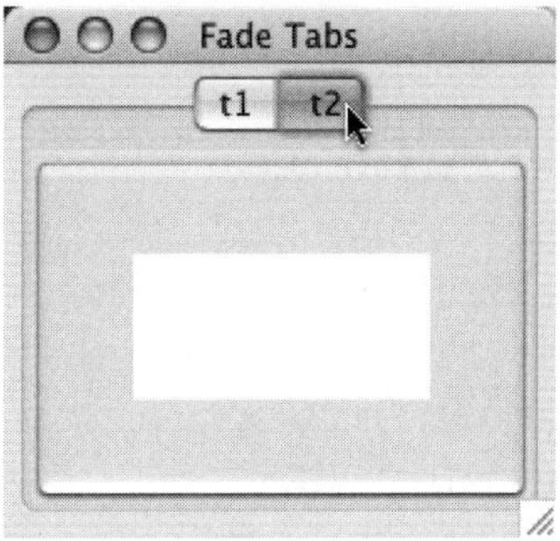

Figure 1-24. Tab transition at mid-point

Another Example

Because `TransitionTabbedPane` makes it so easy to build new animations, I thought I'd add another one. This is the old venetian blinds effect, where vertical bars cover the old screen and uncover the new one; Example 1-19 puts it together.

Example 1-19. Creating a venetian blinds effect

```java
public class VenetianPane extends TransitionTabbedPane {
    public void paintTransition(Graphics2D g2, int step,
            Rectangle size, Image prev) {

        int length = getAnimationLength();
        int half = length/2;

        // create a blind
        Rectangle blind = new Rectangle();

        // calculate the fade out part
        if(step >= 0 && step < half) {
            // draw the saved version of the old tab component
            if(prev != null) {
                g2.drawImage(prev,(int)size.getX(),(int)size.getY(),null);
            }
            // calculate the growing blind
            blind = new Rectangle(
                (int)size.getX(),
                (int)size.getY(),
                step,
                (int)size.getHeight());
        }

        // calculate the fade in part
        if(step >= half && step < length) {
            // calculate the shrinking blind
            blind = new Rectangle(
                (int)size.getX(),
                (int)size.getY(),
                length-step,
                (int)size.getHeight());
            blind.translate(step-half,0);
        }

        // draw the blinds
        for(int i=0; i<size.getWidth()/half; i++) {
            g2.setColor(Color.white);
            g2.fill(blind);
            blind.translate(half,0);
        }

    }
}
```

Just like InOutPane, VenetianPane selectively draws the old tab and then calculates the placement of animated rectangles. In this case, there is a blind rectangle that spans the entire screen from top to bottom, but has the width of the current step. As a result of the step growing, this rectangle gets bigger with each frame. For the second half of the animation, it shrinks and moves to the right, making it appear to fade into nothing. Once the blind is calculated, VenetianPane draws the blind multiple times to cover the entire tab content area, creating the effect seen in Figure 1-25.

Figure 1-25. Tab transition with a venetian blinds effect

This hack is quite extensible. With the power of Java2D you could add translucency, blurs, OS X-like genie effects, or anything else you can dream up. As a future enhancement, you could include more animation settings to control the frame rate and transition time. If you do create more, please post them on the Web for others to share.

HACK #9 Blur Disabled Components

This hack explores creating how to perform a blur transformation on a Swing component.

Every Swing component draws to the screen via the paintComponent( ) method. This is true even for components that offload the actual drawing to Look and Feel UI objects. Because all drawing goes through the paintComponent( ) method at some point, this point is where you can do some interesting things by manipulating the graphics object during the paint process.

Swing components draw to the Graphics object passed in through the paintComponent( ) method. This means that if you replace the Graphics object with a custom version, you can capture a component's drawing into a bitmap instead of going straight to the screen.

Blurring is a pixel-level operation, meaning the actual blurring is done pixel-by-pixel in a bitmap. By drawing the component to a bitmap, blurring that bitmap, and then drawing the bitmap *in the place* of the component, you can effectively have a blurred component without disturbing the rest of the Swing painting routines. The particular implementation in this hack uses a blurred effect to replace the normal graying of a component when it is disabled.

The first step is to capture the button into a bitmap, as shown in Example 1-20.

Example 1-20. Creating a blurrable button

```
public class BlurJButton extends JButton {

    public BlurJButton(String text) {
        super(text);
    }

    public void paintComponent(Graphics g) {
        if(isEnabled( )) {
            super.paintComponent(g);
            return;
        }

        BufferedImage buf = new BufferedImage(getWidth(),getHeight( ),
                    BufferedImage.TYPE_INT_RGB);
        super.paintComponent(buf.getGraphics( ));

        // Blur the buffered image (see next section)

    }
}
```

The BlurJButton class extends a normal JButton and overrides the paintComponent( ) method. If the button is enabled (neither disabled nor grayed out), then it calls the superclass's normal version of paintComponent( ) and returns. If the button is disabled, however, then BlurJButton creates a new BufferedImage with the same dimensions as the component.

> A BufferedImage is simply an image backed by a bunch of bytes in memory. It is a generic kind of image that gives you a lot of flexibility. I set the type of the image to TYPE_INT_RGB, rather than TYPE_INT_ARGB, because the latter adds an alpha channel. An alpha channel lets you create transparency effects, but since the blur doesn't need transparency, that feature would cost you unneeded memory.

Finally, the BlurJButton calls the paintComponent( ) on its superclass, the standard JButton, passing in the graphics obtained from the buffer. This is the key to the hack. By passing in buf.getGraphics( ) instead of the g variable, the button will be drawn entirely to the image buffer, thus enabling the blurring:

```
float[] my_kernel = {
        0.10f, 0.10f, 0.10f,
        0.10f, 0.20f, 0.10f,
        0.10f, 0.10f, 0.10f };
ConvolveOp op = new ConvolveOp(new Kernel(3,3, my_kernel));
Image img = op.filter(buf,null);
g.drawImage(img,0,0,null);
```

Blurring is a complex operation where each pixel is averaged with the pixels next to it to create a new pixel. The actual math is not tricky, but it's very tedious, and you need to take special care around the edges of the buffer. Fortunately, Java2D provides a class that handles all of the messy details. All you have to provide is a series of float values, called a *kernel*.

The kernel is a bunch of numbers between 0 and 1 that will be multiplied against the value of each pixel and its neighboring pixels. In the previous case, there is a 3×3 matrix of values where the target pixel (the one being blurred) is in the center. Multiplying 1 times the pixel value will produce the same pixel value, and therefore the same color. 0 times the pixel value will produce 0, or black. Something in between will produce a darker version of the pixel. Once the kernel is multiplied by the pixels, the values are added together. The kernel in this example has values of 0.10 for every slot except for the center one, which is 0.20. If you add those up, you will find that it comes to exactly 1. This means that the final pixel color will have the same brightness as it did originally (averaged over the entire image), but its color will be a mixture of all of the pixels around it. If the sum of the pixels came out to be less than 1, then the resulting image would be darker than the original. If the sum was greater than 1, then the image would be lighter. This system gives you a lot of flexibility. In fact, many paint programs implement a great number of their filters simply by using different convolution kernels.

 Try changing the values in the kernel to get effects other than blurring.

Once the kernel is created, it is passed into a new ConvolveOp, which does all of the actual calculations. op.filter(buff,null) tells the operation to begin. The null value in the second argument tells the operation to create a new buffer of the same size as the input buffer, buf. Once the blur operation is complete, the final bitmap is drawn to the real screen with the line g.drawImage(img,0,0,null).

With the class in place, you can test it out in code with something like this main( ) method:

```
public static void main(String[] args) {
    JFrame frame = new JFrame("Blurred Button Hack");
    final JButton button = new BlurJButton("A Blurred Button");
    JButton control = new JButton("Switch");
    control.addActionListener(new ActionListener( ) {
        public void actionPerformed(ActionEvent evt) {
            button.setEnabled(!button.isEnabled( ));
        }
    });

    frame.getContentPane( ).add(button);
    frame.getContentPane( ).add("South",control);
    frame.pack( );
    frame.show( );
}
```

This is a standard JFrame containing a BlurJButton as well as a normal button for control. The control button has an ActionListener that toggles the blurred button's enabled state. The initial state—with the button unblurred—is shown in Figure 1-26. When you blur the button, it looks like Figure 1-27.

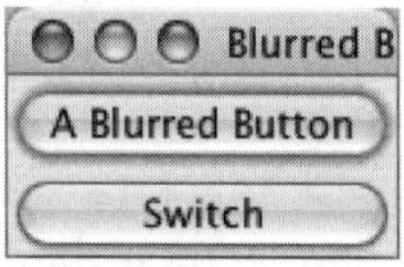

Figure 1-26. Enabled button with no blur effect

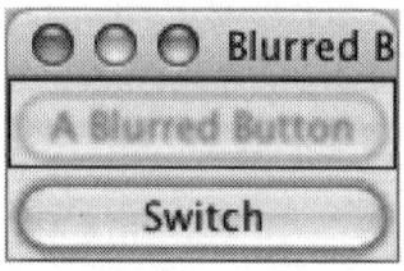

Figure 1-27. Disabled button with blur effect

This technique of rendering to an intermediate buffer can be very powerful. You could extend this hack by doing other pixel-level operations, such as watercolor effects, edge detection, contrast adjustments, or even animated waves and rotations. Anything you can do to a bitmap you can apply to a Swing component.

Building a Drop-Down Menu Button

This hack shows how to build a color chooser as a proper drop-down component. It will behave like `JComboBox` but without the extension headaches of Sun's version of the class.

Most custom Swing components are created with simple subclasses of the standard base classes in `javax.swing`. This works fine most of the time, but every now and then you need to build something where there is no easy standard component to start with. Even worse, sometimes the obvious choice for your starting point is a component so convoluted that you can't figure out where to start. Still, you'd rather not reimplement the wheel. No, I'm not talking about `JTree` or `JTable`—I'm referring to the `JComboBox`. It seems like such a simple component, but the implementation is fiendishly complex.

Most large applications use components that feel like the `JComboBox`, but do something entirely different, like select a color or show a history list. A quick search through the `JComboBox` API doesn't turn up any obvious extension points. You could customize it with some cell renderers, but if you need a component that doesn't show a list of data, you are pretty much out of luck. The source to `JComboBox` is not very helpful either. The work is spread out over several UI classes in the various Look and Feel (L&F) packages. If you did customize one of those, your component would look out of place when used in a different L&F. The only real option is to write your own combo box, which is pretty easy except for the actual drop-down part. You need to show a component on top of the others, poking out of the frame occasionally, but without any decorations of its own. It should be just a borderless floating box. Digging through Swing's source code reveals the secret ingredient: a `JWindow`.

`JWindow` is a subclass of `Window` but not of `Frame`. This means it has no decorations on the side, and it is hidden from the Dock and Taskbar. This is exactly what you want from a pop up. Care must be taken when creating it, however, as you must ensure the window appears only on top of the existing components, and that it disappears when something else gains focus or the window moves. Fortunately, you can do all of this with one composite component and a few event listeners.

`DropDownComponent` will be a composite of the visible component, a down arrow trigger button, and the hidden component that will appear in the pop up. By thinking of your custom component as a composite of existing components, you can make it very flexible. Additionally, subclasses must be able to add different components to make something new out of the same pieces.

Example 1-21 is the start of a DropDownComponent class. It extends JComponent directly and implements both the action and ancestor listener interfaces. It assembles the visible and drop-down components passed into its constructor with an arrow trigger and the listeners.

Example 1-21. Skeleton for a drop-down combo box

```java
public class DropDownComponent extends JComponent
    implements ActionListener, AncestorListener {

    protected JComponent drop_down_comp;
    protected JComponent visible_comp;
    protected JButton arrow;
    protected JWindow popup;

    public DropDownComponent(JComponent vcomp, JComponent ddcomp) {
        drop_down_comp = ddcomp;
        visible_comp = vcomp;

        arrow = new JButton(new MetalComboBoxIcon( ));
        Insets insets = arrow.getMargin( );
        arrow.setMargin( new Insets( insets.top, 1, insets.bottom, 1 ) );
        arrow.addActionListener(this);
        addAncestorListener(this);

        setupLayout( );
    }
}
```

The arrow is just a JButton with a MetalComboBoxIcon. Reusing this arrow lets the code pick up any Metal Look and Feel customizations. The last line of the constructor calls another method in the class, setupLayout( ), to position the arrow next to the visible component while letting the component still grow:

```java
    protected void setupLayout( ) {
        GridBagLayout gbl = new GridBagLayout( );
        GridBagConstraints c = new GridBagConstraints( );
        setLayout(gbl);

        c.weightx = 1.0;  c.weighty = 1.0;
        c.gridx = 0;  c.gridy = 0;
        c.fill = c.BOTH;
        gbl.setConstraints(visible_comp,c);
        add(visible_comp);

        c.weightx = 0;
        c.gridx++;
        gbl.setConstraints(arrow,c);
        add(arrow);
    }
```

So far, this is all standard Swing code. The tricky part is dealing with the JWindow pop up. The pop up must be positioned right below the visible component and be on top of the screen. You also need to look for lost focus events to know when to hide the pop up again. To handle the pop up, use the actionPerformed( ) method:

```
public void actionPerformed(ActionEvent evt) {
    // build pop-up window
    popup = new JWindow(getFrame(null));
    popup.getContentPane( ).add(drop_down_comp);
    popup.addWindowFocusListener(new WindowAdapter( ) {
        public void windowLostFocus(WindowEvent evt) {
            popup.setVisible(false);
        }
    });
    popup.pack( );

    // show the pop-up window
    Point pt = visible_comp.getLocationOnScreen( );
    pt.translate(0,visible_comp.getHeight( ));
    popup.setLocation(pt);
    popup.toFront( );
    popup.setVisible(true);
    popup.requestFocusInWindow( );
}
```

The actionPerformed( ) method will be called whenever the arrow button triggers it. It creates a new JWindow, adds the drop-down child component, positions the window, and then shows it on top of any other components. The JWindow has an anonymous listener that will close the window if it loses focus. Notice that the JWindow constructor takes the result of getFrame( ). getFrame( ) finds the parent frame of the composite drop-down component. The JWindow accepts this frame as its owner, meaning it will be positioned relative to the parent frame and be moved along with it. More importantly, it can receive focus events. Windows without owners can't get focus events because they are effectively out of the focus system. These events are important as they let you know when to hide the window again. Without the frame returned from getFrame( ), the pop up would stay visible and stationary, even if the parent frame gets focus or moves. Here's the code for getFrame( ):

```
protected Frame getFrame(Component comp) {
    if(comp == null) {
        comp = this;
    }
    if(comp.getParent( ) instanceof Frame) {
        return (Frame)comp.getParent( );
    }
    return getFrame(comp.getParent( ));
}
```

With the code so far, you can show the pop-up window. To close it, you must listen for ancestor events to find out when something above the drop-down in the component tree has changed. They all just call hidePopup( ) to safely turn it off:

```
public void ancestorAdded(AncestorEvent event){
    hidePopup( );
}

public void ancestorRemoved(AncestorEvent event){
    hidePopup( );
}

public void ancestorMoved(AncestorEvent event){
    if (event.getSource( ) != popup) {
        hidePopup( );
    }
}

public void hidePopup( ) {
    if(popup != null && popup.isVisible( )) {
        popup.setVisible(false);
    }
}
```

Adding a Color Selection Panel

With the DropDownComponent finished, you can finally build something with it. For this hack, I've chosen a color selector. This is a small widget that lets the user pick one of 12 standard colors without having to open up a full color chooser. Most word processors and spreadsheets have a component like this, so there's no reason for Swing not to have one, too.

ColorSelectionPanel, shown in Example 1-22, is just a JPanel with a 4×3 grid of buttons. Each button represents one of the most common 10 colors, plus black and white. When a color button is clicked, it will call selectColor( ) to fire off a color selection event.

Example 1-22. A color selection panel to be used in the drop-down component

```
public class ColorSelectionPanel extends JPanel {
    public ColorSelectionPanel( ) {
        GridBagLayout gbl = new GridBagLayout( );
        GridBagConstraints c = new GridBagConstraints( );
        setLayout(gbl);

        // reusable listener for each button
        ActionListener color_listener = new ActionListener( ) {
            public void actionPerformed(ActionEvent evt) {
                selectColor(((JButton)evt.getSource()).getBackground( ));
            }
        };
```

Example 1-22. A color selection panel to be used in the drop-down component (continued)

```
// set up the standard 12 colors
Color[] colors = new Color[12];
colors[0] = Color.white;
colors[1] = Color.black;

colors[2] = Color.blue;
colors[3] = Color.cyan;
colors[4] = Color.gray;
colors[5] = Color.green;
colors[6] = Color.lightGray;
colors[7] = Color.magenta;
colors[8] = Color.orange;
colors[9] = Color.pink;
colors[10] = Color.red;
colors[11] = Color.yellow;

// lay out the grid
c.gridheight = 1;
c.gridwidth = 1;
c.fill = c.NONE;
c.weightx = 1.0;
c.weighty = 1.0;

for(int i=0; i<3; i++) {
    for(int j=0; j<4; j++) {
        c.gridx=j;
        c.gridy=i;
        JButton button = new ColorButton(colors[j+i*4]);
        gbl.setConstraints(button,c);
        add(button);
        button.addActionListener(color_listener);
    }
}

}

// fire off a selectedColor property event
protected Color selectedColor = Color.black;
public void selectColor(Color newColor) {
    Color oldColor = selectedColor;
    selectedColor = newColor;
    firePropertyChange("selectedColor",oldColor, newColor);
}

}
```

ColorSelectionPanel uses a custom JButton called ColorButton (shown in Example 1-23). It has no text and a small size so that you can fit 12 of them inside the drop-down window. The button's background comes from the color it represents, and the button draws its own border, so there is no need to draw a grid.

Example 1-23. Custom JButton for color selection

```java
public class ColorButton extends JButton {
    public ColorButton(Color col) {
        super( );
        this.setText("");
        Dimension dim = new Dimension(15,15);
        this.setSize(dim);
        this.setPreferredSize(dim);
        this.setMinimumSize(dim);
        this.setBorderPainted(true);
        this.setBackground(col);
    }
}
```

To put the color selector together, you just need to pack the
ColorSelectionPanel and a status button into a DropDownComponent. You also
need to add a property change listener to detect when the user has selected a
new color and then hide the pop up. This is all handled by Example 1-24.

Example 1-24. Assembling a working color selection widget

```java
public class DropDownTest extends JPanel {

    public static void main(String[] args) {

        final JButton status = new JButton("Color");
        final JPanel panel = new ColorSelectionPanel( );
        final DropDownComponent dropdown = new DropDownComponent(status,panel);
        panel.addPropertyChangeListener("selectedColor",
            new PropertyChangeListener( ) {
            public void propertyChange(PropertyChangeEvent evt) {
                dropdown.hidePopup( );
                status.setBackground((Color)evt.getNewValue( ));
            }
        });

        JFrame frame = new JFrame("Drop Down Test");
        frame.setDefaultCloseOperation(frame.EXIT_ON_CLOSE);
        frame.getContentPane( ).setLayout(new BorderLayout( ));
        frame.getContentPane( ).add("North",dropdown);
        frame.getContentPane( ).add("Center",new JLabel("Drop Down Test"));
        frame.pack( );
        frame.setSize(300,300);
        frame.show( );

    }

}
```

After building the DropDownComponent and putting it in a standard JFrame,
your color selector will look like Figure 1-28.

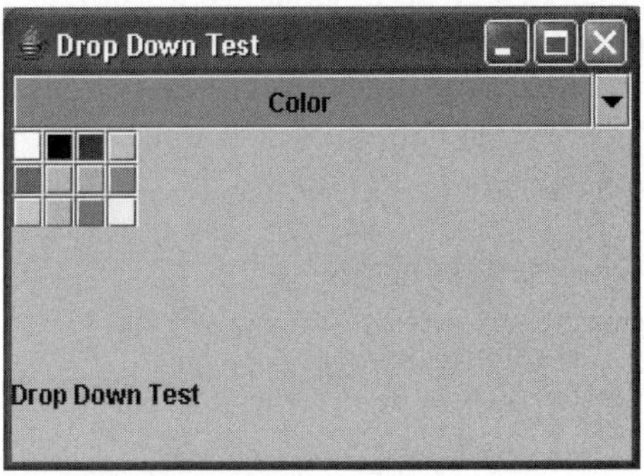

Figure 1-28. A drop-down color chooser in a test JFrame

One nice thing about assembling the drop-down from standard components is that it will still look good when used with a different Look and Feel. Everything the user sees on the screen is some subclass of the standard JButton, but it is just presented in a non-traditional manner. If you switch to another theme where standard buttons are shaped differently, the custom component adapts automatically.

HACK #11

Create Menus with Drop Shadows

This hack explores a simple way to create drop shadows on menus throughout an entire application with minimal code changes.

Many modern operating systems provide menus with interesting effects to make them jump off the screen. One of the most common is the drop shadow. Some programs even provide shadows themselves when the host operating system does not. For years, a lack of low-level graphics support has denied Swing programs access to these kinds of cool effects. But not any more! Most of the effects can be duplicated with Swing's robust theming ability.

Most custom effects require either subclassing a component or messing with graphics overlays. I tried a variety of techniques to create this hack, but I kept coming across the same problem over and over. If I wanted to draw a shadow, I had to change the sizing of each menu item, plus its background, plus the pop-up frame itself. That is a lot of components to manage. It would be a lot simpler if I could tell the components to make themselves a little bit bigger and give me the extra slice of screen real estate to draw in. The solution was right under my nose: the border. Every Swing component can use a custom border, without subclassing, and the border will automatically resize the component to fit. If the border is lopsided, then it will create a kind of shadow effect. Perfect!

Every standard Swing component is actually drawn by a UI helper class, and pop-up menus are no exception. I took the BasicPopupMenuUI in the javax. swing.plaf.basic package and created a subclass called CustomPopupMenuUI (shown in Example 1-25). It only does two things special: adds a custom border to the pop up's parent panel and sets the panel to be transparent.

Example 1-25. Extending the pop-up menu's UI

```
public class CustomPopupMenuUI extends BasicPopupMenuUI {
    public static ComponentUI createUI(JComponent c) {
        return new CustomPopupMenuUI( );
    }

    public Popup getPopup(JPopupMenu popup, int x, int y) {
        Popup pp = super.getPopup(popup,x,y);
        JPanel panel = (JPanel)popup.getParent( );
        panel.setBorder(new ShadowBorder(3,3));
        panel.setOpaque(false);
        return pp;
    }
}
```

The getPopup( ) method generates the actual menu object in the superclass. This version grabs the pop up's parent—a JPanel—and adds the custom ShadowBorder with offsets of 3 pixels, both horizontally and vertically. It also calls setOpaque(false). This tells the component that it does not have to completely fill its boundaries and that the parent component may show through. For most components, this turns off its background, which is the desired effect here.

With the custom pop-up class done, it's time to create the border. ShadowBorder, shown in Example 1-26, is a subclass of AbstractBorder, which handles all of the messy details of border management and lets the developer get down to the actual drawing code pretty quickly.

Example 1-26. Adding a shadowed border

```
class ShadowBorder extends AbstractBorder {
    int xoff, yoff;
    Insets insets;
    public ShadowBorder(int x, int y) {
        this.xoff = x;
        this.yoff = y;
        insets = new Insets(0,0,xoff,yoff);
    }

    public Insets getBorderInsets( Component c ) {
        return insets;
    }
```

Example 1-26. Adding a shadowed border (continued)

```
    public void paintBorder(Component comp, Graphics g,
            int x, int y, int width, int height) {
        g.setColor(Color.black);
        g.translate(x,y);
        // draw right side
        g.fillRect(width-xoff, yoff, xoff, height-yoff);
        // draw bottom side
        g.fillRect(xoff, height-yoff, width-xoff, yoff);
        g.translate(-x,-y);
    }
}
```

The ShadowBorder constructor takes x- and y-offsets and creates an Insets object. These insets have to be returned by the getBorderInsets( ) method in order for other components to size themselves appropriately. Because the insets class uses a 0 for the first two arguments, the extra space will be on the right and bottom only, not the top and left. This will create an offset shadow in the lower-right direction, similar to most native operating system drop shadows.

The actual painting code is very simple: set the color to black, translate the graphics origin to be relative to the x and y passed in, draw the shadow, and translate back. The shadow is composed of two filled-in rectangles, one on the bottom of the component and one on its right side. Note that the drawing begins offset slightly. The right side starts at yoff instead of 0, and the bottom side starts at xoff. These adjustments will create a tiny square of empty space in the lower left and upper right. Those squares will allow the background to show through. Because the background panel was already turned off in the CustomPopupMenuUI's getPopup( ) method, this will let the other components underneath the menu shine through. The drop shadow effect is complete.

The code in Example 1-27 installs the CustomPopupMenuUI into the UIManager. This will ensure that all menus throughout the program use the custom menu. Finally, the test program creates a sample set of menus and some dummy components in the main frame. The finished program looks like Figure 1-29.

Example 1-27. Putting the custom combo box into action

```
public class MenuTest {
    public static void main(String[] args) throws Exception {
        UIManager.put("PopupMenuUI","CustomPopupMenuUI");

        JFrame frame = new JFrame( );
        JMenuBar mb = new JMenuBar( );
        frame.setJMenuBar(mb);
```

Example 1-27. Putting the custom combo box into action (continued)

```
JMenu menu = new JMenu("File");
mb.add(menu);
menu.add(new JMenuItem("Open"));
menu.add(new JMenuItem("Save"));
menu.add(new JMenuItem("Close"));
menu.add(new JMenuItem("Exit"));
menu = new JMenu("Edit");
mb.add(menu);
menu.add(new JMenuItem("Cut"));
menu.add(new JMenuItem("Copy"));
menu.add(new JMenuItem("Paste"));
menu.add(new JMenuItem("Paste Special.."));
frame.getContentPane().setLayout(new BorderLayout());
frame.getContentPane().add("North",new JButton("Button"));
frame.getContentPane().add("Center",new JLabel("a label"));
frame.getContentPane().add("South",new JCheckBox("checkbox"));
frame.pack();
frame.setSize(200,150);
frame.show();
    }
}
```

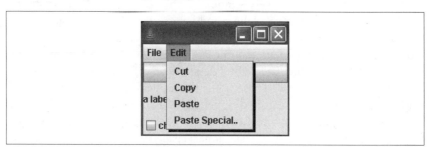

Figure 1-29. Menu with a drop shadow

Add Translucence to Menus

In this hack I will show you how to add true translucency to your menus with only a slight modification to your program.

Computer interfaces are pretty sophisticated these days. Years ago, we considered ourselves lucky to simply have menu bars at all; now, we need menus with sophisticated effects like animation, shadows, and translucency.

You've already seen how to achieve visual effects by overriding the paint( ) method of a parent component and then rendering the children into a buffer [Hack #9]. It would be nice to do the same thing here, but there's just one small problem. Overriding the paint( ) method of the JMenu wouldn't do any good because the JMenu doesn't draw what we think of as a menu—a list of menu items that pop up when you click on the menu's title. The JMenu actually only draws the title at the top of a menu. The rest of the menu is drawn by a JPopupMenu created as a member of the JMenu. Unfortunately this member is marked private, which means you can't substitute your own JPopupMenu subclass for the standard version.

Fortunately there is a way out. Like all Swing components, the menu components delegate their actual drawing to a separate set of Look and Feel classes in the javax.swing.plaf package. If you override the right plaf classes for the menu items and pop-up menu, then you should be able to create the desired translucent effect. It just takes a little subclassing.

Make the Custom Menu Item

All MenuItems are implemented by some form of the javax.swing.plaf. MenuItemUI class. When creating custom UI classes, it is always best to start by subclassing something in the javax.swing.plaf.basic package (in this case, BasicMenuItemUI) because it handles most of the heavy lifting for you, as shown in Example 1-28.

Example 1-28. Extending the basic UI

```
public class CustomMenuItemUI extends BasicMenuItemUI {

    public static ComponentUI createUI(JComponent c) {
        return new CustomMenuItemUI( );
    }

    public void paint(Graphics g, JComponent comp) {
        // paint to the buffered image
        BufferedImage bufimg = new BufferedImage(
            comp.getWidth( ),
            comp.getHeight( ),
            BufferedImage.TYPE_INT_ARGB);
        Graphics2D g2 = bufimg.createGraphics( );
        // restore the foreground color in case the superclass needs it
        g2.setColor(g.getColor( ));
        super.paint(g2,comp);
        // do an alpha composite
        Graphics2D gx = (Graphics2D) g;
        gx.setComposite(AlphaComposite.getInstance(
            AlphaComposite.SRC_OVER,0.8f));
        gx.drawImage(bufimg,0,0,null);
    }

}
```

No constructor is required because all UI classes have a no-arg constructor automatically. All UI classes also need a static createUI( ) method to create a new instance of the class, as you can see in the example. In the paint( ) method, instead of drawing on the graphics object passed in, the code creates a buffered image with the same dimensions as the component, and then calls super.paint( ). This will draw the component onto the buffered image instead of the screen. Once the painting is done, it can apply a transform and then draw the image buffer onto the real Graphics. In this case, the transform is an alpha composite of 0.8. This means that instead of drawing the buffer as is, it will draw the buffer partially transparent (80% solid, in this case). This will draw the bufferedimage into the real graphics with a translucent effect. You can vary the strength of the translucency by modifying the second parameter to the AlphaComposite.getInstance( ) method (1 results in a solid, 0 is totally transparent).

Add a Custom JMenu

If you stopped with just the custom menu items, the menus would seem a bit translucent, but the rest of the window wouldn't shine through. This is because the menu items are inside of another component; in fact, they're inside of three! The JMenu puts all of the menu items inside of a JPopupMenu, which is placed inside of a JPanel, and then the whole deal is put in a layered pane at the top of the frame. The layered pane is already transparent, so you don't need to worry about it, but the JPanel and JPopupMenu are going to be a problem. Example 1-29 handles the custom UI for these.

Example 1-29. Handling translucence for JPanels and JPopupMenus

```
public class CustomPopupMenuUI extends BasicPopupMenuUI {

    public static ComponentUI createUI(JComponent c) {
        return new CustomPopupMenuUI( );
    }

    public void installUI(JComponent c) {
        super.installUI(c);
        popupMenu.setOpaque(false);
    }

    public Popup getPopup(JPopupMenu popup, int x, int y) {
        Popup pp = super.getPopup(popup,x,y);
        JPanel panel = (JPanel)popup.getParent( );
        panel.setOpaque(false);
        return pp;
    }

}
```

The custom pop-up menu UI used here is similar to the CustomMenuItemUI (from Example 1-28). It has a static create UI menu and no constructor. The pop-up menu is already stored as a protected member of the BasicPopupMenuUI parent class, so I can access it easily. The installUI( ) method is called right after the JPopupMenu is created, so this is the best place to put a call to setOpaque(false). For most L&Fs, this will make the component transparent.

That takes care of the pop-up menu, but what about the parent JPanel? The JPanel is created and initialized deep within the javax.swing.PopupFactory class, so it's pretty well out of reach. This is one place where having access to the JRE source code is invaluable. Without that, this entire hack would have been impossible to figure out. Fortunately, we have access to the finished JPopupMenu from within the getPopup method. I overrode that to call the superclass and then grab the newly minted parent of the pop-up menu and cast it to a JPanel. Now, I can finally set it to be transparent, too.

Test It Out

With your two custom UI classes in place, test them out with Example 1-30, which shows a frame containing two sets of menus and a few components. Before creating any components, the program installed the custom UI classes with two calls to UIManager.put( ).

Any time you want to override part of a L&F, you can use UIManager.put( ).

Example 1-30. Testing out the translucent menus

```
public class MenuTest {
    public static void main(String[] args) throws Exception {
        UIManager.put("PopupMenuUI","CustomPopupMenuUI");
        UIManager.put("MenuItemUI","CustomMenuItemUI");

        JFrame frame = new JFrame();
        JMenuBar mb = new JMenuBar();
        frame.setJMenuBar(mb);
        JMenu menu = new JMenu("File");
        mb.add(menu);
        menu.add(new JMenuItem("Open"));
        menu.add(new JMenuItem("Save"));
        menu.add(new JMenuItem("Close"));
        menu.add(new JMenuItem("Exit"));
        menu = new JMenu("Edit");
        mb.add(menu);
```

Example 1-30. Testing out the translucent menus (continued)

```
        menu.add(new JMenuItem("Cut"));
        menu.add(new JMenuItem("Copy"));
        menu.add(new JMenuItem("Paste"));
        menu.add(new JMenuItem("Paste Special.."));
        frame.getContentPane().setLayout(new BorderLayout());
        frame.getContentPane().add("North",new JButton("Button"));
        frame.getContentPane().add("Center",new JLabel("a label"));
        frame.getContentPane().add("South",new JCheckBox("checkbox"));
        frame.pack();
        frame.setSize(200,150);
        frame.show();
    }

}
```

With all of the code in place, you can compile it and get something that
looks like Figure 1-30.

Figure 1-30. Translucent menu

One bug you will notice is that after you open the menu and start moving the
cursor between menu items, the background won't shine through anymore.
This is because Swing, in an effort to speed up the UI, only repaints the parts
it knows have changed. It repaints the menu item, but not the frame contents below (the button and label, in this case) because it thinks they are
obscured by the menu item. Of course, the menu item is translucent, so the
components should shine through, but Swing doesn't know that. To fix the

problem, you'll need to develop a full repaint manager **[Hack #53]** that will force Swing to always repaint the entire component tree, instead of just the menu items. It's a bit slower, but worth it if you really want this effect:

```
UIManager.put("MenuItemUI","CustomMenuItemUI");
RepaintManager.setCurrentManager(new FullRepaintManager( ));
```

One more bug is that the menu must fit within the frame. There are two kinds of menus in Swing: heavyweight and lightweight. Lightweight menus are normal Swing components. Heavyweight menus, on the other hand, are drawn in their own top-level window. This means that there are two windows being drawn: one for the real frame and one for the menu. If you use heavyweight menus, the effect will stop completely because the windows themselves can't be transparent. Normally, Swing will use lightweight menus, but if the menu has to be drawn outside of the frame—which can happen if you have a small window or a really large menu—then it will switch to heavyweight menus automatically and nothing can switch it back until the application restarts. This means you should always make sure your menus fit inside of your windows.

Future Ideas

This hack shows just one example of how you can completely change a component's behavior by customizing its Look and Feel class. Java2D gives you the power to create a wide variety of graphical hacks. As an extension of this technique, you could try blurring the components underneath the menu or create a properly smoothed drop shadow.

Lists and Combos
Hacks 13–20

Lists are underrated and underappreciated, and developers who don't appreciate JLists often use JTables when they don't need to. But lists seem to be making a comeback in desktop applications, and with good reason. A lot of the data we deal with are single-dimension collections—search results, recent URLs, downloaded files, etc.—and by making the onscreen version of them more appealing and more usable, a list is the right way to present this data to the user.

HACK #13 Filter JLists
Make your 1,000-item list a lot more manageable.

One of the nicest things you can do with a large list is to make it manageable with a *filter box*. This is a text area that, as you type into it, removes list elements so that only those that contain the typed text are visible.

The hack to do this basically involves having a list model with two representations of its contents: everything that is in the list, and a subset with just the items to be displayed (i.e., those from the first list that match the filter). The model's get methods are then rewired to use only the second list.

The implementation in this hack, FilteredJList, is a single class with two inner subclasses: FilterModel and FilterField. The list owns the field, so a caller can create the JList fairly typically and then just ask for the field and add it wherever it makes sense in the layout.

Start by declaring FilteredJList as a subclass of JList, and provide a constructor and some convenience methods, as seen in Example 2-1.

Example 2-1. FilterList constructor and convenience methods

```java
public class FilteredJList extends JList {

    private FilterField filterField;
    private int DEFAULT_FIELD_WIDTH = 20;

    public FilteredJList( ) {
        super( );
        setModel (new FilterModel( ));
        filterField = new FilterField (DEFAULT_FIELD_WIDTH);
    }

    public void setModel (ListModel m) {
        if (! (m instanceof FilterModel))
            throw new IllegalArgumentException( );
        super.setModel (m);
    }

    public void addItem (Object o) {
        ((FilterModel)getModel( )).addElement (o);
    }

    public JTextField getFilterField( ) {
        return filterField;
    }
```

Notice that along with holding onto the FilterField, the JList also creates its own FilterModel in the constructor, and overrides setModel( ) to ensure that you can't push in an incompatible model. It also contains an addItem( ) method, which really just delegates to the FilterModel.

FilterModel, shown in Example 2-2, is where the magic happens.

Example 2-2. Inner class to provide a filtered model

```java
class FilterModel extends AbstractListModel {
    ArrayList items;
    ArrayList filterItems;
    public FilterModel( ) {
        super( );
        items = new ArrayList( );
        filterItems = new ArrayList( );
    }
    public Object getElementAt (int index) {
        if (index < filterItems.size( ))
            return filterItems.get (index);
        else
            return null;
    }
    public int getSize( ) {
        return filterItems.size( );
    }
```

Example 2-2. Inner class to provide a filtered model (continued)

```
    public void addElement (Object o) {
        items.add (o);
        refilter();
    }
    private void refilter() {
        filterItems.clear();
        String term = getFilterField().getText();
        for (int i=0; i<items.size(); i++)
            if (items.get(i).toString().indexOf(term, 0) != -1)
                filterItems.add (items.get(i));
        fireContentsChanged (this, 0, getSize());
    }
}
// FilterField inner class listed below
}
```

This model has two ArrayLists for its contents: items contains all the items that have been added to the model; filterItems contains only the items that match the filter. The getSize() and getElementAt() methods, required by ListModel, draw not from the real items list, but from the filterItems list. The filterItems list is reconstituted via calls to the refilter() method, which fires off a ListDataEvent to inform the JList that the contents have changed and require a repaint.

> The refilter() method works on the String representation of the list contents—if your objects are more sophisticated, you might need to adapt the matching logic; e.g., searching the content of email messages represented as objects.

There's also an addItem() method, patterned after the equivalent method in DefaultListModel that, unlike AbstractListModel, assumes mutability (i.e., the ability to add and remove list contents). A more complete implementation of this model would probably need to provide equivalents for all of DefaultListModel's add and remove methods. Notice that addItem() calls refilter() on each add, so that an added item is immediately added to the visible list, assuming that it matches the search term.

The FilterField, shown in Example 2-3, is fairly trivial, and it is responsible for forcing a refilter when its contents change.

Example 2-3. Text field that refilters the model on each keystroke

```
// inner class provides filter-by-keystroke field
class FilterField extends JTextField implements DocumentListener {
    public FilterField (int width) {
        super(width);
```

Example 2-3. Text field that refilters the model on each keystroke (continued)

```
        getDocument( ).addDocumentListener (this);
    }
    public void changedUpdate (DocumentEvent e) {
        ((FilterModel)getModel()).refilter( );
    }
    public void insertUpdate (DocumentEvent e) {
        ((FilterModel)getModel()).refilter( );
    }
    public void removeUpdate (DocumentEvent e) {
        ((FilterModel)getModel()).refilter( );
    }
}
```

The FilterField's DocumentListener calls for a refilter on each of the possible DocumentEvents. For efficiency, it might be faster for the model to provide a refilter method that starts with the filtered list and narrows it down further. This could be called by insertUpdate( ) because adding characters to the filter term can only make it more restrictive, meaning there is no point considering any items that aren't already matches.

To test the FilterJList, Example 2-4 shows a simple main( ) method that populates the list with some names and puts the list and its filter field in a JFrame.

Example 2-4. Simple test GUI for FilteredJList

```
public static void main (String[] args) {
    String[] listItems = {
        "Chris", "Joshua", "Daniel", "Michael",
        "Don", "Kimi", "Kelly", "Keagan"
    };
    JFrame frame = new JFrame ("FilteredJList");
    frame.getContentPane().setLayout (new BorderLayout( ));
    // populate list
    FilteredJList list = new FilteredJList( );
    for (int i=0; i<listItems.length; i++)
        list.addItem (listItems[i]);
    // add to gui
    JScrollPane pane =
        new JScrollPane (list,
                         ScrollPaneConstants.VERTICAL_SCROLLBAR_ALWAYS,
                         ScrollPaneConstants.HORIZONTAL_SCROLLBAR_NEVER);
    frame.getContentPane( ).add (pane, BorderLayout.CENTER);
    frame.getContentPane().add (list.getFilterField( ),
                                BorderLayout.NORTH);
    frame.pack( );
    frame.setVisible(true);
}
```

When run, all the list items are displayed initially, as in Figure 2-1.

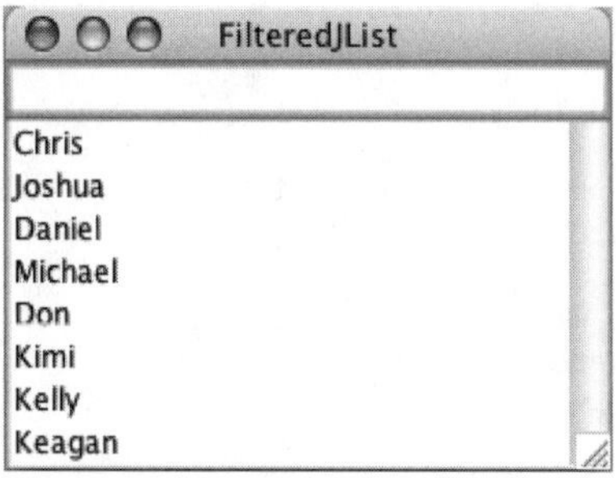

Figure 2-1. Unfiltered contents of a list

But when you type an uppercase *K* (the indexof search in refilter( ) is case-sensitive), the list immediately shrinks to three items, shown in Figure 2-2.

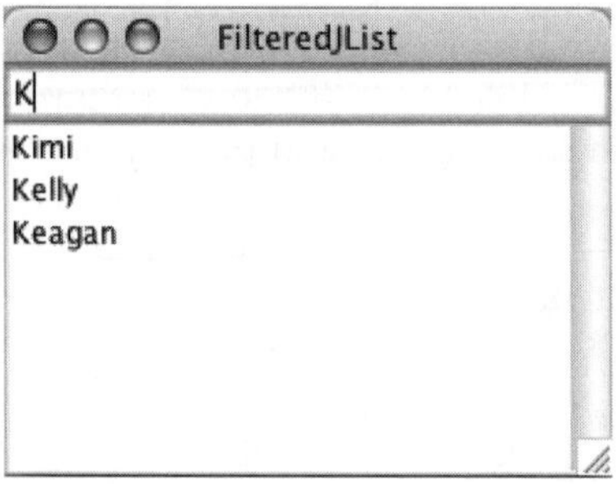

Figure 2-2. Filtering on a keystroke

The only matches for *K* are "Kimi," "Kelly," and "Keagan." Now type an *e*, and "Kimi" will be filtered out, as in Figure 2-3.

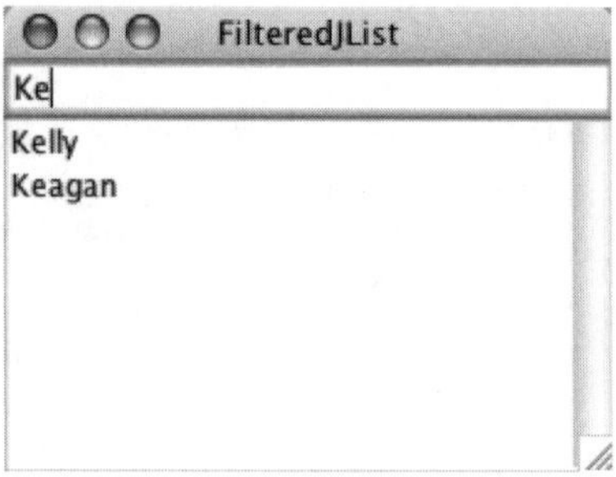

Figure 2-3. Refiltering on successive keystrokes

Add a Filter History

Remember previous searches and research with one click.

Chances are good that if you've searched for something once, it's important enough that you might well search for it again. In Apple's Safari browser, a search widget at the upper right has a little magnifying glass that remembers your last 10 searches. Click the magnifying glass and a pop up appears with the previous searches. Select one and it populates the field and does the search immediately.

Here's an implementation of the same idea, grafted onto the previous hack. In other words, this remembers previous filters. It doesn't remember every keystroke—why bother remembering the searches "J" and "Jo" when you're really just interested in "Joe"—and only adds a search term to the filter when the user presses return.

In the previous hack, you just needed to have a text field and a JList. Now a JButton needs to be attached to the text field, so the two are bundled together in the inner class FilterField. This class is responsible for:

- Telling the model to refilter on each keystroke in the JTextField, as before.
- Remembering the JTextField's contents as a saved search anytime the Return or Enter key is pressed.
- Catching clicks on the JButton and popping up a menu with previous searches.
- Populating the JTextField with a previous search when one is selected from the list. It doesn't need to explicitly tell the model to refilter because changing the text area will fire a DocumentEvent that is already accounted for by the JTextField's DocumentListener.

Example 2-5 shows the new FilterField class.

Example 2-5. List filtering component with text field and history button

```
class FilterField extends JComponent
    implements DocumentListener, ActionListener {
    LinkedList prevSearches;
    JTextField textField;
    JButton prevSearchButton;
    JPopupMenu prevSearchMenu;
    public FilterField (int width) {
        super( );
        setLayout(new BorderLayout( ));
        textField = new JTextField (width);
        textField.getDocument( ).addDocumentListener (this);
        textField.addActionListener (this);
```

Example 2-5. List filtering component with text field and history button (continued)

```
        prevSearchButton =
            new JButton (new ImageIcon ("mag-glass.png"));
        prevSearchButton.setBorder(null);
        prevSearchButton.addMouseListener (new MouseAdapter() {
                public void mousePressed (MouseEvent me) {
                    popMenu (me.getX(), me.getY());
                }
            });
        add (prevSearchButton, BorderLayout.WEST);
        add (textField, BorderLayout.CENTER);
        prevSearches = new LinkedList ();
    }
    public void popMenu (int x, int y) {
        prevSearchMenu = new JPopupMenu();
        Iterator it = prevSearches.iterator();
        while (it.hasNext())
            prevSearchMenu.add (
                new PrevSearchAction(it.next().toString()));
        prevSearchMenu.show (prevSearchButton, x, y);
    }
    public void actionPerformed (ActionEvent e) {
        // called on return/enter, adds term to prevSearches
        if (e.getSource() == textField) {
            prevSearches.addFirst (textField.getText());
            if (prevSearches.size() > 10)
                prevSearches.removeLast();
        }
    }
    public void changedUpdate (DocumentEvent e) {
        ((FilterModel)getModel()).refilter();
    }
    public void insertUpdate (DocumentEvent e) {
        ((FilterModel)getModel()).refilter();
    }
    public void removeUpdate (DocumentEvent e) {
        ((FilterModel)getModel()).refilter();
    }

}
```

Notice how this version of the class uses a MouseListener on the JButton instead of an ActionListener. Either will work, but the MouseEvent provides the location of the mouse click as a Point in the JButton's coordinate space, which is useful for showing the pop-up menu at the exact point of the mouse click. There is an ActionListener implementation, but it's for the JTextField so that when the user presses the Return key, the filter text is saved to the JPopupMenu (and, if there are more than 10 items, the oldest saved search is removed).

The items in the JPopupMenu are instances of PrevSearchAction, which subclasses Swing's Action. This is convenient because they provide a String representation to be shown in the pop-up menu, yet get an actionPerformed( ) when their menu item is selected, which gives them a chance to reset the filter text. Here's what the PrevSearchAction inner class looks like:

```
class PrevSearchAction extends AbstractAction {
    String term;
    public PrevSearchAction (String s) {
        term = s;
        putValue (Action.NAME, term);
    }
    public String toString( ) { return term; }
    public void actionPerformed (ActionEvent e) {
        getFilterField( ).textField.setText (term);
    }
}
```

When a previous search is recalled, it looks like Figure 2-4.

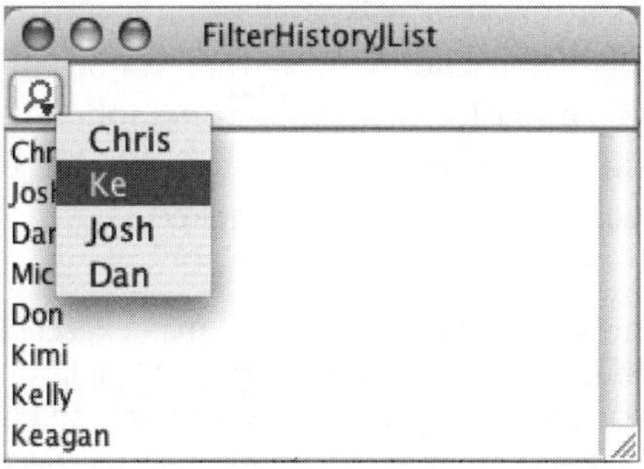

Figure 2-4. Pop-up menu with previous searches

And when the mouse clicks on one of the menu items, the field is populated and the list is filtered. Figure 2-5 shows the result.

Figure 2-5. List filtered by pop-up selection

The general idea of this pop up can be modified to work in similar ways for different kinds of searches, such as popping up a list of which field the search is to be applied to if the list items are complex. An example of this is a mail program in which the pop up might show the options Subject, To, From, etc., meaning that the search is limited to finding the specified term in only the selected field.

HACK #15   Make JLists Checkable

Avoid losing 50 selections to an unshifted click.

One horrible UI problem is dealing with vast collections of things that need to be presented to the user and made selectable. If, like me, you've ever had 1,000 emails in your inbox, you know what I mean. Worse, what if you pick a bunch of items to delete, but your finger slips off the key used for multi-selection (Alt on Windows, Command on the Mac, etc.) and you lose all of your previous selections? Overriding the native selection behavior can make this situation somewhat more palatable.

Because a list like this behaves differently than a normal list, it should look different, too, so I've opted for a checkbox metaphor. Each item is shown with a checkbox, and as you click more items, they get checked, and if you select an already-checked item, it gets unchecked.

> This turns out to be a little harder than expected. I once did it without JList, creating my own scrolling layout of JPanels and faking the list behavior. It turned up a funny Swing bug because I was using GridBagLayout for the fake list, and it started totally bombing out after about 500 items were added to the list. This was because GridBagLayout has a bug where it can't have more than 512 rows. Considering the bug (number 4254022 on the Java Bug Parade) was filed in 1999 and is still open, I'm figuring it won't get fixed by the time you read this.

The basis of the checkable list is a JList. The tricky part here is that there isn't a way (that I've found) to steal the mouse clicks from the JList and consume them before the normal calls to the ListSelectionModel are made. Instead, the strategy is to set up a ListSelectionListener and just fix everything after JList has done its thing.

To implement the checkbox functionality, subclass JList and give it a custom ListSelectionListener and a ListCellRenderer. A complete listing is shown in Example 2-6.

Example 2-6. A checkbox-metaphor JList

```java
public class CheckBoxJList extends JList
    implements ListSelectionListener {

    static Color listForeground, listBackground;
    static {
        UIDefaults uid = UIManager.getLookAndFeel().getDefaults();
        listForeground = uid.getColor ("List.foreground");
        listBackground = uid.getColor ("List.background");
    }

    HashSet selectionCache = new HashSet();
    int toggleIndex = -1;
    boolean toggleWasSelected;

    public CheckBoxJList() {
        super();
        setCellRenderer (new CheckBoxListCellRenderer());
        addListSelectionListener (this);
    }

// valueChanged() listing below

    public static void main (String[] args) {
        JList list = new CheckBoxJList ();
        DefaultListModel defModel = new DefaultListModel();
        list.setModel (defModel);
        String[] listItems = {
            "Chris", "Joshua", "Daniel", "Michael",
            "Don", "Kimi", "Kelly", "Keagan"
        };
        Iterator it = Arrays.asList(listItems).iterator();
        while (it.hasNext())
            defModel.addElement (it.next());
        // show list
        JScrollPane scroller =
            new JScrollPane (list,
                            ScrollPaneConstants.VERTICAL_SCROLLBAR_ALWAYS,
                            ScrollPaneConstants.HORIZONTAL_SCROLLBAR_NEVER);
        JFrame frame = new JFrame ("Checkbox JList");
        frame.getContentPane().add (scroller);
        frame.pack();
        frame.setVisible(true);
    }

}
```

There are two important sections to consider. The first is the valueChanged()
method that implements ListSelectionListener. The following list describes
what happens in that method.

1. Only react if `ListSelectionEvent.isValueAdjusting()` returns false. If it's true, then the event is part of a series—perhaps the user is shift-dragging over several items to multiselect them—and you don't want to do anything until the series of events has completed.

2. Remove the `ListSelectionListener` so that changes to the list made by your code don't fire off events, which would lead to a recursive, stack-blowing fiasco.

3. Cache all the selections that resulted from `JList`'s handling of the event. These will be added or removed from the final selections later.

4. Reselect all the items that were selected before the `valueChanged()` call.

5. Go through the new selections and add them to the selection if they weren't selected before. On the other hand, if they were selected previously, deselect them.

6. Cache all these selections for the next call to `valueChanged()`.

7. Add the `ListSelectionListener` again.

The listing for `valueChanged` is shown in Example 2-7.

Example 2-7. A ListSelectionListener for the checkable JList

```java
public void valueChanged (ListSelectionEvent lse) {
    if (! lse.getValueIsAdjusting()) {
        removeListSelectionListener (this);

        // determine if this selection has added or removed items
        HashSet newSelections = new HashSet();
        int size = getModel().getSize();
        for (int i=0; i<size; i++) {
            if (getSelectionModel().isSelectedIndex(i)) {
                newSelections.add (new Integer(i));
            }
        }

        // turn on everything that was selected previously
        Iterator it = selectionCache.iterator();
        while (it.hasNext()) {
            int index = ((Integer) it.next()).intValue();
            getSelectionModel().addSelectionInterval(index, index);
        }

        // add or remove the delta
        it = newSelections.iterator();
        while (it.hasNext()) {
            Integer nextInt = (Integer) it.next();
            int index = nextInt.intValue();
            if (selectionCache.contains (nextInt))
                getSelectionModel().removeSelectionInterval (index, index);
```

Example 2-7. A ListSelectionListener for the checkable JList (continued)

```
        else
            getSelectionModel().addSelectionInterval (index, index);
    }

    // save selections for next time
    selectionCache.clear();
    for (int i=0; i<size; i++) {
        if (getSelectionModel().isSelectedIndex(i)) {
            selectionCache.add (new Integer(i));
        }
    }

    addListSelectionListener (this);
    }
}
```

The other important part of this class is a ListCellRenderer that shows the
list items with checkboxes, and which is used as a visual cue that the list has
checkbox-like behavior. Aside from adding a checkbox to the renderer component and setting its state appropriately, you should hack the coloring of
the cell to avoid highlighting (because you are already using checkboxes).
The key here is to grab the platform's colors for unselected list cell fore-
grounds and backgrounds, which you can get via the UIDefaults class and
the property names List.foreground and List.background. This cell renderer
always resets the list cells to these unselected colors, leaving just the checkboxes as an indication of what's selected—and does it in the correct colors.
The renderer is implemented as an inner class and is listed in Example 2-8.

Example 2-8. ListCellRenderer for checkbox-based JList

```
class CheckBoxListCellRenderer extends JComponent
    implements ListCellRenderer {
    DefaultListCellRenderer defaultComp;
    JCheckBox checkbox;
    public CheckBoxListCellRenderer() {
        setLayout (new BorderLayout());
        defaultComp = new DefaultListCellRenderer();
        checkbox = new JCheckBox();
        add (checkbox, BorderLayout.WEST);
        add (defaultComp, BorderLayout.CENTER);
    }

    public Component getListCellRendererComponent(JList list,
                                    Object  value,
                                    int index,
                                    boolean isSelected,
                                    boolean cellHasFocus){
```

Example 2-8. ListCellRenderer for checkbox-based JList (continued)

```
        defaultComp.getListCellRendererComponent (list, value, index,
                                            isSelected, cellHasFocus);
        checkbox.setSelected (isSelected);
        Component[] comps = getComponents( );
        for (int i=0; i<comps.length; i++) {
            comps[i].setForeground (listForeground);
            comps[i].setBackground (listBackground);
        }
        return this;
    }
}
```

When you click on items in the list, their selection state is shown with checkboxes, as seen in Figure 2-6.

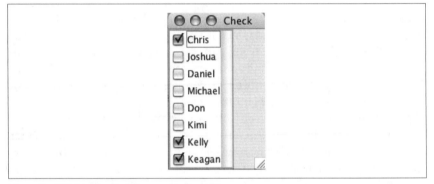

Figure 2-6. Using the checkbox-metaphor JList

Notice how the checkboxes are all you need to see what's selected. In an early version of this hack, I went out of my way to maintain the usual selection colors and it looked lousy, probably because there were two competing metaphors to show the selection: the highlight and the checkbox. Since this hack totally changes how the JList works, it's appropriate to radically change its appearance, too.

Make Different List Items Look Different
HACK #16

An in-progress download shouldn't look like a completed one.

What made me love lists again were the OmniWeb browser and (later) Safari—particularly, their download managers. By way of negative example, take the download manager for Internet Explorer 5 for Mac...please. This GUI was a table of filenames, URLs, sizes, etc., with columns not even intelligently resized for their widths. OmniWeb, on the other hand, showed a running download with a progress bar, and a finished download with the file location and file size. Safari goes a step further with context-appropriate buttons: an X to cancel an in-progress download, a magnifying glass to locate an already-downloaded file, etc. But it's the same idea: *different things shouldn't look the same.*

To do this in Swing, you need a hack that goes against everything in all the other Swing books: you need to stop subclassing JComponent when you write a ListCellRenderer. Instead, delegate the getListCellRendererComponent( ) call to one of several components, choosing whichever best represents the item to be rendered.

In fact, the whole tradition of subclassing JComponent for ListCellRenderers is a pretty hateful practice because they're not really used as Components anyway! They're certainly not added to the JList. Instead, a list cell is rendered off screen and those pixels are blitted to the JList. So, provided that what you return in getListCellRendererComponent is what you want the cell to look like, it really doesn't matter how you get there.

By way of demonstration, this hack shows the items in a given directory with different layouts, depending on the file type. All of the cells use an icon on the left, with a name in bold at the top of a two-line layout. However, if the item is a folder, the bottom line contains a count of the children in that folder. If the item is a text file—it ends with one of the various extensions associated with text files (e.g., *.txt*, *.html*, *.java*)—then there's a different layout that uses two cells on the second line to show file size and word count. And if the item is determined to be an image file, then a layout with room for a little two-row image icon on the right is used.

So, there are four different prototypes, and getListCellRendererComponent( ) needs to choose one, set its fields and highlight colors, and return it. Example 2-9 is quite long, in part because of the icky GridBagLayout work required to make the four prototypes look interesting. This is one time when I really wish I had a visual Swing GUI builder.

Example 2-9. A JList with multiple cell-rendering layouts

```
public class PolymorphicJList extends JList {

    static Color listForeground, listBackground,
        listSelectionForeground, listSelectionBackground;
    static {
        UIDefaults uid = UIManager.getLookAndFeel().getDefaults();
        listForeground  =  uid.getColor ("List.foreground");
        listBackground  =  uid.getColor ("List.background");
        listSelectionForeground = uid.getColor ("List.selectionForeground");
        listSelectionBackground = uid.getColor ("List.selectionBackground");
    }
```

Example 2-9. A JList with multiple cell-rendering layouts (continued)

```java
ImageIcon fileIcon, textFileIcon, directoryIcon,
    imageFileIcon, pngFileIcon, gifFileIcon,
    jpegFileIcon;
JComponent fileCellPrototype, textCellPrototype,
    imageCellPrototype, directoryCellPrototype;
JLabel fileNameLabel, textNameLabel,
    directoryNameLabel, imageNameLabel,
    fileSizeLabel,
    textSizeLabel, textWordCountLabel,
    directoryCountLabel,
    imageSizeLabel, imageIconLabel;

public PolymorphicJList (File dir) {
    super();
    buildPrototypeCells();
    setCellRenderer (new PolyRenderer());
    setModel (new DefaultListModel());
    if (! dir.isDirectory())
        dir = new File (dir.getParent());
    buildModelFromDir (dir);
}

public static void main (String[] args) {
    File dir = new File (".");
    if (args.length > 0)
        dir = new File (args[0]);
    JList list = new PolymorphicJList (dir);
    JScrollPane pain =
        new JScrollPane (list,
                        ScrollPaneConstants.VERTICAL_SCROLLBAR_ALWAYS,
                        ScrollPaneConstants.HORIZONTAL_SCROLLBAR_NEVER);
    JFrame frame = new JFrame ("PolymorphicJList");
    frame.getContentPane().add (pain);
    frame.pack();
    frame.setVisible(true);
}

protected void buildModelFromDir (File dir) {
    File[] files = dir.listFiles();
    DefaultListModel mod = (DefaultListModel) getModel();
    for (int i=0; i<files.length; i++) {
        if (isTextFile (files[i]))
            mod.addElement (new TextFileItem (files[i]));
        else if (isImageFile (files [i]))
            mod.addElement (new ImageFileItem (files[i]));
        else if (files[i].isDirectory())
            mod.addElement (new DirectoryItem (files[i]));
        else
            mod.addElement (new FileItem (files[i]));
    }
}
```

Example 2-9. A JList with multiple cell-rendering layouts (continued)

```
protected boolean isImageFile(File f) {
    if (f.isDirectory())
        return false;
    String name = f.getName();
    return name.endsWith (".gif") || name.endsWith (".GIF") ||
        name.endsWith (".jpg") || name.endsWith (".JPG") ||
        name.endsWith (".jpeg") || name.endsWith (".JPEG") ||
        name.endsWith (".bmp") || name.endsWith (".BMP") ||
        name.endsWith (".png") || name.endsWith (".PNG");
}

protected boolean isTextFile(File f) {
    if (f.isDirectory())
        return false;
    String name = f.getName();
    return name.endsWith (".txt") || name.endsWith (".html") ||
        name.endsWith (".xml") || name.endsWith (".xhtml") ||
        name.endsWith (".java") || name.endsWith (".c") ||
        name.endsWith (".cpp") || name.endsWith (".c++") ||
        name.endsWith (".m") || name.endsWith (".h");
}

protected void buildIcons() {
    String SEP = System.getProperty ("file.separator");
    fileIcon = new ImageIcon ("images" + SEP + "generic.gif");
    textFileIcon = new ImageIcon ("images" + SEP + "text.gif");
    directoryIcon = new ImageIcon ("images" + SEP + "folder.gif");
    imageFileIcon = new ImageIcon ("images" + SEP + "image.gif");
    pngFileIcon = new ImageIcon ("images" + SEP + "png.gif");
    gifFileIcon = new ImageIcon ("images" + SEP + "gif.gif");
    jpegFileIcon = new ImageIcon ("images" + SEP + "jpeg.gif");
}

protected void buildPrototypeCells() {
    buildIcons();
    fileCellPrototype = new JPanel();
    fileCellPrototype.setLayout (new GridBagLayout());
    addWithGridBag (new JLabel(fileIcon), fileCellPrototype,
                    0, 0, 1, 2,
                    GridBagConstraints.WEST,
                    GridBagConstraints.BOTH, 0, 0);
    fileNameLabel = new JLabel();
    Font defaultLabelFont = fileNameLabel.getFont();
    Font nameFont =
        defaultLabelFont.deriveFont (Font.BOLD,
                                    defaultLabelFont.getSize()+2);
    fileNameLabel.setFont (nameFont);
    addWithGridBag (fileNameLabel, fileCellPrototype,
                    1, 0, 1, 1,
                    GridBagConstraints.NORTH,
                    GridBagConstraints.HORIZONTAL, 1, 0);
```

Example 2-9. A JList with multiple cell-rendering layouts (continued)

```
        fileSizeLabel = new JLabel();
        addWithGridBag (fileSizeLabel, fileCellPrototype,
                        1, 1, 1, 1,
                        GridBagConstraints.SOUTH,
                        GridBagConstraints.HORIZONTAL, 1, 0);
        opacify (fileCellPrototype);
        // text file
        textCellPrototype = new JPanel();
        textCellPrototype.setLayout (new GridBagLayout());
        addWithGridBag (new JLabel(textFileIcon), textCellPrototype,
                        0, 0, 1, 2,
                        GridBagConstraints.WEST,
                        GridBagConstraints.BOTH, 0, 0);
        textNameLabel = new JLabel();
        textNameLabel.setFont (nameFont);
        addWithGridBag (textNameLabel, textCellPrototype,
                        1, 0, 2, 1,
                        GridBagConstraints.NORTH,
                        GridBagConstraints.HORIZONTAL, 1, 0);
        textSizeLabel = new JLabel();
        textWordCountLabel = new JLabel();
        addWithGridBag (textSizeLabel, textCellPrototype,
                        1, 1, 1, 1,
                        GridBagConstraints.NORTH,
                        GridBagConstraints.HORIZONTAL, 0, 0);
        addWithGridBag (textWordCountLabel, textCellPrototype,
                        2, 1, 1, 1,
                        GridBagConstraints.SOUTH,
                        GridBagConstraints.HORIZONTAL, 1, 0);

        opacify (textCellPrototype);
        // directory
        directoryCellPrototype = new JPanel();
        directoryCellPrototype.setLayout (new GridBagLayout());
        addWithGridBag (new JLabel(directoryIcon), directoryCellPrototype,
                        0, 0, 1, 2,
                        GridBagConstraints.WEST,
                        GridBagConstraints.BOTH, 0, 0);
        directoryNameLabel = new JLabel();
        directoryNameLabel.setFont (nameFont);
        addWithGridBag (directoryNameLabel, directoryCellPrototype,
                        1, 0, 1, 1,
                        GridBagConstraints.NORTH,
                        GridBagConstraints.HORIZONTAL, 1, 0);
        directoryCountLabel = new JLabel();
        addWithGridBag (directoryCountLabel, directoryCellPrototype,
                        1, 1, 1, 1,
                        GridBagConstraints.SOUTH,
                        GridBagConstraints.HORIZONTAL, 1, 0);
        opacify (directoryCellPrototype);
```

Example 2-9. A JList with multiple cell-rendering layouts (continued)

```
        // image
        imageCellPrototype = new JPanel( );
        imageCellPrototype.setLayout (new GridBagLayout( ));
        addWithGridBag (new JLabel(imageFileIcon), imageCellPrototype,
                        0, 0, 1, 2,
                        GridBagConstraints.WEST,
                        GridBagConstraints.BOTH, 0, 0);
        imageNameLabel = new JLabel( );
        imageNameLabel.setFont (nameFont);
        addWithGridBag (imageNameLabel, imageCellPrototype,
                        1, 0, 1, 1,
                        GridBagConstraints.NORTH,
                        GridBagConstraints.HORIZONTAL, 1, 0);
        imageSizeLabel = new JLabel( );
        addWithGridBag (imageSizeLabel, imageCellPrototype,
                        1, 1, 1, 1,
                        GridBagConstraints.SOUTH, GridBagConstraints.HORIZONTAL,
                        1, 0);
        imageIconLabel = new JLabel( );
        addWithGridBag (imageIconLabel, imageCellPrototype,
                        2, 0, 1, 2,
                        GridBagConstraints.EAST,
                        GridBagConstraints.VERTICAL, 0, 0);
        opacify (imageCellPrototype);
    }

    private void addWithGridBag (Component comp, Container cont,
                                 int x, int y,
                                 int width, int height,
                                 int anchor, int fill,
                                 int weightx, int weighty) {
        GridBagConstraints gbc = new GridBagConstraints( );
        gbc.gridx = x;
        gbc.gridy = y;
        gbc.gridwidth = width;
        gbc.gridheight = height;
        gbc.anchor = anchor;
        gbc.fill = fill;
        gbc.weightx = weightx;
        gbc.weighty = weighty;
        cont.add (comp, gbc);
    }

    private void opacify (Container prototype) {
        Component[] comps = prototype.getComponents( );
        for (int i=0; i<comps.length; i++) {
            if (comps[i] instanceof JComponent)
                ((JComponent)comps[i]).setOpaque(true);
        }
    }
```

Example 2-9. A JList with multiple cell-rendering layouts (continued)

```
    // FileItem, ImageFileItem, TextFileItem, and
    // DirectoryItem classes listed below

    // PolyRenderer class listed below

}
```

Whew! That's a mighty big hack. The main `PolymorphicListCellRenderer`
class builds the prototype cells with help from an `addWithGridBag( )` method
to make the layout take only a hundred lines instead of a thousand. It also
calls `setOpaque( )` on every child of the prototype containers, which ensures
that setting the background color will work for highlighting a cell. It then
builds the list model from the directory passed to the list constructor, iterating over the items in the directory and creating appropriate `FileItems`,
`ImageItems`, etc., for each one. It also holds onto some file-type icons (a
folder icon, a text file icon) that the renderer will need.

In Example 2-10, `FileItem`, `ImageFileItem`, `DirectoryItem`, and `TextFileItem`
are inner classes that are used as the contents of the list model. The constructor for each one initializes the values that will be shown by the renderer, such as word count or the little icon image. The renderer can do
`instanceof` on the value it's asked to render, in order to determine which
prototype to use for which kind of item.

Example 2-10. Objects to represent contents of list model

```java
class FileItem extends Object {
    File file;
    public FileItem (File f) {
        file = f;
    }
}

class ImageFileItem extends FileItem {
    ImageIcon icon;
    public ImageFileItem (File f) {
        super(f);
        initIcon( );
    }
    void initIcon( ) {
        icon = new ImageIcon (file.getPath( ));
        // scale to 32 pix in largest dimension
        Image img = icon.getImage( );
        float factor = 1.0f;
        if (img.getWidth(null) > img.getHeight(null))
            factor = Math.min (32f / img.getWidth(null), 1.0f);
```

Example 2-10. Objects to represent contents of list model (continued)

```
        else
            factor = Math.min (32f / img.getHeight(null), 1.0f);
        Image scaledImage =
            img.getScaledInstance ((int) (img.getWidth(null) * factor),
                                   (int) (img.getHeight(null) * factor),
                                   Image.SCALE_FAST);
        icon.setImage(scaledImage);
    }
}

class DirectoryItem extends FileItem {
    int childCount;
    public DirectoryItem (File f) {
        super(f);
        initChildCount();
    }
    public int getChildCount() { return childCount; }
    void initChildCount () {
        if (! file.isDirectory())
            childCount = -1;
        else
            childCount = file.listFiles().length;
        System.out.println (file.getPath() + ": " + childCount + " items");
    }
}

class TextFileItem extends FileItem {
    int wordCount = -1;
    public TextFileItem (File f) {
        super(f);
        initWordCount();
    }
    public int getWordCount() { return wordCount; }
    protected void initWordCount() {
        try {
            StreamTokenizer izer =
                new StreamTokenizer (new BufferedReader
                    (new FileReader(file)));
            while (izer.nextToken() != StreamTokenizer.TT_EOF)
                wordCount++;
        } catch (Exception e) {
            e.printStackTrace();
            wordCount = -1;
        }
        System.out.println (file.getPath() + ": " + wordCount + " words");
    }
}
```

The PolyRenderer inner class is, of course, responsible for the cell rendering. When it's passed a list item to render, it determines the class of the item and picks an appropriate prototype to modify. It sets the text or images of the children of that prototype, and it sets foreground and background colors on all the children depending on the selection state. PolyRenderer is listed in Example 2-11.

Example 2-11. Inner class to render list items based on different prototypes

```
class PolyRenderer extends Object
    implements ListCellRenderer {

    public Component getListCellRendererComponent(JList list,
                                                  Object value,
                                                  int index,
                                                  boolean isSelected,
                                                  boolean cellHasFocus) {
        if (value instanceof DirectoryItem) {
            DirectoryItem item = (DirectoryItem) value;
            directoryNameLabel.setText (item.file.getName());
            directoryCountLabel.setText (item.getChildCount() + " items");
            setColorsForSelectionState (directoryCellPrototype, isSelected);
            return directoryCellPrototype;
        } else if (value instanceof TextFileItem) {
            TextFileItem item = (TextFileItem) value;
            // populate values
            textNameLabel.setText (item.file.getName());
            textSizeLabel.setText (item.file.length() + " bytes  ");
            textWordCountLabel.setText (item.getWordCount() + " words");
            setColorsForSelectionState (textCellPrototype, isSelected);
            return textCellPrototype;
        } else if (value instanceof ImageFileItem) {
            ImageFileItem item = (ImageFileItem) value;
            // pouplate values
            imageNameLabel.setText (item.file.getName());
            imageSizeLabel.setText (item.file.length() + " bytes");
            imageIconLabel.setIcon (item.icon);
            setColorsForSelectionState (imageCellPrototype, isSelected);
            return imageCellPrototype;
        } else {
            FileItem item = (FileItem) value;
            // pouplate values
            fileNameLabel.setText (item.file.getName());
            fileSizeLabel.setText (item.file.length() + " bytes");
            setColorsForSelectionState (fileCellPrototype, isSelected);
            return fileCellPrototype;
        }
    }
    private void setColorsForSelectionState (Container prototype,
                                             boolean isSelected) {
```

Example 2-11. Inner class to render list items based on different prototypes (continued)

```
        Component[] comps = prototype.getComponents( );
        for (int i=0; i<comps.length; i++) {
            if (isSelected) {
                comps[i].setForeground (listSelectionForeground);
                comps[i].setBackground (listSelectionBackground);
            } else {
                comps[i].setForeground (listForeground);
                comps[i].setBackground (listBackground);
            }
        }
    }
}
```

If you supply an argument, the main( ) method will assume it to be the path to a directory and will show that directory's contents in the list. If you don't supply an argument, the current directory is assumed. Figure 2-7 displays what it looks like when I show my home directory in the PolymorphicJList.

Figure 2-7. Showing my home directory as a JList with multiple cell layouts

As you can see, there's an obvious difference between the layout and contents for the folders, text files, and generic files. Because I didn't have any pictures in my home folder at the time, I reran the demo and pointed into one of my iPhoto folders, which created the list shown in Figure 2-8.

As you can see, image files get a little icon of their contents, while folders just show their item count. They look different because they *are* different.

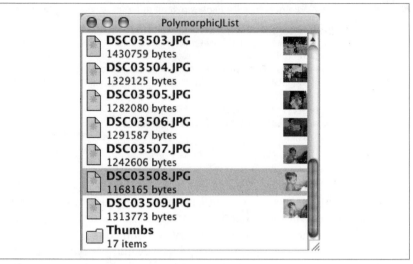

Figure 2-8. Showing a directory of images with special cell layout

Reorder a JList with Drag-and-Drop

Let users put things where they want.

You may be so used to immutable lists that the idea of reordering a list with drag-and-drop seems unnatural. The first time I saw it—rearranging the order of network devices in Mac OS X to establish a priority (e.g., try Ethernet, then wireless, then modem)—I thought it was kind of odd. In fact, Apple felt it necessary to put a label on the list to tell users they could drag-and-drop the list items to rearrange them. Now that I'm used to it, it's totally cool, and I'd like to see it done in more places.

To implement this functionality in a JList, you basically just have to implement the full set of AWT drag-and-drop interfaces because the list will be both the source of the drag and the target of the drop. The other thing you need to do is to use some cell rendering tricks to provide a visual cue as to where the drop will occur.

The ReorderableJList, shown in Example 2-12, is a JList that uses a DefaultListModel, which is mutable for the obvious reason that it will need to change in response to drag-and-drops. The bulk of it is concerned with implementing the drag-and-drop interfaces DragSourceListener, DropTargetListener, and DragGestureListener. It has an inner class implementing Tranferable to hold the item being dropped, although this isn't absolutely necessary. I could have just held the dragged item in an instance variable and nulled the Transferable in the drag-and-drop calls, but it doesn't hurt to do it the nice way.

Example 2-12. A JList that can be reordered with drag-and-drop

```java
public class ReorderableJList extends JList
    implements DragSourceListener, DropTargetListener, DragGestureListener {

    static DataFlavor localObjectFlavor;
    static {
        try {
            localObjectFlavor =
                new DataFlavor (DataFlavor.javaJVMLocalObjectMimeType);
        } catch (ClassNotFoundException cnfe) { cnfe.printStackTrace( ); }
    }
    static DataFlavor[] supportedFlavors = { localObjectFlavor };
    DragSource dragSource;
    DropTarget dropTarget;
    Object dropTargetCell;
    int draggedIndex = -1;

    public ReorderableJList ( ) {
        super( );
        setCellRenderer (new ReorderableListCellRenderer( ));
        setModel (new DefaultListModel( ));
        dragSource = new DragSource( );
        DragGestureRecognizer dgr =
            dragSource.createDefaultDragGestureRecognizer (this,
                                        DnDConstants.ACTION_MOVE,
                                                            this);
        dropTarget = new DropTarget (this, this);
    }

    // DragGestureListener
    public void dragGestureRecognized (DragGestureEvent dge) {
        System.out.println ("dragGestureRecognized");
        // find object at this x,y
        Point clickPoint = dge.getDragOrigin( );
        int index = locationToIndex(clickPoint);
        if (index == -1)
            return;
        Object target = getModel( ).getElementAt(index);
        Transferable trans = new RJLTransferable (target);
        draggedIndex = index;
        dragSource.startDrag (dge,Cursor.getDefaultCursor( ),
                            trans, this);
    }
    // DragSourceListener events
    public void dragDropEnd (DragSourceDropEvent dsde) {
        System.out.println ("dragDropEnd( )");
        dropTargetCell = null;
        draggedIndex = -1;
        repaint( );
    }
```

Example 2-12. A JList that can be reordered with drag-and-drop (continued)

```
    public void dragEnter (DragSourceDragEvent dsde) {}
    public void dragExit (DragSourceEvent dse) {}
    public void dragOver (DragSourceDragEvent dsde) {}
    public void dropActionChanged (DragSourceDragEvent dsde) {}
    // DropTargetListener events
    public void dragEnter (DropTargetDragEvent dtde) {
        System.out.println ("dragEnter");
        if (dtde.getSource( ) != dropTarget)
            dtde.rejectDrag( );
        else {
            dtde.acceptDrag(DnDConstants.ACTION_COPY_OR_MOVE);
            System.out.println ("accepted dragEnter");
        }

    }
    public void dragExit (DropTargetEvent dte) {}
    // dragOver( ) listed below
    // drop( ) listed below
    public void dropActionChanged (DropTargetDragEvent dtde) {}

    // main( ) method to test - listed below

    // RJLTransferable listing below

    // ReorderableListCellRendering listing below
}
```

The constructor creates the list model and sets the cell renderer (an inner class that will be described soon) and creates a DragGestureRecognizer to react to whatever input is judged by the host platform to be a drag (usually clicking and holding down the mouse button while then moving the mouse). It also creates a DragSource and a DropTarget.

When a drag begins, dragGestureRecognized( ) gets called. Your responsibility at this point is to start the drag by creating a Transferable and handing it to the DragSource object via startDrag( ). In this case, you can use the DragGestureEvent to get a Point, from which you can figure out which list item was clicked on. You can get the Object from the model, but the DragSource wants it to be wrapped by a Transferable. Normally, Transferable is used in drag-and-drop to negotiate with the DropTarget on a DataFlavor, and it can express the transferred data. Of course, much of that is irrelevant in this case because the list is already perfectly capable of handling the object, considering the list already had it before the drag began. For this demo, I've created a fairly trivial Transferable, called RJLTransferable, which only knows how to represent plain old Java objects (usually called POJOs). RJLTransferable is shown in Example 2-13.

Example 2-13. Simple Transferable object for a reorderable JList

```
class RJLTransferable implements Transferable {
    Object object;
    public RJLTransferable (Object o) {
        object = o;
    }
    public Object getTransferData(DataFlavor df)
        throws UnsupportedFlavorException, IOException {
        if (isDataFlavorSupported (df))
            return object;
        else
            throw new UnsupportedFlavorException(df);
    }
    public boolean isDataFlavorSupported (DataFlavor df) {
        return (df.equals (localObjectFlavor));
    }
    public DataFlavor[] getTransferDataFlavors () {
        return supportedFlavors;
    }
}
```

With the drag underway, most of the DragSourceListener methods are irrelevant. What you're interested in is the DropTargetListener methods. First, there's dragOver( )—listed in Example 2-14—which indicates a drag-in-progress over your component. In this case, you want to do two things. First, if the source of the drag isn't this object itself, reject the drag—this code is only for drag-and-drop within the JList, not for accepting drops from other components in your GUI. Second, you need to figure out which list item the drag is hovering over by getting a Point from DropTargetDragEvent.getLocation( ), translating it to an index with JList.locationToIndex( ), and then getting that item from the model. Save that target cell to the instance variable dropTargetCell and then call repaint( ), which will give the cell renderer a chance to animate the drop.

Example 2-14. Handling drag-over events in a reorderable JList

```
public void dragOver (DropTargetDragEvent dtde) {
    // figure out which cell it's over, no drag to self
    if (dtde.getSource( ) != dropTarget)
        dtde.rejectDrag( );
    Point dragPoint = dtde.getLocation( );
    int index = locationToIndex (dragPoint);
    if (index == -1)
        dropTargetCell = null;
    else
        dropTargetCell = getModel( ).getElementAt(index);
    repaint( );
}
```

The ReorderableListCellRenderer, shown in Example 2-15, checks this instance variable to see if the value it is passed is the dropTargetCell. If it is, it sets a boolean called isTargetCell. You can use this in an overridden paintComponent( ) method to paint a line in the component's top inset. When the list is repainted, which will happen every time the mouse moves over the JList during a drag, the cell that you're dragging over will draw a line at the top of itself to indicate that the drop will put the dragged item before this one.

Example 2-15. Custom cell renderer to animate potential drops on a reorderable JList

```
class ReorderableListCellRenderer
    extends DefaultListCellRenderer {
    boolean isTargetCell;
    boolean isLastItem;
    public ReorderableListCellRenderer( ) {
        super( );
    }
    public Component getListCellRendererComponent (JList list,
                                              Object value,
                                              int index,
                                              boolean isSelected,
                                              boolean hasFocus) {
        isTargetCell = (value == dropTargetCell);
        isLastItem = (index == list.getModel().getSize( )-1);
        boolean showSelected = isSelected &
                            (dropTargetCell == null);
        return super.getListCellRendererComponent (list, value,
                                              index, showSelected,
                                              hasFocus);
    }
    public void paintComponent (Graphics g) {
        super.paintComponent(g);
        if (isTargetCell) {
            g.setColor(Color.black);
            g.drawLine (0, 0, getSize( ).width, 0);
        }
    }
}
```

The other major thing to handle is the drop itself. In some ways, this is like the drag-over case: you need to reject the drop if the source is anything other than this JList, and you need to figure out which list item the drop has occurred over. Given this, you can pull the object out of the Transferable (which is handed to you in the DropTargetDropEvent), delete it from its previous location in the list, and insert it in its new location. The only catch is that if the dragged item was located before its dropped destination, then the correct drop index will be one less than you'd expect. After all, by deleting it from the list, everything after its old location has now moved up one index. All of this is handled by the drop( ) method, shown in Example 2-16.

Example 2-16. Handling the drop on the reorderable JList

```
public void drop (DropTargetDropEvent dtde) {
    System.out.println ("drop( )!");
    if (dtde.getSource( ) != dropTarget) {
        System.out.println ("rejecting for bad source (" +
                            dtde.getSource().getClass().getName( ) + ")");
        dtde.rejectDrop( );
        return;
    }
    Point dropPoint = dtde.getLocation( );
    int index = locationToIndex (dropPoint);
    System.out.println ("drop index is " + index);
    boolean dropped = false;
    try {
        if ((index == -1) || (index == draggedIndex)) {
            System.out.println ("dropped onto self");
            dtde.rejectDrop( );
            return;
        }
        dtde.acceptDrop (DnDConstants.ACTION_MOVE);
        System.out.println ("accepted");
        Object dragged =
            dtde.getTransferable( ).getTransferData(localObjectFlavor);
        // move items - note that indicies for insert will
        // change if [removed] source was before target
        System.out.println ("drop " + draggedIndex + " to " + index);
        boolean sourceBeforeTarget = (draggedIndex < index);
        System.out.println ("source is" +
                            (sourceBeforeTarget ? "" : " not") +
                            " before target");
        System.out.println ("insert at " +
                            (sourceBeforeTarget ? index-1 : index));
        DefaultListModel mod = (DefaultListModel) getModel( );
        mod.remove (draggedIndex);
        mod.add ((sourceBeforeTarget ? index-1 : index), dragged);
        dropped = true;
    } catch (Exception e) {
        e.printStackTrace( );
    }
    dtde.dropComplete (dropped);
}
```

Finally, you need to call dropComplete( ) to tell the DropTargetDropEvent whether the drag-and-drop succeeded.

The main( ) method shown in Example 2-17 provides the same list of people shown in the other hacks. By way of example, click and hold the mouse on *Chris,* and then drag the mouse toward the bottom of the list. As you drag, potential drops will be indicated by the horizontal line, as seen in Figure 2-9.

Example 2-17. Testing the reorderable JList

```
public static void main (String[] args) {
    JList list = new ReorderableJList ( );
    DefaultListModel defModel = new DefaultListModel( );
    list.setModel (defModel);
    String[] listItems = {
        "Chris", "Joshua", "Daniel", "Michael",
        "Don", "Kimi", "Kelly", "Keagan"
    };
    Iterator it = Arrays.asList(listItems).iterator( );
    while (it.hasNext( ))
        defModel.addElement (it.next( ));
    // show list
    JScrollPane scroller =
        new JScrollPane (list,
                        ScrollPaneConstants.VERTICAL_SCROLLBAR_ALWAYS,
                        ScrollPaneConstants.HORIZONTAL_SCROLLBAR_NEVER);
    JFrame frame = new JFrame ("Checkbox JList");
    frame.getContentPane( ).add (scroller);
    frame.pack( );
    frame.setVisible(true);
}
```

Figure 2-9. Dragging to reorder a JList

Once dropped between the last two items, the item moves to its new location, as seen in Figure 2-10.

One limitation of this approach is that I haven't found a simple way to provide for dropping after the last list element (the moved item goes before the item you drop it on).

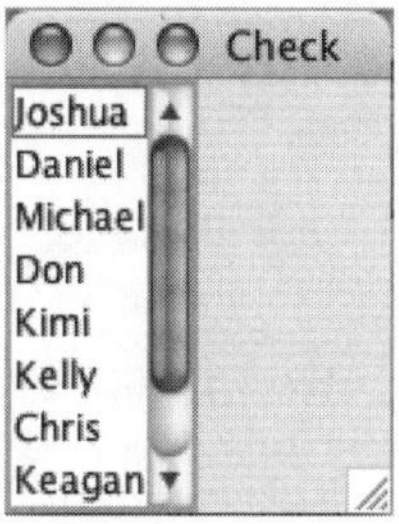

Figure 2-10. Item dropped into new position in a JList

Animate Your JList Selections

Fading in and catching the eye.

Not every GUI involves windows and mouse pointers, and the visual language of a GUI can be very different depending on what is provided by the environment. Typically, GUIs for things like console video games and set-top boxes don't use a mouse metaphor, so there's no onscreen pointer that the user is tracking. As a result, these systems often give the user more profound feedback when they move around a list—highlights slide from one item to another, selected items fade in while deselected items fade out, etc.—so there's something the eye can track. You can do the same thing in Swing, with more cell-rendering hackery. You might not need it now, but it'll be handy if you ever design a kiosk with Swing.

One way to show a changed selection is to show a brief animation of the cell selection. Instead of just being highlighted instantly, you fade the selected cell from its unselected background and foreground colors to its selected colors over the course of a short time (really short, like a half-second, so it isn't annoying).

To do this, you'll need to create an animator thread that kicks off every time the selection changes. This short-lived thread repeatedly updates a highlight color and calls repaint( ). The cell renderer can then use the updated highlight color as it redraws the cells in the list. Example 2-18 shows this technique.

Example 2-18. Animating the JList cell selection

```
import java.awt.*;
import javax.swing.*;
import javax.swing.event.*;
import java.util.*;
```

Example 2-18. Animating the JList cell selection (continued)

```java
public class AnimatedJList extends JList
    implements ListSelectionListener {

    static java.util.Random rand = new java.util.Random( );

    static Color listForeground, listBackground,
        listSelectionForeground, listSelectionBackground;
    static float[] foregroundComps, backgroundComps,
        foregroundSelectionComps, backgroundSelectionComps;

    static {
        UIDefaults uid = UIManager.getLookAndFeel().getDefaults( );
        listForeground =  uid.getColor ("List.foreground");
        listBackground =  uid.getColor ("List.background");
        listSelectionForeground =  uid.getColor ("List.selectionForeground");
        listSelectionBackground =  uid.getColor ("List.selectionBackground");
        foregroundComps =
            listForeground.getRGBColorComponents(null);
        foregroundSelectionComps =
            listSelectionForeground.getRGBColorComponents(null);
        backgroundComps =
            listBackground.getRGBColorComponents(null);
        backgroundSelectionComps =
            listSelectionBackground.getRGBColorComponents(null);
    }
    public Color colorizedSelectionForeground,
        colorizedSelectionBackground;

    public static final int ANIMATION_DURATION = 1000;
    public static final int ANIMATION_REFRESH = 50;

    public AnimatedJList( ) {
        super( );
        addListSelectionListener (this);
        setCellRenderer (new AnimatedCellRenderer( ));
    }

    public void valueChanged (ListSelectionEvent lse) {
        if (! lse.getValueIsAdjusting( )) {
            HashSet selections = new HashSet( );
            for (int i=0; i < getModel().getSize( ); i++) {
                if (getSelectionModel( ).isSelectedIndex(i))
                    selections.add (new Integer(i));
            }
            CellAnimator animator = new CellAnimator (selections.toArray( ));
            animator.start( );
        }
    }
}
```

Example 2-18. Animating the JList cell selection (continued)

```java
public static void main (String[] args) {
    JList list = new AnimatedJList ();
    DefaultListModel defModel = new DefaultListModel();
    list.setModel (defModel);
    String[] listItems = {
        "Chris", "Joshua", "Daniel", "Michael",
        "Don", "Kimi", "Kelly", "Keagan"
    };
    Iterator it = Arrays.asList(listItems).iterator();
    while (it.hasNext())
        defModel.addElement (it.next());
    // show list
    JScrollPane scroller =
        new JScrollPane (list,
                        ScrollPaneConstants.VERTICAL_SCROLLBAR_ALWAYS,
                        ScrollPaneConstants.HORIZONTAL_SCROLLBAR_NEVER);
    JFrame frame = new JFrame ("Checkbox JList");
    frame.getContentPane().add (scroller);
    frame.pack();
    frame.setVisible(true);
}

class CellAnimator extends Thread {
    Object[] selections;
    long startTime;
    long stopTime;
    public CellAnimator (Object[] s) {
        selections = s;
    }
    public void run() {
        startTime = System.currentTimeMillis();
        stopTime = startTime + ANIMATION_DURATION;
        while (System.currentTimeMillis() < stopTime) {
            colorizeSelections();
            repaint();
            try { Thread.sleep (ANIMATION_REFRESH); }
            catch (InterruptedException ie) {}
        }
        // one more, at 100% selected color
        colorizeSelections();
        repaint();
    }

    // colorizeSelections() listing below

    // AnimatedCellRenderer listing below
}
```

Like several previous hacks, this hack starts with some static code to get the platform colors for selected and unselected foreground and background colors. But this time, it also saves them off into arrays of their red, green, and blue components.

The component sets up a ListSelectionListener, which fires off a CellAnimator every time it gets the last of a series of ListSelectionEvents. The CellAnimator is a thread that runs for a short time only (defined by the class variable ANIMATION_DURATION), repeatedly calling colorizeSelections() and then sleeping briefly.

colorizeSelections(), shown in Example 2-19, calculates a float to express how much of the animation duration has elapsed. It then applies this as a proportion to the distance between the start and end values for each of the red, green, and blue components. For example, if the unselected background color is white (255, 255, 255), and the selected color is pure blue (0, 0, 255), then halfway through the animation the color should be (127, 127, 255), where 127 is halfway between the start and end values of the red and green components, and blue doesn't change.

Example 2-19. Determining animation color for selected cells

```
public void colorizeSelections() {
    // calculate % completion relative to start/stop times
    float elapsed = (float) (System.currentTimeMillis() - startTime);
    float completeness = Math.min ((elapsed/ANIMATION_DURATION), 1.0f);
    // calculate scaled color
    float colorizedForeComps[] = new float[3];
    float colorizedBackComps[] = new float[3];
    for (int i=0; i<3; i++) {
        colorizedForeComps[i] =
            foregroundComps[i] +
            (completeness *
             (foregroundSelectionComps[i] - foregroundComps[i]));
        colorizedBackComps[i] =
            backgroundComps[i] +
            (completeness *
             (backgroundSelectionComps[i] - backgroundComps[i]));
    }
    colorizedSelectionForeground =
        new Color (colorizedForeComps[0],
                   colorizedForeComps[1],
                   colorizedForeComps[2]);
    colorizedSelectionBackground =
        new Color (colorizedBackComps[0],
                   colorizedBackComps[1],
                   colorizedBackComps[2]);
}
```

The cell renderer in Example 2-20 is very simple: it just looks to see if the cell it's rendering is selected; if so, it sets its foreground and background to the colorized values. It also sets the cell to be opaque, meaning that the renderer wants the responsibility of drawing all the pixels, which is necessary to make the background color fill the cell. In a more complex cell layout, you might need to apply the foreground and background colors to all the cell's children and make them opaque, too.

Example 2-20. Rendering the animated list cells

```
class AnimatedCellRenderer extends DefaultListCellRenderer {
    public Component getListCellRendererComponent(JList list,
                                                  Object value,
                                                  int index,
                                                  boolean isSelected,
                                                  boolean hasFocus) {
        Component returnMe =
            super.getListCellRendererComponent (list, value, index,
                                                isSelected, hasFocus);
        if (isSelected) {
            returnMe.setForeground (colorizedSelectionForeground);
            returnMe.setBackground (colorizedSelectionBackground);
            /* this might be necessary if you have more
               elaborate cells
            if (returnMe instanceof Container) {
                Component[] children =
                    ((Container)returnMe).getComponents ( );
                System.out.println (children.length + " children");
                for (int i=0;
                    (children != null ) && (i<children.length);
                    i++) {
                    children[i].setForeground (colorizedSelectionForeground);
                    children[i].setBackground (colorizedSelectionBackground);
                }
            }
            */
            if (returnMe instanceof JComponent)
                ((JComponent) returnMe).setOpaque(true);
        }
        return returnMe;
    }
}
```

When you run the code, clicking on a cell makes it briefly fade into the selection color, as seen in Figure 2-11.

One potential improvement: if your list allows multiple selections, then all the selected cells will animate, and it would make more sense to animate just the one that the user has clicked on. You could do this by figuring out (by caching previous selections [Hack #15]) which item is the new selection, and

Figure 2-11. Fading in a cell selection

setting a flag so that the cell renderer applies only the colorized foreground and background colors to that cell.

HACK #19   Turn Methods into List Renderers

By using a little bit of reflection, you can make a generic `ListCellRenderer` that can render data using any method at runtime.

JLists, like JTable and JTree, use a decorator pattern to customize how they look. This system of cell renderers works well, but it can require you to build a unique renderer class for each type of object you want to put into your lists. Often, all you really want to do is call a particular method on the objects in your list, but writing a complete class to just call one method is a lot of work for such a small task. This hack shows you how to use reflection to create a generic cell renderer that can be reused on any object without subclassing.

Building a Generic Renderer

The default JList cell renderer will just call toString( ) on the objects in the list and draw the resulting string to the screen. This is fine for simple uses where you really are just looking at a list of strings or objects with appropriate toString( ) methods. More complicated applications—and they all become more complicated eventually—require more complicated objects, and those objects might not have a convenient or useful toString( ) method. Eventually, you have to write a custom renderer for the particular object you wish to store. But there is another way: reflection.

Reflection lets you programmatically discover and access methods and fields in a java class at runtime. For this hack, you will use reflection to call an arbitrary method. This will allow the programmer using your generic renderer to specify a method using a string. This method will be used to render the component. Because you will be using reflection, you don't need to know the kind of objects in the list. As long as a method with the requested name exists, you can call it and get a value out. This will work even if some of the objects in the JList have different types. But let's not get ahead of ourselves. First, you need a basic cell renderer, as seen in Example 2-21.

Example 2-21. A basic cell renderer

```
public class GenericListCellRenderer extends DefaultListCellRenderer {
    protected String method;
    public GenericListCellRenderer(String method) {
        super( );
        this.method = method;
    }

    public Component getListCellRendererComponent(JList list, Object value,
        int index, boolean isSelected, boolean cellHasFocus) {

        JLabel label = (JLabel)super.getListCellRendererComponent(
            list,value,index, isSelected, cellHasFocus);
        label.setText("my text");
        return label;
    }
}
```

Example 2-21 declares a subclass of the DefaultListCellRenderer—the standard implementation of a ListCellRenderer. The GenericListCellRenderer class takes a method string in its constructor. This string is the name of the method to call on the list value objects.

All ListCellRenderers have a getListCellRendererComponent( ) method, which returns a component to do the actual drawing. Most implementations (DefaultListCellRenderer included) use JLabels as the drawing components because they are relatively lightweight and can have both text and icons. The previous code gets the JLabel component from the superclass and sets the text to *my text*. Once added to a JList, this code will be called for each item in the list, meaning they will all be drawn as *my text*. This works, but it isn't very useful. Now it's time to add some reflection:

```
try {
    Method meth = value.getClass( ).getMethod(method,null);
    if(meth != null) {
        Object retval = meth.invoke(value,null);
        label.setText(""+retval);
    }
} catch (Exception ex) {
    System.out.println("got an execption: " + ex);
    ex.printStackTrace( );
    label.setText(""+value);
}
return label;
```

The previous code replaces the label.setText( ) method in the original renderer. It retrieves the specified method from the current list value and stores it in a Method object. This object represents the abstract method itself. If you did new String("text").getClass( ).getMethod("toString",null), then you would get an object that represents the toString( ) method on any string. Once you have this method, you can call it on the actual object at hand. meth.invoke( ) will invoke the method on the real list item, returning a value into retval. Both getMethod( ) and invoke( ) take an additional argument, which is null in the previous code. This argument is actually an array representing the arguments to the method being called. For this hack to work, you must assume that the method has no arguments, so null is used.

Once you have the return value of the method in hand, you can call setText( ). I set it to ""+retval because that will automatically handle nulls and call toString( ) on the value itself. The reflection code can throw an exception, so it's all wrapped up on a try-catch block. If the reflection fails, then it will set the text using toString( ) on the list item as a backup, which is what the standard renderer would do.

Putting It All Together

To use this new renderer, you need to create a JList and set its CellRenderer property. The following code creates a frame with one JList in it, creates a custom renderer for the toString( ) method, then packs and shows the frame on screen. The list contains an array of strings, representing common subatomic particles:

```
public static void main(String[] args) {
    String[] data = { "Proton", "Neutron", "Electron" };
    JList list = new JList(data);

    GenericListCellRenderer renderer =
        new GenericListCellRenderer("toString");
    list.setCellRenderer(renderer);

    JFrame frame = new JFrame("Cell Renderer Hack");
    frame.getContentPane( ).add(list);
    frame.pack( );
    frame.setVisible(true);
}
```

The generic renderer can call any method on the list item objects as long as the method has no arguments and doesn't return void. It will even work with primitives. You could call hashCode( ), which returns an int, like this:

```
GenericListCellRenderer renderer =
    new GenericListCellRenderer("hashCode");
```

Using toString( ) on the strings will be the same as the default renderer, simply drawing *Proton*, *Neutron*, and *Electron* in the list (see Figure 2-12).

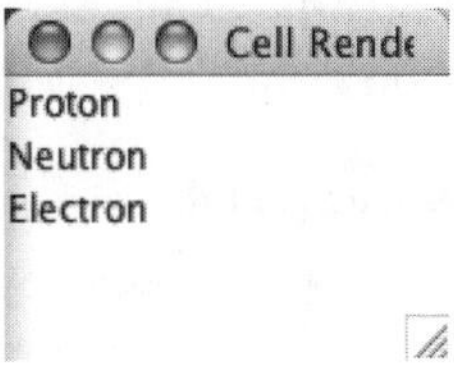

Figure 2-12. Renderer using the toString( ) method

The resulting change would look like Figure 2-13.

Figure 2-13. Renderer using the hashCode( ) method

Using reflection for cell renderers is a very powerful concept because you can reuse potentially complicated code with very little additional effort. Using it to display strings is just a trivial example. Imagine you had a bunch of objects representing entries from an RSS feed. Instead of creating a custom renderer or wrapping the entries in objects with a custom toString( ) method, you could use the GenericListCellRenderer with getTitle( ) to automatically call the getTitle( ) method on the entry objects—no new subclasses or extra code. Just a single string and the renderer takes care of the rest. That is the power of reflection.

Create a Collections-Aware JComboBox

You've moved on from Vector; your combo boxes should, too.

JComboBox is one of Swing's oldest components. Unfortunately, it accepts arrays of objects and Vectors only. Now that Collections objects like List have been part of the JDK for years, it would be nice to use them directly in a combo box without shuffling objects in and out of arrays. Fortunately, the JComboBox uses an MVC (Model-View-Controller) architecture, so you can solve this problem with a simple implementation of a ComboBoxModel.

To start, you need to figure out what the custom model should do. For our purposes, it needs to accept a List in the constructor and preserve any ordering supplied. Another nifty feature would be automatic updates. If you add or delete values to the List, the combo box should update itself automatically. Example 2-22 is a good start.

Example 2-22. A basic combo box to accept lists

```java
public class ListComboBoxModel implements ComboBoxModel {
    protected List data;

    public ListComboBoxModel(List list) {
        this.listeners = new ArrayList();
        this.data = list;
        if(list.size() > 0) {
            selected = list.get(0);
        }
    }

    protected Object selected;
    public void setSelectedItem(Object item) {
        this.selected = item;
    }
    public Object getSelectedItem() {
        return this.selected;
    }

    public Object getElementAt(int index) {
        return data.get(index);
    }
    public int getSize() {
        return data.size();
    }

    protected List listeners;
    public void addListDataListener(ListDataListener l) {
        listeners.add(l);
    }
    public void removeListDataListener(ListDataListener l) {
        this.listeners.remove(l);
    }
}
```

This implementation is pretty much what you'd expect. Each method in ComboBoxModel is implemented (along with its parent interface, ListDataModel). The constructor saves a reference to the List and selects the first element if there is one. The selectedItem accessor works as expected, using the selected variable. getElementAt() and getSize() both pass the work on to the underlying List, and the ListDataListener methods work with a second List for managing the listeners. The important thing to notice here is that the code saves the reference to the List that was passed in, rather than creating a copy. This means that the model will always be in sync with the underlying list implementation. If you call list.add("new item"), it will show up in the combo box automatically.

To test this, use the simple class in Example 2-23.

Example 2-23. Testing the List-based JComboBox

```
public class CBTest {
    public static void main(String[] args) {
        JFrame frame = new JFrame("Hack #4: Create a Collections-Aware
                                JComboBox");
        Container root = frame.getContentPane( );
        root.setLayout(new BoxLayout(root,BoxLayout.X_AXIS));

        // List combo box
        final List list = new ArrayList( );
        list.add("Blinky");
        list.add("Pinky");
        list.add("Inky");

        final ListComboBoxModel mod2 = new ListComboBoxModel(list);
        JComboBox cb2 = new JComboBox( );
        cb2.setModel(mod2);
        root.add(cb2);

        final JButton bt2 = new JButton("Add Item");
        bt2.addActionListener(new ActionListener( ) {
            public void actionPerformed(ActionEvent evt) {
                list.add("Clyde");
            }
        });
        root.add(bt2);
        // show the frame
        frame.pack( );
        frame.setVisible(true);
    }
}
```

The program creates a JComboBox that uses the new ListComboBoxModel. First, it creates a list, populates it with data, passes it to the ListComboBoxModel constructor, and then sends that to the new JComboBox( ). There is also a button that adds a new item to the list when clicked.

When you compile and run this program, it...doesn't work! The addition to the List doesn't show up in the combo box. A look over the API might remind you of the ListDataListener class. When setModel( ) is called, the

JComboBox registers itself as a listener so that it can update itself when the model changes. This means the ListComboBoxModel needs to fire off an event when the underlying List changes.

The problem here is that Java doesn't provide a standard event mechanism for collections. No problem—we can write our own. Because ActionEvents are the most common ones in Swing, just reuse those with a command string of "update". Here's the new event handling code added to the bottom of ListComboBoxModel:

```
public class ListComboBoxModel implements ComboBoxModel, ActionListener {
//..... the rest of the code

// event code
    public void actionPerformed(ActionEvent evt) {
        if(evt.getActionCommand( ).equals("update")) {
            this.fireUpdate( );
        }
    }

    public void fireUpdate( ) {
        ListDataEvent le = new ListDataEvent(this,
            ListDataEvent.CONTENTS_CHANGED,
            0,
            data.size( ));
        for(int i=0; i<listeners.size( ); i++) {
            ListDataListener l = (ListDataListener)listeners.get(i);
            l.contentsChanged(le);
        }
    }
}
```

The actionPerformed( ) method implements ActionListener. It just looks for events with the "update" command and calls fireUpdate( ). That sends a ListDataEvent to all of the model's listeners, which includes the JComboBox itself.

Here is the modified JButton from the sample program:

```
bt2.addActionListener(new ActionListener( ) {
        public void actionPerformed(ActionEvent evt) {
            list.add("Clyde");
            mod2.actionPerformed(new ActionEvent(bt2,0,"update"));
        }

    }
});
```

Running the program again, everything works as expected, as seen in Figure 2-14. When you press the button, *Clyde* is added to the list and the combo box updates itself.

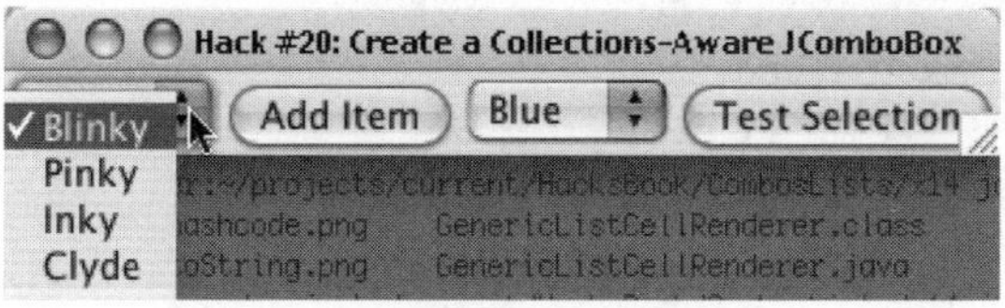

Figure 2-14. The collections-aware combo box

Because the List is backing the new model, you have to consider it to be live. This means you have to address any changes that need to be done on the event-dispatch thread in order to avoid threading issues (like race conditions). In this program, the code modifies the List from another action listener, which means the code is already on the event thread; however, if this was not the case, you would have to use another mechanism, such as SwingUtilities.invokeLater( ).

Now that you have a combo box that's aware of Lists, it makes sense to add another that understands Maps. Many times when you create a UI, you will want the user to select from a set of values. These values are very meaningful to your program, but because they often come from a database, they are short strings like "Calc_Rng", which won't mean anything to your users. They expect to see something like *Calculate Range*. What we need is a simple structure to map between the user-friendly descriptions and the real values. Sounds like a job for Map (Dora fans unite)!

Because Map is a collection, the implementation will be similar to what you've already seen; in fact, you can build it with a subclass of ListComboBoxModel. There are a few issues to tackle first, though. A Map defines a set of mappings between keys and values; it does not define the order of the keys themselves. This will make getElementAt(index) hard to implement because there is no notion of order in Maps. Further, the combo box only knows about the keys it uses for display, and not the underlying values, so you will need another way of pulling the real values out of the model. With these issues in mind, take a look at Example 2-24.

Example 2-24. Map-based combo box model

```
public class MapComboBoxModel extends ListComboBoxModel {

    protected Map map_data;
    protected List index;

    public MapComboBoxModel(Map map) {
        this.map_data = map;
```

Example 2-24. Map-based combo box model (continued)

```
        index = new ArrayList( );
        buildIndex( );
        if(index.size( ) > 0) {
            selected = index.get(0);
        }
    }

    protected void buildIndex( ) {
        index = new ArrayList(map_data.keySet( ));
    }

    public Object getElementAt(int i) {
        return index.get(i);
    }

    public int getSize( ) {
        return map_data.size( );
    }

    public void actionPerformed(ActionEvent evt) {
        if(evt.getActionCommand( ).equals("update")) {
            buildIndex( );
            fireUpdate( );
        }
    }

    public Object getValue(Object selectedItem) {
        return map_data.get(selectedItem);
    }
    public Object getValue(int selectedItem) {
        return getValue(index.get(selectedItem));
    }
}
```

The MapComboBoxModel accepts a collection in its constructor—this time a
Map—saving it for later reference. To maintain the order of the keys, the class
uses a List called index. The constructor calls buildIndex( ) to populate the
List with the Map's set of keys, and then sets the selected item—just like in
the List version. getElementAt( ) uses the index to get the display values and
getSize( ) uses the size of the Map itself.

actionPerformed( ) is different from the List version and calls buildIndex( )
before fireUpdate( ). This ensures that the index is always in sync with the
underlying map and that the JComboBox reflects that. There is no implementation of fireUpdate( ) or managing the listeners because the parent class,
ListComboBoxModel, takes care of those.

The final additions are the two getValue( ) methods, which allow you to retrieve the actual values out of the Map, based on an index or key. One uses the actual selected item and the other uses the index returned by JComboBox. getSelectedIndex( ).

Here's a slight modification to the test program to try this out:

```
// Map Combo Box
final Map map = new HashMap( );
map.put("Red",   "#ff0000");
map.put("Green", "#00ff00");
map.put("Blue",  "#0000ff");

final MapComboBoxModel mod3 = new MapComboBoxModel(map);
final JComboBox cb3 = new JComboBox( );
cb3.setModel(mod3);
root.add(cb3);
final JButton bt3 = new JButton("Test Selection");
bt3.addActionListener(new ActionListener( ) {
    public void actionPerformed(ActionEvent evt) {
        System.out.println("Human color: " + cb3.getSelectedItem( ));
        System.out.println("Computer color: " +
            mod3.getValue(cb3.getSelectedIndex( )));
    }
});
root.add(bt3);
```

This HashMap maps human-readable color names into the hex values that my program wants. The associated button will test the currently selected color, printing both the description the user sees and the underlying hex value.

 Again, you would have to send an ActionEvent to the model to keep it in sync if you added new elements.

The one downside to this approach is that you have no control over the order of the items displayed to the user. It depends on how the Map decides to store them. To impose order on them, you could sort the index in the buildIndex method (e.g., alphabetically), but I think I'll leave that as a future enhancement.

CHAPTER THREE

Tables and Trees

Hacks 21–27

A table component was one of the most obvious missing features in AWT, and among the most welcome additions when Swing came out. However, the JTable may be used too much—it's easy to throw an Object[][] at the constructor and get a full-blown GUI table, and some developers don't question the wisdom of this sort of coding.

But despite the generosity of the Swing JTable API, there are a few things still missing. Wouldn't it be nice if the table model keep itself sorted, or if the column widths had a non-ugly default that takes their contents into account? Well, you didn't buy this book to argue API theory—the point here is to hack things into shape. So, let's get started.

HACK #21

Size Your Columns to Suit Your JTable's Contents

A one-digit column does not need 100 pixels of dead space. You know this; your JTables should, too.

Does Figure 3-1 look like your typical JTable?

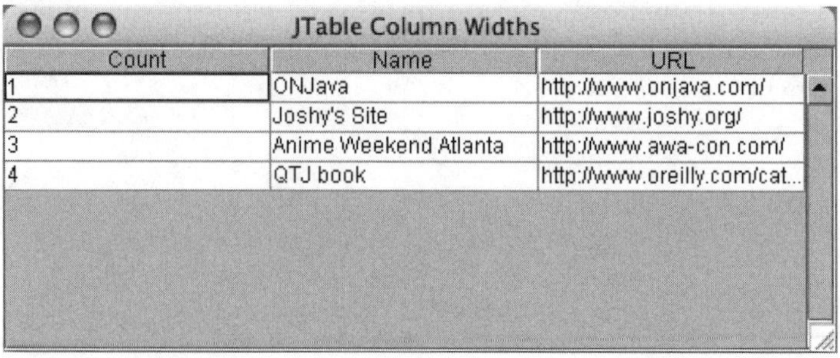

Count	Name	URL
1	ONJava	http://www.onjava.com/
2	Joshy's Site	http://www.joshy.org/
3	Anime Weekend Atlanta	http://www.awa-con.com/
4	QTJ book	http://www.oreilly.com/cat...

(JTable Column Widths)

Figure 3-1. JTable with default column sizing

If it does, then we have a usability problem to discuss. By default, the columns of a JTable are all the same size. For this data, that's obviously a *terrible* decision—there's far too much space reserved for the numbers in the count column, and not nearly enough in the URL column. So, how are you going to fix this?

If you said "turn on the horizontal scrollbar," please close this book, grasp it with both hands, and firmly smack yourself in the head with it. *No*, you are *not* turning on the horizontal scrollbar! Use the pixels available to you before you resort to the user-annoying desperation of horizontal scrolling. In this case, the count column has lots of pixels to spare; you just need to reallocate this extra space to the URL column.

Resetting Column Widths

What makes programmatic column resizing difficult for many Swing programmers is that they can't even find the right methods to use. If all you ever work with is JTable (and maybe a few custom cell renderers), you'll notice that the JavaDoc for those classes says nothing about column widths. The problem may be that the JTable is so generous with helpful methods that you'd never even notice that it's made up of TableColumn objects. Take a look at that TableColumn's JavaDoc, and you'll find getters and setters for minimum, maximum, and preferred widths for columns.

As with components that defer to layout managers, the right property to reset is the preferred width—let the column tell the JTable how wide it would like to be, but let the JTable make the final decision based on the information available to it (after all, there could be other columns contending for space, there might not be enough space for all the columns' preferred size, etc.).

Given that the key to this hack will be calling setPreferredWidth( ) on the TableColumns, the obvious question is: what value should you use for the preferred width? Here's a strategy: assuming you already have the table data, use the width of the widest item in the column. And how do you get that? By using the table's cell renderers to actually figure out how big each cell should be.

ColumnResizer, shown in Example 3-1, has a single static method, adjustColumnPreferredWidths( ), which takes a JTable as its only argument.

> Yes, the name is a mouthful, but it's helpful to express exactly what the method does.

Example 3-1. Adjusting column sizes to suit their contents

```
public class ColumnResizer {

    public static void adjustColumnPreferredWidths(JTable table) {
        // strategy - get max width for cells in column and
        // make that the preferred width
        TableColumnModel columnModel = table.getColumnModel();
        for (int col=0; col<table.getColumnCount(); col++) {
            int maxwidth = 0;
            for (int row=0; row<table.getRowCount(); row++) {
                TableCellRenderer rend =
                    table.getCellRenderer(row, col);
                Object value = table.getValueAt (row, col);
                Component comp =
                    rend.getTableCellRendererComponent (table,
                                                        value,
                                                        false,
                                                        false,
                                                        row,
                                                        col);
                maxwidth = Math.max (comp.getPreferredSize( ).width,
                                     maxwidth);
            } // for row

            TableColumn column = columnModel.getColumn (col);
            column.setPreferredWidth (maxwidth);

        } // for col
    }
}
```

For each column in the table, the method goes through all the rows and
renders each cell. It keeps a running tally of the widest component in the
column, and after considering all the rows, it sends this maximum width to
setPreferredWidth( ).

Example 3-2 demonstrates a unit test class to exercise ColumnResizer.
TestColumnResizer simply puts the JTable into a JFrame, pack( )s it, and shows
it. After a five-second delay, it calls adjustColumnPreferredWidths( ) to reset
the preferred column widths, and it revalidate( )s the table to get a repaint.

Example 3-2. Testing automatic column sizing

```
public class TestColumnResizer {

    final static Object[][] TABLE_DATA = {
        {new Integer(1), "ONJava", "http://www.onjava.com/"},
        {new Integer(2), "Joshy's Site", "http://www.joshy.org/"},
        {new Integer(3), "Anime Weekend Atlanta", "http://www.awa-con.com/"},
        {new Integer(4), "QTJ book",
            "http://www.oreilly.com/catalog/quicktimejvaadn/"}
    };
```

Example 3-2. Testing automatic column sizing (continued)

```java
final static String[] COLUMN_NAMES = {
    "Count", "Name", "URL"
};

public static void main (String[] args) {
    // 142 mac l&f has a header bug - force metal for today
    try {
        UIManager.setLookAndFeel (
            UIManager.getCrossPlatformLookAndFeelClassName( ));
    } catch (Exception e) { e.printStackTrace( );}

    DefaultTableModel mod =
        new DefaultTableModel (TABLE_DATA, COLUMN_NAMES);
    JTable table = new JTable (mod);
    JScrollPane pane =
        new JScrollPane (table,
                    ScrollPaneConstants.VERTICAL_SCROLLBAR_ALWAYS,
                    ScrollPaneConstants.HORIZONTAL_SCROLLBAR_NEVER);
    JFrame frame = new JFrame ("JTable Column Widths");
    frame.getContentPane( ).add (pane);
    frame.pack( );
    frame.setVisible (true);

    try {
        Thread.sleep (5000);
    } catch (Exception e) { e.printStackTrace( ); }

    // now get smart about col widths
    final JTable fTable = table;
    SwingUtilities.invokeLater(new Runnable( ) {
            public void run( ) {
                ColumnResizer.adjustColumnPreferredWidths (fTable);
                fTable.revalidate( );
            }
        });
    }
}
```

Notice that the column width adjustment and revalidate( ) have to be done with a Swing worker thread because the table shouldn't be updated from anything other than the AWT event-dispatch thread.

When run, this initially produces the ugly table seen back in Figure 3-1; after five seconds, it resets automatically to the much more pleasing column widths of Figure 3-2.

If you resize the JFrame, the columns will gain and lose space proportionally, so the URL column will always have much more space than the count column, making it more likely the table will be well-suited to further contents you might add.

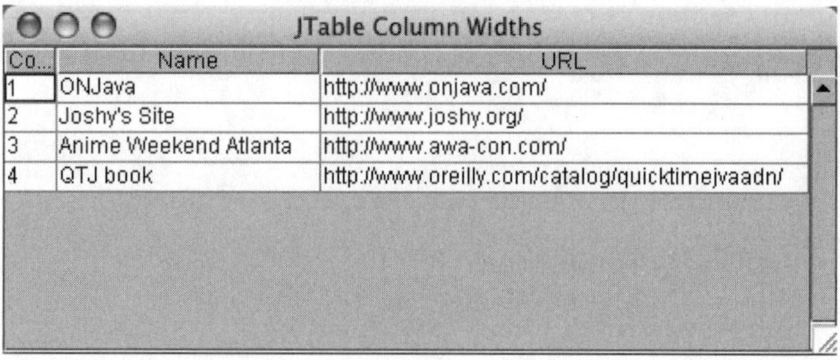

Figure 3-2. JTable columns resized to suit their contents

Accounting for Header Cells

There's a problem with the new weighting of the column widths: since the one-digit contents of the count column are so narrow, the count column header has been crushed to the point where Swing needs to show it with ellipses. Not so good.

The problem, of course, is that the width of the header was never considered in the preferred width calculation. You can do that yourself by changing the logic to prefer the wider of the widest content cell and the header cell. This means you need to get the header cell renderer (either from the TableColumn or the JTableHeader), then render a cell and get its width.

To do this, replace these two lines:

```
TableColumn column = columnModel.getColumn (col);
column.setPreferredWidth (maxwidth);
```

with these:

```
TableColumn column = columnModel.getColumn (col);
TableCellRenderer headerRenderer = column.getHeaderRenderer( );
if (headerRenderer == null)
    headerRenderer = table.getTableHeader().getDefaultRenderer( );
Object headerValue = column.getHeaderValue( );
Component headerComp =
        headerRenderer.getTableCellRendererComponent (table,
                                                headerValue,
                                                false,
                                                false,
                                                0,
                                                col);
maxwidth = Math.max (maxwidth,
                     headerComp.getPreferredSize( ).width);
column.setPreferredWidth (maxwidth);
```

When you run this version of ColumnResizer, the table should look like Figure 3-3.

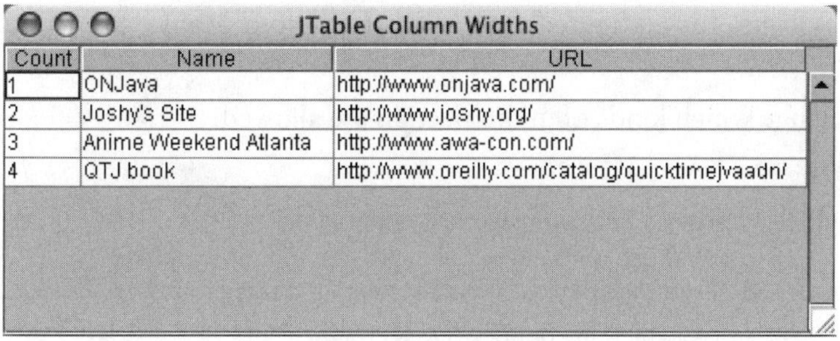

Count	Name	URL
1	ONJava	http://www.onjava.com/
2	Joshy's Site	http://www.joshy.org/
3	Anime Weekend Atlanta	http://www.awa-con.com/
4	QTJ book	http://www.oreilly.com/catalog/quicktimejvaadn/

JTable Column Widths

Figure 3-3. Accounting for header width in JTable column resizing

Having done this, it's still possible to crush either table cells or headers if you resize (programatically or by dragging the frame's corner) to a point where there's just not enough room for all the content. If you really wanted to keep header cells intact, you could alter the previous code to set the TableColumn's minimum width to the preferred width of the header cell, assuming the header isn't much wider than the content. Ultimately, it's really a question of what data you're putting in the table and what looks right to you.

Hacking the Hack

"But," you might be saying, "what if I don't have my table data in advance?" If you have some idea of what the data is probably going to be like, you could create your table, add this "prototype" data as a row, size the columns, and then remove the prototype...all before ever making the table visible. That would give your users reasonable default sizing, and then they could resize columns by dragging header borders as desired. Of course, you could always hook up a TableModelListener and resize the columns every time data is inserted, deleted, or updated, but having the column widths jump around magically can be *very* annoying.

HACK #22 Add Column Selection to JTables

So, why can't I select a column by clicking on its header?

Here's something that seems strange about JTables: you can click on the column headers, but only for the purpose of reordering columns—not for selecting the contents of that column. I don't know about you, but considering that I almost never reorder columns, it seems like the default behavior is backward. And if your users have had their expectations set by working with Excel or other spreadsheets, they'll surely expect the ability to select an entire column.

The to-do list for adding column selectability to a JTable consists of two items:

- Change which kinds of multiselection are allowed.
- Wire up a MouseListener.

Example 3-3 shows a very simple implementation.

Example 3-3. A JTable that allows column selection by clicking on column headers

```
public class ColumnSelectableJTable extends JTable {

    public ColumnSelectableJTable (Object[][] items, Object[] headers) {
        super (items, headers);
        setColumnSelectionAllowed (true);
        setRowSelectionAllowed (false);
        // set up action listener on table header
        final JTableHeader header = getTableHeader();
        header.addMouseListener (new MouseAdapter() {
                public void mouseReleased (MouseEvent e) {
                    if (! e.isShiftDown())
                        clearSelection();
                    int pick = header.columnAtPoint(e.getPoint());
                    addColumnSelectionInterval (pick, pick);
                }
            });

    }

}
```

The constructor is deliberately simple, taking only a two-dimensional array of contents and a one-dimensional array of headers. Of course, JTable has many more constructor signatures than this, but this is the one that will be easiest to expose to a test class (do I have to mention that building out the other constructors is left to the reader as an exercise?).

The next step is changing the defaults for multi-cell selection. The default is to allow row selection—exactly what you *don't* want. So, enable column selection and disable row selection. Next, you want to catch clicks on the headers so you can select columns in response to them. Unfortunately, the JTableHeader component doesn't have an addActionListener() method, so the best you can do is add a MouseListener instead. Of its various methods, you only need to override mouseReleased(), which signals the end of a click-and-release.

To implement the column selection, check the event to see if the Shift key is down. If it is, then the user wants to do a multiple selection, meaning that he intends to add the clicked column to any that are already selected. If not, then you can clear out any existing selection. Next, you need to figure out just which column was clicked. You can do this by asking the event for the Point at which the click occurred. This will be in the coordinate space of the JTableHeader, making it suited for calling JTableHeader.columnAtPoint(). That returns an index, which you can select by calling JTable. addColumnSelectionInterval(), specifying a one-column range that begins and ends at the selected column.

To run this code, I've put together a class that sends some trivial table data to a ColumnSelectableJTable and shows the whole thing in a JFrame. This test is shown in Example 3-4.

Example 3-4. Testing the column-selectable JTable

```
public class TestColumnSelectableJTable extends Object {

    private static final  Object[][] items= {
        {"Monday", "Cheeseburgers", "French Fries", "Peaches"},
        {"Tuesday", "Catfish", "Rice", "Starfruit"},
        {"Wednesday", "Tortellini", "Garlic Bread", "Pears"},
        {"Thursday", "Chicken", "Potatoes", "Strawberries"},
        {"Friday", "Pizza", null, "Fruit Cocktail"}
    };

    private static final Object[] headers = {
        "Day", "Main course", "Side dish", "Fruit"
    };

    public static void main (String[] args) {
        JFrame f = new JFrame ("Selectable columns");
        ColumnSelectableJTable table =
            new ColumnSelectableJTable(items, headers);
        JScrollPane scroller =
            new JScrollPane (table,
                        ScrollPaneConstants.VERTICAL_SCROLLBAR_ALWAYS,
                        ScrollPaneConstants.HORIZONTAL_SCROLLBAR_ALWAYS);
        f.getContentPane().add (scroller);
        f.pack();
        f.setVisible(true);
    }
}
```

When run, this table's columns are selectable either by clicking on a cell in the column or on a header of any of the columns, as seen in Figure 3-4.

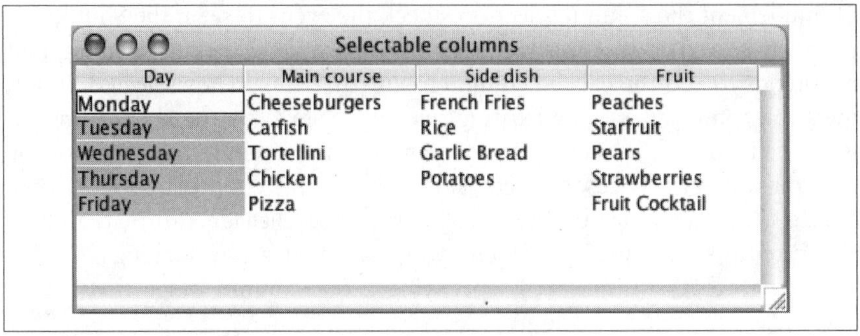

Figure 3-4. Selecting JTable columns by clicking on headers

HACK #23 Let Your JTables Do the Sorting

Why doesn't Swing already offer this? Oh well, here's how to do it yourself.

It's hard to imagine you'll do much serious work with JTables without needing to sort the contents by one of the columns, or support changing between columns to use as the sort criteria. In fact, given how generous the Swing API usually is, it's kind of surprising that it doesn't already offer it. Oh well, it's not that hard to do for yourself.

There are a couple of approaches you could take to solve this problem. You could create a subclass of TableModel, one that keeps an internal Comparator to do the sorting and resorts every time an add( ) or remove( ) type method is called. The drawback to this approach is choosing which of the model classes to subclass. If you go too high up the hierarchy by implementing TableModel or subclassing DefaultTableModel, you would miss some typical Swing functionality that developers expect, like the ability to add and remove rows provided by DefaultMutableTableModel. On the other hand, if you subclass DefaultMutableTableModel, other developers will be unhappy because subclassing your class requires them to pick up public add( ) and delete( ) type methods that expose their data in ways they don't want.

So, consider an alternative: two table models, one that the JTable sees and another that the developer sees. Specifically, the developer will pass her TableModel to the constructor of the sorting model, which will wire up for events on the model. Then, the developer will set the sorting model as the JTable's model. Changes in the base model will force the sorting model to resort its contents and then fire off events to JTable to drive updates to the onscreen representation.

There are more details in the actual implementation of course, particularly when it comes to doing the sorting. Example 3-5 shows the code for the SortableTableModel.

Example 3-5. Self-sorting TableModel

```
public class SortableTableModel implements TableModel,
    TableModelListener {

    EventListenerList listenerList = new EventListenerList();
    TableModel delegatedModel;
    int[] sortedIndicies;
    int sortColumn;
    Comparator comparator;
    Comparator[] comparators;

    public SortableTableModel (TableModel tm) {
        delegatedModel = tm;
        delegatedModel.addTableModelListener (this);
        comparators = new Comparator [tm.getColumnCount()];
        sortedIndicies = new int [0];
        setSortColumn (0);
    }

    // listener stuff
    public void addTableModelListener (TableModelListener l) {
        listenerList.add (TableModelListener.class, l);
    }

    public void removeTableModelListener (TableModelListener l) {
        listenerList.remove (TableModelListener.class, l);
    }

    public void fireTableModelEvent (TableModelEvent e) {
        Object[] listeners = listenerList.getListenerList();
        for (int i = listeners.length-2; i>=0; i-=2) {
            if (listeners[i] == TableModelListener.class) {
                ((TableModelListener) listeners[i+1]).tableChanged(e);
            }
        }
    }

    // contents stuff

    public Class getColumnClass(int columnIndex)
        if (delegatedModel.getRowCount() > 0)
            return delegatedModel.getValueAt(0, columnIndex).getClass();
        else
            return Object.class;
    }

    // getColumnCount(), getColumnName(), getRowCount(),
    // getValueAt(), isCellEditable(), setValueAt() listings below

    // internal helpers
    public void setComparatorForColumn (Comparator c, int i) {
```

Example 3-5. Self-sorting TableModel (continued)

```
        // range check
        if (i > comparators.length) {
            Comparator[] newComparators = new Comparator[i+1];
            System.arraycopy (comparators, 0,
                              newComparators, 0,
                              comparators.length);
            comparators = newComparators;
        }
        // add the comparator
        comparators[i] = c;
    }

    public void setSortColumn (int i) {
        sortColumn = i;

        // reset current comparator, possibly to null, which
        // will make us use "natural ordering" for those values
        comparator = null;
        if ((comparators != null) &&
            (comparators.length > 0))
            // is there one in the list of comparators?
            comparator = comparators[sortColumn];

        // now do the sort
        resort();
    }

    public int getSortColumn () {
        return sortColumn;
    }

    // resort() method listed below
    // SortingDelegate inner class listed below
    // SortingDelegateComparator inner class listed below

    public void tableChanged (TableModelEvent e) {
                        switch (e.getType()) {
                        case TableModelEvent.DELETE: {
                            resort();
                            fireAllChanged();
                            break;
                        }
                        case TableModelEvent.INSERT: {
                            resort();
                            fireAllChanged();
                            break;
                        }
                        case TableModelEvent.UPDATE: {
                            resort();
                            fireAllChanged();
                            break;
```

Example 3-5. Self-sorting TableModel (continued)

```
                                    }

                                    }

    }

    protected void fireAllChanged( ) {
        TableModelEvent e = new TableModelEvent (this);
        fireTableModelEvent (e);
    }
}
```

The instance variables in this class include a list of event listeners to support the `TableModelListener` methods specified by the `TableModel` interface, the model passed in by the caller, a map of sorted indices, the index of the column to sort by, the current `Comparator` to sort with, and an array of `Comparators` arranged by the column each one sorts (the value may be `null` if the column is a primitive or another type that doesn't need a custom `Comparator`).

The `sortedIndicies` array is crucial to maintaining the relationship between the two tables. The values in this array indicate a mapped row in the `delegatedModel`. Thus, if a caller asks for a value in row 2, this model will get the value of `sortedIndicies[2]` and get that row from the `delegatedModel`. All the methods of `TableModel` that work with rows—`getValueAt( )`, `isCellEditable( )`, and `setValueAt( )`—use this look up, so the real key to keeping the model working is to keep this map accurate, which in turn means to redo the sort:

- Whenever the contents of the underlying model change
- Whenever a caller changes the sorting criteria of this model

The constructor is largely trivial, setting the `delegatedModel` instance, adding a `TableModelListener` to it so the sorting model can resort on updates to the `delegatedModel`'s contents, and initializing the structures for the comparators and the row mapping. Supporting the listeners is also essentially boilerplate; here, I've used the `EventListenerList` and backward-counting event firing **[Hack #94]**, as is done commonly throughout Swing.

The implementation of `getColumnClass( )` is important; it ensures that `TableCellRenderers` will get used when appropriate. Swing's implementation of `AbstractTableModel` literally just returns `Object.class` in all cases, which causes everything to render as `JLabels` of the `Object`'s `toString( )`. Yuck. This version actually looks at the `delegatedModel` and, if it has any data, returns the class of the object in the first row of the designated column.

Next in the source, you'll find a series of methods that involve the contents of the model:

- getColumnCount( )
- getColumnName( )
- getRowCount( )
- getValueAt( )
- isCellEditable( )
- setValueAt( )

All of these methods delegate to the wrapped model, with the caveat that any that work with rows look up the mapped row from the sortedIndicies array, as seen in Example 3-6.

Example 3-6. Table model methods that delegate calls to the wrapped model

```
public int getColumnCount( ) {
    return delegatedModel.getColumnCount( );
}
public String getColumnName (int index) {
    return delegatedModel.getColumnName (index);
}
public int getRowCount( ) {
    return delegatedModel.getRowCount( );
}
private int getDelegatedRow (int row) {
    return sortedIndicies [row];
}
public Object getValueAt (int rowIndex, int columnIndex) {
    return delegatedModel.getValueAt (getDelegatedRow(rowIndex),
                                      columnIndex);
}
public boolean isCellEditable (int rowIndex, int columnIndex) {
    return delegatedModel.isCellEditable (rowIndex, columnIndex);
}
public void setValueAt (Object aValue, int rowIndex, int columnIndex) {
    delegatedModel.setValueAt (aValue, rowIndex, columnIndex);
}
```

But how do the contents get sorted? Any class that implements Comparable can be sorted by Collections.sort( ) or one of the Arrays.sort( ) methods, and thus doesn't require any special handling. However, you probably want to handle sorting any arbitrary class, which requires working with custom Comparators—what the comparators array is for. In setComparatorForColumn( ), you range-check the size of the array, and then cache the passed Comparator into the array index that corresponds to the column. For example, setComparatorForColumn (myComparator, 2) should set comparators[2] to myComparator.

This caches the comparators, but only one is used for sorting at any given time. In setSortColumn( ), you cache the index of the sort column, but then you need to pull up the corresponding Comparator. Set the comparator—the one that will be used to perform the sort—to null, and then check the comparators list to see if there is a Comparator at the given index. If so, it will become the new comparator.

Now, you're ready to handle the sorting. When you need to sort, either because the sort index has changed or because the underlying model has changed, you call the resort( ) method, shown in Example 3-7.

Example 3-7. Resorting based on the current comparator

```
protected void resort( ) {
    // does sortedIndicies need to grow or shrink?
    if (sortedIndicies.length != delegatedModel.getRowCount( )) {
        sortedIndicies = new int [delegatedModel.getRowCount( )];
    }
    // build up a list of SortingDelegates
    ArrayList sortMe = new ArrayList( );
    for (int i=0; i<delegatedModel.getRowCount( ); i++) {
        SortingDelegate sd =
            new SortingDelegate (delegatedModel.getValueAt(i, getSortColumn( )),
                                i);
        sortMe.add (sd);
    }
    // now sort him with the SortingDelegateComparator
    SortingDelegateComparator sdc =
        new SortingDelegateComparator (comparator);
    Collections.sort (sortMe, sdc);

    // fill sortedIndicies array
    // index -> value represents mapping from original
    // row to sorted row
    for (int i=0; i<sortMe.size( ); i++) {
        sortedIndicies[i] =
            ((SortingDelegate) sortMe.get(i)).row;
    }

    // fire change event
    fireAllChanged( );
}
```

This starts by resetting the size of the sortedIndicies array, which will be wrong if the number of rows in the delegatedModel has changed. Next, build up an array list of SortingDelegates, an inner class containing a value from the delegatedModel (in the column to be sorted) and a mapped row number. This class is shown in Example 3-8.

Example 3-8. Inner class to map sortable objects to their position in the current sort

```
public class SortingDelegate extends Object {
    public Object value;
    public int row;
    public SortingDelegate (Object v, int r) {
        value = v;
        row = r;
    }
}
```

This can be sorted by the SortingDelegateComparator, another inner class that maps the compare( ) call that is the heart of Java Collections-based sorting (shown in Example 3-9). It takes a Comparator (namely the sorting column's Comparator, if any) and on each compare( ), it looks to see if that Comparator is null; if not, it uses Comparator.compare( ) to do the sorting comparison. In this case, objects should be Comparable, which means the sorter can use Comparable.compareTo( ) to apply "natural ordering" (intuitive numeric ordering for all number types, ASCII ordering for strings, etc.). It throws an exception if there's neither a Comparator to use nor Comparable values.

Example 3-9. Comparator for delegated sorting

```
class SortingDelegateComparator extends Object implements Comparator {
    Comparator comp;
    public SortingDelegateComparator (Comparator c) {
        comp = c;
    }
    public int compare (Object o1, Object o2) {
        Object v1 = ((SortingDelegate)o1).value;
        Object v2 = ((SortingDelegate)o2).value;
        if (comp != null)
            return comp.compare (v1, v2);
        else if (v1 instanceof Comparable)
            return ((Comparable)v1).compareTo (v2);
        else
            throw new IllegalArgumentException ("Can't compare objects "+
                                                "for sorting");

    }
}
```

With the list of SortingDelegates now sorted, you can walk the list and pull out the row field of each object, putting it in the sortedIndicies array. The array is again ready to map all the method calls that refer to rows. You need to fire an event to tell the sorting model's listeners—presumably just the JTable—that contents have updated. Since the resort could affect none, some, or all of the rows, fire off an event saying the whole table has updated.

The final thing to deal with is the events you get from the wrapped model. These can be deletes, inserts, or updates—in all cases, this implementation calls for a total resort and fires off the "everything changed" event.

A test class for this model needs to exercise the sorting and updating caused both by changing the sort criteria and by changing the underlying model. Also, to test the custom Comparator stuff, it needs to have at least one column whose contents aren't Comparable and thus need a Comparator.

TestSortableTableModel provides these with a simple three-column table with canned content and buttons to resort by each of those columns. A fourth button adds another row of data. The third column is a java.awt.Color, which gets its own simple Comparator. The code for the test class is shown in Example 3-10.

Example 3-10. Testing the self-sorting TableModel

```
public class TestSortableTableModel extends JPanel
    implements ActionListener {

    DefaultTableModel myModel;
    SortableTableModel mySortableModel;
    JButton sort1, sort2, sort3, bonus;

    static Object[] headers = {
        "Letter", "Number", "Color"
    };
    static Object[][] data = {
        {"A", new Integer(2), Color.gray.darker().darker()},
        {"B", new Integer (3), Color.gray},
        {"C", new Integer (1), Color.gray.darker()},
    };

    static Object[] bonusData = {
        "D", "0", Color.red
    };

    public TestSortableTableModel (DefaultTableModel m) {
        super (new BorderLayout());
        myModel = m;
        mySortableModel = new SortableTableModel (myModel);
        mySortableModel.setComparatorForColumn (new MyColorComparator(), 2);
        JTable table = new JTable (mySortableModel);
        table.setDefaultRenderer (java.awt.Color.class, new ColorRenderer());
        JScrollPane scroller =
            new JScrollPane (table,
                    ScrollPaneConstants.VERTICAL_SCROLLBAR_ALWAYS,
                    ScrollPaneConstants.HORIZONTAL_SCROLLBAR_ALWAYS);
        table.setPreferredScrollableViewportSize (new Dimension (400, 200));
        setLayout(new BorderLayout());
        add (scroller, BorderLayout.CENTER);
```

Example 3-10. Testing the self-sorting TableModel (continued)

```
        // add sort buttons
        JPanel buttonPanel = new JPanel();
        sort1 = new JButton ("Sort 1");
        buttonPanel.add(sort1);
        sort1.addActionListener(this);
        sort2 = new JButton ("Sort 2");
        buttonPanel.add(sort2);
        sort2.addActionListener(this);
        sort3 = new JButton ("Sort 3");
        buttonPanel.add(sort3);
        sort3.addActionListener(this);
        bonus = new JButton ("More data");
        buttonPanel.add(bonus);
        bonus.addActionListener(this);
        add (buttonPanel, BorderLayout.SOUTH);

    }

    public void actionPerformed (ActionEvent e) {
        if (e.getSource() == sort1) {
            mySortableModel.setSortColumn (0);
        } else if (e.getSource() == sort2) {
            mySortableModel.setSortColumn (1);
        } else if (e.getSource() == sort3) {
            mySortableModel.setSortColumn (2);
        } else if (e.getSource() == bonus) {
            myModel.addRow (bonusData);
        }

    }

    public static void main (String[] args) {
        DefaultTableModel aModel =
            new DefaultTableModel(data, headers) ;
        JFrame frame = new JFrame ("Sortable Table");
        frame.getContentPane().add (new TestSortableTableModel(aModel),
                            BorderLayout.CENTER);
        frame.pack();
        frame.setVisible(true);
    }

}
```

The test class declares its models: a SortableTableModel to pass to the JTable and a DefaultMutableTableModel for the developer to play with. It then declares the default table headers and data as Object arrays. The constructor takes a TableModel (as called by main( ), it will be a DefaultMutableTableModel built from the canned data), from that builds a SortableTableModel, and then creates a JTable. It also sets a custom Comparator for the color column on the sortable model, and a custom renderer for the colors on the table. It then adds and wires up some buttons for sorting and adding extra rows, and puts it all in a JFrame.

The color Comparator is an idea that doesn't entirely make sense—how can you say that green is greater than or less than blue? What this comparator does is look only at brightness, by converting from the RGB color space to HSB and grabbing the brightness value. To make this work for the test, the canned data simply uses shades of gray. Given this scheme, the sort will arrange colors in order from darkest to lightest (least bright to most bright). The comparator and a simple "fill the cell" renderer for colors are shown in Example 3-11.

Example 3-11. The Comparator and TableCellRenderer handle color values in sorting a table test

```java
class MyColorComparator implements Comparator {
    float[] hsb = new float[3];
    public int compare (Object o1, Object o2) {
        if ((! (o1 instanceof Color)) ||
            (! (o2 instanceof Color)))
            return 0;
        else {
            Color c1 = (Color) o1;
            Color c2 = (Color) o2;
            Color.RGBtoHSB ( c1.getRed( ),
                            c1.getGreen( ),
                            c1.getBlue( ),
                            hsb);
            float bright1 = hsb[2];
            Color.RGBtoHSB ( c2.getRed( ),
                            c2.getGreen( ),
                            c2.getBlue( ),
                            hsb);
            float bright2 = hsb[2];
            if (bright1 == bright2)
                return 0;
            else
                return ((bright1-bright2) < 0) ? -1 : 1;
        }
    }
    public boolean equals (Object obj) {
        return super.equals (obj);
    }
}


class ColorRenderer extends DefaultTableCellRenderer {
    public Component getTableCellRendererComponent (JTable table,
                                                    Object value,
                                                    boolean isSelected,
                                                    boolean hasFocus,
                                                    int row,
                                                    int col) {
```

Example 3-11. The Comparator and TableCellRenderer handle color values in sorting a table test (continued)

```
Component returnMe =
    super.getTableCellRendererComponent (table, value,
                                         isSelected,
                                         hasFocus, row, col);


    if (value instanceof Color) {
        Color color = (Color) value;
        returnMe.setBackground (color);
        if (returnMe instanceof JLabel) {
            JLabel jl = (JLabel) returnMe;
            jl.setOpaque(true);
            jl.setText ("");
        }
    }
    return returnMe;
    }
}
```

When run, the table will be sorted by column 0, which contains Strings, as seen in Figure 3-5.

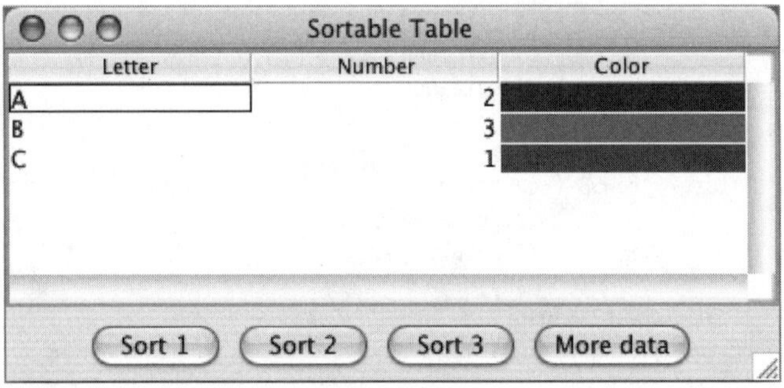

Figure 3-5. JTable sorted automatically by its first column

If you click the Sort 2 button (yes, the numbering is human-readable, and thus it's one greater than actual column indices), the table will immediately sort by the Integers in the middle column, as seen in Figure 3-6.

The color column is next. Click Sort 3 to see the table sort by the colors, as seen in Figure 3-7.

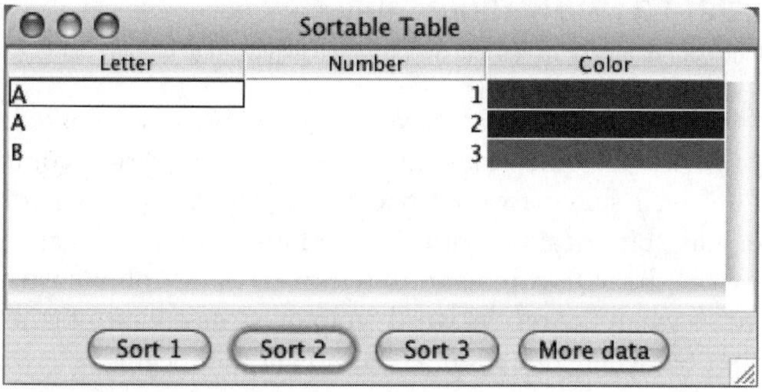

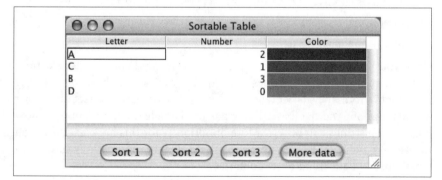

Figure 3-6. Sorting JTable by its second column

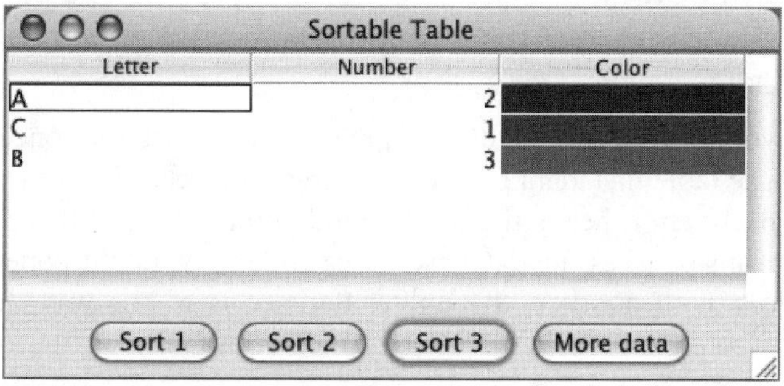

Figure 3-7. Sorting JTable by its third column

Finally, add in another row with the "More data" button. Because its color is solid red (maximum brightness), it will appear last when sorting by color. This is seen in Figure 3-8.

Figure 3-8. Adding data to a self-sorting table model

Create a JDBC Table Model

#24   Bring your database tables into Swing with a minimum of hassle.

If you've worked with databases, you've probably also worked with the tools they provide for quick table maintenance and queries: command-line tools that are well suited to brief hack-and-slash work, but hard to work with once you start dealing with any serious amount of data. It's hard enough to write the SQL command to return 10 or 20 columns in a query—it's even worse when the results word-wrap over the course of a dozen lines, and you can't tell where one result ends and another begins.

Wouldn't it be nice to be able to throw the contents of any database table into a Swing JTable? Give it a few JDBC strings, toss it in a JFrame, and *pow!*—instant GUI.

Building Connectivity

If you've worked with both JDBC and Swing, you'll grasp the concept in one sentence: use table metadata to build a Swing TableModel from the database table. If you haven't, here's the background you'll need: JDBC provides an abstract means of accessing databases. Java code to work with one database should work with another, the only difference is in the way that JDBC achieves a Connection to the database, which is usually a matter of providing Strings for:

- A driver class, which provides implementations of the various java.sql interfaces.
- A URL with which to connect to the database. This implies the use of sockets, though that's not necessarily the case. Some small embeddable databases can live in the same JVM as your application.
- An optional username.
- An optional password.

Once you have the Connection, you can begin to send commands (creation, deletion, and altering of tables) or queries to the database by creating Statements from the Connection. You can also use the Connection to get metadata about the database, like what kinds of features it supports, how long certain strings can be, etc. More importantly for this hack, it allows you to discover what tables are in the database, what columns they have, and what types of data are in those columns.

So, given just a Connection and the name of a table in the database, you can build a Java representation of its contents with two queries. The first query gets column metadata for the table and builds up arrays of the column names and their types. These can be mapped reasonably well to Java classes, at least for whatever types you intend to support. The second query gets all the data from the table. For each row, it gets each column's value. This is put into a two-dimensional array, which represents the entire contents of the table.

With these two queries done, you have everything you need to support the abstract methods of AbstractTableModel:

- getRowCount( ) is the length of the contents array that you create.
- getColumnCount( ) is 0 if you have no contents, or the length of the first item in the contents array (which is itself an array because contents is a two-dimensional array).
- getValueAt( ) is the value at contents[row][col].

AbstractTableModel has utterly trivial implementations of getColumnClass( ) and getColumnName( ), so the first always returns Object.class, the second returns "A", "B", "C", etc.; holding onto column metadata from the first query allows you to provide more useful implementations of these methods, too.

Example 3-12 shows how the JDBCTableModel is implemented.

Example 3-12. Populating a Swing TableModel from a database connection

```
import javax.swing.*;
import javax.swing.table.*;
import java.sql.*;
import java.util.*;

/** an immutable table model built from getting
    metadata about a table in a jdbc database
 */
public class JDBCTableModel extends AbstractTableModel {

    Object[][] contents;
    String[] columnNames;
    Class[] columnClasses;

    public JDBCTableModel (Connection conn,
                           String tableName)
        throws SQLException {
        super();
        getTableContents (conn, tableName);
    }

    protected void getTableContents (Connection conn,
                                     String tableName)
        throws SQLException {
```

Example 3-12. Populating a Swing TableModel from a database connection (continued)

```java
// get metadata: what columns exist and what
// types (classes) are they?
DatabaseMetaData meta = conn.getMetaData( );
System.out.println ("got meta = " + meta);
ResultSet results =
    meta.getColumns (null, null, tableName, null) ;
System.out.println ("got column results");
ArrayList colNamesList = new ArrayList( );
ArrayList colClassesList = new ArrayList( );
while (results.next( )) {
    colNamesList.add (results.getString ("COLUMN_NAME"));
    System.out.println ("name: " +
                        results.getString ("COLUMN_NAME"));

    int dbType = results.getInt ("DATA_TYPE");
    switch (dbType) {
    case Types.INTEGER:
        colClassesList.add (Integer.class); break;
    case Types.FLOAT:
        colClassesList.add (Float.class); break;
    case Types.DOUBLE:
    case Types.REAL:
        colClassesList.add (Double.class); break;
    case Types.DATE:
    case Types.TIME:
    case Types.TIMESTAMP:
        colClassesList.add (java.sql.Date.class); break;
    default:
        colClassesList.add (String.class); break;
    };
    System.out.println ("type: " +
                        results.getInt ("DATA_TYPE"));
}
columnNames = new String [colNamesList.size( )];
colNamesList.toArray (columnNames);
columnClasses = new Class [colClassesList.size( )];
colClassesList.toArray (columnClasses);

// get all data from table and put into
// contents array

Statement statement =
    conn.createStatement ( );
results = statement.executeQuery ("SELECT * FROM " +
                                  tableName);
ArrayList rowList = new ArrayList( );
while (results.next( )) {
    ArrayList cellList = new ArrayList( );
    for (int i = 0; i<columnClasses.length; i++) {
        Object cellValue = null;
```

Example 3-12. Populating a Swing TableModel from a database connection (continued)

```
            if (columnClasses[i] == String.class)
                cellValue = results.getString (columnNames[i]);
            else if (columnClasses[i] == Integer.class)
                cellValue = new Integer (
                                    results.getInt (columnNames[i]));
            else if (columnClasses[i] == Float.class)
                cellValue = new Float (
                                    results.getInt (columnNames[i]));
            else if (columnClasses[i] == Double.class)
                cellValue = new Double (
                                    results.getDouble (columnNames[i]));
            else if (columnClasses[i] == java.sql.Date.class)
                cellValue = results.getDate (columnNames[i]);
            else
                System.out.println ("Can't assign " +
                                        columnNames[i]);
            cellList.add (cellValue);
        }// for
        Object[] cells = cellList.toArray( );
        rowList.add (cells);
    } // while
    // finally create contents two-dim array
    contents = new Object[rowList.size( )] [];
    for (int i=0; i<contents.length; i++)
        contents[i] = (Object []) rowList.get (i);
    System.out.println ("Created model with " +
                    contents.length + " rows");

    // close stuff
    results.close( );
    statement.close( );
}

// AbstractTableModel methods

public int getRowCount( ) {
    return contents.length;
}

public int getColumnCount( ) {
    if (contents.length == 0)
        return 0;
    else
        return contents[0].length;
}

public Object getValueAt (int row, int column) {
    return contents [row][column];
}

// overrides methods for which AbstractTableModel
// has trivial implementations
```

Example 3-12. Populating a Swing TableModel from a database connection (continued)

```java
    public Class getColumnClass (int col) {
        return columnClasses [col];
    }

    public String getColumnName (int col) {
        return columnNames [col];
    }
}
```

The constructor dumps off its real work to getTableContents( ), which is responsible for the two queries just described. It gets a DatabaseMetaData object from the Connection, from which you can then get the column data with a getColumns( ) call. The arguments to this method are the catalog, schema pattern, table name pattern, and column name pattern; this implementation ignores catalogs and schema, although you might need to have callers specify them if you have a complex database. getColumns( ) returns a ResultSet, which you iterate over just like you would with the results of a regular JDBC query.

Getting the column name is easy: just call getString("COLUMN_NAME"). The type is a little more interesting, as the getInt("DATA_TYPE") call will return an int, which represents one of the constants of the java.sql.Types class. In this example, I've simply mapped Strings and the basic number types to appropriate Java classes. TIMESTAMP is SQL's concept of a point in time (a DATE and a TIME), so it gets to be a Java Date. Knowing these types will make it easier to call the right getXXX( ) method when retrieving the actual table data.

The second query is a simple SELECT * FROM tableName. With no WHERE restriction on the query, this will create a ResultSet with every row in the table. I shouldn't have to mention that if tableName is a table with millions of records, your resulting TableModel is not going to fit into memory. You knew that, right?

Again, you need to iterate over a ResultSet. Each time that results.next( ) returns true, meaning there's another result, you pull out every column you know about from the earlier metadata query. This means calling a getXXX( ) method and passing in the column name, where you know which getXXX( ) to use from your earlier investigation of the type of each column. You can go ahead and put numeric data into its proper wrapper class (Integer, Double, etc.) because that works well with the class-based rendering system of JTables. A caller might decide to use a TableCellRenderer that applies a Format class to all Doubles in the table to display them only to a certain number of decimal points, or to render Dates with relative terms like "Today" and "25 hours ago." Strongly typing the data in your model will help with that.

With the queries done, you just convert the ArrayLists to real arrays (which offer quick lookups for the get methods). The implementations of the AbstractTableModel methods mentioned previously, as well as the improved implementations of getColumnClass( ) and getColumnName( ), are trivial uses of the columnNames, columnClasses, and contents arrays built up by this method.

Testing Things Out

Before you say "I can't run this hack, I don't have a database," relax! The open source world has you covered. And no, it's not some big thing like JBoss. HSQLDB, more commonly known by its old name, Hypersonic, is a JDBC relational database engine written in Java. It is really small and can be run as a standalone server or within your JVM. If you are database-less, grab HSQLDB from *http://hsqldb.sourceforge.net/*.

Whatever your database, you'll need a driver classname, URL, username, and password to make a connection to the database. If you have your own database, I trust you already know this. If you just downloaded HSQLDB one paragraph ago, then you'll be using the following information:

- Driver: org.hsqldb.jdbcDriver
- URL: jdbc:hsqldb:file:testdb
- User: sa
- Password: (none)

This assumes you'll be running Hypersonic as part of your application, meaning you'll need to extend your classpath to pick up the *hsqldb.jar* file. Also note that this will create some *testdb* files in your current directory that you can clean up when done. You can also provide a full path to some other directory; see HSQLDB's docs for more info.

The test runner expects to pick up the connection strings as properties named jdbctable.driver, jdbctable.url, jdbctable.user, and jdbctable.pass. To make things easier, there are two ways to pass these in: either as system properties (usually specified with -D arguments to the *java* command), or in a file called *jdbctable.properties*. The book code has a sample of the latter with HSQLDB values as defaults.

To test the JDBCTableModel, the TestJDBCTable creates an entirely new table in the database. The model gets the Connection and the name of this table and loads the data from the database. Then the test class simply creates a new JTable from the model and puts it in a JFrame. Example 3-13 shows the source for this demo.

Example 3-13. Testing the JDBC-based table

```java
import javax.swing.*;
import javax.swing.table.*;
import java.sql.*;
import java.util.*;
import java.io.*;

public class TestJDBCTable {

    public static void main (String[] args) {
        try {
            /*
                driver, url, user, and pass can be passed in as
                system properties "jdbctable.driver",
                "jdbctable.url", "jdbctable.user", and
                "jdbctable.pass", or specified in a file
                called "jdbctable.properties" in current
                directory
            */
            Properties testProps = new Properties( );
            String ddriver = System.getProperty ("jdbctable.driver");
            String durl = System.getProperty ("jdbctable.url");
            String duser = System.getProperty ("jdbctable.user");
            String dpass = System.getProperty ("jdbctable.pass");

            if (ddriver != null)
                testProps.setProperty ("jdbctable.driver", ddriver);
            if (durl != null)
                testProps.setProperty ("jdbctable.url", durl);
            if (duser != null)
                testProps.setProperty ("jdbctable.user", duser);
            if (dpass != null)
                testProps.setProperty ("jdbctable.pass", dpass);
            try {
                testProps.load (new FileInputStream (
                                new File ("jdbctable.properties")));
            } catch (Exception e) {} // ignore FNF, etc.
            System.out.println ("Test Properties:");
            testProps.list (System.out);

            // now get a connection
            // note care to replace nulls with empty strings
            Class.forName(testProps.getProperty
                            ("jdbctable.driver")).newInstance( );
            String url = testProps.getProperty ("jdbctable.url");
            url = ((url == null) ? "" : url);
            String user = testProps.getProperty ("jdbctable.user");
            user = ((user == null) ? "" : user);
            String pass = testProps.getProperty ("jdbctable.pass");
            pass = ((pass == null) ? "" : pass);
```

Example 3-13. Testing the JDBC-based table (continued)

```
        Connection conn =
            DriverManager.getConnection (url, user, pass);

        // create db table to use
        String tableName = createSampleTable(conn);

        // get a model for this db table and add to a JTable
        TableModel mod =
            new JDBCTableModel (conn, tableName);
        JTable jtable = new JTable (mod);
        JScrollPane scroller =
            new JScrollPane (jtable,
                    ScrollPaneConstants.VERTICAL_SCROLLBAR_AS_NEEDED,
                    ScrollPaneConstants.HORIZONTAL_SCROLLBAR_AS_NEEDED);
        JFrame frame = new JFrame ("JDBCTableModel demo");
        frame.getContentPane().add (scroller);
        frame.pack();
        frame.setVisible (true);

        conn.close();

    } catch (Exception e) {
        e.printStackTrace();
    }
}

public static String createSampleTable (Connection conn)
    throws SQLException {

    Statement statement = conn.createStatement();
    // drop table if it exists
    try {
        statement.execute ("DROP TABLE EMPLOYEES");
    } catch (SQLException sqle) {
        sqle.printStackTrace(); // if table !exists
    }

    statement.execute ("CREATE TABLE EMPLOYEES " +
                    "(Name CHAR(20), Title CHAR(30), Salary INT)");
    statement.execute ("INSERT INTO EMPLOYEES VALUES " +
                    "('Jill', 'CEO', 200000 )");
    statement.execute ("INSERT INTO EMPLOYEES VALUES " +
                    "('Bob', 'VP', 195000 )");
    statement.execute ("INSERT INTO EMPLOYEES VALUES " +
                    "('Omar', 'VP', 190000 )");
    statement.execute ("INSERT INTO EMPLOYEES VALUES " +
                    "('Amy', 'Software Engineer', 50000 )");
    statement.execute ("INSERT INTO EMPLOYEES VALUES " +
                    "('Greg', 'Software Engineer', 45000 )");
```

Example 3-13. Testing the JDBC-based table (continued)

```
        statement.close( );

        return "EMPLOYEES";
    }
}
```

The `createSampleTable( )` method is something you could rewrite to insert your own types and values easily. In fact, because it returns the name of the table you've created, you could create many different tables in your database and test out how the model handles them. Or, use a loop to create lots of rows and see how long it takes to load them.

At any rate, when run, the `TestJDBCTable` produces a `JFrame` with the database table's contents, as seen in Figure 3-9.

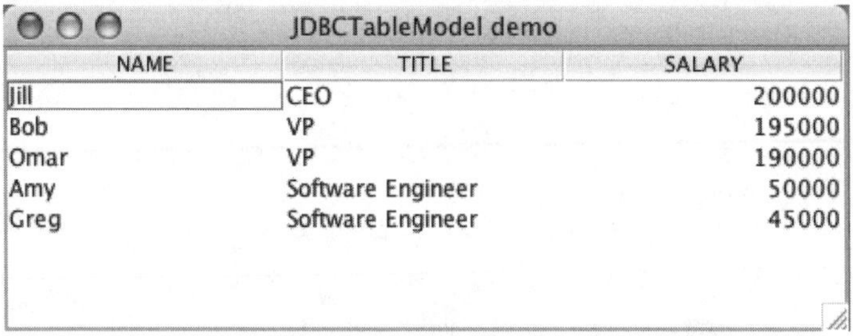

NAME	TITLE	SALARY
Jill	CEO	200000
Bob	VP	195000
Omar	VP	190000
Amy	Software Engineer	50000
Greg	Software Engineer	45000

JDBCTableModel demo

Figure 3-9. JTable populated from a database

HACK #25 Export Table Data to an Excel Spreadsheet

I don't want an entire spreadsheet API, I just want to get a table of values into Excel.

Most corporate intranet applications require interfacing with standard office software, which usually means Microsoft Word and Excel. Interfacing with Microsoft products can be tricky business. Whole suites of products have been created just to address this issue. One of the most commonly requested features is generating a report from the data in a `JTable`. You could use a library like Poi (*http://jakarta.apache.org/poi/*) to read and write Excel files natively, but most of the time that's overkill—you probably don't need to support Excel formulas or complicated formatting. All most users really want to do is dump tabular data into a file that will open in Excel with a double-click. And with a little bit of cleverness, you can do just that.

Dealing with Formatting

Excel uses a complicated database-oriented format for its native *.xls* files. This format defines the formulas, colors, charts and every other advanced feature Excel has supported over the years. Writing to the native *.xls* format is complicated but, fortunately, Excel supports other formats. The one I'm going to target is known as a *tab-delimited* text file, so called because tabs separate each field. This format is just plain text, so it will be super easy to write from Java, and open up in Excel with just a double-click.

Tab-delimited files separate each field with a tab character and each row with a standard Unix line break, \n. Since Swing defines a convenient getValueAt( ) method in the TableModel interface, it's very easy to just loop through the table cells and write it out to a file, as seen in Example 3-14.

Example 3-14. Exporting tab-delimited data from a TableModel

```java
public class ExcelExporter  {
    public ExcelExporter( ) { }
    public void exportTable(JTable table, File file) throws IOException {
        TableModel model = table.getModel( );
        FileWriter out = new FileWriter(file);

        for(int i=0; i < model.getColumnCount( ); i++) {
            out.write(model.getColumnName(i) + "\t");
        }
        out.write("\n");

        for(int i=0; i< model.getRowCount( ); i++) {
            for(int j=0; j < model.getColumnCount( ); j++) {
                out.write(model.getValueAt(i,j).toString( )+"\t");
            }
            out.write("\n");
        }
        out.close( );
        System.out.println("write out to: " + file);
    }
}
```

This code defines an ExcelExporter class with a single method exportTable( ), taking a JTable and a file. All JTables contain an implementation of the TableModel interface that holds the actual data. The code first retrieves the table model and opens a new FileWriter to the file. I used a FileWriter instead of a FileInputStream because Writers automatically handle text encoding issues. This means you don't have to worry about the language the program is running on. Using a Writer ensures that the code will work with any encoding from simple ASCII to triple-byte Korean Unicode.

The TableModel also defines the names of the columns, which are typically printed at the top of each column in the final spreadsheet. The code loops through the column names and prints them to the writer, following each column name with a \t, which represents the tab character, and finally an \n (the Unix newline character, which will work fine on both Mac OS X and Windows) at the end of the line. After that, it loops through each data row in turn, again separating fields with tabs and rows with the newline. After writing the fields, it closes the file and prints a status message. And with that, the core of the table export is done.

The main method in Example 3-15 creates a JTable with sample data and a button to generate an Excel file. First, it creates sample data as string arrays, and then it builds a new DefaultTableModel (the standard TableModel implementation that comes with Swing), nesting it inside of a JTable and then a JScrollPane.

Example 3-15. Testing JTable data export

```
public static void main(String[] args) {
    String[][] data = {
        { "Housewares",  "$1275.00" },
        { "Pets",         "$125.00" },
        { "Electronics", "$2533.00" },
        { "Menswear",     "$497.00" }
    };
    String[] headers = { "Department", "Daily Revenue" };

    JFrame frame = new JFrame("JTable to Excel Hack");
    DefaultTableModel model = new DefaultTableModel(data,headers);
    final JTable table = new JTable(model);
    JScrollPane scroll = new JScrollPane(table);

    JButton export = new JButton("Export");
    export.addActionListener(new ActionListener() {
        public void actionPerformed(ActionFvent evt) {
            try {
                ExcelExporter exp = new ExcelExporter();
                exp.exportTable(table, new File("results.xls"));
            } catch (IOException ex) {
                System.out.println(ex.getMessage());
                ex.printStackTrace();
            }
        }
    });

    frame.getContentPane().add("Center",scroll);
    frame.getContentPane().add("South",export);
    frame.pack();
    frame.setVisible(true);
}
```

The export button has a simple action listener that calls exportTable( ) on a new ExcelExporter. The trick to getting Excel to open the file with a double-click on the desktop is to name the file with an *.xls* extension. It won't be a real Excel file, but the operating system will think that it is and pass it to Excel anyway. Then Excel will look at the file, realize it's actually a tab-delimited text file, and load it with the right import filter.

Figure 3-10 shows what the program looks like.

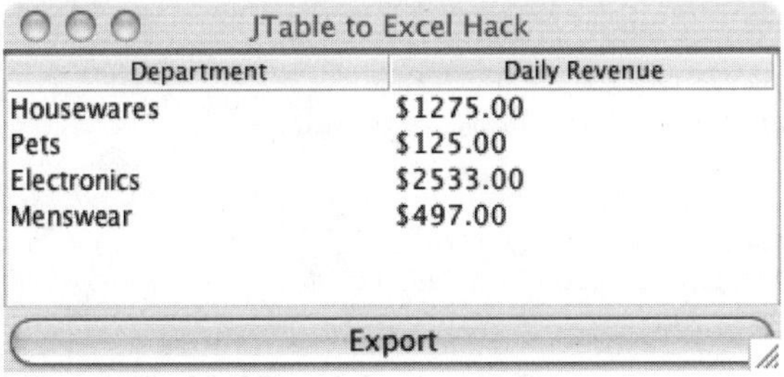

Figure 3-10. An Excel-exporting JTable

HACK #26 Search Through JTables Easily

Use this nifty TableModel decorator to search your JTables with minimal fuss.

Tables have a tendency to get very big; thousands of rows are not uncommon. But this causes some severe navigational issues for your users, like extremely small scrollbar handles, which make it difficult for them to find the information they need. One way to get around these navigational issues is to allow your users to search the table data rather than displaying it all. This hack shows you how to simply search your tables using the Apache open source Lucene search engine.

JTable Search Strategy

Rather than a custom TableModel with integrated Lucene functionality, you can build a TableModel decorator instead. This will allow you to search pre-existing TableModels without modifying them directly.

This works by keeping a set of links to an internal table model based on search criteria. For example, say you have 10 rows in your original table model, and you have a search that limits the results to 5 of those rows. Your inner TableModel will remain unchanged, but your TableModel decorator will have links to only five of the inner TableModel rows—making it look like it only has five rows of data.

Decorating the TableModel

Start by creating a class called TableSearcher that implements TableModel.

Next, create a simple decorator (or wrapper) that implements all of the TableModel methods and forwards the calls to the inner model. Depending on your IDE, you may be able to automate the process (IntelliJ IDEA does it for me). You'll have to modify a few of the methods, but most are going to remain unchanged. You don't have to touch the getColumnName( ) and getColumnClass( ) methods, for example. Just forward them to the inner TableModel:

```
public String getColumnName(int column) {
    return tableModel.getColumnName(column);
}

public Class getColumnClass(int column) {
    return tableModel.getColumnClass(column);
}
```

The getColumnCount( ) method is slightly different in that you have to check if the TableModel is null. This is because the table calls getColumnCount( ) first and calls other column methods only if there are valid columns. Here is the code with the null check:

```
public int getColumnCount( ) {
    return (tableModel == null) ? 0 : tableModel.getColumnCount( );
}
```

Creating Logical Links to the Inner Table Model

Now, you need to introduce the idea of links between the inner table model and this table model. Create a Collection called rowToModelIndex. In it, you'll store Integers corresponding to the inner table model row number, at the index that corresponds to this table model's row. So, if the fifth row in the inner model is the first row in this model, you would store an Integer value of 5 as the first in the rowtoModelIndex.

This method clears the searching state by making a one-to-one mapping of the inner table model to this table model:

```
private void clearSearchingState( ){
    searchString = null;
    rowToModelIndex.clear( );
    for (int t=0; t<tableModel.getRowCount( ); t++){
        rowToModelIndex.add(new Integer(t));
    }
}
```

Now, you need to change the row reference methods to indirect through the row to model index before hitting the inner table model:

```
public int getRowCount( ) {
    return (tableModel == null) ? 0 : rowToModelIndex.size( );
}
public boolean isCellEditable(int row, int column) {
    return tableModel.isCellEditable(getModelRow(row), column);
}

public Object getValueAt(int row, int column) {
    return tableModel.getValueAt(getModelRow(row), column);
}

public void setValueAt(Object aValue, int row, int column) {
    tableModel.setValueAt(aValue, getModelRow(row), column);
}
```

Indexing

Lucene is a document indexing and searching tool, available from *http://
lucene.apache.org/*. To incorporate it into a Java application, you simply need
to put its JAR file, typically named something like *lucene-version.jar*, into
your classpath. For this hack, you'll need the following import statements:

```
import org.apache.lucene.store.*;
import org.apache.lucene.document.*;
import org.apache.lucene.analysis.*;
import org.apache.lucene.index.*;
import org.apache.lucene.search.*;
import org.apache.lucene.queryParser.*;
```

Most developers use Lucene with documents, but you can fake it to index a
table model instead. First, you need to create a Lucene index, where all of
the internal Lucene links are stored. You should use a RAMDirectory rather
than a file-based directory in order to keep everything portable. You'll also
need an Analyzer that helps communicate between data and the index, as
well as an IndexWriter that actually writes to the index:

```
directory = new RAMDirectory( );
analyzer = new WhitespaceAnalyzer( );
IndexWriter writer = new IndexWriter(directory, analyzer, true);
```

For the purposes of indexing, think of every row as a document and every
column as a word or a set of words (called a Field in Lucene-speak) for that
document. Now, loop through the table model's rows, creating a new
Document for each row and add Fields per column:

```
for (int row=0; row < tableModel.getRowCount( ); row++){
    Document document = new Document( );
    //add fields
    writer.addDocument(document);
}
```

First, add a field with the row index in the inner table model. You'll use this to link back to that row later in the row-to-model index. Each field needs a name and a value, so create a constant called ROW_NUMBER that you'll refer to later when retrieving the links:

```
Document document = new Document( );
document.add(new Field(ROW_NUMBER, "" + row, true, true, true));
//more indexing to come
writer.addDocument(document);
```

Then, iterate through all of the columns and add a Field for each column name/value pair:

```
for (int column=0; column < tableModel.getColumnCount( ); column++){
    String columnName = tableModel.getColumnName(column);
    String columnValue = String.valueOf(
        tableModel.getValueAt(row, column)
    ).toLowerCase( );
    document.add(new Field(columnName, columnValue, true, true, true));
}
```

Searching

There are two parts to the searching. First, you have to hit the Lucene index with a search string. This will give you a list of rows in the inner table model that match the search. Then you need to reset the row-to-model index, pointing to those rows.

Getting results from the index. To actually get the search results, you need an IndexSearcher that speaks to the index and returns your search results:

```
IndexSearcher is = new IndexSearcher(directory);
```

You want to make sure all of the fields get searched, so iterate through the table model and put all of the column names in an array that you'll pass into the Lucene search call:

```
String[] fields = new String[tableModel.getColumnCount( )];
for (int t=0; t<tableModel.getColumnCount( ); t++){
    fields[t]=tableModel.getColumnName(t);
}
```

Next, create a Query object to pass to the IndexSearcher; there is a helper method on MultiFieldQueryParser to do just that. Pass it the fields you want to search, your search String, and the analyzer:

```
Query query = MultiFieldQueryParser.parse(searchString, fields, analyzer);
```

Then run the search. Hits is the object type returned by the search call. You'll process the hits in the next section when you map the results back to the inner table model:

```
Hits hits = is.search(query);
```

Recreating the inner table model links. Start by clearing the row-to-model index to get rid of the previous results:

```
rowToModelIndex.clear( );
```

The Hits object contains a number of Documents, just like the ones you put into the index. Remember, you put a field in each Document with the name ROW_NUMBER. So, now you can iterate through the Documents and get the row number from the field value:

```
for (int t=0; t<hits.length( ); t++){
    Document document = hits.doc(t);
    Field field = document.getField(ROW_NUMBER);
    Integer rowNumber = new Integer(field.stringValue( ));
}
```

The last step is to add an Integer to the row-to-model index with the row number retrieved from the document. Then, tie up all the loose ends by firing a table model update.

Try It Out

Because you're creating this table model as a decorator, it's extremely easy to use. The normal code to set up a JTable and a custom table model MyTableModel looks like this:

```
JTable table = new JTable( );
MyTableModel myTableModel = new MyTableModel( );
table.setTableModel(myTableModel);
```

All you need to do is wrap the MyTableModel with a TableSearcher and set the table model for the JTable as the TableSearcher:

```
JTable table = new JTable( );
MyTableModel myTableModel = new MyTableModel( );
TableSearcher tableSearcher = new TableSearcher(myTableModel);
table.setTableModel(tableSearcher);
```

Then, you just need to call the search method at the appropriate time. Usually, you'll have a search field to enter the search and a search button to start the search, so just attach an action listener to them both to fire off a search:

```
final JTextField searchField = new JTextField( );
JButton searchButton = new JButton("Go");

ActionListener searchListener = new ActionListener( ) {
    public void actionPerformed(ActionEvent e) {
        searchTableModel.search(searchField.getText().trim().toLowerCase( ));
        searchField.requestFocus( );
    }
};
```

```
searchButton.addActionListener(searchListener);
searchField.addActionListener(searchListener);
```

Finishing Touches

You've got the bare bones down, but there are a few things you'll want to add to make everything a little more functional. Here are a couple of ideas.

Listen to inner table updates. If the inner table model changes, you need to know about it. Otherwise, your search results will not jive with the inner table model. The simple solution is to add a TableModelListener to the inner table to rebuild the index, and then rerun the search against the new index. Here's the code:

```
private class TableModelHandler implements TableModelListener {
    public void tableChanged(TableModelEvent e) {
        // If we're not searching, just pass the event along.
        if (!isSearching()) {
            clearSearchingState();
            reindex();
            fireTableChanged(e);
            return;
        }
        // Something has happened to the data that may
        // have invalidated the search.
        reindex();
        search(searchString);
        fireTableDataChanged();
    }
}
```

You should consider extending this hack if you have serious performance considerations. You could narrow down the area of the table that changed to fire more accurate events to the table.

Clear search results for blank search. When users search with an empty string, they typically expect that to clear the search. The easiest way to do this is to check for an empty string in the search method. If they search with an empty string, clear the search and rerun the method that indexes all of the inner table model without a search:

```
public void search(String searchString){
    if (searchString == null || searchString.equals("")){
        clearSearchingState();
        fireTableDataChanged();
        return;
    }

    //rest of search method
}
```

If you wanted to hack further, you could make this and other small functions like it each separate decorators. Then you could combine them at will, depending on the needs of your application.

Wrapping Up

This table model decorator is now part of the main Lucene distribution. It's part of a new *lucene-contrib* project for Swing. In addition to this table model decorator, there is also a list decorator. I imagine the search logic is going to beef up, so definitely check out the Lucene site for more information. You can get read-only web access to the Lucene repository at *http://svn.apache.org/repos/asf/lucene/java/trunk/contrib/swing/*. Also note that because these models are officially part of *lucene-contrib*, they are going to be distributed with all new Lucene builds. So, they are going to come free with Lucene in the future.

—*Jonathan Simon*

HACK #27 Animate JTree Drops

Who said working with tree paths was hard? Now you can reorganize tree hierarchies with drag-and-drop.

JTrees are great for representing hierarchy, but they're not so hot as control widgets. You might want to drag items inside a tree, or accept a drop from some other part of your application, and it turns out not to be well suited to that. The problem is that the JTree isn't really a container, so from the Swing programmer's point of view, you see the tree's visual representation, but not the nodes within it.

The goal of this hack is to take a JTree, like the one shown in Figure 3-11, and allow you to reorganize it through drag-and-drop. The bulk of the work will be in animating and handling the drop. The payoff is that making a single tree reorderable will also get you most of the way to making it a good drag-and-drop participant with the rest of your application, since supporting drag-and-drop within the JTree requires you to make the tree a drag source and a drop target.

The Code

If any of the forgoing sounds familiar, it should. Bringing drag-and-drop to the JTree is very similar to supporting it for the JList. In fact, the JTree and the JList have a lot in common—both use cell renderers, both are typically put in JScrollPanes, etc.

Figure 3-11. JTree with drag-and-drop reordering

In fact, the code for this hack started as a straight port of the reorderable JList hack **[Hack #17]**, with obvious changes for the different helper classes (TreeCellRenderer instead of ListCellRenderer) and different handling of the model, since tree models are hierarchical.

To recap what needs to be done:

- The tree needs to implement the DragGestureListener (to start a drag), the DropTargetListener (to handle the drop), and the DragSourceListener (only to get the end-of-drop callback).

- The drag-and-drop implementations need to use the coordinates provided by drag-and-drop events to map to nodes of the tree as either the node to drag or as potential drop targets.

- The renderer needs to use information about whether a to-be-rendered cell is the drop target and to offer suitable visual feedback.

- The drop handling needs to remove the dragged node from its old location and insert it at its new location.

Example 3-16 shows the main class (minus two inner classes that will be introduced shortly).

Example 3-16. JTree with drag-and-drop support

```
public class DnDJTree extends JTree
    implements DragSourceListener, DropTargetListener, DragGestureListener {

    static DataFlavor localObjectFlavor;
    static {
        try {
```

Example 3-16. JTree with drag-and-drop support (continued)

```
        localObjectFlavor =
            new DataFlavor (DataFlavor.javaJVMLocalObjectMimeType);
    } catch (ClassNotFoundException cnfe) { cnfe.printStackTrace( ); }
}
static DataFlavor[] supportedFlavors = { localObjectFlavor };
DragSource dragSource;
DropTarget dropTarget;
TreeNode dropTargetNode = null;
TreeNode draggedNode = null;

public DnDJTree ( ) {
    super( );
    setCellRenderer (new DnDTreeCellRenderer( ));
    setModel (new DefaultTreeModel(new DefaultMutableTreeNode("default")));
    dragSource = new DragSource( );
    DragGestureRecognizer dgr =
        dragSource.createDefaultDragGestureRecognizer (this,
                                DnDConstants.ACTION_MOVE,
                                            this);
    dropTarget = new DropTarget (this, this);
}

// DragGestureListener
public void dragGestureRecognized (DragGestureEvent dge) {
    System.out.println ("dragGestureRecognized");
    // find object at this x,y
    Point clickPoint = dge.getDragOrigin( );
    TreePath path = getPathForLocation (clickPoint.x, clickPoint.y);
    if (path == null) {
        System.out.println ("not on a node");
        return;
    }
    draggedNode = (TreeNode) path.getLastPathComponent( );
    Transferable trans = new RJLTransferable (draggedNode);
    dragSource.startDrag (dge,Cursor.getDefaultCursor( ),
                        trans, this);
}
// DragSourceListener events
public void dragDropEnd (DragSourceDropEvent dsde) {
    System.out.println ("dragDropEnd( )");
    dropTargetNode = null;
    draggedNode = null;
    repaint( );
}
public void dragEnter (DragSourceDragEvent dsde) {}
public void dragExit (DragSourceEvent dse) {}
public void dragOver (DragSourceDragEvent dsde) {}
public void dropActionChanged (DragSourceDragEvent dsde) {}
// DropTargetListener events
public void dragEnter (DropTargetDragEvent dtde) {
    System.out.println ("dragEnter");
```

Example 3-16. JTree with drag-and-drop support (continued)

```
        dtde.acceptDrag(DnDConstants.ACTION_COPY_OR_MOVE);
        System.out.println ("accepted dragEnter");
    }
    public void dragExit (DropTargetEvent dte) {}
    public void dragOver (DropTargetDragEvent dtde) {
        // figure out which cell it's over, no drag to self
        Point dragPoint = dtde.getLocation( );
        TreePath path = getPathForLocation (dragPoint.x, dragPoint.y);
        if (path == null)
            dropTargetNode = null;
        else
            dropTargetNode = (TreeNode) path.getLastPathComponent( );
        repaint( );
    }
    public void drop (DropTargetDropEvent dtde) {
        System.out.println ("drop( )!");
        Point dropPoint = dtde.getLocation( );
        // int index = locationToIndex (dropPoint);
        TreePath path = getPathForLocation (dropPoint.x, dropPoint.y);
        System.out.println ("drop path is " + path);
        boolean dropped = false;
        try {
            dtde.acceptDrop (DnDConstants.ACTION_MOVE);
            System.out.println ("accepted");
            Object droppedObject =
                dtde.getTransferable( ).getTransferData(localObjectFlavor);
            MutableTreeNode droppedNode = null;
            if (droppedObject instanceof MutableTreeNode) {
                // remove from old location
                droppedNode = (MutableTreeNode) droppedObject;
                ((DefaultTreeModel)getModel( )).
                    removeNodeFromParent(droppedNode);
            } else {
                droppedNode = new DefaultMutableTreeNode (droppedObject);
            }
            // insert into spec'd path.  if dropped into a parent
            // make it last child of that parent
            DefaultMutableTreeNode dropNode =
                (DefaultMutableTreeNode) path.getLastPathComponent( );
            if (dropNode.isLeaf( )) {
                DefaultMutableTreeNode parent =
                    (DefaultMutableTreeNode) dropNode.getParent( );
                int index = parent.getIndex (dropNode);
                ((DefaultTreeModel)getModel( )).insertNodeInto (droppedNode,
                                                            parent, index);
            } else {
                ((DefaultTreeModel)getModel( )).insertNodeInto (droppedNode,
                                            dropNode,
                                            dropNode.getChildCount( ));
            }
            dropped = true;
        } catch (Exception e) {
```

Example 3-16. JTree with drag-and-drop support (continued)

```
            e.printStackTrace( );
        }
        dtde.dropComplete (dropped);
    }
    public void dropActionChanged (DropTargetDragEvent dtde) {}

    // main( ) method (unit test) goes here

    // inner classes go here
}
```

In several places in this code—dragGestureRecognized( ), dragOver( ), and drop( )—you can see the use of JTree's getPathForLocation( ), which uses an *x,y* pair from the event to get a TreePath. The last node of this path is the item under the cursor, or null if the cursor is over some non-node part of the JTree. In dragGestureRecognized( ), this is used to start the drag. In dragOver( ) and drop( ), it's used to determine which node will potentially be the drop target. The difference between these two is that dragOver( ) remembers the drop target node for use in repainting, while drop( ) actually handles the drop. Specifically, drop( ) gets the Transferable from the DropTargetDropEvent and, if it is a MutableTreeNode, moves it within the TreeModel. If it isn't a node, it's assumed that this is from some other part of your GUI, and wraps it with a new MutableTreeNode. That block of code isn't used in this demo, but it might be useful when you extend this code.

One other thing to note about drop( ) is that it has different handling based on whether the drop is occurring on a leaf or a branch. On a leaf, the dropped item is inserted before the target. On a branch—i.e., a parent to other nodes—the dropped item is inserted as the last child of the branch.

The RJLTransferable class shown here is used as a fairly straightforward Transferable wrapper around local Java objects:

```
class RJLTransferable implements Transferable {
    Object object;
    public RJLTransferable (Object o) {
        object = o;
    }
    public Object getTransferData(DataFlavor df)
        throws UnsupportedFlavorException, IOException {
        if (isDataFlavorSupported (df))
            return object;
        else
            throw new UnsupportedFlavorException(df);
    }
    public boolean isDataFlavorSupported (DataFlavor df) {
        return (df.equals (localObjectFlavor));
    }
```

```
public DataFlavor[] getTransferDataFlavors () {
    return supportedFlavors;
}
}
```

The other helper inner class is where a lot of the "good stuff" happens. DnDJTreeCellRenderer, listed in the following code, has to be aware of what node is the potential drop target—this is an instance variable set by dragOver( ) in the main class—and if the node to be rendered is the drop target, it draws it differently:

```
class DnDTreeCellRenderer
    extends DefaultTreeCellRenderer {
    boolean isTargetNode;
    boolean isTargetNodeLeaf;
    boolean isLastItem;
    int BOTTOM_PAD = 30;
    public DnDTreeCellRenderer() {
        super();
    }
    public Component getTreeCellRendererComponent (JTree tree,
                                                   Object value,
                                                   boolean isSelected,
                                                   boolean isExpanded,
                                                   boolean isLeaf,
                                                   int row,
                                                   boolean hasFocus) {
        isTargetNode = (value == dropTargetNode);
        isTargetNodeLeaf = (isTargetNode &&
                            ((TreeNode)value).isLeaf( ));
        // isLastItem = (index == list.getModel().getSize( )-1);
        boolean showSelected = isSelected &
                            (dropTargetNode == null);
        return super.getTreeCellRendererComponent (tree, value,
                                                   isSelected, isExpanded,
                                                   isLeaf, row, hasFocus);

    }

    public void paintComponent (Graphics g) {
        super.paintComponent(g);
        if (isTargetNode) {
            g.setColor(Color.black);
            if (isTargetNodeLeaf) {
                g.drawLine (0, 0, getSize( ).width, 0);
            } else {
                g.drawRect (0, 0, getSize().width-1, getSize( ).height-1);
            }
        }
    }
}
}
```

The special rendering is a two-step process. First, getTreeCellRendererComponent( ) figures out if the cell to be rendered is the drop target, and if so, it sets a local boolean. It sets another boolean to indicate that the drop target cell is a leaf. Having set these booleans, it returns the superclass's implementation. In short order, the renderer's paint( ) method is called. In the paint( ), you can use the booleans to apply special rendering. In this version, a drop target that is a leaf gets a line drawn in its top inset, suggesting that the dropped item will be inserted before this node. If rendering a drop target that is a branch—i.e., it's not a leaf—then the special rendering puts a box around the component.

Running the Code

The main method, shown in Example 3-17, builds a reorderable tree and puts it in a JFrame.

Example 3-17. Testing the drag-and-drop JTree

```
public static void main (String[] args) {
    JTree tree = new DnDJTree( );
    DefaultMutableTreeNode root = new DefaultMutableTreeNode("People");
    DefaultMutableTreeNode set1 = new DefaultMutableTreeNode("Set 1");
    DefaultMutableTreeNode set2 = new DefaultMutableTreeNode("Set 2");
    DefaultMutableTreeNode set3 = new DefaultMutableTreeNode("Set 3");
    set1.add (new DefaultMutableTreeNode ("Chris"));
    set1.add (new DefaultMutableTreeNode ("Kelly"));
    set1.add (new DefaultMutableTreeNode ("Keagan"));
    set2.add (new DefaultMutableTreeNode ("Joshua"));
    set2.add (new DefaultMutableTreeNode ("Kimi"));
    set3.add (new DefaultMutableTreeNode ("Michael"));
    set3.add (new DefaultMutableTreeNode ("Don"));
    set3.add (new DefaultMutableTreeNode ("Daniel"));
    root.add (set1);
    root.add (set2);
    set2.add (set3);
    DefaultTreeModel mod = new DefaultTreeModel (root);
    tree.setModel (mod);
    // expand all
    for (int i=0; i<tree.getRowCount( ); i++)
        tree.expandRow (i);
    // show tree
    JScrollPane scroller =
        new JScrollPane (tree,
                     ScrollPaneConstants.VERTICAL_SCROLLBAR_ALWAYS,
                     ScrollPaneConstants.HORIZONTAL_SCROLLBAR_NEVER);
    JFrame frame = new JFrame ("DnD JTree");
    frame.getContentPane( ).add (scroller);
    frame.pack( );
    frame.setVisible(true);
}
```

Figure 3-12 shows the animation of a drag. In this case, the "Chris" node is about to be dropped on top of the "Michael" node.

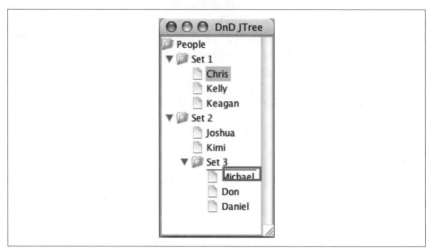

Figure 3-12. Dragging a node within a JTree

Because the drop is occurring over a leaf, the custom rendering shows a line on top of the "Michael" node, meaning that "Chris" will be inserted before "Michael". The result of the drop is shown in Figure 3-13.

Figure 3-13. Dropping a node within a JTree

In case that wasn't such a good idea, Figure 3-14 shows the "Chris" node being dragged back to where it was. In this case, the drag is over the "Set 1" branch, which causes it to be drawn with a box around it, suggesting that the drop will be "into" the branch.

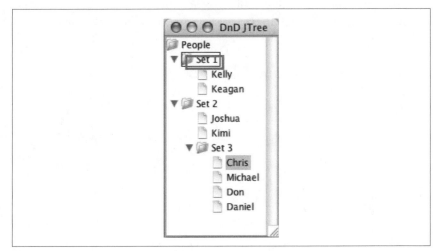

Figure 3-14. Dragging a node to a branch

The drop makes the dragged node the last child of the "Set 1" branch, as shown in Figure 3-15.

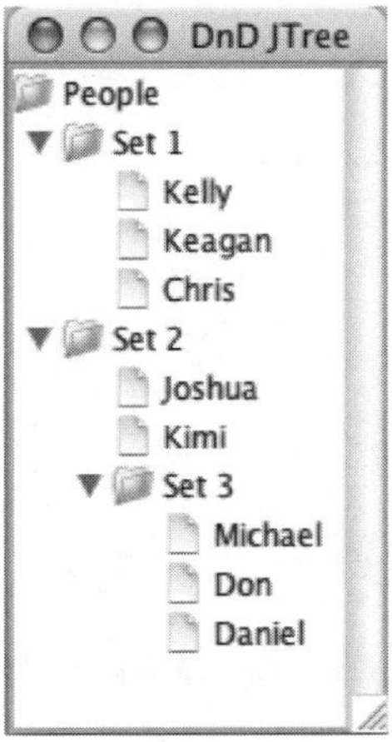

Figure 3-15. Dropping a node onto a branch

This code is primarily focused on making a single JTree reorderable. If you want to make drag-and-drop work between widgets in your GUI, the biggest change you'll need to make is to have the drop( ) method not remove the dragged node from the tree's model, since you can't assume that the dragged item is even a node in this tree. A little bit of checking the event source makes it easy enough to find what scenario you're dealing with.

File Choosers
Hacks 28–32

Ah, the poor JFileChooser. It's probably not anybody's favorite class in Swing, and it's quite likely the anti-favorite of many developers. Prior to Java 1.4, the Metal version had an "icon view" button that actually didn't do anything—not that it was worth writing home about once it was implemented. Little glitches like this make JFileChooser the whipping boy of many Swing developers. Apple's Java guidelines for Mac OS X actually advocate giving up on the JFileChooser altogether and going back to the AWT FileDialog!

This chapter is here to...well, if not to praise the JFileChooser, then certainly not to bury it either. This is Swing after all, and that means there are all sorts of places that you can hack in and embellish functionality to give the user more power, or to make a component smarter about the contents it displays.

HACK #28 Add a Right-Click Context Menu to the JFileChooser

Improve the native platform fidelity of the JFileChooser by adding a contextual menu that lets the user create new folders and delete files.

The standard JFileChooser that comes with Swing is quite limited. It doesn't follow shortcuts or any other linked files. It doesn't have image previews or even a right-click menu. These are all features that users expect to see. Worse, these are the kinds of details that continue to reinforce the belief that Swing apps are inferior to native ones.

This hack will tackle the first limitation, the lack of a context menu. Some platform file choosers—Windows Explorer in particular—provide users with a context menu, also known as a right-click menu. This provides fast access to commonly used functions like Delete and New Folder. Java 5.0 finally added a context menu to the file chooser, but if you want to target the millions of users out there with older versions of Java, then you need your own implementation. This hack creates a right-click menu on the JFileChooser to give the user those missing features.

The goal of this task is to create a contextual menu. This means it's a menu that pops up when you hit the right mouse button (or Control-click on one-button mice). It also is *contextual*, or context sensitive. This means the menu changes—or does something different—depending on what you currently have selected. In this case, there will be two actions: Delete will delete the currently selected file or directory, if one is selected; New Folder will create a new folder (called, not surprisingly, *New Folder*) in the current directory. Both of these actions depend on the current state of the file selection, so they are considered context sensitive.

The Problem

For the most part, Swing is quite extensible, but often only in ways that the Swing team thought of beforehand. The JFileChooser has ways to change the rendering of file icons, filtering the file list, adding components, and changing the text. It does not have any way to add pop-up menus, though. In short, we'll have to hack it, and there's no better way to start than by reusing another hack.

Chapter 8 has a hack for adding pop-up menu support to any frame; see "Create a Global Right-Click" **[Hack #57]**. By reusing its RightClickGlassPane, you can start off with a pop-up menu in place. That just leaves making a connection between the pop up and the file chooser component. Sounds easy, right? Well, if it were easy, it wouldn't be in this book!

First, create a JFileChooser subclass and attach the right-click glass pane:

```
public class ContextMenuFileChooser extends JFileChooser {

    protected Component right_click_pane;

    public ContextMenuFileChooser( ) {
        super( );
        JPopupMenu popup = new JPopupMenu( );
        popup.add(new DeleteAction(this));
        popup.add(new NewFolderAction(this));
        right_click_pane = new RightClickGlassPane(this,popup);
    }
}
```

This code defines a new subclass of JFileChooser—ContextMenuFileChooser. The constructor builds a custom subclass of the RightClickGlassPane and a new JPopupMenu pre-filled with two custom actions: one for deleting files and one for creating new folders.

With the `RightClickGlassPane` initialized, you need to install it in the actual window that contains the `JFileChooser`. While you can create your own window, the most common usage of `JFileChooser` is to show it with the `showDialog()` method; this method creates a new window and installs the chooser in it automatically. However, this means that you have no access to the real window until it's already on screen. Fortunately, the Swing team thought of this (let's give them some credit) and provided the `createDialog()` function. This protected method can be overridden to modify the dialog *before* it shows up on screen. A new implementation of `createDialog()` to add to `ContextMenuFileChooser` is shown here:

```
protected JDialog createDialog(Component parent) {
    JDialog dialog = super.createDialog(parent);

    // create the right-click glass pane.
    dialog.setGlassPane(right_click_pane);
    right_click_pane.setVisible(true);

    return dialog;
}
```

With this code in place, you can right-click anywhere on the file chooser to see the context menu. It's pretty useless, however, since the menu items don't actually do anything. You still have to create the Delete and New Folder actions. The `JFileChooser` API makes this pretty easy, though:

```
class DeleteAction extends AbstractAction {
    protected JFileChooser chooser;
    public DeleteAction(JFileChooser chooser) {
        super("Delete");
        this.chooser = chooser;
    }
    public void actionPerformed(ActionEvent evt) {
        File file = chooser.getSelectedFile();
        if(file != null) {
            file.delete();
            chooser.rescanCurrentDirectory();
        }
    }
}
```

The new `DeleteAction` above is a standard `AbstractAction` subclass, with a small change: it requires a `JFileChooser` in its constructor. The action needs the chooser to tell it which file has been selected. In the `actionPerformed()` implementation, you can see that the action gets the selected file, deletes it, and then tells the chooser to refresh itself. That's it! Pretty simple.

The NewFolderAction is similar and just as simple:

```
class NewFolderAction extends AbstractAction {
    protected JFileChooser chooser;
    public NewFolderAction(JFileChooser chooser) {
        super("New Folder");
        this.chooser = chooser;
    }
    public void actionPerformed(ActionEvent evt) {
        File cwd = chooser.getCurrentDirectory();
        if(cwd != null) {
            File new_dir = new File(cwd,"New Folder");
            new_dir.mkdir();
            chooser.rescanCurrentDirectory();
        }
    }
}
```

With these two actions in place, the custom file chooser will do exactly what
we want it to do: pop up a right-click menu and perform the two actions
when selected.

There's one glaring problem with this solution, though. The menu pops up
no matter where the user clicks in the dialog. This means the menu can
appear even when it's not over the file selection area. The only way to fix
this glitch is to trigger the pop-up menu only when it's over the correct
component. To do this, create an anonymous inline subclass of
RightClickGlassPane that overrides the redispatchMouseEvent( ) method. In
this new method, check to see if a right mouse click is over the correct components before showing the menu:

```
right_click_pane = new RightClickGlassPane(this,popup) {
    protected void redispatchMouseEvent(MouseEvent e, boolean repaint) {
        Component component = getRealComponent(e.getPoint());
        if(component == null) { return; }
        String chooser_class =
            "javax.swing.plaf.metal.MetalFileChooserUI$5";
        if(component.getClass().getName().equals(chooser_class)) {
            super.redispatchMouseEvent(e,repaint);
        } else {
            doDispatch(e);
        }
    }
};
```

There's one caveat here. In order to detect the file selection component, you
have to know which class actually draws the file selection on screen. The
JFileChooser doesn't expose this component, and digging through the
source code only reveals that it's an anonymous inner class. With a runtime
debugger, I found out that the name of the class we want is javax.swing.
plaf.metal.MetalFileChooserUI$5—at least when you are using the Metal

L&F. By testing for that classname, you can detect the file selection widget; however, this will only work under the Metal L&F. For other L&Fs (or versions of Metal other than JDK 1.4), you'll need to look for a different classname. A better implementation of this hack would test for class strings from all of the most common Look and Feels on the major Java platforms.

 I'll leave that task to you as an exercise. Have a ball!

With all the code in place, you can create a main( ) method that tests out the new ContextMenuFileChooser:

```java
public static void main(String[] args) {
    final JFileChooser jfc = new ContextMenuFileChooser( );
    jfc.showOpenDialog(null);
    System.exit(0);
}
```

Figure 4-1 shows what the finished JFileChooser looks like.

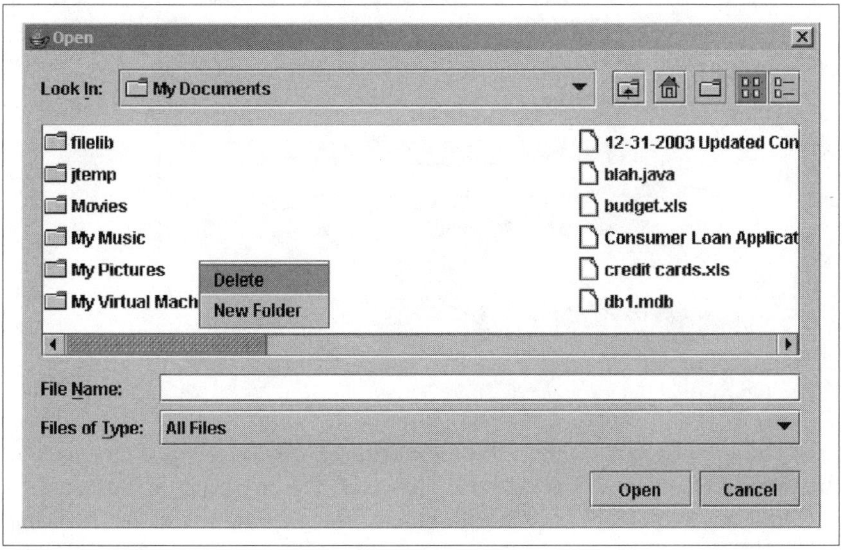

Figure 4-1. Context-sensitive menu

 This hack won't work with JDK 1.5 because that JFileChooser already provides its own context menu.

Display Shortcuts in the JFileChooser

HACK #29 This hack will customize the JFileChooser to recognize shortcut (linked) folders and overlay them with a link graphic, mimicking the native Windows File Explorer.

Another of JFileChooser's glaring bugs is the lack of any support for linked directories. This is hardly surprising, as Java itself has no understanding of linked directories. Most operating systems support linked files, however, and often indicate to the user that a file is linked—for example, by drawing an arrow overlaid on top of the folder or directory icon. Compare the typical JFileChooser in Figure 4-2 to the standard Windows file chooser in Figure 4-3. There's more than a small difference! No wonder it's hard to get folks to move to Swing.

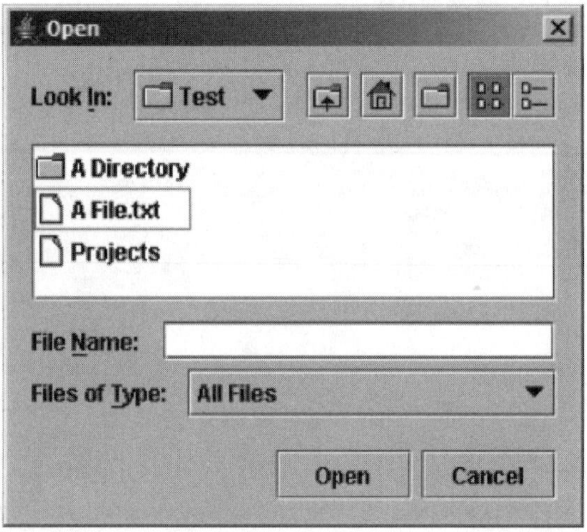

Figure 4-2. Normal JFileChooser

Like every Swing component, the look of the JFileChooser is controlled by the installed Look and Feel (L&F). However, the JFileChooser also uses a custom class similar to a table cell renderer for drawing the actual files and folders. That class, FileView, is the best place to start hacking the JFileChooser's display.

The FileView contains five methods that determine the names, icons, and other attributes that are actually displayed in a JFileChooser. By overriding these methods, you can change the look or text of any file. To draw shortcuts as linked folders, you just need to override the getIcon( ) and isTraversable( ) methods. getIcon( ) returns the icon to use when drawing the file.

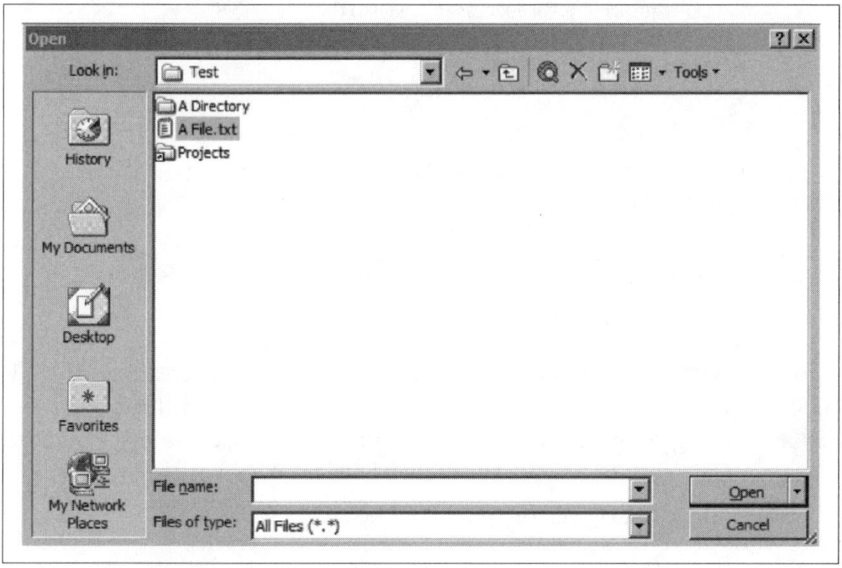

Figure 4-3. Standard Windows file chooser

isTraversable( ) tells the file chooser if a given file is a directory type of object, meaning the user can click and open it to list new files. These two methods will transform a *shortcut.lnk* file into a shortcut directory with the right icon.

 For the sake of brevity, this is a Windows-specific hack. You should be able to modify this hack easily to work with symlinks on Unix and Linux, as well as Mac OS X. Consider it homework!

To get started, create the ShortcutFileView class. This extends FileView, overriding the isTraversable( ) method to return true if the isDirLink( ) method indicates that the file is indeed a link (determined by looking for the *.lnk* extension). If the file is not a link, isDirLink( ) will return null.

Notice that isTraversable( ) returns a Boolean instead of a boolean. This allows a null to be returned in addition to the true/false values that boolean would allow.

Any method of FileView subclasses that return null will cause the file chooser to defer to its default file view, instead of using the custom view:

```
class ShortcutFileView extends FileView {

    public boolean isDirLink(File f) {
```

```
        if(f.getName().toLowerCase().endsWith(".lnk")) {
            return true;
        }
        return false;
    }

    public Boolean isTraversable(File f) {
        if(isDirLink(f)) {
            return new Boolean(true);
        }
        return null;
    }
}
```

Below is a sample program to test the ShortcutFileView. It creates a new file chooser, sets the file view to a new ShortcutFileView, and then opens the dialog. It is important to set the view before the showOpenDialog() because file choosers cannot be changed after they have been shown on screen:

```
public class DisplayShortcutTest {
    public static void main(String[] args) throws Exception {
        JFileChooser chooser = new JFileChooser();
        chooser.setFileView(new ShortcutFileView());
        chooser.showOpenDialog(null);
    }
}
```

This program changes the look of shortcuts to look like folders and be clickable, but they still don't have the link icon. This will require a bit more work. The second method to override in the file view is the getIcon() method. The plan is to get a standard folder icon then draw it onto a new icon with the overlaid link graphic. This part will create a new JFileChooser and get a reference to its normal file view. The following FileChooserUI code forces the file chooser to initialize its Look and Feel subsystem, ensuring that the FileView will be valid:

```
public Icon getIcon(File f) {
    if(isDirLink(f)) {

        JFileChooser chooser = new JFileChooser();
        FileChooserUI fcui = (FileChooserUI) UIManager.getUI(chooser);
        fcui.installUI(chooser);
        FileView def = fcui.getFileView(chooser);
```

Once you have the file view, you need to pull out a folder icon. You can do this by asking for the icon of a known folder, in this case C:\windows:

```
        // get the standard icon for a folder
        File tmp = new File("C:\\windows");
        Icon folder = def.getIcon(tmp);
```

```
        int w = folder.getIconWidth( );
        int h = folder.getIconHeight( );
```

Once you have the icon, you can build a new image to draw it on, and then overlay the link graphic:

```
        // create a buffered image the same size as the icon
        Image img = new BufferedImage(w,h,
                            BufferedImage.TYPE_4BYTE_ABGR);
        Graphics g = img.getGraphics( );

        // draw the normal icon
        folder.paintIcon(chooser,g,0,0);

        // draw the shortcut image on top of the icon
        Image shortcut = new ImageIcon("shortcut.png").getImage( );
        g.drawImage(shortcut,0,0,null);

        // clean up and return
        g.dispose( );
        return new ImageIcon(img);
    }
    return super.getIcon(f);
}
```

That's it. With the new icon created, your file chooser should look like Figure 4-4.

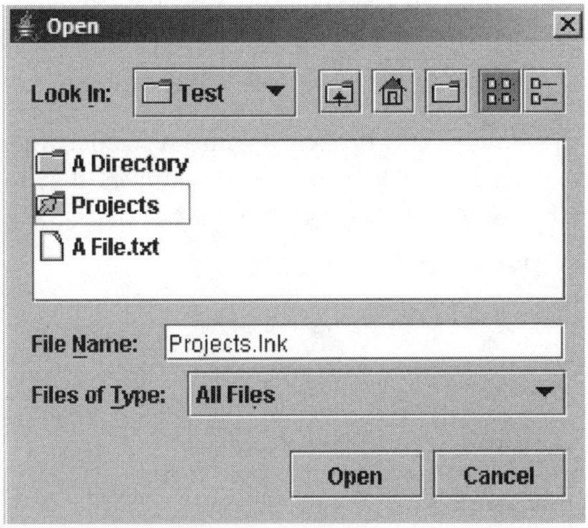

Figure 4-4. JFileChooser showing a shortcut

Real Windows Shortcut Support

Support Windows shortcuts by actually opening and parsing files with the under-documented LNK format.

It's one thing to properly display Windows shortcuts **[Hack #29]** by looking for the *.lnk* extension and changing the default icon to look like a link. But there's a glaring flaw: when you click on the shortcut it doesn't actually link anywhere! This hack will make the shortcuts really work by hacking into the undocumented shortcut files themselves.

Since links are not supported natively by the filesystem, Windows fakes it by storing the shortcut metadata (path, icon, and other information) in a *.lnk* file. When you click on the shortcut, the windows file manager reads the LNK file, extracts the target file/directory path, and then opens a new window at the real location. Your Java program can do the exact same thing using a custom FileSystemView. The only tricky part is actually parsing the LNK files.

Microsoft has never documented the LNK file format, preferring native Windows developers to use system APIs for all manipulation. Creative hackers on the Web have reverse engineered most of the format, which fortunately includes the parts you need to extract target filepaths.

Jesse Hager has compiled a great PDF describing the format in detail. I used that document to write the code in this hack. You can read the full document at *http://www.i2s-lab.com/ Papers/The_Windows_Shortcut_File_Format.pdf*.

The LNK files are binary data broken up into a header followed by a few optional blocks of data. The format provides offsets that make parsing it easy. The following code is the beginning of a LNK parser:

```
public class LnkParser {

    public LnkParser(File f) throws Exception {
        parse(f);
    }

    public void parse(File f) throws Exception {
        // read the entire file into a byte buffer
        FileInputStream fin = new FileInputStream(f);
        ByteArrayOutputStream bout = new ByteArrayOutputStream( );
        byte[] buff = new byte[256];
        while(true) {
            int n = fin.read(buff);
            if(n == -1) { break; }
            bout.write(buff,0,n);
```

```
    }
    fin.close( );
    byte[] link = bout.toByteArray( );
```

The class defines one important method, parse( ), which accepts a File object representing the LNK file. The first step is to load the entire file into a byte buffer.

> I have seen some versions of this code use a more stream-oriented approach with loops that read byte by byte. Since LNK files are always pretty small (usually under 5k), I felt the extra memory was worth it to allow cleaner code using index offsets.

Next comes the header parsing:

```
// get the flags byte
byte flags = link[0x14];

// get the file attributes byte
final int file_atts_offset = 0x18;
byte fileatts = link[file_atts_offset];
byte is_dir_mask = (byte)0x10;
if((fileatts & is_dir_mask) > 0) {
    is_dir = true;
} else {
    is_dir = false;
}
```

The header has a lot of values in it, but we are only interested in the values at byte 0x14 (the flags) and at 0x18 (the file attributes). Each of these values is 8 bits (a byte), where each bit represents something, such as whether the LNK points to a file or a directory. Because they are always at the same place, you can just jump directly to them in the array and store the values. To access a bit you need a *mask*, which is a number that lets you hide all of the bits in a value that you *don't* want, leaving only the bit you do want. To use it, you AND (a bitwise operation specified by the & character) the value and the mask together. Then you can just test if the final value is greater than zero to see if that bit was set. If the 4th bit of the file attributes byte is set (i.e., is equal to 1), then the target of this shortcut is a directory. The fileatts and is_dir_mask are ANDed together. If the final value is greater than zero, then the bit must have been set and the program sets the is_dir variable to true; otherwise, it sets is_dir to false.

```
// if the shell settings are present, skip them
final int shell_offset = 0x4c;
int shell_len = 0;
if((flags & 0x1) > 0) {
```

```
        // the plus 2 accounts for the length marker itself
        shell_len = bytes2short(link,shell_offset) + 2;
    }
```

LNK files have an optional block for shell settings, which are irrelevant for the purposes of getting the target path. If the shell settings are present (indicated by the 0th bit of the flags), then jump to the shell block, get its length from the next 2 bytes, and then skip to the end. The if((flags & 0x1) >0) section ANDs the flags value and a mask to get the 0th bit and see if there is a shell block. If the shell block is not present, then you can just set the offset to 0 and continue. bytes2short() is a simple routine that converts two bytes into a short.

```
        // get to the file block
        int file_start = 0x4c + shell_len;

        // get the local volume and local system values
        int local_sys_off = link[file_start+0x10] + file_start;
        real_file = getNullDelimitedString(link,local_sys_off);
        p("real filename = " + real_file);
```

The file block starts 0x4c (76 in hexadecimal) bytes after the previous block (or the headers if there was no previous block). Once you are at the file block, you can pull out the 0x10th byte to find the offset to the local system target filename.

> If the directory was on a network drive, you would have to look for a different offset, but I've assumed the file was local to keep the code simple. A more robust implementation would support both local and remote files.

Once you have the offset to the filename, pull it out as a null-delimited string and save it in the real_file variable.

I referenced these two utility functions earlier. getNullDelimitedString looks through the byte array starting at the requested offset. When it finds a null value (0), it will return a substring from the starting offset to the last valid character; that substring contains the filepath. bytes2short uses bit-shifting to turn two bytes into a short integer:

```
    static String getNullDelimitedString(byte[] bytes, int off) {
        int len = 0;
        // count bytes until the null character (0)
        while(true) {
            if(bytes[off+len] == 0) {
                break;
            }
            len++;
        }
```

```
    return new String(bytes,off,len);
}

// convert two bytes into a short
// note, this is little-endian because it's for an
// Intel-only OS.
static int bytes2short(byte[] bytes, int off) {
    return bytes[off] | (bytes[off+1]<<8);
    }
```

> If you learned low-level programming on RISC machines like
> I did, you might be surprised that the second byte is being
> shifted instead of the first. You must remember that short-
> cut files are designed for Windows, which only runs on little-
> endian processors. After writing this hack, I remembered
> how much I hate bit flipping and byte manipulation. I proba-
> bly switched to Java so early so that I would never have to
> deal with data at the byte level again!

Now, the class just needs some getters to let the outside world use the
parser. These two methods expose the is_dir and real_file variables that
the parse( ) method sets:

```
private boolean is_dir;
public boolean isDirectory( ) {
    return is_dir;
}

private String real_file;
public String getRealFilename( ) {
    return real_file;
}
```

LNK Parser written, it's now time to hand the shortcut information over to
the file chooser. JFileChoosers divide the file manipulation duties into two
helper classes. The FileView class controls the look of files **[Hack #29]**, such as
names, icons, etc. The FileSystemView provides the JFileChooser with information about the filesystem itself, including which files are directories. For
controlling directories, the two methods implemented here are particularly
relevant:

```
public class ShortcutFileSystemView extends FileSystemView {

public Boolean isTraversable(File f) {
    if(isDirLink(f)) {
        return new Boolean(true);
    }
    return super.isTraversable(f);
}
```

```
public File[] getFiles(File dir, boolean useFileHiding) {
    if(isDirLink(dir)) {
        dir = getRealFile(dir);
    }

    return super.getFiles(dir,useFileHiding);
}
```

The JFileChooser will call isTraversable( ) on each file to see if it is really a folder. This does not control whether it uses a folder icon, but whether the user can open up and follow the file as a directory. This implementation simply calls the isDirLink( ) method (detailed shortly) to test the current file. If it's not a shortcut then it defers to the parent class.

getFiles( ) returns the directory listing of the given file. JFileChooser provides this to let developers mess with the file listing. You could use this to prevent hidden files from showing or to restrict the user from areas of the filesystem they shouldn't be allowed to access. For this hack, the getFiles( ) method will look for shortcuts and replace them with the real files they point to by calling the getRealFile( ) method:

```
private boolean isDirLink(File f) {
    try {
        if(f.getName().toLowerCase( ).endsWith(".lnk")) {
            if(new LnkParser(f).isDirectory( )) {
                return true;
            }
        }
    } catch (Exception ex) {
        System.out.println("ex: " + ex);
        ex.printStackTrace( );
    }
    return false;
}

private File getRealFile(File file) {
    try {
        return new File(new LnkParser(file).getRealFilename( ));
    } catch (Exception ex) {
        System.out.println("ex: " + ex);
        ex.printStackTrace( );
        return null;
    }
}
```

isDirLink( ) and getRealFile( ) are very simple. They just call the appropriate function on the LnkParser and catch exceptions. By moving all of the actual LNK handling code into the LnkParser, you could add support easily to other kinds of links here just by adding a few more if statements.

To support drawing the icons, just modify the ShortcutFileView from the previous hack to call the LnkParser as well:

```
public boolean isDirLink(File f) {
    try {
        if(f.getName().toLowerCase().endsWith(".lnk")) {
            LnkParser parser = new LnkParser(f);
            if(parser.isDirectory()) {
                return true;
            }
        }
    } catch (Exception ex) {
        System.out.println("exception: " + ex.getMessage());
        ex.printStackTrace();
    }
    return false;
}
```

And finally, here's a test class that will build a new shortcut enabled file chooser. It creates a normal file chooser, and then sets the FileSystemView to the new shortcut subclass. It also sets the modified version of the ShortcutFileView:

```
public class ShortcutTest {
    public static void main(String[] args) throws Exception {
        FileSystemView fsv = new ShortcutFileSystemView();
        JFileChooser chooser = new JFileChooser();
        chooser.setFileSystemView(fsv);
        chooser.setFileView(new ShortcutFileView());
        chooser.showOpenDialog(null);
    }
}
```

Figure 4-5 shows the JFileChooser displaying a shortcut that will behave like a real Windows shortcut when clicked.

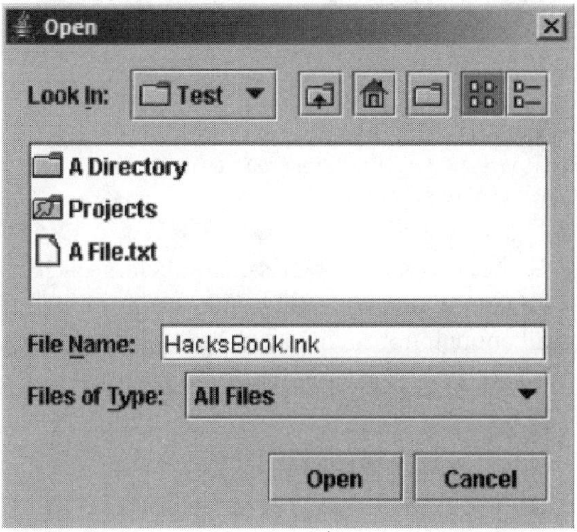

Figure 4-5. A JFileChooser with a live shortcut

Add Image Preview to File Choosers

#31 This hack will show you how to add an image previewer to a JFileChooser, and it will set you on the way toward building your own customizations.

We've already talked about JFileChooser's numerous limitations. Not surprisingly, many applications have their own custom choosers and extensions to support things like image previews. The standard JFileChooser was designed to mimic only the most common features, but it does provide a way to add your own enhancements.

The standard JFileChooser looks like most native file choosers. It has a directory selector, a list of files, and select and close buttons. There may also be a toolbar of sorts. If you want to build your own customized file chooser, you could do it the same way platform-specific file choosers are implemented—through L&F code. This would entail subclassing javax.swing. plaf.basic.BasicFileChooserUI, working around the private methods, and possibly reimplementing the whole thing, none of which is easy or fun. Fortunately, the JFileChooser API provides a simple extension hook in the form of the setAccesory( ) method. This method lets you add any JComponent to an existing JFileChooser, thereby adding your own features without mucking around in file chooser code.

In this hack, you'll learn how to create an image previewer. This is a component that shows a thumbnail view of the currently selected file—if that file is an image. It will also show the dimensions of the image. Because Java 1.4 provides robust image support with the javax.imageio API, this should be pretty easy. The first step is a custom ImagePreview component:

```
public class ImagePreview extends JPanel implements PropertyChangeListener {
    private JFileChooser jfc;
    private Image img;

    public ImagePreview(JFileChooser jfc) {
        this.jfc = jfc;
        Dimension sz = new Dimension(200,200);
        setPreferredSize(sz);
    }
```

The code defines the ImagePreview class, a subclass of JPanel. I've hardcoded the size of the component to 200×200—large enough to tell what the image is, but small enough not to impact the file chooser very much.

ImagePreview also implements PropertyChangeListener so it can detect when the user selects a file:

```
public void propertyChange(PropertyChangeEvent evt) {
    try {
        System.out.println("updating");
```

```
        File file = jfc.getSelectedFile( );
        updateImage(file);
    } catch (IOException ex) {
        System.out.println(ex.getMessage( ));
        ex.printStackTrace( );
    }
}
```

PropertyChange is the single method of the PropertyChangeListener interface. This will be called by the JFileChooser each time the user selects (or deselects) a file. When that happens, ImagePreview will call its updateImage( ) method on that file:

```
public void updateImage(File file) throws IOException {
    if(file == null) {
        return;
    }

    img = ImageIO.read(file);
    repaint( );
}
```

In this method, file will be null if jfc.getSelectedFile( ) in propertyChange( ) returned null. This indicates the user deselected a file or pressed the Cancel button. In either case, there is no image to display. If the file is not null, then updateImage( ) will try to read it with ImageIO.read( ). The javax.imageio interface is quite robust and complex, but the most common operations—reading and writing files—can be performed with the static methods in ImageIO. If the file is not an image file, then read( ) will return null, which means updateImage( ) doesn't have to handle that case. After reading the image, the method calls repaint( ) to tell Swing that the ImagePreview may need to be redrawn.

The paintComponent( ) method contains the guts of ImagePreview. First, it fills in the background with gray. Without this call, the background would be just the contents of the current buffer, which could be anything, like other components on the screen or the previous state of the ImagePreview:

```
public void paintComponent(Graphics g) {
    // fill the background
    g.setColor(Color.gray);
    g.fillRect(0,0,getWidth(),getHeight( ));
```

Next comes the actual image-drawing code:

```
if(img != null) {
    // calculate the scaling factor
    int w = img.getWidth(null);
    int h = img.getHeight(null);
    int side = Math.max(w,h);
    double scale = 200.0/(double)side;
```

```
        w = (int)(scale * (double)w);
        h = (int)(scale * (double)h);

        // draw the image
        g.drawImage(img,0,0,w,h,null);
```

Notice the if(img != null) line. If ImageIO.read( ) returned null, then the img variable will be null as well. With this if statement, you don't need to check for file extensions or do image format detection. The ImageIO class will take care of it all. Before it paints the image, the code will calculate which side of the image is longer (length or height). By scaling the image down relative to the longer side, your code doesn't have to worry about the image being clipped; it will always be small enough to fit inside the 200×200 square component.

With the image in place, you just need to draw the text for the width and height near the bottom. Since the image could be in any color scheme, there is no way to guarantee that the color picked for the text would show up against the image. To handle this, I draw the text in black first, and then draw it a second time shifted up and to the left by one pixel. This creates a subtle shadow effect and ensures that the white text is always visible, even if it's on a white background:

```
        // draw the image dimensions
        String dim = w + " x " + h;
        g.setColor(Color.black);
        g.drawString(dim,31,196);
        g.setColor(Color.white);
        g.drawString(dim,30,195);
    } else {
```

Finally, if the image is null, an error message is printed:

```
    } else {

        // print a message
        g.setColor(Color.black);
        g.drawString("Not an image",30,100);
    }
```

With the ImagePreview class set up, you're ready to test things out. This code creates a standard JFileChooser and adds a new ImagePreview to it with the setAccessory( ) method. It also adds the preview as a property change listener so it can detect user file selections:

```
public static void main(String[] args) {
    JFileChooser jfc = new JFileChooser( );
    ImagePreview preview = new ImagePreview(jfc);
    jfc.addPropertyChangeListener(preview);
    jfc.setAccessory(preview);
    jfc.showOpenDialog(null);
}
```

With the code all in place, the running program will look like Figure 4-6.

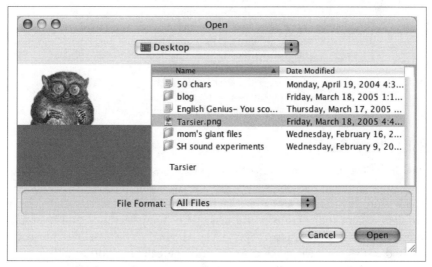

Figure 4-6. A file chooser that previews images

As a nice enhancement, you could modify ImagePreview to show previews of other kinds of files (e.g., PDF or SVG). You could even preview text files by showing the first few lines of the document. Because setAccessory( ) lets you set any JComponent, you could create a panel that does something completely different, like connecting to a network drive, à la iDisk, or setting import preferences like encoding and line endings.

HACK #32 Preview ZIP and JAR Files

This hack will show you how to customize the file chooser to let users navigate and load files from inside a ZIP or JAR file archive.

Most modern operating systems now have built-in support for compressed files, usually in the form of ZIP files. You can open up a ZIP file and navigate the contents from within the standard file browser or dialog box, all without actually uncompressing anything. Surprisingly, JFileChooser doesn't support ZIP files, even though Java has built-in ZIP support in the java.util.zip package. And, since JAR files are in the same format, you get two-for-one today!

Before you read any further, I want to warn you that this is one of the longest and most complicated hacks in the book. I don't want to scare you away, but the code is pretty dense. Of course, you wouldn't expect any less from a hacks book, right? What you will learn from this hack, however, will let you build custom filesystem views for any type of data-source, including FTP, WebDAV, or even SQL databases. I think the complexity is worth it. Plus, you'll learn more about how the File object really works and how to hack it to pieces.

Build File Proxies

The JFileChooser uses a FileSystemView to access the real filesystem. This view, unfortunately, assumes the existence of actual java.io.File objects. There is no way to represent a filesystem without Files, which wouldn't be a problem except that File is a real class with many methods, not a simple interface. Fortunately, File is not declared final. You can override each method with your own version to redirect the calls to another object, and that's exactly how this hack works. By creating proxies around the real ZIP file objects, you can fool the FileSystemView into working with items that aren't real files.

ZIP files are represented in the java.util.zip package by a ZipFile object that contains one ZipEntry for each compressed file it contains. To show the compressed files in the chooser, each ZipEntry is wrapped inside of a ZipEntryFileProxy, which extends the real File class. It contains a reference to the ZipEntry, the enclosing ZipFile, a path string, and the File object of the actual ZIP file, as shown in Example 4-1.

Example 4-1. A ZIP file proxy

```
import java.util.zip.*;

public class ZipEntryFileProxy extends File {
    ZipFileProxy zip;
    ZipFile zipfile;
    String name, path;
    File parent;
    ZipEntry entry;

    public ZipEntryFileProxy(ZipFileProxy zip, ZipFile zipfile,
                             String path, File parent) {
        super("");
        this.zip = zip;
        this.zipfile = zipfile;
        this.path = path;
        this.parent = parent;
        this.entry = zipfile.getEntry(path);
```

Example 4-1. A ZIP file proxy (continued)

```
        // determine if the entry is a directory
        String tmp = path;

        if(entry.isDirectory( )) {
            tmp = path.substring(0,path.length( )-1);
        }

        // then calculate the name
        int brk = tmp.lastIndexOf("/");
        name = path;
        if(brk != -1) {
            name = tmp.substring(brk+1);
        }
    }
```

The constructor is pretty straightforward. It saves references to the passed-in object and then does some calculations on the path. If the entry is a directory, then the path will end with a slash. The code chops off this trailing slash, if present, and then looks for the name of the entry. Files inside of a ZIP are stored as a list of complete pathnames with slashes, not as a tree of objects like a real filesystem. Thus, the name of a file—what you would normally think of as its filename—is actually just the last part of a complete path, including the parent directories. To parse this and get the real filename, the code looks for the last slash in the filename and pulls out the trailing string.

The rest of the ZipEntryFileProxy class overrides a portion of the standard File methods. Each call returns a value based on the saved data from the ZIP file, rather than the actual File parent class:

```
public boolean exists( ) { return true; }

public int hashCode( ) {
    return name.hashCode( ) ^ 1234321;
}

public String getName( ) { return name; }
public String getPath( ) { return path; }
public boolean isDirectory() { return entry.isDirectory( ); }
public boolean isAbsolute( ) { return true; }
public String getAbsolutePath( ) { return path; }
public File getAbsoluteFile( ) { return this; }
public File getCanonicalFile( ) { return this; }
public File getParentFile( ) { return parent; }

public boolean equals(Object obj) {
    if(obj instanceof ZipEntryFileProxy) {
        ZipEntryFileProxy zo = (ZipEntryFileProxy)obj;
```

```
                if(zo.getAbsolutePath().equals(getAbsolutePath())) {
                    return true;
                }
            }
            return false;
        }

        public InputStream getInputStream() throws IOException {
            return zipfile.getInputStream(entry);
        }

        public File[] listFiles() {
            Map children = (Map)zip.hash.get(path);
            File[] files = new File[children.size()];
            Iterator it = children.keySet().iterator();
            int count = 0;
            while(it.hasNext()) {
                String name = (String)it.next();
                files[count] = new ZipEntryFileProxy(zip, zipfile, name,this);
                count++;
            }
            return files;
        }
    }
```

There are two special things to note in this code. First, the code adds one method that wasn't in the original File class: getInputStream(). There is no way to get an InputStream out of a normal File. Instead, you must create a FileInputStream, which of course doesn't know anything about ZIP files, so that won't work. As a workaround, ZipEntryFileProxy adds the method getInputStream() to get a proper input stream. The disadvantage of this solution is that any code that uses the file chooser will need to be aware of ZIP files; it cannot simply assume that the file chooser only returns real files. This means you would have to modify any existing code that uses the JFileChooser to check if the file is really a ZipEntryFileProxy; if it is, you need to do a cast, and then grab the input stream appropriately. Otherwise, your program will throw lots of exceptions as the FileInputStream tries to open a file that doesn't exist in a form it can understand.

The other thing to note is that listFiles() creates new ZipEntryFileProxy objects for each child file (if the file is a directory) by pulling the names out of a HashTable stored in the ZipFileProxy (which represents the ZIP file). The ZipFileProxy (Example 4-2) wraps the entire ZIP file, whereas the ZipEntryFileProxy maps to files stored *within* the ZIP file, though they are both custom subclasses of java.io.File. The ZipFileProxy constructor accepts a File object pointing to the real ZIP file on disk. After saving a few references, the constructor calls parse() to set up a HashMap of the file entries within the ZIP.

Example 4-2. ZipFileProxy class

```java
public class ZipFileProxy extends File {
    protected Map hash;
    private ZipFile zipfile;
    private File real_file;

    public ZipFileProxy(File file) {
        super(file.getAbsolutePath());
        try {
            this.hash = new HashMap();
            this.real_file = file;
            zipfile = new ZipFile(file,ZipFile.OPEN_READ);
            hash.put("",new HashMap());
            Enumeration en = zipfile.entries();
            parse(en);
        } catch (IOException ex) {
            System.out.println(ex.getMessage());
            ex.printStackTrace();
        }
    }
    public String getPath() { return real_file.getPath(); }
    public boolean exists() { return real_file.exists(); }
    public String getName() { return real_file.getName(); }

    public File[] getFiles(String dir) {
        Map children = (Map)hash.get(dir);
        File[] files = new File[children.size()];
        Iterator it = children.keySet().iterator();
        int count = 0;
        while(it.hasNext()) {
            String name = (String)it.next();
            files[count] = new ZipEntryFileProxy(this, zipfile, name, this);
            count++;
        }
        return files;
    }

    /* create a hashtable of the entries and their paths */
    private void parse(Enumeration en) {
        while(en.hasMoreElements()) {
            ZipEntry ze = (ZipEntry)en.nextElement();
            String full_name = ze.getName();
            String name = full_name;
            if(ze.isDirectory()) {
                name = full_name.substring(0,full_name.length()-1);
            }

            int brk = name.lastIndexOf("/");

            String parent = "";
            if(brk != -1) {
                parent = name.substring(0,brk+1);
            }
```

Example 4-2. ZipFileProxy class (continued)

```
            String node_name = name;
            if(brk != -1) {
                node_name = full_name.substring(brk+1);
            }

            if(ze.isDirectory( )) {
                HashMap children = new HashMap( );
                hash.put(full_name,children);
            }
            Map parent_children = (Map)hash.get(parent);
            parent_children.put(full_name,"");
        }
    }

}
```

Just like `ZipEntryFileProxy`, `ZipFileProxy` wraps a real file object and passes most method invocations to the superclass. The special code here is in parse( ), which loops through each entry in the ZIP file, breaks each pathname into its constituent parts, and builds up a set of nested `HashTables`. Each directory entry is represented by a `HashMap` of child filenames. A master map holds the directory entries. This nested structure is what lets the `ZipEntryFileProxy` find its place in the virtual tree of files.

Build a Custom Filesystem View

Now that you have a tree of virtual `File` objects, you can implement the real `FileSystemView`. As shown in Example 4-3, `ZipFileSystemView` overrides each of its parent class's methods, redirecting them to ZIP-specific code if the file is an instance of a `ZipEntryFileProxy`.

Example 4-3. ZipFileSystemView class

```
public class ZipFileSystemView extends FileSystemView {

    public ZipFileSystemView( ) throws IOException { }

    public File createNewFolder(File file) { return null; }

    public File createFileObject(File dir, String filename) {
        if(dir instanceof ZipEntryFileProxy) {
            ZipEntryFileProxy zdir = (ZipEntryFileProxy) dir;
            return new ZipEntryFileProxy(zdir.zip, zdir.zipfile, filename, dir);
        }
        return super.createFileObject(dir,filename);
    }
```

Example 4-3. ZipFileSystemView class (continued)

```java
    public File getChild(File dir, String filename) {
        if(dir instanceof ZipEntryFileProxy) {
            ZipEntryFileProxy zdir = (ZipEntryFileProxy) dir;
             return new ZipEntryFileProxy(zdir.zip,zdir.zipfile,
                                    dir.getPath( )+filename,dir);
        }
        return super.getChild(dir,filename);
    }

    public String getSystemDisplayName(File f) {
        if(f instanceof ZipEntryFileProxy) {
            return f.getName( );
        }
        return super.getSystemDisplayName(f);
    }

    public File getParentDirectory(File dir) {
        if(dir instanceof ZipEntryFileProxy) {
            return dir.getParentFile( );
        }
        return super.getParentDirectory(dir);
    }

    public File[] getFiles(File dir, boolean useFileHiding) {
        if(dir.getName( ).endsWith(".zip")) {
            ZipFileProxy proxy = new ZipFileProxy(dir);
            File[] fs = proxy.getFiles("");
            return fs;
        }

        if(dir instanceof ZipEntryFileProxy) {
            return dir.listFiles( );
        }

        return super.getFiles(dir,useFileHiding);
    }

    public Boolean isTraversable(File f) {
        if(f.getName( ).endsWith(".zip")) {
            return new Boolean(true);
        }
        if(f instanceof ZipEntryFileProxy) {
            boolean b = ((ZipEntryFileProxy)f).isDirectory( );
            return new Boolean(b);
        }
        return super.isTraversable(f);
    }

}
```

Note the isTraversable( ) method, which returns true if the file ends with *.zip* or is an instance of ZipEntryFileProxy. Without this, the JFileChooser would never let the user navigate inside of ZIP files.

Put It All Together

The class in Example 4-4 creates a JFileChooser with a ZipFileSystemView. The only custom code beyond the view itself is a check to see if the selected file is a ZipEntryFileProxy. If so, the program will cast the file to a ZipEntryFileProxy and call getInputStream( ). If not, it will just create a FileInputStream as normal.

Example 4-4. A sample program

```
public class ZipTest {

    public static void main(String[] args) throws Exception {
        FileSystemView fsv = new ZipFileSystemView( );
        JFileChooser chooser = new JFileChooser(".");
        chooser.setFileSystemView(fsv);
        chooser.showOpenDialog(null);
        File file = chooser.getSelectedFile( );
        System.out.println("Got the file: " + file + " " + file.getClass( ));

        InputStream in = null;
        if(file instanceof ZipEntryFileProxy) {
            in = ((ZipEntryFileProxy)file).getInputStream( );
        } else {
            in = new FileInputStream(file);
        }
    }
}
```

As you can see, this method of extending the JFileChooser to support an alternative filesystem is quite hackish. Sadly, it's the only way to do such a thing without writing a completely custom file chooser. This is probably why so many IDE authors have just chucked the entire JFileChooser and FileSystemView API in favor of a custom dialog. However, if you wish to remain within the standard API, you can certainly do it, as this hack proves. As a future enhancement, you might make this class more generic, handling the nasty details of file wrapping while delegating the actual alternative filesystem to a subclass. This would create an API more like TreeModel, from which other developers can create their own implementations easily.

Windows, Dialogs, and Frames

Hacks 33–40

For four chapters, we've hacked away at Swing widgets, from JLabels to JTables, without worrying too much about the context in which they're shown to the user. And yet, every Swing widget must ultimately be contained in some kind of window to be on the screen at all. It's not an exaggeration to say that many competent Swing programmers don't even know or care about the hierarchy of AWT Windows, Dialogs, and Frames or their Swing equivalents, JWindow, JDialog, and JFrame. Yet, it's these same programmers who don't know that commercial components like splash screens are all possible in Swing; they see dialogs and frames and assume everything has a titlebar. This is hardly true, though—you can easily remove the decorations of a dialog, or just work with the window superclass.

Suffice it to say there's much you can do with windows and their subclasses. So much so, in fact, that it fills two chapters. This chapter will deal with hacks that deal with placing, moving, and resizing windows in ways that are fairly consistent with the design of the window classes. The next chapter will be a lot more aggressive in breaking the rules.

HACK #33

Window Snapping

Make your windows snap to the edges of the screen by using a special event listener.

Back in the prehistoric days of desktop software, as graphics programs were being invented, they solved the problem of managing the drawing tools by creating mini-windows called *palettes* (and their later variation, toolbars). Eventually, the programs had so many palettes that the users grew frustrated trying to organize them. Lining them up on the edge of the screen was particularly nasty, so fledgling young programmers took it upon themselves to create *snappable windows*. These were windows that were magnetic (metaphorically speaking) and could align themselves to the screen's edges. This hack demonstrates how to recreate this technique with Java.

The idea is simple: you check whenever the user moves the window. If the window is off the screen, then move it back to the edge. Moving the window is pretty easy. The trickier part is knowing when the window has moved. Fortunately, AWT has an answer: the ComponentListener interface.

In Java, every UI component (in both AWT and Swing) fires events whenever it moves, resizes, is shown, or is hidden. Any class can receive these events by implementing the ComponentListener interface. For the purposes of this hack, you only need the componentMoved event, so start by subclassing ComponentAdapter, which provides default no-operation implementations of all of ComponentListener's declared methods. Then just override the componentMoved( ) method, as seen in Example 5-1.

Example 5-1. A ComponentListener to snap a window into place

```
public class WindowSnapper extends ComponentAdapter {

    public WindowSnapper( ) { }

    private boolean locked = false;
    private int snap_distance = 50;

    public void componentMoved(ComponentEvent evt) {
        if(locked) return;
        Dimension size = Toolkit.getDefaultToolkit().getScreenSize( );
        int nx = evt.getComponent().getX( );
        int ny = evt.getComponent().getY( );
        // top
        if(ny < 0+snap_distance) {
            ny = 0;
        }
        // left
        if(nx < 0+snap_distance) {
            nx = 0;
        }
        // right
        if(nx > size.getWidth() - evt.getComponent().getWidth( ) -
                snap_distance) {
            nx = (int)size.getWidth()-evt.getComponent().getWidth( );
        }
        // bottom
        if(ny > size.getHeight() - evt.getComponent().getHeight( ) -
                snap_distance) {
            ny = (int)size.getHeight()-evt.getComponent().getHeight( );
        }

        // make sure we don't get into a recursive loop when the
        // set location generates more events
```

Example 5-1. A ComponentListener to snap a window into place (continued)

```
        locked = true;
        evt.getComponent( ).setLocation(nx,ny);
        locked = false;
    }

}
```

Every time componentMoved( ) is called, it gets the screen size and current coordinates of the window. Because window coordinates are already relative to the screen's origin, there is no need to translate them. Next comes four if statements to determine whether the window is at least partially off screen. The first two handle the top and lefthand sides of the screen. If the user moves the component off screen, or even moves within snap_distance of the screen's edges, this method moves the window directly to 0. The second two ifs handle the bottom and righthand sides of the screen, which is essentially the same as the first two except they have to account for the size of the window as well. Finally, the window is moved to the correct location.

You should also take note of the locked variable. This is used to avoid a potential infinite loop. Essentially, the componentMoved( ) method will be called every time the window moves. The componentMoved( ) method will also call setLocation( ) on the window, which will then trigger another move event. Left unchecked, these methods will be called over and over, locking the paint thread, and crashing your program with an out-of-memory error. It would be nice to look at the event and tell if the user moved the window or if the code did, but the API doesn't provide such a function. The solution: detect recursive calls by using a lock variable. If locked is false, then this is a real move event done by the user, and it's OK to do the snapping. Then, just before setLocation( ) is called, the code sets locked to true. If componentMoved( ) is called again, the code knows that further movement should be ignored. After setLocation( ) returns, locked is set back to false.

To test out the WindowSnapper, you have to add it as a ComponentListener to a window:

```
    public static void main(String[] args) {
        JFrame frame = new JFrame("Hack #33: Window Snapping");
        JLabel label = new JLabel(
           "Move this window's titlebar to demonstrate screen edge snapping.");
        frame.getContentPane( ).add(label);
        frame.pack( );

        frame.addComponentListener(new WindowSnapper( ));
        frame.setVisible(true);
    }
```

However, this hack has one major flaw. Because the component events are read-only, it is impossible to intercept the move and position the window before it has been drawn on screen. Thus the window will flash as the user moves it. Creating a custom event queue would seem to be the answer because you could then modify the events before they are sent to the components, but this won't work for move events on windows (or any subclass like JFrame). Windows are real structures provided by the operating system, rather than purely Java objects. The window events are created by the OS itself and passed into the JVM from the C level, meaning there is no way to capture these before they take effect. Still, in many of your applications, the flashing may be an acceptable trade-off for snapping.

HACK #34   Make a Draggable Window

Drag a window by clicking on its background using a special event listener.

Most windows let you move them by dragging the titlebar. Some program windows, however, don't have titlebars. In the age of eye-candy interfaces (see iTunes and WinAmp for prime examples) it is very common to have a window—possibly non-rectangular—without any titlebar or window controls at all. This makes for a pretty window, but how do you move it? Simply by dragging any available space on the window. Though not terribly intuitive, such programs are commonplace, and this book wouldn't be called *Swing Hacks* without providing a Java implementation of draggable windows, even when no titlebar is used.

The simplest approach to this problem is to create a listener that simply catches all drags and moves the window:

```
public class MoveMouseListener implements MouseListener, MouseMotionListener
{
    JComponent target;
    JFrame frame;
    public MoveMouseListener(JComponent target, JFrame frame) {
        this.target = target;
        this.frame = frame;
    }

    public void mouseClicked(MouseEvent e) {}
    public void mouseEntered(MouseEvent e) {}
    public void mouseExited(MouseEvent e) {}
    public void mousePressed(MouseEvent e) {}
    public void mouseReleased(MouseEvent e) {}
    public void mouseMoved(MouseEvent e) {}
    public void mouseDragged(MouseEvent e) {
        frame.setLocation(new Point(e.getX(),e.getY()));
    }
}
```

This class implements MouseListener and MouseMotionListener with no-ops for all methods except mouseDragged( ), which moves the frame to the current mouse location. However, this approach has two problems. First, the mouse coordinates are going to be relative to the component, rather than the screen. Thus, a click on a 50×50 button in the bottom right of the screen might return (25, 25) when it should really be more like (1000, 700). The other problem is that the code moves the origin of the frame to the mouse cursor. This would look strange because the window would immediately jump so that its upper-left corner is right under the cursor. The proper behavior is for the window to stay in the same position *relative* to the cursor as the cursor moves around.

The solution to the first problem (getting screen coordinates rather than component coordinates) is to convert mouse coordinates to absolute screen coordinates. The following method does just that (we'll use this shortly in mouseDragged( )):

```
Point getScreenLocation(MouseEvent e) {
    Point cursor = e.getPoint( );
    Point target_location = this.target.getLocationOnScreen( );
    return new Point(
        (int)(target_location.getX()+cursor.getX( )),
        (int)(target_location.getY()+cursor.getY( )));
}
```

Solving the second issue (keeping the window static relative to the mouse) requires saving an initial offset between window and cursor, and then maintaining that offset throughout the drag. You should add a new mousePressed( ) implementation that saves the current screen location of the mouse cursor (start_drag) and the current location of the window (start_loc). The distance between the two points can be used to form an offset:

```
Point start_drag;
Point start_loc;
public void mousePressed(MouseEvent e) {
    this.start_drag = this.getScreenLocation(e);
    this.start_loc = this.getFrame(this.target).getLocation( );
}
```

Next, the listener should maintain the offset difference throughout the drag operation by calculating a new offset each time the mouse moves. Here is the new mouseDragged( ) method:

```
public void mouseDragged(MouseEvent e) {
    Point current = this.getScreenLocation(e);
    Point offset = new Point(
        (int)current.getX()-(int)start_drag.getX( ),
        (int)current.getY()-(int)start_drag.getY( ));
    JFrame frame = this.getFrame(target);
```

```
        Point new_location = new Point(
            (int)(this.start_loc.getX()+offset.getX()),
            (int)(this.start_loc.getY()+offset.getY()));
        frame.setLocation(new_location);
    }
```

Using the utility method, it gets the current mouse position in screen coordinates, and then calculates the distance between that position and where the mouse started. Finally, it adds this offset to the starting location for the window to set the window's final location.

Every now and then, the event queue will drop a mouse event. If the code was adding the deltas (change in position) from each drag event, then eventually the user would start to see errors as a result of these dropped events. Because this code always recalculates the window position relative to the start of the drag, these errors don't have an effect. Plus, since Swing sends all mouse events to a dragged component—even if the cursor moves outside the bounds of the component—you don't have to worry about the user dragging off the edge of the window and shutting down the whole process.

This method of window dragging has two strengths. First, since the work is done in a listener, you can add this listener to any existing Swing component without subclassing. Any old program can become draggable! Second, only drags on the attached component affect the window—you can make the background of the window draggable without affecting any of the foreground components (like the Play button on an MP3 player).

To test out the mouse listener, try adding it to the Calendar hack [Hack #4]. Change the main( ) function like this:

```
    public static void main(String[] args) {
        JFrame frame = new JFrame( );
        CalendarHack ch = new CalendarHack( );
        ch.setDate(new Date( ));
        frame.getContentPane( ).add(ch);

        frame.setUndecorated(true);
        MoveMouseListener mml = new MoveMouseListener(ch, frame);
        ch.addMouseListener(mml);
        ch.addMouseMotionListener(mml);

        frame.pack( );
        frame.setVisible(true);
    }
```

The only additions are the four bold lines in the middle of the method. The first line turns off the standard window decorations, and the second creates the MoveMouseListener with references to the CalendarHack component and its frame. The last two lines add the listener so that it receives all of the mouse events before the frame is shown on screen.

The final hack looks like Figure 5-1, with the titlebar and window controls hidden and the entire component draggable.

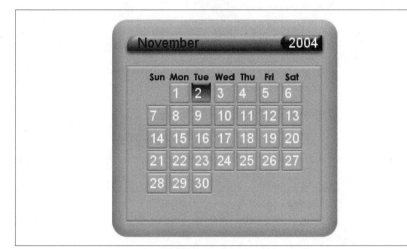

Figure 5-1. A draggable calendar

Add Windows Resize Icons

**HACK
#35**

The Windows resize icons aren't built into Java. Here's how to make your own.

Windows has two standard icons to let users know that they can resize a window. I can't tell you why there are two or how to decide between them, but I can tell you how to reproduce both of them in Java. Note that this hack is concerned with *painting* the icons accurately—it will be up to your code to handle events on components that use these icons and handle them appropriately.

A Tale of Two Icons

First take a look at the two icons. Figure 5-2 shows the icon used by Windows Explorer, MS Paint, and other applications; Figure 5-3 shows the icon used by Word and other Office applications.

The Icon Interface

The easiest and most flexible way to implement these icons is through the Icon interface. Using Icon allows you to change an icon's appearance easily if you need to match new system defaults. It's also a lot easier to implement transparency with an Icon than by making an image from the corner icon using a screen capture and editing it in a professional graphics application like Photoshop.

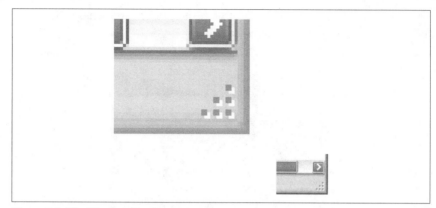

Figure 5-2. The Windows Explorer resize icon

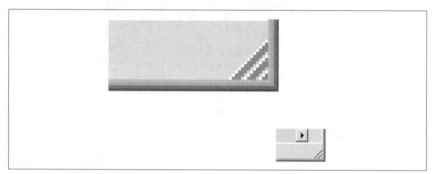

Figure 5-3. The Windows MS Office resize icon

Icon is pretty simple, and it has only three methods:

```
void paintIcon(Component c, Graphics g, int x, int y);

int getIconWidth( );

int getIconHeight( );
```

The getIconWidth( ) and getIconHeight( ) methods should be pretty easy to implement—you just need the pixel size of your custom icons. The paintIcon( ) method is where all the interesting stuff happens.

The Explorer Icon

Figure 5-4 shows a huge blowup of what we'll call the Explorer icon.

At a glance, you can see the six squares in a triangular pattern with a subtle white 3D effect on the squares. The easiest thing to handle is the size, so start with that. This icon is 12×12 pixels (one square in Figure 5-4 equals one pixel).

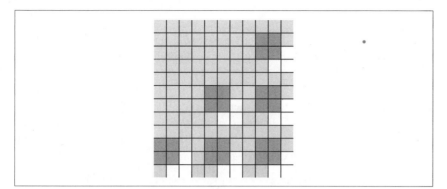

Figure 5-4. The Windows Explorer icon zoomed in

Here are the width and height methods. Start by creating constants for height and width, and write the getters:

```
private static final int WIDTH = 12;
private static final int HEIGHT = 12;

public int getIconHeight( ) {
    return WIDTH;
}

public int getIconWidth( ) {
    return HEIGHT;
}
```

To implement paintIcon( ), you'll need to recreate this icon using the graphic primitives provided by AWT. So, you need to carefully analyze how the original was created. After close inspection, you'll find that each square actually has three separate colors: the top-right color, the bottom-right color, and the left color. Here are the color constants you need:

```
private static final Color SQUARE_COLOR_LEFT = new Color(184, 180, 163);
private static final Color SQUARE_COLOR_TOP_RIGHT = new Color(184, 180, 161);
private static final Color SQUARE_COLOR_BOTTOM_RIGHT = new Color(184, 181, 161);
```

To recreate the icon, it will help to have a method to paint the gray squares. Notice that the method also caches Graphics' previous color and resets the graphics color at the end of the method, which is generally a good practice:

```
private void drawSquare(Graphics g, int x, int y){
    Color oldColor = g.getColor( );
    g.setColor(SQUARE_COLOR_LEFT);
    g.drawLine(x,y, x,y+1);
    g.setColor(SQUARE_COLOR_TOP_RIGHT);
    g.drawLine(x+1,y, x+1,y);
    g.setColor(SQUARE_COLOR_BOTTOM_RIGHT);
    g.drawLine(x+1,y+1, x+1,y+1);
    g.setColor(oldColor);
}
```

The code looks strange because of all of the drawLine( ) calls that really should be drawPoint( ) calls. Because there is no drawPoint() method, you can accomplish the same thing by drawing a line to and from the same point.

You could paint each square and then add the 3D effect with more lines, but this is a good time to take advantage of the non-transparent nature of computers. It's easier just to paint the white 3D effect as white squares and paint over the corners when you draw the gray squares.

Continuing as before, create a constant for the 3D effect color (white):

```
private static final Color THREE_D_EFFECT_COLOR = new Color(255, 255, 255);
```

The constant is used by a helper method to paint the white squares. It caches the old paint color, sets the graphics to paint white, draws the square, and resets the graphics color:

```
private void draw3dSquare(Graphics g, int x, int y){
    Color oldColor = g.getColor( );
    g.setColor(THREE_D_EFFECT_COLOR);
    g.fillRect(x,y,2,2);
    g.setColor(oldColor);
}
```

Now, think of the icon as a grid with rows and columns representing the locations for the squares. It's really a 3×3 grid that's partially filled in like this:

```
|   |   | X |
|   | X | X |
| X | X | X |
```

Keep track of the rows and columns with variables to make painting easier. Also, keep track of the space between the rows and columns in pixels:

```
int firstRow = 0;
int firstColumn = 0;
int rowDiff = 4;
int columnDiff = 4;
```

The row difference works out to be four because the square is two pixels wide, plus one pixel for the white effect, plus one pixel for spacing. The same deal applies for the column difference. From there, it's easy to calculate the other rows and columns based on the starting row and column and their distances from each other:

```
int secondRow = firstRow + rowDiff;
int secondColumn = firstColumn + columnDiff;
int thirdRow = secondRow + rowDiff;
int thirdColumn = secondColumn + columnDiff;
```

Next, paint the white squares: one in the first row, two in the second, and three in the third. Notice that the white squares are offset by one pixel because the column and row variables (firstRow, secondRow, etc.) reference the gray squares. These squares provide the 3D effect.

```
//first row
draw3dSquare(g, firstColumn+1, thirdRow+1);

//second row
draw3dSquare(g, secondColumn+1, secondRow+1);
draw3dSquare(g, secondColumn+1, thirdRow+1);

//third row
draw3dSquare(g, thirdColumn+1, firstRow+1);
draw3dSquare(g, thirdColumn+1, secondRow+1);
draw3dSquare(g, thirdColumn+1, thirdRow+1);
```

Finally, paint the gray squares on top of the white squares:

```
//first row
drawSquare(g, firstColumn, thirdRow);

//second row
drawSquare(g, secondColumn, secondRow);
drawSquare(g, secondColumn, thirdRow);

//third row
drawSquare(g, thirdColumn, firstRow);
drawSquare(g, thirdColumn, secondRow);
drawSquare(g, thirdColumn, thirdRow);
```

The Office Icon

Figure 5-5 shows the MS Office corner icon in detail.

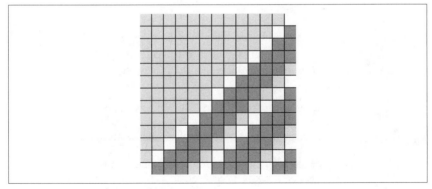

Figure 5-5. The Windows MS Office icon zoomed in

This icon is easier—it's just a couple of straight lines. Also, it's 13×13 pixels, which is bigger than the last icon. So, start with the trivial size methods:

```
private static final int WIDTH = 13;
private static final int HEIGHT = 13;

public int getIconHeight( ) {
    return WIDTH;
}

public int getIconWidth( ) {
    return HEIGHT;
}
```

The paintIcon( ) method is also pretty straightforward. Start by painting the three white lines, and follow up with the dark gray lines. Here's the code:

```
public void paintIcon(Component c, Graphics g, int x, int y) {

    g.setColor(WHITE_LINE_COLOR);
    g.drawLine(0,12, 12,0);
    g.drawLine(5,12, 12,5);
    g.drawLine(10,12, 12,10);

    g.setColor(GRAY_LINE_COLOR);
    g.drawLine(1,12, 12,1);
    g.drawLine(2,12, 12,2);
    g.drawLine(3,12, 12,3);

    g.drawLine(6,12, 12,6);
    g.drawLine(7,12, 12,7);
    g.drawLine(8,12, 12,8);

    g.drawLine(11,12, 12,11);
    g.drawLine(12,12, 12,12);

}
```

Notice you don't have to paint the light gray color because it's actually the panel background color. Any area you don't explicitly paint over picks up the background color, which is exactly what you want here.

 These icons are approximations; some things will be different between applications and systems. They were taken directly, pixel by pixel, from Windows Explorer and Microsoft Office 2000 running on Windows XP Professional. Different applications are slightly different, even on the same version of Windows. Double check platforms you are deploying to and make sure the colors are correct. Meanwhile, it's still a really good working icon, even if a couple of pixels are off by a few shades.

—Jonathan Simon

Add Status Bars to Windows

HACK #36

Lots of applications use a bottom-of-window panel to communicate status. But Swing doesn't provide a consistent way to do this. So, you need to provide it yourself.

Many applications in Microsoft Windows use a status bar—an area at the bottom of each window (to the left of the resize box if there is one) that can be used to communicate summary information to the user in a compact form. Typical contents of a status bar might include what a web browser is doing (e.g., "Connecting to www.oreilly.com"), or, as in Figure 5-6, a summary of the contents of a folder, showing the number of contained items, their size, etc.

| 26 objects (Disk free space: 1.37 GB) | 42.3 MB | 🖳 My Computer |

Figure 5-6. Windows Explorer's status bar

Standard Status Bars

This is the standard MS Windows setup for a status bar:

- An icon on the far right letting users know they can resize the application
- A label on the left for free form text
- Several labels on the right for details (e.g., 42.3 MB in Figure 5-6)

There is also a bit of custom painting involved to get the top and bottom shading right. First, you'll do the panel shading, and then loop back to the previous list and add all of the necessary components to the status bar.

This hack copies the Windows Explorer status bar in Windows XP. Different applications are slightly different. The purpose of this hack isn't to start a religious war about which application to copy. You can just make minor changes if you want to copy a different application's status bar (such as Word or Outlook, which are different than Windows Explorer and also from each other).

Start by creating a class called JStatusBar extending JPanel:

```
public class JStatusPanel extends JPanel {
  //more to come
}
```

Then add a constructor and set the preferred height to be 23 pixels (the height of the Windows Explorer status bar—count 'em up if you don't trust me). You can ignore the preferred width of the status bar since you'll be

adding the status bar to your frame with a BorderLayout or similar layout
that will stretch this component to the width of the window:

```
public JStatusPanel( ){
    setPreferredSize(new Dimension(getWidth( ), 23));
}
```

Painting Panel Details

Figure 5-7 shows the Windows Explorer status bar zoomed in around the
42.3 MB label. There are a couple of gray lines at the top and bottom, as
well as a blue line at the bottom, used to achieve a subtle gradation effect.

Figure 5-7. Explorer's status bar zoomed in

You can achieve this effect easily by overriding paintComponent( ) and drawing the lines yourself. Here is the overridden paintComponent( ) code:

```
public void paintComponent(Graphics g) {
    super.paintComponent(g);

    int y = 0;
    g.setColor(new Color(156, 154, 140));
    g.drawLine(0, y, getWidth( ), y);
    y++;
    g.setColor(new Color(196, 194, 183));
    g.drawLine(0, y, getWidth( ), y);
    y++;
    g.setColor(new Color(218, 215, 201));
    g.drawLine(0, y, getWidth( ), y);
    y++;
    g.setColor(new Color(233, 231, 217));
    g.drawLine(0, y, getWidth( ), y);

    y = getHeight( ) - 3;
    g.setColor(new Color(233, 232, 218));
    g.drawLine(0, y, getWidth( ), y);
    y++;
    g.setColor(new Color(233, 231, 216));
    g.drawLine(0, y, getWidth( ), y);
    y = getHeight( ) - 1;
    g.setColor(new Color(221, 221, 220));
    g.drawLine(0, y, getWidth( ), y);
}
```

The first section draws the gray lines at the top. Midway through, y is reset based on the panel height, and then the bottom lines are drawn.

Add the Corner Icon

Next, you need to add the resize icon—preferably made to resemble real Windows resize icons **[Hack #36]**. Make a JLabel for the corner icon and add the icon to it. Since this hack is mimicking the Explorer status bar, use the TriangleSquareWindowsCornerIcon. Also, remember to set the label opacity to false. This makes the status panel background show through the icon:

```
JLabel resizeIconLabel = new JLabel(new TriangleSquareWindowsCornerIcon( ));
resizeIconLabel.setOpaque(false);
```

Now, you need to add the label to the panel. You need the resize icon to be at the right, on the bottom of the bar. For this to work, set the JStatusBar layout to a BorderLayout. Then create another panel called rightPanel and set its layout to BorderLayout as well. Add the rightPanel to the status bar, to the east; add the resize icon to the rightPanel, to the south. Don't forget to set the rightPanel's opacity to false as well. This will place the icon on the bottom right of the status bar:

```
JPanel rightPanel = new JPanel(new BorderLayout( ));
rightPanel.setOpaque(false);
rightPanel.add(resizeIconLabel, BorderLayout.SOUTH);
add(rightPanel, BorderLayout.EAST);
```

While you're at it, create another panel and name it contentPanel. Add this to the center of the status bar. You'll use this in the next few sections to add the rest of the components:

```
contentPanel = new JPanel( );
contentPanel.setOpaque(false);
add(contentPanel, BorderLayout.CENTER);
```

Add the Left Component

Now that the contentPanel is in place, you need to configure it to hold all of the components you're going to add to the status bar. Remember that the status bar has several components on the righthand side (just to the left of the resize icon) that don't resize.

> It's actually possible for these components to resize, but standard Windows behavior is to have the size stay the same and center text.

There are also a bunch of separators between each of the righthand components. And on the left, the status bar has a main component that takes up all of the space left over after the righthand components (yes, it's rather confusing; read this section again and you'll get it).

You could get most of this behavior with a bunch of nested panels and layouts. But it's easier to use a single layout manager that can handle all of these, such as FormLayout from JGoodies. I don't want to get *too* detailed about FormLayout, so feel free to check out *http://www.jgoodies.com* for more info. You'll need to download JGoodies Forms from the JGoodies site and put its JAR file (*forms-1.0.5.jar* as of this writing) in your classpath. Here is the code to create a new FormLayout and set it on the contentPanel:

```
layout = new com.jgoodies.forms.layout.FormLayout(
    "2dlu, pref:grow",
    "3dlu, fill:10dlu, 2dlu");

contentPanel.setLayout(layout);
```

FormLayout is essentially an advanced grid, typically configured by passing in strings that describe the row and column contents in a heavily condensed syntax. So, you need to configure the grid columns and rows and then add the components to the appropriate locations. It's a simplistic approach that is really powerful.

The first line—2dlu, pref:grow—creates two columns: one column is two dialog units (dlu in the code) wide and another column that grows. This is for the left component (which needs to grow), and is it going to be added to the second column (the first column is there simply to create a space). The dialog unit system used for this space is based on the pixel size of the dialog font, meaning it can grow and shrink as fonts and resolutions change. Overall, this creates better and more consistently sized components and windows than using absolute pixel measurements.

The second line—3dlu, fill:10dlu, 2dlu—creates the rows for the layout. In this case, it adds a three dialog unit space at the top, a two dialog unit space at the bottom, and fills the rest of the space with the component you add.

Now, add the left component. When you add components to a FormLayout-enabled panel, you need to use a JGoodies CellConstraints object. You can use the simple CellConstraints that takes an x- and y-coordinate. In this case, the coordinate is (2,2) because FormLayout starts counting at 1 and you're skipping the first column and row to create space. Here is the code:

```
public void setMainLeftComponent(JComponent component){
    contentPanel.add(component, new CellConstraints(2, 2));
}
```

Add a Separator Panel

Before you can add the components to the right side, you need to make a separator panel. This is actually a really simple component that draws a gray line and a white line in the middle of the panel. Look on the right and left of the 42.3 MB text in Figure 5-7 to see what the separators should look like.

Example 5-2 shows the SeparatorPanel code.

Example 5-2. A panel to separate sections of the status bar

```java
public class SeparatorPanel extends JPanel {
    private Color leftColor;
    private Color rightColor;

    public SeparatorPanel(Color left, Color right) {
        this.leftColor = left;
        this.rightColor = right;
        setOpaque(false);
    }

    protected void paintComponent(Graphics g) {
        g.setColor(leftColor);
        g.drawLine(0,0, 0,getHeight( ));
        g.setColor(rightColor);
        g.drawLine(1,0, 1,getHeight( ));
    }

}
```

And the Rest...

Now that the right panel has been added and you've got the code for the SeparatorPanel, you can add the rest of the components to the status bar. You'll be adding two columns to the layout—one for the SeparatorPanel and one for the actual component. In order to add the components at the correct location, you'll need to cache the x- and y-coordinates and increment the coordinates as you add components. So, create two fields— layoutCoordinateX and layoutCoordinateY—to keep track of the current coordinates:

```java
public void addRightComponent(JComponent component, int dialogUnits){
    layout.appendColumn(new ColumnSpec("2dlu"));
    layout.appendColumn(new ColumnSpec(dialogUnits + "dlu"));

    layoutCoordinateX++;
    contentPanel.add(
        new SeparatorPanel(Color.GRAY, Color.WHITE),
        new CellConstraints(layoutCoordinateX, layoutCoordinateY)
    );
```

```
    layoutCoordinateX++;
    contentPanel.add(
        component,
        new CellConstraints(layoutCoordinateX, layoutCoordinateY)
    );
}
```

 Notice that the size is passed into this method in dialog units rather than pixels. You could easily change this to pixels if you want, but I find dialog units to be a much easier way to layout this kind of component.

Running the Hack

Example 5-3 is the code for a complete simulation frame. You just need to create the JStatusBar and add the left, main, and right components. All of the layout and painting logic is encapsulated completely in JStatusBar. The bold lines in the middle of the StatusBarSimulator are where the status bar is created and the three components are added. Also, notice that all of the labels are center aligned—this mimics the standard Windows practice. You can see the finished product in Figure 5-8.

Your application is about to self destruct.   12/31/99 | 11:59 PM

Figure 5-8. The status bar from StatusBarSimulator

Example 5-3. Using the JStatusBar in a JFrame

```
public class StatusBarSimulator {

    public static void main(String[] args) {
        try {
            UIManager.setLookAndFeel(new WindowsLookAndFeel());
        } catch (Exception e){

        }

        JFrame frame = new JFrame();
        frame.setBounds(200,200, 600, 200);
        frame.setTitle("Status bar simulator");

        Container contentPane = frame.getContentPane();
        contentPane.setLayout(new BorderLayout());

        JStatusBar statusBar = new JStatusBar();
        JLabel leftLabel =
            new JLabel("Your application is about to self destruct.");
        statusBar.setMainLeftComponent(leftLabel);
```

Example 5-3. Using the JStatusBar in a JFrame (continued)

```
    JLabel dateLabel = new JLabel("12/31/99");
    dateLabel.setHorizontalAlignment(SwingConstants.CENTER);
    statusBar.addRightComponent(dateLabel, 30);

    JLabel timeLabel = new JLabel("11:59 PM");
    timeLabel.setHorizontalAlignment(SwingConstants.CENTER);
    statusBar.addRightComponent(timeLabel, 30);

    contentPane.add(statusBar, BorderLayout.SOUTH);

    frame.setDefaultCloseOperation(JFrame.EXIT_ON_CLOSE);
    frame.show( );

    }

}
```

—Jonathan Simon

HACK #37   Save Window Settings

Make sure your windows always show up right where you left them, even after a program restarts, by saving the window position and size automatically.

Swing is a rich toolkit that can be used to create many kinds of programs, but there are certain features that virtually all applications need, like window settings and preferences. This hack shows how to automatically store and retrieve window locations and dimensions in an existing program without using custom Frame subclasses, or even making many changes to your existing code.

Saving the size and location of a window is actually pretty easy. You can just store them in a file and retrieve them later. The difficulty is identifying each window, and doing it in a way that's as noninvasive as possible.

The Window Saver Class

The first step is to create a class that handles all of the work. Because managing windows will be a global function of the entire program, start with a simple singleton with a factory interface, as shown in Example 5-4.

Example 5-4. Singleton for saving window settings

```
public class WindowSaver implements AWTEventListener {

    private static WindowSaver saver;
    private Map framemap;
```

Example 5-4. Singleton for saving window settings (continued)

```
private WindowSaver( ) {
    framemap = new HashMap( );
}

public static WindowSaver getInstance( ) {
    if(saver == null) {
        saver = new WindowSaver( );
    }
    return saver;
}
```

The WindowSaver constructor creates a private map to store all of an application's frames. When each frame is loaded, the saver will store a reference to it in this map. Later, when the application needs to save or reload each window, it will use the map to find each frame again. The constructor is private so that only one instance (and one map) of the program ever exists in the JVM.

The WindowSaver also implements AWTEventListener. This is how it can find each frame. Swing has a global event queue that allows you to get every event throughout the JVM. You can access this queue by registering an AWTEventListener to the global toolkit like this:

```
Toolkit tk = Toolkit.getDefaultToolkit( );
tk.addAWTEventListener(WindowSaver.getInstance( ),
    AWTEvent.WINDOW_EVENT_MASK);
```

AWTEventListener defines a single method, eventDispatched(AWTEvent). Through this method, you can look for each window as it is opened.

Each window produces several events for actions such as closing, opening, resizing, hiding, etc. Some events, such as activation, happen each time a window is shown on the screen. The WINDOW_OPEN event will be called only once per window, right when the window is first shown. This is perfect for our purposes because that particular event will happen after an application has created and initialized each window, but before the window is shown on screen, making it the ideal place to set window size and location:

```
public void eventDispatched(AWTEvent evt) {
    try {
        if(evt.getID( ) == WindowEvent.WINDOW_OPENED) {
            ComponentEvent cev = (ComponentEvent)evt;
            if(cev.getComponent( ) instanceof JFrame) {
                JFrame frame = (JFrame)cev.getComponent( );
                loadSettings(frame);
            }
        }
    }catch(Exception ex) {
        p(ex.toString( ));
    }
}
```

This code listens for WINDOW_OPEN events and then retrieves the reference to the JFrame that was created. Finally, it calls loadSettings( ) on the frame:

```
public static void loadSettings(JFrame frame) throws IOException {
    Properties settings = new Properties( );
    settings.load(new FileInputStream("configuration.props"));
    String name = frame.getName( );
    int x = getInt(settings,name+".x",100);
    int y = getInt(settings,name+".y",100);
    int w = getInt(settings,name+".w",500);
    int h = getInt(settings,name+".h",500);
    frame.setLocation(x,y);
    frame.setSize(new Dimension(w,h));
    saver.framemap.put(name,frame);
    frame.validate( );
}
```

loadSettings( ) demonstrates the real trickery of this hack. Every object in Java has a unique hash code, but hash codes are poor identifiers because they will be different each time the program is run. That makes them useless for saving preferences or referring to windows. Fortunately, Swing defines a little-known property for each component: name. You can name any component in your program with a unique string, and name will be the same every time the program runs. This makes it ideal for saving properties.

loadSettings( ) creates a new properties object, populates it with the contents of a configuration.props file, and then retrieves the name of the given frame. For each property you want to retrieve (the frame coordinates and size), just prepend the property with the name of the component. If the application developer named a frame control-panel, then the x-coordinate would be stored in control-panel.x.

After getting each property, loadSettings( ) sets the location and size of the frame, and then adds the frame to the global frame map so that it can be retrieved later. As a final step, it calls validate( ) on the frame to make sure Swing updates the frame's location and size properly. Here is getInt( ), which is a utility method to retrieve integers from property strings and which substitutes a default value if the string is missing:

```
public static int getInt(Properties props, String name, int value) {
    String v = props.getProperty(name);
    if(v == null) {
        return value;
    }
    return Integer.parseInt(v);
}
```

So, that takes care of loading frame properties.

Once registered to the global event queue, the WindowSaver class will automatically adjust each frame when it is first opened, ensuring that windows are always positioned properly every time the program is run. Saving the window settings, however, is a different matter. This should really happen only when the program closes—assuming the application developer wants window settings saved at all. There might be a standard location for say, dialog boxes, that should always be observed, regardless of how the user moved the windows around last time the program was run. It's probably best to allow applications to explicitly request settings be saved:

```
file.add(new AbstractAction("Quit") {
    public void actionPerformed(ActionEvent evt) {
        try {
            WindowSaver.saveSettings();
            System.exit(0);
        } catch (Exception ex) {
            System.out.println(ex);
        }
    }
});
```

This code adds a Quit menu item that quits the application, but that also calls a saveSettings() method, which again creates a properties object and populates it with the contents of configuration.props. However, instead of looking for window events, it loops through the frame map containing each of the frame references and retrieves the window settings:

```
public static void saveSettings() throws IOException {
    Properties settings = new Properties();
    settings.load(new FileInputStream("configuration.props"));

    Iterator it = saver.framemap.keySet().iterator();
    while(it.hasNext()) {
        String name = (String)it.next();
        JFrame frame = (JFrame)saver.framemap.get(name);
        settings.setProperty(name+".x",""+frame.getX());
        settings.setProperty(name+".y",""+frame.getY());
        settings.setProperty(name+".w",""+frame.getWidth());
        settings.setProperty(name+".h",""+frame.getHeight());
    }
    settings.store(new FileOutputStream("configuration.props"),null);
}
```

After looping through all of the frames, saveSettings() saves the properties back out to the configuration.props file, ready to be loaded the next time the user launches the application.

To demonstrate WindowSaver, you can create a main() method that registers the WindowSaver, builds a simple frame with a button and a Quit menu, and then shows the frame on screen. When the window is opened, the settings will be pulled from the properties file. When the user quits the program, the settings will be saved back to the properties file:

```
public static void main(String[] args) throws Exception {
    Toolkit tk = Toolkit.getDefaultToolkit();
    tk.addAWTEventListener(WindowSaver.getInstance(),
        AWTEvent.WINDOW_EVENT_MASK);

    final JFrame frame = new JFrame("Hack X");
    frame.setName("WSTes.main");
    frame.getContentPane().add(new JButton("a button"));
    JMenuBar mb = new JMenuBar();
    JMenu menu = new JMenu("File");
    menu.add(new AbstractAction("Quit") {
        public void actionPerformed(ActionEvent evt) {
            try {
                WindowSaver.saveSettings();
                System.exit(0);
            } catch (Exception ex) {
                System.out.println(ex);
            }
        }
    });
    mb.add(menu);
    frame.setJMenuBar(mb);
    frame.pack();
    frame.show();
}
```

HACK #38 Earthquake Dialog

Make sure your users really know they got their password wrong.

One of the funny ways that Mac OS X uses animation in its UI is when the user logs in. If she enters an incorrect login and/or password, the whole login dialog shakes violently for a second, like a road sign thwacked with a bat, or a cartoon character who has just run full-speed into a solid object (say, a picture of a tunnel painted over a wall).

We like this effect a lot, so we thought we'd bring it to Swing. It's a pretty straightforward bit of animation, so we jazzed it up...with *trigonometry*!

Exterior Animation

Here's an initial queston: do you want to subclass JDialog and add the animation effect to that class, or create a class that animates the shaking on another JDialog? I thought that subclassing would be a bad choice because JOptionPane generates some very convenient JDialogs, and you wouldn't want to lose those. So, you'll have to have another class animate your dialogs.

I've called it `DialogEarthquakeCenter` because it'll be a class that monitors the shaking, just like seismologists do in their earthquake centers.

Obviously, the `DialogEarthquakeCenter` needs a reference to the dialog that it will be shaking. It also needs a few other values, which I've set as constants:

SHAKE_DISTANCE
> The maximum distance in each direction the dialog should move.

SHAKE_CYCLE
> The time in milliseconds for a complete cycle: center, right, center, left, back to center.

SHAKE_DURATION
> Total time in milliseconds to shake the dialog.

SHAKE_UPDATE
> How often (in milliseconds) to update the dialog's position and repaint. You might increase this if the CPU use is excessive, but animation smoothness decreases with less-frequent updates.

Beyond that, all you'll need to keep track of is where the dialog started (so you can put it back at the end of the animation), a running clock of how far you are into the animation, and where the dialog is located. Example 5-5 shows the code to put all this into action.

Example 5-5. A class to shake a JDialog back and forth

```
public class DialogEarthquakeCenter extends Object {

    public static final int SHAKE_DISTANCE = 10;
    public static final double SHAKE_CYCLE = 50;
    public static final int SHAKE_DURATION = 1000;
    public static final int SHAKE_UPDATE = 5;

    private JDialog dialog;
    private Point naturalLocation;
    private long startTime;
    private Timer shakeTimer;
    private final double HALF_PI = Math.PI / 2.0;
    private final double TWO_PI = Math.PI * 2.0;

    public DialogEarthquakeCenter (JDialog d) {
        dialog = d;
    }

    public void startShake( ) {
        naturalLocation = dialog.getLocation( );
        startTime = System.currentTimeMillis( );
        shakeTimer =
            new Timer(SHAKE_UPDATE,
                    new ActionListener( ) {
```

Example 5-5. A class to shake a JDialog back and forth (continued)

```
                    public void actionPerformed (ActionEvent e) {
                        // calculate elapsed time
                        long elapsed = System.currentTimeMillis( ) -
                            startTime;
                        // use sin to calculate an x-offset
                        double waveOffset = (elapsed % SHAKE_CYCLE) /
                            SHAKE_CYCLE;
                        double angle = waveOffset * TWO_PI;

                        // offset the x-location by an amount
                        // proportional to the sine, up to
                        // shake_distance
                        int shakenX = (int) ((Math.sin (angle) *
                                             SHAKE_DISTANCE) +
                                             naturalLocation.x);
                        dialog.setLocation (shakenX, naturalLocation.y);
                        dialog.repaint( );

                        // should we stop timer?
                        if (elapsed >= SHAKE_DURATION)
                            stopShake( );
                    }
                }
                );
        shakeTimer.start( );
    }

    public void stopShake( ) {
        shakeTimer.stop( );
        dialog.setLocation (naturalLocation);
        dialog.repaint( );
    }

    public static void main (String[] args) {
        JOptionPane pane =
            new JOptionPane ("You've totally screwed up your login\n" +
                            "Go back and do it again... and do you think\n" +
                            "you could remember your password this time?",
                            JOptionPane.ERROR_MESSAGE,
                            JOptionPane.OK_OPTION);
        JDialog d = pane.createDialog (null, "Shakin'!");
        DialogEarthquakeCenter dec = new DialogEarthquakeCenter (d);
        d.pack( );
        d.setModal (false);
        d.setVisible(true);
        dec.startShake( );

        // wait (forever) for a non-null click and then quit
        while (pane.getValue( ) == JOptionPane.UNINITIALIZED_VALUE ) {
            try { Thread.sleep(100); }
            catch (InterruptedException ie) {}
```

Example 5-5. A class to shake a JDialog back and forth (continued)

```
        }
        System.exit(0);
    }
}
```

The class includes the constants described earlier, along with:

- A reference to the JDialog to be animated
- The dialog's natural location (i.e., its location before the animation begins)
- The time that the animation began (for calculating offsets)
- A javax.swing.Timer to run the animation
- Some trigonometry constants

The advantage of the Swing Timer is, of course, that it keeps the repainting on the event-dispatch thread and thus keeps it thread-safe. There's a little bit of non-Swing code executed by the timer to calculate the position, but it's not so bad that you have to worry about blocking the GUI **[Hack #92]**.

The constructor is trivial—it just remembers the dialog as an instance variable. The real fun begins in the startShake( ) method. It starts by storing the current time and location; the time is for use in the animation, and the location is for cleaning up later. Next, it creates the javax.swing.Timer and sets it to fire every SHAKE_UPDATE milliseconds.

Now for some math and the methodology behind moving the dialog. Ignoring friction, air resistance, and other real-world factors—this is a dialog box in the fantasy world of the desktop after all—I opted for *simple harmonic motion*, which is motion that can be expressed by a sine function and is not driven or dampened externally. Values of the sine function range from -1 to 1, so the dialog's horizontal offset can be expressed at the sine of some value from 0 to 2π, multiplied by the maximum offset (namely SHAKE_DISTANCE).

Trig? Really?

Let me take a moment to explain why I'm forcing you to think about trigonometry in a Swing book. When you knock something back and forth, like a tuning fork or a pendulum, it doesn't move at a constant speed to one extreme, then stop and immediately move at a constant speed in the other direction. It slows down as it reaches the extreme, stops momentarily, and then accelerates in the other direction, moving faster until it crosses the center, at which point it starts decelerating. You need more than simple addition to model this—and trig is the ticket.

So, that's what happens in the actionPerformed( ) callback. The method takes the elapsed time and figures out how far into a cycle it is (given a cycle time of SHAKE_CYCLE), expressed as a double between 0 and 1. Multiply this by 2π, and you've got an angle you can pass to Math.sin( ). Multiply that by SHAKE_DISTANCE, and you'll have an x-offset in the range -SHAKE_DISTANCE $\leq n \leq$ SHAKE_DISTANCE. Add that to the naturalLocation's x-value, keep the natural y-value, and you have the new location for the dialog. Call setLocation( ) with this point and repaint( ).

actionPerformed( )'s only other responsibility is to check to see if the animation time has expired and, if so, to call the stopShake( ) method, which is public and could thus be called by an outsider to end the animation prematurely. stopShake( ) stops the Timer, returns the dialog to its natural location, and repaint( )s.

Shake, Rattle, and Roll

I've provided a main( ) method to demonstrate the DialogEarthquakeCenter. To show its flexibility, I made it shake a JOptionPane dialog, to prove you can still use option dialogs as well as normal dialogs, although you do need to work with option dialogs slightly differently:

```
public static void main (String[] args) {
    JOptionPane pane =
        new JOptionPane ("You've totally screwed up your login\n" +
                         "Go back and do it again... and do you think\n"  +
                         "you could remember your password this time?",
                         JOptionPane.ERROR_MESSAGE,
                         JOptionPane.OK_OPTION);
    JDialog d = pane.createDialog (null, "Shakin'!");
    DialogEarthquakeCenter dec = new DialogEarthquakeCenter (d);
    d.pack( );
    d.setModal (false);
    d.setVisible(true);
    dec.startShake( );

    // wait (forever) for a non-null click and then quit
    while (pane.getValue( ) == JOptionPane.UNINITIALIZED_VALUE ) {
        try { Thread.sleep(100); }
        catch (InterruptedException ie) {}
    }
    System.exit(0);
}
```

The main( ) method builds a JOptionPane dialog through what can only be called "the other way." Most developers will call JOptionPane.show... Dialog( ) because it's convenient to get the dialog on screen immediately and provide the user's selection as a return value, and because it's not necessary to ever have a reference to the dialog. With `DialogEarthquakeCenter`, however, you need that reference. So, instead, you provide the usual `JOptionPane` values (message, message type, user options, etc.) to the `JOptionPane` constructor, and then derive a dialog with `createDialog( )`. Don't worry—you still end up with the same option dialog.

Next, you create a `DialogEarthquakeCenter` from that dialog. Then you can return to the dialog, `pack( )` it, and make it visible. One hazard of working with the `JOptionPane` dialog is that it is modal, meaning it will block the AWT event-dispatch thread when shown; thus, it won't shake because `DialogEarthquakeCenter` won't get any animation callbacks from `Timer`. To get around this, I just made the dialog non-modal—after all, the user probably isn't going to be able to click it when it's moving. Another option might be for the `DialogEarthquakeCenter` constructor to remember if its dialog is modal, and to reset this state in `stopShake( )`.

Unfortunately, there's not a great way to show the effect of this animation in book form. The best I can suggest is that you compile and run the hack for yourself. While you're at it, change some of the constant values to see the effect of longer or shorter shake cycles, distances, and durations.

HACK #39   Spin Open a Detail Pane

You don't want to bombard the user with details, but you don't want to hide them either. Here's a way to let the user pop open a More Info widget.

You have to be careful not to weigh down your GUIs with so much information that the user can't see what really matters. On the other hand, there are times that the user may want more information than is obvious on one screen or panel. A simple way of dealing with this is to put a More Info button that pops up a new window. That leads to the annoyance of having too many windows on the screen, none associated in any way with their source.

Mac OS X has a nice idea: the spin open disclosure widget. It works like this: you have a component of some sort—perhaps a simple label or a complex panel—with a triangle-shaped spinner below it. When the user clicks the spinner, a whole new widget opens up below the spinner, offering more information. In fact, the new widget can have significant functionality: to set file permissions from the Finder, you open a Get Info window and spin open an Ownership and Permissions section to set your own access (if you own the file), and a second Details spinner lets you set access levels for the owner, group, and others.

The Invisible Man

This hack is fairly simple and relies on one fact: you can add a component to a layout and alternately make it visible and invisible. Its position relative to other components is preserved when it's invisible, but it takes up no onscreen space. So, a spin-open container consists of three components:

- The top component, which is always visible
- The spinner
- The bottom component, whose visibility can be set by clicking on the spinner

The layout of these three is pretty straightforward, as seen in Example 5-6, which lists the MoreInfoPanel class but omits an inner class (for now).

Example 5-6. Laying out the three panel components

```
public class MoreInfoPanel extends JPanel {

    public Component topComponent;
    protected SpinWidget spinWidget;
    public Component bottomComponent;

    public static final int SPIN_WIDGET_HEIGHT = 14;

    public MoreInfoPanel (Component tc, Component mic) {
        topComponent = tc;
        spinWidget = new SpinWidget( );
        bottomComponent = mic;
        doMyLayout( );
    }

    protected void doMyLayout( ) {
        setLayout (new BoxLayout (this, BoxLayout.Y_AXIS));
        add (topComponent);
        add (spinWidget);
        add (bottomComponent);
        resetBottomVisibility( );
    }

    protected void resetBottomVisibility( ) {
        if ((bottomComponent == null) ||
            (spinWidget == null))
            return;
        bottomComponent.setVisible (spinWidget.isOpen( ));
        revalidate( );
        if (isShowing( )) {
            Container ancestor = getTopLevelAncestor( );
            if ((ancestor != null) && (ancestor instanceof Window))
                ((Window) ancestor).pack( );
```

Example 5-6. Laying out the three panel components (continued)

```
                repaint( );
        }
    }

    public void showBottom (boolean b) {
        spinWidget.setOpen (b);
    }

    public boolean isBottomShowing ( ) {
        return spinWidget.isOpen( );
    }
    // See below for SpinWidget inner class
}
```

The constructor simply assigns the top and bottom Components to local variables, creates a SpinWidget (see Example 5-7), and calls doMyLayout( ). The latter method puts the components into a vertical BoxLayout and calls the convenience method resetBottomVisibility( ).

resetBottomVisibility( ) is responsible for setting the visibility of the bottom component based on whether the SpinWidget is currently open or closed. It then finds and re-pack( )s its parent Window, so that if the bottom component is wider than the top, the enclosing window will resize to fit the now-visible contents. Of course, this behavior might not be appropriate in some cases: you might put a MoreInfoPanel in a complex GUI and not want to re-pack( ) the parent Window. Imagine an IDE in which you browse items in a list or tree on the left, and show varying levels of detail on the right with nested MoreInfoPanels. The right pane might want to get sizing-related events when its child MoreInfoPanels change sizes, but it wouldn't be appropriate for them to try to resize the entire JFrame. This might call for hacking the hack to set up an event-listener system, so that you could deliver sizing-related events to a specific parent.

Now for the SpinWidget, shown in Example 5-7. I wrote this as a custom JPanel that draws the triangles with graphics primitives. This has the advantage of being self-contained, but if you'd rather just use a JButton with hand-drawn triangle GIFs, go for it.

Example 5-7. Inner class spin triangle

```
public class SpinWidget extends JPanel {
    boolean open;
    Dimension mySize = new Dimension (SPIN_WIDGET_HEIGHT,
                                      SPIN_WIDGET_HEIGHT);
    final int HALF_HEIGHT = SPIN_WIDGET_HEIGHT / 2;
    int[] openXPoints =
        { 1, HALF_HEIGHT, SPIN_WIDGET_HEIGHT-1};
```

Example 5-7. Inner class spin triangle (continued)

```java
    int[] openYPoints =
        { HALF_HEIGHT, SPIN_WIDGET_HEIGHT-1, HALF_HEIGHT};
    int[] closedXPoints =
        { 1, 1, HALF_HEIGHT};
    int[] closedYPoints =
        { 1, SPIN_WIDGET_HEIGHT-1, HALF_HEIGHT };
    Polygon openTriangle =
        new Polygon (openXPoints, openYPoints, 3);
    Polygon closedTriangle =
        new Polygon (closedXPoints, closedYPoints, 3);

    public SpinWidget() {
        setOpen (false);
        addMouseListener (new MouseAdapter() {
                public void mouseClicked (MouseEvent e) {
                    handleClick();
                }
            });
    }

    public void handleClick() {
        setOpen (! isOpen());
    }

    public boolean isOpen() {
        return open;
    }

    public void setOpen (boolean o) {
        open = o;
        resetBottomVisibility();
    }

    public Dimension getMinimumSize() { return mySize; }
    public Dimension getPreferredSize() { return mySize; }

    // don't override update(), get the default clear
    public void paint (Graphics g) {
        if (isOpen())
            g.fillPolygon (openTriangle);
        else
            g.fillPolygon (closedTriangle);
    }
}
```

As you can see, the code does some work to create the points for the two tri-angle polygons, which are used in the paint() method. Other than that, it's a simple state machine with two boolean states: when it gets a click, it switches states. The call to setOpen() calls the enclosing class's resetButtonVisibility(), which will make the bottom component visible.

Now You See Me

To show a non-trivial use of the MoreInfoPanel, the TestMoreInfoPanel class shown in Example 5-8 creates a JOptionPane dialog, hijacks its content pane, and puts that into a MoreInfoPanel as the top component. The bottom component is a JTextArea with a more detailed (or obnoxious, in this case) description of the warning in the dialog. This MoreInfoPanel is then reset as the dialog's content pane. The initial result looks like Figure 5-9.

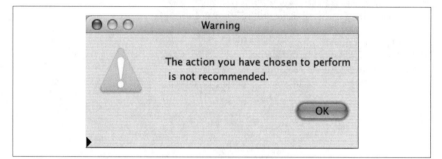

Figure 5-9. A Warning dialog with a closed MoreInfoPanel

Example 5-8. A spin-open dialog using a MoreInfoPanel

```java
import java.awt.*;
import javax.swing.*;

public class TestMoreInfoPanel {

    public static void main (String[] args) {
        JOptionPane pane =
            new JOptionPane ("The action you have chosen to perform\n is " +
                            "not recommended.",
                            JOptionPane.WARNING_MESSAGE);
        JDialog dialog = pane.createDialog (null, "Warning");
        Container grabbedContent = dialog.getContentPane( );
        JTextArea area =
            new JTextArea ("No, seriously dude, you are about to totally "+
                            "bake your computer, if not your entire " +
                            "network, if you don't bail right now.  Think " +
                            "I'm kidding?  Would I go to such lengths to " +
                            "provide such an elaborate warning message if " +
                            "I were kidding?  No, no, wait... you know " +
                            "what?  Go ahead.  Click OK and blow everything " +
                            "to kingdom come.  See if I care.",
                            5, 40);
        area.setLineWrap (true);
        area.setWrapStyleWord (true);
```

Example 5-8. A spin-open dialog using a MoreInfoPanel (continued)

```
JScrollPane scroller =
    new JScrollPane (area,
                     ScrollPaneConstants.VERTICAL_SCROLLBAR_ALWAYS,
                     ScrollPaneConstants.HORIZONTAL_SCROLLBAR_NEVER);
MoreInfoPanel mip = new MoreInfoPanel (grabbedContent, scroller);
dialog.setContentPane (mip);
dialog.pack( );
dialog.setVisible(true);
// dialog blocks on setVisible (JOptionPane makes it modal)
System.exit(0);
    }
}
```

When the user clicks the triangle at the bottom left, the More Info text area appears, as seen in Figure 5-10.

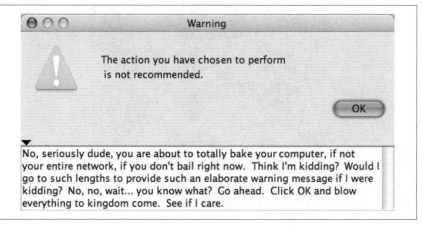

Figure 5-10. The Warning dialog after opening the MoreInfoPanel

HACK #40   Minimize to a Mini-Frame

When you want your program to have a smaller window but still be on the screen, try building a mini-mode.

Since the advent of iTunes, it seems that all consumer-oriented applications must have meticulous interfaces that can dynamically adjust themselves. Gone are the days of simply minimizing an application. Now your program must have a small version rather than (or in addition to) hiding when minimized. The smaller version contains limited controls but can fit nicely at the bottom of the screen. This hack shows how to create a dynamic frame that can switch properly between sizes for a more modern-looking interface.

I Shall Call Him...Mini-Me

Switching a frame between two sizes is quite easy: just call setSize( ) and you're done. Doing it well is a bit more difficult, however. When you minimize the window, you also need to remove the window decorations, hide the menu bar, and remove the components that shouldn't be visible in the mini-view. This is a bit trickier, not the least of which because you can't turn off the window decorations of a frame once it has been created. But I'm getting ahead of myself. First, you need a sample application.

Let's take a simple clock program. The normal window looks like Figure 5-11. The goal is to provide a mini version that looks like Figure 5-12.

Figure 5-11. A normal application window

Figure 5-12. A mini application window

This program has a clock, a panel with more configuration options (represented here with just the label More configuration), a menu bar, and a pop-up menu for later use. Example 5-9 creates the interface and puts the components in the right places, but it doesn't do anything with them yet.

Example 5-9. The beginning of a clock with a mini version

```
public class MiniMizeHack implements MouseListener, ActionListener {

    public JFrame frame;
    public JPanel panel;
    public JPopupMenu popup;
```

Example 5-9. The beginning of a clock with a mini version (continued)

```java
public JMenuBar menubar;
public JLabel top;
public JLabel bottom;

public MiniMizeHack( ) {
    top = new JLabel(new ImageIcon("image.png"));
    bottom = new JLabel("More configuration here");

    frame = new JFrame("Mini Mize Hack");
    panel = new JPanel( );
    panel.setLayout(new BorderLayout( ));
    panel.add("Center",bottom);
    panel.add("North",top);
    frame.getContentPane( ).add(panel);

    menubar = new JMenuBar( );
    JMenu menu = new JMenu("File");
    menu.add(new JMenuItem("Open"));
    menu.add(new JMenuItem("Quit"));
    menubar.add(menu);

    JMenu window = new JMenu("Window");
    JMenuItem mini = new JMenuItem("Minimize");
    mini.addActionListener(this);
    window.add(mini);
    menubar.add(window);
    frame.setJMenuBar(menubar);

    popup = new JPopupMenu( );
    JMenuItem restore = new JMenuItem("Restore");
    restore.addActionListener(this);
    popup.add(restore);
}

public void mousePressed(MouseEvent e) {
    maybeShowPopup(e);
}

public void mouseReleased(MouseEvent e) {
    maybeShowPopup(e);
}
public void mouseExited(MouseEvent e) { }
public void mouseEntered(MouseEvent e) { }
public void mouseClicked(MouseEvent e) { }
private void maybeShowPopup(MouseEvent e) {
    if (e.isPopupTrigger( )) {
        popup.show(e.getComponent( ),
                e.getX(), e.getY( ));
    }
}
```

The code declares a `MiniMizeHack` class, which creates the UI and adds itself as an `ActionListener` to the Minimize and Restore menu items. The mouse listener implementation is there to control the pop-up menu, but because the `MiniMizeHack` class hasn't been added as a listener to any components, the pop up won't do anything yet.

Minimize the Frame

The `actionPerformed()` method does the actual switching. This is the meat of the hack. It tests if the bottom component is visible. If the component is visible, then this method calls `switchToMini()` and reshapes the frame to be smaller. If the bottom component is *not* visible, then `actionPerformed()` calls `switchToNormal()` to reverse the changes:

```
public void actionPerformed(ActionEvent evt) {
    if(bottom.isVisible()) {
        switchToMini();
    } else {
        switchToNormal();
    }
}
```

The magic happens in the `switchToMini()` method. A big part of a mini window is that it doesn't have any borders, or at the least it uses custom ones. Swing does not let you turn off a frame's borders and window decorations after the frame has been shown on screen because it might have already allocated immutable system resources. The only way around this limitation is to seamlessly replace the old frame with a new one:

```
private Dimension normal_size;
public void switchToMini() {
    // nuke the old frame and build a new one
    Point location = frame.getLocation();
    normal_size = frame.getSize();
    frame.setVisible(false);
    frame = new JFrame();
    frame.setUndecorated(true);
    frame.getContentPane().add(panel);
```

The `switchToMini()` method starts by saving the current frame location and size, and then hides the frame and replaces it with a new one. Now, it can safely call `setUndecorated(true)` on the frame. The `frame.getContentPane().add(panel)` line will add the main panel to the new frame. It is not necessary to remove the panel from the old frame because Swing will take care of it automatically. There is also no need to remove the menu bar because it had never been added to the new frame.

Now, the code can hide the bottom component (the label representing the extra clock configuration) and add the mouse listener to activate the pop up on right-clicks. If you are using Java 5.0, you can add another line to make the frame always be on top. This can be annoying to some users, however, so a real program would have a preference to control that feature:

```
// hide the extra components
bottom.hide( );

// add the pop up
panel.addMouseListener(this);

// stay on top
frame.setAlwaysOnTop(true);

// show the frame again
frame.pack( );
frame.setLocation(location);
frame.setVisible(true);
```

With the frame prepared, the code packs it, gives it the location of the original frame, and makes it visible again.

Restore the Frame

When the user triggers the pop-up menu and selects Normal, the switchToNormal( ) method will be called. This method reverses what the switchToMini( ) method did:

```
public void switchToNormal( ) {
    // nuke the old frame and build a new one
    Point location = frame.getLocation( );
    frame.setVisible(false);
    frame = new JFrame( );
    frame.setUndecorated(false);
    frame.getContentPane( ).add(panel);

    // show the extra components
    bottom.show( );
    frame.setJMenuBar(menubar);

    // hide the pop up
    panel.removeMouseListener(this);

    // turn off stay on top
    frame.setAlwaysOnTop(false);

    // show the frame again
    frame.pack( );
    frame.setSize(normal_size);
    frame.setLocation(location);
    frame.setVisible(true);
}
```

switchToNormal( ) will first save the location of the frame, hide the frame, and replace it with a new, fully decorated one. It then turns the menu bar and bottom component back on, removes the pop-up listener, turns off Always on Top (only for Java 5.0), and restores the frame.

To launch the application, you need to add only a main( ) method to create a mini and show it on screen:

```
public static void main(String[] args) {
    MiniMizeHack mini = new MiniMizeHack( );
    mini.frame.pack( );
    mini.frame.setSize(300,300);
    mini.frame.setVisible(true);
}
```

Swing doesn't do everything by default, but it makes a lot of things possible. This hack showed how to create the sort of dynamic frame actions that users expect today. One enhancement you would probably want to add is the draggable background [Hack #34] because a window without a titlebar may be difficult to move by itself. You might also want to use small buttons instead of a pop-up menu to control the toggling since most users will be familiar with the min, max, and close buttons.

Transparent and Animated Windows

Hacks 41–47

In the previous chapter, our window hacks generally played by the rules—we simulated the earthquake dialog [Hack #38] by animating calls to setLocation( ), and switched to a mini-size window [Hack #40] by calling setSize( ) and removing some window decorations.

This chapter's hacks approach from outside the Window API per se, by hacking the windows with Java 2D, stuffing things into the glass pane of a JDialog or JFrame, and more. Some of them are practical, some are just pretty, but all of these hacks offer something unexpected.

HACK #41 Transparent Windows

Create translucent and shaped windows, while avoiding native code, with clever use of a screenshot.

One of the most commonly requested Swing features is transparent windows. Also called *shaped windows*, these are windows that have transparent portions, allowing the desktop background and other programs to shine through. Java doesn't provide any way of creating transparent windows without using the Java Native Interface (JNI) (and even then the native platform must support transparency as well), but that's not going to stop us. We can cheat using one of my favorite techniques, the screenshot.

The process of faking a transparent window is basically:

1. Take a screenshot before the window is shown.

2. Use that screenshot as the background of the window.

3. Adjust the position so that the screenshot and the real screen line up, creating the illusion of transparency.

This is the easy part. The hard part is updating the screenshot when the window moves or changes.

To start off, create a JPanel subclass that can capture the screen and paint it as the background, as shown in Example 6-1.

Example 6-1. A transparent background component

```
public class TransparentBackground extends Jcomponent {
    private JFrame frame;
    private Image background;

    public TransparentBackground(JFrame frame) {
        this.frame = frame;
        updateBackground( );
    }

    public void updateBackground( ) {
        try {
            Robot rbt = new Robot( );
            Toolkit tk = Toolkit.getDefaultToolkit( );
            Dimension dim = tk.getScreenSize( );
            background = rbt.createScreenCapture(
            new Rectangle(0,0,(int)dim.getWidth( ),
                            (int)dim.getHeight( )));
        } catch (Exception ex) {
            p(ex.toString( ));
            ex.printStackTrace( );
        }
    }

    public void paintComponent(Graphics g) {
        Point pos = this.getLocationOnScreen( );
        Point offset = new Point(-pos.x,-pos.y);
        g.drawImage(background,offset.x,offset.y,null);
    }
}
```

First, the constructor saves a reference to the parent JFrame; then it calls updateBackground( ), which captures the entire screen using java.awt.Robot. createScreenCapture( ), and saves the capture in the background variable. paintComponent( ) gets the panel's absolute position on screen and then fills the panel with the background image, shifted to account for the panel's location. This makes the fake background image line up with the real background, giving the appearance of transparency.

You can run this with a simple main( ) method, dropping a few components onto the panel and putting it into a frame:

```
public static void main(String[] args) {
    JFrame frame = new JFrame("Transparent Window");
    TransparentBackground bg = new TransparentBackground(frame);
    bg.setLayout(new BorderLayout( ));
    JButton button = new JButton("This is a button");
    bg.add("North",button);
```

```
        JLabel label = new JLabel("This is a label");
        bg.add("South",label);
        frame.getContentPane( ).add("Center",bg);
        frame.pack( );
        frame.setSize(150,100);
        frame.show( );
    }
```

The code produces a window that looks like Figure 6-1.

Figure 6-1. Transparent windows in action

The code is pretty simple, but it has two big flaws. First, if the window is moved, the background won't be refreshed automatically. paintComponent( ) only gets called when the user resizes the window. Second, if the screen ever changes, it won't match up with the background anymore.

You really don't want to update the screenshot often, though, because that involves hiding the window, taking a new screenshot, and then reshowing the window—all of which is disconcerting to the user. Actually detecting when the rest of the desktop changes is almost impossible, but most changes happen when the foreground window changes focus or moves. If you accept this idea (and I do), then you can watch for those events and only update the screenshot when that happens:

```
public class TransparentBackground extends JComponent
        implements ComponentListener, WindowFocusListener,
        Runnable {
    private JFrame frame;
    private Image background;
    private long lastupdate = 0;
    public boolean refreshRequested = true;
```

```
public TransparentBackground(JFrame frame) {
    this.frame = frame;
    updateBackground();
    frame.addComponentListener(this);
    frame.addWindowFocusListener(this);
    new Thread(this).start();
}

public  void componentShown(ComponentEvent evt) { repaint(); }
public  void componentResized(ComponentEvent evt) { repaint(); }
public  void componentMoved(ComponentEvent evt) { repaint(); }
public  void componentHidden(ComponentEvent evt) { }

public void windowGainedFocus(WindowEvent evt) { refresh(); }
public void windowLostFocus(WindowEvent evt) { refresh(); }
```

First, make the panel, TransparentWindow, implement ComponentListener, WindowFocusListener, and Runnable. The listener interfaces will let the panel catch events indicating that the window has moved, been resized, or the focus changes. Implementing Runnable will let the panel create a thread to handle custom repaint( )s.

The implementation of ComponentListener involves the four methods beginning with component. They each simply call repaint( ) so that the background will be updated whenever the user moves or resizes the window. Next are the two window focus handlers, which just call refresh( ), as shown here:

```
public void refresh() {
    if(frame.isVisible()) {
        repaint();
        refreshRequested = true;
        lastupdate = new Date().getTime();
    }
}

public void run() {
    try {
        while(true) {
            Thread.sleep(250);
            long now = new Date().getTime();
            if(refreshRequested &&
                ((now - lastupdate) > 1000)) {
                if(frame.isVisible()) {
                    Point location = frame.getLocation();
                    frame.hide();
                    updateBackground();
                    frame.show();
                    frame.setLocation(location);
                    refresh();
                }
```

```
                lastupdate = now;
                refreshRequested = false;
            }
        }
    } catch (Exception ex) {
        p(ex.toString());
        ex.printStackTrace();
    }
}
```

refresh() ensures that the frame is visible and schedules a repaint. It also sets the refreshRequested boolean to true and saves the current time, which will become very important shortly.

The run() method sleeps constantly, waking up every quarter-second to see if a refresh has been requested, and whether it has been more than a second since the last refresh. If more than a second has passed and the frame is actually visible, then run() will save the frame location, hide it, update the background, then put the frame back in place and call refresh(). This ensures that the background is never updated more than needed.

So, why all of this rigmarole about using a thread to control refreshing? One word: recursion. The event handlers could simply call updateBackground() and repaint() directly, but hiding and showing the window to generate the screenshot would cause more focus-changed events. These would then trigger another background update, causing the window to hide again, and so on, creating an infinite loop. The new focus events are generated a few milliseconds after refresh() is processed, so simply checking for an isRecursing flag wouldn't stop a loop.

Additionally, any user action that would change the screen will probably create lots of events, not just one. It's just the *last* event that should trigger updateBackground(), not the first. To handle all these issues, the code creates a thread that watches for repaint requests and only processes a new screenshot if it hasn't already been done in the last 1,000 milliseconds. If the user generates events continuously for five seconds (searching for that lost browser window, for example), then only when everything else has settled down for a second will the refresh actually happen. This ensures that users won't have a window disappear out from under them while they are moving things around.

Another annoyance is that the window still has its border, which sort of ruins the effect of having a transparent background. Unfortunately, removing the borders with setUndecorated(true) would also remove the titlebar and window controls. This probably isn't too much of a problem, though, because the types of applications that typically use shaped windows usually have draggable backgrounds [Hack #34].

Here's a simple test program to put this into action:

```
public static void main(String[] args) {
    JFrame frame = new JFrame("Transparent Window");
    frame.setUndecorated(true);

    TransparentBackground bg = new TransparentBackground(frame);
    bg.snapBackground();
    bg.setLayout(new BorderLayout());

    JPanel panel = new JPanel() {
        public void paintComponent(Graphics g) {
            g.setColor(Color.blue);
            Image img = new ImageIcon("mp3.png").getImage();
            g.drawImage(img,0,0,null);
        }
    };
    panel.setOpaque(false);

    bg.add("Center",panel);

    frame.getContentPane().add("Center",bg);
    frame.pack();
    frame.setSize(200,200);
    frame.setLocation(500,500);
    frame.show();
}
```

The code creates a faux MP3 player interface using a JPanel subclass and a PNG image with transparency. Note the call to frame.setUndecorated(true), which turns off the border and titlebar. The call to panel.setOpaque(false) turns off the default background (usually plain gray), allowing the screenshot background to shine through the transparent parts of the image (Figure 6-2). This produces a window that looks like Figure 6-3—a vision of Java programs to come?

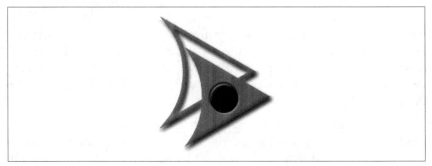

Figure 6-2. Template for an MP3 player

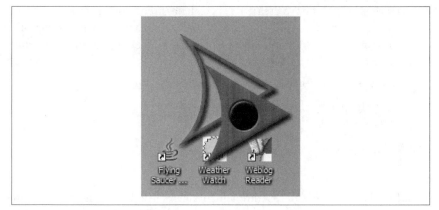

Figure 6-3. Running the MP3 player

Make Your Frame Dissolve

Create animated frame dissolves using two screenshots and some clever graphics code.

Dissolve is a term from old motion pictures where the director would switch scenes by fading, or *dissolving*, from one image to another. Eventually directors came up with more interesting dissolves like the vertical wipe, the venetian effect (little thin strips that look like venetian blinds), and the classic fade to black. With a little bit of screenshot hackery, you can create similar effects in Swing, allowing your program to fade away or do some other interesting animation when the user quits.

AWT doesn't support real transparent or shaped windows (though you can fake it with a screenshot pasted into a window that fills the screen **[Hack #41]**. Most dissolves involve applying some graphic effect to both the starting and ending images, which in this case means the application window itself and the rest of the user's desktop under the window. With this in mind, the basic plan is four steps:

1. Capture an image of the window.
2. Capture an image of the entire screen *without* the window.
3. Cover up the entire screen with a new window.
4. Show the dissolve animation.

To keep this simple, I have created a special class that does a simple fade-to-transparent animation. Once the class is built, you can create more complicated animations by overriding the paint method, leaving the messy details to the parent class. Here's the basic skeleton:

```
class Dissolver extends JComponent implements Runnable {
    Frame frame;
    Window fullscreen;
    int count;
    BufferedImage frame_buffer;
    BufferedImage screen_buffer;

    public Dissolver( ) { }
```

Dissolver is a JComponent that implements Runnable so that it can have an animation loop. It has member variables for the application frame to dissolve (frame), the window that covers up the screen (fullscreen), an animation counter (count), and the two buffers for storing the frame and the desktop background image (frame_buffer and screen_buffer).

Prepare the Dissolve

Dissolver has one method to start the dissolve process called dissolveExit( ), which takes the JFrame you want to dissolve and generates everything else it needs internally:

```
public void dissolveExit(JFrame frame) {
    try {
        this.frame = frame;
        Robot robot = new Robot( );

        // cap screen w/ frame to frame buffer
        Rectangle frame_rect = frame.getBounds( );
        frame_buffer = robot.createScreenCapture(frame_rect);

        // hide frame
        frame.setVisible(false);

        // cap screen w/o frame
        Dimension screensize = Toolkit.getDefaultToolkit( )
                                    .getScreenSize( );
        Rectangle screen_rect = new Rectangle(0,0,
            screensize.width, screensize.height);
        screen_buffer = robot.createScreenCapture(screen_rect);

        // create big window w/o decorations
        fullscreen = new Window(new JFrame( ));
        fullscreen.setSize(screensize);
        fullscreen.add(this);
        this.setSize(screensize);
        fullscreen.setVisible(true);
```

```
        // start animation
        new Thread(this).start( );
    } catch (Exception ex) {
        System.out.println(ex);
        ex.printStackTrace( );
    }
}
```

dissolveExit( ) saves a reference to the frame and creates a new java.awt.
Robot to handle the screen captures. Then it captures just the area of the
screen containing the frame by calling robot.createScreenCatpure( ), using
the rectangle returned by frame.getBounds( ). After making this screen capture, it hides the frame and then captures the entire screen into the second
buffer. Finally, it creates a new Window that covers the entire screen, adds the
Dissolver as the window's only child, and starts the animation on a new
thread.

There are two tricky things to look out for here. First, the code uses a Window
instead of a JFrame so that the window won't show up in a task list or the
dock. This also means it won't have any window decorations that would
ruin the illusion of transparency. Second, the Window constructor requires
you to pass in another window or frame. This is because every window is
attached to a parent window and will only be visible when the parent is (on
certain platforms). Using the existing application frame won't work because
it's just been hidden, but if you create a new, empty JFrame, the window will
show up fine.

Run the Animation

dissolveExit( ) creates a new thread around the run( ) method (see the following code). This method will request a repaint on the component every
100 milliseconds, looping 20 times and then quitting. This will create a two-
second dissolve animation, but you can certainly tweak these values to your
own tastes:

```
public void run( ) {
    try {
        count = 0;
        Thread.currentThread( ).sleep(100);
        for(int i=0; i<20; i++) {
            count = i;
            fullscreen.repaint( );
            Thread.currentThread( ).sleep(100);
        }
    } catch (InterruptedException ex) { }
    System.exit(0);
}
```

Do the Drawing

Now that the component will be repainted for each frame of the animation, you can finally do some drawing. Fading to nothing is really easy with Swing. You just need to draw the background image first, and then draw the frame on top using a Composite. A Composite is a class that knows to adjust the standard mechanism in some way. An AlphaComposite will draw partially transparent images depending on the alpha value you pass in. An alpha value of 1 will draw the image fully opaque, while a value of 0 will be completely transparent. Values between 1 and 0 will draw the image partially transparent. Always be sure to save the old composite so you can return the Graphics object to its original state when you are done:

```
public void paint(Graphics g) {
    Graphics2D g2 = (Graphics2D)g;
    // draw the screen, offset in case the window isn't at 0,0
    g.drawImage(screen_buffer,-fullscreen.getX(),
        -fullscreen.getY(),null);

    // draw the frame
    Composite old_comp = g2.getComposite();
    Composite fade = AlphaComposite.getInstance(
        AlphaComposite.SRC_OVER,1.0f-((float)count)/20f);
    g2.setComposite(fade);
    g2.drawImage(frame_buffer,frame.getX(),frame.getY(),null);
    g2.setComposite(old_comp);
}
```

The class in Example 6-2 creates a frame with one button called quit. When you press the Quit button, the dissolve will be activated, fading the window into nothing and then calling System.exit(). If you compile and run the code, it will look something like Figure 6-4.

Figure 6-4. A fade dissolve

Example 6-2. A simple test class

```
public class DissolveHack {

    public static void main(String[] args) {

        final JFrame frame = new JFrame("Dissolve Hack");
        JButton quit = new JButton("Quit");
        quit.addActionListener(new ActionListener( ) {
            public void actionPerformed(ActionEvent evt) {
                new Dissolver( ).dissolveExit(frame);
            }
        });

        frame.getContentPane( ).add(quit);
        frame.pack( );
        frame.setLocation(300,300);
        frame.setSize(400,400);
        frame.setVisible(true);
    }
}
```

Create a Genie Effect

One of my favorite bits of eye candy from Mac OS X is the minimize dissolve. When you click on the minimize button in any application, the window will shrink and slide into the dock. This is called the genie effect, and it not only looks cool, but it also gives you feedback about where a window has gone. Example 6-3 is a subclass of Dissolver that overrides the paint( ) method to create a spinning, shrinking window that somewhat mimics the genie effect.

Example 6-3. Adding a genie effect to your toolbox

```
class SpinDissolver extends Dissolver {

    public void paint(Graphics g) {
        Graphics2D g2 = (Graphics2D)g;
        // draw the screen, offset in case the window isn't at 0,0
        g.drawImage(screen_buffer,-fullscreen.getX( ),
            -fullscreen.getY( ),null);

        // save the current transform
        AffineTransform old_trans = g2.getTransform( );

        // move to the upper-lefthand corner of the frame
        g2.translate(frame.getX( ), frame.getY( ));

        // move the frame off toward the left
        g2.translate(-((count+1) * (frame.getX( )+frame.getWidth( ))/20),0);
```

Example 6-3. Adding a genie effect to your toolbox (continued)

```
        // shrink the frame
        float scale = 1f / ((float)count+1);
        g2.scale(scale,scale);

        // rotate around the center
        g2.rotate(((float)count)/3.14/1.3,
            frame.getWidth()/2, frame.getHeight()/2);

        // finally draw the frame
        g2.drawImage(frame_buffer,0,0,null);

        // restore the current transform
        g2.setTransform(old_trans);
    }
}
```

This dissolver will shrink the window and spin it, while moving it toward the left at the same time. This make the window look like it is spinning off into oblivion, as in Figure 6-5.

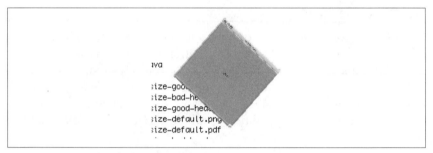

Figure 6-5. A spin dissolve

This hack shows off just a few of the really cool effects you can accomplish with just a bit of Java2D code in your Swing application. Because the parent Dissolve class takes care of most of the tricky parts, you can easily create your own subclasses that focus on just the animation itself. You might want to try some other animations, such as the circle and linear wipes common to old movies, or a better genie effect that works when you quit your application. Java2D gives you the power to do virtually any linear transform (shear, scale, rotate, etc.), plus composites and convolutions. For even more effects, you could use Java3D or JOGL to create three-dimensional effects like spinning cubes and perspective transforms.

Create Custom Tool Tips

Replace the standard rollover tool tip with an attractive custom version, including a border and rounded corners.

Every Swing component can have a *tool tip*, a little snippet of explanatory text that pops up when you let your mouse cursor linger over the component. These tool tips are often useful, but they usually look quite boring. This hack shows how to create visually interesting tool tips with a custom subclass.

In Swing, all tool tips are instances of the JToolTip class. To create your own version, you need only subclass JToolTip and override the paintComponent() method. In this hack, we'll create a tool tip with a rectangle that has a beveled border and a white background. The actual drawing can be taken care of with a few Java2D drawing commands. Example 6-4 is the code to draw the tool tip's background and border.

Example 6-4. A nice-looking tool tip

```
class CustomToolTip extends JToolTip {

    public void paintComponent(Graphics g) {

        // create a round rectangle
        Shape round = new RoundRectangle2D.Float(4,4,
            this.getWidth( )-1-8,
            this.getHeight( )-1-8,
            15,15);

        // draw the white background
        Graphics2D g2 = (Graphics2D)g;
        g2.setRenderingHint(RenderingHints.KEY_ANTIALIASING,
            RenderingHints.VALUE_ANTIALIAS_ON);
        g2.setColor(Color.white);
        g2.fill(round);

        // draw the gray border
        g2.setColor(Color.gray);
        g2.setStroke(new BasicStroke(5));
        g2.draw(round);
        g2.setRenderingHint(RenderingHints.KEY_ANTIALIASING,
            RenderingHints.VALUE_ANTIALIAS_DEFAULT);

        // draw the text
        String text = this.getComponent().getToolTipText( );
        if(text != null) {
            FontMetrics fm = g2.getFontMetrics( );
            int h = fm.getAscent( );
```

Example 6-4. A nice-looking tool tip (continued)

```
        g2.setColor(Color.black);
        g2.drawString(text,10,(this.getHeight( )+h)/2);
    }
}
```

This code creates a round rectangle shape that is then reused to draw the background and border. Notice that anti-aliasing is turned on for drawing the shape, but it's turned back to the default (which could be on or off) before drawing the text. It would look strange to have anti-aliased text if the rest of the interface was still using standard aliased text—using the default is a safer idea.

Because this tool tip needs extra space around the text to draw the border, you will need to modify the tool tip's preferred size. The getPreferredSize( ) method here adds an extra 20 pixels in each direction:

```
public Dimension getPreferredSize( ) {
    Dimension dim = super.getPreferredSize( );
    return new Dimension((int)dim.getWidth( )+20,
            (int)dim.getHeight( )+20);
}
```

The tool tip has rounded corners, but with the code as it stands, you would still see the slivers of gray that fill out the component's real corners. In order to hide the gray and let the components below shine through, you need to make the tool tip transparent. You can do this by setting opaque to false in the tool tip's constructor. The tool tip component is not a direct child of the frame that contains the tool tip. There is another component between the tool tip and the frame that will be visible even if the tool tip is transparent. You can make this extra component transparent with an additional setOpaque(false) call on the tool tip's parent at the start of the paintComponent( ) method:

```
public CustomToolTip( ) {
    super( );
    // make the tool tip not fill in its background
    this.setOpaque(false);
}

public void paintComponent(Graphics g) {

    // set the parent to not be opaque
    Component parent = this.getParent( );
    if(parent != null) {
        if(parent instanceof JComponent) {
            JComponent jparent = (JComponent)parent;
            if(jparent.isOpaque( )) {
```

```
                jparent.setOpaque(false);
            }
        }
    }

    // ... the rest of the drawing code
```

Install the Tool Tip

To install the custom tool tip, you need to override the createToolTip( ) method of the component you wish to modify. An example using a custom JButton is shown in Example 6-5.

Example 6-5. Installing a custom tool tip

```
class CustomJButton extends JButton {
    JToolTip _tooltip;

    public CustomJButton( ) {
        _tooltip = new CustomToolTip( );
        _tooltip.setComponent(this);
    }

    public JToolTip createToolTip( ) {
        return _tooltip;
    }

}
```

Because the tool tip is specified by the custom JButton class, all you need to do is create some components and set their tool tip text. The code in Example 6-6 creates two buttons and three labels in a frame. The buttons have custom tool tips that will display—complete with the now transparent corners—on top of the rest of the screen, as shown in Figure 6-6.

Figure 6-6. A tool tip with a custom border

Example 6-6. Testing out custom tool tips

```java
public class ToolTipsHack {

    public static void main(String[] args) {
        JButton button;

        JFrame frame = new JFrame("Tool Tips Hack");
        BoxLayout layout =  new BoxLayout(
            frame.getContentPane( ),
            BoxLayout.Y_AXIS);
        frame.getContentPane( ).setLayout(layout);

        button = new CustomJButton( );
        button.setText("Open");
        button.setToolTipText("Open an existing file");
        frame.getContentPane( ).add(button);

        button = new CustomJButton( );
        button.setText("Save");
        button.setToolTipText("Save the currently open file");
        frame.getContentPane( ).add(button);

        frame.getContentPane( ).add(new JLabel("a label"));
        frame.getContentPane( ).add(new JLabel("a label"));
        frame.getContentPane( ).add(new JLabel("a label"));

        frame.pack( );
        frame.show( );
    }
}
```

HACK #44   Turn Dialogs into Frame-Anchored Sheets

One of Mac OS X's best ideas is binding the dialog to the window it blocks. This hack shows you how to mimic this in Swing.

One of my favorite features in Mac OS X is the *sheet*. This is a dialog box replacement that slides down from a window's titlebar. Figure 6-7 shows an example of a sheet in Apple's Safari web browser.

Why Sheets Rock

Looking at it, you might think, "what's the big deal" or "how is this any different than a regular dialog?" Oh, it's far better:

A sheet is visually anchored to the window that it blocks
    On platforms where dialogs have titlebars and close boxes, the relationship between a dialog and the window it blocks is not necessarily intuitive. On a related point....

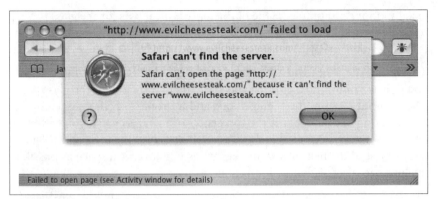

Figure 6-7. Sheet in Mac OS X Safari browser

A sheet doesn't have a close box

Dialog close boxes are one of the most hateful and stupid concepts in Windows and its many Linux imitators. What does the close box mean? Cancel? The default option? What does it mean when the dialog has multiple options of equal plausibility and thus no default? Perhaps the worst thing about the close box was back in the AWT era when Java developers—too lazy to add and wire-up an OK button to their dialogs—just figured users could dismiss the dialog with the close box. Mac OS 8 and 9 dialogs didn't have close boxes, so when a Java application brought up such a dialog, *the application blocked itself forever.* Duh. Sheets mean having to click one of the provided buttons, so the user's choices are unambiguous.

A sheet is used to block one window

This is an obvious side effect of being visually tied to a single window, but that's probably the most common case. As a side effect, this gives greater prominence to dialogs that block all windows for a single application ("Are you sure you want to Quit and lose all unsaved changes in all documents?") and dialogs that block all applications ("Are you sure you want to Shut Down?").

So, if you agree that it's an excellent GUI concept, the next question is "how do I mimic sheets in Swing?"

Use the Glass Pane

One way to imitate the Mac OS X sheet is to use the *glass pane*—a layer in the LayeredPane used by all RootPaneContainers, including JApplets, JFrames, JInternalFrames, JWindows, and JDialogs. In terms of z-order—the ordering of layers on "top" of one another from the user's perspective—the glass pane is "above" the content pane and the menu bar in the LayeredPane. It is usually empty and unfilled. One of the more typical uses for the glass pane is to add a MouseListener and MouseMotionListener to deny events to the content pane and thereby block it.

To imitate the sheet with the glass pane, the idea is to take the contents you'd usually put into a JDialog and place them instead into the glass pane. This will put them in the frame, above and in front of the frame's contents. To position your contents at the top center of the glass pane, you can use a GridBagLayout that gives the sheet a NORTH anchor, and then add a "glue" component in the next row that takes up as much vertical space as possible, pushing the sheet to the top of the pane.

Example 6-7 shows a subclass of JFrame that exposes a showJDialogAsSheet( ) method, which grabs the JDialog's content pane JComponent and inserts it into the glass pane as the sheet.

Example 6-7. Adding a sheet in a JFrame's glass pane

```
import javax.swing.*;
import javax.swing.border.*;
import java.awt.*;
import java.awt.event.*;

public class SheetableJFrame extends JFrame {

    JComponent sheet;
    JPanel glass;

    public SheetableJFrame (String name) {
        super(name);
        glass = (JPanel) getGlassPane();
    }

    public JComponent showJDialogAsSheet (JDialog dialog) {
        sheet = (JComponent) dialog.getContentPane();
        sheet.setBackground (Color.red);
        glass.setLayout (new GridBagLayout());
        sheet.setBorder (new LineBorder(Color.black, 1));
        glass.removeAll();
        GridBagConstraints gbc = new GridBagConstraints();
        gbc.anchor = GridBagConstraints.NORTH;
        glass.add (sheet, gbc);
        gbc.gridy=1;
        gbc.weighty = Integer.MAX_VALUE;
        glass.add (Box.createGlue(), gbc);
        glass.setVisible(true);
        return sheet;
    }
```

Example 6-7. Adding a sheet in a JFrame's glass pane (continued)

```
    public void hideSheet( ) {
        glass.setVisible(false);
    }
}
```

Simple enough, isn't it? To test this component, just create a JFrame and a
JDialog to insert into the frame. The SheetTest class in Example 6-8, which
exercises the SheetableJFrame, fills the frame with interesting content by
making a JLabel from an image file. It then creates a JDialog the easy way—
by making JOptionPane do it.

> If you're used to calling JOptionPane's various
> show*XXX*Dialog( ) methods, you might be unfamiliar with the
> idea of constructing and holding on to a JOptionPane and
> creating dialogs from it. This approach isn't common, but
> it's useful if you want to hold on to the JDialog, maybe for
> reuse (e.g., you have memory or performance concerns with
> repeatedly creating and disposing of dialogs) or because you
> don't want to block as soon as you show it. In the case of
> this demo, the advantage is to get a dialog to play with, with-
> out having to layout and wire up everything yourself.

Example 6-8. Testing the SheetableJFrame

```
import javax.swing.*;
import java.awt.*;
import java.awt.event.*;
import java.beans.*;

public class SheetTest extends Object
    implements PropertyChangeListener {

    JOptionPane optionPane;
    SheetableJFrame frame;

    public static void main (String[] args) {
        new SheetTest( );
    }

    public SheetTest ( ) {
        frame = new SheetableJFrame ("Sheet test");
        // put an image in the frame's content pane
        ImageIcon icon = new ImageIcon ("keagy-lunch.png");
        JLabel label = new JLabel (icon);
        frame.getContentPane( ).add(label);
        // build JOptionPane dialog and hold onto it
        optionPane = new JOptionPane ("Do you want to save?",
                                JOptionPane.QUESTION_MESSAGE,
                                JOptionPane.YES_NO_OPTION);
```

Example 6-8. Testing the SheetableJFrame (continued)

```
            frame.pack( );
            frame.setVisible(true);
            optionPane.addPropertyChangeListener (this);
            // pause for effect, then show the sheet
            try {Thread.sleep(1000);}
            catch (InterruptedException ie) {}
            JDialog dialog =
                optionPane.createDialog (frame, "irrelevant");
            frame.showJDialogAsSheet (dialog);
        }

        public void propertyChange (PropertyChangeEvent pce) {
            if (pce.getPropertyName( ).equals (JOptionPane.VALUE_PROPERTY)) {
                System.out.println ("Selected option " +
                                    pce.getNewValue( ));
                frame.hideSheet( );
            }
        }
    }
}
```

The other thing that's interesting about holding onto a JOptionPane is that it—not the dialog—is what fires events when the user clicks one of the buttons. These are fired as PropertyChangeEvents with the property name value, which you should refer to as JOptionPane.VALUE_PROPERTY. In this case, what you want to listen for is any change in the value, which indicates that something has been clicked and means it's time to hide the sheet.

When you run SheetTest, the image comes up in a SheetableJFrame and, after a one-second pause for effect, the sheet appears at top center, as seen in Figure 6-8.

Figure 6-8. JDialog shown as a "sheet" in the glass pane

When you click either of the options, the event listener hides the glass pane, which makes the sheet disappear.

This is a pretty simple case of using the glass pane—in fact, the test is a few lines longer than the implementation of the sheet. The only thing that's missing is the charming animation of the sheet sliding in [Hack #45]....

HACK #45 Animating a Sheet Dialog

By animating the sheet's appearance and disappearance, you give the user a better clue that his attention is required. Plus, it looks cool.

Another really great thing about the sheet functionality in Mac OS X is that it doesn't just suddenly appear—it slides out from the titlebar, as if unrolling from under the bar. This animation further reinforces the relationship between the sheet and the window because the short animation catches your eye and alerts you to the fact that something about the window has changed dramatically—namely, that it is now blocked by the sheet dialog.

Animate the Sheet

You already know how to get components into the glass pane [Hack #44], so you should expect that the key to sheet animation is to perform the animation in the glass pane, on top of the other components. Of course, you might have also guessed that the tricky part of this is going to be showing successively larger parts of the dialog as the animation progresses.

To make this work, you first need to create a custom component for the animating version of the sheet, separate from the sheet itself. Then, on each pass of the animation cycle, change the size of the custom component. It will always have the same width—the width of the real sheet—but its height will be some percentage of the height of the original, based on how much of the animation time has elapsed. This approach can work for both directions of the animation: when the sheet is incoming, the height will get progressively greater; when the sheet is going out, the height will decrease.

To actually draw the animating sheet during the animation, you can use `BufferedImage.getSubimage()` to grab a portion of the real sheet, and then draw that into its own `Graphics` via `paint()` callbacks. When the animation completes, the animating sheet is removed from the glass pane and the real sheet is added.

An interesting side effect of this is that the user can't click the buttons as the sheet appears or retracts because it's just an image of the sheet, not the sheet itself. Of course, the animation is so short (one second in Example 6-9, and Mac OS X's actually comes out faster than that), that it's unlikely a user could track the moving sheet with her mouse and successfully click a button anyway.

One advantage of using a custom component like this is that the kinds of things that worked for basic sheets **[Hack #44]** all work here as well. For example, you could use a simple GridBagLayout (wow, there's a phrase you don't hear often) to get the sheet centered atop the glass pane. As the sheet is a real component, it should also handle resizing appropriately.

Setting aside the details of the custom component needed to create the animated version of the sheet, Example 6-9 shows the reworked version of the sheet frame, which I've called AniSheetableJFrame.

Example 6-9. JFrame for animating sheet appearance and disappearance

```java
import javax.swing.*;
import javax.swing.border.*;
import java.awt.*;
import java.awt.event.*;
import java.awt.image.*;

public class AniSheetableJFrame extends JFrame
    implements ActionListener {

    public static final int INCOMING = 1;
    public static final int OUTGOING = -1;
    public static final float ANIMATION_DURATION = 1000f;
    public static final int ANIMATION_SLEEP = 50;

    JComponent sheet;
    JPanel glass;
    AnimatingSheet animatingSheet;
    boolean animating;
    int animationDirection;
    Timer animationTimer;
    long animationStart;
    BufferedImage offscreenImage;

    public AniSheetableJFrame (String name) {
        super(name);
        glass = (JPanel) getGlassPane( );
        glass.setLayout (new GridBagLayout( ));
        animatingSheet = new AnimatingSheet( );
        animatingSheet.setBorder (new LineBorder(Color.black, 1));
    }
```

Example 6-9. JFrame for animating sheet appearance and disappearance (continued)

```java
public JComponent showJDialogAsSheet (JDialog dialog) {
    sheet = (JComponent) dialog.getContentPane( );
    sheet.setBorder (new LineBorder(Color.black, 1));
    glass.removeAll( );
    animationDirection = INCOMING;
    startAnimation( );
    return sheet;
}

public void hideSheet( ) {
    animationDirection = OUTGOING;
    startAnimation( );
}

private void startAnimation( ) {
    glass.repaint( );
    // clear glasspane and set up animatingSheet
    animatingSheet.setSource (sheet);
    glass.removeAll( );
    GridBagConstraints gbc = new GridBagConstraints( );
    gbc.anchor = GridBagConstraints.NORTH;
    glass.add (animatingSheet, gbc);
    gbc.gridy=1;
    gbc.weighty = Integer.MAX_VALUE;
    glass.add (Box.createGlue( ), gbc);
    glass.setVisible(true);

    // start animation timer
    animationStart = System.currentTimeMillis( );
    if (animationTimer == null)
        animationTimer = new Timer (ANIMATION_SLEEP, this);
    animating = true;
    animationTimer.start( );
}

private void stopAnimation( ) {
    animationTimer.stop( );
    animating = false;
}

// used by the Timer
public void actionPerformed (ActionEvent e) {
    if (animating) {
        // calculate height to show
        float animationPercent =
            (System.currentTimeMillis( ) - animationStart) /
            ANIMATION_DURATION;
        animationPercent = Math.min (1.0f, animationPercent);
        int animatingHeight = 0;
```

Example 6-9. JFrame for animating sheet appearance and disappearance (continued)

```
        if (animationDirection == INCOMING) {
            animatingHeight =
                (int) (animationPercent * sheet.getHeight( ));
        } else {
            animatingHeight =
                (int) ((1.0f - animationPercent) * sheet.getHeight( ));
        }
        // clip off that much from sheet and blit it
        // into animatingSheet
        animatingSheet.setAnimatingHeight (animatingHeight);
        animatingSheet.repaint( );

        if (animationPercent >= 1.0f) {
            stopAnimation( );
            if (animationDirection == INCOMING) {
                finishShowingSheet( );
            } else {
                glass.removeAll( );
                glass.setVisible(false);
            }
        }
    }
}

    private void finishShowingSheet( ) {
        glass.removeAll( );
        GridBagConstraints gbc = new GridBagConstraints( );
        gbc.anchor = GridBagConstraints.NORTH;
        glass.add (sheet, gbc);
        gbc.gridy=1;
        gbc.weighty = Integer.MAX_VALUE;
        glass.add (Box.createGlue( ), gbc);
        glass.revalidate( );
        glass.repaint( );
    }

    // inner class AnimatedSheet goes here
}
```

Looking at this code method by method, the constructor's only new task is to create an instance of the AnimatingSheet inner class that will be used by the animation.

showJDialogAsSheet( ) again hijacks the content pane from the JDialog and sets it aside as the sheet instance variable. But instead of putting sheet in the glass pane immediately, it sets the animationDirection to INCOMING and calls startAnimation( ). The hideSheet( ) method makes similar changes: instead of messing with the glass pane directly, it simply sets the direction to OUTGOING and calls startAnimation( ).

startAnimation( ) begins by refreshing the glass pane with a repaint( ). It then informs the AnimatingSheet of its new source (i.e., the sheet) and adds the AnimatingSheet to the layout. It then sets up a javax.swing.Timer to get callbacks to an actionPerformed( ) method that performs each step of the animation. The ANIMATION_SLEEP parameter affects how smooth the animation will look—shorter sleeps will result in a higher frame rate, but higher CPU use.

I've set this value as low as 2 ms and haven't had a problem, but I'm on a pretty fast box (a dual 1.8 GHz G5 Power Mac). You might want to play with this value to get an ideal performance-to-smoothness ratio.

stopAnimation( ) just stops the Timer, as you might expect.

The actionPerformed( ) method is used by the Timer callbacks. It has two tasks: calculating the height of the sheet to show, and wrapping up the animation if it has run its course. Notice that the progress calculation doesn't assume that it has been called back in accordance with the ANIMATION_SLEEP. It calculates the current time offset from when the animation began, and calculates a progress from that, which in turn allows it to figure out how much of the sheet to show. This is a really good practice because if your computer can't keep up with your desired rate, the Timer will combine multiple callbacks into one. By just using the current time (instead of a possibly incorrect assumption about frame rate), you'll keep up with the specified rate and duration. On screen, combined callbacks will look like dropped frames, but a choppier animation is preferable to one that takes longer than it should.

If actionPerformed( ) decides that the animation has finished, it calls stopAnimation( ) and then cleans up the glass pane by either removing its contents (if the direction is OUTGOING) or by calling finishShowingSheet( ) (if direction is INCOMING). The finishShowingSheet( ) method clears the glass pane and puts the real sheet in place, just like showJDialogAsSheet( ) did in the last lab.

Self-Painting

So, the frame is responsible for adding, removing, and animating the AnimatedSheet, and for adding the real sheet when the incoming animation completes. What that leaves for the AnimatedSheet is the ability to paint itself (from a region of the original dialog) and report an accurate size for the benefit of the glass pane's LayoutManager.

Example 6-10 shows the code for the AnimatingSheet inner class.

Example 6-10. Inner class to paint sheet during animation

```
class AnimatingSheet extends JPanel {
    Dimension animatingSize = new Dimension (0, 1);
    JComponent source;
    BufferedImage offscreenImage;
    public AnimatingSheet () {
        super();
        setOpaque(true);
    }
    public void setSource (JComponent source) {
        this.source = source;
        animatingSize.width = source.getWidth();
        makeOffscreenImage(source);
    }
    public void setAnimatingHeight (int height) {
        animatingSize.height = height;
        setSize (animatingSize);
    }
    private void makeOffscreenImage(JComponent source) {
        GraphicsConfiguration gfxConfig =
            GraphicsEnvironment.getLocalGraphicsEnvironment()
                            .getDefaultScreenDevice()
                            .getDefaultConfiguration();
        offscreenImage =
            gfxConfig.createCompatibleImage(source.getWidth(),
                                            source.getHeight());
        Graphics2D offscreenGraphics =
            (Graphics2D) offscreenImage.getGraphics();
        source.paint (offscreenGraphics);
    }
    public Dimension getPreferredSize() {  return animatingSize; }
    public Dimension getMinimumSize() { return animatingSize; }
    public Dimension getMaximumSize() { return animatingSize; }
    public void paint (Graphics g) {
        // get the bottom-most n pixels of source and
        // paint them into g, where n is height

        BufferedImage fragment =
            offscreenImage.getSubimage (0,
                                    offscreenImage.getHeight() -
                                        animatingSize.height,
                                    source.getWidth(),
                                    animatingSize.height);
        // g.drawImage (fragment, 0, 0, this);
        g.drawImage (fragment, 0, 0, this);
    }
}
```

The constructor is more or less trivial, so take a look at the setSource( ) method. This method stores the source JComponent (the sheet that the frame created from a dialog) as an instance variable, and calculates a width for the AnimatingSheet. This width will be constant through the animation, so it's assigned at this step.

The makeOffscreenImage( ) that setSource( ) calls takes the source JComponent and draws an offscreen BufferedImage. It does this by calling GraphicsConfiguration.createCompatibleImage( ) with the size of the source. Using createCompatibleImage( ) is highly recommended for creating off-screen images because it will keep you from getting surprised by greater or lesser color depths on platforms other than your own. makeOffscreenImage( ) then gets the Graphics2D for this image and tells source to paint itself onto the Graphics2D. The offscreen image now contains an image of the source component.

setAnimatingHeight( ), called by the frame's Timer just before it repaint( )s the AnimatingSheet, stores away two values that will be needed by the paint( ) callback: the height in pixels to be painted and the new size of the animat-ing sheet. This new size is returned by getPreferredSize( ), getMinimumSize( ), and getMaximumSize( ), so the layout manager will know how much space to provide for it.

And now for the big payoff: paint( ) is called as a result of the frame's Timer callback making a repaint( ) call. It uses BufferedImage.getSubimage( ) to get the pixels for the bottom-most animatingHeight pixels of the offscreen image. It then draws this sub-image into the Graphics at 0,0. The image's size matches the newly reported preferred size of the AnimatingSheet compo-nent, so the sub-image fills it completely.

And that's it. The frame is responsible for managing what's in the glass pane—animating sheet, real sheet, or nothing—and for running the anima-tion. The AnimatingSheet is just responsible for adjusting its size when called by the animation, and for painting an appropriate representation suitable to that size, which it does by grabbing sub-images from an offscreen image of the real component.

The SheetTest class has only one meaningful change from the version in the last hack: the SheetableJFrame becomes an AniSheetableJFrame. Run it once to see the effect, and then play with the ANIMATION_DURATION and ANIMATION_ SLEEP values to see what it looks like when you change the duration or the smoothness of the animation. For the screenshot sequence in Figure 6-9, I used a duration of 10,000 ms (10 seconds) so I could get multiple shots and show the progress of the animation.

Figure 6-9. Successive screenshots of an animated glass pane sheet

Slide Notes Out from the Taskbar

Pop up a note above the taskbar when your application wants attention.

On Windows, long-running applications sometimes will slide in a window above the taskbar to call attention to themselves when an interesting event occurs, such as a finished download or an IM buddy's appearance.

If you want to do this in Java, you need to deal with a pretty significant problem: neither AWT nor Swing has any concept of the taskbar (where it is, how big it is, whether it's auto-hiding, or anything else). As a result, you don't know where to draw the window, and just taking a guess or hardcoding something is hazardous—too high and the window floats inexplicably on the desktop, too low and it gets buried under the taskbar.

Furthermore, how is this going to work on other operating systems? On the Mac, the proper way to get attention is to bounce your application's dock icon. Since there's no API exposing that functionality, can you at least use a Windows-like slide-in window above the dock? Sure...if you can figure out how tall the dock is (it's user configurable), or whether the dock is even on the bottom of the screen (it might be on the right or left, too).

Fortunately, it is possible to figure out what unobstructed space is available to you on the main display. After that, it's just a matter of offscreen imaging and animation.

Figure Out Where You Are

The key to figuring out your available space is to get the local GraphicsEnvironment, which describes the display, and then call getMaximumWindowBounds( ). This method, introduced in Java 1.4, returns a Rectangle representing the largest centered Window that could fit on the display, accounting for objects that intrude on the display's usable space, like the Windows taskbar or the Mac's monolithic menu bar.

This means that on Windows, the Rectangle will have an upper-left corner at 0,0; on the Mac, it will be at 0,22, which leaves space for the Mac's menu bar. Meanwhile, the height of the Rectangle won't be the height of your display unless you have your taskbar set to auto-hide, or you have moved it to the right or left.

So, now you have the beginnings of the slide-in above-taskbar window. By subtracting the height of the window from the y-coordinate of the last usable row, you can place the window directly above the taskbar or dock. To do the slide-in, you'll need to do an animation loop in which progressively larger portions of the complete window are blitted into a smaller onscreen version. This is very similar to the animated sheet [Hack #45] you've already seen. It's so similar, in fact, that you can reuse the inner class from that hack to do the progressive redrawing.

A simple implementation, SlideInNotification, is shown in Example 6-11.

Example 6-11. Sliding in a window immediately above the taskbar or dock

```java
import javax.swing.*;
import java.awt.*;
import java.awt.event.*;
import java.awt.image.*;

public class SlideInNotification extends Object {

    protected static final int ANIMATION_TIME = 500;
    protected static final float ANIMATION_TIME_F =
        (float) ANIMATION_TIME;
    protected static final int ANIMATION_DELAY = 50;

    JWindow window;
    JComponent contents;
    AnimatingSheet animatingSheet;
    Rectangle desktopBounds;
    Dimension tempWindowSize;
    Timer animationTimer;
    int showX, startY;
    long animationStart;

    public SlideInNotification () {
        initDesktopBounds();
    }

    public SlideInNotification (JComponent contents) {
        this();
        setContents (contents);
    }
```

Example 6-11. Sliding in a window immediately above the taskbar or dock (continued)

```
protected void initDesktopBounds() {
    GraphicsEnvironment env =
        GraphicsEnvironment.getLocalGraphicsEnvironment();
    desktopBounds = env.getMaximumWindowBounds();
    System.out.println ("max window bounds = " + desktopBounds);
}

public void setContents (JComponent contents) {
    this.contents = contents;
    JWindow tempWindow = new JWindow();
    tempWindow.getContentPane().add (contents);
    tempWindow.pack();
    tempWindowSize = tempWindow.getSize();
    tempWindow.getContentPane().removeAll();
    window = new JWindow();
    animatingSheet = new AnimatingSheet ();
    animatingSheet.setSource (contents);
    window.getContentPane().add (animatingSheet);
}

public void showAt (int x) {
    // create a window with an animating sheet
    // copy over its contents from the temp window
    // animate it
    // when done, remove animating sheet and add real contents

    showX = x;
    startY = desktopBounds.y + desktopBounds.height;

    ActionListener animationLogic = new ActionListener() {
            public void actionPerformed(ActionEvent e) {
                long elapsed =
                    System.currentTimeMillis() - animationStart;
                if (elapsed > ANIMATION_TIME) {
                    // put real contents in window and show
                    window.getContentPane().removeAll();
                    window.getContentPane().add (contents);
                    window.pack();
                    window.setLocation (showX,
                            startY - window.getSize().height);
                    window.setVisible(true);
                    window.repaint();
                    animationTimer.stop();
                    animationTimer = null;
                } else {
                    // calculate % done
                    float progress =
                        (float) elapsed / ANIMATION_TIME_F;
                    // get height to show
                    int animatingHeight =
                        (int) (progress * tempWindowSize.getHeight());
```

Example 6-11. Sliding in a window immediately above the taskbar or dock (continued)

```
                animatingHeight = Math.max (animatingHeight, 1);
                animatingSheet.setAnimatingHeight (animatingHeight);
                window.pack( );
                window.setLocation (showX,
                                    startY - window.getHeight( ));
                window.setVisible(true);
                window.repaint( );
            }
        }
      };
    animationTimer =
        new Timer (ANIMATION_DELAY, animationLogic);
    animationStart = System.currentTimeMillis( );
    animationTimer.start( );
  }

  // AnimatingSheet inner class listed below

}
```

After setting the constants for the speed of the animation and the frame rate (i.e., how frequently to call for repaints), the constructors are used to determine the usable screen space (given the GraphicsEnvironment strategy just detailed) and optionally to set the contents of the slide-in window.

setContents( ) is a little tricky because you need to figure out the size of the contents (a JComponent) before you can start the animation loop that draws fragments of them. You can do this by putting them into a temporary window and packing it, which forces all of its contents to be validated and made displayable. Next, you create the real Window to show on screen, but instead of adding the contents, you add an AnimatingSheet—the inner class that shows progressively larger parts of the contents as the animation runs. When the animation is finished, the AnimatingSheet will be removed and the real contents added.

To slide in the window, a caller invokes the showAt( ) method, passing in an arbitrary x-coordinate. Nothing in Java tells you what is showing on the taskbar or dock, so there's no way, short of going native to get your slide-in window to appear above a specific taskbar/dock icon. The showAt( ) method is where you need to figure out the y-coordinate where the animation will begin, namely the last usable row. Given the Rectangle that represented the largest possible onscreen window, you add its y-coordinate to its height. The y-coordinate accounts for top-of-screen obstructions like the Mac menu bar, and the height counts all the space from there to the taskbar or dock, if any.

showAt( ) contains a large, anonymous inner class ActionListener that performs the animation logic that will be called back by a javax.swing.Timer.

Slide Notes Out from the Taskbar

As with most animations, the first thing you do is to figure out how much time has elapsed in the animation. If the animation is finished, you take out the AnimatingSheet, insert the real contents, pack the Window and reset its location to its final visible location, show it, and shut down the Timer.

If the animation time has not fully elapsed, you calculate how far into the animation you are, as a percentage (a float between 0.0 and 1.0), and from that you get how many vertical pixels you want to show on this pass. Send this value to AnimatingSheet's setAnimatingHeight( ) method, pack( ) the window (which picks up the preferred height you just set), set the location to the starting y-coordinate minus the window's new height, and repaint.

The AnimatingSheet inner class was already described in the previous hack, but to recap, it represents some vertically cropped fragment of a source component. When you set the source, it creates an offscreen Image of the component's pixels. Then, when you call setAnimatingHeight( ) from the animation loop, it resets its preferred, minimum, and maximum size to use that height (this is why it can be packed by the Window during the animation). Then, when paint( ) is called, it uses BufferedImage.getSubimage( ) to get a portion of the offscreen image that it can blit into the Graphics with a typical double-buffer-like drawImage( ) call.

This version, shown in Example 6-12, has two differences from the earlier version of AnimatingSheet:

- Because this window scrolls in the opposite direction of the drop-down sheets, the getSubimage( ) call gets the top-most *n* pixels instead of the bottom-most pixels.

- On Windows, I found the offscreen buffer was black unless explicitly cleared out first. This wasn't a problem on Mac OS X.

Example 6-12. The AnimatingSheet inner class is used in creating notifications that slide in and out

```
class AnimatingSheet extends JPanel {
    Dimension animatingSize = new Dimension (0, 1);
    JComponent source;
    BufferedImage offscreenImage;
    public AnimatingSheet () {
        super();
        setOpaque(true);
    }
    public void setSource (JComponent source) {
        this.source = source;
        animatingSize.width = source.getWidth();
        makeOffscreenImage(source);
    }
```

Example 6-12. The AnimatingSheet inner class is used in creating notifications that slide in and out (continued)

```java
public void setAnimatingHeight (int height) {
    animatingSize.height = height;
    setSize (animatingSize);
}
private void makeOffscreenImage(JComponent source) {
    GraphicsEnvironment ge =
        GraphicsEnvironment.getLocalGraphicsEnvironment( );
    GraphicsConfiguration gfxConfig =
        ge.getDefaultScreenDevice().getDefaultConfiguration( );
    offscreenImage =
        gfxConfig.createCompatibleImage(source.getWidth( ),
                                        source.getHeight( ));
    Graphics2D offscreenGraphics =
        (Graphics2D) offscreenImage.getGraphics( );
    // windows workaround
    offscreenGraphics.setColor (source.getBackground( ));
    offscreenGraphics.fillRect (0, 0,
                                source.getWidth(), source.getHeight( ));
    // paint from source to offscreen buffer
    source.paint (offscreenGraphics);
}
public Dimension getPreferredSize( ) { return animatingSize; }
public Dimension getMinimumSize( ) { return animatingSize; }
public Dimension getMaximumSize( ) { return animatingSize; }
public void update (Graphics g) {
    // override to eliminate flicker from
    // unnecessary clear
    paint (g);
}
public void paint (Graphics g) {
    // get the top-most n pixels of source and
    // paint them into g, where n is height
    // (different from sheet example, which used bottom-most)
    BufferedImage fragment =
        offscreenImage.getSubimage (0,
                                    0,
                                    source.getWidth( ),
                                    animatingSize.height);
    g.drawImage (fragment, 0, 0, this);
}
}
}
```

Running the Hack

The SlideInNotification will take any JComponent as its contents. To make things a little interesting, the TestSlideInNotification class, shown in Example 6-13, grabs an icon from the JOptionPane class and makes a JLabel of that and a little nonsense text.

Example 6-13. Testing the slide-in notification

```java
import javax.swing.*;

public class TestSlideInNotification {

    public static void main (String[] args) {
        Icon errorIcon = UIManager.getIcon ("OptionPane.errorIcon");
        JLabel label = new JLabel ("Your application asplode",
                                   errorIcon,
                                   SwingConstants.LEFT);
        SlideInNotification slider = new SlideInNotification (label);
        slider.showAt (450);
    }
}
```

When you run this application, one thing to make note of is the standard output because the SlideInNotification class has one System.out.println( ) left in to show the discovered dimensions. Here's what Windows reports with a taskbar showing:

```
max window bounds = java.awt.Rectangle[x=0,y=0,width=800,height=570]
```

and what it reports with the taskbar set to auto-hide:

```
max window bounds = java.awt.Rectangle[x=0,y=0,width=800,height=600]
```

Meanwhile, on the Mac, the bounds with a dock on the bottom of the screen look like this:

```
max window bounds = java.awt.Rectangle[x=0,y=22,width=1280,height=707]
```

and with the dock over on the right, they look like this:

```
max window bounds = java.awt.Rectangle[x=0,y=22,width=1244,height=746]
```

Notice that in each case, the first usable y-coordinate is 22, accounting for the unusable space under the Mac's monolithic menu bar. Notice also in the second case that I've lost usable horizontal space because the dock is on the right. By the way, if you're doing the math and can't figure out why nothing adds up to 1024×768, it's because I have a wide-screen monitor and my screen size is 1280×768.

Of course, don't stare too long at the console output, or you'll miss the appearance of the slide-in window. Figure 6-10 shows the window in mid-animation on Windows, with and without a visible taskbar.

Figure 6-10. Slide-in window on Windows with taskbar showing (left) and set to auto-hide (right)

Figure 6-11 shows the slide-in window on Mac OS X. It's less appropriate on the Mac, and it will be obscured if the user has dock magnification turned on, but it's not really bad either.

Figure 6-11. Slide-in window on Mac OS X with dock on bottom of screen (left) and not on bottom (right)

Hacking the Hack

To expand this hack, the first thing you'd probably want to do is add some kind of MouseListener so that if the user clicks to acknowledge the appearance of the slide-in window, you could react to it by removing the slide-in window, bringing your application's main window to the front, etc. Then again, you can put live components in here, so there's no reason you couldn't just generate a JOptionPane, make a JDialog from it, grab the content pane of that JDialog, and show it in the slide-in window. That would give you real, active Swing buttons and handy JOptionPane return values. After all, that's what the sheet example did.

#47 Indefinite Progress Indicator

Despite its numerous advanced widgets, Swing offers no efficient way to show that a task of unknown length is in progress. This hack presents two solutions to address this issue.

Have you ever watched an application do something, but not tell you what that something is? Other applications let you know what's going on but don't really tell you how long they will need to complete the task. For instance, the Microsoft Windows copy dialog is famous for its silly (and lengthy) nonprogress indicators. As a user, I find this very annoying; as a programmer, I know how difficult it can be to determine the duration of a task.

The Swing Solution

To address this issue, developers created particular widgets meant to show a task of unknown length is in progress. You can see such a widget in Mozilla's installer. It displays an indefinite progress bar—also called a *Cylon*—in which a small rectangle bounces back and forth between the two horizontal edges. I have also seen indefinite progress bars filling like regular progress bars, going backward once filled and starting all over again. The

idea of an indefinite progress bar is great, but most existing implementations are just wrong. Users know what a progress bar looks like, and they
also know how it is supposed to behave. It is a bad idea to present a familiar
widget acting in a very surprising way. Unfortunately, the Swing designers
followed this trend and added the setIndeterminate(boolean) method to
JProgressBar. Check out Example 6-14.

Example 6-14. An indefinite progress bar

```
import javax.swing.*;
public class CylonBar {
  public static void main(String[] args) {
    JFrame f = new JFrame("Progress");
    JProgressBar p = new JProgressBar();
    p.setIndeterminate(true);
    f.getContentPane().add(p);
    f.pack();
    f.setDefaultCloseOperation(JFrame.EXIT_ON_CLOSE);
    f.setVisible(true);
  }
}
```

This short example creates a new window containing an indefinite progress
bar. When you launch the program, you can see a small rectangle bouncing
back and forth within the progress bar's bounds, as in Figure 6-12. The
result is much better on Mac OS X because it uses the native Look and Feel
automatically, as shown in Figure 6-13. Despite this visual improvement,
though, the result is still far from perfect.

Figure 6-12. The indefinite progress bar offered by Swing

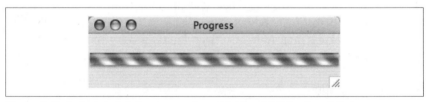

Figure 6-13. Swing's indefinite progress bar with Mac OS X Look and Feel

There are several better ways to show that a task of unknown length is in
progress.

Picture as Indicator

The first solution relies on cycling the brightness of a picture in a panel. Instead of moving a rectangle back and forth, you can increase and decrease the brightness of a picture. The result is much more appealing and lets you choose an adequate picture regarding the current running task. Figure 6-14 shows the AnimatedPanel in action.

A	B	C	D	E	F	G	H	I	J
1	2	3	4	5	6	7	8	9	10
2	4	6	8	10	12	14	16	18	20
3	6	9	12	15	18	21	24	27	30
4	8	12	16	20	24	28	32	36	40
5	10	15	20	25	30	35	40	45	50
6	12	18	24	30	36	42	48	54	60
7	14	21	28	35	42	49	56	63	70
8	16	24	32	40	48	56	64	72	80
9	18	27	36	45	54	63	72	81	90
10	20	30	40	50	60	70	80	90	100

Figure 6-14. The first tab demonstrates the use of a picture as an indefinite progress indicator

When you click the Start button, the contents of the Animated tab are replaced by a panel containing a picture and a message. With the picture's brightness cycles, as shown in Figure 6-15, you can see the most bright state on the left and the less bright state on the right.

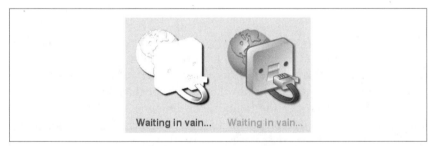

Figure 6-15. AnimatedPanel displays a picture and cycles its brightness

To change the brightness of the picture dynamically, AnimatedPanel starts an animation thread responsible for computing the brightness over the time:

```
public void start() {
    this.animator = new Thread(new HighlightCycler(), "Highlighter");
    this.animator.start();
}

class HighlightCycler implements Runnable {
    private int way = 1;
    private final int LOWER_BOUND = 10;
    private final int UPPER_BOUND = 35;
    private int value = LOWER_BOUND;

    public void run() {
        while (true) {
            try {
                Thread.sleep(1000 / (UPPER_BOUND - LOWER_BOUND));
            } catch (InterruptedException e) {
                return;
            }

            value += this.way;
            if (value > UPPER_BOUND) {
                value = UPPER_BOUND;
                this.way = -1;
            } else if (value < LOWER_BOUND) {
                value = LOWER_BOUND;
                this.way = 1;
            }

            synchronized (convolvedImage) {
                setBrightness((float) value / 10);
                setGradientFactor((float) value / UPPER_BOUND);
            }
        }
    }
}
```

When the start() method of the panel is called, a new thread is spawned to run HighlightCycler. The animation loop is very simple, and it increases or decreases the variable value until its value reaches LOWER_BOUND or UPPER_ BOUND. Then, setBrightness() is invoked to change the brightness of the picture. Given the values of the bounds, the brightness swings between 1.0 (unchanged) and 3.5 (the picture is 3.5 times brighter). You can notice this call is synchronized with the object convolvedImage, which is one of the two BufferedImages contained in AnimatedPanel. This image is the result of a filter applied on originalImage, the picture that contains the unchanged original picture. As applying the filter can take some time, the code synchronizes on convolvedImage to ensure the previous filtering is done before running a new one. This code shows how to change the brightness of the picture:

```
private void setBrightness(float multiple) {
  float[] brightKernel = { multiple };
  RenderingHints hints = new RenderingHints(RenderingHints.KEY_RENDERING,
      RenderingHints.VALUE_RENDER_QUALITY);
  BufferedImageOp bright = new ConvolveOp(new Kernel(1, 1, brightKernel),
      ConvolveOp.EDGE_NO_OP, hints);
  bright.filter(originalImage, convolvedImage);
  repaint();
}
```

The parameter multiple tells the method how many times brighter than the
original the resulting image must be. To achieve this effect, you can simply
perform a convolve operation on the original image. The kernel contains a
single value, multiple. When the filter( ) method is invoked, every pixel
value of the original image is multiplied by the value of the kernel, making it
brighter. The result is stored in convolveImage. It is now easy to use the
AnimatedPanel in an application:

```
Icon icon = UIHelper.readImageIcon("network.png");
AnimatedPanel animated = new AnimatedPanel("Waiting in vain...", icon);
getContentPane( ).add(animated);
animated.start( );
```

Besides the start( ) method, you can call stop( ) to interrupt the animation
thread when the task is done. This panel can be very efficient when used
with a CardLayout. As this layout lets you stack components, you can put a
form on top of the animated panel. When the user performs an action, you
can display the animated panel and start the animation. At the end of the
task, you just need to stop the animation and hide the animated panel.

The example file *Demo.java* contains a complete example
using CardLayout.

The Glass Pane as an Indicator

Using the AnimatedPanel proves to be efficient in form-oriented applications. Unfortunately, it does not help much when the running task must not
be interrupted by any action performed by the user. In this case, you need a
way to disable the entire GUI while displaying an indefinite progress indicator. This can be done with a glass pane, as shown in Figure 6-16.

InfiniteProgressPanel is an animated glass pane you can set up on any
Swing frame:

```
InfiniteProgressPanel  glassPane = new InfiniteProgressPanel( );
setGlassPane(glassPane);
glassPane.start( );
```

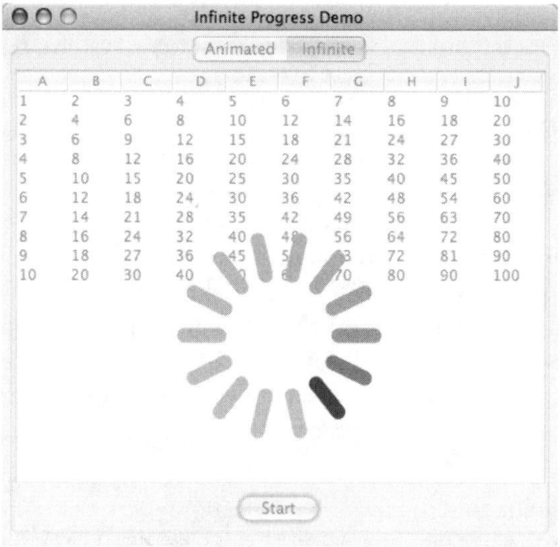

Figure 6-16. InfiniteProgressPanel draws a white veil to disable the UI visually

When you start( ) the panel, a fade-in animation is played during the ramp-up phase. When stop( ) is called, a fade-out animation is played. Between the two, a circular shape is rotated at the center of the glass pane. All the while, a white translucent veil is drawn over the underlying UI to disable it visually.

The implementation of InfiniteProgressPanel relies on many parameters, which you can specify with the various constructors:

text
> The optional message to be displayed below the circular shape

barsCount
> The number of bars composing the circular shape

shield
> The opacity of the white veil, also known as the shield

fps
> The requested amount of frames per second during the animation

rampDelay
> The time, in milliseconds, that fade-in and fade-out animations should last

Build the Circular Shape

Everything begins when the start( ) method is invoked:

```
public void start( )
{
  addMouseListener(this);
  setVisible(true);
  ticker = buildTicker( );
  animation = new Thread(new Animator(true));
  animation.start( );
}
```

Before running the animation, this method takes care of adding a mouse listener that is responsible for catching all the mouse events and preventing them from being forwarded to the underlying user interface. Thus, the user will not be able to perform any action. The second step is to set the glass pane to be visible. Finally, the ticker, the circular shape, is built and the animation is started. Building the shape is done with two methods:

```
private Area buildPrimitive( )
{
  Rectangle2D.Double body = new Rectangle2D.Double(6, 0, 30, 12);
  Ellipse2D.Double   head = new Ellipse2D.Double(0, 0, 12, 12);
  Ellipse2D.Double   tail = new Ellipse2D.Double(30, 0, 12, 12);

  Area tick = new Area(body);
  tick.add(new Area(head));
  tick.add(new Area(tail));

  return tick;
}

private Area[] buildTicker( )
{
  Area[] ticker = new Area[barsCount];
  Point2D.Double center = new Point2D.Double((double) getWidth( ) / 2,
                                             (double) getHeight( ) / 2);
  double fixedAngle = 2.0 * Math.PI / ((double) barsCount);

  for (double i = 0.0; i < (double) barsCount; i++)
  {
    Area primitive = buildPrimitive( );

    AffineTransform toCenter = AffineTransform.getTranslateInstance(
        center.getX(), center.getY( ));
    AffineTransform toBorder =
        AffineTransform.getTranslateInstance(45.0, -6.0);
    AffineTransform toCircle =
        AffineTransform.getRotateInstance(-i * fixedAngle,
        center.getX(), center.getY( ));
```

```
    AffineTransform toWheel = new AffineTransform( );
    toWheel.concatenate(toCenter);
    toWheel.concatenate(toBorder);

    primitive.transform(toWheel);
    primitive.transform(toCircle);

    ticker[(int) i] = primitive;
  }

  return ticker;
}
```

The buildTicker( ) method returns an array of Areas, where each Area is one of the bars composing the resulting shape. A bar is built in buildPrimitive( ) by merging two circles and a rectangle. The role of buildTicker( ) is simply to create the requested amount of bars and to move them to their final location. To do that, the code applies several AffineTransform operations: toCenter first translates the bar to the center of the glass pane, toBorder then moves the bar to the perimeter of the circle you want to create, and toCircle finally rotates the bar around the glass pane's center.

Paint the Indicator

Once ticker has been built, paintComponent( ) only needs to get each bar and fill it on the graphics surface of the glass pane:

```
public void paintComponent(Graphics g)
{
  if (started)
  {
    int width  = getWidth( );
    int height = getHeight( );

    Graphics2D g2 = (Graphics2D) g;
    g2.setRenderingHints(hints);

    g2.setColor(new Color(255, 255, 255, (int) (alphaLevel * shield)));
    g2.fillRect(0, 0, getWidth(), getHeight( ));

    for (int i = 0; i < ticker.length; i++)
    {
      int channel = 224 - 128 / (i + 1);
      g2.setColor(new Color(channel, channel, channel, alphaLevel));
      g2.fill(ticker[i]);
    }
  }
}
```

To make things clearer, this code does not contain the painting of the text. To allow the glass pane to be visible even when the animation is not started, the application first checks the value of started. When false, start( ) has not been called yet and nothing must be drawn. In the other case, the white veil is first painted all over the glass pane. The fourth parameter of the Color object used by fillRect( ) defines the opacity. Opacity depends on two parameters here: shield and alphaLevel. The latter is computed by the animation thread to fade in and fade out the glass pane. As alphaLevel is between 0 and 255, and you multiply it by shield, which is in the range 0.0 to 1.0, to obtain the opacity of the veil. Finally, the for loop computes a new color for each bar and paints it. The colors are computed so as to create a circular gradient and give an impression of movement when the circular shape is rotated.

Run the Animation Thread

The most complicated part of InfiniteProgressPanel is the Animator thread since its run( ) method handles the fade-in and -out animations, as well as the main animation. The only constructor of Animator requires a boolean parameter called rampUp. When true, the thread will play both main and fade-in animations. Otherwise, the fade-out animation is played. This is what happens when you call InfiniteProgressPanel.stop( ). Here is the code of Animator.run( ) to handle the main animation:

```
public void run( )
{
  Point2D.Double center;
  center = new Point2D.Double((double) getWidth( ) / 2,
                              (double) getHeight( ) / 2);
  double fixedIncrement = 2.0 * Math.PI / ((double) barsCount);
  AffineTransform toCircle;
  toCircle = AffineTransform.getRotateInstance(fixedIncrement,
                                               center.getX( ),
                                               center.getY( ));

  long start = System.currentTimeMillis( );
  if (rampDelay == 0)
    alphaLevel = rampUp ? 255 : 0;

  started = true;
  boolean inRamp = rampUp;

  while (!Thread.interrupted( ))
  {
    if (!inRamp)
    {
```

```
    for (int i = 0; i < ticker.length; i++)
        ticker[i].transform(toCircle);
}

repaint();

// fade-in/out animation

try
{
    Thread.sleep(inRamp ? 10 : (int) (1000 / fps));
} catch (InterruptedException ie) {
    break;
}
Thread.yield();
    }
}
```

The first step of this method is to create an instance of AffineTransform that will be used to rotate the bar by a fixed increment. By applying this transformation to the bars, each bar will move clockwise to the location of the next bar. The rotation cannot happen during the fade-in animation, when rampUp, and therefore inRamp, are true. After having rotated the ticker and repainted the glass pane, the thread goes to sleep. The length of the sleep is defined by the request amount of frames per second. The more frames you specify, the more CPU resources the animation will need. Finally, the fade-in and fade-out animations, not shown here, are performed by computing alphaLevel according to the elapsed time since the beginning of the animation, stored in the variable start. The alpha level is computed so that it goes, during the fade in, from 0 to 255 in rampDelay milliseconds. The same rule applies to the fade-out animation.

Displaying nice-looking, indefinite progress indicators is not very difficult in Swing, even though it requires some work. Using a circular shape is definitely the best way to show an infinite progress indicator because you can walk around it indefinitely, even if you always go in the same direction.

—Romain Guy

Text
Hacks 48–55

Text handling pervades the Swing API, from the labeling of a JButton to handling styled text in a JTextArea. When we talk about hacking Swing's text handling, we often mean two different things: hacking into the representation of the text (say, by making it searchable), or hacking into how that text is displayed. This chapter will help you see that Swing text isn't just about little JTextFields for entering your username.

HACK #48

Make Text Components Searchable

This hack will show you how to add incremental search to a text area as a simple document listener, making it very easy to integrate with your existing software.

Many years ago, text editors had either no searching capabilities or a straight word search only. You would type a word into a dialog box and the program would search for that word, moving to its first location in the document. If you were lucky, there was a command to search again, instead of starting the process over. Then one day Emacs introduced a new kind of searching. The program would search as you typed in each character, updating the cursor with each keystroke. To search again, you only had to hit the Return key. If you wanted a less specific search, you could just hit the Backspace key and remove letters. Everything updated in real time. Incremental searching was born.

Most GUI toolkits—Java Swing included—do not provide incremental search. Java does, however, give you the tools to build your own incremental search. The 1.4 release of Java finally added a long requested feature: regular expressions. These are complex but concise patterns that are internally compiled into searching and matching code. With a single regular expression (known more commonly as a *regex*) you could match email addresses, split a complex data field, parse SQL expressions, or recognize different date formats. This hack has much more humble needs, but Java 1.4's built-in regex support will make the search implementation very easy.

The plan for this hack is to create a searching utility object that targets a JTextComponent (the common subclass for all Swing text components such as JTextArea and JTextField). It will also listen for action and document change events from a search component (usually a JTextField) to do the actual searching. By constructing it with class agnostic listeners, you can add it easily to existing programs without changing much code.

A Basic Search Class

The code in Example 7-1 defines the IncrementalSearch class, which implements the DocumentListener and ActionListener interfaces. Programs with search usually have a search field above the search target. The IncrementalSearch constructor accepts a JTextComponent as the target, and the document listener events will provide access to the search field itself. In addition to the usual suspects, you'll need to import the Swing event, Swing text, and regex classes.

Example 7-1. Starting the basic incremental search class

```
import javax.swing.event.*;
import javax.swing.text.*;
import java.util.regex.*;

public class IncrementalSearch
    implements DocumentListener, ActionListener {

    protected JTextComponent content;
    public IncrementalSearch(JTextComponent comp) {
        this.content = comp;
    }

    /* DocumentListener implementation */
    public void insertUpdate(DocumentEvent evt) {
        runNewSearch(evt.getDocument( ));
    }
    public void removeUpdate(DocumentEvent evt) {
        runNewSearch(evt.getDocument( ));
    }
    public void changedUpdate(DocumentEvent evt) {
        runNewSearch(evt.getDocument( ));
    }
```

You can see that all three document listener methods just call runNewSearch( ), passing in the document. This forces the search to start over if the user types new text, hits the Backspace key, or replaces a selection. So far, there is nothing tricky here. The complexity lies in the runNewSearch( ) function, which handles the actual searching.

Running the Search

The runNewSearch( ) method pulls out the query string from the document. Notice that it passes 0 and the length of the document into the getText( ) method. All of the Document methods operate in terms of a starting and ending index. You deal with chunks of text only with these indices rather than getting and setting Strings, which would entail lots of byte copying. Copying isn't a big deal for this hack, but it could be a problem for large documents (think several hundred kilobytes). Here is the runNewSearch( ) method:

```
protected Matcher matcher;

private void runNewSearch(Document query_doc) {
    try {
        String query = query_doc.getText(0,query_doc.getLength( ));

        Pattern pattern = Pattern.compile(query);
        Document content_doc = content.getDocument( );
        String body = content_doc.getText(0,content_doc.getLength( ));

        matcher = pattern.matcher(body);
        continueSearch( );

    } catch (Exception ex) {
        p("exception: " + ex);
        ex.printStackTrace( );
    }
}
```

After getting the text, runNewSearch( ) creates a new pattern from the query (which requires no modification since it is a simple search), and then retrieves the target document and text. With the search text, target body text, and pattern in hand, it creates a Matcher and calls continueSearch( ). The Matcher is the class that will do the actual searching with an internally compiled regex:

```
private void continueSearch( ) {
    if(matcher != null) {
        if(matcher.find( )) {
            content.getCaret( ).setDot(matcher.start( ));
            content.getCaret( ).moveDot(matcher.end( ));
            content.getCaret( ).setSelectionVisible(true);
        }
    }
}
```

The continueSearch( ) method just calls find( ) on the matcher, if it exists. If find( ) returns true, meaning it found a match somewhere, it sets the selection. Selections are defined by a caret with a dot. The dot represents the selection point. By setting the dot at the start of the match and then moving it with the moveDot( ) function, it will create a selection between the start and ending points. Finally, setSelectionVisible(true) scrolls the target component, if needed, to make the selection visible on screen.

The action listener implementation will call continueSearch( ) whenever an action is performed. Both JButtons and JTextFields produce actions—the former when they are clicked, and the latter when the user hits the Return key. Listening for action events is an easy way of providing a hook to repeat the search:

```
/* ActionListener implementation */
public void actionPerformed(ActionEvent evt) {
    continueSearch( );
}
```

Since the matcher object remembers its place, each time find is called it will continue searching from the current location. This means the user can just hit Enter over and over to loop through the results in the document, highlighting each one as it goes along.

Adding Search to Swing Components

The following code creates a typical search interface. There is a large JTextArea below a text field. The IncrementalSearch is attached to the text area through its constructor. The search field is connected via the document and action listeners. Once the class is put all together, it will look like Figure 7-1.

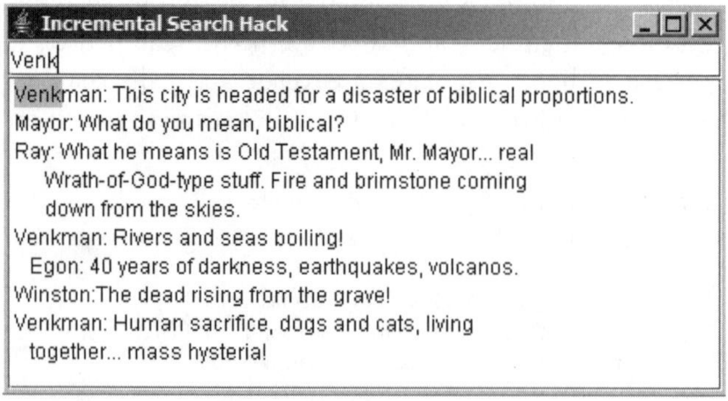

Figure 7-1. Incremental repeatable search of a JTextArea

```
public static void main(String[] args) {
    JTextArea text_area = new JTextArea(10,20);
    JScrollPane scroll = new JScrollPane(text_area);
    IncrementalSearch isearch = new IncrementalSearch(text_area);

    JTextField search_field = new JTextField( );
    search_field.getDocument( ).addDocumentListener(isearch);
    search_field.addActionListener(isearch);

    JFrame frame = new JFrame("Incremental Search Hack");
    frame.getContentPane( ).add("North",search_field);
    frame.getContentPane( ).add("Center",scroll);
    frame.pack( );
    frame.show( );
}
```

As the user types, the search selection will update on every keystroke. Return (or Enter) will jump to the next result, and Backspace will make the search less specific.

Hacking the Hack

You could expand this hack with support for case-insensitive searching, or allow users to type in more complicated regular expressions instead of straight text-matching. Because the component is built as an event listener, it's very easy to drop your search routines into existing applications. Event listeners are probably the best way to add new features, such as incremental searching.

H A C K   Force Text Input into Specific Formats
#49   Use Java's powerful pattern matching to enforce rules on typed input

Validating input is an important GUI task, and some applications will validate your input when you tab off a field or even validate it on every keystroke. After all, it's a lot easier to deal with bogus data by not letting it into your system in the first place.

One technique for validating user input is to use a regular expression and then evaluate the input against it. For example, a field that can be uppercase letters only must always match the expression [A-Z]*, and one that can be any combination of uppercase, lowercase, numbers, and spaces must match [A-Za-z0-9]* (notice the space after 9).

Java's regex feature lets you create TextComponents that enforce matching against an expression. The basic idea is to watch for changes in the underlying Document and do your pattern match then.

Constraining a Document

Hopefully, you won't be surprised to know that you don't need to touch the view classes—JTextField, JTextArea, etc.—to add text constraint functionality. Text entry is happening in the model—in other words the Document—so that's where you tie in your regex code. This hack, listed in Example 7-2, subclasses PlainDocument to run the regex check on every call to insertString( ).

Example 7-2. A document allowing input that matches only a regex

```java
import javax.swing.text.*;
import java.util.regex.*;

public class RegexConstrainedDocument extends PlainDocument {

    Pattern pattern;
    Matcher matcher;

    public RegexConstrainedDocument () { super(); }
    public RegexConstrainedDocument (AbstractDocument.Content c) { super(c); }
    public RegexConstrainedDocument (AbstractDocument.Content c, String p) {
        super (c);
        setPatternByString (p);
    }
    public RegexConstrainedDocument (String p) {
        super();
        setPatternByString (p);
    }

    public void setPatternByString (String p) {
        Pattern pattern = Pattern.compile (p);
        // checks the document against the new pattern
        // and removes the content if it no longer matches
        try {
            matcher = pattern.matcher (getText(0, getLength( )));
            System.out.println ("matcher reset to " +
                                getText (0, getLength( )));
            if (! matcher.matches( )) {
                System.out.println ("does not match");
                remove (0, getLength( ));
            }
        } catch (BadLocationException ble) {
            ble.printStackTrace( ); // impossible?
        }
    }

    public Pattern getPattern( ) { return pattern; }

    public void insertString (int offs, String s, AttributeSet a)
        throws BadLocationException {
```

Example 7-2. A document allowing input that matches only a regex (continued)

```
        // consider whether this insert will match
        String proposedInsert =
            getText (0, offs) +
            s +
            getText (offs, getLength() - offs);
        System.out.println ("proposing to change to: " +
                            proposedInsert);
        if (matcher != null) {
            matcher.reset (proposedInsert);
            System.out.println ("matcher reset");
            if (! matcher.matches()) {
                System.out.println ("insert doesn't match");
                return;
            }
        }
        super.insertString (offs, s, a);
    }
}
```

This class holds onto a `Pattern` and a `Matcher` to perform the regex matching. The pattern can be set in the constructor, or later with a call to
`setPatternByString()`. In either case, the method compiles the pattern and
creates a `Matcher` with the `Document`'s text. Changing the pattern could, of
course, create a mismatch with any existing text in the `Document`, so the
`Matcher` immediately calls `matches()` and if the text does not match, it
deletes all the text from the `Document`.

Perhaps the more typical case is when the `Document.insertString()` method is
called. This will happen on every keystroke in a `JTextComponent`. Assuming the
`Matcher` is not null, meaning that the `Pattern` has been set at some point, you
simply need to call `Matcher.matches()` against the `Document`'s new contents to
see if they comply with the regex constraints. If not, return early, never calling the superclass's `insert()` method, and thus disallowing the input.

Adding Constrained Text Fields

Since the `Document` isn't actually visible, you need to put it in something in
order to test it. The `TestRegexConstrainedDocument` class creates a `JTextField`
for you to type in a regular expression to enforce, and a longer `JTextField`
for text to test. You create this latter `JTextField` with the seldom-seen constructor that takes a `Document`, an initial-value `String`, and a width (specified
in columns). Obviously, you use a `RegexConstrainedDocument` for the first
argument. There's also a Set `JButton` that takes the `String` value of the regex
field and sets that as the new pattern to match the document against, with
`RegexConstrainedDocument`'s `setPatternByString()` method. The rest is mostly
layout code. The test class is shown in Example 7-3.

Example 7-3. GUI to test the RegexConstrainedDocument in a JTextField

```java
import java.awt.*;
import java.awt.event.*;
import javax.swing.*;

public class TestRegexConstrainedDocument extends JPanel
    implements ActionListener {

    JTextField regexField, filterField;
    JButton regexButton;
    RegexConstrainedDocument regexDoc;

    public TestRegexConstrainedDocument() {
        setLayout (new BoxLayout (this, BoxLayout.Y_AXIS));
        // top - regex stuff
        JPanel topPanel = new JPanel();
        JLabel rLabel = new JLabel ("regex:" );
        topPanel.add (rLabel);
        regexField = new JTextField (20);
        topPanel.add(regexField);
        regexButton = new JButton ("Set");
        regexButton.addActionListener (this);
        topPanel.add (regexButton);
        add (topPanel);
        // bottom - filterfield
        regexDoc =
            new RegexConstrainedDocument ();
        filterField = new JTextField (regexDoc, "",  50);
        add (filterField);
    }

    public void actionPerformed (ActionEvent e) {
        System.out.println ("actionperformed");
        if (e.getSource() == regexButton) {
            System.out.println ("regexbutton");
            regexDoc.setPatternByString (regexField.getText());
        }
    }

    public static void main (String[] args) {
        JComponent c = new TestRegexConstrainedDocument();
        JFrame f = new JFrame ("Regex filtering");
        f.getContentPane().add (c);
        f.pack();
        f.setVisible(true);
    }
}
```

When run, the displayed GUI looks like Figure 7-2. Notice that by using the regex [A-Z]*, you can enter uppercase letters and spaces, but nothing else.

When you type a comma, a question mark, or lowercase letters, they are ignored.

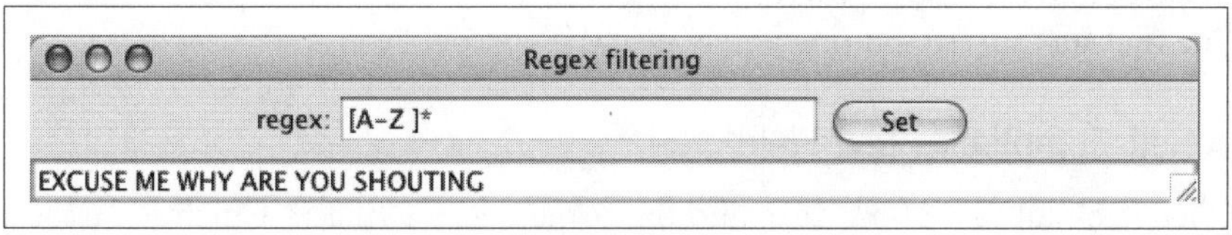

Figure 7-2. Filtering JTextField input with a regular expression

You can do smart things with this tool, but also really stupid things. Let's say you want to restrict input to the characters that will be in a North American phone number of the form 123-456-7890. You can set the pattern to [0-9\-]*, which will allow the user to type in only numbers and the hyphen.

Now you're feeling clever, but you don't like the fact that this still allows users to type patterns that aren't phone numbers, like 1111111 or -1-1-1-1. So, you set the pattern to an exact description of the phone number pattern:

    [0-9]{3}-[0-9]{3}-[0-9]{4}

But now your users can't enter *anything*! Why? Because although that regular expression does specify the phone number pattern, no substring of it will ever match. This expression specifies exactly 12 characters, so when you type the first one, there's only one character—it doesn't match the pattern, so it's rejected.

The moral of the story here is to be thoughtful. You might decide to wire up a FocusListener so you impose the regex pattern only when the user moves off the field, and change the "delete everything" behavior to something a little less forceful; for example, you could pop up a dialog telling the user that her input isn't in the right format. Just don't be surprised when regular expressions give you results that are logical, but sometimes unexpected.

HACK #50   Auto-Completing Text Fields

Typing in a whole URL is a pain. When the user starts to type, complete his text with previously entered options, and let the user select one instead of typing the whole URL.

The auto-completing text field is instantly familiar from its use in browsers, where it is probably most needed. Nobody wants to have to try to type—or for that matter even remember—a huge URL to some page they've visited before, particularly not something like those Amazon.com URLs with inexplicable 20-digit numbers and bunches of seemingly arbitrary characters. On the other hand, not everything needs to be saved as a bookmark.

The text field that pops up a window of recently viewed sites is a happy compromise. It jogs your memory by showing you completion options, and it saves lots of typing by letting you simply click one of the options and having that text inserted immediately into the text field.

A Self-Completing Text Field

This hack takes a JTextField and has it manage a JWindow, which contains a JList of possible completion values. The real work is done by an inner class that manages the list of completions and has a javax.util.regex.Pattern object to match each potential completion against the field's current text. Example 7-4 is what you need to get going.

Example 7-4. A JTextField that manages a pop-up list of completions

```
import java.awt.*;
import javax.swing.*;
import javax.swing.event.*;
import javax.swing.text.*;
import java.util.*;
import java.util.regex.*;

public class CompletableJTextField extends JTextField
    implements ListSelectionListener {

    Completer completer;
    JList completionList;
    DefaultListModel completionListModel;
    JScrollPane listScroller;
    JWindow listWindow;

    public CompletableJTextField (int col) {
        super (col);
        completer = new Completer( );
        completionListModel = new DefaultListModel( );
        completionList = new JList(completionListModel);
        completionList.setSelectionMode (ListSelectionModel.SINGLE_SELECTION);
        completionList.addListSelectionListener (this);
        listScroller =
            new JScrollPane (completionList,
                            ScrollPaneConstants.VERTICAL_SCROLLBAR_AS_NEEDED,
                            ScrollPaneConstants.HORIZONTAL_SCROLLBAR_NEVER);
        listWindow = new JWindow( );
        listWindow.getContentPane( ).add (listScroller);
    }

    public void addCompletion (String s) {
        completer.addCompletion (s); }
```

Example 7-4. A JTextField that manages a pop-up list of completions (continued)

```java
    public void removeCompletion (String s) {
        completer.removeCompletion (s); }

    public void clearCompletions (String s ) {
        completer.clearCompletions (); }

    public void valueChanged (ListSelectionEvent e) {
        if (e.getValueIsAdjusting()) { return; }
        if (completionList.getModel().getSize() == 0) {return;}
        listWindow.setVisible (false);
        final String completionString =
            (String) completionList.getSelectedValue();
        Thread worker = new Thread() {
                public void run() {
                    setText (completionString);
                }
            };
        SwingUtilities.invokeLater (worker);
    }

    /** inner class does the matching of the JTextField's
        document to completion strings kept in an ArrayList
     */
    class Completer implements DocumentListener {
        private Pattern pattern;
        private ArrayList completions;
        public Completer() {
            completions = new ArrayList();
            getDocument().addDocumentListener (this);
        }

        public void addCompletion (String s) {
            completions.add (s);
            buildAndShowPopup();
        }

        public void removeCompletion (String s) {
            completions.remove (s);
            buildAndShowPopup();
        }

        public void clearCompletions () {
            completions.clear();
            buildPopup();
            listWindow.setVisible(false);
        }

        private void buildPopup() {
            completionListModel.clear();
            System.out.println ("buildPopup for " + completions.size() +
                                " completions");
```

Example 7-4. A JTextField that manages a pop-up list of completions (continued)

```java
        Iterator it = completions.iterator();
        pattern = Pattern.compile (getText() + ".+");
        while (it.hasNext()) {
            // check if match
            String completion = (String) it.next();
            Matcher matcher = pattern.matcher (completion);
            if (matcher.matches()) {
                // add if match
                System.out.println ("matched "+ completion);
                completionListModel.add (completionListModel.getSize(),
                                            completion);
            } else {
                System.out.println ("pattern " +
                                        pattern.pattern() +
                                        " does not match " +
                                        completion);
            }
        }
    }

    private void showPopup() {
        if (completionListModel.getSize() == 0) {
            listWindow.setVisible(false);
            return;
        }
        // figure out where the text field is,
        // and where its bottom left is
        java.awt.Point los = getLocationOnScreen();
        int popX = los.x;
        int popY = los.y + getHeight();
        listWindow.setLocation (popX, popY);
        listWindow.pack();
        listWindow.setVisible(true);
    }

    private void buildAndShowPopup() {
        if (getText().length() < 1)
            return;
        buildPopup();
        showPopup();
    }

    // DocumentListener implementation
    public void insertUpdate (DocumentEvent e) { buildAndShowPopup(); }
    public void removeUpdate (DocumentEvent e) { buildAndShowPopup(); }
    public void changedUpdate (DocumentEvent e) { buildAndShowPopup(); }

    }
}
```

The `CompletableJTextField` constructor is responsible for setting up the JList and its model; for wiring up the field as a `ListSelectionListener`; and for packing the list into a `JScrollPane`, which sits in an initially invisible JWindow. It also creates an instance of the inner class `Completer`, which is responsible for managing the list of completions. Note that this version of the hack supplies only one of the typical `JTextField` constructor signatures; you'd probably want to provide others to make the component more convenient for callers.

There are three methods for adding, removing, and clearing completions, but these just decorate calls to the `Completer` inner class.

Skip ahead to the `Completer` at this point because it's the guts of the implementation. This class has an `ArrayList` of all the `Strings` to be considered as completions of the field text, and a regex `Pattern` to do matching. When you want to add and delete possible completions, you need to add or delete them from the `ArrayList` and then manage the `ListModel` in the outer class and show the JWindow. Clearing is similar, but you clear the `ListModel` and hide the window.

`buildModel()` is a convenience class to do the list model management. It starts by clearing the list model, then creates a regex `Pattern` with the field text, concatenated with ".* ", which means the pattern is "what's in the field, plus zero or more other characters." To match against possible completions, you get an `Iterator` of them and then go through them, each time creating a `Matcher` of the field text and looking for a match. If it matches, add it to the list model.

With the list model rebuilt, you show the updated list to the user by rechecking the field's onscreen location, putting the window directly below that, and calling `setVisible(true)`.

The inner class also provides a `DocumentListener` implementation that simply rebuilds and shows the completion list window on any kind of change to the field's underlying `Document`.

Mouse clicks on the list in this window is handled by a `valueChanged()` method in the outer class. Unfortunately, this has to deal with the fact that the choice of an item fires off a chain of `ListSelectionEvents`, only one of which you're interested in. The chain of events always begins with one for which `valueIsAdjusting` is `true`. This is meant to indicate that the user is dragging through the list to make multiple selections, and it is sent even though this list is single-select. At any rate, it's not the last event, so ignore it. Another selection event is sent when the list is cleared out and has no items; this isn't worth acting on, so ignore it, too. Having screened those cases out, you should have a nonadjusting `ListSelectionEvent` and a non-zero list size.

You can hide the window at this point and look at the selection value. Since the Completer just puts Strings in the list model, you can pull out the selected value and set that as the text of the field. And you're done.

Well, not quite. If you call setText( ) directly in valueChanged( ), you'll be thrown an IllegalStateException. The problem is that you're attempting to change the value of the Document while it's already being changed. In other words, firing off the DocumentEvent is part of the document edit that began with the user's keystroke that led to the completion menu appearing; this edit needs to complete before another is attempted. As you can see in this hack, the workaround is to create a worker thread to set the field with the clicked text, and to invoke that worker on a later cycle through the event loop. This arrangement returns immediately and lets the first edit finish, then sets the field later.

Test Out Auto-Complete

To test this class, you need to put the CompletableJTextField in a GUI and provide a way to give it some completions. The TestCompletableJTextField class in Example 7-5 does just that, offering a second JTextField where you can enter strings that will be offered as completions to text typed into the CompletableJTextField. When run, the test GUI originally looks like Figure 7-3.

Example 7-5. A GUI to exercise the CompletableJTextField

```
import java.awt.*;
import java.awt.event.*;
import javax.swing.*;

public class TestCompletableJTextField extends JPanel
    implements ActionListener {

    CompletableJTextField completableField;
    JTextField completionField;

    public TestCompletableJTextField () {
        super();
        setLayout (new BoxLayout (this, BoxLayout.Y_AXIS));
        completableField = new CompletableJTextField (75);
        add (completableField);
        JPanel bottom = new JPanel ();
        bottom.add (new JLabel ("Completion:"));
        completionField = new JTextField (40);
        completionField.addActionListener (this);
        bottom.add (completionField);
        JButton addButton = new JButton ("Add");
        addButton.addActionListener (this);
```

Example 7-5. A GUI to exercise the CompletableJTextField (continued)

```
        bottom.add (addButton);
        add (bottom);
    }

    public void actionPerformed (ActionEvent e) {
        completableField.addCompletion (completionField.getText( ));
        completionField.setText ("");
    }

    public static void main (String[] main) {
        JFrame f = new JFrame ("Completions...");
        f.getContentPane().add (new TestCompletableJTextField( ));
        f.pack( );
        f.setVisible (true);
    }
}
```

Figure 7-3. Empty CompletableJTextField

To test things out, I added the addresses of some of O'Reilly's web sites: *www.onjava.com*, *www.onlamp.com*, *www.java.net*, and *webservices.xml.com*. Figure 7-4 shows that after I type w, all four sites match.

Figure 7-4. All completions showing after typing one character

In Figure 7-5, I type a second w; *webservices.xml.com* no longer matches, so it disappears from the list.

As I continue my typing (www.on), only two matches remain, as seen in Figure 7-6.

At this point, I clicked *www.onjava.com*. This text is placed into the field and the list window disappears, as seen in Figure 7-7.

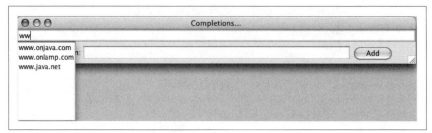

Figure 7-5. One completion removed after typing two characters

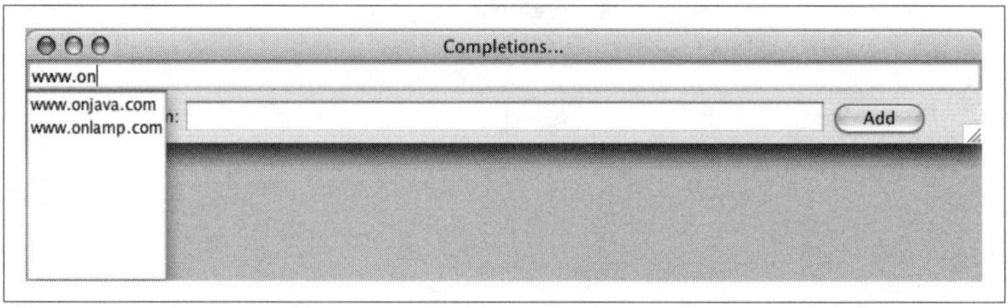

Figure 7-6. Another completion removed after typing six characters

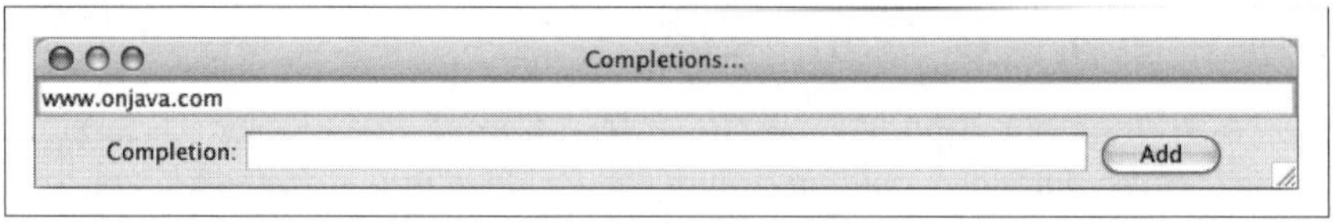

Figure 7-7. Text field filled in by clicking on completion from list

One question you might ask about this implementation is "why stuff a JList in a JWindow you have to manage, when you could just use a JPopupMenu?" Good question, but one with a pretty straightforward answer: the JPopupMenu is modal, so once it appears, clicking on it is the *only* option. That's not the desired behavior here, where clicking in the menu is optional, and the more likely circumstance at any time is that the user will continue typing. So, the better approach is to let her keep typing and just keep track of the possible completions.

HACK #51 Write Backward Text

Baffle your friends by turning their text into its mirror image.

The fact that everything in Swing goes through the Java2D rendering pipeline makes it really easy to apply all sorts of effects to Swing components. Text offers some fun possibilities. For one, you can challenge the user by turning his text into a mirror image of itself.

Messing with JLabel

The easiest text component to distort is the simple JLabel. The BackwardsJLabel class in Example 7-6 subclasses JLabel and uses an AffineTransform in the paint( ) method to do the flip.

Example 7-6. Rendering a JLabel as a mirror image

```
import java.awt.*;
import javax.swing.*;
import java.awt.geom.*;
import javax.swing.text.Document;

public class BackwardsJLabel extends JLabel {

    public BackwardsJLabel () { super( ); }
    public BackwardsJLabel (Icon image) {super (image);}
    public BackwardsJLabel (Icon image, int align) {super (image, align);}
    public BackwardsJLabel (String text) { super (text);}
    public BackwardsJLabel (String text, Icon icon, int align) {
        super (text, icon, align);
    }
    public BackwardsJLabel (String text, int align) { super (text, align);}

    public void paint (Graphics g) {
        if (g instanceof Graphics2D) {
            Graphics2D g2 = (Graphics2D) g;
            AffineTransform flipTrans = new AffineTransform( );
            double widthD = (double) getWidth( );
            flipTrans.setToTranslation (widthD, 0);
            flipTrans.scale (-1.0, 1);
            g2.transform (flipTrans);
            super.paint(g);
        } else {
            super.paint(g);
        }
    }
}
```

The constructors make trivial calls to their parent classes, so the key is the overridden paint( ) method. It first checks that you have a Graphics2D and does the cast. Any Graphics2D has an AffineTransformation that defines transforms that are to be applied as the Graphics2D is rendered. The AffineTransform of a Component will usually have some important transforms already defined in it, so it's best not to replace its transform, but rather to use the Graphics2D.transform( ) method to modify the existing AffineTransform with one of your own making.

But what kind of transform do you want to do? A mirror image consists of two separate trasnformations: scaling the x-coordinates by a factor of -1 (flipping them around the axis, so that the pixels furthest to the right are now furthest to the left), and translating by the width of the component (so the pixels move from negative coordinates, where they wouldn't be seen, back into positive space). This transformation is illustrated in Figure 7-8.

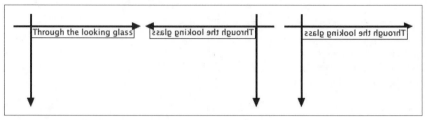

Figure 7-8. Mirror image as scale-and-translate AffineTransform

Mirror, Mirror on the Wall

The following main( ) method provides a trivial setup of a frame in which you can view the backward JLabel. The result is shown in Figure 7-9.

Figure 7-9. JLabel rendered as mirror image

```
public static void main (String[] args) {
    BackwardsJLabel field =
        new BackwardsJLabel ("Through the looking glass");
    JFrame frame = new JFrame("Backwards Text");
    frame.getContentPane( ).add (field);
    frame.pack( );
    frame.setVisible(true);
}
```

Because the transformation is simple and limited to the paint( ) method, it seems like something you could do anywhere. You can easily create a BackwardsJTextField that uses exactly the same paint( ) method in a trivially overridden JTextField—honestly, it's so trivial that it's not worth listing here; just set up the trivial "call super" constructors, copy over this paint( ) method, and tweak the main( ) method to show the text field instead of the label. The result will look like Figure 7-10.

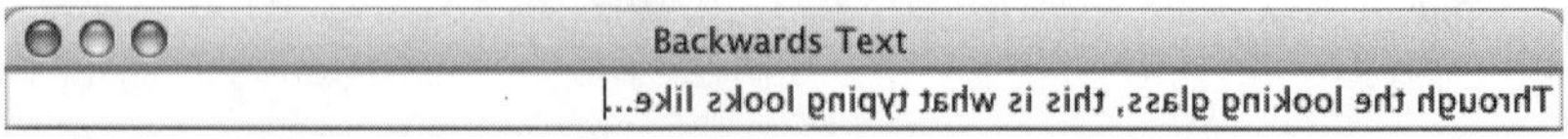

Figure 7-10. JTextField rendered as mirror image

This looks amusing and, when you type, the new text is indeed backward. But the novelty wears off quickly; messing with the display screws up the drawing of the caret and text highlighting, along with the handling of mouse clicks to set the insert point. In playing around with JTextArea, we found that we hosed word wrap, too, so we were stuck on the top line.

So, it's a cute trick, but let's reserve it for labels, OK?

HACK #52 Use HTML and CSS in Text Components

Spruce up your plain JLabels and buttons using HTML and CSS effects, such as underlines, color, and even embedded tables.

You may know that you can display HTML using a subclass of JTextPane, but did you also know that Swing supports simple HTML and CSS in virtually every text component? As long as you can trick it into showing it as HTML instead of the markup, you can do some pretty nifty things.

Here's the Trick

Every text component in Swing can display HTML, but the component needs to *know* that the text is HTML, rather than a string that just happens to contain a bunch of angle brackets. Since there is no setHTMLText(true) method on JTextComponent, you have to resort to being a little trickier. If the string passed to the component's constructor (or setText( )) method starts with <html>, then the component will switch to HTML mode. Here is a quick example:

```
JButton b1a = new JButton("<html><i>my button</i>");
```

This code will produce a button that looks like Figure 7-11.

Figure 7-11. Italic text

You don't need to match the <html> with an </html> tag at the end. Swing's HTML parser is pretty tolerant of malformed HTML, so for simple things you can just type whatever is shortest. The mode can only be set once, so if you put plain text into the component first and then HTML later, it will still be in plain text mode. You should note that slower computers will exhibit a noticeable delay the first time a component is shown with HTML. This is because Swing has to load up all of the javax.swing.text.html classes; however, they are cached for any further instances.

Use HTML and CSS in Text Components

To avoid this initial delay, you could load a hidden component in a separate thread during program startup.

HTML can be used as a shortcut for text effects that would be cumbersome
or impossible with standard Font objects. For example, Font doesn't provide
a way to draw underlined text, but with HTML you can do this:

```
JLabel l1 = new JLabel("<html><u>underlined</u></html>");
```

This produces the text seen in Figure 7-12.

Figure 7-12. Underlined text

HTML also lets you get multi-lined text and mixed fonts:

```
JButton b2 = new JButton("<html><i>my</i> button</html>");
```

This produces the button seen in Figure 7-13.

Figure 7-13. Mixed styles

You can even add line break tags:

```
JLabel l2 = new JLabel("<html>my multi-<br>line text</html>");
```

Using this, you get the button seen in Figure 7-14.

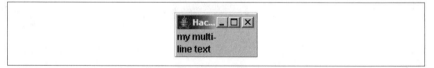

Figure 7-14. Multi-lined text

You can use HTML in more than just labels and buttons. JCheckBox,
JRadioButton, and even JComboBox support it. Here is an example of each:

```
JCheckBox cb1 = new JCheckBox("<html>The <i>real</i> thing");
JRadioButton rb1 = new JRadioButton(
    "<html>Even <font color=\"#ff0000\">better</font>");
```

```
String[] vals = { "<html><i>better</i>",
    "<html><u>yet again</u>" };
JComboBox combo1 = new JComboBox(vals);
```

This creates the collection of HTML-styled components seen in Figure 7-15.

Figure 7-15. Some other HTML components

Swing supports most features of basic HTML: paragraphs, lists, simple tables, and colors. It also supports basic CSS, which can give you greater control over borders, padding, and other visual attributes. This next example creates a header followed by list items of large colored text surrounded by a border. Since there is so much markup, I put it into a StringBuffer first:

```
StringBuffer sb = new StringBuffer( );
sb.append("<html><head><style type='text/css'>");
sb.append("li { font-style: italic; font-size: 30pt; }");
sb.append("li { font-family: serif; color: #ff5555; }");
sb.append("ul { border-width: 4px; border-style: solid;
            border-color: #ff0000; } ");
sb.append("ul { background-color: #ffeeee; }");
sb.append("</style></head>");
sb.append("<h3>H3 Header</h3>");
sb.append("<ul><li>large serifed text</li><li>as list items</li>");
sb.append("</html>");

JLabel l3 = new JLabel(sb.toString( ));
```

This produces the label seen in Figure 7-16.

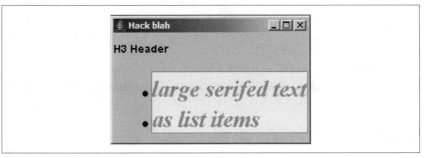

Figure 7-16. Borders and lists

There is no definitive list of every CSS layout feature the HTMLEditorKit supports, but you can get a good overview in the JavaDoc for the javax.swing.text.html.CSS class.

CSS also gives you the ability to define a style and reuse it with multiple components, putting you one step closer to the kind of separation of content and style that we take for granted on the Web. In this example, both labels share the same CSS declaration. If you change the declaration, it would change both labels. This declaration could even be stored in a properties file, letting non-programmers affect the look of your application:

```
StringBuffer css = new StringBuffer( );
css.append("<html><head><style type='text/css'>");
css.append("body { color: #4444ff; font-weight: normal;}");
css.append("</head><body>");

JLabel 14 = new JLabel(css+"Cartman");
JLabel 15 = new JLabel(css+"Stan");
```

This produces the labels seen in Figure 7-17.

Figure 7-17. Shared CSS styles

Putting HTML in Swing components is a little-known feature that packs a big punch. You can use it to quickly create layout effects that are cumbersome or impossible to do with traditional text.

HACK #53   Use Global Anti-Aliased Fonts

Think Swing apps always look ugly because of the chunky fonts? Finally, you can do something about it!

Java 1.2 introduced Java2D, complete with the ability to draw anti-aliased text. Unfortunately, anti-aliasing is off by default and turning it on requires a programmatic change on each UI component. This hack shows how to turn on anti-aliasing for an entire frame without customizing each component. It also introduces a special repaint manager that is the key to several other hacks in this book, such as the partial translucent menus [Hack #12].

The Problem

To turn on anti-aliasing, you simply need to set a rendering hint:

```
Graphics2D g2 = (Graphics2D)g;
g2.setRenderingHint(RenderingHints.KEY_ANTIALIASING,
                    RenderingHints.VALUE_ANTIALIAS_ON);
```

Unfortunately, the Graphics object is not very long-lived. There is no global place to set a hint because there's a new Graphics object for every repaint( ). Any property you set would be gone by the next paint call. The usual workaround is to subclass the component you want to anti-alias and override the paint( ) method:

```
class AAButton extends JButton {
    public void paint(Graphics g) {
        Graphics2D g2 = (Graphics2D)g;
        g2.setRenderingHint(RenderingHints.KEY_ANTIALIASING,
                            RenderingHints.VALUE_ANTIALIAS_ON);
        super.paint(g2);
    }
}
```

This will work, but it means you have to create a custom subclass for *every component in your application*. Not a very appealing solution.

Mac OS X provides anti-aliased rendering through a system property, but this only works because Apple thoughtfully added it to their JVM. Developers on other platforms are left out. Java 5.0 provides a standard system property for anti-aliasing, but that doesn't help the millions of 1.3 and 1.4 JVMs out there. Another option would be to use some form of code injection to modify each paint method at the bytecode level, but this requires an AOP tool, custom build scripts, and other things that are probably overkill for such a simple feature. There has to be a better way—and there actually is.

A long, long time ago (in a research lab far, far away) I worked on a scalable UI toolkit for Java called SubArctic. One of its key features was that a component would paint onto a canvas object called a Drawable—what we would call a Graphics object in Swing. This Drawable would be passed from parent to child in a recursive tree traversal. Drawables could be hacked to do all sorts of complicated things, and since a child always drew on the Drawable from its parent, the parent could make a change without the child knowing about it. Thus, you could create a parent panel that rotated all graphics by 45 degrees and a standard child component (like a button or scrollbar) would work without modification. This scheme was incredibly flexible. We had hacks for drop shadows, bit-level operations (blur, sharpen, b/w), affine transformations (rotate, shear), or just about any other crazy idea you could come up with. I have long wanted to do this in Swing, but there has always been one obstacle: in Swing, a child's paint( ) method is not always called by its parent's paintChildren( ) method.

Swing provides three sub-paint methods: paint( ) calls paintBackground( ), paintComponent( ), and paintChildren( ), passing a Graphics object to each. Ideally, if you overrode paintChildren( ) in a custom panel class to add the rendering hint, then all of the children would draw anti-aliased text. Then you could just make this custom panel be the root of your frame and the rendering hint would magically apply to all of the children in the window. This would be one change per frame, instead of one per component (a definite improvement).

That sounds all nice and good, except that it doesn't work. The assumption that a child's paint( ) method is always called by its parent's paintChildren( ) method is wrong. Swing lies! In an effort to speed up rendering, Swing tracks which components have changed and need redrawing. They are, in Swing parlance, marked as *dirty*. The system repaints all of the dirty components and leave the others untouched. If Swing detects that a child component is dirty, but that its parent is not, then it will jump directly to the child's paint( ) method, bypassing the parent's paintChildren( ) method completely. Crummy, huh?

You could work around this by marking each component with setOpaque(false). Then, Swing would have no guarantee that the component covers its parent completely, and the parent would have to be repainted as well. Unfortunately, setOpaque( ) was really meant for custom components, and standard widgets like JButton may draw erratically if opacity changes. To make matters worse, this varies by L&F, something you don't want to account for. In addition, you would have to call setOpaque(false) on every component in the application. This is less intrusive than subclassing, but still a huge amount of work. Next option, please!

What you really want to do is just have the entire component hierarchy be marked dirty when any component changes. Then the whole frame will be repainted, and each child's paint( ) method will be called from its parent's paintChildren( ) method, making the anti-aliased panel idea work. The key to this strategy is a little-known class called the RepaintManager.

RepaintManager is a Swing utility class used to track the dirty components in a window and to tell Swing what to repaint. The guys at Sun Microsystems made this a public class to facilitate debugging, not for the strange hack we are about to attempt, but strange hacks are the point of this book, so let's get started.

RepaintManager has a lot of methods, but we're only interested in one of them: addDirtyRegion( ), which is called each time a component wants to make a portion of itself dirty. The version seen in Example 7-7 will still mark it dirty, but then it will mark the entire frame dirty as well, triggering a full repaint( ).

Example 7-7. Tricking RepaintManager

```
import javax.swing.RepaintManager;
import javax.swing.JComponent;
import java.awt.Container;

public class FullRepaintManager extends RepaintManager {
    public void addDirtyRegion(JComponent comp, int x, int y, int w,
                               int h) {
        super.addDirtyRegion(comp,x,y,w,h);
        JComponent root = getRootJComponent(comp);
        // to avoid a recursive infinite loop
        if(comp != root) {
            super.addDirtyRegion(root,0,0,root.getWidth( ),
                                 root.getHeight( ));
        }
    }
    public JComponent getRootJComponent(JComponent comp) {
        Container parent = comp.getParent( );
        if(parent instanceof JComponent) {
            return getRootJComponent((JComponent)parent);
        }
        return comp;
    }

}
```

The addDirtyRegion( ) implementation first calls the super version and then looks for the highest ancestor that is still an instance of JComponent (because you don't really want the frame itself marked dirty). Then, it calls addDirtyRegion( ) a second time on the root component, marking the entire window dirty. Once this is done, the repaint thread will take over and repaint the entire window, ensuring that any custom JPanel hacks (in this case, setting the anti-aliased rendering hint) will be handled normally. By creating a custom repaint manager like this, you now have a reusable tool to use in other hacks.

Now that we have our full screen repainting, let's use it. Example 7-8 is the code to an AntiAliasedPanel along with a simple main( ) method for testing.

Example 7-8. Testing out anti-aliasing on a global scale

```
public class AntiAliasedPanel extends JPanel {

    public void paintChildren(Graphics g) {
        Graphics2D g2 = (Graphics2D)g;
        g2.setRenderingHint(RenderingHints.KEY_ANTIALIASING,
                            RenderingHints.VALUE_ANTIALIAS_ON);
        super.paintChildren(g2);
    }
```

Example 7-8. Testing out anti-aliasing on a global scale (continued)

```
    public static void main(String[] args) {
        RepaintManager.setCurrentManager(new FullRepaintManager( ));
        JPanel panel = new AntiAliasedPanel( );
        JFrame frame = new JFrame("Hack 100: Anti-Aliased text");
        frame.getContentPane( ).add(panel);

        JLabel label = new JLabel("This is anti-aliased text");
        label.setFont(label.getFont( ).deriveFont(40f));
        panel.add(label);

        frame.pack( );
        frame.setVisible(true);
    }
}
```

AntiAliasedPanel is just a standard JPanel subclass with the paintChildren( ) method overridden to turn on anti-aliasing. The main( ) method first sets the current RepaintManager to the custom version. Then it creates a JFrame with the AntiAliasedPanel as its root, adding a JLabel with large type. Figure 7-18 shows what the anti-aliased label looks like. I've also shown a standard label in Figure 7-19 for comparison.

Figure 7-18. With anti-aliasing

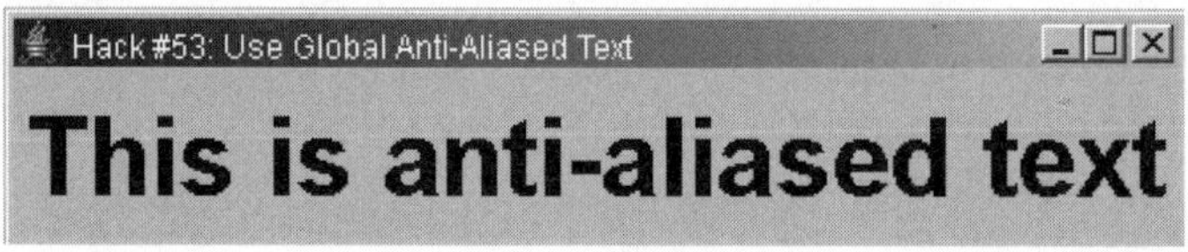

Figure 7-19. Without anti-aliasing

The disadvantage of this scheme is that we have defeated all of Swing's speed optimizations, but I think it's worth it for the possibilities we've opened up. This hack just sets the anti-aliasing rendering hint, but we could also use custom JPanels to do other things with the Graphics object, such as blurring, rotation, or animation. For more examples of this approach, take a look at the partially translucent menus **[Hack #48]** and custom tool tip **[Hack #43]** hacks.

Anti-Aliased Text Without Code

HACK
#54

Draw anti-aliased text without any code changes at all using two clever tricks introduced in Java 5.0.

Since Java 1.2, UI programmers can draw anti-aliased text. Unfortunately, anti-aliasing must be enabled for every Swing component by writing a few lines of code for each of them **[Hack #53]**. This hack describes a clever way to turn on anti-aliasing for an entire frame by adding a customized repaint manager. As every programmer seeks for effortless solutions, we will discover how to do the same without writing any lines of code.

The Java 5.0 Trick

Sun Microsystems released Java 5.0, a.k.a. Tiger, in September 2004. Among many improvements, like a new theme for the Metal L&F, this release of J2SE paves the way for application-wide text anti-aliasing support in Mustang, the upcoming release of Java. To this end, the Swing team added a special field in the hidden class com.sun.java.swing.SwingUtilities2. Meant for internal purposes only, this class is left undocumented by Sun's engineering teams.

If you look closely at its source code, provided in *src.zip* with Sun's JVM, you'll discover a very interesting method: drawTextAntialiased(JComponent c). This method returns a boolean value used by Swing's painting framework to know whether the specified component must be drawn with anti-aliased text. Here is its complete source code:

```
private static boolean drawTextAntialiased(JComponent c) {
    if (!AA_TEXT_DEFINED) {
        if (c != null) {
            return ((Boolean)c.getClientProperty(
                        AA_TEXT_PROPERTY_KEY)).booleanValue();
        }
        return false;
    }
    return AA_TEXT;
}
```

As you can see, there are two ways to enable anti-aliased text. In the first case, the static variable AA_TEXT_DEFINED is set to false, and a check is performed against the component's properties. Hence, a component in which the property AA_TEXT_PROPERTY_KEY is set to true will be anti-aliased. You can set this property to a given component with the following line of code:

```
myComponent.putClientProperty(SwingUtilities2.AA_TEXT_PROPERTY_KEY,
    new Boolean(true));
```

Add this line of code in any of your applications, compile it, and launch it with J2SE 5.0 and you'll see the magic happen. While extremely useful, this trick is not enough since we sure don't want to do that for every component instance in our UI. The source code of drawTextAntialiased( ) gives us a clue to understand how to globally enable anti-aliased text. When AA_TEXT_ DEFINED is set to true, the value AA_TEXT is returned. Both are defined at the beginning of *SwingUtilities2.java*:

```
static {
  fontCache = new LSBCacheEntry[CACHE_SIZE];
  Object aa = java.security.AccessController.doPrivileged(
    new GetPropertyAction("swing.aatext"));
  AA_TEXT_DEFINED = (aa != null);
  AA_TEXT = "true".equals(aa);
  AA_FRC = new FontRenderContext(null, true, false);
}
```

The variables we are interested in are computed according to the value of the object aa. This object is the value of a JVM property called swing.aatext, and it is supposed to be a String object. AA_TEXT_PROPERTY_KEY is true only when this property has been set, and AA_TEXT is true when the value of the property is the String value "true". Given this information, we just need to set the swing.aatext property of the JVM to enable anti-aliasing. This can be done on the command line with the help of the –D switch, as in this example:

```
java –Dswing.aatext=true WebHunter
```

Figure 7-20 is what an application looks like with swing.aatext properly set. I have also shown a screenshot of the same application without this property for comparison (in Figure 7-21).

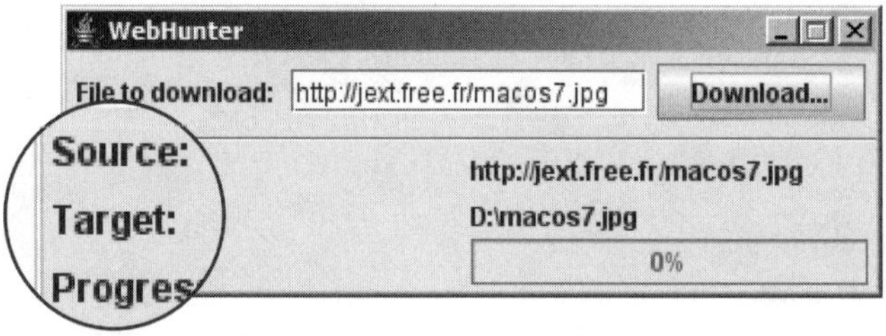

Figure 7-20. Anti-aliased text with J2SE 5.0 swing.aatext property

This trick is very useful and extremely simple to set up. Best of all, it requires no change in the source code of the application, allowing use of it even with applications you did not write. Unfortunately, this hack has two major drawbacks. First, it works only with Sun's J2SE 5.0 and is not guaranteed to be available with other vendors' implementations. Also, remember

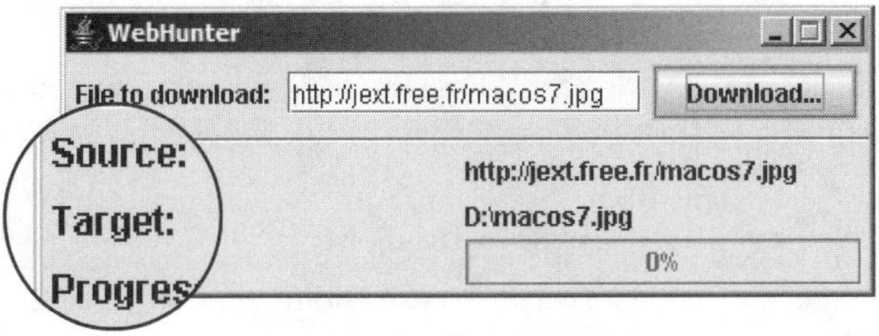

Figure 7-21. Anti-aliased text without J2SE 5.0 swing.aatext property

that SwingUtilities2 is an undocumented and hidden class for which no support will ever be provided. This means that it can be changed without notice. Using it might break your applications in a future release of Java.

—Romain Guy

HACK #55 Anti-Aliased Text with a Custom Look and Feel

Another way to get smooth text is to use a custom Look and Feel to avoid the fragile Java 5.0 APIs.

When the Java 5.0 anti-aliasing trick **[Hack #54]** was first discovered, some discussions arose on the Web. Many people strongly disagree with using it because it can be broken at any time by Sun Microsystems. Should we be deprived of anti-aliased text because of such a silly problem? Frédéric Lavigne, author of the famous Skin L&F and webmaster of *www.javootoo.com*, a great repository of Look and Feels for Swing, didn't think so and found an elegant and clever way to get the same result.

The Wrap Look and Feel

His idea is to use a custom Look and Feel whose sole purpose is to enable anti-aliasing hints on the Graphics instances used to draw the UI. He implemented his idea in the Wrap Look and Feel, which can be downloaded at *wraplf.l2fprod.com*. Another Look and Feel, SmoothMetal, enables anti-aliasing in your application. Yet, you are stuck with Metal Look and Feel when using it. Wrap Look and Feel acts as a decorator for the current Look and Feel. Thus, you can choose any Look and Feel you want and wrap it with Wrap Look and Feel to enable anti-aliasing. Doing so requires a single line of code:

```
import com.l2fprod.common.swing.plaf.wrap.Wrapper;
Wrapper.wrap( );
```

No matter which Swing Look and Feel you set, the wrap( ) method will handle it properly. One line of code is good, but not good enough. We'd be better off with no line of code at all. Frédéric feels the same way and provides the excellent Wrapit class you can use to install the Wrap Look and Feel at runtime:

```
java -classpath wraplf.jar;. Wrapit WebHunter
```

The Wrapit class contains a main( ) entry point that will install the Wrap Look and Feel and then call the main( ) entry point of the class passed as the first argument on the command line. This Look and Feel is a powerful tool you can use to enhance the appearance of any Java application, whether you have the source code or not.

—*Romain Guy*

Rendering
Hacks 56–64

Sometimes it's not what you put into your GUI, but how you draw it. The hacks in this chapter are based in some way on using (or abusing) how AWT and Swing render the graphic contents of a GUI. In several cases, we use Java2D to bring graphic transformations and color-handling to Swing components. In others, we use AWT's font handling to change components; not just JTextComponents, but any components that need to draw text to render themselves. And in still other cases, we mess with the process by which Swing renders its contents.

HACK #56 Create a Magnifying Glass Component

Zoom in on those pixels with a little creative abuse of the AWT's debugging-oriented Robot class.

Some graphics programs use a component that shows a magnified view of what the cursor is currently hovering over. This can be very helpful for doing pixel-accurate editing of a picture.

It should be simple enough to do in Swing—get pixels from one component and put them in another—but there are some missing pieces. Specifically, how do you get the pixels out of the source component as an Image so you can drawImage( ) them into the magnified component? You could do this if you owned the source component and set it up with a double-buffer because creating the offscreen buffer would require creating an Image, which is exactly what you needed anyway. But for an arbitrary JComponent, you can't assume that level of access to the source's pixels.

But there's another option back in AWT: the Robot class, introduced in J2SE 1.3. It has a createScreenCapture( ) method that can grab the screen, or just part of it, and return it as a Java2D BufferedImage. This is what we need to get things going.

Build the Magnifying Glass

The DetachedMagnifyingGlass will need to keep track of the Component it's viewing, the current mouse location in that component, a zoom factor, and its own size. It will also need an instance of the AWT Robot for taking screen grabs. The other thing it needs to do is to have a MouseMotionListener, so that it will get updates on the cursor's position and, when it changes, do a new grab and repaint( ).

The DetachedMagnifyingGlass code is shown in Example 8-1.

Example 8-1. JComponent to provide a magnified view of another JComponent

```java
public class DetachedMagnifyingGlass extends JComponent
    implements MouseMotionListener {

    double zoom;
    JComponent comp;
    Point point;
    Dimension mySize;
    Robot robot;

    public DetachedMagnifyingGlass (JComponent comp,
                                    Dimension size,
                                    double zoom) {
        this.comp = comp;
        // flag to say don't draw until we get a MouseMotionEvent
        point = new Point (-1, -1);
        comp.addMouseMotionListener(this);
        this.mySize = size;
        this.zoom = zoom;
        // if we can't get a robot, then we just never
        // paint anything
        try {
            robot = new Robot( );
        } catch (AWTException awte) {
            System.err.println ("Can't get a Robot");
            awte.printStackTrace( );
        }
    }

    public void paint (Graphics g) {
        if ((robot == null) || (point.x == -1))
        {
            g.setColor (Color.blue);
            g.fillRect (0, 0, mySize.width, mySize.height);
            return;
        }
        Rectangle grabRect = computeGrabRect( );
        BufferedImage grabImg = robot.createScreenCapture (grabRect);
        Image scaleImg =
            grabImg.getScaledInstance (mySize.width, mySize.height,
                                       Image.SCALE_FAST);
```

Example 8-1. JComponent to provide a magnified view of another JComponent

```
        g.drawImage (scaleImg, 0, 0, null);
    }

    private Rectangle computeGrabRect( ) {
        // width, height are size of this comp / zoom
        int grabWidth = (int) ((double) mySize.width / zoom);
        int grabHeight = (int) ((double) mySize.height / zoom);
        // upper-left corner is current point
        return new Rectangle (point.x, point.y, grabWidth, grabHeight);
    }

    public Dimension getPreferredSize( ) { return mySize; }
    public Dimension getMinimumSize( ) { return mySize; }
    public Dimension getMaximumSize( ) { return mySize; }

    // MouseMotionListener implementations
    public void mouseMoved (MouseEvent e) {
        Point offsetPoint = comp.getLocationOnScreen( );
        e.translatePoint (offsetPoint.x, offsetPoint.y);
        point = e.getPoint( );
        repaint( );
    }
    public void mouseDragged (MouseEvent e) {
        mouseMoved (e);
    }
}
```

Looking at the code, the constructor takes the source component, a size for the magnified component, and a zoom level. It assigns these to its instance variables, and sets up a MouseMotionListener to get updates regarding the cursor position, which is initialized to a "don't paint me" dummy value of (-1, -1). It also builds the AWT Robot. Since this can fail on some OSes or under certain security situations, the robot == null case will have to be handled gracefully in the painting routine.

The paint( ) method begins by checking for the two conditions that indicate the mangnified component can't be painted: if there's no Robot or if the cursor has never entered the source component. In either of these cases, the magnified component simply fills itself with blue and returns.

On the other hand, if valid data is available, the magnifier needs to figure out what portion of the source component to grab. For simplicity, you can compute a rectangle whose upper left is the current cursor location. The width and height of the rectangle are computed by multiplying the zoom factor by the magnifying component's height and width. So, for a zoom of 1.0, the grab is exactly the size of the magnifier. For a zoom of 0.5, it grabs half the width and half the height, and for 2.0, it grabs twice the width and height.

With a grab rectangle calculated, call Robot.createScreenCapture( ) to grab those pixels and return them as a BufferedImage. Unless your zoom factor is 1.0, this image will be larger or smaller than the DetachedMagnifyingGlass component, so you need to use getScaledInstance( ) to scale it to your component size. In terms of a scaling behavior, the code uses the SCALE_FAST constant because the moving mouse will be calling for many repaints, and thus many grabs and scales, every second. Finally, with your properly sized image in memory, you paint to the Graphics to get the grabbed data into your component.

> One TODO item I haven't shown here, but that might pro-
> vide a performance boost, would be to flush( ) the various
> temporary images after you've called drawImage( ).

To ensure the AWT LayoutManagers respect the size that's set for the component, have getPreferredSize( ), getMinimumSize( ), and getMaximumSize( ) all
return the size that was originally sent to the constructor, since the size of
the magnifier component is critical in computing what to grab from the
source component.

The last bit of code in this class is a MouseMotionListner, which is used to
track the mouse's location. You need to do this so you'll always have an up-
to-date point when the paint( ) method is called. You'll only get events
when the cursor is over the source component, and it's easy enough to cache
the point in the MouseEvent, but there's a catch: that point is relevant to the
coordinate system of the source component, not the screen, so unless the
component is at the upper-left corner of the screen, you will be grabbing the
wrong pixels in paint( ). The fix is to translate the point from the source
component's coordinate system to the screen's coordinate system. Do this
by getting the component's onscreen location with getLocationOnScreen( ),
and then translate the Point with MouseEvent.translate( ).

Testing the Magnifier Out

To take DetachedMagnifyingGlass out for a spin, Example 8-2 shows a
TestDetachedMagnifyingGlass class, which opens an image in a JFrame and
sets a DetachedMagnifyingGlass next to it.

Example 8-2. Testing the MagnifyingGlassComponent

```
public class TestDetachedMagnifyingGlass extends Object {

    public TestDetachedMagnifyingGlass(File f) {
        // image frame
        ImageIcon i = new ImageIcon (f.getPath( ));
        JLabel l = new JLabel (i);
```

Example 8-2. Testing the MagnifyingGlassComponent (continued)

```
        JFrame imgFrame = new JFrame ("Image");
        imgFrame.getContentPane( ).add(l);
        imgFrame.pack( );
        imgFrame.setVisible(true);
        // magnifying glass frame
        JFrame magFrame = new JFrame ("Mag");
        DetachedMagnifyingGlass mag =
            new DetachedMagnifyingGlass (l, new Dimension (150, 150), 2.0);
        magFrame.getContentPane( ).add (mag);
        magFrame.pack( );
        magFrame.setLocation (new Point (
                        imgFrame.getLocation().x + imgFrame.getWidth( ),
                        imgFrame.getLocation( ).y));
        magFrame.setVisible(true);
    }

    public static void main (String[] args) {
        JFileChooser chooser = new JFileChooser( );
        chooser.showOpenDialog(null);
        File f = chooser.getSelectedFile( );
        new TestDetachedMagnifyingGlass (f);
    }
}
```

This class simply brings up a `JFileChooser` to pick an image file, which it loads into an `ImageIcon` and then into a `JLabel`. It then creates a `DetachedMagnifyingGlass` from the `JLabel`, with a size of 150×150 and a magnification factor of 2.0, and moves it to the immediate right of the source component.

Figure 8-1 shows what the test looks like when run.

Figure 8-1. Use of the DetachedMagnifyingGlass

Hacking the Hack

The only problem with the Robot approach is that it doesn't limit itself to capturing from the source component—it'll take any onscreen pixels from any application. That means that when you approach the edges of the source component, you can pick up pixels from the desktop or other apps, as seen in Figure 8-2.

Figure 8-2. Capturing pixels outside of the target component

Is this a problem? Some users will mind it, some won't. To get rid of it, you'll need to smarten up computeGrabRect( ) to bounds-check its right and bottom edges (the top left is the cursor position, so it can never overshoot the top or left of the component) by adding the untranslated point to the proposed grab width and seeing if that is greater than the width of the source component, and then doing the same for the height. This will take some refactoring, since computeGrabRect( ) doesn't have access to the untranslated point. Also, if you're not necessarily going to be painting the entire magnified component every time, you'll have to erase it at the top of paint( ), so you don't have "crud" from the previous repaint left over after this repaint.

Create a Global Right-Click

Give your application a right-click context menu without having to add a listener to every component.

Oftentimes, an application needs to have a pop-up menu that is accessible from more than one component. Sometimes the entire window should be right-clickable. Unfortunately, doing this the normal way in Swing would require adding a mouse listener to every component in the window, which isn't a very appealing solution, especially if your UI code is spread across many classes. It would be much nicer if there were a single place to add the context menu. This hack shows how to use a single glass pane to provide a right-clickable menu to the entire application.

A glass pane is an invisible JComponent that covers an entire JFrame. The glass pane can be used to catch events or draw on top of the rest of the application. For this hack, we will use a glass pane to capture right-click events and trigger a pop up, alleviating the need to register a mouse listener with every component in the frame. The basic idea is for the glass pane to intercept all mouse events and forward them on to the application, except for the right-click. Right-clicks will trigger the pop-up menu instead. This way there is only one listener per frame, instead of potentially hundreds.

To start off, you need a component that has a reference to the content pane of the frame and a pre-built pop-up menu. This is the beginning of just such a class:

```
public class RightClickGlassPane extends JComponent
    implements MouseListener, MouseMotionListener {

    private JPopupMenu popup;
    private Container contentPane;

    public RightClickGlassPane(Container contentPane, JPopupMenu menu) {
        addMouseListener(this);
        addMouseMotionListener(this);
        this.contentPane = contentPane;
        popup = menu;
    }

    public void paint(Graphics g) {
    }

    // catch all mouse events and redispatch them
    public void mouseMoved(MouseEvent e) {
        redispatchMouseEvent(e, false);
    }
```

```
public void mouseDragged(MouseEvent e) {
    redispatchMouseEvent(e, false);
}
public void mouseClicked(MouseEvent e) {
    redispatchMouseEvent(e, false);
}
public void mouseEntered(MouseEvent e) {
    redispatchMouseEvent(e, false);
}
public void mouseExited(MouseEvent e) {
    redispatchMouseEvent(e, false);
}
public void mousePressed(MouseEvent e) {
    redispatchMouseEvent(e, false);
}
public void mouseReleased(MouseEvent e) {
    redispatchMouseEvent(e, false);
}
```

In the RightClickGlassPane constructor, the code saves a reference to the content pane and pop-up menu that were passed into it. Then it registers itself as both a MouseListener and MouseMotionListener so that it can capture all mouse events and send them to the redispatchMouseEvent( ) method. The RightClickGlassPane also overrides the paint( ) method to do nothing, ensuring that the glass pane is invisible.

The redispatchMouseEvent( ) method is the key to the right-click glass pane. It must first check for a right-click (actually the pop-up trigger, which will also handle Control-click on the Mac), and then either show the pop up at the mouse location or forward the event to the correct component. Event forwarding is the hard part.

Each mouse event contains the current mouse coordinates, along with the state of the mouse buttons and any modifier keys (such as Control or Shift). Mouse coordinates are always relative to the component being clicked. This means that a 10,10 position relative to a JButton in the middle of the screen wouldn't be the same location as 10,10 relative to another JButton lower down on the screen. In order to account for coordinate differences, redispatchMouseEvent( ) needs to convert between coordinate systems using the SwingUtilities.convertPoint( ) method:

```
private void redispatchMouseEvent(MouseEvent e, boolean repaint) {

    // if it's a pop up
    if(e.isPopupTrigger()) {
        // show the pop up and return
        popup.show(e.getComponent(), e.getX(), e.getY());
    } else {
        // since it's not a pop up we need to redispatch it.
```

```
    // get the mouse click point relative to the content pane
    Point containerPoint = SwingUtilities.convertPoint(this,
        e.getPoint(),contentPane);

    // find the component that is under this point
    Component component = SwingUtilities.getDeepestComponentAt(
        contentPane, containerPoint.x, containerPoint.y);

    // return if nothing was found
    if (component == null) {
        return;
    }

    // convert point relative to the target component
    Point componentPoint = SwingUtilities.convertPoint(
        this, e.getPoint(), component);

    // redispatch the event
    component.dispatchEvent(new
        MouseEvent(component, e.getID(),
        e.getWhen(), e.getModifiers(),
        componentPoint.x, componentPoint.y,
        e.getClickCount(), e.isPopupTrigger()));
    }
}
```

In the else statement, the current mouse position is converted to be relative
to the contentPane, which is at the root of the window. Next, the method
determines which component was clicked using the SwingUtilities.
getDeepestComponentAt( ) method, and then it converts the point to be relative to the target component. Finally, it uses a special method on Component
called dispatchEvent( ), which will rebroadcast a new mouse event to the
target component as if it were the original event. The target component will
never know the difference; it just won't ever receive right-clicks. The following main( ) method creates a sample screen with a few widgets and the custom RightClickGlassPane:

```
public static void main(String[] args) {
    // create a frame with some components in it
    JFrame frame = new JFrame("Right Click Test");
    JButton button = new JButton("this is a button");
    JTextField tf = new JTextField("this is a textfield");
    JPanel panel = new JPanel();
    panel.add(button);
    panel.add(tf);
    frame.getContentPane().add(panel);

    JPopupMenu popup = new JPopupMenu();
    popup.add(new JMenuItem("Dogs"));
    popup.add(new JMenuItem("Cats"));
    popup.add(new JMenuItem("Mass Hysteria"));
```

```
// create the right-click glass pane.
Component rc = new RightClickGlassPane(frame.getContentPane( ),popup);
// set as glasspane and make it visible
frame.setGlassPane(rc);
rc.setVisible(true);

// pack and show the frame
frame.pack( );
frame.setSize(400,200);
frame.show( );
}
```

While most of this is boilerplate, be sure to notice the call to rc.setVisible( ). This is where the glass pane is turned on. If the glass pane is not visible, then your code won't ever receive events and work its magic.

This hack only demonstrates intercepting a mouse click, but it could be used for any other type of event capturing, such as remapping one key to another, recording mouse events, blocking mouse events **[Hack #58]**, or creating completely synthetic events to fool the program.

HACK #58 Block a Window Without a Modal Dialog

Block the input in a single window during long operations without stopping your entire application.

Since the dawn of GUIs, most toolkits have had the concept of a modal dialog box. This is a small window that restricts input to itself, blocking access to the rest of the program (or entire operating system in some cases). Modal windows often produce the desired effect, but sometimes you need a window that can block itself without blocking access to the whole application. The most common use for such a window is a long running process, like rendering frames of a movie or waiting for the network to respond. In this case, you would like to let the user still interact with the rest of the application but block the one window that represents the work in progress. Swing doesn't provide a modal window like this, but since when has that stopped us?

Blocking Basics

To block a window, you could disable the components within it, but then you would need to recursively find each component and disable it manually. This is a big headache, and would make for a very ugly window (all those grayed-out components). All you really want to do is capture all input to the window and block that. Swing provides a great way to do this: the glass pane. The glass pane sits on top of all other components in a window, making it the perfect place to implement blocking behavior.

Since you want your glass pane to be transparent, it's best to start with a plain JComponent that doesn't draw anything. Example 8-3 defines a WindowBlocker class that extends JComponent and implements the MouseInputListener (a compound interface that combines the MouseListener and MouseMotionListener).

Example 8-3. Listening for mouse events

```
public class WindowBlocker extends JComponent
    implements MouseInputListener {

    public WindowBlocker( ) {
        addMouseListener(this);
        addMouseMotionListener(this);
    }

    public void mouseMoved(MouseEvent e) {
    }
    public void mouseDragged(MouseEvent e) {
    }
    public void mouseClicked(MouseEvent e) {
    }
    public void mouseEntered(MouseEvent e) {
    }
    public void mouseExited(MouseEvent e) {
    }
    public void mousePressed(MouseEvent e) {
        Toolkit.getDefaultToolkit().beep( );
    }
    public void mouseReleased(MouseEvent e) {
    }
```

So far, the code is pretty simple. The WindowBlocker catches all mouse events and does nothing, sending the events to that great bit bucket in the sky. When the user presses the mouse, the computer will beep, indicating that the window is busy. The component still won't actually receive events because it is invisible by default. When you are ready to start blocking events, you should make the component visible. That's where the block( ) method comes in:

```
    private Cursor old_cursor;
    public void block( ) {
        old_cursor = getCursor( );
        setCursor(Cursor.getPredefinedCursor(Cursor.WAIT_CURSOR));
        setVisible(true);
    }

    public void unBlock( ) {
        setCursor(old_cursor);
        setVisible(false);
    }
```

Before setting the component to visible, you should save the current mouse image and then change it to a busy cursor. The cursor will only be in effect over the component you call setCursor( ) on, so only the blocked window will get the busy signal. All other windows will still use their normal cursors. When unblock( ) is called, you can restore the cursor and hide the WindowBlocker component again.

Build a Test Process

To test the window blocker, you will need some sort of long-running process. The class in Example 8-4, LongProcess, will start a 10-second countdown when its actionPerformed( ) method is called. It will also print the current time left in a status label. Note that the call to setText( ) on the status label is inside of a SwingUtilities.invokeLater( ) method. This makes sure that setText( ) is called from the Swing event thread, avoiding any threading issues or deadlock.

Example 8-4. Filling up clock cycles

```
class LongProcess implements ActionListener, Runnable {
    JLabel status;
    WindowBlocker blocker;
    public LongProcess(JLabel status, WindowBlocker blocker) {
        this.blocker = blocker;
        this.status = status;
    }

    public void actionPerformed(ActionEvent evt) {
        blocker.block( );
        new Thread(this).start( );
    }

    public void setText(final String text) {
        SwingUtilities.invokeLater(new Runnable( ) {
            public void run( ) {
                status.setText(text);
            }
        });
    }

    public void run( ) {
        for(int i=10; i>0; i--) {
            // set the label
            final String text = "("+i+") seconds left";
            setText(text);
```

Example 8-4. Filling up clock cycles (continued)

```
            // sleep for 1 second
            try {
                Thread.currentThread( ).sleep(1000);
            } catch (Exception ex) {
            }
        }
        // set the final status string
        setText("Process Complete");
        blocker.unBlock( );
    }
}
```

Putting It All Together

With your window blocking and long-process classes ready, you can put them together in a simple program. The main( ) method in Example 8-5 creates a text area, a button, and a status label. Then it makes a WindowBlocker and installs it with frame.setGlassPane( ). The LongProcess is added as an action listener to the Start button, so when the user presses Start Processing, the process will launch and call WindowBlocker.block( ). Once the process ends, it will call WindowBlocker.unBlock( ), releasing the window.

Example 8-5. Testing the blocking window

```
public static void main(String[] args) {
    JFrame frame = new JFrame("Blocking Window");
    JTextArea jta = new JTextArea(10,40);
    JScrollPane scroll = new JScrollPane(jta);
    JButton start = new JButton("Start Processing");
    JLabel status = new JLabel("status");

    WindowBlocker blocker = new WindowBlocker( );
    frame.setGlassPane(blocker);
    start.addActionListener(new LongProcess(status,blocker));

    Container comp = frame.getContentPane( );
    comp.add("North",  start);
    comp.add("Center", scroll);
    comp.add("South",  status);

    frame.pack( );
    frame.show( );
}
```

Create a Color Eyedropper

#59   Enhance your color pickers with an eyedropper tool that grabs a color from anywhere on the screen.

Most paint tools give you an eyedropper, but I've never seen a Java program do it. Getting a screen pixel requires native access, which is usually blocked off from Java programs. Java 1.3 introduced a new method to the Robot class, getPixelColor( ), which can retrieve the color anywhere on the screen. The problem is that you don't get mouse events once the cursor leaves your JFrame. This is fine if you only want to select colors from your own application, but a color chooser needs to select from anywhere on the screen. Java 5.0 introduces new APIs for getting complete mouse events, but that doesn't help us today.

The answer to this tricky problem, of course, is to cheat! This hack makes a screenshot and then paints it into a JFrame called ColorChooserDemo, which fills the entire screen. The screenshot is indistinguishable from the real desktop except that nothing in the background updates. However, since the screenshot is only needed while the user selects a color, this should be OK. ColorChooserDemo also has a JLabel in the center of the screen, which displays the currently selected color. Once the user has finished selecting a color by releasing the mouse, the entire frame will disappear and the component that launched the chooser—usually a JButton—will get the color through setBackground( ). While it's running, ColorChooserDemo looks like Figure 8-3.

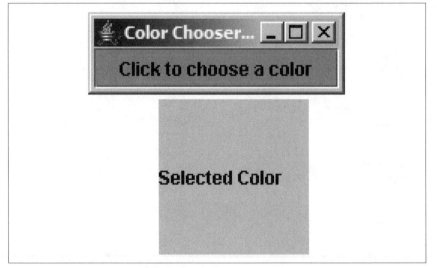

Figure 8-3. Running the ColorChooserDemo

The first step is to set up the required components. The ColorChooserDemo is a subclass of JFrame with member variables to hold the screenshot (background_image), the panel to draw the image (image_panel), the JLabel to display the current color under the cursor (label), and a few support variables. The beginnings of this class are shown in Example 8-6.

Example 8-6. Skeleton of the ColorChooserDemo class

```
public class ColorChooserDemo extends JFrame
    implements MouseListener, MouseMotionListener {

    JPanel image_panel;
    Dimension screen_size;
    JComponent comp = null;
    Image background_image = null;
    Robot robot;
    JLabel label;

    public ColorChooserDemo(JComponent comp) {
        // get the screen dimensions
        screen_size = Toolkit.getDefaultToolkit().getScreenSize();

        // set up the frame (this)
        this.addMouseListener(this);
        this.addMouseMotionListener(this);
        this.comp = comp;
        this.setUndecorated(true);
        this.setSize(screen_size.width, screen_size.height);

        // set up the panel that holds the screenshot
        image_panel = new JPanel() {
            public void paintComponent(Graphics g) {
                super.paintComponent(g);
                g.drawImage(background_image,0,0,null);
            }
        };
        image_panel.setPreferredSize(screen_size);
        this.getContentPane().add(image_panel);

        // set up the display label
        label = new JLabel("Selected Color");
        label.setOpaque(true);
        label.setSize(100,100);
        image_panel.setLayout(null);
        image_panel.add(label);
        label.setLocation((int)screen_size.getWidth()/2 - 50,
            (int)screen_size.getHeight()/2 - 50);
    }
```

In its constructor, the ColorChooserDemo accepts a JComponent to store the selected color in. Next, the code gets the current screen size from the AWT Toolkit, and then follows the usual litany of listeners and setters. Note the call to setUndecorated(true), which turns off the window controls. This adds to the illusion that the user is clicking on the real system desktop and not a screenshot.

The image_panel is a standard JPanel with the paintComponent( ) method overridden to draw the screenshot image over its background. It is also set to fill the screen with setPreferredSize(screen_size), and then is added to the frame.

Before returning, the ColorChooserDemo constructor creates a 100×100 pixel JLabel to display the current selected color. By default, the label would let its parent component (the screenshot) show through instead of filling its background with the selected color, so the code calls setOpaque(true) to make sure the background is visible. Finally, the label is moved to the middle of the screen, calculated by dividing the screen dimensions in half and subtracting half of the label size. Of course a LayoutManager would mess with the explicit coordinates set here, so image_panel's layout is set to null. This gets rid of the default layout manager, BorderLayout, and allows the absolute positioning to work.

Now that the chooser frame and its components are set up, the frame needs to make the actual screenshot. ColorChooserDemo overrides the show( ) method to make the screenshot before the frame pops up on screen. The show( ) method uses the robot.createScreenCapture( ) to capture and save the screen to the background_image variable before passing control to the superclass, as shown in the following code:

```
public void show( ) {
    try {
        // make the screenshot before showing the frame
        Rectangle rect = new Rectangle(0,0,
            (int)screen_size.getWidth( ),
            (int)screen_size.getHeight( ));
        this.robot = new Robot( );
        background_image = robot.createScreenCapture(rect);
        super.show( );
    } catch (AWTException ex) {
        System.out.println("exception creating screenshot:");
        ex.printStackTrace( );
    }
}
```

Once the ColorChooserDemo frame is visible, the user can begin selecting colors by clicking and dragging anywhere on the (now fake) screen. The mousePressed( ), mouseDragged( ), and mouseReleased( ) methods of the mouse/

mouse-motion listener implementation update the selected color on each mouse event. setSelectColor( ) does the actual update by setting the background color on both the label (which the user can see) and the component that was passed into the constructor (currently hidden behind frame):

```
// update the selected color on mouse press, dragged, and release
public void mousePressed(MouseEvent evt) {
    setSelectedColor(robot.getPixelColor(evt.getX(), evt.getY()));
}
public void mouseDragged(MouseEvent evt) {
    setSelectedColor(robot.getPixelColor(evt.getX(), evt.getY()));
}
// for released we want to hide the frame as well
public void mouseReleased(MouseEvent evt) {
    setSelectedColor(robot.getPixelColor(evt.getX(),evt.getY()));
    this.setVisible(false);
}

// update both the display label and the component that was passed in
public void setSelectedColor(Color color) {
    comp.setBackground(color);
    label.setBackground(color);
}

// no-ops for the rest of the mouse-event listener
public void mouseClicked(MouseEvent evt) { }
public void mouseEntered(MouseEvent evt) { }
public void mouseExited(MouseEvent evt) { }
public void mouseMoved(MouseEvent evt) { }
```

When the user releases the mouse, the mouseReleased( ) method will do one last color update and then hide the frame. This way, when the user is done selecting a color, the final color will be visible as the background of the launching component, as seen in Figure 8-4.

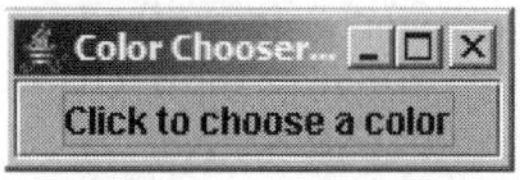

Figure 8-4. After a color is chosen

Launching the demo just requires a component to call show( ) on the ColorChooserDemo:

```
public static void main(String[] args) {
    JFrame frame = new JFrame("Color Chooser Hack");
    final JButton button = new JButton("Click to choose a color");
    button.addActionListener(new ActionListener() {
        public void actionPerformed(ActionEvent evt) {
            JFrame frame = new ColorChooserDemo(button);
            frame.show();
```

```
        }
    });

    frame.getContentPane( ).add(button);
    frame.pack( );
    frame.setVisible(true);
}
```

And that's it! Now you can add full-screen color choosing to any component without requiring native access at all. As an improvement, you could make the preview actually show a magnified view of where the cursor is instead of just the selected color.

Changing Fonts Throughout Your Application
Get a quick font face-lift, without having to write a whole Look and Feel.

With no standards documents to obey and more flexible user expectations, web designers get much more freedom with their fonts than Swing developers expect. They get to set font styles with CSS, while we're expected to just leave well enough alone. Sure, you can change fonts on a component-by-component basis with setFont( ), but it's not like you can just say "from now on, I want all JLabels to use the Cheese Deluxe Demi-Bold font." Well, OK, you could create a subclass of JLabel to set that font in its constructor, but your change wouldn't be picked up by any of JLabel's subclasses, like the default renderers for list, table, and tree cells. Fortunately, there is a much easier way than fighting with single inheritance.

Swing components get many of their defaults (e.g., fonts, icons, borders), from a Hashtable owned by the UIManager class. Actually, it is a subclass of Hashtable, called UIDefaults, which offers strongly typed methods like getFont( ), getBorder( ), getColor( ), etc., each of which takes a key object.

Now, since this is just a Hashtable, you can put stuff in just as easily as you can get it out. All you have to do is know what the key is. As it turns out, for fonts, the keys are Strings that end with a .font suffix. So, for demonstration purposes, you can iterate through the keys of the UIDefaults, and every time you find one that ends in .font, put the Font of your choice back into the UIDefaults.

Changing the Default Fonts

The goal of the ChangeAllFonts example is to change the default font of all Swing components, by changing all the appropriate keys it can find in UIDefaults. It starts by getting a font name from the command line and creating a 12-point plain Font instance.

Next, it gets the UIDefaults object as a Hashtable and gets an Enumeration of its keys. It walks the enumeration and, for every key ending in .font, it uses put( ) to replace the previous font with the user-selected font.

Finally, it creates a simple GUI with several typical JComponents and shows them in a JFrame. This short example is shown in Example 8-7.

Example 8-7. Changing default fonts via UIDefaults

```
public class ChangeAllFonts {

    final static String[] LIST_ITEMS =
    { "JList", "with", "new Font" };

    public static void main (String[] args) {
        try {
            // get user's font
            if (args.length < 1) {
                System.out.println (
                    "Usage: ChangeAllFonts font-name");
                return;
            }
            String fontName = args[0];
            Font font = new Font (fontName, Font.PLAIN, 12);

            // put this font in the defaults table for every
            // ui font resource key
            Hashtable defaults = UIManager.getDefaults( );
            Enumeration keys = defaults.keys( );
            while (keys.hasMoreElements( )) {
                Object key = keys.nextElement( );
                if ((key instanceof String) &&
                    (((String) key).endsWith(".font"))) {
                    System.out.println (key);
                    defaults.put (key, font);
                }
            }

            // now bring up a GUI to show this off
            JPanel panel = new JPanel( );
            panel.setLayout (new BoxLayout (panel, BoxLayout.Y_AXIS));
            panel.add (new JLabel ("JLabel with font " + fontName));
            panel.add (new JTextField ("JTextField with font " +
                    fontName));
            panel.add (new JButton ("JButton with font " +
                    fontName));
            JList list = new JList (LIST_ITEMS);
            JScrollPane pane =
                new JScrollPane (list,
                    ScrollPaneConstants.VERTICAL_SCROLLBAR_ALWAYS,
                    ScrollPaneConstants.HORIZONTAL_SCROLLBAR_NEVER);
            panel.add (pane);
```

Example 8-7. Changing default fonts via UIDefaults (continued)

```
                JFrame frame = new JFrame ("Changing default fonts");
                frame.setDefaultCloseOperation (WindowConstants.EXIT_ON_CLOSE);
                frame.getContentPane( ).add(panel);
                frame.pack( );
                frame.setVisible(true);

        } catch (Exception e) {
            e.printStackTrace( );
        }
    }
}
```

Fonts 'R' Us

To run the code, you specify the name of your desired font on the command line as the only argument to the class. If the font you want to use has one or more spaces in its name, you'll need to enclose the font name in quotes, as in the example:

```
cadamson% java ChangeAllFonts "Comic Sans MS"
```

This produces a GUI whose components all use the 12-point plain Comic Sans MS font, as seen in Figure 8-5.

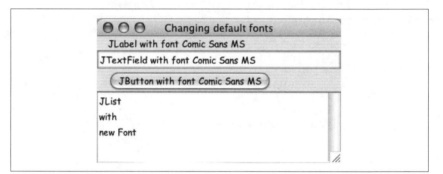

Figure 8-5. Changing default fonts for Swing widgets

You should also note the standard output when running this example, since the code prints out every .font key it finds. The output is too long to list here, but the first few items look like this:

```
CheckBox.font                      ToolBar.font
Tree.font                          ColorChooser.font
Viewport.font                      ToggleButton.font
ProgressBar.font                   Panel.font
RadioButtonMenuItem.font           TextArea.font
FormattedTextField.font
```

These are all JComponents, but they're notably lacking the "J" that starts the name of typical Swing components (Tree.font for JTree, TextArea.font for JTextArea, etc.).

Now that you know the keys for the UIDefaults table, instead of blindly changing all of them to the same font, you can customize a look by applying different fonts—or different sizes and styles of one or two base fonts—to different widgets.

Load New Fonts at Runtime

Who cares what fonts your users have? Bundle the fonts you want your application to use and load those fonts dynamically!

Using fonts with any predictability used to be a nightmare in Java. For a while, you could only depend on having access to one serif, one sans-serif, and one monospaced font, and the constants you'd use to get those fonts changed between Java 1.0 and 1.1. Fortunately, you're now free to use any font installed on the user's machine and load it by name.

Of course, not everyone has the same fonts. Even different installations of the same operating system will have different fonts available. I still use some TrueType fonts I've been toting from machine to machine for 15 years, and it's a safe bet that very few other people will have those same fonts.

This would seem to limit your Swing application to using only the fonts you know are installed with an operating system—maybe Arial and Times New Roman on Windows, Lucida Grande and Palatino on Mac OS X, etc. But it's not so. You can load font files at runtime and make them available to your Java application, even if the font isn't installed on the user's machine.

The Wonders of createFont( )

Using dynamically loaded fonts comes down to a single, critical, often overlooked AWT method in the Font class: createFont( ). This method, introduced in Java 1.3, takes two parameters: a font format (as an int), which to date has no legal value other than Font.TRUETYPE_FONT, and an InputStream.

This stream is typically a FileInputStream from a *.ttf* TrueType file, or some equivalent. By equivalent, I meant that you could presumably put the font on the network and get a stream from a URL or put the font file inside a *.jar*, find it along the classpath with ClassLoader.getResourceAsStream( ), and load from that.

Mac OS X's font suitcases—a holdover from the Classic Mac OS—aren't supported. Your fonts need to be in *.ttf* files.

FontLoadingDemo, shown in Example 8-8, offers a straightforward application of this font-loading technique. It takes the path to a *.ttf* file as its command-line argument, creates an InputStream, and creates a Font. It then derives a plain, 32-point instance of the font, and uses that to put a sample JLabel in a JFrame.

Example 8-8. Loading fonts at runtime

```
public class FontLoadingDemo {

    public static void main (String[] args) {
        try {
            // get font from path in args[0]
            if (args.length < 1) {
                System.out.println (
                    "usage: FontLoadingDemo path-to-ttf");
                return;
            }
            File f = new File (args[0]);
            FileInputStream in = new FileInputStream (f);
            Font dynamicFont =
                Font.createFont (Font.TRUETYPE_FONT, in);
            Font dynamicFont32Pt =
                dynamicFont.deriveFont (32f);

            // draw something with it
            JLabel testLabel =
                new JLabel ("Dynamically loaded font \"" +
                        dynamicFont.getName( ) + "\"");
            testLabel.setFont (dynamicFont32Pt);
            JFrame frame = new JFrame ("Font Loading Demo");
            frame.getContentPane( ).add (testLabel);
            frame.pack( );
            frame.setVisible(true);
        } catch (Exception e) {
            e.printStackTrace( );
        }
    }
}
```

Testing Font Loading

All you need to run this demo is a *.ttf* file of a TrueType font, preferably one not already installed on your system so you'll know that the demo works. There are many free and shareware fonts on the Web; I found the Marriage

Script font at *http://www.free-fonts.com/*. Once you have a *.ttf* file, run the demo like this:

```
cadamson% java FontLoadingDemo marriage_script.ttf
```

Running the demo pops up a window like the one seen in Figure 8-6.

Figure 8-6. Marriage font loaded on the fly

With this technique, and a consistent scheme for bundling your application resources (i.e., stuffing all your fonts in a JAR file, perhaps with other resources like images, sounds, and localizations), you have the freedom to use whatever fonts you like in your GUI, without worrying about what end users do or don't have installed.

H A C K #62 Build a Colorful Vector-Based Button

Build a resolution-independent OS X-style button using scalable graphics code.

The button in this hack is *resolution independent*, meaning that it can resize and rescale automatically as the user's windows and display change, stretching and tiling the graphics to fill the new space. The button doesn't depend on being any particular size to look good. As higher-quality and higher-resolution monitors become more common, users will start to expect attractive interfaces that scale and reflow with their increasingly expansive displays. This hack shows how to create an attractive `JButton` that will scale with both size and resolution, opening the door for a completely vector-drawn Swing Look and Feel.

Use Scaling to Your Advantage

Since this button must scale with the size of the screen, you can use a variable called `scale`. Every piece of drawing code for this button is done relative to `scale`'s value. If the scale value changes, the entire button will change accordingly. The scale value itself is based on the current font size of the component. If the component's font is resized (due to a DPI change, for example), then the scale value will change accordingly, resizing the entire button. With a scale value in place, this hack is simply a matter of recreating the Aqua button look with Java2D calls. The goal is a button that looks like Figure 8-7.

Figure 8-7. A green vector JButton

Not a simple task, but it's not impossible either. All the work is done in
Example 8-9.

Example 8-9. Creating liquid buttons

```
public class VectorButton extends JButton implements MouseListener {
    public VectorButton() {
        this.addMouseListener(this);
    }

    public Dimension getPreferredSize() {
        String text = getText();
        FontMetrics fm = this.getFontMetrics(getFont());
        float scale = (50f/30f)*this.getFont().getSize2D();
        int w = fm.stringWidth(text);
        w += (int)(scale*1.4f);
        int h = fm.getHeight();
        h += (int)(scale*.3f);
        return new Dimension(w,h);
    }

    public void paintComponent(Graphics g) {
        Graphics2D g2 = (Graphics2D)g;
        g2.setRenderingHint(RenderingHints.KEY_ANTIALIASING,
            RenderingHints.VALUE_ANTIALIAS_ON);
        g2.setColor(this.getBackground());
        g2.fillRect(0,0,this.getWidth(),this.getHeight());

        float scale = (50f/30f)*this.getFont().getSize2D();

        drawLiquidButton(this.getForeground(),
            this.getWidth(), this.getHeight(),
            getText(), scale,
            g2);
    }
}
```

The previous code is the essence of VectorButton. It is just a subclass of
JButton, overriding getPreferredSize() and paintComponent() and adding a
mouse listener implementation.

A custom version of getPreferredSize( ) is required because, by default, a JButton will size itself based on the current Look and Feel. For this hack, we want the button sized based on the scale value. You can see that scale is calculated by multiplying the current font size against a scaling factor. I chose the factor 50/30 by testing different values and simply seeing what looked right. The actual factor doesn't matter as long as you're consistent, which is why scale is calculated the same way for both getPreferredSize( ) and paintComponent( ). The paintComponent( ) method just turns on anti-aliasing, fills the background, calculates scale, and then calls drawLiquidButton( ) where the real work is done.

drawLiquidButton( ) is a wrapper for a series of custom drawing functions that create each part of the liquid button. In order to emulate the Aqua look, you'll need to use a series of rounded rectangles and gradient fills.

> To make the code more understandable, I broke it up into
> functions for the shadow, body, text, highlight, and border.

As you go through the code, you will notice that scale is multiplied by a small adjustment value like 0.1f or 0.04f. These numbers were chosen largely through trial and error, just by trying different values to see what looked good. Finding those values took a long time but really added to the quality of the finished button. If you decide to build your own vector widget, it will really pay to spend the time tweaking your drawing, too. Here's the method implementation:

```
protected void drawLiquidButton(Color base,
            int width, int height,
            String text, float scale,
            Graphics2D g2) {

    // calculate inset
    int inset = (int)(scale*0.04f);
    int w = width - inset*2 - 1;
    int h = height - (int)(scale*0.1f) - 1;

    g2.translate(inset,0);
    drawDropShadow(w,h,scale,g2);

    if(pressed) {
        g2.translate(0, 0.04f*scale);
    }
```

```
drawButtonBody(w,h,scale,base,g2);
drawText(w,h,scale,text,g2);
drawHighlight(w,h,scale,base,g2);
drawBorder(w,h,scale,g2);

if(pressed) {
    g2.translate(0, 0.04f*scale);
}
g2.translate(-inset,0);
}
```

The inset value used represents the space between the start of the button and the upper left of the real JButton boundaries. Without an inset, the drawn button would be too close to the component borders, and the shadow would get cut off. The test for if(pressed) translates everything but the shadow just a tiny bit down. This will create the pressed-in effect common to buttons in most Look and Feels.

Next comes the different drawing functions. The shadow is created by overlapping two rounded rectangles with different shades of gray and alpha. Using an alpha value allows the shadows to blend well:

```
protected void drawDropShadow(int w, int h,
        float scale, Graphics2D g2) {
    g2.setColor(new Color(0,0,0,50));
    fillRoundRect(g2,
        (-.04f)*scale,
        (.02f)*scale,
        w+.08f*scale, h+0.08f*scale,
        scale*1.04f, scale*1.04f);
    g2.setColor(new Color(0,0,0,100));
    fillRoundRect(g2,0,0.06f*scale,w,h,scale,scale);
}
```

The body of the button is a gradient that goes from top to bottom. Since the developer could change the color of the button, the gradient is calculated from darker and lighter versions of the base color. The body has two parts. The outer round rectangle forms the bulk of the button, while the inner round rectangle is smaller and lighter, creating a subtle glowing effect:

```
protected void drawButtonBody(int w, int h, float scale,
        Color base, Graphics2D g2) {

    Color grad_top = base.brighter();
    Color grad_bot = base.darker();
    GradientPaint bg = new GradientPaint(
        new Point(0,0), grad_top,
        new Point(0,h), grad_bot);
    g2.setPaint(bg);
```

```
    this.fillRoundRect(g2,
        (0)*scale,
        (0)*scale,
        w,h,1*scale,1*scale);

    // draw the inner color
    Color inner = base.brighter();
    inner = alphaColor(inner,75);
    g2.setColor(inner);
    this.fillRoundRect(g2,
        scale*(.4f),
        scale*(.4f),
        w-scale*.8f, h-scale*.5f,
        scale*.6f,scale*.4f);
}

// generate the alpha version of the specified color
protected static Color alphaColor(Color color, int alpha) {
    return new Color(color.getRed(), color.getGreen(),
        color.getBlue(), alpha);
}
```

Finally, you get to handle the actual drawing of the text. The text position is calculated by centering the width and height of the text based on the current font metrics. The text is actually drawn twice: first with a translucent gray offset by a few pixels, and then again in black. This creates a very slight drop shadow on the text itself, making it appear raised above the button surface:

```
protected void drawText(int w, int h, float scale,
        String text, Graphics2D g2) {

    // calculate the width and height
    int fw = g2.getFontMetrics().stringWidth(text);
    int fh = g2.getFontMetrics().getAscent() -
        g2.getFontMetrics().getDescent();
    int textx = (w-fw)/2;
    int texty = h/2 + fh/2;

    // draw the text
    g2.setColor(new Color(0,0,0,70));
    g2.drawString(text,(int)((float)textx+scale*(0.04f)),
        (int)((float)texty + scale*(0.04f)));
    g2.setColor(Color.black);
    g2.drawString(text, textx, texty);
}
```

The highlight is another set of round rectangles, this time going from mostly opaque to completely transparent. Since they are drawn after the text, the highlight will appear to float above the button, giving it a glossy sheen. Finally, a black border is drawn around the entire button in drawBorder().

```
protected void drawHighlight(int w, int h, float scale,
        Color base, Graphics2D g2) {

    // create the highlight
    GradientPaint highlight = new GradientPaint(
        new Point2D.Float(scale*0.2f,scale*0.2f),
        new Color(255,255,255,175),
        new Point2D.Float(scale*0.2f,scale*0.55f),
        new Color(255,255,255,0)
    );
    g2.setPaint(highlight);
    this.fillRoundRect(g2, scale*0.2f, scale*0.1f,
        w-scale*0.4f, scale*0.4f, scale*0.8f, scale*0.4f);
    this.drawRoundRect(g2, scale*0.2f, scale*0.1f,
        w-scale*0.4f, scale*0.4f, scale*0.8f, scale*0.4f);
}

protected void drawBorder(int w, int h,
        float scale, Graphics2D g2) {

    // draw the border
    g2.setColor(new Color(0,0,0,150));
    this.drawRoundRect(g2,
        scale*(0f),
        scale*(0f),
        w,h,scale,scale);
}
```

You may have noticed in the code some calls to fillRoundRect( ) instead of Graphics2D.fillRoundRect( ). All of this code deals with floats, and the Graphics2D version of the round rectangle methods only take ints. Rather than fill the code with a million (int) casts, it's just easier to perform a few casts in the fillRoundRect( ) and drawRoundRect( ) utility methods:

```
// float version of fill round rect
protected static void fillRoundRect(Graphics2D g2,
            float x, float y,
            float w, float h,
            float ax, float ay) {

    g2.fillRoundRect(
        (int)x, (int)y,
        (int)w, (int)h,
        (int)ax, (int)ay
    );
}

// float version of draw round rect
protected static void drawRoundRect(Graphics2D g2,
            float x, float y,
            float w, float h,
            float ax, float ay) {
```

```
g2.drawRoundRect(
    (int)x, (int)y,
    (int)w, (int)h,
    (int)ax, (int)ay
);
}
```

Finally, you may have noticed the pressed boolean in drawLiquidButton( ). JButton provides a way of knowing when the button has been selected, but there is no way to know when it is pressed or released during the clicking process. Most applications have no need for this information, but because this hack involves rendering changes, you'll need to know the pressed state in order to draw the button properly. Since JButton doesn't tell you the current state, you have to detect it with a mouse listener that looks for press and release events:

```
/* mouse listener implementation */
protected boolean pressed = false;
public void mouseExited(MouseEvent evt) { }
public void mouseEntered(MouseEvent evt) { }
public void mouseClicked(MouseEvent evt) { }
public void mouseReleased(MouseEvent evt) {
    pressed = false;
}
public void mousePressed(MouseEvent evt) {
    pressed = true;
}
```

Hacking the Hack

The VectorButton takes an awful lot of drawing code. This isn't so much because it scales, but simply because recreating the work of Apple's talented graphic designers with Swing code is difficult. One possible improvement would be to use SVG files instead of direct Java2D code. This would let you develop the actual look of the button in a graphics program instead of the slow code/compile/run cycle we are all used to as programmers. It would also let you pass the work on to a real graphic designer while you focus on speed and functionality.

VectorButton shows the potential of vector-based interfaces, but it's just the tip of the iceberg. Imagine if you had an entire Look and Feel based on vectors, where all the buttons scaled according to the font size. Then you could change the font size to scale the entire application—while it's running! You could even do proper DPI calculations based on the physical size and shape of the user's screen to make your application look identical on any device, scaling from PDAs all the way up to high resolution HDTVs.

Add a Third Dimension to Swing

User interfaces have stuck to 2D drawing for many years. Today, Swing and Java3D give you a chance to go one step further and add 3D widgets to your UI.

Have you ever wondered how to add nice 3D components into your Swing applications? Java3D is a free API provided by Sun Microsystems for Linux and Windows, and by Apple for Mac OS X, that lets you create 3D scenes. Although well documented, Java3D seems impossible to use with Swing—at least at first glance.

The Problems with Java3D

Imagine you decided to create a new, astonishing application called AmazonPick that would let the user search for books on the Amazon.com store. Your eye-candy user interface would even display the currently selected book as a 3D object; whenever the user selects another book, the 3D object would flip to show the new cover on its opposite side. Figure 8-8 shows how the application should look.

Figure 8-8. AmazonPick shows books as full 3D objects

Unfortunately, you won't be able to obtain these results without a little imagination. For instance, take a close look at Figure 8-8 and notice the gradient background of the window. Displaying such a background is very easy with Swing and the opaque properties of Swing components, as seen in the rather simple class in Example 8-10.

Example 8-10. A demo program for 3D components

```
public BooksDemo( )
{
  super("AmazonPick");

  JButton cover1 = UIHelper.createButton("", "cover1_small_button", true);
  JButton cover2 = UIHelper.createButton("", "cover2_small_button", true);
  JButton cover3 = UIHelper.createButton("", "cover3_small_button", true);

  JPanel buttons = new JPanel( );
  buttons.add(cover1);
  buttons.add(cover2);
  buttons.add(cover3);
  buttons.setOpaque(false);

  setContentPane(new GradientPanel( ));
  getContentPane( ).setLayout(new BorderLayout( ));
  getContentPane( ).add(buttons, BorderLayout.SOUTH);

  pack( );
  setResizable(false);
  setDefaultCloseOperation(EXIT_ON_CLOSE);

  UIHelper.centerOnScreen(this);
}
```

This code creates three buttons, each containing a picture of a book loaded by the utility class UIHelper, and then puts them in a JPanel. This panel is itself added to the content pane of the window, at the south side. With the help of the setContentPane( ) method, the default content pane is replaced by a new panel—an instance of GradientPanel—that is capable of drawing a nice gradient. To make sure the gradient remains visible in the buttons panel, you need to make the panel transparent. This can be achieved easily by calling setOpaque(false), which will prevent the component—in our case, the panel—from drawing its background, letting underlying components shine through.

Now, we have to take a slight diversion into AWT and Swing vagaries. With J2SE, you can use two different graphical toolkits to create an application: AWT and Swing. The main difference between those two is that AWT widgets are heavyweight whereas Swing widgets are lightweight. These names come from the very nature of these components. Whatever platform you are running your application on, AWT widgets are drawn using the underlying OS native toolkit. Swing, on the contrary, is completely decoupled from the OS and all the painting is done by Java itself. As a result, AWT widgets are the least common denominator between the various operating systems supported by Java. This also means that advanced features like transparency are pure fantasy with AWT: Swing lets you create transparent components very easily, but AWT does not.

The bad news is that Java3D offers an AWT component only, Canvas3D, to display a 3D scene. So you'll have to mix some Swing and AWT code. Here is how you can add such a component in the Swing UI:

```
Canvas3D c3d = new Canvas3D(SimpleUniverse.getPreferredConfiguration( ));
c3d.setSize(CANVAS3D_WIDTH, CANVAS3D_HEIGHT);
getContentPane( ).add(centerPanel, BorderLayout.CENTER);
createScene( );
```

createScene( ) is responsible for building the 3D scene the Canvas3D will display. Running this code will produce a rather ugly result, as shown in Figure 8-9.

Figure 8-9. A Canvas3D cannot be made transparent

As you can see, you end up with a black background in the Canva3D. Because the only way to get rid of a component's background is to call setOpaque(false)—which is defined by JComponent and thus isn't available to AWT components—you are stuck with this ugly background. Indeed, as a lightweight component, the canvas cannot be made transparent. Things get even worse when you try to add a menu bar to the application because of the order in which components are painted: lightweight first, heavyweight next. Figure 8-10 shows an example of what happens when a pop-up menu is drawn by Swing. Because it is a lightweight component, it is drawn before Canvas3D, when it should be drawn after the canvas.

Figure 8-10. Lightweight components are drawn behind heavyweight components

Thankfully, this new problem (it's all AWT's fault!) was so annoying that the Swing team decided to add a workaround for it. You can simply force all pop-up menus of your applications to be created as heavyweight components instead of lightweight components. A single line of code is enough to fix the problem:

```
JPopupMenu.setDefaultLightWeightPopupEnabled(false);
```

If you invoke this method before you create the first JMenu or JPopupMenu, you ensure your menus will be drawn on top of heavyweight components. So, this takes care of one issue, but you still need to deal with the black background problem.

Faking Transparency

Because you cannot change the opacity of the Canvas3D, you are left with only two possible solutions. The first is to get rid of Swing, go back to AWT, and offer a crappy interface to the users. Because this doesn't seem like too great an option, we'll just have to fake transparency.

A Java3D scene is represented as a graph in which every node is an object or a group of objects. A close look at the package com.sun.j3d.utils.geometry reveals the existence of the Background class, which you can use to change the background of the 3D scene. For instance, you can create an Alpine scene just by adding a background with a photo of the Alps as its texture. Therefore, to fake transparency, you just have to use the window's content panel as texture for a new Background object that you then add to the scene graph. This is how AmazonPick creates the Java3D scene and adds a special background:

```
public void createScene( )
{
    BranchGroup objRoot = new BranchGroup( );
    objRoot.addChild(createBackground( ));
    // creates the whole scene
}
```

In Java3D, the scene is an instance of BranchGroup. By adding the Background created by the method createBackground( ) as a child of the scene node, you can set the background of the scene. The background itself is created like this:

```
protected Background createBackground( )
{
    BufferedImage image;
    image = new BufferedImage(c3d.getParent().getWidth( ),
                              c3d.getParent().getHeight( ),
                              BufferedImage.TYPE_INT_RGB);
    getContentPane().paint(image.getGraphics( ));

    BufferedImage subImage;
    subImage = new BufferedImage(CANVAS3D_WIDTH,
                                 CANVAS3D_HEIGHT,
                                 BufferedImage.TYPE_INT_RGB);
    Graphics2D subGraphics = (Graphics2D) subImage.getGraphics( );
    subGraphics.drawImage(image, null, -c3d.getX( ), -c3d.getY( ));

    ImageComponent2D backImage;
    backImage = new ImageComponent2D(ImageComponent2D.FORMAT_RGB,
                                     subImage)
    Background bg = new Background(backImage);
    BoundingSphere bounds = new BoundingSphere( );
    bounds.setRadius(100.0);
    bg.setApplicationBounds(bounds);

    return bg;
}
```

The texture is created in two steps. The first is to create a BufferedImage called image on which you paint the content panel of the window. Notice that the picture has the same dimensions as the content panel. Calling the paint( ) method of the component you want to see through the Java3D scene is less efficient than taking a screen capture with the help of java.awt.Robot; however, it is a lot easier because it works even when the Canvas3D has already been added to the window. This allows, for instance, changing the texture when the window is resized and the gradient changes due to the new dimensions.

Once the content panel has been fully drawn in image, you must clip it to retrieve the exact part covered by the Canvas3D. This is done with another BufferedImage called subImage. This new picture has the same dimensions as the 3D scene. The second step is to draw image on subImage (without forgetting to change the origin of the drawing when you call drawImage( )). When the two last parameters of this method are both 0, the image is drawn on the target surface with its top-left corner at the target's top-left corner. With the coordinates $-$c3d.getX( ) and $-$c3d.getY( ), the pixel of image drawn at the top-left corner of subImage is the pixel where the Canvas3D is located on screen. This ensures the code paints the exact part of the content panel that lies behind the 3D scene.

Then, a Background object is created with subImage as a texture. To achieve this, you need to create an ImageComponent2D from the BufferedImage—and don't forget to make the pixel formats compatible! Since subImage has its pixels stored as RGB integers, you must do the same for ImageComponent2D. A bounding sphere is finally attached to the background. Java3D uses this sphere to know where the background object needs to be rendered and where it should not be rendered. In this case, the background will appear within a sphere of a radius of 100 units. This value is large enough to prevent any rendering problem. Figure 8-11 shows the final result, with a "transparent" 3D scene and no bugginess with pop-up menus.

—Romain Guy

Turn the Spotlight on Swing

HACK #64

Users often get lost when using applications, as if they were in total darkness. Why don't you turn on a spotlight to show them the way?

Most applications involve a fair amount of data manipulation. The user creates, edits, deletes, and moves around data items. When the amount of data becomes important, it is vital for the user to be able to search for items easily. Yet, search result displays are often irritatingly complicated, and the results are a pain to browse through. This hack describes how to draw a user's attention to only the parts of the UI you want him to look at.

Figure 8-11. All the problems provoked by mixing Java3D and Swing have been solved

The Metaphor

If you have ever been to a comic show, to the theatre, or to the circus, you've probably noticed how spotlights are used to move your focus to a particular location on the stage. A search operation can be compared to a theatre stage, where actors have been replaced by search results. You just need to get the user to focus on the right location.

Take a look at an example application, shown in Figure 8-12, which displays a predefined set of books and lets you search for one or more of them by entering a search query in the text field at the bottom of the window.

Since the application is just a demo, you can only enter one of the following queries: *books, sci-fi, adams,* and *pratchett*. Each query, when validated by the Enter key, will find the related books and spotlight them, as shown in Figure 8-13.

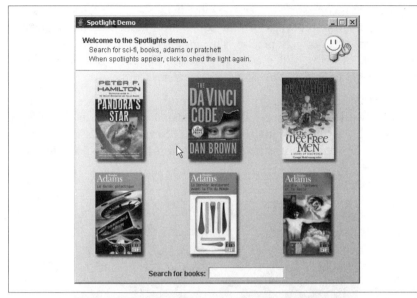

Figure 8-12. The bookshelf application must let the user search for books

Figure 8-13. Searching for "sci-fi" highlights Science Fiction books

You can even go one step further: the more light you shed, the less darkness there is. For instance, when several books are found, it is likely that the search query was not very precise. This means the user will be more interested in lots of items. When the query yields only a few results, it is likely that the user wants to see only a few specific items.

As you create several spotlights—one per result—the interface is less darkened than with only one spotlight. If you take a close look at Figure 8-13, you'll be able to perceive the other books. Nevertheless, a single search result will prevent the user from seeing the other books, as shown in Figure 8-14.

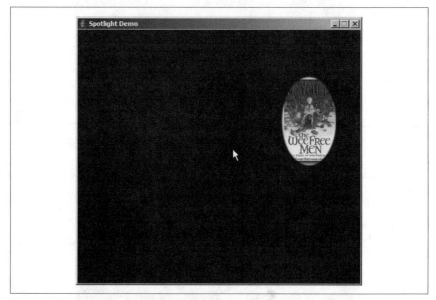

Figure 8-14. With only one spotlight, it is almost impossible to see the other books

Add the Spotlight

The implementation of spotlights for Swing is divided into two classes, SpotlightPanel and Spotlight. The first class is a glass pane that needs to be set up on a frame, and the second defines the location and the shape of a spotlight. Here is an example of how to use spotlights:

```
SpotlightPanel  glassPane = new SpotlightPanel( );
setGlassPane(glassPane);
Spotlight s1 = glassPane.addSpotlight(0, 0, 25, 50);
Spotlight s2 = glassPane.addSpotlight(100, 100, 30);
```

Here, you create two spotlights: s1 and s2. The first is an ellipse 25-pixels wide, 50-pixels high, and located at the top-left corner of the frame; the second is a circle with a radius of 30 pixels and located 100 pixels away from the top and the left of the frame's border. Each spotlight is implemented as an ellipse with the class Ellipse2D.Double, as shown in Example 8-11.

Example 8-11. Representing a spotlight with an Ellipse2D

```
public class Spotlight
{
  protected Ellipse2D.Double spot;
  protected Rectangle2D.Double bounds;

  public Spotlight(int x, int y, int w, int h)
  {
      this.spot = new Ellipse2D.Double(x, y, w, h);
  }

  public Ellipse2D getSpot( )
  {
      return spot;
  }

  public double getArea( )
  {
      return Math.PI * spot.getWidth() * spot.getHeight() / 4.0;
  }
}
```

As you can see in the code, the Spotlight class is fairly simple and contains only two public methods. The first one, getSpot( ), returns the Ellipse2D instance used to draw the spotlight. It can also be used to dynamically change the location and the size of the spotlight. Once you've installed a few spotlights, you will be able to get Ellipse2D to animate them. By moving them around, shrinking them, or growing them, you can create stunning effects. The second method of this class, getArea( ), is used by SpotlightPanel to define the amount of darkness according to the total area occupied by the spotlights on the window. Thus, if you have enough spotlights to cover 80% of the window with light, SpotlightPanel will use a darkness of 20%. In short, getArea( ) computes the geometrical area of the spotlight's ellipse.

The SpotlightPanel panel class (shown in Example 8-12) only needs a few methods as well. You must be able to create spotlights, to remove a particular spotlight, to remove all spotlights, and to paint spotlights on the screen. You also need two constructors. If you look at the previous figures, you should see that the spotlights' borders are blurred to get a nicer rendering.

Unfortunately, the blurring method used in the painting algorithm is very slow and prevents smooth animation of the spotlights. To account for this, you need a special constructor to instruct the panel to draw blurred borders, along with a constructor that leaves blurring at its default (*on* in this class, although you may want to leave it *off* normally). When you need still spotlights, activate the blur to get a nicer result. On the contrary, when you want to animate the spotlights, deactivate the blur to get full-speed animations.

Example 8-12. Constructors of the SpotlightPanel class

```
public class SpotlightPanel extends JComponent implements MouseListener
{
  protected boolean blur;
  protected List spotlights;
  protected ConvolveOp blurOp;
  protected RenderingHints hints;

  public SpotlightPanel( )
  {
    this(true);
  }

  public SpotlightPanel(boolean blur)
  {
    this.blur = blur;
    spotlights = new ArrayList( );
    blurOp = new ConvolveOp(getBlurKernel(3), ConvolveOp.EDGE_NO_OP, null);
    hints = new RenderingHints(RenderingHints.KEY_RENDERING,
                        RenderingHints.VALUE_RENDER_QUALITY);
    hints.put(RenderingHints.KEY_ANTIALIASING,
            RenderingHints.VALUE_ANTIALIAS_ON);
    hints.put(RenderingHints.KEY_FRACTIONALMETRICS,
            RenderingHints.VALUE_FRACTIONALMETRICS_ON);
  }

  // other methods omitted
}
```

The default constructor enables the blur. You can use the second constructor and pass it false to deactivate this option. The rendering of the blur effect is done with the help of a ConvolveOp. You learned about the inner workings of a blur operation when you blurred disabled components **[Hack #9]**. The constructor also creates an instance of ArrayList in which all the spotlights are stored:

```
public Spotlight addSpotlight(int x, int y, int w, int h)
{
  if (spotlights.size( ) == 0)
  {
```

```
        setVisible(true);
        addMouseListener(this);
    }

    Spotlight spot = new Spotlight(x, y, w, h);
    spotlights.add(spot);
    return spot;
}
```

When a new spotlight is added, the panel is made visible immediately, and a new mouse listener is registered on the glass pane. This mouse listener simply waits for a mouseClicked( ) event to clear the spotlights and hide the glass pane. This feature is necessary to let the user decide when she wants to get back to the application and hide the search results. The other methods related to spotlight management are removeSpotlight(Spotlight s) and clearSpotlights( ). Both remove the mouse listener and hide the glass pane when all the spotlights have been removed.

The most important work is done in the paintSpotlights( ) method, called by the paintComponent( ) method:

```
protected void paintSpotlights(Graphics g)
{
  if (spotlights.size( ) > 0)
  {
    int width = getWidth( );
    int height = getHeight( );

    double screenArea = width * height;
    double spotsArea = 0.0;

    Rectangle2D screen = new Rectangle2D.Double(0, 0, width, height);
    Area mask = new Area(screen);

    for (int i = 0; i < spotlights.size( ); i++)
    {
      Spotlight spot = (Spotlight) spotlights.get(i);
      spotsArea += spot.getArea( );
      mask.subtract(new Area(spot.getSpot( )));
    }

    Graphics2D g2 = (Graphics2D) g;
    Color shieldColor = new Color(0.0f, 0.0f, 0.0f, 1.0f - (float)
(spotsArea / screenArea));

    if (blur)
    {
      BufferedImage buffer = new BufferedImage(width, height,
        BufferedImage.TYPE_INT_ARGB);
      Graphics2D g2buffer = (Graphics2D) buffer.createGraphics( );
```

```
      g2buffer.setRenderingHints(hints);
      g2buffer.setColor(shieldColor);
      g2buffer.fill(mask);

      g2.drawImage(buffer, blurOp, 0, 0);
    } else {
      g2.setRenderingHints(hints);
      g2.setColor(shieldColor);
      g2.fill(mask);
    }
  }
}
```

The very first step is to compute the area of the glass pane and the total area occupied by the spotlights. When the spotlights list is browsed to compute the area, a particular shape is created. An Area is a Java2D shape that encloses another shape, and on which you can then perform geometrical boolean operations like subtracting or merging shapes. In this example, spotlights can be seen as ellipsoidal holes in a black rectangle. Therefore, you first create an Area, called mask, with a Rectangle2D the size of the glass pane and subtract each spotlight to this shape. Using an Area has many advantages, the more interesting being the possibility to overlap the spotlights, as shown in Figure 8-15.

Figure 8-15. By subtracting ellipses to a rectangle, you can easily overlap the spotlights

The next step is to draw the shape containing the spotlights. Before doing that, though, you need to compute the opacity of mask. When you create a new Color instance, you can define the opacity as a number between 0.0 (fully transparent), and 1.0 (fully opaque). To compute the required opacity, the program first divides the area of the spotlights by the total area. Thereby, if spotlights occupy 20% of the total area, you obtain the value 0.2. Subtract this from 1.0 to compute the final opacity. In this example, the opacity would be 0.8, or 80%.

The final step of the rendering depends on whether blurring is activated. When blurring is off, the mask is simply filled with shieldColor. Note that the rendering hints defined in the constructor are used at this moment to draw anti-aliased shapes. If blurring is activated, an extra step is required. Instead of drawing the spotlights directly onto the glass pane's graphics surface, an offscreen buffer is created, with the same size as the panel itself. After having drawn mask on this offscreen buffer, the resulting picture is drawn onto the panel's graphics surface. All the magic happens when you call the drawImage( ) method with a ConvolveOp as the second parameter. The method applies our blur filter on the picture while drawing it.

—Romain Guy

Drag-and-Drop
Hacks 65–69

Several years ago, the Swing team introduced a pair of APIs for data transfer: java.awt.datatransfer and java.awt.dnd (Drag and Drop). The former abstracts the concept of data exchange to and from your application (participating with either Java or native applications) and provides clipboard-based copy-and-paste functionality. The latter particularizes these abstractions to the specifics of drag-and-drop behavior. While many developers use these APIs for working with unstyled clipboard text only, you can do much more. Both Drag and Drop events and the clipboard support images, URLs, Files, and even custom Java objects.

HACK #65 Drag-and-Drop with Files

Drag files from your application directly to the desktop, complete with translucent icons.

This hack shows you how to go much further than mere clipboard access by digging into the lower levels of the Drag and Drop APIs and building a program that can save files directly to the desktop via dragging, complete with proper file icons and drag feedback.

When you use an editor to write a large document, you often save it to a particular location on your filesystem—in a *Projects* folder perhaps. This is because you will keep the file around for a long time, so you want to store it for later use. Small documents, however, are often created for transient reasons. I often write a few paragraphs and then immediately post it to a weblog or attach it to an email. Some applications (particularly those on Mac OS X) let you save something quickly by dragging a small marker into another application or the desktop. The marker represents the file and lets you quickly move the entire file into another context (a blog editor, for example) without thinking about where to save the file (and trying to remember where you stashed it 10 minutes later).

Since drag-to-save behavior is not a standard part of the Java platform, you will have to build it from scratch using the Drag and Drop APIs. First, you will need a class that can trigger the drop action. The plan is to detect the gesture, create a temp file to be saved, and then start the real drag with the appropriate cursor and user feedback. Here's a starting point:

```
class FileDragGestureListener extends DragSourceAdapter
    implements DragGestureListener {
    JTextArea text;
    Cursor cursor;
    public FileDragGestureListener(JTextArea text) {
        this.text = text;
    }
}
```

The FileDragGestureListener implements DragGestureListener and extends the DragSourceAdapter. Swing sends all drag events to a DragSource listener.

> Extending the DragSourceAdapter, instead of implementing DragSource directly, lets your class avoid implementing all of the required methods. DragSourceAdapter gives you empty, no-op implementations of all the methods in DragSource.

FileDragGestureListener accepts a component to grab the text from. Any provider of text would work, but I chose a JTextArea because it's the most likely to be used in a text editor.

All operating systems define a *drag gesture*, which usually means something like "click and drag for more than 10 pixels," though it varies from platform to platform. Swing will detect the drag gesture and send an event to a DragGestureListener, which is why FileDragGestureListener also implements that interface. DragGestureListener defines one method: dragGestureRecognized( ). This is where the real work of this hack is done:

```
public void dragGestureRecognized(DragGestureEvent evt) {
    try {

        // generate the temp file
        File proxy_temp = File.createTempFile("tempdir",".dir",null);
        File temp = new File(proxy_temp.getParent(),"myfile.txt");
        FileOutputStream out = new FileOutputStream(temp);
        out.write(text.getText().getBytes());
        out.close();
```

The implementation of dragGestureRecognized( ) starts by creating a temp file to store the text. Actually, first it creates a fake temp file, proxy_temp, using the File.createTempFile( ) method. Then it creates the real temp file in the same directory and writes the text data to the file. You could skip the proxy_temp part, but then if the user drags to the desktop, he will end up with a filename like *myfile158392.txt* instead of *myfile.txt*. Using the proxy file lets you create a file with a useful name, while still keeping the file in the default temp directory.

Now that the file is done, it's time to create an icon:

```
// get the right icon
FileSystemView fsv = FileSystemView.getFileSystemView( );
Icon icn = fsv.getSystemIcon(temp);

Toolkit tk = Toolkit.getDefaultToolkit( );
Dimension dim = tk.getBestCursorSize(
    icn.getIconWidth(),icn.getIconHeight( ));
BufferedImage buff = new BufferedImage(dim.width,dim.height,
                        BufferedImage.TYPE_INT_ARGB);
icn.paintIcon(text,buff.getGraphics( ),0,0);
```

In most operating systems, each type of file has a different icon, such as a little piece of paper for a text file or musical notes for MP3 files. You could bundle such icons with your program, but then they wouldn't look right on all operating systems. FileSystemView provides a platform-independent way to get the appropriate icon for any file type with the getSystemIcon( ) method.

Once you have the icon, you just need the underlying image. You could cast the icon to an ImageIcon because most platforms use those—but the odd platform here or there might not. It's much safer to draw the icon into a new buffered image. Drawing into a new image also lets you convert the icon to the right cursor size without resizing it. Without this step, the operating system might resize the image on its own, resulting in a messy drag icon that looks horrible. Note the BufferedImage is created with TYPE_INT_ARGB. This preserves any transparency that may be in the native system icons (e.g., on Mac OS X).

With the file and image in place, it's time to start the drag:

```
// set up drag image
if(DragSource.isDragImageSupported( )) {
    evt.startDrag(DragSource.DefaultCopyDrop, buff,
            new Point(0,0),
            new TextFileTransferable(temp),
            this);
} else {
    cursor = tk.createCustomCursor(buff,new Point(0,0),"billybob");
    evt.startDrag(cursor, null, new Point(0,0),
            new TextFileTransferable(temp),
            this);
}

// end the try/catch block and handle exceptions
```

Some operating systems support the idea of a *drag image*. This is a small image underneath the cursor representing what is being dragged. For OS X, this is usually a translucent version of the file icon. Windows doesn't support drag images, so you can just make the cursor itself be the file icon. That's not quite as nice, but it gives the user the same effect. In the previous code, DragSource.isDragImageSupported( ) lets you know which way to go. If drag images are supported, then it starts a new drag with evt.startDrag( ), passing in the default copy cursor, the drag image, the cursor hotspot on the drag image, a Transferable for the temp file (more on this later), and a DragSource. FileDragGestureListener just passes in this because it also extends the DragSourceAdapter. If drag images are not supported, then the code creates a custom cursor using the icon and starts the drag using the new cursor.

Once the drag is started, Swing will provide you with callbacks each time the user moves the cursor and enters or exits an area where the file could be dropped. To provide feedback about whether a file can be dropped over the current location, you should override the dragEnter( ) and dragExit( ) methods in DragSourceAdapter to switch the cursor and reflect the current drop target:

```
public void dragEnter(DragSourceDragEvent evt) {
    DragSourceContext ctx = evt.getDragSourceContext( );
    ctx.setCursor(cursor);
}

public void dragExit(DragSourceEvent evt) {
    DragSourceContext ctx = evt.getDragSourceContext( );
    ctx.setCursor(DragSource.DefaultCopyNoDrop);
}
```

Earlier, I mentioned the TextFileTransferable class. The Drag and Drop APIs, along with the clipboard, define something known as a Transferable. This is a wrapper around some data that describes the flavor of the data and provides access to the data itself. You can think of a flavor as a MIME type. Thus, a transferable for images would support the DataFlavor.imageFlavor flavor, and a text transferable would support the stringFlavor. You can create your own flavors, too, but it's always better to use the standard ones if you can.

The TextFileTransferable (in Example 9-1) holds a single text file and can transfer it using the javaFileListFlavor, which represents a java.util.List containing File objects.

Example 9-1. Building a temporary file holder

```
class TextFileTransferable implements Transferable {
    File temp;

    public TextFileTransferable(File temp) throws IOException {
        this.temp = temp;
    }

    public Object getTransferData(DataFlavor flavor) {
        List list = new ArrayList();
        list.add(temp);
        return list;
    }

    public DataFlavor[] getTransferDataFlavors() {
        DataFlavor[] df = new DataFlavor[1];
        df[0] = DataFlavor.javaFileListFlavor;
        return df;
    }

    public boolean isDataFlavorSupported(DataFlavor flavor) {
        if(flavor == DataFlavor.javaFileListFlavor) {
            return true;
        }
        return false;
    }
}
```

TextFileTransferable implements Transferable and only recognizes the
javaFileListFlavor. getTransferData( ) returns the single file wrapped in an
ArrayList. getTransferDataFlavors( ) returns an array with only one element: javaFileListFlavor. And isDataFlavorSupported returns true if the
specified flavor is a javaFileListFlavor.

With all of the components in place, it's time to make a simple application
to pull it all together (see Example 9-2).

Example 9-2. Testing out drag-and-drop

```
public class FileDropper {
    public static void main(String[] args) throws IOException {
        JFrame frame = new JFrame("Hack #65: Drag-and-Drop with Files");
        frame.setDefaultCloseOperation(frame.EXIT_ON_CLOSE);

        FileSystemView fsv = FileSystemView.getFileSystemView();
        Icon icon = fsv.getSystemIcon(File.createTempFile("myfile.",".txt"));
        ImageIcon iicn = (ImageIcon)icon;
```

Example 9-2. Testing out drag-and-drop (continued)

```
        frame.getContentPane().setLayout(new BorderLayout());
        JTextArea text = new JTextArea();

        JLabel label = new JLabel("myfile.txt",icon,SwingConstants.CENTER);
        DragSource ds = DragSource.getDefaultDragSource();
        DragGestureRecognizer dgr = ds.createDefaultDragGestureRecognizer(
            label,
            DnDConstants.ACTION_MOVE,
            new FileDragGestureListener(text));

        frame.getContentPane().add("North",label);
        frame.getContentPane().add("Center",text);

        frame.pack();
        frame.setSize(400,300);
        frame.setVisible(true);
    }
}
```

FileDropper creates a new frame with a label and a text area. The label gets a
text file icon, the same as the drag operation from earlier. The crucial part of
the code is the ds.createDefaultDragGestureRecognizer() call. This ties the
system-wide drag class to your custom recognizer. Without this call, the system would know nothing about your customizations, and nothing would
happen when the user tries to drag the label to another application or the
desktop. With the call, though, the cursor will switch to show a small text
icon and the user can successfully drag the file to any place that accepts it
(see Figure 9-1). Now you can save files or transfer them without ever going
to a Save File dialog or having to navigate hierarchies of folders.

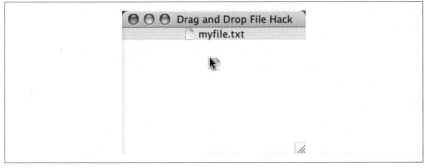

Figure 9-1. Drag-and-drop a file

HACK #66   Handle Dropped URLs

Drag-and-drop is like a box of chocolates; you never know what you're going to get....

Bookmark menus are so 1995. Today, you should expect to be able to drag URLs to other applications and have those applications open web pages, store the address in a bookmark database, start an email in response to a mailto: URL, etc. Java's networking chops are well-established and aren't the problem here. The issue is actually getting the URL itself from the drop.

To accept drops of native objects, your GUI needs to designate some Component as the onscreen drop target. Your code then implements the DropTarget interface, which means your implementation will get callbacks when the user drags the mouse into your component, over it, out of it, etc. Most of DropTarget's methods can be left as no-ops; for now, only the drop( ) method matters.

What's interesting about native drag-and-drop (and copy-and-paste, for that matter) is that there's not necessarily one way to represent the data being transferred. Instead, you do a sort of negotiation with the Transferable passed to you by the DropTargetDropEvent: it specifies, in order of robustness, which DataFlavors it can deliver, or you ask whether specific DataFlavors are supported.

In the demo code in Example 9-3, I have a method called dumpDataFlavors( ), which shows the DataFlavors offered to you by the drop. You can use System.out.println( ) on a particular flavor to get its MIME type, which describes the contents of the drop, and a representation class, which indicates how those contents will be provided to you by Transferable. getTransferData( ). For example, some browsers will give you a java.net. URL, whose DataFlavor looks like this:

```
java.awt.datatransfer.DataFlavor[mimetype=application/x-java-url;
    representationclass=java.net.URL]
```

One thing that's surprising is the number of DataFlavors offered by popular web browsers. Table 9-1 is a short listing of some of the browsers I tested.

Table 9-1. Browsers and their supported DataFlavors

Browser	Supported DataFlavors
Firefox 1.0 / Windows XP	78
MSIE 6.0 / Windows XP	53
Safari 1.3 / Mac OS X	53
Firefox 1.0 / Mac OS X	30
MSIE 5.2.3 / Mac OS X	53

Fortunately, a few DataFlavors appear on the lists for each browser, so your drop can just handle these common cases.

The URLDropTargetDemo class in Example 9-3 presents a large Drop Here label and a JTextField to show the dropped URL. I could have opened a stream from that URL and rendered its contents in Swing's HTMLEditorKit, but the result looks so bad with real-world web pages that it wasn't worth it. Besides, your app might be doing something other than opening web pages, such as storing bookmarks or starting emails.

Example 9-3. A drop target for URLs

```java
public class URLDropTargetDemo extends JPanel
    implements DropTargetListener {

    DropTarget dropTarget;
    JLabel dropHereLabel;
    JTextField statusField;
    static DataFlavor urlFlavor;
    static {
        try {
            urlFlavor =
                new DataFlavor ("application/x-java-url; class=java.net.URL");
        } catch (ClassNotFoundException cnfe) {
            cnfe.printStackTrace( );
        }
    }

    public URLDropTargetDemo( )  {
        super(new BorderLayout( ));
        dropHereLabel = new JLabel ("Drop here",
                                    SwingConstants.CENTER);
        dropHereLabel.setFont (getFont( ).deriveFont (Font.BOLD, 24.0f));
        add (dropHereLabel, BorderLayout.CENTER);
        // set up drop target stuff
        dropTarget = new DropTarget (dropHereLabel, this);
        statusField = new JTextField (30);
        statusField.setEditable(false);
        add (statusField, BorderLayout.SOUTH);
    }

    public static void main (String[] args) {
        JFrame frame = new JFrame ("URL DropTarget Demo");
        URLDropTargetDemo demoPanel = new URLDropTargetDemo( );
        frame.getContentPane( ).add (demoPanel);
        frame.pack( );
        frame.setVisible(true);
    }
```

Example 9-3. A drop target for URLs (continued)

```
// drop target listener events
public void dragEnter (DropTargetDragEvent dtde) {}

public void dragExit (DropTargetEvent dte) {}

public void dragOver (DropTargetDragEvent dtde) {}

public void drop (DropTargetDropEvent dtde) {
    System.out.println ("drop");
    dtde.acceptDrop (DnDConstants.ACTION_COPY_OR_MOVE);
    Transferable trans = dtde.getTransferable( );
    dumpDataFlavors (trans);
    boolean gotData = false;
    try {
        // try for application/x-java-url flavor
        if (trans.isDataFlavorSupported (urlFlavor)) {
            URL url = (URL) trans.getTransferData (urlFlavor);
            statusField.setText (url.toString( ));
            statusField.setCaretPosition (0);
            gotData = true;
        } else if (trans.isDataFlavorSupported (DataFlavor.stringFlavor)) {
            // try for string flavor
            String s =
                (String) trans.getTransferData (DataFlavor.stringFlavor);
            statusField.setText (s);
            gotData = true;
        }
    } catch (Exception e) {
        e.printStackTrace( );
    } finally {
        System.out.println ("gotData is " + gotData);
        dtde.dropComplete (gotData);
    }
}

public void dropActionChanged (DropTargetDragEvent dtde) {}

private void dumpDataFlavors (Transferable trans) {
    System.out.println ("Flavors:");
    DataFlavor[] flavors = trans.getTransferDataFlavors( );
    for (int i=0; i<flavors.length; i++) {
        System.out.println ("*** " + i + ": " + flavors[i]);
    }
}
}
```

A static initializer sets up a flavor for getting real java.net.URLs (MIME type application/x-java-url) from applications that provide them. The only other DataFlavor you'll need is a string flavor that exists as a constant in the DataFlavor class itself.

The constructor does all the work needed to accept drops. Really, this just consists of creating a DropTarget, which requires a Component (the "Drop here" label), and a class implementing the DropTargetListener interface.

In the drop( ) method, you need to acceptDrop( ) to begin the process of handling the drop. Pull out the Transferable from the DropTargetDropEvent, and look to see if it supports any DataFlavors that your application can support. In this demo, I implemented this with simple if/else statements to try the urlFlavor and the constant stringFlavor. Each block knows what the drop can be cast to, so one block casts to a URL, while the other casts to a String.

When your code is finished handling the drop—successfully or not—you need to call dropComplete( ) on the DropTargetDropEvent, and pass a boolean to indicate whether the drop was successful. The host OS can use this information to finish animating the drop; for example, by flying the drag image back to its source if the drop failed.

Drag Away

When you run the application, the big drop target is obvious, as seen in Figure 9-2. In this case, a URL is being dragged from the Shiira web browser on Mac OS X.

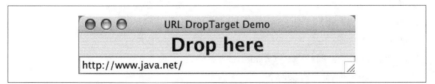

Figure 9-2. Dragging a URL to a Swing component

Once you drop a URL on the target, the dropped URL replaces the text in the JTextField (as seen in Figure 9-3).

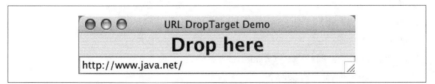

Figure 9-3. Swing component after handling a dropped URL

Handle Dropped Images

#67   I spy, with my little drop() method, something that doesn't support DataFlavor.imageFlavor...arrrgh!

Handling drag-and-drop from native applications **[Hack #66]** can be tricky because they're not particularly consistent about how they represent the data being transferred to your application. Now, let's say you want to accept dropped images—not image files, but actual images inside of browser windows, digital photo viewers, word processing and page-layout applications, etc. There's a constant in DataFlavor for images, so surely you can count on that being a flavor offered to you by the Transferable, right?

No, of course not. That would be too easy.

Using the dumpDataFlavors() strategy of the earlier URL hack, I checked out the DataFlavors offered by images dropped from some popular Windows and Mac applications. The results are pretty interesting—check out Table 9-2.

Table 9-2. DataFlavor offerings for images on various platforms

Application/platform	DataFlavors
Preview 2.1 / Mac OS X	1
GraphicConverter 4.6 / Mac OS X	1
Finder / Mac OS X	1
Safari 1.3 / Mac OS X	55
Firefox 1.0 / Mac OS X	57
QuickTime Player 6.5 / Mac OS X	1
AppleWorks 6.2.9 / Mac OS X	1
MarinerWrite 3.6.4 / Mac OS X	1
iPhoto 4.0.3 / Mac OS X	1
Explorer / Windows XP	1
MSIE 6.0 / Windows XP	27
Firefox 1.0 / Windows XP	80
Paint / Windows XP	N/A
Windows Picture and Fax Viewer / Windows XP	N/A
Windows Media Player / Windows XP	N/A
QuickTime Player 6.5.1 / Windows XP	N/A
QuickTime Picture Viewer 6.5.1 / Windows XP	N/A

The first thing you should notice is the poor support for dragging and dropping images in Windows: Paint, Picture and Fax Viewer, and the QuickTime applications are not drag sources, and dragging an image from the playlist of Windows Media Player to the Swing application in this hack actually crashes Java.

Furthermore, the supported DataFlavors are all over the map. A lot of these provide references to image files in the form of either a javaFileListFlavor (as do the Windows and Mac desktops), a list of URIs (the MIME type text/uri-list defined by RFC 2483 and supported by many of the browsers), or a single URL. To top it off, some of the older Mac applications send a single, hard-to-handle DataFlavor that will require special QuickTime-based handling [Hack #68].

Thanks to Swing's support for common image types like GIF, JPEG, and PNG, a file reference is good enough because you can easily make an ImageIcon from a URL or filepath to any of these types.

Grabbing the Drop

Example 9-4 shows a basic application that accepts a drop and tries to obtain from the drop (in order of preference):

1. A java.awt.Image
2. A java.util.List of java.io.Files
3. A String, formatted per the uri-list spec
4. A java.net.URL

Example 9-4. Handling dropped images from other applications

```
public class ImageDropTargetDemo extends JPanel
    implements DropTargetListener {

    DropTarget dropTarget;
    JLabel dropHereLabel;
    static DataFlavor urlFlavor, uriListFlavor, macPictStreamFlavor;
    static {
        try {
            urlFlavor =
                new DataFlavor ("application/x-java-url; class=java.net.URL");
            uriListFlavor =
                new DataFlavor ("text/uri-list; class=java.lang.String");
        } catch (ClassNotFoundException cnfe) {
            cnfe.printStackTrace( );
        }
    }
```

Example 9-4. Handling dropped images from other applications (continued)

```java
public ImageDropTargetDemo( ) {
    super(new BorderLayout( ));
    dropHereLabel = new JLabel ("   Drop here   ",
                                SwingConstants.CENTER);
    dropHereLabel.setFont (getFont( ).deriveFont (Font.BOLD, 24.0f));
    add (dropHereLabel, BorderLayout.CENTER);
    // set up drop target stuff
    dropTarget = new DropTarget (dropHereLabel, this);
}

public static void main (String[] args) {
    JFrame frame = new JFrame ("Image DropTarget Demo");
    ImageDropTargetDemo demoPanel = new ImageDropTargetDemo( );
    frame.getContentPane( ).add (demoPanel);
    frame.pack( );
    frame.setVisible(true);
}

// drop target listener events

public void dragEnter (DropTargetDragEvent dtde) {}

public void dragExit (DropTargetEvent dte) {}

public void dragOver (DropTargetDragEvent dtde) {}

// drop( ) method listed below

public void dropActionChanged (DropTargetDragEvent dtde) {}

public void showImageInNewFrame (ImageIcon icon) {
    JFrame frame = new JFrame( );
    frame.getContentPane( ).add (new JLabel (icon));
    frame.pack( );
    frame.setVisible(true);
}

public void showImageInNewFrame (Image image) {
    showImageInNewFrame (new ImageIcon (image));
}

private void dumpDataFlavors (Transferable trans) {
    System.out.println ("Flavors:");
    DataFlavor[] flavors = trans.getTransferDataFlavors( );
    for (int i=0; i<flavors.length; i++) {
        System.out.println ("*** " + i + ": " + flavors[i]);
    }
}
}
```

As in "Handle Dropped URLs" [Hack #66], this program uses static initializers to set up two custom DataFlavors: one for URLs and another for lists of URIs provided as Strings. Constants for images (specifically, java.awt.Images) and lists of files (java.util.Lists of java.io.Files) are provided for you by the DataFlavor class.

You register for drag-and-drop by creating a DropTarget with an onscreen component and an implementation of the DropTargetListener class. The key to the DropTargetListener is to meaningfully implement the drop( ) method, taking a DropTargetDropEvent and accepting the drop, trying to get the data from the event's Transferable, and reporting back to the event on whether the data was handled successfully. To prove that it worked, this application shows the dropped image in a new JFrame.

Of course, the devil is in the details, meaning the drop( ) method, which is listed in Example 9-5.

Example 9-5. Handling the image drop

```
public void drop (DropTargetDropEvent dtde) {
    System.out.println ("drop");
    dtde.acceptDrop (DnDConstants.ACTION_COPY_OR_MOVE);
    Transferable trans = dtde.getTransferable( );
    System.out.println ("Flavors:");
    dumpDataFlavors (trans);
    boolean gotData = false;
    try {
        // try to get an image
        if (trans.isDataFlavorSupported (DataFlavor.imageFlavor)) {
            System.out.println ("image flavor is supported");
            Image img = (Image) trans.getTransferData (DataFlavor.imageFlavor);
            showImageInNewFrame (img);
            gotData = true;
        } else if (trans.isDataFlavorSupported (
                        DataFlavor.javaFileListFlavor)) {
            System.out.println ("javaFileList is supported");
            java.util.List list = (java.util.List)
                trans.getTransferData (DataFlavor.javaFileListFlavor);
            ListIterator it = list.listIterator( );
            while (it.hasNext( )) {
                File f = (File) it.next( );
                ImageIcon icon = new ImageIcon (f.getAbsolutePath( ));
                showImageInNewFrame (icon);
            }
            gotData = true;
        } else if (trans.isDataFlavorSupported (uriListFlavor)) {
            System.out.println ("uri-list flavor is supported");
            String uris = (String)
                trans.getTransferData (uriListFlavor);
```

Example 9-5. Handling the image drop (continued)

```
            // url-lists are defined by rfc 2483 as crlf-delimited
            StringTokenizer izer = new StringTokenizer (uris, "\r\n");
            while (izer.hasMoreTokens ()) {
                String uri = izer.nextToken();
                System.out.println (uri);
                ImageIcon icon = new ImageIcon (uri);
                showImageInNewFrame (icon);
            }
            gotData = true;
        } else if (trans.isDataFlavorSupported (urlFlavor)) {
            System.out.println ("url flavor is supported");
            URL url = (URL) trans.getTransferData (urlFlavor);
            System.out.println (url.toString());
            ImageIcon icon = new ImageIcon (url);
            showImageInNewFrame (icon);
            gotData = true;
        }
    } catch (Exception e) {
        e.printStackTrace();
    } finally {
        System.out.println ("gotData is " + gotData);
        dtde.dropComplete (gotData);
    }
}
```

drop() asks the Transferable for supported DataFlavors in the order you'd prefer to deal with them. First, obviously, is DataFlavor.imageFlavor. If this is supported, you can trivially cast the data object returned by Transferable. getTransferData() to an Image.

The next easiest thing to deal with is the Java file list, denoted by the MIME type application/x-java-file-list, and handled by the DataFlavor constant javaFileListFlavor. Given Swing's support for various image file formats, you can cast the transfer data to a java.util.List, iterate over its members, cast each one to a File, and make an ImageIcon from each file's path. URLs work pretty much the same way: cast the transfer data to a java.net.URL and make an ImageIcon from it.

URI lists take just a little work on your part. RFC 2483 defines these as being some number of URIs, separated by CRLF pairs. It's trivial to take the URI list as a string and send it to a StringTokenizer to pick out each URI, which can then be passed to the ImageIcon constructor.

Shut Up and Drag

Start up the demo and drag over an image from your favorite application, as shown in Figure 9-4.

Figure 9-4. Dragging an image from a native application to a Swing component

When dropped, you'll see the image appear in its own JFrame. In Figure 9-5, I've dragged small images from several different applications, resulting in each being opened in its own frame.

Figure 9-5. Image dropped from a native application and opened in Swing

This *won't* work if you're dragging an image from one of the Mac OS X applications that only supplies one DataFlavor. You'll have to deal with Picts [Hack #68] in that situation.

 ## HACK #68 Handling Dropped Picts on Mac OS X

For Mac applications that provide only the legacy Pict flavor of drops, QuickTime for Java offers a Mac-specific solution.

You should already recognize the existence of hard-to-handle DataFlavors [Hack #67] passed by certain Mac applications. Of the Mac apps I tested, several old apps (many using the Carbon APIs, which were developed to migrate classic Mac apps to OS X) support only one DataFlavor. When I drop from GraphicConverter, QuickTime Player, AppleWorks, and MarinerWrite, the only supported DataFlavor was reported as:

```
java.awt.datatransfer.DataFlavor[mimetype=image/x-pict;
    representationclass=java.io.InputStream]
```

For those of you who don't use Macs, Pict is part of QuickDraw, the original Mac graphics API. The term is wildly overloaded—Pict can refer to a file format, a resource hidden in an application file, a wrapper around vector drawing commands, and as a wrapper around optionally compressed pixel data. It's in this latter form that Pict is a preferred format for passing image data on the Mac clipboard because Picts are easy for Mac applications to render and convert (through the QuickDraw library, of course).

Unfortunately, Java doesn't know the first thing about Picts, so it's frustrating to see that Pict is the only supported DataFlavor. Worse, the data is supplied as an InputStream, instead of a file or a URL, meaning you have to handle it in Java, instead of handing off to non-Java code that might be able to convert the Pict to something that can handle the format more gracefully.

Fortunately, there is a Java solution to the problem, and it's called Quick-Time for Java (QTJ). This API is a Java wrapper around the native Quick-Time multimedia API. It's available for Mac OS X and Windows, but since a Windows application isn't going to pass you a Pict, you only need to worry about the Mac OS X case. One advantage of all this API-wrangling: QTJ is installed by default on Mac OS X, so you can count on it being there.

Everything in this hack is Mac-specific. Since Picts are only going to be an issue on Mac OS X, don't bother with this on programs that you're sure won't need to deal with Mac OS X drops.

First, you'll need to define a DataFlavor for Pict data in Java input streams:

```
macPictStreamFlavor =
    new DataFlavor ("image/x-pict; class=java.io.InputStream");
```

Next, take the code from the hack on handling standard dropped images **[Hack #67]** and give drop( ) a new else if( ) {...} block to deal with this flavor. This block will use a QTJPictHelper class, so you need to make that available (I'll show you this helper class soon). Since you don't want to need to have this class at compile time—that would make life harder for Windows and Linux users, who might not have the *QTJava.zip* file to compile against—this code uses reflection to load the QTJPictHelper class and invoke its pictStreamToJavaImage( ):

```
} else if (trans.isDataFlavorSupported (macPictStreamFlavor)) {
    System.out.println ("mac pict stream flavor is supported");
    InputStream in =
        (InputStream) trans.getTransferData (macPictStreamFlavor);
    // for the benefit of the non-mac crowd, this is
    // done with reflection.  directly, it would be:
    // Image img = QTJPictHelper.pictStreamToJavaImage (in);
```

```
        Class qtjphClass = Class.forName ("QTJPictHelper");
        Class[] methodParamTypes = { java.io.InputStream.class };
        Method method =
            qtjphClass.getDeclaredMethod ("pictStreamToJavaImage",
                                          methodParamTypes);
        InputStream[] methodParams = { in };
        Image img = (Image) method.invoke (null, methodParams);
        showImageInNewFrame (img);
        gotData = true;
    }
```

OK, now for the fun part: converting the input stream from Pict data to a
Java image. This code is drawn from techniques in the book *QuickTime for
Java: A Developer's Notebook* (O'Reilly), which has a whole chapter on
QuickDraw and how to call it from Java. The gist of the technique is to use a
GraphicsImporter, which handles various types of image data, to read the
Pict. From this you can get a GraphicsImporterDrawer that allows you to get
a QTImageProducer, which is an AWT ImageProducer and, of course, can pro-
duce a normal java.awt.Image.

Example 9-6 shows the QTJPictHelper helper class I mentioned earlier.
Unlike most examples in the book, this listing includes the import statements because the QTJ stuff will be new to most readers.

Example 9-6. Using QTJ to handle Mac Pict data in a Transferable

```
import java.awt.*;
import java.io.*;

import quicktime.*;
import quicktime.qd.*;
import quicktime.std.*;
import quicktime.std.image.*;
import quicktime.std.movies.media.*;
import quicktime.app.view.*;

public class QTJPictHelper extends Object {

    static Image pictStreamToJavaImage (InputStream in)
        throws IOException {
        Image image = null;
        // create a buffer for bytes read from stream
        byte[] buffy = new byte [2048];
        // must have empty 512-byte header so GraphicsImporter
        // will think it's a file
        int off = 512;
        int totalRead = 0;
        // loop, attempting to read as many bytes as will fit
        // in the array, growing array as necessary
        int bytesRead = 0;
        while ((bytesRead = in.read (buffy, off, buffy.length-off)) > -1) {
```

Example 9-6. Using QTJ to handle Mac Pict data in a Transferable (continued)

```
                totalRead += bytesRead;
                off += bytesRead;
                if (off == buffy.length) {
                    // reallocate new array
                    byte[] buffy2 = new byte [buffy.length * 2];
                    System.arraycopy (buffy, 0, buffy2, 0, buffy.length);
                    buffy = buffy2;
                }
            }
            try {
                // hand it to QTJ GraphicsImporter
                QTSession.open( );
                Pict pict = new Pict (buffy);
                DataRef ref = new DataRef (pict,
                                          StdQTConstants.kDataRefQTFileTypeTag,
                                          "PICT");
                GraphicsImporter gi =
                    new GraphicsImporter (StdQTConstants.kQTFileTypePicture);
                gi.setDataReference (ref);
                QDRect rect = gi.getSourceRect ( );
                Dimension dim = new Dimension (rect.getWidth( ),
                                               rect.getHeight( ));
                GraphicsImporterDrawer gid =
                    new GraphicsImporterDrawer (gi);
                QTImageProducer ip = new QTImageProducer (gid, dim);

                // create AWT image
                image = Toolkit.getDefaultToolkit( ).createImage (ip);

            } catch (QTException qte) {
                qte.printStackTrace( );
            } finally {
                QTSession.close( );
            }
            return image;
        }
    }
```

To compile this code, you need the *QTJava.zip* file (yes, QTJ is old enough to pre-date JAR files) in your classpath. On Mac OS X, you'd compile with something like this:

```
javac -classpath /System/Library/Java/Extensions/QTJava.zip
    QTJPictHelper.java
```

The implicit QTJ hack in this code is that the GraphicsImporter has to be fooled into believing that a block of memory is actually a Pict file as it would appear on disk, and Pict files have a 512-byte header that the importer skips over. So, the first thing this code does is to build a byte array from the input stream, starting with 512 empty bytes.

Next is the QTJ stuff. It's OK if you don't totally understand it—QTJ code is pretty twisted. That's why there's a whole book on it. First, you open a QTSession, which initializes QuickTime and allocates resources. You have to do this before any QTJ call. It can throw a QTException, as can most other QTJ calls, so the whole thing is wrapped in a try-catch block.

Next, you create a Pict object from the byte array and pass that to DataRef, which is a sort of generic media reference. In this case, you pass in flags to tell the DataRef exactly what it's pointing to. The second and third arguments indicate that we're using the old-style Mac OS file type and that its value is PICT. You might be wondering why being a Pict object isn't self-descriptive enough. It's because many QTJ objects are just pointers to blocks of memory and the functions that work with them. The DataRef signature used here takes a QTHandleRef as an argument. QTHandleRef is subclassed by Pict, but it is little more than a pointer; the only level on which the DataRef understands the Pict, in fact, is as a block of memory. My point here: QTJ code is weird and often C-like.

Create a GraphicsImporter for the Pict format, and point it to the DataRef. You have now read the Pict "file" from memory. Now, you can get the size of the imported image and create a QTImageProducer, with help from a GraphicsImporterDrawer (a sort of QT-to-Java bridge for still images, also used by QTJ's Swing JComponents). Since this is a normal, everyday ImageProducer, you can create an image with Component.createImage( ) or Toolkit.createImage( ).

Finally, you need to call QTSession.close( ) to deallocate QuickTime resources. It's OK to do it many times in a program, although it's probably more efficient to open( ) it once and close( ) it once; e.g., in your quit handler or a shut-down hook.

Take a Breath and Run

The code works exactly as in the previous hack—all you've done is support one more DataFlavor. In Figure 9-6, I've dropped two images from Quick-Time Player onto the Java app, and both are shown in their own windows.

Actually, this is a little more interesting than it looks because the larger image isn't a still image; it's the current frame of an MPEG-4 movie that I dragged and dropped into the Java app. The single frame is transported as a Pict, and using QTJ lets you get it into the Java world. This hack only scratches the surface of QTJ's potential—if you want to do Java Media on the Mac, you should check out *QuickTime for Java: A Developer's Notebook*, by Chris Adamson (yours truly), published by O'Reilly.

Figure 9-6. Handling dropped images by supporting Pict format

Translucent Drag-and-Drop

The Java implementation of drag-and-drop offers poor visual feedback. This hack shows how to provide more information and a better-looking response to the user.

A good way to create user-friendly interfaces is to provide the ability to drag-and-drop almost anything from, within, and onto those interfaces. Mac OS X is a perfect example of a good drag-and-drop use. Every time I try to drag something to drop it onto something else, it just works. AWT, and therefore Swing, let applications implement drag-and-drop but lack something Mac OS X already offers: really cool visual feedback to let the user know what's going on.

A Rather Boring Cursor

J2SE has offered drag-and-drop facilities since version 1.2. All the necessary classes and interfaces can be found in the package java.awt.dnd. Although not very easy to use at first, this package provides powerful features you can use to greatly improve the usability of your applications. Unfortunately, the Java drag-and-drop framework offers little visual feedback. In fact, the only feedback the user can get is a simple mouse cursor. For instance, you can show that a drag-and-drop operation is in progress with the following line of code:

```
dropTarget.setCursor(DragSource.DefaultMoveDrop);
```

Figure 9-7 shows what the visual feedback looks like on Windows.

```
protected GhostGlassPane glassPane;
protected String action;

private List listeners;

public GhostDropAdapter(GhostGlassPane glassPane, String action) {
    this.glassPane = glassPane;
    this.action = action;
    this.listeners = new ArrayList();
}

public void addGhostDropListener(GhostDropListener listener) {
    if (listener != null)
        listeners.add(listener);
}
```

Figure 9-7. Default drag-and-drop visual feedback on Windows

Not only does this look bad, it also conveys very little information. Mac OS X users are used to a much richer environment, and why should Windows or Linux users expect less? As an example of what can be done, Safari—Mac OS X's default web browser—shows a translucent thumbnail of the picture you are dragging. Figure 9-8 shows what this looks like in action.

Figure 9-8. Mac OS X provides great looking visual feedback for drag-and-drop

The quality of the interaction is greatly enhanced by the quantity of information provided by the visual feedback. Another example is dragging a link from the web browser to the desktop, where a translucent text box containing the link title and the URL is shown. Wouldn't it be great to be able to do the same in your application? Thankfully, Swing is perfectly suited for that kind of job.

Translucence Rocks

Implementing a stylish drag-and-drop requires being able to draw a translucent picture over any component. Every Swing frame contains several layers on which components are painted. These layers serve many purposes, among which is the drawing of pop-up menus over the regular components. The higher-level layer is called the glass pane. A glass pane is a transparent container you can use to draw over the entire UI, as seen in the hack that turned dialogs into frame-anchored "sheets" **[Hack #44]**. You will use it to display translucent pictures during a drag-and-drop operation, as seen in Figure 9-9.

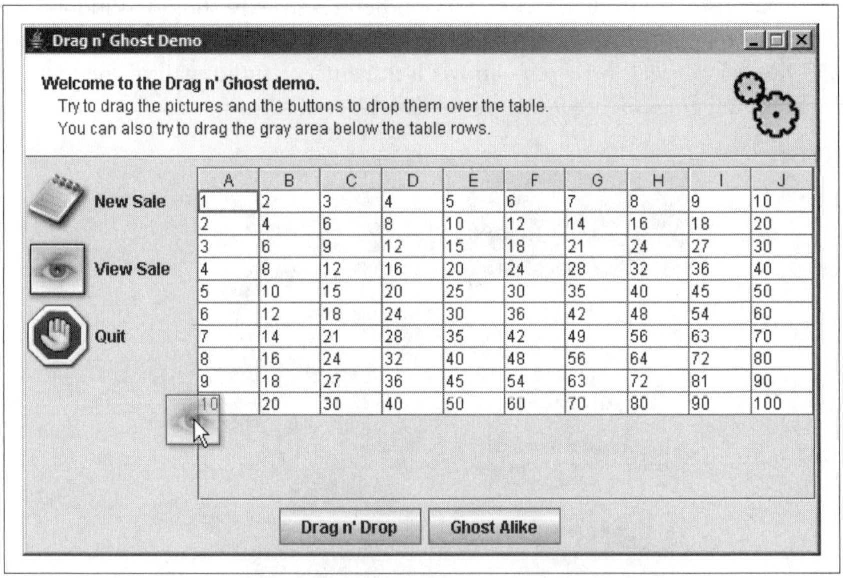

Figure 9-9. A translucent picture as visual feedback for drag-and-drop

Yet, translucent pictures do not cover all the needs of effective drag-and-drop visual feedback. When the user drops a file on your application, you can use a picture to indicate what the type of the file is. However, what picture will you use when the user wants to drag a text box into another box, and expect the contents of the first box to be copied to the second? The best solution is simply to display a translucent copy of the component itself, referred to as a *ghost* in the code. Figure 9-10 shows a ghost in mid-drag.

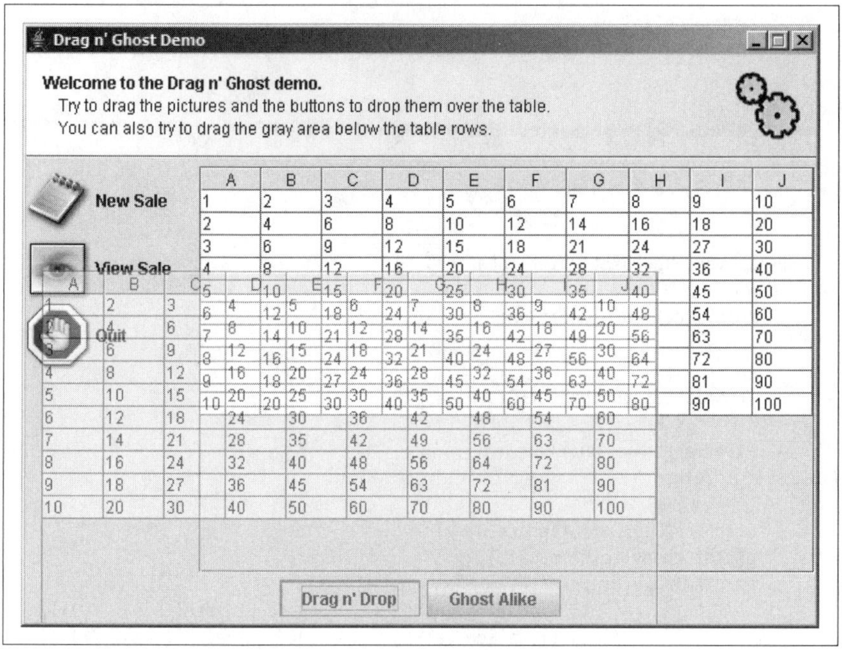

Figure 9-10. A ghost is a translucent copy of a Swing component

This time, you will not use the package java.awt.dnd; you'll need your own framework for this level of sophistication. By breaking out of the pre-built box, you gain full control of drag-and-drop.

Drawing a Ghost

The very first thing you need is a glass pane able to draw a translucent picture over the UI. A glass pane is nothing more than a transparent JPanel. The code of GhostGlassPane is very simple, as shown in Example 9-7.

Example 9-7. Creating a glass pane for ghosting

```java
import java.awt.*;
import java.awt.image.*;
import javax.swing.*;

public class GhostGlassPane extends JPanel
{
    private AlphaComposite composite;
    private BufferedImage dragged = null;
    private Point location = new Point(0, 0);
```

Example 9-7. Creating a glass pane for ghosting (continued)

```java
public GhostGlassPane( )
{
    setOpaque(false);
    composite = AlphaComposite.getInstance(AlphaComposite.SRC_OVER, 0.5f);
}

public void setImage(BufferedImage dragged)
{
    this.dragged = dragged;
}

public void setPoint(Point location)
{
    this.location = location;
}

public void paintComponent(Graphics g)
{
    if (dragged == null)
        return;

    Graphics2D g2 = (Graphics2D) g;
    g2.setComposite(composite);
    g2.drawImage(dragged,
                (int) (location.getX( ) - (dragged.getWidth(this)  / 2)),
                (int) (location.getY( ) - (dragged.getHeight(this) / 2)),
                null);
}
}
```

This glass pane has two properties: the picture to be displayed and its location. To make the picture translucent, use an AlphaComposite instance. Besides colors, strokes, and painters, Java2D drawings can be affected by composites that define how the newly drawn pixels are mixed with the underlying pixels. In this case, you want the new pixels—i.e., the picture— to be drawn at 50% of their initial opacity. You can change the second parameter of getInstance( ) to choose the opacity. The valid value range is from a totally opaque 0.0 to a totally transparent 1.0. An AlphaComposite can be used to define how the alpha channels of the source (the pixels being drawn), and the target (the existing pixels) are mixed together. You can select the mixing mode with the first parameter of getInstance( ) and refer to the documentation of AlphaComposite to get a comprehensive list of possible modes. It turns out that the AlphaComposite.SRC_OVER composite gives the best result for our job.

The only job of the paintComponent( ) will be to draw the dragged picture. Therefore, there is no need to call super.paintComponent( ), as it will perform unnecessary operations.

> Do not forget to set the composite in this method, or you might draw the picture fully opaque.

The center of the picture is painted at the location specified in setLocation( ). This means assuming the location given is the location of the mouse cursor. Now, you've got a fully functional glass pane, and you just need to add it to a Swing frame:

```
glassPane = new GhostGlassPane( );
setGlassPane(glassPane);
```

Also, do not forget that a glass pane is not visible by default: you will have to call setVisible(true) when a drag-and-drop operation is initiated. The final step is the activation of drag-and-drop on components requiring it. You can use a picture as drag-and-drop feedback:

```
JLabel label = new JLabel("New Sale");
GhostDropAdapter pictureAdapter;
pictureAdapter = new GhostPictureAdapter(glassPane,
                                         "new_sale",
                                         "images/new_sale.png")
label.addMouseListener(pictureAdapter);
label.addMouseMotionListener(new GhostMotionAdapter(glassPane));
```

You can also use a ghost feedback:

```
JButton button = new JButton("Ghost Feedback"));
GhostDropAdapter componentAdapter;
componentAdapter = new GhostComponentAdapter(glassPane, "button_pushed");
button.addMouseListener(componentAdapter);
button.addMouseMotionListener(new GhostMotionAdapter(glassPane));
```

Whatever choice you make, you need two adapters to perform drag-and-drop. The first one is an adapter for the MouseListener interface. It can be either a GhostPictureAdapter, to handle pictures, or a GhostComponentAdapter, to handle a component ghost. The role of this adapter is to handle the beginning and the end of a drag-and-drop gesture. When a drop action is performed, an event is fired to every GhostDropListener registered by the adapter. The code in Example 9-8 shows how GhostComponentAdapter works. The code of GhostPictureAdapter is almost the same, and it's left to you to check out (all the code for this book is online; visit *http://www.oreilly.com/catalog/swinghks*).

Example 9-8. Handling component ghosts

```java
import java.awt.*;
import java.awt.event.*;
import java.awt.image.*;
import javax.swing.*;

public class GhostComponentAdapter extends GhostDropAdapter
{
    public GhostComponentAdapter(GhostGlassPane glassPane, String action) {
        super(glassPane, action);
    }

    public void mousePressed(MouseEvent e)
    {
        Component c = e.getComponent( );

        BufferedImage image = new BufferedImage(c.getWidth( ),
                                        c.getHeight( ),
                                        BufferedImage.TYPE_INT_ARGB);
        Graphics g = image.getGraphics( );
        c.paint(g);

        glassPane.setVisible(true);

        Point p = (Point) e.getPoint().clone( );
        SwingUtilities.convertPointToScreen(p, c);
        SwingUtilities.convertPointFromScreen(p, glassPane);

        glassPane.setPoint(p);
        glassPane.setImage(image);
        glassPane.repaint( );
    }

    public void mouseReleased(MouseEvent e)
    {
        Component c = e.getComponent( );

        Point p = (Point) e.getPoint().clone( );
        SwingUtilities.convertPointToScreen(p, c);

        Point eventPoint = (Point) p.clone( );
        SwingUtilities.convertPointFromScreen(p, glassPane);

        glassPane.setPoint(p);
        glassPane.setVisible(false);
        glassPane.setImage(null);

        fireGhostDropEvent(new GhostDropEvent(action, eventPoint));
    }
}
```

When a mouse-press event is fired by the drag-and-drop source, a new off-screen picture is created. This picture has the exact same dimensions as the source component itself. Then the component is asked to paint itself on the Graphics surface of the picture. The code obtains a ghost—a copy of the component—which is passed to the glass pane.

You might wonder why the SwingUtilities class is used. Since the code listens to the events fired by a component, the mouse location it receives is bound to the component's coordinate system. For instance, when the mouse is pressed with the cursor at the top-left corner of the component, the location is 0,0. Unfortunately, you cannot use this location with the glass pane. As the pane covers the whole frame, you need to translate the location from the component's coordinate system to the glass pane's coordinate system. There is no way to achieve this in one step, which is why the code first translates the location to the screen coordinates and then to the glass pane coordinates. The glass pane can then safely paint the picture at the given location.

The second adapter required for performing a full drag-and-drop operation is an adapter for the MouseMotionListener interface. The framework needs it to change the location of the picture, or the ghost, when the mouse moves over the window. The code is pretty simple:

```
public void mouseDragged(MouseEvent e)
{
  Component c = e.getComponent();
  Point p = (Point) e.getPoint().clone();
  SwingUtilities.convertPointToScreen(p, c);
  SwingUtilities.convertPointFromScreen(p, glassPane);
  glassPane.setPoint(p);
  glassPane.repaint();
}
```

As before, you need to convert the location of the mouse event into the right coordinate system. Once you get a valid location, the pane is repainted. The full source code of this hack is available in this book's downloadable source code. The only part of the drag-and-drop framework you have not seen is the GhostDropListener and its GhostDropEvent. Both are very easy to understand when you remember that the drop location given by the event is expressed in screen coordinates. Therefore, you must translate it into the target component's coordinates if you need to perform some checks. The complete example provides an AbstractGhostDropManager that implements GhostDropListener to provide two methods to handle drag-and-drop targets more easily.

—*Romain Guy*

Audio
Hacks 70–78

Sound is underrated as a useful tool for building good user interfaces. A lot of developers balk at the thought of sound support, imagining an office full of noisy machines, emitting a beeping cacophony more like a 1980s video-game arcade than a place of business. But on the other hand, don't you appreciate it when you get a nice little audible cue? For example:

- When your IM buddy logs in
- When your CD has finished burning
- When your gigantic upload has finished
- When someone is trying to hack into your network and you're not even looking at the screen

And beyond these kinds of uses, don't forget the whole realm of applications that are, by their nature, all about sound: music players, sound editors, voice chat, and VoIP, etc. Clearly, java.awt.Toolkit.beep( ) is not going to cut it.

Java has two built-in options for playing simple sounds in memory: applet AudioClips and JavaSound. Because of their limitations, this chapter will also look at two extensions: Java Media Framework (JMF) and QuickTime for Java (QTJ). Later in the chapter, you'll find more sophisticated JavaSound coverage, including how to visualize an in-memory sound clip, and how to play sounds too big to fit in memory.

Play a Sound in an Applet

If you're forced to write to the old Applet API for sound, here's how you do it.
Good luck.

Let me be very clear up front: applet-based sound sucks. If you are in a hurry to get sound into your application and can count on your users having Java 1.3 or better, go ahead and use JavaSound instead **[Hack #71]**. Applet-based sound is going to be most useful to those who must deliver applets (and only applets) to very old browsers and JVMs. And it's not going to be pretty.

Java 1.0 and 1.1 shipped with no support for application-based sound. None. The only sound support was for applets, presumably so they could punt the responsibilities for audio to the enclosing browser. The idea in the early JDKs is built around an AudioClip, a class found in the java.awt. applet package—as David Flanagan says in *Java Foundation Classes in a Nutshell* (O'Reilly), "only because there is no better place for it."

The Code

To demonstrate AudioClips, Example 10-1 shows a hacked up little applet.

Example 10-1. Playing an AudioClip in an applet

```
public class AppletSound extends Applet
    implements ActionListener {

    JButton fileButton, loadButton, playButton, loopButton, stopButton;
    JLabel urlLabel;
    JTextField urlField;
    AudioClip clip;

    public AppletSound( ) {
        setLayout (new GridLayout (2,1));
        // first row layout
        JPanel topPanel = new JPanel( );
        urlLabel = new JLabel ("URL:");
        topPanel.add (urlLabel);
        urlField = new JTextField (25);
        urlField.addActionListener (this);
        topPanel.add (urlField);
        loadButton = new JButton ("Load");
        loadButton.addActionListener (this);
        topPanel.add (loadButton);
        fileButton = new JButton ("File");
        fileButton.addActionListener (this);
        topPanel.add (fileButton);
        add (topPanel);
```

Example 10-1. Playing an AudioClip in an applet (continued)

```java
        // second row layout
        JPanel bottomPanel = new JPanel( );
        playButton = new JButton ("Play");
        playButton.addActionListener (this);
        bottomPanel.add (playButton);
        stopButton = new JButton ("Stop");
        stopButton.addActionListener (this);
        bottomPanel.add (stopButton);
        loopButton = new JButton ("Loop");
        loopButton.addActionListener (this);
        bottomPanel.add (loopButton);
        add (bottomPanel);
    }

    public void stop( ) {
        clip.stop( );
    }

    public void actionPerformed (ActionEvent e) {
        Object source = e.getSource( );
        if (source == fileButton) {
            JFileChooser chooser = new JFileChooser( );
            int pick = chooser.showOpenDialog(this);
            if (pick == JFileChooser.APPROVE_OPTION) {
                try {
                    File file = chooser.getSelectedFile( );
                    urlField.setText (file.toURL().toString( ));
                } catch (MalformedURLException murle) {
                    murle.printStackTrace( );
                }
            }
        } else if (source == loadButton ) {
            try {
                System.out.println ("field: " + urlField.getText( ));
                URL clipURL = new URL (urlField.getText( ));
                System.out.println ("loading " + clipURL);
                clip = getAudioClip (clipURL);
                System.out.println ("got clip");
            } catch (MalformedURLException murle) {
                murle.printStackTrace( );
            }
        } else if (source == playButton ) {
            clip.play( );
        } else if (source == stopButton ) {
            clip.stop( );
        } else if (source == loopButton ) {
            clip.loop( );
        }
    }
```

Example 10-1. Playing an AudioClip in an applet (continued)

```java
    public static void main (String args[]) {
        JFrame f = new JFrame ("Applet Sound");
        f.getContentPane().add (new AppletSound());
        f.pack();
        f.setVisible(true);
    }
}
```

If you've never worked with an applet, you need to be aware that they can't simply be launched from the command line with the java command. They need to live in some sort of applet-aware container, typically a browser, with their size and parameters specified by HTML tags. Example 10-2 shows a simple *index.html* file to show the AppletAudio applet in a web page.

Example 10-2. HTML to display AppletSound applet

```html
<html>
<head><title>Applet Sound</title></head>
<body>
<p>Playing sound with <code>java.applet</code></p>
<APPLET
  CODE="AppletSound.class"
  WIDTH="600"
  HEIGHT="75">
</APPLET>
</body>
</html>
```

Notice how the applet doesn't have a setVisible(true) line anywhere. The applet is an AWT panel that does its own layout; its constructor will be called from the browser plug-in (or equivalent) to get its pixels into the browser window.

The constructor of this applet is concerned exclusively with layout. It provides a JTextField for a URL, a Load JButton to load an AudioClip from that URL; a File JButton that can be used instead of typing in a file:/// URL by hand; and Play, Stop, and Loop JButtons to control the AudioClip.

actionPerformed() is the guts of this applet. If you click the File button, it simply shows a JFileChooser, converts the chosen file to a URL, and puts that in the TextField.

The handler for the Load button is also critical. When this button is clicked, the applet gets the text from the JTextField, makes a URL out of the text, and passes that URL to getAudioClip(). getAudioClip() is an Applet method that's a shortcut for getting an AppletContext object, which describes the environment the applet runs in and calls its getAudioClip().

The last three buttons—Play, Stop, and Loop—are handled trivially in actionPerformed( ) with calls to the Applet methods play( ), stop( ), and loop( ), respectively.

I've also provided a main( ) method here. Applets don't need them, but since an applet is just a JPanel, why not just put it in a JFrame and run it, right? What's the worst that could happen?

No Browser, No Sound

Since there's a main( ) method, just type java AppletAudio on the command line and the applet will come up in its own frame, as seen in Figure 10-1.

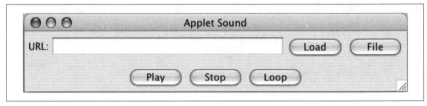

Figure 10-1. AudioClip player launched as an application

Click the File button and choose a file to have its URL placed in the field. Now, click Play.

Nothing happens. If you have an output console, you should see something like:

```
java.lang.NullPointerException
        at java.applet.Applet.getAppletContext(Applet.java:171)
        at java.applet.Applet.getAudioClip(Applet.java:279)
        at AppletSound.actionPerformed(AppletSound.java:71)
        at javax.swing.AbstractButton.fireActionPerformed(
            AbstractButton.java:1819)
    ...
```

I'll save you the time of typing a URL by hand and hitting Load; the same thing happens.

What's happening is that the implicit call to getAppletContext( ) is failing because there is no applet context; i.e., the environment in which the applet is executed. An applet expects to run in a browser or something similar that provides access to cached images and sounds and the ability to get documents via URLs. Obviously, the four-line main( ) method doesn't attempt to provide such facilities.

So, to provide a suitable environment, use a browser to open the *index.html* file. It also works to use the JDK's appletviewer from the command line. Either way, this should open a web page that looks like Figure 10-2.

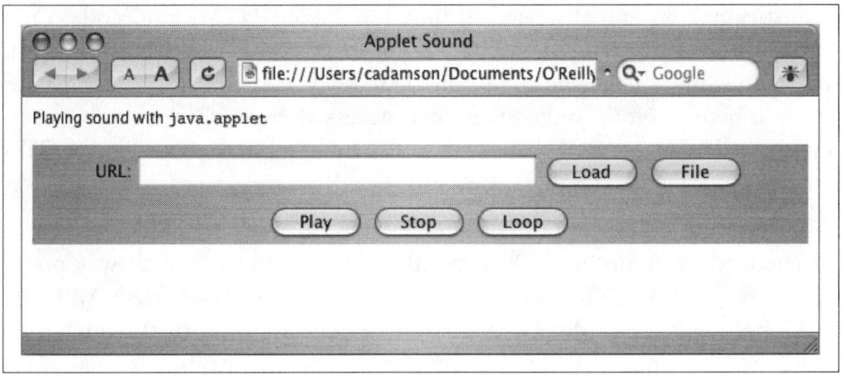

Figure 10-2. Applet to play AudioClips

Click File and...nothing happens. If you have an output window open, you'll see the reason:

```
[aeris:HacksBook/Media/52] cadamson% appletviewer index.html
apple.awt.EventQueueExceptionHandler Caught Throwable : java.security.
AccessControlException: access denied (java.util.PropertyPermission user.
home read)
java.security.AccessControlException: access denied (java.util.
PropertyPermission user.home read)
        at java.security.AccessControlContext.checkPermission(
            AccessControlContext.java:269)
        at java.security.AccessController.checkPermission(
            AccessController.java:401)
        at java.lang.SecurityManager.checkPermission(
            SecurityManager.java:524)
        at java.lang.SecurityManager.checkPropertyAccess(
            SecurityManager.java:1276)
        at java.lang.System.getProperty(System.java:573)
        at sun.awt.shell.ShellFolderManager.get(ShellFolderManager.java:51)
        at sun.awt.shell.ShellFolder.get(ShellFolder.java:245)
        at javax.swing.filechooser.FileSystemView.getDefaultDirectory(
            FileSystemView.java:362)
        at javax.swing.JFileChooser.setCurrentDirectory(
            JFileChooser.java:525)
        at javax.swing.JFileChooser.<init>(JFileChooser.java:321)
        at javax.swing.JFileChooser.<init>(JFileChooser.java:273)
        at AppletSound.actionPerformed(AppletSound.java:56)
```

Thanks to restrictive applet security, you can't open a JFileChooser in an applet without going and rewriting your permissions file or pointing to a new, more permissive set of policies. Typing a URL by hand and trying to load it fails in the same way and for the same reason. It probably makes sense to assume the worst of an applet, but it makes it hard for an applet to do anything useful, doesn't it?

Realistically, you actually need to host the applet (HTML and code) on a web server and access it via a URL. If you have access to a web server, put *index.html* and *AppletAudio.class* in their own web directory, along with some known-to-work audio files, then access it remotely with a browser. Type in a URL to one of those audio files by hand and try to load it. This time, it should work (finally).

But what formats are supported? Back in Java 1.0 and 1.1, AudioClips had to be encoded in mono at 8,000 Hz with μ-law encoding...which was pretty awful. In Java 1.4.2, a few simple container formats are supported. AIFF and WAV both work, but Mac OS X doesn't support the *.au* format, which used to be the only option (Windows can play *.au*, by the way). Also, AudioClip can't play WAVs and AIFFs whose contents are compressed in any way. And neither Mac nor Windows supports MP3 as AudioClips.

You can also load audio from sites other than the one hosting your applet, which seems contrary to the stringent applet security seen earlier.

So, using java.awt.applet's AudioClip means your application has to be an applet, it can only run a handful of audio formats, and your media can't be local unless you go through the hassle of overriding the SecurityManager for the applet.

As you might imagine, early Java developers demanded a replacement.

HACK #71   Play a Sound with JavaSound

Get a small clip to play from memory with a lot less hassle.

The JavaSound API was developed to answer complaints about the inadequacies of the AudioClip class in the applet package...not the least of which was the fact that it couldn't be used in applications. JavaSound consists of two packages—javax.sound.sampled and javax.sound.midi—plus two service provider interface (spi) sub-packages for adding support for new devices, formats, converters, etc.

JavaSound was introduced as an extension to Java 1.2 (I know, I know, "Java 2 Standard Edition, version 1.2"), and it became part of Core Java in 1.3. In other words, you're pretty safe assuming that it's present on your user's machine. That's one big point in its favor.

Putting JavaSound to Work

To show off JavaSound, the code in Example 10-3 exhibits a short application that allows the user to pick a file from the local filesystem and play it. A dialog shows the selected filename; OK it when the audio completes to exit the program.

Example 10-3. Playing audio with JavaSound

```java
public class CoreJavaSound extends Object
    implements LineListener {

    File soundFile;
    JDialog playingDialog;
    Clip clip;

    public static void main (String[] args) {
        JFileChooser chooser = new JFileChooser( );
        chooser.showOpenDialog(null);
        File f = chooser.getSelectedFile( );
        try {
            CoreJavaSound s = new CoreJavaSound (f);
        } catch (Exception e) {
            e.printStackTrace( );
        }
    }

    public CoreJavaSound (File f)
        throws LineUnavailableException, IOException,
                UnsupportedAudioFileException {
        soundFile = f;
        // prepare a dialog to display while playing
        JOptionPane pane = new JOptionPane ("Playing " + f.getName( ),
                                        JOptionPane.PLAIN_MESSAGE);
        playingDialog = pane.createDialog (null, "Application Sound");
        playingDialog.pack( );

        // get and play sound
        Line.Info linfo = new Line.Info (Clip.class);
        Line line = AudioSystem.getLine (linfo);
        clip = (Clip) line;
        clip.addLineListener (this);
        AudioInputStream ais = AudioSystem.getAudioInputStream(soundFile);
        clip.open (ais);
        clip.start( );
    }

    // LineListener
    public void update (LineEvent le) {
        LineEvent.Type type = le.getType( );
        if (type == LineEvent.Type.OPEN) {
            System.out.println ("OPEN");
        } else if (type == LineEvent.Type.CLOSE) {
            System.out.println ("CLOSE");
            System.exit (0);
```

Example 10-3. Playing audio with JavaSound (continued)

```
    } else if (type == LineEvent.Type.START) {
        System.out.println ("START");
        playingDialog.setVisible(true);
    } else if (type == LineEvent.Type.STOP) {
        System.out.println ("STOP");
    }
  }
}
```

The JavaSound API for working with sampled sounds is an elaborate—perhaps even baroque—set of abstractions about the various parts of a sound system. The point of entry is an AudioSystem, whose various static methods let you get at the different sound resources. These include Lines, which are audio feeds (input or output); Mixers, which combine lines; AudioInputStreams, which represent incoming audio data; and format conversions. Line has a sub-interface called DataLine, which has a sub-interface called Clip, which represents a line that can be loaded into memory and played immediately, instead of streaming out from its source. If your data is small enough to fit in memory while being played, this is a particularly convenient class to work with.

 If your audio is not small enough to fit in memory, check out how to play JavaSound files of any length **[Hack #76]** later in this chapter.

To play audio in JavaSound, you need to set up a DataLine and call its start( ) method. Easier said than done, though—this is the baroque part.

There are a couple of ways to get a Line. In the most basic case, you just indicate that you want a line that can work with a given class. Because this example works with Clips, it asks for a Line.Info object suitable for use with Clips. Then you pass that info object to the AudioSystem to get a Line, which can be cast to a Clip since that's what you asked for in the first place.

Before setting up the media data, this example sets up a LineListener, which will provide events when the media is opened, starts playing, stops playing, and is closed.

OK, you've got a Clip, so here's how to get some audio data into it. You create an AudioInputStream from the static getAudioInputStream( ) method, then pass it to Clip's open( ) method. This makes the clip operational: it prefetches any needed system resources and enters a "ready to play" state. Now, you can just play the audio with the start( ) method, inherited from DataLine.

The example sets up a LineListener on the Clip and looks at the type of received events for four values defined in the LineEvent.Type class: OPEN, CLOSE, START, and STOP. All of these are logged to standard out, and then an appropriate action is taken: START makes the dialog visible, STOP hides the dialog and closes the clip (this is called when you OK the dialog), and CLOSE exits the application (and is called as a side effect of clip.close() in the handling of STOP).

There are a lot more classes in the package, and you can write really confusing code with them—and I haven't even mentioned MIDI. But for the stated goal of playing a small audio file with a minimum of fuss, that's how you do it with JavaSound.

Listen Up

When you run the demo program, it brings up a regular JFileChooser. You need to pick a sound file from one of JavaSound's supported file formats... of which there are only three: WAV, AIFF, and AU (not MP3, WMA, or Ogg). You knew there had to be a catch, right? Moreover, by default, Java-Sound only plays uncompressed sound files, so if the data in the file is in ALAW, ULAW, MACE, etc., it won't play.

If JavaSound can read it, it will start playing the chosen file immediately. The demo also shows a dialog like Figure 10-3, showing the name of the chosen audio file.

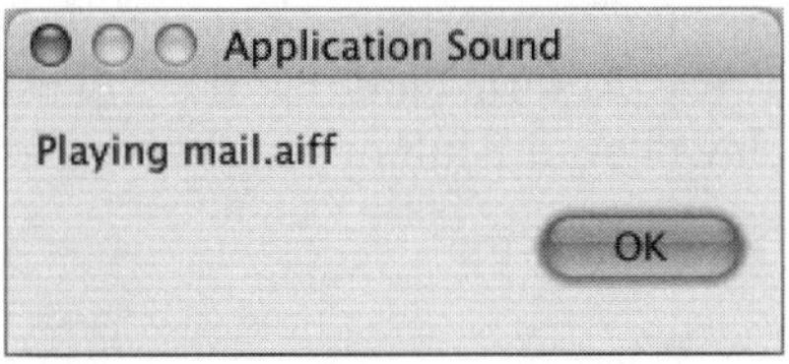

Figure 10-3. Dialog showing current sound file

Clicking the OK button clears the dialog and unblocks the AWT so that when the clip finishes playing, the STOP event can remove the dialog from the screen and close the clip, which exits the demo.

Working with the AudioSystem and having to pass around description objects is a little strange, especially with JavaSound's habit of using public inner classes as descriptor objects, but thanks to the Clip class, it does offer a pretty reasonable way to play small audio clips from your program.

The downside to JavaSound is the small number of supported formats. Java-Sound, at least out of the box, isn't well suited to handle having random sound formats thrown at it. That's not a problem if you're supplying your own sounds for your application—just stick with AIFF or WAV. But it does make JavaSound less than useful in a media browser or some other application that is going to have to deal with random formats encountered on the Net or the user's local storage. Of course, that's part of the idea of the spi sub-package: Sun provides the framework, and third parties make their formats available to Java by implementing spi interfaces.

HACK #72 Play a Sound with Java Media Framework

Use the Java Media Framework for better performance and support for more audio formats.

Java Media Framework (JMF) is Sun's attempt to bring a broadly focused multimedia framework to Java, supporting audio, video, and other time-based media types. The idea is to provide Java desktop applications with these features across operating systems. Like JavaSound, it's meant to be extended so that Sun or third parties could add support for new file formats or codecs (the compression/decompression encoding schemes used inside those files).

JMF offers another way to provide sound from an application. The advantages of doing so are that JMF *may* provide access to many more sound files than JavaSound will alone, and that JMF is somewhat easier to code than JavaSound, particularly for simple tasks. The disadvantages are that JMF capabilities vary wildly by platform, and that the end user will have to install JMF separately, which will be difficult or simply not allowed for some users.

Installing JMF

Download and install JMF from its home page at *http://java.sun.com/products/java-media/jmf/index.jsp* and you should be ready to go—no reboot required. The installers should have put everything into the correct path and set up your environment. If you have trouble getting JMF programs to run, or if you used the all-Java version that doesn't have a special installer, you can try adding the following environment variable:

```
JMFHOME="C:\Program Files\JMF2.1.1"
```

Next, add the two JMF Java libraries to your classpath:

```
CLASSPATH="$JMFHOME\lib\jmf.jar;$JMFHOME\lib\sound.jar;.;$CLASSPATH"
PATH="$JMFHOME\lib;$PATH"
```

The Code

The demo in Example 10-4 is basically a port of the CoreJavaSound demo used in playing audio with JavaSound [Hack #71], except that the event-handling has been simplified to a "quit when done" implementation. JMF's playback metaphor involves Players, which simply play media, and Processors, which may take action on the media, such as adding effects or transcoding to other formats. This allows the simple stuff to stay simple: to play a file, you wire it up to a Player, tell everything to get initialized ("realized" in JMF parlance), and call start( ). Notice that while the other imports are omitted as usual, this listing shows the import javax.media.* that will bring in the JMF classes used here.

Example 10-4. Playing audio with Java Media Framework

```
import javax.media.*;

public class JMFSound extends Object
    implements ControllerListener {

    File soundFile;
    JDialog playingDialog;

    public static void main (String[] args) {
        JFileChooser chooser = new JFileChooser( );
        chooser.showOpenDialog(null);
        File f = chooser.getSelectedFile( );
        try {
            JMFSound s = new JMFSound (f);
        } catch (Exception e) {
            e.printStackTrace( );
        }
    }

    public JMFSound (File f)
        throws NoPlayerException, CannotRealizeException,
            MalformedURLException, IOException {
        soundFile = f;
        // prepare a dialog to display while playing
        JOptionPane pane = new JOptionPane ("Playing " + f.getName( ),
                                    JOptionPane.PLAIN_MESSAGE);
        playingDialog = pane.createDialog (null, "JMF Sound");
        playingDialog.pack( );

        // get a player
        MediaLocator mediaLocator =
            new MediaLocator(soundFile.toURL( ));
        Player player =
            Manager.createRealizedPlayer (mediaLocator);
```

Example 10-4. Playing audio with Java Media Framework (continued)

```
        player.addControllerListener (this);
        player.prefetch( );
        player.start( );
        playingDialog.setVisible(true);
    }

    // ControllerListener implementation
    public void controllerUpdate (ControllerEvent e) {
        System.out.println (e.getClass().getName( ));
        if (e instanceof EndOfMediaEvent) {
            playingDialog.setVisible(false);
            System.exit (0);
        }
    }
}
```

The major change from the CoreJavaSound demo is in the constructor, after the dialog is readied. You create a MediaLocator, a sort of generic means of referring to the source location of media, from a URL of the selected file.

The MediaLocator allows you to create a Player with a one-line call to Manager.createRealizedPlayer(MediaLocator). A lot occurs in this call: the Manager, a sort of central point of access to JMF resources, creates a Player, wires it up to the MediaLocator, calls prefetch( ) to process some of the media data (to reduce startup delay), and calls realize( ) to allocate system-dependent media resources. The result is a ready-to-play Player.

To add event-awareness, add a listener with addControllerListener( ), Controller being a superclass of Player. Finally, you can play the media with start( ).

The ControllerListener interface defines a single method, controllerUpdate( ), which receives a ControllerEvent. In JMF, the class of the event is used for determining behavior; there are more than a dozen you might choose to deal with. To get the "end of the media" event, you just check to see if the event is an EndOfMediaEvent object, which in this case is handled by hiding the dialog and quitting the application.

Take JMF for a Spin

Functionally, the application is largely identical to the CoreJavaSound demo: a JFileChooser asks you to pick a file. When you do, it starts playing and a dialog box shows you the filename. When the audio completes, the application quits.

The one thing that's really different is that you can play many more file formats than you can with just JavaSound. Or maybe you can't. It all depends on what operating system you're running on. The JMF install offers an all-Java version and "performance packs" for some operating systems, which use native code. The latter offer not only better performance for the media formats supported by the all-Java version, they also integrate with the native media library on the host operating system to play other media files, ones that couldn't be opened with the all-Java version alone.

This might make you deceive yourself: if you develop a JMF application on Windows and it works with your media, it won't necessarily work on another operating system, either because Sun never made a performance pack for that system (Mac OS X), or because even with the performance pack, the native libraries don't support that format. If you go the JMF route, you need to rigorously test cross-platform, or you may very well have an application that really only works on one OS.

HACK #73   Play a Sound with QuickTime for Java

Using QuickTime, you can play even more kinds of sounds, but only on two operating systems.

QuickTime for Java offers another way to significantly improve the media capabilities of your application. Its list of supported formats is huge (see *http://www.apple.com/quicktime/products/qt/specifications.html* for the current list) and always growing as Apple continues to improve it. That's a big advantage over JMF, which was dropped into maintenance mode in 1999 and largely ignored since then.

The huge disadvantage with QuickTime for Java is that it works on Windows and Mac only. That's because QTJ, as it's typically called, is really just an object-oriented (OO) wrapper to call C functions in the native QuickTime library. That gives you native-speed performance, but it also means the wrappers don't do anything without an underlying native implementation.

QuickTime Beating Up on JavaSound

For the purposes of this hack, let's say you only need to support Mac and Windows, or that you need to open files from the iTunes Music Store (QTJ can do it, which is apparently the only way to do it in Java), or for whatever reason QTJ looks like the right solution. Example 10-5 shows a port of the JavaSound audio player to a QTJ-based implementation.

Example 10-5. Playing audio with QuickTime for Java

```
import quicktime.std.*;
import quicktime.std.clocks.*;
import quicktime.std.movies.*;
import quicktime.*;
import quicktime.io.*;
import quicktime.app.time.*;

public class QTJSound extends Object {

    File soundFile;
    JDialog playingDialog;
    Movie movie;

    public static void main (String[] args) {
        JFileChooser chooser = new JFileChooser();
        chooser.showOpenDialog(null);
        File f = chooser.getSelectedFile();
        try {
            QTJSound s = new QTJSound (f);
        } catch (Exception e) {
            e.printStackTrace();
        }
    }

    public QTJSound (File f)
        throws QTException {
        soundFile = f;
        // prepare a dialog to display while playing
        JOptionPane pane = new JOptionPane ("Playing " + f.getName(),
                                    JOptionPane.PLAIN_MESSAGE);
        playingDialog = pane.createDialog (null, "QTJ Sound");
        playingDialog.pack();

        // get and play sound
        QTSession.open();
        QTFile qtf = new QTFile (f);
        OpenMovieFile omf = OpenMovieFile.asRead (qtf);
        movie = Movie.fromFile (omf);
        MyDemoCloser closer = new MyDemoCloser (movie);
        TaskAllMovies.addMovieAndStart ();
        movie.start();
        playingDialog.setVisible(true);
    }

    class MyDemoCloser extends ExtremesCallBack {

        public MyDemoCloser (Movie m) throws QTException {
            super (m.getTimeBase(),
                    StdQTConstants.triggerAtStop);
            callMeWhen();
        }
```

Example 10-5. Playing audio with QuickTime for Java (continued)

```
    public void execute( ) {
        playingDialog.setVisible (false);
        System.out.println ("dialog closed");
        // note: this can hang on Windows - consider
        // using QTSession.exitMovies( ) instead
        QTSession.close( );
        System.out.println ("closed QTSession");
        System.exit(0);
    }
  }
}
```

Some of this code looks very un-Java-like and there's a reason: QTJ is an object-oriented wrapper around a straight-C API. Whenever I see the C versions of things I do in QTJ, I'm grateful they got it as OO as they did. Nevertheless, there are differences: where a Java developer would expect to deal with listeners, QTJ makes you wrangle CallBack objects, which have to reregister themselves every time they're called or else they're forgotten. And the number of imports for a small class is quite atypical—QTJ is highly granular in its class organization.

Take a look at the constructor. After doing the file-selection dialog, it calls QTSession.open( ). This is a call that initializes QuickTime resources and must be made before any other QTJ call, or an exception will be thrown. You'll be responsible for shutting down QuickTime later, of course.

The basic thing you want to do is to use the file to create a Movie. Don't worry, this isn't turning into a video hack; QuickTime uses the term *movie* for any playable or displayable thing it works with: audio, video, audio and video, Flash, static images, etc. To create the Movie, you need an OpenMovieFile, which you get by making a QTFile from java.io.File and then using the static asRead( ) to get an OpenMovieFile.

The demo sets up a callback by creating an instance of the inner class MyDemoCloser, calls the cryptic TaskAllMovies.addMovieAndStart( ) (more on that later), and finally starts the audio with Movie.start( ). If the source is a URL, or a file on really slow media, it might help to call Movie.prePreroll( ) and Movie.preroll( ) before starting, to let QuickTime pre-allocate needed system resources and read in some data.

Setting up a callback to close everything down requires use of an ExtremesCallBack, which is an object that gets called when either the beginning or end of the movie is reached. Its constructor takes the movie's timebase (which is an object representing the movie's time-keeping system) and a flag to indicate what conditions the callback should be called in. The flag is an int, but it really contains bit values that can be ORed together. For example, if the media could play in both directions and you wanted to be notified when it reached the beginning of the movie too, you'd pass StdQTConstants.triggerAtStop | StdQTConstants.triggerAtStart.

Next, you have to use callMeWhen( ) to register the callback. This signs you up for one callback—if you're called and are still interested in future events, you have to reregister with another callMeWhen( ).

When the sound finishes, the callback calls execute( ). This is when you shut everything down, as in the other hacks. Notice that you close down Quick-Time with QTSession.close( ), the obvious counterpart to QTSession.open( ). There are some issues about how well it works on Windows: it sometimes hangs for me, and you may want to use the safer QTSession.exitMovies( ), which only closes down some of QTJ, but the rest seems to get taken care of by QTJ itself, as I've never had a problem.

And one more bit of arcane QTJ lore: the code makes a call to TaskAllMovies.addMovieAndStart( ). This helps deal with the fact that movies have to explicitly be given CPU time, with calls to a task( ) method, in order to work. TaskAllMovies is a convenience Thread that can periodically make this tasking call for all your movies. If you've read Chris' book on QTJ, you would think that this isn't necessary, as having the AWT event-dispatch thread usually provides tasking calls. The problem is that the dialog box that's showing while the audio plays is modal; thus, it *blocks the event loop*, which in turn blocks the tasking you usually get for free with AWT. So, you have to set it up yourself.

QTJ is full of weird gotchas like this. What do you expect when it's largely a port from C?

Compiling QuickTime Code

Yep, this hack has special compile instructions. First, you have to be sure that your machine even has QuickTime for Java on it. It's installed by default with Mac OS X, so this is only an issue for Windows-based developers. On Windows, if you don't have QuickTime at all, get it from *http://www.apple.com/quicktime/* and do a custom install: QuickTime for Java will be one of the non-default optional pieces, and you just need to checkmark it to include it in your install. If you do have QuickTime, run the QuickTime Updater from your Start menu or your tray to do a "custom" update, which will show the same list of optional pieces as the main installer.

The install or update will put *QTJava.zip* into the *lib/ext* of any Java home folders it finds. It should also put a copy in *C:\windows\system32* and add a system-wide environment variable QTJAVA pointing to one of these files, with the path in quotes (which may or may not be good for you, depending on what else you do with environment variables).

Here's the fun part about compiling: you must explicitly point your compile-time classpath to one of these *QTJava.zip* files for javac (or jikes, or whatever) to find the QTJ classes. If you don't, you'll get a bunch of compile-time errors like:

```
QTJSound.java:4: package quicktime.std does not exist
import quicktime.std.*;
       ^
QTJSound.java:5: package quicktime.std.clocks does not exist
import quicktime.std.clocks.*;
       ^
QTJSound.java:6: package quicktime.std.movies does not exist
import quicktime.std.movies.*;
```

So, assuming you want to work with a copy of Java installed in *Program Files\Java\j2re1.4.2_06* (which is my current path...yours may vary), you compile this demo with the following command:

```
C:\>javac
   -classpath "c:\Program Files\Java\j2re1.4.2_06\lib\ext\QTJava.zip"
   QTJSound.java
```

> This should be typed as one line—I've word-wrapped to accommodate the book's margins.

You can substitute any other path to a *QTJava.zip* file for the classpath if you find it more convenient, or just write an Ant build file to automate everything for you.

On Mac OS X, the location of *QTJava.zip* is never a mystery because the system installer puts it in */System/Library/Java/Extensions.QTJava.zip*. So, you compile with:

```
[aeris:HacksBook/Media/52] cadamson% javac -classpath
   /System/Library/Java/Extensions/QTJava.zip
   QTJSound.java
```

In either case, you'll probably be relieved to know that you don't have to specify the classpath when *running* a QTJ application.

Running the Code

Like the JMF port [Hack #72], QTJSound looks and feels more or less the same as the original CoreJavaSound [Hack #71]. The big difference is in the supported sound file formats. QuickTime will open not just uncompressed WAVs and AIFFs, but compressed data in those formats, along with MP3s, AACs, 3GPP mobile audio files, iTunes Music Store files, audio tracks of various audio/video formats like QuickTime movies (*.mov*), MPEG-4, even audio CD tracks (but only on the Mac).

That's obviously the big win with QuickTime for Java: you get support for a lot more formats. The price you pay is that your code only runs on two operating systems and that it can be difficult to write. The ideal would be if the obvious points of extensibility in JavaSound and JMF had been exploited, so that more formats would be available when using those APIs. With a notable exception [Hack #74], that hasn't happened yet.

> By the way, to learn more about QuickTime for Java, check out *QuickTime for Java: A Developer's Notebook* (O'Reilly).

HACK #74   Add MP3 Support to JMF

MP3s are everywhere, and by installing a plug-in you can use them with Java Media Framework, too.

It used to be said that every program will continue to grow until it includes an email reader. Today we could say the same for MP3 players. They are everywhere, and any program that has plug-ins will eventually be given a music player. Playing MP3s in Java used to be quite an ordeal, involving a suite of toolkits and codecs from different sources. Fortunately, it's a lot easier to play an MP3 file these days, and this hack shows how.

JMF came out in 1998, supporting playback of a number of audio and video formats, but not MP3. Support for this popular format arrived with JMF 2.0 in 1999. Unfortunately, in 2002, Sun removed MP3 support from JMF because of licensing problems. Finally, in November of 2004, Sun released a fully licensed MP3 plug-in for public download on their web site. With this plug-in, you can play any MP3 file with only four lines of code.

Add a Plug-In to JMF

First, install Java Media Framework [Hack #72]. To add MP3 support, download the plug-in from *http://java.sun.com/products/java-media/jmf/mp3/download.html*. The download page offers an *.exe* installer for Windows and a ZIP for other platforms. In both cases, there is an *mp3plugin.jar* file that the install docs say you need to place in the *ext/lib* directory of any JRE you want to provide the plug-in to. With the JAR in your classpath, you install the plug-in with the following command:

```
java com.sun.media.codec.audio.mp3.JavaDecoder
```

On Mac OS X, the proper way to add JAR files to the class-path is to put them in */Library/Java/Extensions*, instead of using the actual *ext/lib* directory, which is hard to find and will be wiped out by system installers and updates anyways.

Simplicity Is Nice

Example 10-6 is the code for pretty much the simplest MP3 playing program you can create. You will need to import javax.media.* in addition to the usual java.io classes.

Example 10-6. A very basic MP3 player

```java
import javax.media.*;

public class MP3Player {

    public static void main(String[] args) throws Exception {
        File file = new File("test.mp3");
        MediaLocator mrl = new MediaLocator(file.toURL());
        Player player = Manager.createPlayer(mrl);
        player.start();
    }
}
```

Those four lines in main( ) do it all. The MediaLocator takes care of loading and buffering the file as long as you can give it a URL. The player controls the actual music output. It has the basic functions you would expect, like start( ) and stop( ). If you compile and run this program with a test MP3 file, audio should start playing immediately.

Distribute Your Program

If you need to distribute your program, it's best to include platform install-ers and instruct users to install them first.

Licensing restrictions from Sun may apply here!

Even better, if you have a custom install program, make it run the JMF and MP3 installers first. If you don't have an installer or don't know which platform the program will be installed on, use the cross-platform versions (also available from the URLs mentioned in this hack). They are slower but are completely written in Java so they can run on anything.

HACK #75   Build an Audio Waveform Display

With a little understanding of audio data formats, you can easily build a basic graphical audio display.

Representing audio visually is extremely useful. You can use waveform displays to quickly tell audio files apart, like a file thumbnail, or for non-linear editing, such as deleting parts of the file and processing.

Figure 10-4 shows a waveform displayed in Audacity, a free, open source audio editing application. This hack shows you how to build a basic waveform display from raw audio data.

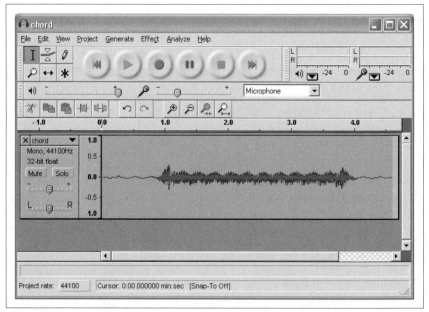

Figure 10-4. Audacity with an audio waveform displayed

The end result of this hack is displayed in Figure 10-5. You'll start by reading in the entire audio file using an AudioInputStream. Then you'll convert the raw data from the stream into useful audio samples, organized by channel. With the converted channel audio data, you'll create a single waveform panel. Then you'll wrap up the complete audio display by combining several waveform panels to display multi-channel audio.

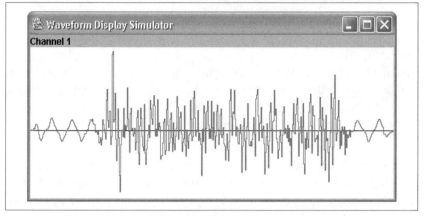

Figure 10-5. The waveform display you'll build in this hack

Some Basic Definitions

You'll need to know a few basic terms and concepts about audio before you get started.

Sample
> One measurement of audio data. For Pulse Code Modulated (PCM) encoding, a sample is an instantaneous representation of the voltage of the analog audio. There are other types of encoding, like μ-law and a-law, that are rarely used.

Sampling Rate
> The number of samples in one second. Measured in Hertz (Hz) or kilo-Hertz (kHz). The most common sampling rate is 44.1 kHz (CD quality audio). Often, you'll find 22.05 kHz or 11.025 kHz on the Web, since the files are smaller and the conversion is easier.

Sample Size
> The number of bits in one sample. It is typically a multiple of eight because data is stored in 8-bit bytes. The most common sample size is 16 bits, which is CD quality audio. Often you'll find 8-bit audio because the files are smaller. You'll rarely find anything less then 8-bit audio because the quality is pretty poor. Sample size is sometimes called bit depth.

Channel
> A channel is an independent stream of audio. Stereo is the most common form of multi-channel audio—one independent left and right channel. Higher-end audio formats include 5.1 surround sound (actually six channels) and up.

Frame

A frame is a cross section of samples across all channels in the audio file. So, a 16-bit stereo (two channel) audio file will have 32-bit frames (16 bits per sample * 2 channels per frame = 32 bits per frame).

Load the Raw Data

Java reads raw audio data in 8-bit bytes, but most audio has a higher sample size. So, in order to represent the audio, you'll have to combine multiple bytes to create samples in the audio format. But first, you'll need to load all of the audio into a buffer before you combine the bytes into samples.

Start by getting an audio stream from a file:

```
File file = new File(filename);
AudioInputStream audioInputStream = AudioSystem.getAudioInputStream(file);
```

Now that you have the AudioInputStream, you can read in the audio data. AudioInputStream has a read( ) method that takes an unpopulated byte[] and reads in data the length of the byte[]. To read in the entire audio file in one shot, create a byte[] the length of the entire audio file. The complete length of the file in bytes is:

```
total number of bytes = bytes per frame * total number of frames
```

You can get the number of frames for the whole file (frameLength) and the size of the frame (frameSize) from the AudioInputStream:

```
int frameLength = (int) audioInputStream.getFrameLength( );
int frameSize = (int) audioInputStream.getFormat().getFrameSize( );
```

You can create the byte[] with the length set to frameLength * frameSize:

```
byte[] bytes = new byte[frameLength * frameSize];
```

Finally, you can read in the audio, passing the AudioInputStream the empty byte[] and catching the appropriate exceptions:

```
int result = 0;
try {
    result = audioInputStream.read(bytes);
} catch (Exception e) {
    e.printStackTrace( );
}
```

Convert to Samples and Channels

The raw audio data isn't very useful. It needs to be broken up into channels and samples. From there, it's easy to paint the samples.

The bytes will be converted to samples and represented as ints. You'll need a container to store the samples across all channels. So, create a two dimensional int[][] referencing the channel and samples per channel. You've already seen how to get the frame length from the AuduioInputStream, and you can get the number of channels the same way. Here is the code to initialize the int[][]:

```
int numChannels = audioInputStream.getFormat().getChannels();
int frameLength = (int) audioInputStream.getFrameLength();
int[][] toReturn = new int[numChannels][frameLength];
```

Now, you need to iterate through the byte[], convert the bytes to samples, and place the sample in the appropriate channel in the int[][]. The byte[] is organized by frames, meaning that you'll read in a sample for every channel rather than all of the samples for a specific channel in a row. So, the flow is to loop through the channels and add samples until the byte[] has been iterated completely:

```
int sampleIndex = 0;

for (int t = 0; t < eightBitByteArray.length;) {
    for (int channel = 0; channel < numChannels; channel++) {
        int low = (int) eightBitByteArray[t];
        t++;
        int high = (int) eightBitByteArray[t];
        t++;
        int sample = getSixteenBitSample(high, low);
        toReturn[channel][sampleIndex] = sample;
    }

    sampleIndex++;
}
```

This hack is going to deal exclusively with 16-bit samples. They are by far the most common. Plus, you can get an idea for how sample conversion works while still keeping things pretty straightforward. This code gets much trickier with multiple dynamic sample sizes.

Now for the getSixteenBitSample() method. You can't simply add the bytes together using regular addition because the bits are displaced—in a 16-bit sample the high byte represents bits 0 through 7, and the low byte represents bits 8 through 15. It's more like concatenation, so the type of math shown here won't work:

```
  1010 1101 (high byte)
+ 0011 0010 (low byte)
-----------
  1101 1111
```

What you want is more like this:

```
1010 1101              (high byte)
+           0011 0010  (low byte)
---------------------
1010 1101 0011 0010
```

And in order to get this to work with standard addition, you need to add two 16-bit bytes with bits shifted and placeholder 0s added where necessary. Then you get something like this:

```
1010 1101 0000 0000 (high byte)
+ 0000 0000 0011 0010 (low byte)
---------------------
1010 1101 0011 0010
```

The high byte needs to be *bit shifted*. Bit shifting, the process of sliding bits around, is typically a big no-no in Java—as a result, you've probably never seen the bit-shifting operator before (it's << or >> depending on the direction followed by the number of bits to shift in either direction). However, here it is necessary to use bit shifting, so you will bit shift the high byte 8 bits to the left:

```
high << 8
```

Now, you need to prepend the leading 0s onto the low byte. You can do this using the bit AND operator and using a 16-bit byte consisting of all 0s. It works like this:

```
0000 0000 0000 0000 (all 0's bytes)
+           0011 0010 (low byte)
---------------------
0000 0000 0011 0010
```

Here is the code for the sample conversion:

```
private int getSixteenBitSample(int high, int low) {
    return (high << 8) + (low & 0x00ff);
}
```

Creating a Single Waveform Display

Now that you have the audio sample data organized by channels, it's time to get to painting. To keep everything modular, create a class called SingleWaveformPanel to paint one channel of audio data. In the next section, you'll write a WaveformPanelContainer to use multiple SingleWaveformPanels to handle multi-channel audio.

The waveform painting is going to be drawn by plotting points scaled to the sample data and drawing lines between them. This is simplistic, but it yields good results. Figures 10-4 and 10-5 show the same waveform in Audacity and the simulator for this hack; they're pretty close.

I'm going to gloss over the scaling code because I really want to concentrate on the conversion from audio information to visualization. But to understand why scaling is necessary, remember that CD quality audio has 44,100 samples per second. So, without scaling, you would need 44,100 horizontal pixels for every second of your audio file. Obviously, this is impractical. So, if you dig into the source code for this hack, you can see the scaling and how the scales are determined. Meanwhile, just assume that the waveform is always scaled to fit in the panel.

Start by drawing the center line at 0:

```
g.setColor(REFERENCE_LINE_COLOR);
g.drawLine(0, lineHeight, (int)getWidth( ), lineHeight);
```

Next, mark the origin to start drawing at 0,0:

```
int oldX = 0;
int oldY = (int) (getHeight( ) / 2);
int xIndex = 0;
```

Now, you need to figure out the incremental jump between samples to adjust for the scale factor. This works out to be:

```
number of samples / (number of samples * horizontal scale factor)
```

The following code grabs the increment and paints a line from the origin to the first sample:

```
int increment = getIncrement( )
g.setColor(WAVEFORM_COLOR);

int t = 0;

for (t = 0; t < increment; t += increment) {
    g.drawLine(oldX, oldY, xIndex, oldY);
    xIndex++;
    oldX = xIndex;
}
```

Finish up by iterating through the audio and drawing lines to the scaled samples:

```
for (; t < samples.length; t += increment) {
    double scaleFactor = getYScaleFactor( );
    double scaledSample = samples[t] * scaleFactor;
    int y = (int) ((getHeight( ) / 2) - (scaledSample));
    g.drawLine(oldX, oldY, xIndex, y);

    xIndex++;
    oldX = xIndex;
    oldY = y;
    }
}
```

Create a Container

Now that you have the waveform painting under control, you need to create a container called WaveformPanelContainer for SingleWaveformPanels in order to show multi-channel audio. Figure 10-6 shows the waveform in the simulator.

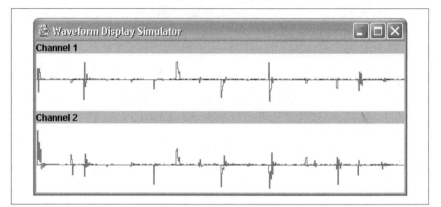

Figure 10-6. Multi-channel (stereo) audio in the simulator for this hack

Example 10-7 is the complete code for the WaveformPanelContainer. AudioInfo is a helper class that contains references to the loaded audio samples and the current channel.

Example 10-7. Testing out the waveform display

```
public class WaveformPanelContainer extends JPanel {
    private ArrayList singleChannelWaveformPanels = new ArrayList();
    private AudioInfo audioInfo = null;

    public WaveformPanelContainer() {
        setLayout(new GridLayout(0,1));
    }

    public void setAudioToDisplay(AudioInputStream audioInputStream){
        singleChannelWaveformPanels = new ArrayList();
        audioInfo = new AudioInfo(audioInputStream);
        for (int t=0; t<audioInfo.getNumberOfChannels(); t++){
            SingleWaveformPanel waveformPanel
                    = new SingleWaveformPanel(audioInfo, t);
            singleChannelWaveformPanels.add(waveformPanel);
            add(createChannelDisplay(waveformPanel, t));
        }
    }
```

Example 10-7. Testing out the waveform display (continued)

```
private JComponent createChannelDisplay(
        SingleWaveformPanel waveformPanel,
        int index) {
    JPanel panel = new JPanel(new BorderLayout());
    panel.add(waveformPanel, BorderLayout.CENTER);

    JLabel label = new JLabel("Channel " + ++index);
    panel.add(label, BorderLayout.NORTH);

    return panel;
    }
}
```

Seeing Is Believing

Now, you're ready to run the hack. The main() method shown here is the simulator code. Notice the creation of the AudioInputStream and the creation of the container with the stream. All painting and management of SingleWaveformPanels is encapsulated within the separate panel classes:

```
public static void main(String[] args) {
    try {

        JFrame frame = new JFrame("Waveform Display Simulator");
        frame.setBounds(200,200, 500, 350);

        File file = new File(args[0]);
        AudioInputStream audioInputStream
            = AudioSystem.getAudioInputStream(file);

        WaveformPanelContainer container = new WaveformPanelContainer();
        container.setAudioToDisplay(audioInputStream);

        frame.getContentPane().setLayout(new BorderLayout());
        frame.getContentPane().add(container, BorderLayout.CENTER);

        frame.setDefaultCloseOperation(JFrame.EXIT_ON_CLOSE);

        frame.show();
        frame.validate();
        frame.repaint();

    } catch (Exception e){
        e.printStackTrace();
    }
}
```

Then, just make sure to pass the audio filename in at the command line. Use something like this:

```
java WaveformDisplaySimulator chord.wav
```

This hack shows you how to do all of the sample conversion and painting you need to display a waveform very simplistically. However, you should address a few key issues before using this in an audio application; for example, this only deals with 16-bit audio. You probably would want to build something a little more generic to deal with other sample sizes. You may also want to deal with compression, so you can display waveforms for MP3 files. That said, this hack still gives you a good idea of how to dig into raw audio data and get your audio visualization on.

—Jonathan Simon

HACK #76   Play Non-Trivial Audio

When loading an entire audio clip into memory is a bad idea (or just impossible), you have to take JavaSound responsibilities into your own hands.

Playing JavaSound audio with a Clip **[Hack #71]** is a pretty convenient way to play a short sound, like a sound effect for a desktop application. The only problem is that the Clip loads all the audio into memory, which could have a couple of bad side effects:

- It makes your application use more memory, which could cause problems.
- The audio you need might not fit into memory at all.

You might have run into this second point if you tried to load a really big audio file into a Clip. For example, I took a 3 minute, 45 second track from a CD and converted it to 8-bit mono PCM in an AIFF file, which ended up being 9.4 MB. You can guess what happened:

```
[aeris:HacksBook/Media/52] cadamson% java CoreJavaSound
javax.sound.sampled.LineUnavailableException: Failed to allocate clip data:
Requested buffer too large.
        at com.sun.media.sound.MixerClip.implOpen(MixerClip.java:536)
        at com.sun.media.sound.MixerClip.open(MixerClip.java:161)
        at com.sun.media.sound.MixerClip.open(MixerClip.java:249)
        at CoreJavaSound.<init>(CoreJavaSound.java:39)
        at CoreJavaSound.main(CoreJavaSound.java:17)
```

Unfortunately, most of the JavaSound code you'll find on the Web deals with Clips only and not with getting a Line for larger files, or potentially endless streams for that matter. Why? Perhaps because JavaSound doesn't do it for you—*you* are responsible for reading bytes and feeding them to JavaSound!

Grabbing a DataLine

This hack is going to play an uncompressed (i.e., PCM) AIFF or WAV file of arbitrary length by getting a DataLine for the data and then repeatedly reading the data from disk and writing it to the DataLine.

> PCM stands for *Pulse Code Modulation*, which means that analog audio has been sampled at regular intervals and quantized (i.e., each sample is expressed as a numeric value). It's the lowest-level, most common denominator data that Java-Sound understands, since it can be delivered directly to a sound system for playback.

The class to do this will be called PCMFilePlayer. Given a file, its responsibilities are to:

1. Verify that the file contains PCM data (signed or unsigned).
2. Get a Line for this format.
3. Kick off a thread to read bytes from the file and write them to the Line, which plays them.

Reading and writing bytes doesn't sound too bad, but JavaSound imposes another requirement on you: you have to send complete frames, not just a bunch of bytes, to the Line. A frame is one complete sample of audio in whatever format you're dealing with. For the PCM formats supported by this hack, a frame can be one of three sizes:

- 1 byte for 8-bit mono sound
- 2 bytes for either 8-bit stereo sound or 16-bit mono sound
- 4 bytes for 16-bit stereo sound

The implication for the read-write loop is that if you read some number of bytes that leave you off an even frame boundary, then you have to save the partial frame you've read, not send it to the Line, and instead append it to the beginning of the next read.

Finally, when you reach the end of the file, you need to call Line.drain( ) to make sure it plays out all the data you've sent it, and then close the Line.

The code for the PCMLinePlayer is shown in Example 10-8.

Example 10-8. Playing uncompressed audio files in JavaSound

```
import javax.sound.sampled.*;

public class PCMFilePlayer implements Runnable {
    File file;
```

Example 10-8. Playing uncompressed audio files in JavaSound (continued)

```java
AudioInputStream in;
SourceDataLine line;
int frameSize;
byte[] buffer = new byte [32 * 1024]; // 32k is arbitrary
Thread playThread;
boolean playing;
boolean notYetEOF;

public PCMFilePlayer (File f)
    throws IOException,
            UnsupportedAudioFileException,
            LineUnavailableException {
    file = f;
    in = AudioSystem.getAudioInputStream (f);
    AudioFormat format = in.getFormat( );
    AudioFormat.Encoding formatEncoding = format.getEncoding( );
    if (! (formatEncoding.equals (AudioFormat.Encoding.PCM_SIGNED) ||
            formatEncoding.equals (AudioFormat.Encoding.PCM_UNSIGNED)))
        throw new UnsupportedAudioFileException (
                            file.getName( ) + " is not PCM audio");
    System.out.println ("got PCM format");
    frameSize = format.getFrameSize( );
    DataLine.Info info =
        new DataLine.Info (SourceDataLine.class, format);
    System.out.println ("got info");
    line = (SourceDataLine) AudioSystem.getLine (info);
    System.out.println ("got line");
    line.open( );
    System.out.println ("opened line");
    playThread = new Thread (this);
    playing = false;
    notYetEOF = true;
    playThread.start( );
}

public void run( ) {
    int readPoint = 0;
    int bytesRead = 0;

    try {
        while (notYetEOF) {
            if (playing) {
                bytesRead = in.read (buffer,
                                    readPoint,
                                    buffer.length - readPoint);
                if (bytesRead == -1) {
                    notYetEOF = false;
                    break;
                }
            }
```

Example 10-8. Playing uncompressed audio files in JavaSound (continued)

```
                    // how many frames did we get,
                    // and how many are left over?
                    int frames = bytesRead / frameSize;
                    int leftover = bytesRead % frameSize;
                    // send to line
                    line.write (buffer, readPoint, bytesRead-leftover);
                    // save the leftover bytes
                    System.arraycopy (buffer, bytesRead,
                                      buffer, 0,
                                      leftover);
                    readPoint = leftover;

                } else {
                    // if not playing
                    // Thread.yield( );
                    try { Thread.sleep (10);}
                    catch (InterruptedException ie) {}
                }
            } // while notYetEOF
            System.out.println ("reached eof");
            line.drain( );
            line.stop( );
        } catch (IOException ioe) {
            ioe.printStackTrace( );
        } finally {
            // line.close( );
        }
    } // run

    public void start( ) {
        playing = true;
        if (! playThread.isAlive( ))
            playThread.start( );
        line.start( );
    }

    public void stop( ) {
        playing = false;
        line.stop( );
    }

    public SourceDataLine getLine( ) {
        return line;
    }

    public File getFile( ) {
        return file;
    }
}
```

Notice in the constructor that, as with the Clip, the way to get an actual Line object is to construct a DataLine.Info object and then pass that to AudioSystem. This time, you construct a DataLine.Info class with both the SourceDataLine class—you need this subclass of Line because it provides the write( ) method with which you supply bytes to the Line—and an AudioFormat object describing the data you'll be supplying. Assuming that doesn't throw a LineUnavailableException (and it shouldn't, because the format is already known to be PCM, which JavaSound always supports), you'll have a line that you can open and start writing bytes to.

As mentioned previously, the key issue for the thread that reads bytes from the file and writes them to the Line is that it has to be aware of frame boundaries. In this code, readPoint indicates the index of the buffer to start reading bytes into. When you have an incomplete frame after reading from the input stream, you copy the bytes from the incomplete frame to the front of the buffer in preparation for the next read. For example, if you have a frame size of 4, and bytesRead % 4 equals 3, then you copy those 3 bytes to the front of the buffer and set readPoint to 3. The next read( ) will start at 3, and the first byte read into the buffer will complete the frame from the previous read( ).

Big Files, Big Sound

Since this is still in the realm of JavaSound, much of what was shown in the Clip-based hack still works. A demo application simply has to provide PCMFilePlayer with a file and then start it. Since PCMFilePlayer exposes its Line through a get method, you can even wire up as a LineListener and get notified of STOP, START, OPEN, and CLOSE LineEvents. Example 10-9 shows the simple GUI, using PCMFilePlayer.

Example 10-9. Playing arbitrarily long uncompressed WAV or AIFF audio

```
import javax.sound.sampled.*;

public class StreamingLineSound extends Object
        implements LineListener {

    File soundFile;
    JDialog playingDialog;
    PCMFilePlayer player;

    public static void main (String[] args) {
        JFileChooser chooser = new JFileChooser( );
        chooser.showOpenDialog(null);
        File f = chooser.getSelectedFile( );
```

Example 10-9. Playing arbitrarily long uncompressed WAV or AIFF audio (continued)

```
        try {
            StreamingLineSound s = new StreamingLineSound (f);
        } catch (Exception e) {
            e.printStackTrace( );
        }
    }

    public StreamingLineSound (File f)
        throws LineUnavailableException, IOException,
            UnsupportedAudioFileException {
        soundFile = f;
        // prepare a dialog to display while playing
        JOptionPane pane = new JOptionPane ("Playing " + f.getName( ),
                                    JOptionPane.PLAIN_MESSAGE);
        playingDialog = pane.createDialog (null, "Streaming Sound");
        playingDialog.pack( );

        player = new PCMFilePlayer (soundFile);
        player.getLine( ).addLineListener (this);
        player.start( );

    }

    // LineListener
    public void update (LineEvent le) {
        LineEvent.Type type = le.getType( );
        if (type == LineEvent.Type.OPEN) {
            System.out.println ("OPEN");
        } else if (type == LineEvent.Type.CLOSE) {
            System.out.println ("CLOSE");
            System.exit (0);
        } else if (type == LineEvent.Type.START) {
            System.out.println ("START");
            playingDialog.setVisible(true);
        } else if (type == LineEvent.Type.STOP) {
            System.out.println ("STOP");
            playingDialog.setVisible(false);
            player.line.close( );
        }
    }
}
```

When run, this class shows a dialog box (seen in Figure 10-7), identical to the one produced in "Play a Sound with JavaSound" [Hack #71]. The only difference is that this one can stay up potentially indefinitely, since the player can keep reading and writing bytes forever.

Figure 10-7. Playing a large AIFF file in JavaSound

HACK #77 Show Audio Information While Playing Sound

Providing visual feedback for JavaSound audio, or at least trying to....

You might want to play a clip without any corresponding visuals; for example, if you were using it to signal the end of a long-running process such as uploading a file. On the other hand, if the sound is the focus of the application, as in a music-player application, you might need to show the user some information about the audio he's playing.

The Code

You already know how to play audio from a file or stream **[Hack #76]**; building on that, you can create a simple GUI that shows some of the basic traits of the audio, by pulling fields out of the AudioFormat object, which can be retrieved from the Line once it has been created. These fields include the audio format, bits/sample, frame size and rate, and *endian*ness (which indicates how two-byte values are to be interpreted: *big-endian* means the first byte is more significant, and *little-endian* means the second is).

More impressively, DataLine provides a getLevel( ) method that returns the current level of the audio being played, as a float from 0.0 (silence) to 1.0 (maximum volume). You can use this to create a graphical level meter by getting the level and coloring in that percentage of a component. For example, if the level is 0.5, you'd fill in half of the component.

Drawing this level meter is pretty straightforward: create a JPanel whose paint( ) method clears the Graphics, gets the line level, and fills a rectangle starting at (0,0) with a height equal to the component's height and a width equal to the level times the component's width. Then you need to set up an animation loop—a javax.swing.Timer is convenient because it avoids any thread-safety issues while doing the painting—to repeatedly call repaint( ) on the meter.

Combine this together and you have the `DataLineInfoGUI`, seen in
Example 10-10. Note that to play the audio, it uses the `PCMFilePlayer` class
from the previous hack, so you can use an arbitrarily long AIFF or WAV, as
long as its contents are uncompressed PCM data.

Example 10-10. Displaying audio format information

```java
import javax.sound.sampled.*;

public class DataLineInfoGUI extends JPanel {

    PCMFilePlayer player;
    JButton startButton;

    public DataLineInfoGUI (File f) {
        super( );
        try {
            player = new PCMFilePlayer (f);
        } catch (Exception ioe) {
            add (new JLabel ("Error: " +
                            ioe.getMessage( )));
            return;
        }
        DataLine line = player.getLine( );
        // layout
        // line 1: name
        setLayout (new BoxLayout (this, BoxLayout.Y_AXIS));
        add (new JLabel ("File:   " +
                        player.getFile().getName( )));
        // line 2: levels
        add (new DataLineLevelMeter (line));
        // line 3: format info as textarea
        AudioFormat format = line.getFormat( );
        JTextArea ta = new JTextArea( );
        ta.setBorder (new TitledBorder ("Format"));
        ta.append ("Encoding: " +
                    format.getEncoding().toString( ) + "\n");
        ta.append ("Bits/sample: " +
                    format.getSampleSizeInBits( ) + "\n");
        ta.append ("Endianness: " +
                    (format.isBigEndian( ) ? " big " : "little") + "\n");
        ta.append ("Frame size: " +
                    format.getFrameSize( ) + "\n");
        ta.append ("Frame rate: " +
                    format.getFrameRate( ) + "\n");
        add (ta);

        // now start playing
        player.start( );
    }
```

Example 10-10. Displaying audio format information (continued)

```java
public static void main (String[] args) {
    JFileChooser chooser = new JFileChooser( );
    chooser.showOpenDialog(null);
    File file = chooser.getSelectedFile( );
    DataLineInfoGUI demo =
        new DataLineInfoGUI (file);

    JFrame f = new JFrame ("JavaSound info");
    f.getContentPane( ).add (demo);
    f.pack( );
    f.setVisible(true);
}

class DataLineLevelMeter extends JPanel {
    DataLine line;
    float level = 0.0f;
    public DataLineLevelMeter (DataLine l) {
        line = l;
        Timer timer =
            new Timer (50,
                        new ActionListener ( ){
                            public void actionPerformed (ActionEvent e) {
                                level = line.getLevel( );
                                repaint( );
                            }
                        });
        timer.start( );
    }
    public void paint (Graphics g) {
        Dimension d = getSize( );
        g.setColor (Color.green);
        int meterWidth = (int) (level * (float) d.width);
        g.fillRect (0, 0, meterWidth, d.height);
    }
}
}
```

This is a pretty straightforward implementation of the strategy sketched out previously: the class is a JPanel with a BoxLayout to which you can add an arbitrary number of rows. The first is the name of the file, the second is the level meter, and the third is a JTextArea to which you can append various fields pulled from the AudioFormat.

The level meter's constructor takes care of setting up its own repaint callbacks, so there's no babysitting required on the part of the caller. All that's left for the constructor is to start the player to begin feeding bytes to the Line.

Testing It Out

Launch the DataLineGUI application and you'll get a file-selection dialog. Choose a suitable AIFF or WAV, and you'll see the GUI shown in Figure 10-8.

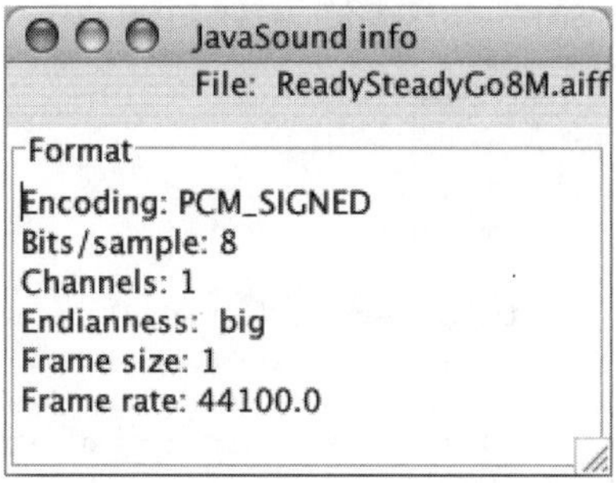

Figure 10-8. Audio player display with format information

This is all well and good for a simple GUI, but there's one problem: *where the heck is our level meter?!* It should be between the filename and the text area, but it's totally not there!

Initially, I suspected my repaint code was hosed, but it all seemed correct. So, right after figuring out the meter width, I added a sanity-check debug line:

```
System.out.println ("level = " + level);
```

And when I ran it, I got a result that I really didn't want to see:

```
[aeris:HacksBook/Media/x11] cadamson% java DataLineInfoGUI
got PCM format
got info
got line
opened line
level = 0.0
level = 0.0
level = 0.0
level = 0.0
level = 0.0
```

And that was on a really loud song, so it wasn't just a slow fade in. I looked around to see if there was something special you have to do for getLevel( ) to work, but there wasn't.

Then I Googled, and found this post to the javasound-interest mailing list from February 2003:

```
Date:         Mon, 17 Feb 2003 22:31:21 -0800
Reply-To:     Discussion list for JavaSound API
              <JAVASOUND-INTEREST@JAVA.SUN.COM>
Sender:       Discussion list for JavaSound API
              <JAVASOUND-INTEREST@JAVA.SUN.COM>
From:         Florian Bomers <Florian.Bomers@SUN.COM>
Organization: Sun Microsystems Inc.
Subject:      Re: DataLine.getLevel()?
Comments: To: knute@frazmtn.com
Content-Type: text/plain; charset=us-ascii

Unfortunately, it is not implemented. (actually, in my private opinion, it
is a questionable method anyway: usually soundcard drivers do not provide
such a primitive, so the Java Sound implementation has to calculate this
"level" on its own. But there are many different algorithms to do so, suited
depending for what the "level" is needed for, and it would possibly eat
unnecessarily processor resources. So I guess it's best if everybody does
the calculation of the "level" on his own on the buffers received by the TDL
or written to the SDL, respectively. Easy and fast algorithms are maximum,
moving average,block average, power).

sorry...
Florian

Knute Johnson wrote:
>
> Anybody know if DataLine.getLevel() is implemented?  All I get is 0.0
> on SourceDataLines and -1.0 on TargetDataLines.
>
> Thanks,
>
> Knute Johnson
```

In fact, a little further research shows that the fact that DataLine.getLevel() always returns UNKNOWN_LEVEL was filed as bug 4297101 in the Java Bug Parade on December 6, 1999. Five years later, it's still not fixed, though it looks like there was at least an attempt to fix it for Tiger (J2SE 5.0)—a fix that was abandoned in August 2003.

 By the way, wouldn't it have saved a lot of people a lot of time if they disclosed in the Javadoc that this method is a no-op? But I digress....

So, the level meter is not going to work—not because of the graphics, but because there's no way to get an accurate level. Or is there?

Hacking the Hack

Florian's message to javasound-interest says it is best if "everybody does the calculation of the 'level' on his own[, based] on the buffers received by the TDL [(TargetDataLine, usually used by capture devices)] or written to the SDL [(SourceDataLine)], respectively."

Setting aside the argument of duplication of effort, note that the buffers he speaks of are available in the hack code; it's what the PCMFilePlayer reads from the file and writes to the Line (specifically, a SourceDataLine, as Florian's message notes). So, in theory at least, this can be done. But it's not going to be pretty.

First, create a new DataLineInfoGUI2 class that is identical to the one from earlier in this hack, except that instead of using a PCMFilePlayer, it uses a PCMFilePlayerLeveler, a class that will be defined next.

This new class is pretty much the same as the old PCMFilePlayer, except that on each time through the while loop, as it reads the buffer and writes it to the line, it will call a method to scan through the buffer and determine a level for this group of samples. So, after reading the bytes from the input stream but before writing them to the line, add:

```
// calculate level
calculateLevel (buffer, readPoint, leftover);
```

As Florian argues in his message, the idea of a level is up for interpretation, but there is a general sense that it should represent the loudness or quietness of the audio at a certain time. Making the problem worse is the fact that the sample values will always be going up and down because the samples represent how much a speaker should be excited or relaxed, and it's the sample's periodic change that creates sound waves we hear. Put another way, even the loudest sounds can have some 0 samples at the bottom of their waves.

As a crude attempt at approximating a level, this hack's implementation gets the maximum amplitude (on either speaker, if the source is stereo) in the entire buffer. To make this a little more fine-tuned, this version of the player figures out a buffer size suitable to provide 1/20 of a second of audio, rather than the flat 32 KB used earlier. To do that, add this after getting the Line in the constructor:

```
// figure out a small buffer size
int bytesPerSec = format.getSampleSizeInBits( ) *
                  (int) format.getSampleRate( );
System.out.println ("bytesPerSec = " + bytesPerSec);
int bufferSize = bytesPerSec / 20;
buffer = new byte[bufferSize];
```

This needs to sync with the line as well—if the line's buffer is nearly full, it won't accept this entire buffer on the write( ) without blocking. So, you can tune the while loop to do a read-and-write only if the Line will accept a bufferful of data. Do this by adding the following block after the if (playing) statement:

```
// only write if the line will take at
// least a buffer-ful of data
if (line.available( ) < buffer.length) {
    Thread.yield( );
    continue;
}
```

Now, the only problem is implementing calculateLevel( )—i.e., doing the actual iteration through the buffer to calculate a maximum value. This, frankly, is a huge pain in the butt, because to determine each sample value, you have to deal with four issues you hadn't cared about before:

- Channels (i.e., mono versus stereo)
- Sample size
- Endianness
- Signing

This is handled in the calculateLevel( ) method of PCMFilePlayerLeveler, listed in Example 10-11.

Example 10-11. Method to calculate a crude "level" of sample bytes in a buffer

```
private void calculateLevel (byte[] buffer,
                             int readPoint,
                             int leftOver) {
    int max = 0;
    boolean use16Bit = (format.getSampleSizeInBits( ) == 16);
    boolean signed = (format.getEncoding( ) ==
                    AudioFormat.Encoding.PCM_SIGNED);
    boolean bigEndian = (format.isBigEndian( ));
    if (use16Bit) {
        for (int i=readPoint; i<buffer.length-leftOver; i+=2) {
            int value = 0;
            // deal with endianness
            int hiByte = (bigEndian ? buffer[i] : buffer[i+1]);
            int loByte = (bigEndian ? buffer[i+1] : buffer [i]);
            if (signed) {
                short shortVal = (short) hiByte;
                shortVal = (short) ((shortVal << 8) | (byte) loByte);
                value = shortVal;
            } else {
                value = (hiByte << 8) | loByte;
            }
```

Example 10-11. Method to calculate a crude "level" of sample bytes in a buffer (continued)

```
                max = Math.max (max, value);
            } // for
        } else {
            // 8 bit - no endianness issues, just sign
            for (int i=readPoint; i<buffer.length-leftOver; i++) {
                int value = 0;
                if (signed) {
                    value = buffer [i];
                } else {
                    short shortVal = 0;
                    shortVal = (short) (shortVal | buffer [i]);
                    value = shortVal;
                }
                max = Math.max (max, value);
            } // for
        } // 8 bit
        // express max as float of 0.0 to 1.0 of max value
        // of 8 or 16 bits (signed or unsigned)
        if (signed) {
            if (use16Bit) { level = (float) max / MAX_16_BITS_SIGNED; }
            else { level = (float) max / MAX_8_BITS_SIGNED; }
        } else {
            if (use16Bit) { level = (float) max / MAX_16_BITS_UNSIGNED; }
            else { level = (float) max / MAX_8_BITS_UNSIGNED; }
        }
    } // calculateLevel
```

This crude implementation just reads all the samples in order, meaning the stereo case—samples alternating between left and right—is ignored. Thus, the maximum value wins, regardless of what channel it's on.

Figuring out the value is still a bit-munging pain because of the three outstanding issues that must be dealt with. For 16-bit audio, the samples should be read two at a time. You arrange the "high" (most significant) and "low" (least significant) bytes based on the endianness of the format, and then cast to a Java int or short based on whether you need to maintain the sign bit (in a 32-bit int, the 16 bits won't be signed; in Java's 16-bit short, the sign will be maintained). Eight-bit audio spares you the endianness hassle, though you still have to be aware of signage, and cast to a byte or short based on whether you need to preserve a sign.

All of this, just to figure out the value of a sample. As you might expect, the only thing left to do on each loop is to compare the sample's value to the maximum for this buffer, and to reset the maximum if this value is higher. At the end, you divide the maximum value against the maximum possible value for that combination of bits and signage to get the level as a value between 0.0 and 1.0.

Running the Hacked Hack

When you run this hack, you finally get a player with a level meter, as seen in Figure 10-9.

```
      ⊖ ⊖ ⊖  JavaSound info
                File:  SpaceLion.aiff
    ┌Format────────────────────┐
    │Encoding: PCM_SIGNED        │
    │Bits/sample: 8              │
    │Channels: 1                 │
    │Endianness: big             │
    │Frame size: 1               │
    │Frame rate: 44100.0         │
    └───────────────────────────┘
```

Figure 10-9. Audio player display with format information and level meter

While this looks OK in a book, it really isn't very satisfactory when you're watching the audio as it plays. It doesn't seem to relate to the music that closely; that is, it seems to follow softer music OK, but it really falls apart on rock music.

Part of the reason is that this "maximum" algorithm is quite crude; an approach such as averaging the samples in the buffer might be more realistic.

But the real problem is that the access JavaSound gives you is doomed to be hopelessly behind what's being played. Think about the available() method, which reports how much you can write to the SourceDataLine's buffer without blocking. What's happening is that you're refilling one end of its buffer, while it drains out the other end to the speakers—or more accurately, to the native sound system (which may have its own buffers, and thus more latency). This arrangement is illustrated in Figure 10-10.

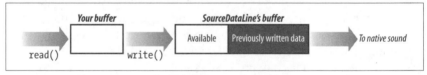

Figure 10-10. Flow of samples through buffers in JavaSound

So, you can calculate the level for the samples in the buffer, but it will be some time until those samples are played, so you have a mismatch of what's being measured and what's actually being played. What you need is access to the SourceDataLine's buffer, so you could run the level check on the bytes that are just about to be played. Until and unless that's available, the suggested workaround isn't really going to work.

Of course, Sun could just go and actually implement getLevel( )...wouldn't that be nice?

HACK #78 Provide Audio Controls During Playback

Let your users take control of JavaSound playback.

To complete this set of JavaSound-related hacks, why not give the user the opportunity to control the sound as it plays? JavaSound provides a very dynamic means of getting at *controls* like *gain* and *pan* (more commonly thought of as volume and balance) through a discovery mechanism that you can use to support any kind of control that might exist, even a control you know nothing about.

On the other hand, JavaSound presents a control not as a GUI widget, but just as an object that can affect the behavior of a Line. This hack will help you provide the GUI side.

The Control class simply defines a getType( ) and toString( ) method. What's more interesting is its subclasses, each of which defines a different kind of control:

BooleanControl
> Controls a value that can be either true or false

EnumControl
> Controls a value that can be one of *n* known values

FloatControl
> Controls a value that is expressed as a floating-point number

CompoundControl
> Controls multiple properties, and itself contains multiple controls

You can get the Controls supported by your Line simply by calling Line. getControls( ), which returns an array of Controls. You can also ask for a specific control by using a constant of the Control.Type subclass, such as BooleanControl.Type.MUTE or FloatControl.Type.MASTER_GAIN. Pass this constant to Line.isControlSupported( ) to see if the control is available for the given line, and then get the control object with Line.getControl( ).

If you look at the subclasses of Control, you'll see that each provides getter and setter methods appropriate to its data type. BooleanControl, for example, has a getValue( ) that returns a boolean and a setValue( ) that takes a boolean. FloatControl has similar methods that work with floats. Each also provides a number of what might be called "verbiage methods" that provide text for building a GUI. For example, FloatControl offers label names for its minimum, maximum, and middle values, and another that describes the units represented by the control (like "dB" for a gain-related control, or "frames per second" for one that is timing-related).

Anyways, you've probably figured out that you can build a GUI by using Swing to provide a view to these Controls. In fact, it's fairly straightforward to take a factory approach to handing out JComponents based on Controls, as shown in Table 10-1.

Table 10-1. Controls and their Swing representation

Control type	Swing representation
BooleanControl	JCheckBox
EnumControl	JComboBox
FloatControl	JSlider

The CompoundControl can't be handled as easily because you can't know how far you'll have to recursively dig into its hierarchy of controls, nor how to represent them in relation to one another. For what it's worth, JavaSound does not define any CompoundControl.Type constants, and it's not clear that any CompoundControls exist in J2SE; the Javadoc only speaks in theory of supporting something like a graphic equalizer, which would need to be a CompoundControl.

Theory to Practice

To handle the different types of controls that can be encountered, one nice approach would be to build a factory: you hand it a Control, and it gives you back a JComponent that you can add to your GUI. Example 10-12 shows a simple implementation of this.

Example 10-12. Factory to generate Swing widgets for JavaSound controls

```
import javax.sound.sampled.*;

public class ControlComponentFactory {

    private ControlComponentFactory() {super();}

    public static JComponent getComponentFor (Control control) {
        System.out.println (control.getType().getClass());
        if (control instanceof BooleanControl)
            return new BooleanControlComponent ((BooleanControl) control);
        else if (control instanceof FloatControl)
            return new FloatControlComponent ((FloatControl) control);
        return new JLabel ("unsupported");
    }
}
```

You might notice that I haven't written a GUI class for EnumControl. That's because in my testing, the array of Controls returned by getControl( ) has never contained an EnumControl, so I don't have a good way to test it. After looking at the implementation of the boolean and float cases, I'll discuss how an EnumControlComponent would work.

The easier case is the BooleanControl, used for controls like Mute, which turns off the sound (but remembers the previous volume, so when un-muted, the sound is as loud as it was before). Example 10-13 shows the implementation of the BooleanControlComponent.

Example 10-13. Swing widget for a JavaSound BooleanControl

```
import javax.sound.sampled.*;

public class BooleanControlComponent extends JPanel
    implements ActionListener {
    BooleanControl control;
    JCheckBox box;
    public BooleanControlComponent (BooleanControl c) {
        control = c;
        box = new JCheckBox ();
        box.setSelected (control.getValue());
        add (box);
        box.addActionListener (this);
    }

    public void actionPerformed (ActionEvent ae) {
        control.setValue (box.isSelected());
    }
}
```

As you can see, this is practically trivial. The GUI contains a single JCheckBox, whose value you set to the value of the control so that it is in a proper state when first shown. Then, when the user clicks it, you just call the BooleanControl's setValue( ) method.

Supporting a FloatControl is a lot harder. As you might expect, the way to represent a range of floating-point values is with a JSlider; the user can slide left to reduce the value and right to increase it. To ensure the GUI's useful-ness, you can put JLabels on the left and right of the slider to show what the minimum and maximum values mean. For example, on a Pan control, which adjusts placement of stereo sound, the minimum value of -1.0 is Left and the maximum value of 1.0 is Right.

What makes it hard is handling a mapping of arbitrary floating-point values to a JSlider's int-based range. Complicating things is the fact that FloatControls can and do use very different ranges for their values, often spanning nega-tive and positive values, and operating in both small and vast ranges of possible values. For example, if you decide to have your JSlider values range from 0 to 1000, it may have to accommodate ranges as disparate as:

- -1.0 to 1.0
- 0.0 to 48000.0
- -80.0 to 13.9794

In fact, those are the ranges of default controls for pan, sampling rate, and master gain, respectively.

And to make things more fun, you have to be able to translate both ways: from control value to slider value (when first creating the widget so its initial onscreen representation is accurate), and from slider value to control value (when the user moves the slider).

But, in the end, it's just math. You can create a setSliderFromControl( ) method to calculate what percent of the control's maximum value is represented by the current value, apply that percent to the range of the JSlider's possible values, and set the JSlider to that. A setControlFromSlider( ) would use the exact same approach, except that it figures out the percentage-of-maximum of the JSlider, and applies that to the control's range. The resulting FloatControlComponent class is shown in Example 10-14.

Example 10-14. Swing widget for a JavaSound FloatControl

```
import javax.sound.sampled.*;

public class FloatControlComponent extends JPanel
    implements ChangeListener {

    FloatControl control;
    JSlider slider;
    float min, max, range;
    final static int SLIDER_MIN = 0;
    final static int SLIDER_MAX = 1000;
    final static float SLIDER_RANGE = SLIDER_MAX - SLIDER_MIN;

    public FloatControlComponent (FloatControl c) {
        control = c;
        min = c.getMinimum( );
        max = c.getMaximum( );
        range = max - min;
        add (new JLabel (control.getMinLabel( )));
        slider = new JSlider (SLIDER_MIN, SLIDER_MAX);
        slider.addChangeListener (this);
        setSliderFromControl( );
        add (slider);
        add (new JLabel (control.getMaxLabel( )));
    }
```

Example 10-14. Swing widget for a JavaSound FloatControl (continued)

```
    private void setSliderFromControl( ) {
        // figure out value as percent of range
        float offsetValue = control.getValue( ) - min;
        float percent = 0.0f;
        if (range != 0.0)
            percent = offsetValue / range;
        // apply that to SLIDER_RANGE
        int sliderValue = (int) (percent * SLIDER_RANGE);
        slider.setValue (sliderValue);
    }

    private void setControlFromSlider( ) {
        // figure out slider percentage
        float sliderPercentage =
            (float) slider.getValue( ) / SLIDER_RANGE;
        // figure out value for that percentage of range
        float rangeOffset = sliderPercentage * range;
        float newValue = rangeOffset + min;
        control.setValue (newValue);
    }

    // ChangeListener implementation
    public void stateChanged (ChangeEvent e) {
        setControlFromSlider( );
    }
}
```

Having provided these two implementations, it should be clear how you would create an EnumControlComponent. The EnumControl.getValues( ) method returns a String array that you would use as the model of an uneditable JComboBox. You'd use getValue( ) to set one of these as the initial value, and then on user events, you could pull out the JComboBox's selection and set the EnumControl with setValue( ).

Check It Out!

The DataLineControlGUI shown in Example 10-15 is a simple JPanel that contains a JLabel with the name of the file to be played on the first line of a GridBagLayout, and then control-name JLabels and factory-generated control widgets on each successive line. The sound is played by the PCMFilePlayer, which was introduced as part of playing uncompressed AIFFs and WAVs of arbitrary lengths [Hack #76].

Example 10-15. Creating an audio player with GUI controls

```java
import javax.sound.sampled.*;

public class DataLineControlGUI extends JPanel {

    PCMFilePlayer player;
    JButton startButton;

    public DataLineControlGUI (File f) {
        super( );
        try {
            player = new PCMFilePlayer (f);
        } catch (Exception ioe) {
            add (new JLabel ("Error: " +
                            ioe.getMessage( )));
            return;
        }
        DataLine line = player.getLine( );
        // layout
        // line 0: name
        setLayout (new GridBagLayout( ));
        GridBagConstraints gbc = new GridBagConstraints( );
        gbc.gridy = 0;
        gbc.fill = GridBagConstraints.HORIZONTAL;
        gbc.gridwidth = 2;
        gbc.anchor = GridBagConstraints.SOUTH;
        add (new JLabel ("File:  " +
                        player.getFile().getName( )), gbc);
        // subsequent lines: controls
        gbc.gridwidth = 1;
        Control[] controls = line.getControls();
        for (int i=0; i<controls.length; i++) {
            gbc.gridx = 0;
            gbc.gridy++;
            gbc.anchor = GridBagConstraints.EAST;
            add (new JLabel(controls[i].getType().toString( )), gbc);
            JComponent controlComp =
                ControlComponentFactory.getComponentFor (controls[i]);
            gbc.gridx = 1;
            gbc.anchor = GridBagConstraints.WEST;
            add (controlComp, gbc);
        }

        // now start playing
        player.start( );
    }
}
```

Example 10-15. Creating an audio player with GUI controls (continued)

```
public static void main (String[] args) {
    JFileChooser chooser = new JFileChooser();
    chooser.showOpenDialog(null);
    File file = chooser.getSelectedFile();
    DataLineControlGUI demo =
        new DataLineControlGUI (file);

    JFrame f = new JFrame ("JavaSound control");
    f.getContentPane().add (demo);
    f.pack();
    f.setVisible(true);
    }
}
```

When run with a suitable audio file, the resulting GUI looks like Figure 10-11. Note that it's possible you might have other control widgets (or an unsupported label for `EnumControls` and `CompoundControls`) if Java-Sound gives you different controls than it did when I wrote and ran this on Java 1.4.2.

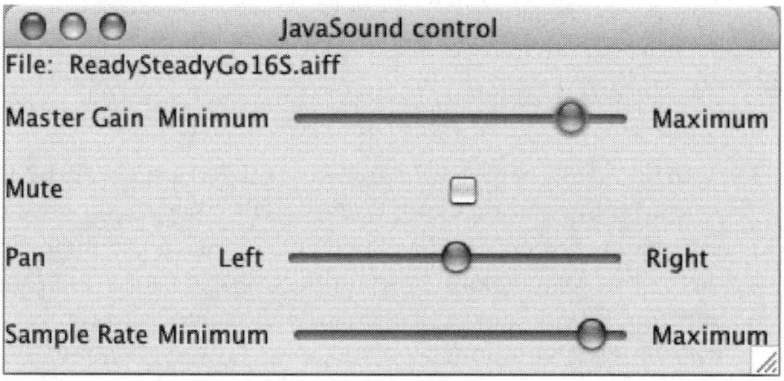

Figure 10-11. JavaSound audio player with GUI controls

Native Integration and Packaging

Hacks 79–87

You can try really hard to develop a desktop application that looks good, feels right, and meets the user's needs, but if a Windows or Mac user has to drop down to a command line and type java -jar MyCoolApp.jar to run it, it's not going to win you any points in the user experience department. There are points of integration with the native platform that you'll often want and need to access from a Swing application, or specific functionality you'll want to provide on a platform-by-platform basis, and that's what this chapter is about.

Actually, this chapter was almost rendered irrelevant by the JDesktop Integration Components (JDIC) project on Java.net (*https://jdic.dev.java.net/*), which is addressing the most serious needs for desktop Java applications: creating platform-appropriate double-clickables, providing access to the native web browser component, associating Java applications with certain kinds of documents, etc. JDIC may solve some of the biggest issues facing Java on the desktop...which leaves us all the more room for creative hackery.

Launch External Programs on Windows

HACK #79

With one simple command you can tell Windows to open files, directories, and URLs on your behalf.

Swing programmers have always had difficulty dealing with native operating systems because of Java's cross-platform nature. Even simple things like opening a web browser require building native hooks with JNI or building on top of custom libraries. This hack will show you how to open files, URLs, and start an email app without using any native libraries or custom C coding.

The Power of Runtime.exec( )

Native integration in Java has always depended on the Java Native Interface, or JNI. Whether you code to JNI directly or use a third-party library, you are still dealing with native C code through a Java layer. This has always been problematic because in order to write a JNI library, you need to know a lot about the internals of the underlying operating system. Most Java developers went to Java to *get away* from that sort of thing, so it's often not worth it for something simple like opening a URL. There is another way of talking to the native OS, though. You can use Runtime.exec( ).

Since 1.0, Java has had the Runtime.exec( ) static function to start another program directly and pass command-line parameters. It's easy to forget about command-line utilities, but for simple things they can be far, far easier than trying to deal with JNI. The disadvantages of calling a native program over a Java API are of course speed, since you are starting a new process, and the fact that the program is not cross-platform. This may be an acceptable tradeoff, however, since you could disable the feature that needs the exec( ) call or provide a different command for other platforms.

Open a Text File

Windows 2000 introduced a small program called start. Originally a separate install, the start program is now just a command built into the cmd.exe that comes with Windows XP. It is a simple command but it can do some powerful things, such as opening a file with the default viewer, showing a directory in the file explorer, or even launching a web browser.

For example, the sample program in Example 11-1 will open a text file with the default viewer (usually Windows Notepad).

Example 11-1. Launching a text file with start

```
import java.io.IOException;
public class ExecTest {
    public static void main(String[] args) throws IOException {
        String cmd = "cmd.exe /c start ";
        String file = "c:\\version.txt";
        Runtime.getRuntime().exec(cmd + file);
    }
}
```

That's it! cmd.exe is the command processor built into Windows (a holdover from the DOS days). Whenever you open a DOS box, you are running cmd.exe. You can manually replicate the previous code by typing "start c:/version.txt" into a command-line window.

Open a URL

You can open a web browser the same way as a text file because Windows associates all URLs, specifically ones that begin with *http*, with a default web browser. If you call start on a URL then the browser will open, as seen in Example 11-2.

Example 11-2. Opening a URL in the default web browser on Windows

```java
import java.io.IOException;
public class ExecTest {
    public static void main(String[] args) throws IOException {
        String cmd = "cmd.exe /c start ";
        String file = "http://www.google.com";
        Runtime.getRuntime( ).exec(cmd + file);
    }

}
```

You can also use the browser support to open up a new email message. Since mailto: is a URL protocol, usually mapped to the user's default email program, if you open up a mailto: URL, Windows will open a new message ready to send (see Example 11-3).

Example 11-3. Using start to open an email application

```java
import java.io.IOException;
public class ExecTest {
    public static void main(String[] args) throws IOException {

        String cmd = "cmd.exe /c start ";
        String file = "mailto:author@mybook.com";
        Runtime.getRuntime( ).exec(cmd + file);
    }

}
```

The previous code will open up a new email message addressed to *author@mybook.com*. The return address will be filled in automatically with the user's own address. You can remove the address (*author@mybook.com*) to open a new blank email.

By default, cmd.exe will open a requested file using the standard viewer for that file's type. For example, cmd.exe /c start music.mp3 will open the song file using the default program, possibly the Windows Media Player or iTunes. If you would rather open the file with a particular program that you specify, then you can simply add the program name before the file.

As another example, cmd.exe /c start version.txt opens a text file in Windows Notepad (assuming that's the default text file viewer). cmd.exe /c start winword.exe version.txt would open the file in MS Word. This requires having Word installed, of course, so I would only recommend hardcoding the program name if you are sure it's really there.

Open a Directory

The start command can also open a directory as well as a file, meaning it will open a file manager window showing the contents of that directory. Program installers often do this after the install is complete to show where the program was placed. The code in Example 11-4 will open a new Explorer window showing the contents of the C: drive.

Example 11-4. Opening a directory on Windows

```java
import java.io.IOException;
public class ExecTest {
    public static void main(String[] args) throws IOException {
        String cmd = "cmd.exe /c start ";
        String file = "c:\\";
        Runtime.getRuntime( ).exec(cmd + file);
    }
}
```

HACK
#80
Open Files, Directories, and URLs
on Mac OS X

Open files, directories, and URLs in external programs right from your Swing app.

We can't let Windows have all of the fun. Mac OS X has a similar and even easier to use program called open, which lets you open any file, directory, or web page directly from the command line. This hack shows you how to embed open in your own program.

Using Open

Back in the late 80s, NeXT, Inc. created the first true integration between a graphical user interface and a Unix-like operating system when they released NeXTSTEP. Part of this OS was a command-line program called open, which could open a file, directory, and (once the Web was invented) a URL. Apple purchased NeXT in the late 90s and NeXTSTEP became the core of Mac OS X. Along with this purchase came the open command, still as useful as ever.

open has a simple syntax: open *filename*. By calling it from within your program, you can open any file with its default application. open will start launching the viewer automatically and return control to your program immediately. As in Microsoft Windows, you can call the program using Runtime.exec():

```
public static void main(String[] args) throws Exception {
    Runtime rt = Runtime.getRuntime();
    rt.exec("open notes.txt");
}
```

This program will open a file in the current directory (*notes.txt*), in the default viewer for text files, usually TextEdit. You can also specify an absolute path for the file:

```
rt.exec("open /Users/josh/Desktop/notes.txt");
```

If you pass a directory instead of a file, then OS X will open that directory in a new Finder window. This can be useful for showing the location of a recently downloaded file or demonstrating where to install new software:

```
// open the current working directory
rt.exec("open .");
// open the applications directory
rt.exec("open /Applications");
```

Finally, you can open any web page using the user's default web browser (probably Safari) by calling open with a URL:

```
// open Yahoo! in the user's web browser
rt.exec("open http://www.yahoo.com/");
```

Handle Spaces

Some filepaths may contain spaces. When you run open from the command line you can escape these spaces using quotes like this:

```
open 'Current Notes.txt'
```

Unfortunately, quotes won't work when you call open from a program because the quotes are actually interpreted by the user's command-line shell, not open itself. When you call open directly from a program, you are bypassing the shell and lose quote interpolation. The solution is to break the command line into an array of arguments manually. That way open knows what is a space and what is the gap between arguments:

```
Runtime rt = Runtime.getRuntime();
String[] cmd = {"open", "Current Notes.txt"};
rt.exec(cmd);
```

Now, you might wonder why open needs to distinguish between argument gaps and real spaces when it takes only one argument to begin with. open

---

actually does have some other arguments. For example, -t will force the file to be opened in TextEdit, and -f will make open read from standard input rather than a file.

The most useful extra argument is probably -a, which lets you force the file to be opened in a particular program rather than just using the default. For example, if you wanted to open a text file in Microsoft Word instead of the default text editor, you could do something like this:

```
public static void main(String[] args) throws Exception {
    Runtime rt = Runtime.getRuntime( );
    String[] cmd = {
        "open",
        "-a",
        "Microsoft Word",
        "mynotes.txt"
    };
    rt.exec(cmd);
}
```

Notice you have to use an array instead of a single string because Microsoft Word has a space in it. If you don't do that, the program will fail with a bus error.

open is a simple but very powerful program because it gives you easy access to launching programs and files without knowing the user's settings. The default applications will be used for each file type, including URLs. You don't have to hardcode this information into your program, thus creating a better experience for your user.

To learn more about the open command, you can type man open into a terminal window.

Make Mac Applications Behave Normally

#81

Setting a few system properties will make your application seem more like other Mac apps.

Of the desktop platforms your application is likely to run on, the Mac is the least like the others. Maybe it's because the various Linux desktops hemmed closely to Windows' ways of thinking, or maybe the GNOME guys had never used a Mac and didn't "think different." But the result is that certain assumptions you might reasonably make on Windows or Linux—like assuming that windows have menu bars and that any corner or edge of a window can be dragged to resize the window—aren't correct on the Mac.

To smooth over the cross-platform differences somewhat, Apple does certain things differently in its Java implementation. For one thing, it will automatically put a Swing application into its native Look and Feel, Aqua, rather than defaulting into cross-platform Metal or Ocean as would happen on other platforms. In other words, you don't have to do anything special to pick up the Mac Look and Feel, although redundantly asking for and setting the native Look and Feel classname doesn't hurt either.

Moreover, Apple provides some key/value pairs that you can set in the Java system properties to get even more Mac-like behavior. Because these properties all start with apple or com.apple, you can set them and not worry that they'll affect the behavior of your application on any other platform.

Using the Apple System Properties

Apple has been changing the names and behaviors of these system properties for a while, and some of them are deprecated or no-op'ed, so I'll just show four of the most useful ones here. To see the whole list, check out the Runtime System Properties of Apple's Java 1.4.1 release notes on *http://developer.apple.com/releasenotes/Java/index.html*.

You can set the properties several ways. The obvious way is to use the -D command-line argument:

```
java -Dapple.awt.showGrowBox=true MyClass
```

However, this becomes tedious to type after you decide to use multiple properties. Another option is to simply call System.setProperty( ) in your code, though you'll need to do so as soon as possible so the desired property gets picked up by the JVM before it's needed. A third option exists as well: if you're bundling the Java application as a double-clickable Mac application, your tool of choice will give you an opportunity to set these values. For example, the JarBundler that Apple provides with its developer tools has a properties pane in which you can enter name/value pairs; these are saved with the application bundle and provided to the JVM as if they'd been set on the command line.

> The downloadable book code contains demo applications for all the tricks shown in this chapter, but since the point in this hack is the one-line System.setProperty( ) call and not 20 lines of code that demonstrate the effect, the demo code is not shown here, just screenshots of the results.

Using the Mac's Menu Bar

One of the most striking differences between the Mac and Windows/Linux GUIs is that the Mac has a single menu bar at the top of the screen, rather than menu bars in each application window. This will break a lot of assumptions if you're coming over from the Windows world (for one thing, an application can still be running without any windows open, since the user can usually spawn a new window from the File menu), but for now, just focus on the fact that menus inside of windows are going to feel very alien to a Mac user. Figure 11-1 shows what a typical Swing window looks like on a Mac with the menu bar in the window.

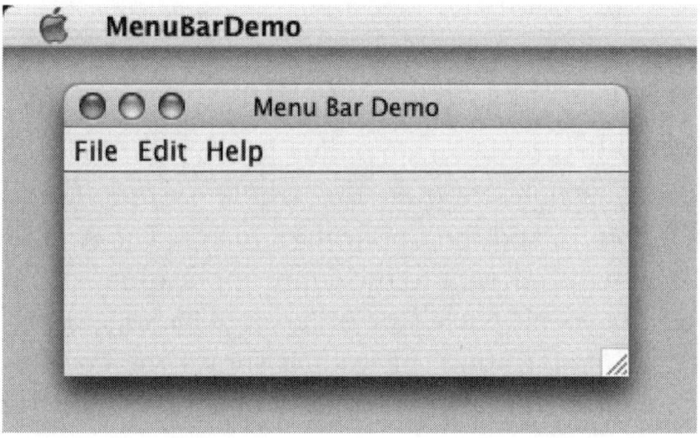

Figure 11-1. Swing application with menu bar in a Mac window

Change that by setting the system property `apple.laf.useScreenMenuBar` to true. This takes all Swing menu bars out of their `JFrame`s and puts them up in the Mac menu bar. Figure 11-2 shows the effect of setting this property on a Swing window.

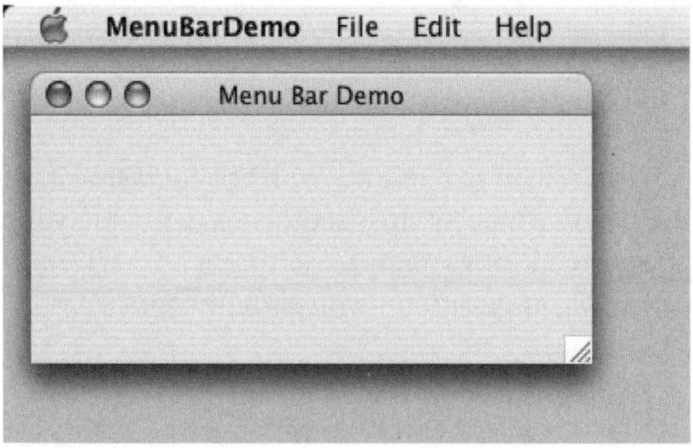

Figure 11-2. Swing application with menus in a Mac menu bar

AWT windows will always use the Mac menu bar.

One thing worth mentioning is that if your application uses different menus in its various windows, this will still seem strange to Mac users, as the menu bar will change based on which of your application's windows has focus. But to be truly Mac-like, you'd have to have the same menu bar all the time, which on Windows/Linux might mean having completely inappropriate menus in some windows. Then again, with good design—and probably some ResourceBundles—you should be able to provide an appropriate menu bar experience to all your users.

Presenting an Appropriate Application Name

On Mac OS X, the first two items (reading left to right) on the menu bar are the Apple menu, which controls the whole system (Software Update, Restart, Log Out, etc.), and the Application menu. The Application menu is meant to contain items relevant to the entire application: an about box, preferences, the ability to hide itself or other applications, and Quit. But the menu isn't named Application; instead, it shows the current application's name. That's great for something short and memorable like Mail or Firefox. But for a Java application, it picks up the name of the application's main( ) class. And when you package your code (like you're supposed to, with the inverted Internet address style), you get a monstrosity like Figure 11-3.

com.mycompany.myproject.mysubproject.MyClass

Figure 11-3. A long Java classname as a Mac application name

Fortunately, you can rein in the insanity with the com.apple.mrj.application. apple.menu.about.name property. Just set this to the name you want to show in the application menu. For example, setting it to MyDemo produces the much more reasonable application menu seen in Figure 11-4.

Figure 11-4. A custom application name for a Java application

Showing the Mac Grow Box

Traditionally, Mac applications have reserved the bottom-right corner as the only space that you can drag to resize a window. It is shown as a diagonally dimpled grow box, often reserving the space above it for a scrollbar. There's also sometimes either a scrollbar or a status bar to the box's left. At any rate, this approach to resizing is very different from having a few pixels for a border on the right, left, and bottom edges—all of which are draggable—as users expect from Microsoft Windows.

By default, the grow box is not shown in Mac Java windows. You can make the grow box appear by setting the property apple.awt.showGrowBox to true. This does, however, have a significant downside, as seen in Figure 11-5.

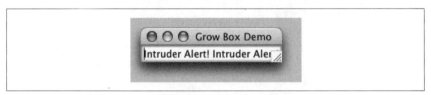

Figure 11-5. Mac grow box intruding on Swing display space

The grow box intrudes into the Java display space. In this case, it clobbers the right-most part of a JTextField.

The proper way to handle this is to reserve some space for the grow box. The simple thing to do—in fact, it's what Apple's Java 1.3.1 did by default—is to reserve 15 pixels of vertical space for the grow box. You could probably just have a subclass of JFrame for your Mac users that puts the usual frame contents in the CENTER of a BorderLayout, and creates a spacer with Box.createVerticalStrut(15) to reserve space for the grow box in the SOUTH. Figure 11-6 shows the corrected window after this approach is applied.

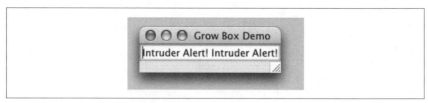

Figure 11-6. Mac grow box with space reserved for it at the bottom of JFrame

Jump on the Brushed Metal Bandwagon

Apparently, Mac applications are no longer cool unless they use the brushed metal L&F of Apple's various iApps, such as iTunes, iChat, etc. Fortunately, it's easy to pick up that appearance for your Java application. Just set the property apple.awt.brushMetalLook to true. This produces windows like the one seen in Figure 11-7.

Figure 11-7. Swing window with brushed metal appearance

Apple's documentation of this feature says that this should be applied to your primary application window only, not supporting dialogs or preference windows, but it's hard to see how that rule can be enforced when this property causes all your windows to pick up the brushed metal look automatically.

Control iTunes on Mac OS X

With a few bits of AppleScript, you can monitor and control Macintosh iTunes from your own application.

You can make some really great applications using plain Java, but the software world isn't what it used to be. The buzzword for new applications is integration. Modern programs are defined not only by what they do, but what they can talk to. The poster child for integration these days is iTunes,

---

so what better way to show off the power of Java than by taking control of iTunes directly from your own Java app!

The task of dealing with native applications is, by nature, platform specific. For example, though Apple ships identical *looking* copies of iTunes for both Windows and Mac, the integration APIs couldn't be more different.

Apple Events

Most well-written Mac OS X applications support an API called Apple Events. Apple Events let a programmer send commands and requests to a running application from another program, through a process often called scripting. The application must be written to support Apple Events and every scriptable feature must be defined explicitly when the program is written. Since it was Apple that wrote iTunes, they did a very good job of exposing virtually every feature through Apple Events. All you need to do is tap into these events.

Apple Events is an API, and you need a programming language to support it. There are a variety of languages to choose from, but the easiest one to start with is AppleScript, as the syntax is simple and OS X ships with a command-line interpreter. There are also direct Java bindings available, but for the kinds of simple things you are likely to want to do with iTunes, exec( )ing the interpreter will be much easier. All you have to do is call osascript with the AppleScript commands you want to run, and OS X will do the rest.

AppleScript is a simple language with a somewhat natural language feel to it. If you want to tell iTunes to toggle the Play/Pause button, you can call this script from the command line:

```
osascript -e 'tell app "iTunes" to playpause'
```

Now *that's* the kind of simple integration I like! Because you can directly execute command-line programs from inside your code, the Java equivalent would look like this:

```
String[] args = { "osascript", "-e",
                  "tell app \"iTunes\" to playpause" };
Process proc = rt.exec(args);
```

That's it. You can make iTunes do virtually anything you want with simple commands like this. One caveat to remember is that iTunes must be running as the same user for this to work. This usually isn't a program for desktop applications, but if you made a web application with this technique, you might need a workaround like a chown script or a daemon that runs next to iTunes. Example 11-5 is the code for a simple program with one button that will toggle the iTunes Play/Pause button.

Example 11-5. Controlling iTunes on the Mac

```java
public class MacITunes implements ActionListener {
    public static void main(String[] args) {
        JFrame frame = new JFrame("Mac iTunes Hack");
        JButton button = new JButton("Play/Pause");
        button.addActionListener(new MacITunes( ));
        frame.getContentPane( ).add(button);
        frame.pack( );
        frame.setVisible(true);
    }

    public void actionPerformed(ActionEvent evt) {
        try {
            Runtime rt = Runtime.getRuntime( );
            String[] args = { "osascript",
                "-e","tell app \"iTunes\" to playpause"};
            Process proc = rt.exec(args);
        } catch (IOException ex) {
            System.out.println("exception : " + ex.getMessage( ));
            ex.printStackTrace( );
        }
    }
}
```

This code creates a JFrame with one button. The button's action listener creates a new java.lang.Runtime object, sets up the command-line arguments, and finally calls osascript to control iTunes. When you click on the button in the Swing application, iTunes will start playing. If you press the button a second time, iTunes will pause. Virtually any feature in iTunes can be scripted this way.

Sometimes you don't want to tell iTunes to do something, but instead want to get information *from* it. osascript can handle this, too. When you call a function that returns a value, osascript will write the value to standard out, which you can pick up from the process's input stream. For example, if you wanted to get the name of the currently playing track, you could change the action listener code to look like this:

```java
public void actionPerformed(ActionEvent evt) {
    try {
        Runtime rt = Runtime.getRuntime( );
        String[] args = { "osascript", "-e",
            "tell app \"iTunes\" to artist of current track as string"};
        Process proc = rt.exec(args);
        InputStream in = proc.getInputStream( );
        String str = new DataInputStream(in).readLine( );
        System.out.println("got: " + str);
```

```
    } catch (IOException ex) {
        System.out.println("exception : " + ex.getMessage());
        ex.printStackTrace();
    }
}
```

The line:

```
tell app "iTunes" to artist of current track as string
```

will call the artist method on the current track. It will return the artist as a string and print it to standard out. You can get the standard output by reading from `proc.getInputStream()`. The code then prints the string as a single line, so you can easily read it with the `readLine()` method on a `DataInputStream`. Once you have the string back, you can print it, put it in a `JLabel`, or do whatever else is appropriate for your program.

Apple has more information available on the iTunes AppleScript API at *http://www.apple.com/applescript/itunes/*. With this API, you can do almost anything. For example, you can get the name of a playing song:

```
tell app "iTunes" to name of current track as string
```

You can also get the album name:

```
tell app "iTunes" to album of current track as string
```

Muting the volume is also a piece of cake:

```
tell application "iTunes" to set mute to true
```

In the same vein, you can obtain the current volume:

```
tell application "iTunes" to sound volume as integer
```

Take a look at the API and see what other interesting things you can do. Many of the other programs that come with Mac OS X can be controlled with Apple Events as well, so there is a lot to play with. You can query the network status, open files and programs, or even tie Mail and iPhoto together to capture, edit, and send photo albums. The possibilities are huge and are all accessible right from your own Swing application.

HACK #83 Control iTunes Under Windows

Use a simple open source library to monitor and control Windows iTunes from your Swing application.

Windows doesn't have a standard scripting API like Apple Events, but it does have another object model that iTunes supports. Using an open source library, this hack will show you how to script iTunes just as easily on Windows as you can on the Mac.

Working with COM

The Component Object Model (COM) is a standard way for Windows components to expose functionality that other programs can call at runtime. com4j (*https://com4j.dev.java.net/*) is an open source library that creates connections from Java programs to COM objects. com4j has two parts: a command-line program to create the Java interfaces that your program will call, and a native library that binds your program to the COM object at runtime.

com4j uses class annotations to do its magic, so you can only use it with Java 5.0 or greater.

To get started, download the com4j package at *https://com4j.dev.java.net/servlets/ProjectDocumentList*. With the com4j stubber and the iTunes executable in your current directory, you can generate the interfaces like this:

```
java -jar tlbimp.jar -o jtunes -p test.jtunes iTunes.exe
```

This command will load the iTunes executable and look for COM definitions. Once they are located, `tlbimp` will generate a bunch of Java interfaces in the `test.jtunes` package and put the *.java* files into the *jtunes* directory. If you look at the generated Java interfaces, you will see a whole slew of methods and objects for playing, querying tracks, and dealing with virtually every other feature of iTunes. com4j will also pull out any embedded documentation and insert the documentation as JavaDoc comments in the generated interfaces.

This process is pretty quick, so you may find it useful to call it from Ant as part of your compile process.

Once you have the interface stubs, you can create a program to control iTunes quite easily. You can use the same program that you did when controlling iTunes on the Mac **[Hack #82]**. Just replace the action listener with the class in Example 11-6.

Example 11-6. A listener to control iTunes on Windows

```
import test.jtunes.*;

public class WinItunes {

    public void actionPerformed(ActionEvent evt) {
        try {
```

Example 11-6. A listener to control iTunes on Windows (continued)

```
        IiTunes itunes;
        itunes = ClassFactory.createiTunesApp( );
        itunes.playPause( );
    } catch (Exception ex) {
        System.out.println("exception : " + ex.getMessage( ));
        ex.printStackTrace( );
    }
  }
}
```

Compile this class along with the interfaces in the test.jtunes package. You will also need the *com4j.jar* in your CLASSPATH and *com4j.dll* files in your PATH. When you run the program, the com4j library will connect to iTunes—launching it if necessary—and execute the playPause( ) method.

> com4j only allows you to call methods from the same thread that you used to create the COM proxy. Typically, you want to update your Swing components with iTunes information, which you can do safely from the Swing event thread only. This means that you should create the COM proxy from the event thread as well (using the ClassFactory method). Unfortunately, this may cause your application to block for a few seconds while iTunes loads (if it's not already running). To avoid this delay, you probably want to do all of your iTunes communication through a custom queue, or use the new concurrency utilities available in Java 5.0. The com4j developers are working on a solution to this problem, so it may be solved by the time you read this.

Get Track Information

As with Apple Events on the Mac [Hack #82], the COM interface gives you a way to query the currently playing track. You can call iTunes.currentTrack( ) to get an IITTrack object. This object has methods to query just about anything you could possible want to know about a track, including the artist, album, playing time, encoding method, and even the import date. Each method on the IITTrack object returns information as Strings or Java primitives, so it's pretty easy to access anything you want and then stuff it into your Swing interface. The following code shows how to get the track number, count, name, album, and artist:

```
IITTrack track;
track = itunes.currentTrack( );
int track_number = track.trackNumber( );
int track_count = track.trackCount( );
```

```
String track_name = track.name();
String album_name = track.album();
String artist_name = track.artist();
```

com4j is a great open source project that unleashes the power of Java code integrated with native applications. The iTunes COM interface provides hooks for virtually everything that iTunes can do. These two things mean you could write a program to sort songs, create new playlists, or even export track listings to your own application that prints CD labels. You can find *fscom/sdk/itunescomsdk.html*, so see what other cool things you can come up with.

HACK #84   Construct Single-Launch Applications

Only allow one instance of a program, notifying the existing instance when the user tries to launch a new one.

Most graphical desktop applications are designed for multitasking. You start your program to work on something, then switch to another program and come back later. Oftentimes you'll leave a large program, like a word processor, running in the background to be used again when you need to open another document, say an email attachment you received. When you click on the attachment, your operating system won't start a new instance of the word processor; instead, it will send a message to the currently running instance to open the new file—saving lots of system resources.

Java programs aren't designed with single-launch behavior in mind. They still use the old Unix style of single use, command-line launching. You start the program to do something and it finishes quickly. If you use the program again it will start a new instance, do the work, and finish. There is never any instance reuse, but modern desktop programs demand it. Because Java doesn't support single-launch applications, this hack shows you how to build it into your programs with a simple use of sockets.

Local Sockets

Building a single-launch application requires two parts. When the program starts, it needs to detect if another copy is already running. If there is, then the program can quit instead of continuing to launch. The new program also needs to tell the first copy about any command-line arguments—the filename to open, for example. You could create a temp file in a known location and look to see if it already exists. This would take care of multiple program instances, but not passing arguments around. Plus, you would need to worry about race conditions and cleaning up the temp file when the last program exits. Thankfully, there's a much better solution: local sockets.

A socket is a network connection defined by a hostname and a port. A *local socket* is a network connection only on the local machine. When you open a socket to listen for connections you are *binding* to that port. Only one program can bind to any given port at one time, so the port itself can serve as your lock. If your program cannot connect to the port, then another program must already be using it. It doesn't matter what the port number is, as long as your program always uses the same one. Here is the beginning of the code to put this into action:

```
public class SingleLauncherApplication implements Runnable {
    public static final int PORT = 38629;
    public JLabel label;
    public ServerSocket server;

    public void launch(String[] args) {
        try {
            server = new ServerSocket(PORT);
            new Thread(this).start();
            firstMain(args);
        } catch (IOException ioex) {
            System.out.println("already running!");
            relaunch(args);
        }
    }
}
```

SingleLauncherApplication is a class with one core method: launch( ). launch( ) takes the same arguments as the standard main( ) method, which is important since you are essentially creating fake versions of main. When launch is called, it will first try to bind to the port by creating a server socket. Notice the PORT constant set to the number 38629. It is important that the port isn't reserved for use by any system services. Some operating systems also restrict user programs to only use ports over 1,000, so I picked this number at random from the 20,000 to 60,000 range. This makes it very unlikely that the port will already be in use by any other program.

If launch( ) can create a ServerSocket, then it will start a new thread, engage run( ), and then call firstMain( ):

```
public void firstMain(String[] args) {
    JFrame frame = new JFrame("Single Launch Application");
    frame.setDefaultCloseOperation(JFrame.EXIT_ON_CLOSE);
    String word = "";
    if(args.length >= 1) {
        word = args[0];
    }
    label = new JLabel("The word of the day is: " + word);
    frame.getContentPane( ).add(label);
    frame.pack( );
    frame.show( );
}
```

firstMain( ) contains the normal startup code that would have gone in main( ) previously. Here, it creates a new JFrame with a single label in it, containing the text "The word of the day is:" followed by the first command-line argument.

Next comes the run( ) method, which is launched in the new thread by launch( ). Its entire purpose in life is to sit on that port and wait for connections. If another instance connects, then it reads in the arguments and calls otherMain( ) to relaunch the application:

```java
public void run( ) {
    System.out.println("waiting for a connection");
    while(true) {
        try {
            // wait for a socket connection
            Socket sock = server.accept( );

            // read the contents into a string buffer
            InputStreamReader in = new InputStreamReader(
                sock.getInputStream( ));
            StringBuffer sb = new StringBuffer( );
            char[] buf = new char[256];
            while(true) {
                int n = in.read(buf);
                if(n < 0) { break; }
                sb.append(buf,0,n);
            }
            // split the string buffer into strings
            String[] results = sb.toString( ).split("\\n");
            // call other main
            otherMain(results);
        } catch (IOException ex) {
            System.out.println("ex: " + ex);
            ex.printStackTrace( );
        }
    }
}
```

server.accept( ) will block until another program connects. When one does, the code will open an input stream for the socket and begin to read out characters and save it in a string buffer. If in.read(buf) returns -1 (n<0), then it knows the other end disconnected and that's all there is. Command-line arguments are just strings, but they may have spaces in them, so the code above will split the string buffer by new lines ("\\n") into an array of strings. Finally, it calls otherMain( ) with the string array:

```java
public void otherMain(final String[] args) {
    if(args.length >= 1) {
        SwingUtilities.invokeLater(new Runnable( ) {
```

```
        public void run( ) {
            label.setText("The word of the day is: " + args[0]);
        }
    });
    }
}
```

otherMain( ) doesn't repeat the startup steps of firstMain( ). Instead it just changes the text of the label to match the new command-line arguments. Because Swing isn't thread-safe, you can't set the label text in the launching thread. Instead, you need to call it from the Swing event thread. The easiest way to do this is with the utility method: SwingUtilities.invokeLater( ). You can pass it an anonymous Runnable( ) that does the actual setText( ) call. Note that the input variable args has to be made final for this to work.

If this is the second instance of the program, then the new ServerSocket( ) will fail, and relaunch( ) is called to send the command-line arguments to the first instance:

```
public void relaunch(String[] args) {
    try {
        // open a socket to the original instance
        Socket sock = new Socket("localhost",PORT);

        // write the args to the output stream
        OutputStreamWriter out = new OutputStreamWriter(
            sock.getOutputStream( ));
        for(int i=0; i<args.length; i++) {
            out.write(args[i]+"\n");
            p("wrote: " + args[i]);
        }

        // cleanup
        out.flush( );
        out.close( );
    } catch (Exception ex) {
        System.out.println("ex: " + ex);
        ex.printStackTrace( );
    }
}
```

relaunch( ) opens a socket to the port on localhost. Since new ServerSocket( ) failed, it knows that the first instance of the program is already waiting on the other side of that port. Once it connects, it writes the command-line arguments to the socket's output stream, separating each argument with a newline (\n). Finally, it flushes the output stream to make sure everything was written, and then closes it. After that, the relaunch( ) and launch( ) methods will return, quitting the second instance of the program. The arguments have now been sent to the first instance.

To actually start this whole class, you simply call the launch method like this:

```
public static void main(String[] args) {
    new SingleLauncherApplication( ).launch(args);
}
```

The first time the program is launched it will create the window with the label. For example, running the following command would result in Figure 11-8.

```
java -cp . SingleLauncherApplication 'anonymous'
```

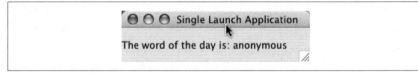

Figure 11-8. Initial launch

Now, start the program again, with the first running:

```
java -cp . SingleLauncherApplication 'perspicacity'
```

Instead of creating a new window, the program will contact the original (and still running) instance and change the text to Figure 11-9.

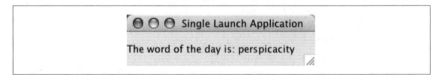

Figure 11-9. After relaunching

HACK   Stuff Stuff in JARs
#85   Hide images, sounds, and more inside JAR files.

Does your application need a special installer? Do you have to put images, sounds, icons, and properties all in their own folders or other special locations relative to your application? Does your application launch with a *.sh* script on Unix or a *.bat* on Windows?

You do? Really? I was just speaking rhetorically. I kind of figured everyone was using JARs by now.

An Obvious Secret

JAR files—the acronym is short for Java ARchive—must be the best-known, least-used feature in Java. Many developers throw a JAR in their classpath to pick up some standard extension API or third-party library, but how many actually distribute their software that way?

And JARs aren't just about code. It's really easy to put the files your program needs into a JAR. This has the added advantage of hiding your images, sounds, default settings, and so forth from end users.

But to load these items, you need to make a change in how you load stuff in your code. Instead of specifying a known path or URL, you ask a ClassLoader to find these resources along the classpath. By doing this, you can get your resources from flat files while you're developing, and then easily switch to getting them from inside a JAR when the code is deployed in the field.

The key is the ClassLoader's getResource( ) and getResources( ) methods, which take a path relative to the loaded class and return a URL and an array of URLs respectively. A getResourceAsStream( ) method converts the URL to an InputStream as a convenience.

To clarify the relative path: say you have a directory that includes your compiled classes in a path like *com/mycompany/mypackage/...*, an *images* directory, and a *sounds* directory. A relative path would be one of the form *images/something.png*, *sounds/something.aiff*, etc. By using a resource on the classpath, there is no difference (to the user) between files in a JAR and files in sub-directories on a filesystem. Either way, you get a URL that you can use by passing it to methods that take URL arguments, by opening an InputStream from it, etc.

Showing Off

Example 11-7 shows an example of this technique. It uses the getResource( ) method to load an image and put it in an ImageIcon, which in turn is used to create a JButton. It also loads in a sound, which is played via JavaSound when you click the button.

Example 11-7. Loading image and sound as resources along the classpath

```
import java.awt.*;
import java.awt.event.*;
import javax.swing.*;
import javax.sound.sampled.*;
import java.net.*;
```

Example 11-7. Loading image and sound as resources along the classpath (continued)

```java
public class JarResourceLoading extends JFrame
    implements ActionListener {

    JButton button;
    ImageIcon buttonIcon;
    Clip buhClip;

    public final static String SOUND_PATH = "sounds/buhbuhbuh.aiff";
    public final static String IMAGE_PATH = "images/keagan-buh.jpeg";

    public JarResourceLoading () {
        super ("Resources from .jar");
        // get image and make button
        URL imageURL = getClass().getClassLoader().getResource (IMAGE_PATH);
        System.out.println ("found image at " + imageURL);
        buttonIcon = new ImageIcon (imageURL);
        button = new JButton ("Click to Buh!", buttonIcon);
        button.setHorizontalTextPosition (SwingConstants.CENTER);
        button.setVerticalTextPosition (SwingConstants.BOTTOM);
        button.addActionListener (this);
        getContentPane( ).add (button);
        // load sound into Clip
        try {
            URL soundURL = getClass().getClassLoader().getResource (SOUND_PATH);
            System.out.println ("found sound at " + soundURL);
            Line.Info linfo = new Line.Info (Clip.class);
            Line line = AudioSystem.getLine (linfo);
            buhClip = (Clip) line;
            AudioInputStream ais = AudioSystem.getAudioInputStream(soundURL);
            buhClip.open(ais);
        } catch (Exception e) {
            e.printStackTrace( );
        }
    }

    public void actionPerformed (ActionEvent e) {
        System.out.println ("click!");
        if (buhClip != null) {
            buhClip.setFramePosition (0);
            buhClip.start( );
        }
        else
            JOptionPane.showMessageDialog (this,
                                           "Couldn't load sound",
                                           "Error",
                                           JOptionPane.ERROR_MESSAGE);
    }

    public static final void main (String[] args) {
        JFrame frame = new JarResourceLoading( );
```

Example 11-7. Loading image and sound as resources along the classpath (continued)

```
        frame.pack( );
        frame.setVisible(true);
    }
}
```

Notice how the paths to the sound and the image are relative:

```
public final static String SOUND_PATH = "sounds/buhbuhbuh.aiff";
```

These paths specify the path from a given starting point. As getResource( ) checks each entry in its classpath—whether they're directories or JAR files (ZIP files are also allowed)—the class loader looks for a directory called *sounds* and, if that's found, for an entry inside it called *buhbuhbuh.aiff*. It's also worth noting that you use the Unix-style forward slashes, regardless of what operating system this is run on.

When you compile and run this code from the source directory, the result looks like Figure 11-10.

Figure 11-10. Application using image and sound loaded with getResource( )

Along with showing this simple GUI, it also prints to standard out the URLs returned by getResource( ). Running from the source directory, the output looks like this:

```
[tonberry:] cadamson% java JarResourceLoading
found image at file:/Users/cadamson/Documents/O'Reilly/books/swing%20hacks/
    HacksBook/PackagingInstalling/97/images/keagan-buh.jpeg
found sound at file:/Users/cadamson/Documents/O'Reilly/books/swing%20hacks/
    HacksBook/PackagingInstalling/97/sounds/buhbuhbuh.aiff
```

Packing Up

So far, this only proves that resource loading is a nice alternative to fully specified paths. The next step is to put the application and its resources in a JAR. You can do this with a single command:

```
jar cf buh.jar JarResourceLoading.class images sounds
```

Now, you run the application from the JAR by pointing the classpath into it. Here's what the output from that looks like:

```
[tonberry:] cadamson% java -classpath buh.jar JarResourceLoading
found image at jar:file:/Users/cadamson/Documents/O'Reilly/books/
    swing%20hacks/HacksBook/PackagingInstalling/97/buh.jar!/images/
    keagan-buh.jpeg
found sound at jar:file:/Users/cadamson/Documents/O'Reilly/books/
    swing%20hacks/HacksBook/PackagingInstalling/97/buh.jar!/sounds/
    buhbuhbuh.aiff
```

Note the different URLs: the image and sound are now found inside *buh.jar*. The format of the jar: URL is also interesting, in that it combines a regular file:-type URL for the JAR file with a path inside that JAR, using a ! character to separate the two parts.

Double-Clicking JARs

There are a few more useful things you can do with JAR files. The first is that you can eliminate the need to specify a main class on the command line by specifying it in the JAR file instead. This has the advantage of making the JAR a double-clickable application on graphical operating systems. To do this, create a Manifest file with a line like the following in it:

```
Main-Class: JarResourceLoading
```

You put this into the JAR with the jar command's m option. Because this option requires an argument (as does c, which creates the JAR file), you specify the JAR file to be created and the Manifest file to be inserted in the order that you use the m and c options. So, you can create the JAR like this:

```
jar cfm buh.jar manifest.txt JarResourceLoading.class images sounds
```

or like this:

```
jar mcf manifest.txt buh.jar JarResourceLoading.class images sounds
```

You could also create the JAR with one command and add the Manifest with another. In any case, you can run the application inside the JAR by double-clicking its icon, or with the command:

```
java -jar buh.jar
```

Granted, this is all pretty burdensome if you have to do it over and over. Presumably, you'll want to automate creating and populating your JAR, and the most popular way to do that is with Apache Ant (*http://ant.apache.org/*). Ant lets you split up and customize the compiling and JAR-building tasks, and its XML syntax is far easier to read than command-line options. Example 11-8 shows a simple Ant *build.xml* file that builds this example and packs it into a JAR, along with a Manifest file that specifies the main class.

Example 11-8. Ant file to compile an application and build a JAR file

```
<project name="jar-resource-loading" default="all" basedir=".">

  <target name="compile">
    <javac srcdir="." destdir="."/>
  </target>

  <target name="package">
    <jar destfile="buh.jar"
        basedir="."
        includes="*.class, images/*, sounds/*"
        manifest="manifest.txt" />
  </target>

  <target name="all" depends="compile, package" />

</project>
```

Because the default target (all) runs the compile and package targets as needed, to compile the application and stuff it and its resources into a JAR, use the command:

```
ant
```

And the Kitchen Sink

Because you can get a URL and thus an InputStream—via URL.openStream( )—from any resource found in a JAR, you can put pretty much any kind of file into the JAR and read it back at runtime. This example used images and sounds for simplicity, since ImageIcon's constructor and AudioSystem.getAudioInputStream( ) both take URL objects directly, but if you're willing to deal with reading the stream yourself, there's no reason you couldn't put other kinds of files in the JAR. You could put a properties file with default settings in the JAR, open a stream, and then read it into a Properties object via the load( ) method. You could put an executable in the JAR and extract it to the local filesystem. You could even put a ZIP file in the JAR, add code to open the ZIP and decompress it to disk, and thus have a self-extracting archive.

Make Quick Look and Feel Changes

Customize Metal with custom fonts, colors, and even system-bound
properties using just a few API calls.

Swing is a very customizable UI toolkit. The most advanced way of changing the look of your application is with a custom Look and Feel (L&F), but
they can be tricky to build. Swing's L&F API is very complicated, often
requiring thousands of lines of code for a complete custom theme. Fortunately, if you want to change just a few colors or fonts, the L&F API provides a much easier way. This hack shows how to create simple visual
changes using UI properties.

Look and Feel Properties

Every Look and Feel that extends the javax.swing.plaf.basic.* classes can
accept special properties that define the behavior of each Swing component.
For example, there is property to control the background color of every
JButton. If you change this property at the start of your program, then every
JButton you create will have that background color.

The UI properties are stored in a static class called the UIManager. To set a
property, just put in the name of the property and a value object like a
Color. To set the background color of a button to green, you would do
something like this:

```
UIManager.put("Button.background", Color.green);
```

> It is important to set these properties before any compo-
> nents are created or they won't pick up the new settings.

Below is the code for a simple program that shows a few components in a
frame. It has a button, label, and text field along the top and a text area in a
scroll pane in the middle. There is also a simple file menu at the top. Before
creating any components, it sets the foreground and background colors for
the button, label, text field, and panel to light and dark green:

```
public static void main(String[] args) throws Exception {

    Color bg = Color.green.brighter();
    Color fg = Color.green.darker();
    UIManager.put("Button.background",bg);
    UIManager.put("Button.foreground",fg);
```

```
UIManager.put("Label.background",bg);
UIManager.put("Label.foreground",fg);
UIManager.put("TextField.background",bg);
UIManager.put("TextField.foreground",fg);
UIManager.put("Panel.background",bg);
UIManager.put("Panel.foreground",fg);

JTextArea jta = new JTextArea( );
jta.setText("text\ntext\ntext\ntext\ntext\ntext"+
    "\ntext\ntext\ntext\ntext\ntext");
JScrollPane scroll = new JScrollPane(jta);

JButton button = new JButton("A Button");
JLabel label = new JLabel("A Label");
JTextField text = new JTextField("A TextField");

JMenuBar mb = new JMenuBar( );
JMenu file = new JMenu("File");
file.add(new JMenuItem("Open"));
file.add(new JMenuItem("Close"));
mb.add(file);

JFrame frame = new JFrame("Custom LaF Defaults");

JPanel top = new JPanel( );
top.setLayout(new BoxLayout(top,BoxLayout.X_AXIS));
top.add(button);
top.add(label);
top.add(text);

JPanel panel = new JPanel( );
panel.setLayout(new BorderLayout( ));
panel.add("North",top);
panel.add("Center",scroll);

frame.getContentPane( ).add(panel);
frame.setJMenuBar(mb);

frame.pack( );
frame.setSize(300,200);
frame.setVisible(true);
}
```

When compiled, this will look like Figure 11-11.

Swing provides over 300 properties that define the colors and fonts of each standard component. This lets you customize almost anything in your program. You can even set a color to be transparent, which may look interesting if you have a pattern background.

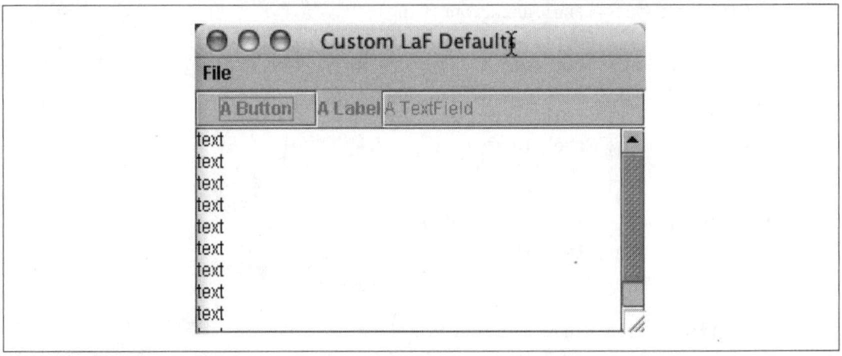

Figure 11-11. A sample program with green components

Text Components

Text components have font settings in addition to their colors. This lets you set a component to use a different font style or size. You can even load a custom font from a file:

```
Font font = Font.createFont(Font.TRUETYPE_FONT,
    new FilcInputStream("dungeon.ttf"));
font = font.deriveFont(Font.BOLD,16f);
UIManager.put("Label.font",font);
```

This would look like Figure 11-12.

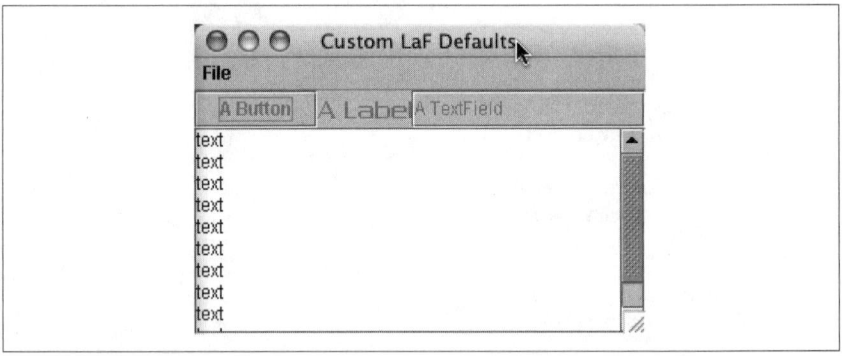

Figure 11-12. A custom font

Most components also have margins that are defined by an Insets object. A text field with large insets:

```
UIManager.put("TextField.margin", new Insets(25,25,25,25));
```

would look like Figure 11-13.

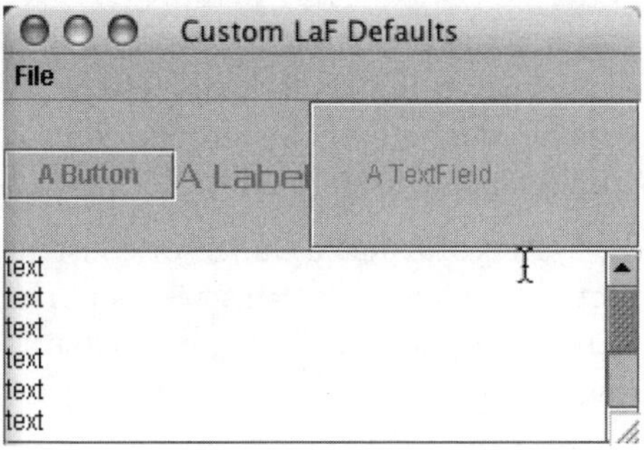

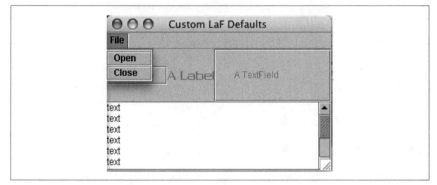

Figure 11-13. A JTextField with large insets

Some components even have borders. Menu items have borders but they are turned off by default. You need to set an extra boolean to make a new border show up, as in Figure 11-14.

```
Border border = BorderFactory.createEtchedBorder(
    EtchedBorder.LOWERED);
UIManager.put("MenuItem.border", border);
UIManager.put("MenuItem.borderPainted", new Boolean(true));
```

Figure 11-14. Menu items with etched borders

Use System Colors

The UIManager lets you change any color in your application to whatever you want. Now, what if you wanted to create a theme that matched the native operating system closer? You could hardcode some color values for each OS, but most windowing systems also let their users customize their colors. Hardcoded values wouldn't take those dynamic colors into account. Fortunately, AWT provides a way out: the SystemColor class.

SystemColor is a special subclass of Color that provides access to most of the standard color settings of any operating system. It also has the special ability to update itself whenever the underlying system color changes. This means if the user switches her native colors from a control panel, your application will automatically update itself to reflect the new settings.

Instead of methods, SystemColor has a bunch of constants that define each type of color from activeCaptionText to windowBorder. The documentation is minor, so you will need to play around with different settings to get the effect you are looking for:

```
Color sysbg = SystemColor.control;
Color sysfg = SystemColor.controlText;
UIManager.put("Button.background",sysbg);
UIManager.put("Button.foreground",sysfg);
```

This code sets the background and foreground of every button to use the control and controlText fields of SystemColor. With my computer set to use the Desert theme, it looks like Figure 11-15.

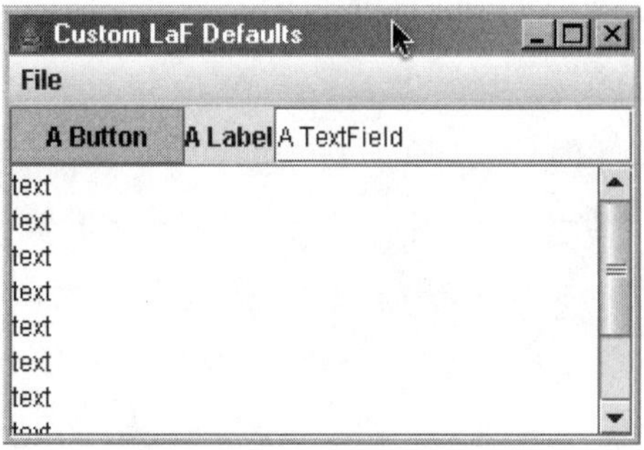

Figure 11-15. Window with the Desert theme

If I change my window theme to high-contrast black, it looks like Figure 11-16.

UIManager properties give developers a simple way to customize the colors, fonts, and borders of almost any Swing component. As an enhancement, you could allow users to customize the colors themselves and store the values in a properties file.

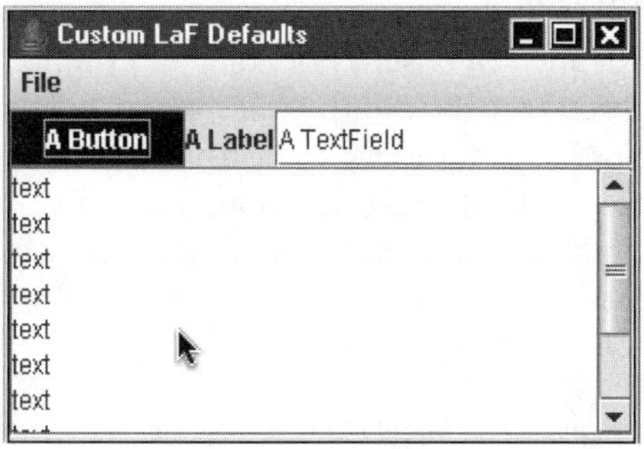

Figure 11-16. *Window with the high-contrast black theme*

Create an Inverse Black-and-White Theme

Create a custom black-and-white theme for monochrome LCD displays using
a few simple UIManager calls.

The UIManager lets you set simple resources for color, fonts, and padding,
but you may have noticed that if you want to theme all of the components,
you need to set properties on each one. Since Swing has over 300 Look and
Feel properties, this could become a problem. Fortunately, there is another
way to make global changes without creating an entire custom L&F. Metal,
the standard cross-platform L&F that comes with Swing, can use themes.
This hack demonstrates how to create a Metal theme that forces the components to use only black and white.

Swing lets you switch between different Look and Feels. You can use a
native Look and Feel (such as the one that comes with Mac OS X) or a third-
party Look and Feel if you have them installed. Swing also comes with a
standard L&F called Metal. Metal is built into the JRE and is always available, making it the ideal L&F to customize.

Like all L&Fs, Metal has many, many classes that you can subclass to make
changes. However, it also comes with an interface called MetalTheme. If you
implement MetalTheme, then you can customize most of Metal without digging into the details. Most of the colors in Metal can be set, in fact, with just
six values. Metal makes it even easier by providing a default implementation called, unsurprisingly, DefaultMetalTheme that you can use as a starting
point.

A Black-and-White Theme

A Metal theme is defined by a series of colors and fonts. The most important ones are the three primary and three secondary colors. These define the standard set of colors used for every widget on screen. Certain components have additional colors, like the text selection, but almost everything is based on these six. Example 11-9 is a theme that uses only white and black. It is useful for embedded devices that can't afford the hardware or memory requirements of a color display.

Example 11-9. A black-and-white Metal theme

```
import javax.swing.plaf.metal.*;
import javax.swing.plaf.ColorUIResource;

public class InverseTheme extends DefaultMetalTheme {

    protected ColorUIResource getPrimary1() {
        return new ColorUIResource(255,255,255);
    }
    protected ColorUIResource getPrimary2() {
        return new ColorUIResource(0,0,0);
    }
    protected ColorUIResource getPrimary3() {
        return new ColorUIResource(255,255,255);
    }

    // component borders
    protected ColorUIResource getSecondary1() {
        return new ColorUIResource(0,0,0);
    }
    // selected components (button down state)
    protected ColorUIResource getSecondary2() {
        return new ColorUIResource(0,0,0);
    }
    // component backgrounds
    protected ColorUIResource getSecondary3() {
        return new ColorUIResource(255,255,255);
    }
}
```

Two of the primary colors are all white, and the third is black. The three secondary colors are just the reverse: two black and one white. This introduces extra contrast. Each color controls a different part of the component. The MetalTheme documentation is very sparse, so the only way to know what a particular color will do is to try it. Without the theme, the screen will look like Figure 11-17.

With the InverseTheme installed, the window will look like Figure 11-18.

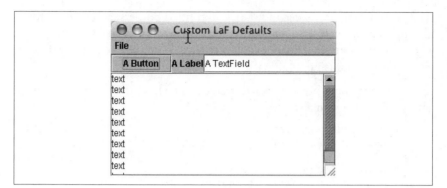

Figure 11-17. Window with no changes

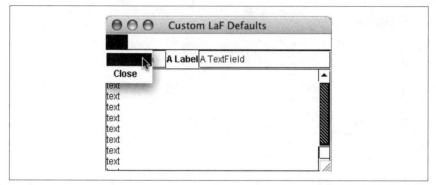

Figure 11-18. Window with an inverse theme

Setting the six colors gets us most of the way, but there are still some problems. In particular, the label is hidden and the text field looks wrong when you select it. To correct these, you'll need to set three more colors:

```
//for label text
public ColorUIResource getSystemTextColor( ) {
    return new ColorUIResource(0,0,0);
}

// background of selected text
public ColorUIResource getTextHighlightColor( ) {
    return new ColorUIResource(0,0,0);
}

// foreground of selected text
public ColorUIResource getHighlightedTextColor( ) {
    return new ColorUIResource(255,255,255);
}
```

The SystemTextColor is used for labels and titled borders, so you have to set this to black as well. The highlighted text, as well as the background of the highlight, are controlled by the HighlightedTextColor and TextHighlightColor, respectively (confusing, I know).

The only remaining problem is the menus. They have their own set of properties, which you can also set:

```
public ColorUIResource getMenuBackground() {
    return new ColorUIResource(255,255,255);
}
public ColorUIResource getMenuForeground() {
    return new ColorUIResource(0,0,0);
}

public ColorUIResource getMenuSelectedBackground() {
    return new ColorUIResource(0,0,0);
}
public ColorUIResource getMenuSelectedForeground() {
    return new ColorUIResource(255,255,255);
}
```

With all of the colors set, you are ready to load up the theme. All you have to do is call MetalLookAndFeel.setCurrentTheme() before you create any Swing components.

```
public static void main(String[] args) {
    MetalLookAndFeel.setCurrentTheme(new InverseTheme());
    //.. set up Swing components now
}
```

If you set it as the first line of the main() method in the demonstration program from the previous hack, you will see your themed window as in Figure 11-19.

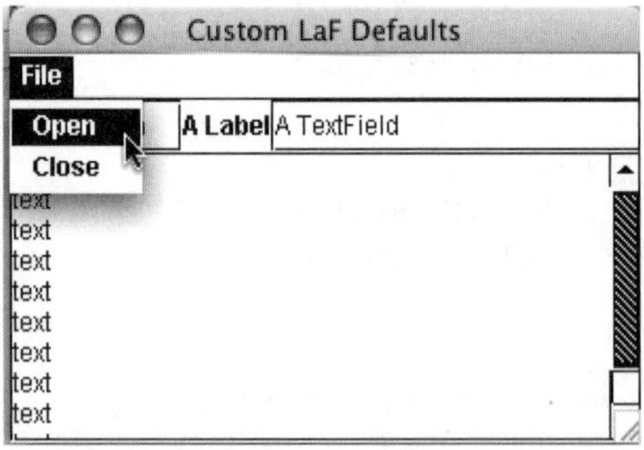

Figure 11-19. A better inverse theme

Miscellany
Hacks 88–100

Not everything about Swing fits into nice little groupings of functionality. Some of the cool stuff you can do involves cursors, event-dispatching, networking, and even the lights on the keyboard. So, here we present some hacks that were just unique (or weird) enough to defy easy categorization.

HACK #88 Display a Busy Cursor

Use the setCursor( ) method and an animation thread to show a frame's busy status.

One of Swing's lesser-known features is the ability to change the mouse cursor on a per-component basis. Because the cursor change happens very quickly, you could combine this ability with some simple threading to create an animated cursor. This hack will show you how to create an animated cursor useful for showing a busy status.

Any Swing component—even a frame—can have a custom cursor. The application as a whole will retain the normal mouse cursor, but when the user moves over the appropriately configured component, the cursor will change to whatever is set for that component. This behavior lends itself nicely to restricting user access during long running processes because the rest of the application can look and feel responsive while the portion that represents the process is visually unusable by the custom cursor.

Pre-Generating Images

The best way to manage a short animation is by pre-generating your images in an array. This lets you loop through the array rather than creating a bunch of nasty conditionals. If you later expand the animation, you can just add more images to the array, leaving the rest of the code untouched.

First, you need to build an AnimatedCursor class and generate the images in the constructor. In this case, the images are instances of the java.awt.Cursor object. I used standard, predefined cursors to keep the code easy, but you could also use cursors derived from custom images. A JFrame is passed into the constructor and stored for later use, as you can see in Example 12-1.

Example 12-1. A simple animated cursor

```
public class AnimatedCursor implements Runnable, ActionListener {
    private boolean animate;
    private Cursor[] cursors;
    private JFrame frame;

    public AnimatedCursor(JFrame frame) {
        animate = false;
        cursors = new Cursor[8];
        this.frame = frame;
        cursors[0] = Cursor.getPredefinedCursor(Cursor.N_RESIZE_CURSOR);
        cursors[1] = Cursor.getPredefinedCursor(Cursor.NE_RESIZE_CURSOR);
        cursors[2] = Cursor.getPredefinedCursor(Cursor.E_RESIZE_CURSOR);
        cursors[3] = Cursor.getPredefinedCursor(Cursor.SE_RESIZE_CURSOR);
        cursors[4] = Cursor.getPredefinedCursor(Cursor.S_RESIZE_CURSOR);
        cursors[5] = Cursor.getPredefinedCursor(Cursor.SW_RESIZE_CURSOR);
        cursors[6] = Cursor.getPredefinedCursor(Cursor.W_RESIZE_CURSOR);
        cursors[7] = Cursor.getPredefinedCursor(Cursor.NW_RESIZE_CURSOR);
    }
}
```

AnimatedCursor implements Runnable because it will be threaded, and it accepts action events to turn on and off the animation. You can reuse the standard directional cursors, one for each compass direction, stored in a Cursor array, which is eight items long.

Running the Animation

Next, you need to build the actual animation thread:

```
public void run( ) {
    int count = 0;
    while(animate) {
        try {
            Thread.currentThread( ).sleep(200);
        } catch (Exception ex) { }

        frame.setCursor(cursors[count % cursors.length]);
        count++;
    }
    frame.setCursor(Cursor.getPredefinedCursor(Cursor.DEFAULT_CURSOR));
}
```

Like most run( ) methods, the previous code does something repeatedly in a loop with a sleep( ) on each pass. In this case, you call setCursor( ) on the frame and increment the count variable. Notice the code line:

```
cursors[count % cursors.length]
```

which will loop over each cursor in the array, wrapping when it reaches the end. The mod operator (%) is indispensable for these types of calculations. The loop also sleeps on every pass. I chose 200 ms because that lets the cursor make a complete revolution every second and a half, which seemed about right; you can adjust it to your taste:

```
public void actionPerformed(ActionEvent evt) {
    JButton button = (JButton)evt.getSource( );
    if(animate) {
        button.setText("Start Animation");
        animate = false;
    } else {
        animate = true;
        button.setText("Stop Animation");
        new Thread(this).start( );
    }
}
```

The actionPerformed( ) method starts and stops the animation thread. It also updates the text on the JButton as further user feedback.

Put It All Together

```
public static void main(String[] args) {
    JFrame frame = new JFrame("Animated Cursor Hack");

    JButton button = new JButton("Start Animation");
    button.addActionListener(new AnimatedCursor(frame));

    frame.getContentPane( ).add(button);
    frame.pack( );
    frame.show( );
}
```

The main( ) method in the preceding code creates a frame with a control button. The AnimatedCursor applies directly to the frame so that the cursor will animate whenever it's over the window. A screen capture cannot really capture the effect, but when you put it together, it will look something like Figure 12-1.

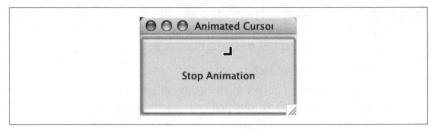

Figure 12-1. An animated cursor

And More...

The most obvious enhancement is to use real images for the cursor, as the many cursor packs available on the Web can attest (type "free cursors" into Google and see what you get). Animated cursors could also be used to indicate other elements of program state, such as network traffic or the current tool in use. With a few images and the help of the setCursor( ) function, you can do almost anything.

H A C K   Fun with Keyboard Lights
#89
Flash the Caps Lock, Num Lock, and Scroll Lock keys for extra user feedback.

The AWT and Swing APIs are huge and full of robust components and frameworks for building big applications. They also have some dark corners where the lesser-known functions live. While cruising through the JavaDoc for java.awt.Toolkit, I ran across a function I had never noticed before, despite it being in the API for over four years. This hack explores building a keyboard busy indicator using the Toolkit.setLockingKeyState( ) function.

The root class of AWT, Toolkit, has a very interesting little function: setLockingKeyState( ). You pass it the KeyEvent for the key you want to lock down and turn it on or off with the boolean. For most keyboards, this means the Caps Lock, Num Lock, and Scroll Lock keys (some keyboards may also have a Kana lock for Kanji support). Now that you have this nifty little function, what should you do with it?

My first thought was a busy cursor. If you've got three lights in a row, why not blink them off and on in sequence? The code in Example 12-2 will flip each light on and off in order, creating a moving bar effect (depending on the order of your keyboard LEDs).

Example 12-2. Lights, camera, action

```
class SpinnerThread extends Thread {
    private boolean go;
    public void quit() {
        go = false;
    }
    public void run() {
        go = true;
        // get a toolkit
        Toolkit tk = Toolkit.getDefaultToolkit();

        // save the old key states
        boolean old_num, old_caps, old_scroll;
        old_num = tk.getLockingKeyState(KeyEvent.VK_NUM_LOCK);
        old_caps = tk.getLockingKeyState(KeyEvent.VK_CAPS_LOCK);
        old_scroll = tk.getLockingKeyState(KeyEvent.VK_SCROLL_LOCK);

        // set all keys to off
        tk.setLockingKeyState(KeyEvent.VK_NUM_LOCK,false);
        tk.setLockingKeyState(KeyEvent.VK_CAPS_LOCK,false);
        tk.setLockingKeyState(KeyEvent.VK_SCROLL_LOCK,false);
```

SpinnerThread is a Runnable implementation, meaning you can launch it with
new Thread(new SpinnerThread()).start( ). The run( ) method starts an infinite loop, ending only when the quit( ) method is called. The first thing to
notice is that the code saves the existing state of the buttons so that it can
restore them later. If you had Caps Lock on you'd probably still want it on
once the busy cursor leaves. Next, it sets all of the key states to false. This
puts them into a known position so that the animation looks right:

```
int key = -1;
boolean state = false;
// loop through 100 times
int counter = 0;
while(go) {
    // select each key every 3rd time
    if(counter%3 == 0) { key = KeyEvent.VK_NUM_LOCK; }
    if(counter%3 == 1) { key = KeyEvent.VK_CAPS_LOCK; }
    if(counter%3 == 2) { key = KeyEvent.VK_SCROLL_LOCK; }
    // flip the state
    state = tk.getLockingKeyState(key);
    tk.setLockingKeyState(key,!state);
    // sleep for 500 msec
    try { Thread.currentThread().sleep(500);
    } catch (InterruptedException ex) {}

    // increment counter
    counter++;
}
```

```
// restore the key settings
tk.setLockingKeyState(KeyEvent.VK_NUM_LOCK,old_num);
tk.setLockingKeyState(KeyEvent.VK_CAPS_LOCK,old_caps);
tk.setLockingKeyState(KeyEvent.VK_SCROLL_LOCK,old_scroll);
```

Next comes the loop, which flips one key each time through the loop, cycling between the three keys. This is what produces the actual animation. Once the loop is finished, the keyboard states are restored.

Revisiting this hack (I first wrote it for a blog on *http://www.java.net*), I have been looking for other interesting ideas. One popped out at me as being truly annoying, so I chose to include it here. The class in Example 12-3 flashes the Scroll Lock key on every keystroke. Thus, your computer will keep in time with your typing. Is this the future of human-computer evolution, or just plain annoying?

The key, so to speak, of this hack is once again the Toolkit object. It contains a very interesting method, addAWTEventListener( ), that lets you add a listener for every event dispatched throughout the JVM. This is equivalent to putting a listener on each component in your entire program. This method is mainly intended for debuggers and testing tools, but I've used it to listen for application-wide keystroke events.

Example 12-3. Scroll Lock keeping up with typing

```
public class KeyboardFlasher implements AWTEventListener {

    public static void main(String[] args) {
        Toolkit tk = Toolkit.getDefaultToolkit( );
        KeyboardFlasher flasher = new KeyboardFlasher( );
        tk.addAWTEventListener(flasher, AWTEvent.KEY_EVENT_MASK);

        JFrame frame = new JFrame("Hack #89: Fun with Keyboard Lights");

        JTextField tf = new JTextField("this is some text");
        frame.getContentPane( ).add(tf);
        frame.pack( );
        frame.setVisible(true);
    }
```

KeyboardFlasher implements the AWTEventListener interface and the main method adds a new flasher to the toolkit as a listener. tk.addAWTEventListener's second argument, AWTEvent.KEY_EVENT_MASK, indicates that the listener should receive key events only. If I wanted the program to also look for mouse clicks, then I would do a bitwise OR (|) of KEY_EVENT_MASK with MOUSE_EVENT_MASK. Finally, the main( ) method creates a text field in a frame to test out generating keyboard events:

```
    public void eventDispatched(AWTEvent evt) {
        if(evt instanceof KeyEvent) {
            KeyEvent kevt = (KeyEvent)evt;
            if(kevt.getID() == KeyEvent.KEY_PRESSED) {
                System.out.println("key event: " + evt);
                if(kevt.getKeyCode() != KeyEvent.VK_SCROLL_LOCK) {
                    flipScrollLock();
                }
            }
        }
    }

    public void flipScrollLock() {
        Toolkit tk = Toolkit.getDefaultToolkit();
        boolean state = tk.getLockingKeyState(KeyEvent.VK_SCROLL_LOCK);
        tk.setLockingKeyState(KeyEvent.VK_SCROLL_LOCK,!state);
    }
```

As an implementation of AWTEventListener, KeyboardFlasher has one required method only, eventDispatched(). This receives all events generated in the system. This implementation first checks that the event is indeed a keyboard event, and then checks if it is a KEY_PRESSED event. This will distinguish between the key going down and the key going up. Then, the method checks to make sure that the key pressed isn't the Scroll Lock key.

 If I didn't add this check, the code would go into an infinite loop, as each flip of the Scroll Lock key would generate a new event and trigger a new flip.

Finally comes flipScrollLock(), which does exactly what it suggests: flips the state of the Scroll Lock key each time it is called. In other words, it takes two strokes to complete a cycle. For a faster effect, you could make the light turn on with the downward stroke and then off again with the upward stroke. You would just need to call flipScrollLock() twice, once for each event.

setLockingKeyState() is one of those nut-ball little functions that seems to have no purpose, but it sure lets us have some fun. What other uses can you think up? A new email alert? A three-bar sound meter? A Wi-Fi strength indicator?

Create Demonstrations with the Robot Class

#90   Use the Robot class to control the mouse cursor and create interactive software features.

One of the coolest things about Swing is that you can often use a class for something completely different than what it was originally intended. The java.awt.Robot class, for example, can move the mouse cursor programmatically. This feature was originally intended for use by automated testing tools (hence the name Robot), but I've found it very useful to demonstrate software features by moving the mouse cursor through the same actions as the user. Instead of just describing something in a help file, you can actually show the user what to do—and this hack explains how.

I, Robot

To create a mouse animation, you need three things:

1. The ability to move the cursor
2. The start and end points of the animation
3. A way to smoothly interpolate the cursor position

The java.awt.Robot class has a variety of methods for capturing program state and controlling the user interface, including Robot.mouseMove( ), which allows you to move the mouse cursor programmatically.

The following code is the implementation of a method moveMouse( ), which takes three arguments: a starting component, an ending component, and a duration for the animation (in milliseconds). Because most demonstrations involve showing the user a particular component, the easiest points to use are the centers of start and end components. The mouse will smoothly move from the center of the starting component to the center of the ending one. We normally think of components as being positioned relative to their parents, but since the Robot class uses absolute mouse positions, you'll need to convert the components to their screen locations:

```
public void moveMouse(JComponent start, JComponent end,
    final int duration) throws Exception {
    final Robot robot = new Robot( );

    // get middle of start
    final Point start_coords = start.getLocationOnScreen( );
    start_coords.translate(start.getWidth( )/2,
        start.getHeight( )/2);
```

```
// get middle of end
final Point end_coords = end.getLocationOnScreen( );
end_coords.translate(end.getWidth( )/2,
    end.getHeight( )/2);

// create interpolation point and offsets
int steps = duration/50;
//Point current = new Point(start_coords);
int distx = (end_coords.x - start_coords.x);
int disty = (end_coords.y - start_coords.y);

// move the mouse over 10 steps
for(int i=1; i<=steps; i++) {
    int x = start_coords.x + i*distx/steps;
    int y = start_coords.y + i*disty/steps;
    robot.mouseMove(x,y);
    try { Thread.currentThread( ).sleep(50);
    } catch (Exception ex) {}
}
}
```

This code creates a new Robot and calculates the center positions of the start and end components using screen coordinates. steps is the number of frames required to fill the specified duration. Since each frame will be 1/20 of a second long, the number of frames is the total duration divided by 50 ms. distx and disty are the distances between the two components in the horizontal and vertical directions. With these values in hand, it is a simple matter to interpolate a new position for each frame and then move the mouse cursor there.

To test the system, you'll need some sort of a demonstration program. The code in Example 12-4 creates a fake file browser with a list of directories, a list of files, and a toolbar with three buttons: Info, New Dir, and Delete. You can see this in Figure 12-2.

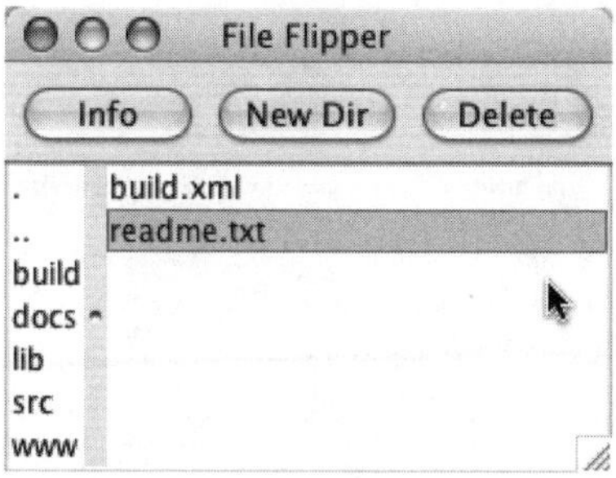

Figure 12-2. Sample program to demonstrate mouse automation

Example 12-4. A simple demonstration for the power of Robot

```
public class AutoMouseHack implements ActionListener {
    public JButton info, new_dir, delete;

    public  void createDemo() {
        JFrame frame = new JFrame("File Flipper");

        String[] dirs = {".","..","build","docs","lib","src","www"};
        String[] files = {"build.xml","readme.txt"};
        JList dir_list = new JList(dirs);
        JList files_list = new JList(files);

        JSplitPane split = new JSplitPane(
            JSplitPane.HORIZONTAL_SPLIT,
            dir_list,files_list);

        info = new JButton("Info");
        new_dir = new JButton("New Dir");
        delete = new JButton("Delete");

        JPanel toolbar = new JPanel();
        toolbar.setLayout(new FlowLayout());
        toolbar.add(info);
        toolbar.add(new_dir);
        toolbar.add(delete);

        frame.getContentPane().setLayout(new BorderLayout());
        frame.getContentPane().add("North",toolbar);
        frame.getContentPane().add("Center",split);

        frame.pack();
        frame.show();
    }
```

The demonstration program also contains a Help screen (shown in Figure 12-3).

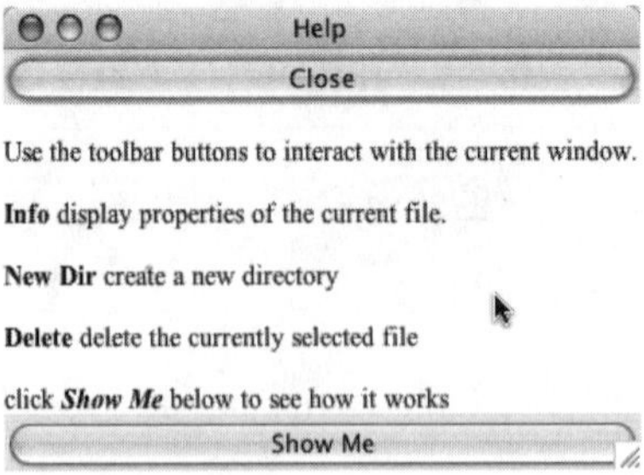

Figure 12-3. Help text

This is an HTML pane with the help text in it, plus Close and Show Me buttons. Clicking Show Me will take control of the mouse cursor and show the animation. Note that the JEditorPane switches to HTML mode automatically if you put in a content type of text/html and start the body text with <html>:

```java
JButton showme;
public void createHelp( ) throws IOException {
    JFrame frame = new JFrame("Help");
    JButton close = new JButton("Close");
    showme = new JButton("Show Me");
    showme.addActionListener(this);

    JEditorPane html = new JEditorPane("text/html",
        "<html><body>" +
        "<p>Use the toolbar buttons to interact with the current window</p>."+
        "<p><b>Info</b> display properties of the current file.</p>" +
        "<p><b>New Dir</b> create a new directory</p>"+
        "<p><b>Delete</b> delete the currently selected file</p>" +
        "<p>click <i><b>Show Me</b></i> below to see how it works</p>"
    );

    frame.getContentPane( ).setLayout(new BorderLayout( ));
    frame.getContentPane( ).add("North",close);
    frame.getContentPane( ).add("Center",html);
    frame.getContentPane( ).add("South",showme);

    frame.pack( );
    frame.setLocation(400,50);
    frame.setVisible(true);
}

public static void main(String[] args) throws Exception {
    AutoMouseHack hack = new AutoMouseHack( );
    hack.createDemo( );
    hack.createHelp( );
}
```

With a demonstration program and some help text, now you can create the actual animation. The moveMouse( ) function moves the mouse cursor from one location to another over a certain amount of time. If you make the cursor start and end on the same component, then it will act as a time delay, making the cursor appear to pause over that component:

```java
public void actionPerformed(ActionEvent evt) {
    try {
        moveMouse(showme, info, 2000);
        moveMouse(info, info, 1000);
        moveMouse(info, new_dir, 1000);
        moveMouse(new_dir, new_dir, 1000);
        moveMouse(new_dir, delete, 1000);
```

```
                moveMouse(delete, delete, 1000);
                moveMouse(delete, showme, 500);
            } catch (Exception ex) {
                System.out.println(""+ex);
            }
        }
```

The event handler moves the cursor from the showme button, which is where the cursor will already be anyway, to the info toolbar button over a period of two seconds. After that, the cursor will hop from button to button taking one second to move with a one second pause over each button. Finally, the cursor rushes back to the showme button in a half-second. It is important to return the cursor to its starting position so that the user won't have to hunt for it after the animation is complete. It's best to always return things to the state you found them.

HACK #91 Check Your Mail with Swing

Add email checking to your application with just a few method calls.

As email becomes a bigger part of our daily lives, I have seen it creep into more and more places. My email program alerts me when there is new mail. I can check my email via the phone. I log in to my web mail from an Internet cafe. Email is everywhere, so why shouldn't it be in your Swing application? This hack shows how to embed in your application an email checker that shows the current number of unread messages and can launch the user's email application.

Dealing with email servers can be a complicated and tricky business. To help address these issues, Sun created the JavaMail API, which is a set of classes defining a vendor-neutral interface for accessing email servers.

Sun's sample implementation provides IMAP support, which is what I will demonstrate here. If you have another kind of email server, such as Exchange, you could install your own service provider and use it the same way.

The code in this hack needs to do two things. First, it must open a connection to the email server periodically and check for new mail. Second, it must launch the user's email program on a double-click. I have encapsulated the email checking and launching code into separate classes, making it very easy to add to an existing program.

The `EmailChecker` class, shown in Example 12-5, is a simple `Runnable` implementation that receives a `JLabel` to its constructor. The run loop will sleep for a certain amount of time (one minute in this case) then call `checkEmail( )`. Every time there is new mail, it will set the text of the label to something like "You have *N* new messages."

Example 12-5. Checking for new messages

```
import java.util.Properties;
import javax.swing.JLabel;
import javax.swing.SwingUtilities;
import javax.mail.*;

public class EmailChecker implements Runnable {
    private JLabel label;
    public EmailChecker(JLabel label) {
        this.label = label;
    }

    public void run( ) {
        while(true) {
            try {
                checkEmail( );
                Thread.currentThread( ).sleep(1000*60); // sleep 1 min
            } catch (Exception ex) {
                System.out.println("exception: " + ex);
                ex.printStackTrace( );
            }
        }
    }
}
```

Next comes the `checkEmail( )` implementation:

```
    public synchronized void checkEmail( ) throws Exception {
        String username = "joshy@code.joshy.org";
        String password = "satans";
        String hostname = "code.joshy.org";
        int port = 143;

        Properties props = System.getProperties( );
        Session sess = Session.getDefaultInstance(props);
        sess.setDebug(true);
```

To actually check the email, you need to first collect the relevant parameters: the username, password, hostname of the email server, and the port (usually 143 for IMAP servers). In addition to this information, you also need a copy of the system properties to allocate an email `Session`.

> In a more advanced version of this hack, you could override
> some of the system properties to change the installed email
> provider or modify other settings.

Once you have the session, you can open an IMAP email store and connect
to it:

```
Store store = sess.getStore("imap");
store.connect(hostname, port, username, password);

Folder inbox = store.getFolder("INBOX");
final int new_count = inbox.getUnreadMessageCount();

SwingUtilities.invokeLater(new Runnable() {
    public void run() {
        label.setText("You have " + new_count + " unread messages.");
        System.out.println("unread messages = " + new_count);
    }
});
} // end checkEmail()
```

This code connects to the email store and then opens the *INBOX* folder.
Some email servers may use a different name for the inbox folder, but
INBOX should suffice for most IMAP servers. Finally, you can get the
unread message count. Once you have obtained the new message count, you
can set the text of the label. It's important to do this on the Swing thread,
however, which is why the code uses SwingUtilities.invokeLater() to perform the operation.

The second task for this hack is to actually launch the user's email program.
Detecting the default email program is difficult and error prone. If you don't
want to use a native library like JDIC, then your only option is to ask the
user where his program is and launch it with Runtime.exec(). Example 12-6
takes care of this, which turns out to be mercifully simple.

Example 12-6. Asking the user for an email program

```
import java.awt.event.MouseAdapter;
import java.awt.event.MouseEvent;

public class EmailLauncher extends MouseAdapter {
    public void mousePressed(MouseEvent evt) {
        if(evt.getClickCount() >= 2) {
            launchEmailReader();
            evt.consume();
        }
    }
```

Example 12-6. Asking the user for an email program (continued)

```
public void launchEmailReader( ) {
    try {
        Runtime rt = Runtime.getRuntime( );
        rt.exec("C:\\Program Files\\Mozilla Thunderbird\\thunderbird.exe");
    } catch (Exception ex) {
        System.out.println(ex.getMessage( ));
        ex.printStackTrace( );
    }
}
}
```

I implemented EmailLauncher as a mouse listener that looks for a double-click, which makes it very easy to add to any component with a simple addMouseListener( ) call. I have hardcoded the path to my email program, but a more advanced version of this hack would use a preferences screen to ask the user.

Example 12-7 is a simple program that creates a frame with one JLabel to show the mail status. It attaches an EmailLauncher to the status label as a mouse listener and then launches the EmailChecker in its own thread just before making the frame visible.

Example 12-7. Testing out the email utilities

```
public class EmailTest {
    public static void main(String[] args) {
        JFrame frame = new JFrame("Hack #91: Check Your Mail with Swing");
        JLabel status = new JLabel("You have XXX unread messages.");
        frame.getContentPane( ).add(status);
        frame.pack( );
        status.addMouseListener(new EmailLauncher( ));

        EmailChecker email = new EmailChecker(status);
        new Thread(email).start( );

        frame.setVisible(true);
    }
}
```

Once you compile the program and run it, you should see something like Figure 12-4.

This is a pretty simple hack, but it should give you inspiration to try other embedded features, such as checking RSS feeds or playing MP3s.

Figure 12-4. Email checker running

For a more graphical effect, you could use the email icons from the windows system fonts. WebDings and WingDings contain the email icons shown in Figures 12-5 and 12-6.

Figure 12-5. "Have Mail" icon

Figure 12-6. "No Mail" icon

However, Windows does strange codepage mapping, so these fonts aren't simple translations of letters to symbols. Instead, you will have to use the true Unicode values for the glyphs you want:

```
SwingUtilities.invokeLater(new Runnable( ) {
    public void run( ) {
        //label.setText("You have " + new_count + " unread messages.");
        if(new_count > 0) {
            label.setFont(new Font("WebDings",
                Font.PLAIN,40));//label.getFont().getSize( )));
            label.setText(""+(char)0xf099);
        } else {
            label.setFont(new Font("WingDings",
                Font.PLAIN,40));//label.getFont().getSize( )));
            label.setText(""+(char)0x2709);
        }
        System.out.println("unread messages = " + new_count);
    }
});
```

This code will set the label to character 0xf099 in the WebDings font (the envelope with a lightning bolt) if there is at least one unread email. If there are no unread emails, it will use character 0x2709 in the WingDings font (a plain envelope).

> Java doesn't support all of the glyphs in certain custom fonts, so be sure to test your applications before going into production whenever you use non-ASCII fonts.

HACK #92 Don't Block the GUI

Thread your heavy lifting so the event-dispatch thread stays responsive.

Practically every AWT and Swing book you'll ever see keeps things simple by responding to button clicks, menu selections, and other actions by doing something in the event listener. That's probably good for helping you learn the various GUI widgets, but it sets you up for a really bad habit: putting increasingly long-lasting calls in your event callbacks.

This is bad because the thread that calls actionPerformed( ), valueChanged( ), and other event-based methods is the same thread that services GUI events throughout AWT and Swing. The AWT Event Dispatch Thread is responsible for polling for events, dispatching them to listeners, and for repainting everything. If you block it on some long-lasting call—such as database or network access, intense calculation, etc.—then mouse clicks and key-presses won't be processed, menus won't be available, portions of your GUI may not get repainted if they become obscured by other windows, etc. Oh, and the user will hate you. Just so you know.

The trick, then, is to keep heavy lifting out of the event-dispatch thread. There's a very straightforward way to do this in Java: move complicated processing to its own thread, and let event dispatching continue immediately after starting this new thread. Then you just have to deal with cleanup when the launched thread finishes up.

AWTBlockDemo, shown in Example 12-8, offers a test bed for exhibiting and fixing the problem. It offers a JTextField along with two JButtons: Load (blocking) and Load (non-blocking). A menu also offers the blocking and non-blocking load as JMenuItems, along with a Quit menu item.

The text field takes a URL. When you click one of the load buttons or menu items, it loads the file at that address into the text area. The text area is prepopulated with the address for java.awt.Component in Sun's JavaDoc, a nice 300 KB file that will take a little while to load, even with a fast network connection.

 If your network is *really* fast, you can put some Thread. sleep( ) calls in the code to simulate a slower network.

The code for the demo is shown in Example 12-8.

Example 12-8. Demonstration of both blocking and not blocking the AWT event-dispatch thread during lengthy actions

```
import java.awt.*;
import java.awt.event.*;
import javax.swing.*;
import java.io.*;
import java.net.*;

public class AWTBlockDemo extends JFrame {

    JButton blockButton, dontBlockButton;
    JMenuItem blockMenuItem, dontBlockMenuItem, quitMenuItem;
    JTextField urlField;
    JTextArea contentArea;
    final static String DEFAULT_URL =
        "http://java.sun.com/j2se/1.4.2/docs/api/java/awt/Component.html";
    Thread loaderThread;

    public AWTBlockDemo ( ) {
        super ("AWT Thread Blocking");
        initMainLayout( );
        initMenus( );
        initActions( );
    }
```

Example 12-8. Demonstration of both blocking and not blocking the AWT event-dispatch thread during lengthy actions (continued)

```java
private void initMainLayout( ) {
    urlField = new JTextField (DEFAULT_URL, 60);
    JPanel topPanel = new JPanel ( );
    topPanel.setLayout (new BoxLayout (topPanel, BoxLayout.Y_AXIS));
    topPanel.add (urlField);
    JPanel buttonPanel = new JPanel( );
    blockButton = new JButton ("Load (blocking)");
    dontBlockButton = new JButton ("Load (non-blocking)");
    buttonPanel.add (blockButton);
    buttonPanel.add (dontBlockButton);
    topPanel.add (buttonPanel);
    contentArea = new JTextArea (25, 60);
    JScrollPane scroller =         .
        new JScrollPane (contentArea,
                        ScrollPaneConstants.VERTICAL_SCROLLBAR_ALWAYS,
                        ScrollPaneConstants.HORIZONTAL_SCROLLBAR_ALWAYS);
    getContentPane().setLayout(new BorderLayout( ));
    getContentPane( ).add (topPanel, BorderLayout.NORTH);
    getContentPane( ).add (scroller, BorderLayout.CENTER);
}

private void initMenus( ) {
    JMenuBar bar = new JMenuBar( );
    JMenu fileMenu = new JMenu ("File");
    blockMenuItem = new JMenuItem ("Load (blocking)");
    dontBlockMenuItem = new JMenuItem ("Load (non-blocking)");
    fileMenu.add (blockMenuItem);
    fileMenu.add (dontBlockMenuItem);
    fileMenu.addSeparator( );
    quitMenuItem = new JMenuItem ("Quit");
    fileMenu.add (quitMenuItem);
    bar.add (fileMenu);
    setJMenuBar (bar);
}

private void initActions( ) {
    quitMenuItem.addActionListener (new QuitAction( ));
    BlockingLoadAction blocker = new BlockingLoadAction( );
    blockButton.addActionListener (blocker);
    blockMenuItem.addActionListener (blocker);
    NonBlockingLoadAction nonBlocker = new NonBlockingLoadAction( );
    dontBlockButton.addActionListener (nonBlocker);
    dontBlockMenuItem.addActionListener (nonBlocker);
}

public static void main (String[] args) {
    AWTBlockDemo awtbd = new AWTBlockDemo( );
    awtbd.pack( );
    awtbd.setVisible (true);
}
```

Example 12-8. Demonstration of both blocking and not blocking the AWT event-dispatch thread during lengthy actions (continued)

```java
public void loadURL(boolean useWorker) {
    try {
        URL url = new URL (urlField.getText( ));
        BufferedReader in =
            new BufferedReader (
                new InputStreamReader (url.openStream( )));
        StringBuffer sbuf = new StringBuffer( );
        char[] buffy = new char [16 * 1024];
        int bytesRead = 0;
        while ((bytesRead = in.read (buffy, 0, buffy.length)) > -1) {
            sbuf.append (buffy, 0, bytesRead);
            // if your net connection is too fast to see blocking
            // add the following here:
            // Thread.sleep (50);
        }
        if (! useWorker) {
            contentArea.setText (sbuf.toString( ));
            contentArea.setCaretPosition(0);
        } else {
            final StringBuffer finalSBuf = sbuf;
            Thread worker = new Thread( ) {
                public void run ( ) {
                    contentArea.setText (finalSBuf.toString( ));
                    contentArea.setCaretPosition(0);
                }
            };
            SwingUtilities.invokeLater (worker);
        }
    } catch (Exception e) {
        CharArrayWriter writer = new CharArrayWriter( );
        e.printStackTrace (new PrintWriter (writer));
        contentArea.setText(writer.toString( ));
        contentArea.setCaretPosition(0);
    }
}

class QuitAction extends AbstractAction {
    public void actionPerformed (ActionEvent e) {
        System.exit(0);
    }
}

class BlockingLoadAction extends AbstractAction {
    public void actionPerformed (ActionEvent e) {
        // note that threaded version doesn't offer a means of
        // being interrupted so it refuses second launch instead
        if (loaderThread != null)
            return;
        loadURL(false);
    }
}
```

Example 12-8. Demonstration of both blocking and not blocking the AWT event-dispatch thread during lengthy actions (continued)

```
class NonBlockingLoadAction extends AbstractAction implements Runnable {
    // note that this doesn't offer a means of being interrupted
    // so it refuses second launch instead
    public void actionPerformed (ActionEvent e) {
        if (loaderThread != null)
            return;
        loaderThread = new Thread ((Runnable) this);
        loaderThread.start( );
    }
    public void run( ) {
        loadURL(true);
        loaderThread = null;
    }
}
}
```

To Block or Not to Block

The demo application is shown in Figure 12-7.

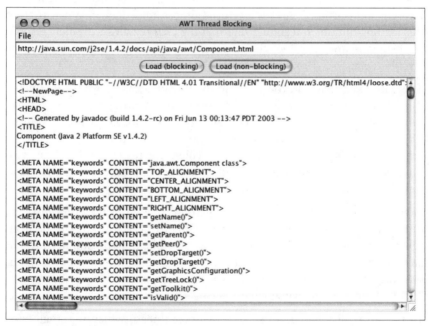

Figure 12-7. Blocking and not blocking AWT event dispatch by loading a URL into a JTextArea

After launching the application, try loading the same address with the blocking and non-blocking Load buttons. In the blocking version, you should see that you can't open the JMenu or reposition the caret in the JTextField. If you've already filled the JTextArea, you'll find that the scrollbar is unresponsive while you're blocking. Drag a window over the demo and then bring the demo to the foreground—on some operating systems, the area previously obscured by the window won't repaint.

Of course, none of this happens when you use the non-blocking version.

Take a look back at Example 12-8. There are separate Actions for the blocking and non-blocking buttons and menu items; but in the end, both of them call loadURL(). The difference is how they call it: the BlockingLoadAction calls loadURL() directly in actionPerformed(), while the NonBlockingLoadAction creates a Thread and runs it. As an aside, both of these methods check to see if there's already a thread running from the NonBlockingLoadAction, as you wouldn't want two of these threads running at once, since the first one would populate the text area only to have it clobbered when the second finished.

But back to the point: because the non-blocking load is only responsible for creating and starting a thread, it returns almost immediately. When you use this loading option, you should find that the GUI remains extremely responsive—menus are viewable, the text field is responsive, you can drag the scrollbar, etc.

The only thing that's a little tricky in the threaded case is what to do when the thread finishes. Swing is not thread-safe, so you're not supposed to make Swing calls from any thread other than the event-dispatch thread. If you do, you'll eventually create crazy bugs that look like NullPointerExceptions or ArrayIndexOutOfBoundsExceptions, but which are really coming from two threads trying to work with one widget at the same time, thus setting and resetting its variables in hard-to-debug race conditions.

Now, you might be thinking, "wasn't getting code off of the event-dispatch thread the whole point of this exercise?" Only to a certain extent—the strategy is to put as little on event dispatch as possible, but you still need to put any Swing calls on it. So, you put the network loading in its own thread, but put the update to the JTextArea back on event dispatch. In other words: "render unto event dispatch what is Swing's...".

You can do your Swing work with a worker thread, which is actually just any Runnable, typically one whose run() method does some Swing work. By calling SwingUtilities' invokeAndWait() or invokeLater()—the difference is in whether you want the Runnable executed immediately or in a few milliseconds, and whether you're willing to handle an InterruptedException—you can put the code in the worker back on the event-dispatch thread. This scheme is effectively a callback method, but instead of being concerned about being called from some event, you're interested in ensuring you're called by a given thread, namely the event-dispatch thread.

In the doRun( ) implementation, you'll notice that there's a flag for whether or not to use a worker. The blocking version doesn't, and doesn't need to, since it's already being called from the event-dispatch thread. The non-blocking version does, but it uses a worker only to reset the contents of the text area after downloading the contents of the URL:

```
final StringBuffer finalSBuf = sbuf;
Thread worker = new Thread( ) {
    public void run ( ) {
        contentArea.setText (finalSBuf.toString( ));
        contentArea.setCaretPosition(0);
    }
};
SwingUtilities.invokeLater (worker);
```

Notice how a final variable is used for the StringBuffer. The anonymous inner thread can see class and instance variables but not local variables like sbuf. It can, however, see a final local variable, so that's what you pass in.

HACK #93 Code Models That Don't Block

Models should know that they're doing work on another thread.

You already know how to keep Swing responsive by moving expensive operations off the event-dispatch thread **[Hack #92]**. However, one downside to that approach is that it uses a separate inner class to coordinate the interaction between the work being done on the other thread and the Swing components. If you reused the same widgets in several places, you wouldn't want to have to write the "start a thread and populate when done" code over and over again. So don't. Why couldn't the model be responsible for this sort of behavior?

Well, the model can—you just have to do a little thinking. Models in Swing are generally in two states: null (no data) or populated with data. What if you had a third state, one that indicated that the model was still loading its data?

Models Aren't Always Dumb

Adapt Example 12-8 to create *AWTBlockModels.java*. To illustrate the loading, this hack has a JProgressBar that you need to declare before the constructor, and which you add at the bottom of initMainLayout( ):

```
progressBar = new JProgressBar (0, 100);
getContentPane( ).add (progressBar, BorderLayout.SOUTH);
```

The strategy in this hack is to make the JTextArea's model responsible for its own threaded loading, so get rid of the loadURL( ) method. That code will move to the models, which subclass javax.swing.text.PlainDocument. First, change the actions to use these documents:

```
class BlockingLoadAction extends AbstractAction {
    public void actionPerformed (ActionEvent e) {
        BlockingURLDocument bud =
            new BlockingURLDocument (urlField.getText( ));
        progressBar.setEnabled (true);
        progressBar.setValue (0);
        contentArea.setDocument (bud);
        progressBar.setValue (100);
    }
}

class NonBlockingLoadAction extends AbstractAction  {
    public void actionPerformed (ActionEvent e) {
        NonBlockingURLDocument nbud =
            new NonBlockingURLDocument (urlField.getText( ));
        contentArea.setDocument (nbud);
        // makeProgressBarUpdaterFor (nbud);
    }
}
```

The actions are pretty much the same, except for the fact that the blocking version sets the JProgressBar before and after setting the JTextArea's document. Why doesn't the non-blocking action touch the progress bar? We'll get back to that.

Example 12-9 is the blocking document, so named because it loads all the data from the URL in its constructor, which will cause the Action's constructor to block until everything is loaded.

Example 12-9. A document that will block while loading a URL

```
class BlockingURLDocument extends PlainDocument {
    public BlockingURLDocument (String urlString) {
        super( );
        try {
            URL url = new URL (urlField.getText( ));
            BufferedReader in =
                new BufferedReader (
                    new InputStreamReader (url.openStream( )));
```

Example 12-9. A document that will block while loading a URL (continued)

```
        StringBuffer sbuf = new StringBuffer( );
        char[] buffy = new char [16 * 1024];
        int bytesRead = 0;
        while ((bytesRead = in.read (buffy, 0, buffy.length)) > -1) {
            sbuf.append (buffy, 0, bytesRead);
            // if your net connection is too fast to see blocking
            // add the following here
            // Thread.sleep (1000);
        }
        remove (0, getLength( ));
        insertString (0, sbuf.toString( ), null);
    } catch (Exception e) {
        CharArrayWriter writer = new CharArrayWriter( );
        e.printStackTrace (new PrintWriter (writer));
        try {
            remove (0, getLength( ));
            insertString (0, writer.toString( ), null);
        } catch (Exception e2) {e2.printStackTrace( );}
    }
  }
}
```

The implementation here is pretty simple: read bytes and stuff them into a StringBuffer until the stream is exhausted, then stuff them into the Document with insertString( ). This makes for clean code because the Document loads its own data. The downside is that the caller, which is on the event-dispatch thread, blocks until all the data is read and inserted into the Document. And, of course, a blocked event-dispatch thread means nothing in your GUI gets repainted, mouse events aren't processed...basically, nobody's happy.

A more enlightened approach requires a Document to load its own data and yet not block the caller. In other words, it will need to return almost immediately, thread whatever work doesn't need to be on event dispatch, and use a worker thread to do the Swing work in a thread-safe manner. Example 12-10 is what a non-blocking document looks like.

Example 12-10. Document that will not block on URL loading

```
class NonBlockingURLDocument extends PlainDocument
    implements Runnable {
    protected int length = -1;
    protected int totalBytesRead = 0;
    protected String urlString;
    protected Thread readThread;
    public NonBlockingURLDocument (String urlString) {
        super( );
        this.urlString = urlString;
```

Example 12-10. Document that will not block on URL loading (continued)

```
        // start thread here
        readThread = new Thread (this);
        readThread.start( );
    }
    public void run( ) {
        try {
            remove (0, getLength( ));
            URL url = new URL (urlField.getText( ));
            URLConnection conn = url.openConnection( );
            length = conn.getContentLength( );
            System.out.println ("length is " + length);
            BufferedReader in =
                new BufferedReader (
                    new InputStreamReader (conn.getInputStream( )));
            char[] buffy = new char [16 * 1024];
            totalBytesRead = 0;
            int bytesRead = -1;
            while ((bytesRead = in.read (buffy, 0, buffy.length)) > -1) {
                final String str = new String (buffy, 0, bytesRead);
                final int finalTBR = totalBytesRead;
                Runnable worker = new Runnable ( ) {
                    public void run( ) {
                        try {
                            insertString (finalTBR, str, null);
                        } catch (BadLocationException ble) {
                            ble.printStackTrace( );
                        }
                    }
                };
                SwingUtilities.invokeLater (worker);
                totalBytesRead += bytesRead;
                System.out.println ("read " + totalBytesRead +
                                    " of " + length +
                                    ", progress == " + getProgress( ));
                // if your net connection is too fast to see updating,
                // make buffy smaller above (maybe 512 bytes) and
                // add the following here:
                // Thread.sleep (500);
            }

        } catch (Exception e) {
            CharArrayWriter writer = new CharArrayWriter( );
            e.printStackTrace (new PrintWriter (writer));
            try {
                remove (0, getLength( ));
                insertString (0, writer.toString( ), null);
            } catch (Exception e2) {e2.printStackTrace( );}
        } finally {
            readThread = null;
        }
    }
```

Example 12-10. Document that will not block on URL loading (continued)

```
    public boolean isAlive( ) {
        return (readThread != null) && (readThread.isAlive( ));
    }
    public float getProgress( ) {
        return (float) totalBytesRead/length;
    }
}
```

In this case, all the loading is done in a run( ) method, so the constructor simply creates a Thread called readThread to wrap the run( ), starts the thread, and then returns, freeing up the event-dispatch thread almost immediately.

So, now it's up to readThread to read the stream and load its contents into the Document. As in the blocking version (Example 12-9), it reads bytes into a buffer, but instead of building a big StringBuffer with which to do a mass-insert, it uses Document's insertString( ) method to put each bufferful into the document. Since insertString( ) will cause the model to fire off events, this will provide for a constant updating of the view; that's why this version calls insertString( ) each time through the loop instead of once at the bottom, as the blocking version did. However, insertString( ) is a Swing method, meaning it's thread-unsafe, so you can't call it directly from the readThread. Instead, you set up a worker and use SwingUtilities. invokeLater( ) to put the insertString( ) call, and only that call, back onto the event-dispatch thread.

Running the Code

If you have a fast Internet connection, it is possible that you'll load the data so fast that you don't mind the blocking or you can't see the incremental updating of the non-blocking version. To make this more dramatic, increase the time that each model sleep( )s, and reduce the size of the buffer used to read bytes from the InputStream. To show the incremental, non-blocking update in Figure 12-8, I set the sleep( ) time to 500 milliseconds and the buffer size to a mere 80 bytes.

Now you have a URL-loading document and a model for JTextComponents that will handle its own threaded loading and can thus be dropped into any JTextComponent without needing to add any other code to manage its threaded operation.

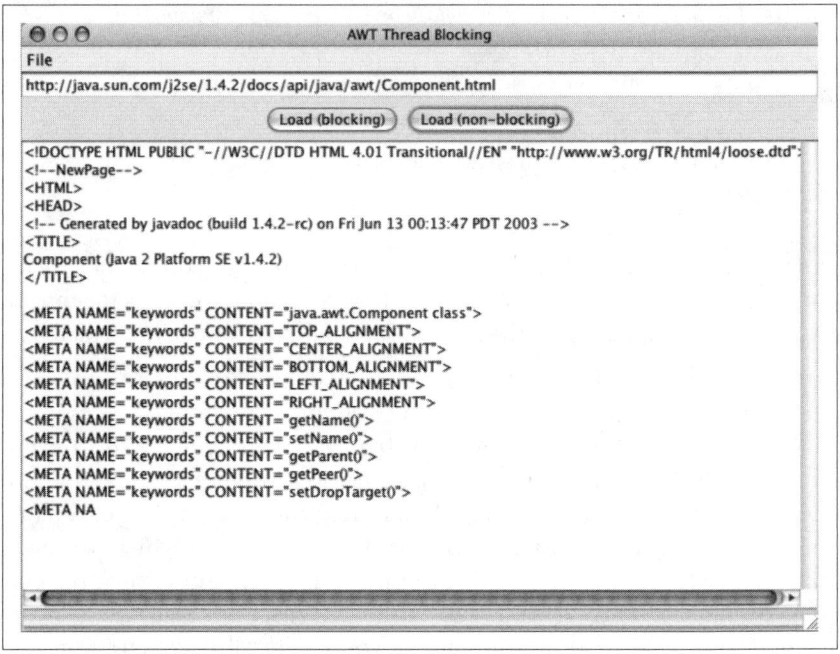

Figure 12-8. Progressive self-update of a JTextArea's document

Exposing the Threading

But what if a caller *wants* to manage threading? You might want to at least expose the fact that a thread is still updating and have the rest of your code be aware of that state.

Notice that the NonBlockingURLDocument exposes a pair of extra methods— isAlive( ) and getProgress( )—that aren't required by Document or anything else in javax.swing.text. These are extra methods I tossed into the demo to support the progress bar mentioned earlier in this hack.

The strategy here is to have an outside caller periodically check in on the NonBlockingURLDocument, get its progress, and update a progress bar. Notice I said periodically: this is a job for javax.swing.Timer! Using the Swing timer, you get regular callbacks, and your code is guaranteed to be on the event-dispatch thread.

So, uncomment the makeProgressBarUpdaterFor( ) call shown earlier, and add this implementation of that method, along with a helper method:

```
private void makeProgressBarUpdaterFor (NonBlockingURLDocument nbud) {
    final NonBlockingURLDocument updatingDoc = nbud;
    updateProgressBar (0);
    ActionListener callback = new ActionListener() {
        public void actionPerformed (ActionEvent ev) {
            progressBar.setEnabled (true);
            int progress = (int) (updatingDoc.getProgress() * 100);
            updateProgressBar (progress);
            if (! updatingDoc.isAlive())
                progressBarUpdater.stop();
        }
    };
    progressBarUpdater = new javax.swing.Timer (2000, callback);
    progressBarUpdater.start();
}

private void updateProgressBar (int progress) {
    // System.out.println ("update progress bar: " + progress);
    if (progress > 0) {
        progressBar.setValue (progress);
    }
    else
        progressBar.setEnabled (false);
}
```

The makeProgressBarUpdaterFor() method creates a Timer that calls back to the given ActionListener every two seconds. The ActionListener gets the progress from the NonBlockingURLDocument and calls updateProgressBar(), which updates the progress bar if the value is positive, and disables the bar if it's negative. Also, if the document is no longer loading, the callback stops the Timer.

You might be thinking "why would I have to check for negative progress?" As it turns out, it's an unfortunate implementation detail: a lot of web servers send -1, meaning unknown, as the HTTP content-length header. If you look around, you'll find sites that do send a valid content length. Figure 12-9 shows an incremental load of *http://www.oreilly.com/*.

This approach used URLs and Documents, but the approach is widely applicable to other kinds of models—list models, tables models, etc.—and would be well suited to other kinds of slow-to-load data. It should be straightforward to see how you could take this approach to create, say, a TableModel that's passed a java.sql.Connection and populates its rows progressively with database queries, without blocking the AWT and without making the user wait to see the first few rows of data.

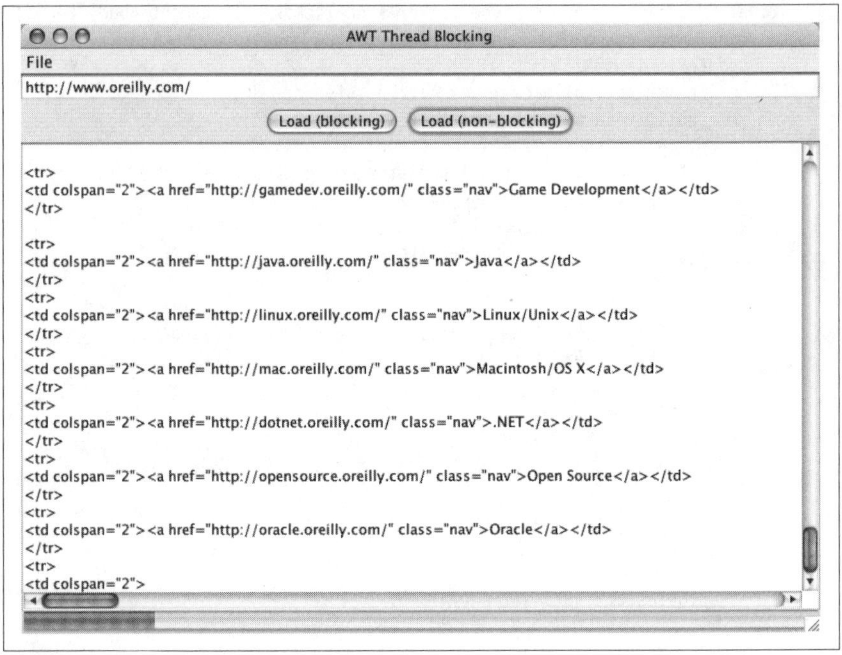

Figure 12-9. Incremental self-loading with a progress bar

H·A·C·K #94   Fire Events and Stay Bug Free

Most developers think that writing an event-firing method is trivial. Most developers are wrong.

As you develop your own Swing components, it's likely that you'll eventually need to have them fire off events; this comes up as soon as you have a model that needs to update a view. If you've strongly typed everything by writing new classes for the model, view, event, and listener, then you'll have to write your own fire method.

Most developers assume this to be trivial. For example, to manage a list of FooListeners, they'll typically maintain a Vector or ArrayList and fire off the event with a block like this:

```
Iterator it = listeners.iterator();
while (it.hasNext())
    ((FooListener).it.next()).handleEvent (fooEvent);
```

And there you have it. It's simple. It's clean. It's elegant. It's *wrong*.

The Problem

To illustrate the problem and its various solutions, consider the listener class in Example 12-11.

Example 12-11. A simple event listener

```
import java.util.*;

public class TestEventListener extends Object
    implements EventListener {
    String id;
    public TestEventListener (String id) {
        this.id = id;
    }
    public void handleEvent (EventObject o) {
        System.out.println (id + " called");
        if (id.equals ("C")) {
            ((TestEventSource) o.getSource()).removeListener (this);
        }
    }
}
```

This listener hangs on to a String and prints that string to standard out when handleEvent( ) is called. Also, if the string is a specific value—C in this case—it removes itself from the event source. If you can see why that's going to be a big deal, congratulations. If not, read on.

Next, define an abstract class to exercise various means of firing the event. This is shown in Example 12-12.

Example 12-12. Abstract class for testing event-firing techniques

```
public abstract class TestEventSource {
    public abstract void addListener (TestEventListener l);
    public abstract void removeListener (TestEventListener l);
    public abstract void fireEvent (java.util.EventObject o);
    public void test() {
        addListener (new TestEventListener ("A"));
        addListener (new TestEventListener ("B"));
        addListener (new TestEventListener ("C"));
        addListener (new TestEventListener ("D"));
        addListener (new TestEventListener ("E"));
        fireEvent(new java.util.EventObject(this));
    }
}
```

This abstract class requires subclasses to include addListener( ), removeListener( ), and fireEvent( ) methods. It also implements a test method that creates five listeners, identified as the letters A through E, and fires an event to each one.

Now, to show why the obvious way of firing the event is wrong, consider the PathologicalIteratingEventSource in Example 12-13. This does exactly what the introduction to this hack advocated—it has an ArrayList to hold the listeners, and it uses an Iterator to fire off the event to the listeners.

Example 12-13. Iterating over listeners to fire events

```java
import java.util.*;

public class PathologicalIteratingEventSource
    extends TestEventSource {

    ArrayList listeners = new ArrayList();

    public void addListener (TestEventListener l) {
        listeners.add (l);
    }

    public void removeListener (TestEventListener l) {
        listeners.remove (l);
    }

    public void fireEvent (EventObject o) {
        Iterator it = listeners.iterator();
        while (it.hasNext()) {
            TestEventListener l = (TestEventListener) it.next();
            l.handleEvent (o);
        }
    }

    public static void main (String[] args) {
        PathologicalIteratingEventSource pies =
            new PathologicalIteratingEventSource();
        pies.test();
    }
}
```

So, what happens when you run it? Here's the output:

```
[tonberry] cadamson% java PathologicalIteratingEventSource
A called
B called
C called
Exception in thread "main" java.util.ConcurrentModificationException
        at java.util.AbstractList$Itr.checkForComodification(
            AbstractList.java:448)
        at java.util.AbstractList$Itr.next(AbstractList.java:419)
        at PathologicalIteratingEventSource.fireEvent(
            PathologicalIteratingEventSource.java:19)
        at TestEventSource.test(TestEventSource.java:11)
        at PathologicalIteratingEventSource.main(
            PathologicalIteratingEventSource.java:27)
```

So, what happened? The problem is obviously with the C listener, the one that removes itself after being called. In fact, this removal is what causes the disaster—the ConcurrentModificationException indicates that you're trying to change the Collection that underlies the Iterator, while iterating over it.

And It Gets Worse

At least Java 1.2 has a fail-fast exception for this. Back in Java 1.1, without Collections, you might have used a for loop instead of an Iterator to count over the listeners. Example 12-14 shows what that might look like.

Example 12-14. Using a for-loop to fire events

```java
import java.util.*;

public class PathologicalForLoopEventSource
    extends TestEventSource {

    ArrayList listeners = new ArrayList( );

    public void addListener (TestEventListener l) {
        listeners.add (l);
    }

    public void removeListener (TestEventListener l) {
        listeners.remove (l);
    }

    public void fireEvent (EventObject o) {
        for (int i=0; i<listeners.size( ); i++) {
            TestEventListener l = (TestEventListener) listeners.get(i);
            l.handleEvent (o);
        }
    }

    public static void main (String[] args) {
        PathologicalForLoopEventSource pfles =
            new PathologicalForLoopEventSource( );
        pfles.test( );
    }
}
```

Good news: this doesn't throw an exception. Bad news: this doesn't throw an exception, as seen in the console output:

```
[tonberry] cadamson% java PathologicalForLoopEventSource
A called
B called
C called
E called
```

The obvious question here is: why didn't D get called? Well, think about it: you iterate over the listeners by index, from 0 to 4. On index 2, the code calls C's handleEvent( ), which removes itself from the ArrayList. As a result, D, which was at index 3, is now at index 2. But having serviced index 2 (which was C), the for loop moves on to index 3, which is now listener E. Thus, D never gets called.

That was a *lot* of fun the first time I got to debug it.

Hacking a Solution

Consider an alternative approach. Counting up gets you in trouble because a listener that removes itself shifts the indices of all subsequent listeners. But if you counted *down*—from the last listener to the first—then a listener could remove itself safely.

In these examples, this would mean counting from index 4 down to 0. On index 2, listener C removes itself, but that doesn't change the indices of the listeners that haven't been called yet, which are at indices 0 and 1.

All you have to do is change the fireEvent( ) method in the BackwardsForLoopEventSource class:

```
public void fireEvent (EventObject o) {
    for (int i=listeners.size( )-1; i>=0; i--) {
        TestEventListener l = (TestEventListener) listeners.get(i);
        l.handleEvent (o);
    }
}
```

Run this modified code and you get the output shown here:

```
[tonberry] cadamson% java BackwardsForLoopEventSource
E called
D called
C called
B called
A called
```

Woo hoo! It works! All five listeners get called.

Does the event order matter? Do you need to require that listeners are called in the order they were added? If so, you might do something else, like going back to the Iterator approach and making a clone that you iterate over. But that's not really necessary.

Surprisingly, the "count backward" approach is how Swing's classes handle this problem. If you look in the source of Swing objects that have fireXXX( ) methods, you'll see they generally use javax.swing.event.EventListenerList. This class maintains a list in which each pair of elements defines a listener: each even-numbered entry is the Class of a listener, and each odd-numbered entry is the listener itself. This means you have to go through the list two entries at a time, checking the class and then firing the event to the listener. It's kind of weird, but the JavaDoc says this provides more thread-safety and serialization support...yeah, great, I'm sure I'll appreciate that the next time I buy some JavaBeans off the shelf at Fry's.

Anyways, take a look at the JavaDoc and you'll see that Sun provides a prototype event-firing method to use with the EventListenerList, and like the previous example, it uses a backward for loop. Example 12-15 shows a simple implementation as a TestEventSource.

Example 12-15. Using an EventListenerList to fire events

```java
import java.util.*;
import javax.swing.event.*;

public class EventListenerListEventSource
    extends TestEventSource {

    EventListenerList listenerList = new EventListenerList( );

    public void addListener (TestEventListener l) {
        listenerList.add (TestEventListener.class, l);
    }

    public void removeListener (TestEventListener l) {
        listenerList.remove (TestEventListener.class, l);
    }

    public void fireEvent (EventObject o) {
        Object[] listeners = listenerList.getListenerList( );
        for (int i = listeners.length-2; i>=0; i-=2) {
            if (listeners[i] == TestEventListener.class) {
                ((TestEventListener) listeners[i+1]).handleEvent(o);
            }
        }
    }

    public static void main (String[] args) {
        EventListenerListEventSource bfles =
            new EventListenerListEventSource( );
        bfles.test( );
    }
}
```

Notice the odd for loop—you start at the second-to-last element and decrement by two each time. On each pass, you take the first object of the pair; if it's the right class to fire the event to, you get the second object of the pair and call its event-handling method. Presumably, you could use this to mix up different kinds of listeners in the same list, calling different methods for different classes.

When run, this test produces the following output. Since the event firing counts down through the listeners, it's functionally the same as the simpler backward for loop shown earlier:

```
[tonberry] cadamson% java EventListenerListEventSource
E called
D called
C called
B called
A called
```

HACK #95   Debug Your GUI

Standard out and err aren't just for log files anymore.

Debugging GUIs often means keeping one or two console windows open, so you can see the debugging messages you print to standard out (via System. out.println( ) and the like), as well as stack traces printed to standard err when exceptions are caught. In the field, you might want to log these to a file with something like java.util.logging, but at design time, or when investigating a bug, you want to see exactly when the exceptions happen, and running tail -f mylog.txt in multiple terminal windows may not be practical, especially if you're trying to get a customer on the phone to do it.

An alternative is for your own application to have debugging windows that collect everything printed to standard out and err, something that you or a user can bring up with a keypress or menu item.

Hijacking Output Streams

Fortunately, taking control of the standard output and error streams is pretty easy. The trick is to repoint it into your own JTextAreas, as shown in Example 12-16.

Example 12-16. Redirecting System.out and System.err to Swing windows

```
import java.awt.*;
import java.awt.event.*;
import javax.swing.*;
import java.io.*;
```

Example 12-16. Redirecting System.out and System.err to Swing windows (continued)

```java
public class StdErrOutWindows extends Object {

    JTextArea outArea, errArea;

    public StdErrOutWindows ( ) {
        // out
        outArea = new JTextArea (20, 50);
        JScrollPane pain =
            new JScrollPane (outArea,
                            ScrollPaneConstants.VERTICAL_SCROLLBAR_ALWAYS,
                            ScrollPaneConstants.HORIZONTAL_SCROLLBAR_ALWAYS);
        JFrame outFrame = new JFrame ("out");
        outFrame.getContentPane( ).add (pain);
        outFrame.pack( );
        outFrame.setVisible(true);
        // err
        errArea = new JTextArea (20, 50);
        pain =
            new JScrollPane (errArea,
                            ScrollPaneConstants.VERTICAL_SCROLLBAR_ALWAYS,
                            ScrollPaneConstants.HORIZONTAL_SCROLLBAR_ALWAYS);
        JFrame errFrame = new JFrame ("err");
        errFrame.getContentPane( ).add (pain);
        errFrame.pack( );
        errFrame.setLocation (errFrame.getLocation( ).x + 20,
                            errFrame.getLocation( ).y + 20);
        errFrame.setVisible (true);
        // set up streams
        System.setOut (new PrintStream (new JTextAreaOutputStream (outArea)));
        System.setErr (new PrintStream (new JTextAreaOutputStream (errArea)));
    }

    public static void main (String[] args) {
        new StdErrOutWindows( );
        // test
        System.out.println ("test to out");
        System.out.println ("another test to out");
        try {
            throw new Exception ("Test exception");
        } catch (Exception e) {
            e.printStackTrace( );
        }
    }

    public class JTextAreaOutputStream extends OutputStream {
        JTextArea ta;
        public JTextAreaOutputStream (JTextArea t) {
            super( );
            ta = t;
        }
```

Example 12-16. Redirecting System.out and System.err to Swing windows (continued)

```java
    public void write (int i) {
        char[] chars = new char[1];
        chars[0] = (char) i;
        String s = new String (chars);
        ta.append(s);
    }
    public void write (char[] buf, int off, int len) {
        String s = new String (buf, off, len);
        ta.append(s);
    }

  }

}
```

The best place to start with this example is actually at the bottom, in the inner class. JTextAreaOutputStream is exactly what it sounds like: an OutputStream that takes the data sent to write( ) and appends it to a JTextArea. You only need to override two methods, the write( ) that takes a single character (as a Unicode int) and the write( ) that takes a character array, as these are called by subclasses, including PrintStream's various print( ) methods. To get the text to the JTextArea, all you have to do is convert it to a String and call JTextArea.append( ) to put it at the end of the log window.

The constructor of this demo class creates JTextAreas and puts them in visible JFrames—your application may want to hide the JFrames until they're needed. Next, it creates JTextAreaOutputStreams to write to the JTextAreas, and it replaces the default System.out and System.err streams with them.

 If you wanted to log output to the default out and err as well as your JTextArea, the JTextAreaOutputStream could hold onto a reference to the default PrintStream and write to that, as well as appending to the JTextArea.

The main( ) method exercises the streams by printing lines to System.out, then throwing an exception, catching it, and printing the stack trace (which goes to System.err). Figure 12-10 shows what it looks like when run.

In this example, I turned on horizontal scrollbars for the JTextAreas with ScrollPaneConstants.HORIZONTAL_SCROLLBAR_ALWAYS. I did this to maintain the formatting of stack traces, so you can read what called what, line-by-line. In my opinion, horizontal scrollbars are often overused, especially with JTables, in a hateful practice of making the user do extra scrolling work to just see the contents of a row, which usually represent a single thing (the to/

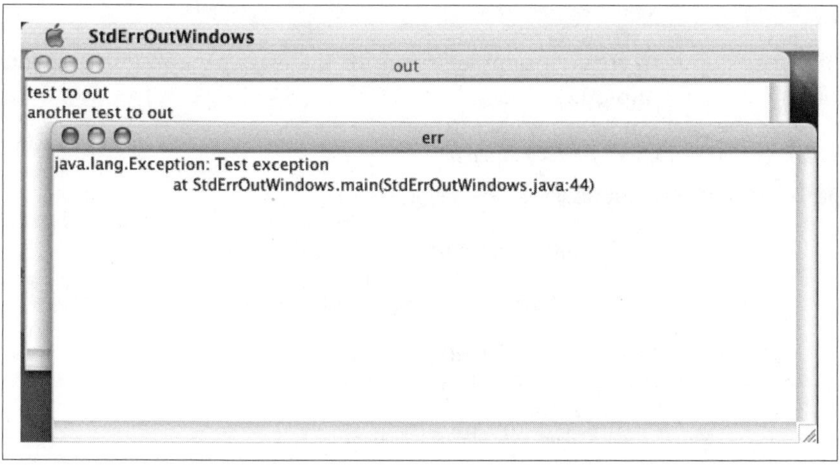

StdErrOutWindows

| out |

test to out
another test to out

| err |

java.lang.Exception: Test exception
                at StdErrOutWindows.main(StdErrOutWindows.java:44)

Figure 12-10. Capturing standard out and err to Swing windows

from/subject of one email message, the details of a downloaded file, etc.). In cases like these, I'll try to see if a JList with a multi-line cell renderer [Hack #16] can keep all the data together in a visually pleasing form. So, when is horizontal scrolling OK? I think it's appropriate when the data you're displaying is not row-oriented, and instead you're scrolling up, down, and across a single cohesive thing, like a large image or, in this case, a stack trace.

Debug Components with a Custom Glass Pane

Show component boundaries at runtime using a glass pane.

Sometimes when I'm building a really complicated Swing layout, I start to lose track of what I'm looking at. Which component is this? Does that panel extend all the way to the end of the frame? A way to visualize the layout would be a useful addition to the usual development tools. This hack explores using a custom glass pane to highlight each component and its classname.

A glass pane is a normally transparent Swing component that is drawn on top of all of the other components in a frame, as you saw when you put dialog-like "sheets" into the glass pane [Hack #44]. It is this ability that forms the center of the hack. The custom glass pane will traverse the entire tree of components in the frame, filling a translucent rectangle over each component. Deeper components will get painted multiple times resulting in a darker color. The glass pane will also watch the mouse cursor to determine which component the user is pointing at. That component's classname will then be drawn in the glass pane as well.

Screens and Glass

The first step is to create a sample screen for the glass pane to draw on top
of, as seen in Example 12-17.

Example 12-17. A screen for the glass pane

```
public class ComponentGlassPane extends JComponent {

    public static void main(String[] args) {

        JFrame frame = new JFrame("Component Boundary Glasspane");

        Container root = frame.getContentPane( );
        root.setLayout(new BoxLayout(root,BoxLayout.Y_AXIS));
        final JButton activate =
            new JButton("Show component boundaries");
        root.add(activate);
        root.add(new JLabel("Juice Settings"));

        JPanel panel = new JPanel( );
        panel.setLayout(new BoxLayout(panel,BoxLayout.X_AXIS));
        panel.add(new JLabel("Flavor"));
        panel.add(new JTextField("           "));
        root.add(panel);

        frame.pack( );
        frame.show( );

        final ComponentGlassPane glass =
            new ComponentGlassPane(frame);
        frame.setGlassPane(glass);

        activate.addActionListener(new ActionListener( ) {
            public void actionPerformed(ActionEvent evt) {
                glass.setVisible(true);
            }
        });

    }
```

This main( ) method creates a frame with a few components and one nested
panel (called panel). The ComponentGlassPane is declared as a subclass of
JComponent so it can be passed to the setGlassPane( ) method on the frame.
The glass pane is not visible initially, which produces the same behavior as if
it wasn't even there. The activate button is used to make the glass pane
visible.

The next step is to create the ComponentGlassPane constructor:

```
private JFrame frame;
private Point cursor;
public ComponentGlassPane(JFrame frame) {
    this.frame = frame;
    cursor = new Point( );
    this.addMouseMotionListener(new MouseMotionAdapter( ) {
        public void mouseMoved(MouseEvent evt) {
            cursor = new Point(evt.getPoint( ));
            ComponentGlassPane.this.repaint( );
        }
    });
    this.addMouseListener(new MouseAdapter( ) {
        public void mouseClicked(MouseEvent evt) {
            ComponentGlassPane.this.setVisible(false);
        }
    });
}
```

This method saves the parent frame that was passed in, and it creates a new point to store the cursor coordinates. Then it adds two mouse listeners to itself. The first listener copies the current mouse coordinates into the cursor object every time the mouse moves. It also requests a repaint, since the user may have moved from one component to another, which would change the currently visible label.

The second mouse listener simply waits for mouse clicks. If the user clicks the mouse, then this listener turns off the visualization effect by hiding the glass pane, and the screen goes back to normal.

So far this has all been pretty straightforward: create a custom JComponent and set it as the glass pane on a JFrame. Now comes the tricky part: painting the translucent rectangles and labels. First, you need to override the paint( ) method to retrieve the root component of the frame and pass it to the rPaint( ) method:

```
public void paint(Graphics g) {
    Container root = frame.getContentPane( );
    rPaint(root,g);
}
```

rPaint( ) stands for recursive paint. It needs to recurse over the entire component tree, painting a rectangle at each step and possibly drawing the label. Because this is so complicated, I'll take it in stages. Here is the initial portion of the method:

```
private void rPaint(Component comp, Graphics g) {
    int x = comp.getX( );
    int y = comp.getY( );
    g.translate(x,y);
    cursor.translate(-x,-y);
```

```
int w = comp.getWidth( );
int h = comp.getHeight( );

// draw background
g.setColor(new Color(1.0f, 0.5f, 0.5f, 0.3f));
g.fillRect(0,0,w,h);
g.setColor(Color.red);
g.drawRect(0,0,w,h);
```

First, the rPaint( ) method gets the x- and y-coordinates of the component and translates the Graphics object and the cursor. The graphics must be translated so that all drawing will happen relative to the origin of the current component. If this weren't called, then all of the rectangles would be shoved into the upper-lefthand corner of the frame. The cursor is also translated, but in the opposite direction. This is because each component's origin must be subtracted from the cursor position to make it relative to the component.

This translation of coordinates is the key to any recursive tree traversal. With this technique, you can start at the top of the tree and do any sort of operation you want to each component, safe in the knowledge that any drawing operations will line up properly.

After coordinate conversion, rPaint( ) grabs the width and height of the current component and then sets the drawing color. Note that this drawing color is composed of four numbers. The first three represent the values of each color component (red, green, and blue) from 0 to 1, where 1 represents 100% of that component and 0 represents 0%. The values 1.0f, 0.5f, and 0.5f produce a medium pink.

The f after each number tells the compiler that this is a floating point number. You could write (float)1.0 to get the same effect.

The last number represents the alpha channel, or transparency, going from 1 for opaque to 0 for completely transparent:

```
// if the mouse is over this component
if(comp.contains(cursor)) {
    // draw the text
    String cls_name = comp.getClass().getName( );
    Graphics2D g2 = (Graphics2D)g;
    Font fnt = g.getFont( );
    FontMetrics fm = g.getFontMetrics( );
    int text_width = fm.stringWidth(cls_name);
    int text_height = fm.getHeight( );
    int text_ascent = fm.getAscent( );
```

```
// draw text background
g.setColor(new Color(1f,1f,1f,0.7f));
g.fillRect(0,0,text_width,text_height);
g.setColor(Color.white);
g.drawRect(0,0,text_width,text_height);

// draw text
g.setColor(Color.black);
g.drawString(cls_name, 0, 0+text_ascent);
}
```

Now that the pink rectangle is filled in, the glass pane needs to draw the name of the current component—but only if the mouse is over that component. That is what the comp.contains(cursor) line does. If contains( ) is true, then rPaint( ) calculates the dimensions of the classname as a string, draws a translucent white background (with 70% opacity), draws a solid white border rectangle, and then finally draws the actual text in solid black:

```
if(comp instanceof Container) {
    Container cont = (Container)comp;
    for(int i=0; i<cont.getComponentCount( ); i++) {
        Component child = cont.getComponent(i);
        rPaint(child,g);
    }
}
```

Next comes the recursion. Without this step, rPaint( ) would just work on the root component and stop. Here it checks if the current component is a java.awt.Container (which would always be true for any Swing component since javax.swing.JComponent subclasses Container). If the component has children, it calls rPaint( ) recursively on each child, thus traversing the entire tree of components:

```
        cursor.translate(x,y);
        g.translate(-x,-y);
} // end rPaint( ) method
```

This last step simply reverses the graphics translation from the beginning of rPaint( ). Had the coordinates been passed in as ints, which are passed-by-value, it would not be necessary to undo the translations. Any changes to a passed-by-value variable are lost when the enclosing method ends. However, since cursor and g are both referenced by name, the changes have to be reversed manually.

If you compile and run this code, you will get a screen that looks like Figure 12-11. When you press the activate button, you will see Figure 12-12. As you move the mouse around, the classname label will update.

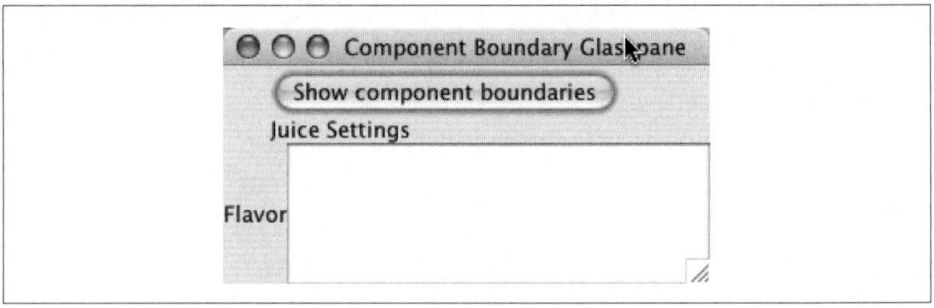

Figure 12-11. The normal window

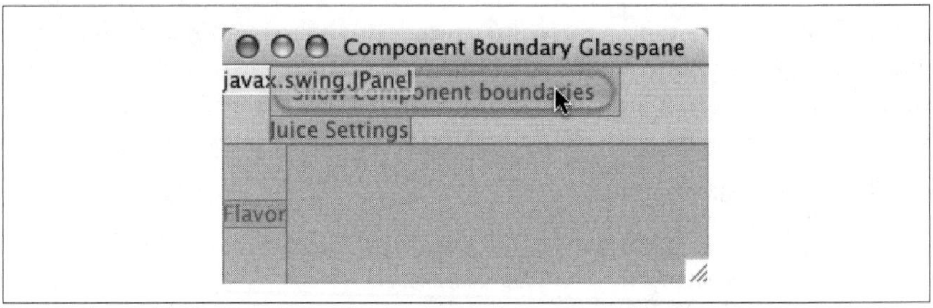

Figure 12-12. The window with the glass pane showing

This hack performs a simple visualization: it creates translucent rectangles with solid labels. The same technique could be used to create a much more dynamic interface displaying more detailed information, such as button state, component IDs, color settings, or any other artifact of Swing components.

One thing to notice here is that there are two or more labels visible at any given time. This is because of the nesting of components—if the cursor is over a text field and that text field is inside of a panel, then technically the cursor is over both components, producing two labels. You could enhance the ComponentGlassPane to only draw one label by creative use of the SwingUtilities.getDeepestComponentAt( ) method.

Mirror an Application
HACK #97
With creative use of the AWT event log, you can bind two instances of an application together over a socket, creating a mirroring effect.

One of the coolest—and severely underrated—features of Java is serialization. Because Java code runs entirely in a virtual machine, it's possible to send objects over the network to another program and have the objects still functional when they get there. One day while perusing the AWT documentation, I came across the AWTEventListener. I wondered what interesting thing you could do by capturing all of the events in a program. I could write them to disk, of course, but it would be even cooler to send them over the network to another copy of the program. That way the two programs could reuse each other's events and become mirrors! With a global event queue and a bit of serialization, this turns out to be quite easy.

To replicate events over the network, you need to do three things:

1. Capture all AWT events. This can be done with an AWTEventListener.
2. Send the event objects over the network.
3. Pick the objects up on the other end of the network and repost them in the second program.

It sounds pretty simple, but there are always a few dragons hiding in the mist.

Set Up a Window

Every test program begins with a frame and a few components. This program is no different, with ApplicationMirrorTest (shown in Example 12-18) creating a frame, button, and text field in its constructor.

Example 12-18. Simple test program for mirroring

```
public class ApplicationMirrorTest {

    public ApplicationMirrorTest( ) {
        JFrame frame = new JFrame( );
        frame.getContentPane().setLayout(new FlowLayout( ));

        final JButton button = new JButton("action generator");
        frame.getContentPane( ).add(button);

        JTextField tf = new JTextField("text field");
        frame.getContentPane( ).add(tf);

        frame.pack( );
        frame.show( );
    }
```

Become a Server or Client

There is only one program, but it must run in two modes: one for sending AWT events and one for receiving. If the program starts and it's the first instance running, then it should wait to receive events. If it's the second instance running, then it should send events instead. But how does the program know if it is the first or second instance? The only real way is to look for a shared resource. If the resource is already taken, then this must be the second instance. As with creating single-launch applications on Windows [Hack #84], a network socket is the best choice for a shared resource because you need it anyway to send the events:

```
public void start() {
    try {
        // send events
        final Socket sock = new Socket("localhost",6754);
        openSender(sock);
    } catch (Exception ex) {
        try {
            openReceiver();
        } catch (Exception ex2) {
            System.out.println("exception: " + ex);
        }
    }
}
```

The start() method here tries to open a socket on a known port number (6754 in this case). If the socket can be opened, then that means there is a program on the other end waiting for a connection, in which case the code can call openSender() to start sending events. If the socket cannot be opened, then there is no other program and this is the first running instance. In that case, you can call openReceiver() and start waiting for another program to connect.

Send Mouse Events

To send events, you first need an output stream to send them. The java.io package helpfully provides the ObjectOutputStream. It will take any Java object, serialize it, and write it to the stream the class represents. Next, you need to capture all relevant events and prepare them to go out. The AWT Toolkit object lets you add listeners for any set of AWT events you wish. You just need to OR together masks for the event types you want:

```
public void openSender(Socket sock) throws Exception {
    final ObjectOutputStream out = new
        ObjectOutputStream(sock.getOutputStream());

    Toolkit.getDefaultToolkit().addAWTEventListener(
        new AWTEventListener() {
            public void eventDispatched(AWTEvent evt) {
                try {
                    if(evt instanceof MouseEvent) {
                        MouseEvent me = (MouseEvent)evt;
                        out.writeObject(evt);
                    }
                } catch (Exception ex) { }
            }
        },
```

```
        AWTEvent.ACTION_EVENT_MASK |
        AWTEvent.MOUSE_EVENT_MASK
    );
}
```

First, openSender( ) creates a new ObjectOutputStream around the socket's output stream. Next, it creates a new AWTEventListener that takes each event and tests if it is a mouse event; if so, this method writes it to the output stream. Notice that the second argument of addAWTEventListener( ) is two event masks ORed together (using the | operator).

Receive Mouse Events

Receiving events is the reverse of sending them. You must open a server socket for the (sending) instance to connect to, and then pull the events off of the network one by one and repost them to the system event queue:

```
public void openReceiver( ) throws Exception  {
    // receive events
    ServerSocket server = new ServerSocket(6754);
    Socket sock = server.accept( );

    EventQueue eq = Toolkit.getDefaultToolkit().getSystemEventQueue( );

    ObjectInputStream in = new ObjectInputStream(sock.getInputStream( ));
    while(true ) {
        AWTEvent evt = (AWTEvent) in.readObject( );
        if(evt instanceof MouseEvent) {
            MouseEvent me = (MouseEvent)evt;
            MouseEvent me2 = new MouseEvent(
                me.getComponent( ),
                me.getID( ),
                me.getWhen( ),
                me.getModifiers( ),
                me.getX( ),
                me.getY( ),
                me.getClickCount( ),
                me.isPopupTrigger( ),
                me.getButton( )
            );
            eq.postEvent(me2);
        }
    }
}
```

Notice that the events are not posted directly to the event queue. Since the objects really belong to the other instance, they won't work in this instance properly—all of the internal object references will be wrong. However, you can make an *exact copy* of the event just by creating a new one with the arguments from the old one. Then the new event will work fine in this second instance.

Put all of this together, with the following main( ) method, and then fire up two copies of your program. The first one will wait for a connection. When the second one starts, it will send every mouse event over the network to the first copy, which will then reuse it. If you click on the button in the second window, you will see the button depress in the first.

```java
public static void main(String[] args) throws Exception {
    ApplicationMirrorTest mirror = new ApplicationMirrorTest( );
    mirror.start( );
}
```

Component Problems

Wait…did this work? No, it didn't. The events still don't work after being sent over the network. A little debugging will show that every part of the reconstituted event works properly except for the getComponent( ) method, which returns null. Why?

The reference to the component doesn't get sent over the wire because that would require sending the component itself. That component, of course, is part of your entire Swing tree, which would also have to be sent over. Pretty soon you'd be sending a few megabytes through the network for every event. To avoid this, the developers of Java made the component reference *transient*, which means the object will be skipped during serialization. That makes the component fast, but it presents a problem: how do you know which component the event goes with?

When you think about it, you wouldn't really want the actual component in the other program anyway. You already have a component on the receiving instance that's showing on screen. You just need to associate the event with the correct component from the sending instance, and match that with the correct component in the receiving instance. Fortunately, every Swing component can have a name attached to it. If both programs use the same names (which they will since they are just different instances of the same code), then you can build a HashMap to keep track of them all. Example 12-19 takes care of these details.

Example 12-19. Associating events with components via the component name

```java
public class ComponentMap extends HashMap implements AWTEventListener {

    public ComponentMap( ) {
        Toolkit tk = Toolkit.getDefaultToolkit( );
        tk.addAWTEventListener(this,
            AWTEvent.COMPONENT_EVENT_MASK);
    }
```

Example 12-19. Associating events with components via the component name (continued)

```
public void eventDispatched(AWTEvent evt) {
    try {
        // p("evt = " + evt);
        ComponentEvent ce = (ComponentEvent)evt;
        // p("storing component: " + ce.getComponent().getName());
        this.put(
            ce.getComponent().getName(),
            ce.getComponent()
            );
    } catch (Exception ex) {
        // p("ex: " + ex);
    }
}

}
```

ComponentMap is a subclass of HashMap, and it adds one key feature. It listens for component events system-wide and stores the components in its HashTable with the component name as the key. Now, instances can look up components using ComponentMap. Of course, this means you need to name all of your components. By default, subclasses of JComponent will have a null value for getName(), so you need to set these names explicitly:

```
Map component_map;
public ApplicationMirrorTest() {
    component_map = new ComponentMap();

    JFrame frame = new JFrame();
    frame.getContentPane().setLayout(new FlowLayout());

    final JButton button = new JButton("action generator");
    button.setName("button");
    frame.getContentPane().add(button);

    JTextField tf = new JTextField("text field");
    tf.setName("textfield");
    frame.getContentPane().add(tf);

    frame.pack();
    frame.show();
}
```

The new version of the ApplicationMirrorTest, which uses all of this new code, creates a ComponentMap to track names, and then sets a name for each component as it's created. Once you have the lookup map, you can modify the sending loop in openSender() to send the component's name before it sends the event:

```
if(evt instanceof MouseEvent) {
    MouseEvent me = (MouseEvent)evt;
```

```
        out.writeObject(me.getComponent().getName());
        out.writeObject(evt);
    }
```

You also need to modify the openReceiver( ) method's loop to read a name in before reading in an event. Once you have the name on the receiving side, you can look up the proper component and associate that with the received event.

With these changes in place, the program will work. Each event on the sending instance side will be captured and sent over the network. On the receiving side, each event will be recreated and reposted. The two programs will stay completely in sync; even rollover effects will happen simultaneously:

```
while(true ) {
    String name = (String) in.readObject();
    AWTEvent evt = (AWTEvent) in.readObject();
    if(evt instanceof MouseEvent) {
        MouseEvent me = (MouseEvent)evt;
        MouseEvent me2 = new MouseEvent(
            //me.getComponent(),
            (Component)component_map.get(name),
            me.getID(),
            me.getWhen(),
            me.getModifiers(),
            me.getX(),
            me.getY(),
            me.getClickCount(),
            me.isPopupTrigger(),
            me.getButton()
        );
        eq.postEvent(me2);
    }
}
```

Add Velocity for Dynamic HTML

#98   Use the Velocity template engine to mimic server-side web technologies in your Swing application.

Servlets, JSPs, and other server-side technologies help separate an application's model from its view and allow you to build flexible and dynamic web applications. Of course, Swing applications have their own benefits, like fast user interaction without the need for web server communication. It would be cool to have the power of those server-side technologies right in your Swing application, but without the overhead of a local web server. You can actually mimic a lot of that functionality using a combination of Apache's Velocity template engine and a Swing HTML panel.

As an example, suppose you want to display the weather for the next three days as part of your application. You need a nice graphic weather display showing your users the current weather, as in Figure 12-13.

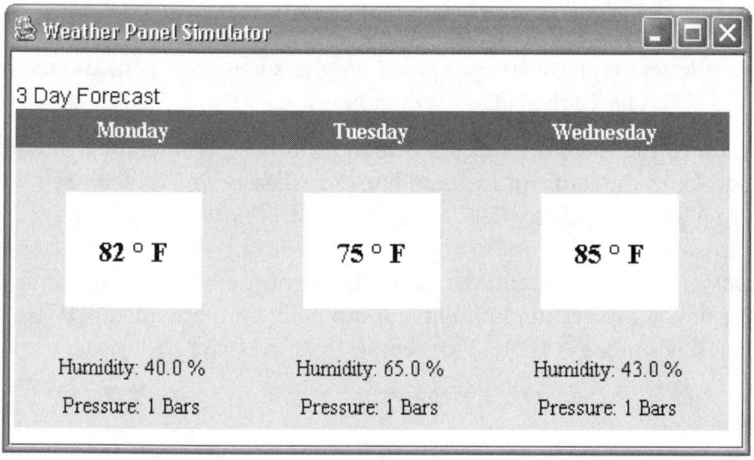

Figure 12-13. A graphical weather page

Velocity and Templates

Velocity is an open source template engine, released under the Apache Jakarta umbrella. At its simplest, Velocity allows you to add intelligent replacement from a text file. At its most extreme, Velocity allows you to call Java methods and use the entire VTL (Velocity Template Language) to create intelligent templates using loops, conditionals, and variables. In other words, you get the power of an MVC infrastructure like JSP, but in a very lightweight local-client technology.

When using Velocity, you have two basic elements to deal with: the *VelocityContext* and the *template*. The VelocityContext holds objects that can be referenced from the template. The template is text with imbedded VTL that controls the Velocity output.

In this simple example, ${name} and ${what} indicate replaceable values:

```
${name} is a total ${what}
```

Here is a simple context:

```
VelocityContext context = new VelocityContext();
context.put("name", Jonathan);
context.put("what", Rockstar);
```

When you run Velocity with this context and this template, it will print out:

```
Jonathan is a total Rockstar
```

Create the HTML

You'll probably want to create your pages in an HTML editor like Dreamweaver. Better yet, have your graphics designers handle design, and then you can add VTL tags to the HTML they create.

For each of the three days in the display, you need temperature, humidity, pressure, and the name of the day. For each measurement, you need a variable in VTL—call these TEMP, HUMIDITY, and PRESSURE—and preface them with DAY and the day number (like DAY1). Figure 12-14 is a screenshot from Dreamweaver, where I built the page with all of the VTL. The dynamic data for the day, temperature, humidity, and pressure are provided by VTL tags: the first day's name is ${DAY1}, its temperature is ${DAY1_TEMP}, etc.

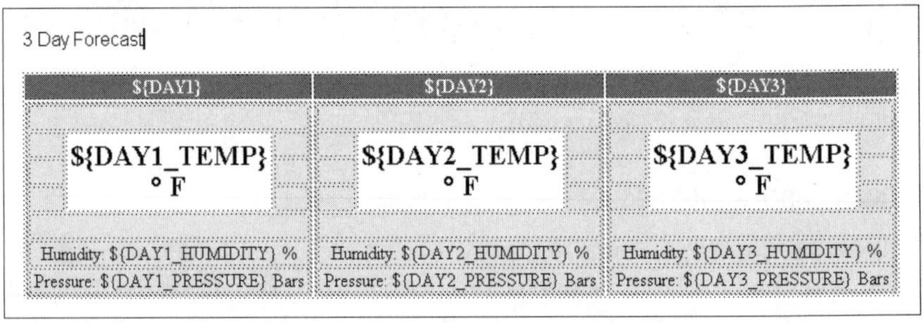

Figure 12-14. Weather web page in Dreamweaver

Create a Data Object

Now, it's time to leave template land and get into some Java code. You need to write a data object to represent the weather for a particular day. You'll find this useful when you build up your context. To keep things simple, Example 12-20 uses an immutable object.

Example 12-20. A simple weather data object

```java
public class Weather {

    private BigDecimal temperature;
    private BigDecimal humidity;
    private BigDecimal pressure;
    private String day;
```

Example 12-20. A simple weather data object (continued)

```java
    public Weather(BigDecimal temperature, BigDecimal humidity, BigDecimal
                    pressure, String day) {
        this.temperature = temperature;
        this.humidity = humidity;
        this.pressure = pressure;
        this.day = day;
    }

    public BigDecimal getTemperature() {
        return temperature;
    }

    public BigDecimal getHumidity() {
        return humidity;
    }

    public BigDecimal getPressure() {
        return pressure;
    }

    public String getDay() {
        return day;
    }

}
```

Of course, you need to display all of this visual wizardry, so create a class
that contains a JEditorPane for displaying the HTML. You can use whichever HTML renderer you choose, but JEditorPane is a good choice because
it's built into Swing. Example 12-21 is a basic container that contains a
JEditorPane and configures it to render HTML.

Example 12-21. Panel to contain the HTML display pane

```java
public class WeatherPanel {
    private JEditorPane htmlPane;

    public WeatherPanel() {
        htmlPane = createHtmlPanel();
    }

    private JEditorPane createHtmlPanel() {
        JEditorPane editorPane = new JEditorPane();
        HTMLEditorKit editorKit = new HTMLEditorKit();
        editorKit.install(editorPane);
        editorPane.setEditorKit(editorKit);
        editorPane.setEditable(false);
        return editorPane;
    }
```

Example 12-21. Panel to contain the HTML display pane (continued)

```java
    public Component getComponent( ) {
        return new JScrollPane(htmlPane);
    }

}
```

Next, you need to add a method to reconfigure the htmlPane with a collection of Weather objects:

```java
    public void displayWeather(String html, Collection weather){
        String result = html;
        try {
            VelocityContext context = createContext(weather);
            result = processString(context, html);
        } catch (Exception e){
            e.printStackTrace( );
        }
        htmlPane.setText(result);
    }
```

You need to read in the HTML file you created, and that's where displayWeatherByFile( ) comes in. You supply it the filename, and it reads the HTML in that file:

```java
    public void displayWeatherByFile(String fileName, Collection weather){
        displayWeather(readFile(fileName), weather);
    }

    private String readFile(String fileName) {
        StringBuffer htmlBuffer = new StringBuffer( );

        try {
            InputStream inputStream = WeatherPanel.class.
    getResourceAsStream(fileName);
            BufferedReader reader =
                new BufferedReader(new InputStreamReader(inputStream));

            while (true){
                String line = reader.readLine( );
                if (line != null){
                    htmlBuffer.append(line);
                } else {
                    break;
                }
            }
        } catch (IOException iox){
            iox.printStackTrace( );
        }
        return htmlBuffer.toString( );
    }
```

Create a Velocity Context

Now, you need to make a VelocityContext to supply dynamic values to your template. Create a method called createContext and loop through the weather collection, which contains three Weather objects:

```
private VelocityContext createContext(Collection weatherCollection) {
    VelocityContext context = new VelocityContext( );
    int index = 1;

    for (Iterator iterator = weatherCollection.iterator( );
        iterator.hasNext( );) {
        Weather weather = (Weather) iterator.next( );
        //add info to context
        index++;
    }

    return context;
}
```

Next, create a variable for each day, since all of the VTL is keyed on a measurement, as well as the day (DAY1, DAY2, or DAY3):

```
String day = "DAY" + index;
```

Now, add the day itself, as well as entries for temperature, humidity, and pressure:

```
context.put(day, weather.getDay( ));
context.put(day + "_TEMP", weather.getTemperature( ));
context.put(day + "_HUMIDITY", weather.getHumidity( ));
context.put(day + "_PRESSURE", weather.getPressure( ));
```

Fill the Template with Values

This is the easiest part. The code below is boilerplate code to initialize the Velocity engine and run a template (htmlText) through Velocity with a context. It then returns the completed HTML as a String:

```
private String processString(VelocityContext context, String htmlText)
    throws Exception {

    StringWriter writer = new StringWriter( );
    Properties properties = new Properties( );
    Velocity.init(properties);
    Velocity.evaluate(context,
        writer,
        null,
        htmlText);
    return writer.getBuffer().toString( );
}
```

Sunny Outside?

Finally, take WeatherPanel for a spin. It's a pretty straightforward simulator, creating a display frame and a collection of Weather objects, and connecting the two. Notice that the WeatherPanel is created and configured with the Weather objects:

```
public WeatherPanelSimulator() {
    JFrame frame = new JFrame("Weather Panel Simulator");
    frame.setBounds(200,200, 500, 350);

    Weather weather1 = new Weather(
        new BigDecimal("82"),
        new BigDecimal("40.0"),
        new BigDecimal(1),
        "Monday");
    Weather weather2 = new Weather(
        new BigDecimal("75"),
        new BigDecimal("65.0"),
        new BigDecimal(1),
        "Tuesday");
    Weather weather3 = new Weather(
        new BigDecimal("85"),
        new BigDecimal("43.0"),
        new BigDecimal(1),
        "Wednesday");

    ArrayList list = new ArrayList();
    list.add(weather1);
    list.add(weather2);
    list.add(weather3);

    WeatherPanel weatherPanel = new WeatherPanel();
    weatherPanel.displayWeatherByFile("html/today.html", list);

    frame.getContentPane().setLayout(new BorderLayout());
    frame.getContentPane().add(
        weatherPanel.getComponent(),
        BorderLayout.CENTER);

    frame.setDefaultCloseOperation(JFrame.EXIT_ON_CLOSE);
    frame.show();

}
```

This technique is really useful for simple dynamic variable replacement. It lets you change the interface at runtime without code changes by changing the HTML, and you can have your graphics designers implement parts of your application directly in HTML.

—*Jonathan Simon*

Get Large File Icons

Using an undocumented Windows-only class, you can retrieve large, full-color file icons from the operating system.

The FileSystemView provides access only to file icons of a default size, which usually means 16×16 pixels. If you look at your desktop, however, you may see icons that are much bigger and with more detail and color. There is no standard way to get the larger icons, but on Windows you can use an undocumented (and unsupported) class to get access to them. Sun's JRE for Windows includes a hidden class called sun.awt.shell.ShellFolder that will let you retrieve larger (32×32) desktop file icons.

> This class is only available in Sun's JRE for Windows, so it won't work with other vendors or on other platforms.

The class in Example 12-22 will take a filename and show its large icon in a window.

Example 12-22. Grabbing a large icon

```
public class LargeIconTest {

    public static void main(String[] args) throws Exception {
        // Create a File instance of an existing file
        File file = new File(args[0]);

        // Get metadata and create an icon
        sun.awt.shell.ShellFolder sf =
                sun.awt.shell.ShellFolder.getShellFolder(file);
        Icon icon = new ImageIcon(sf.getIcon(true));
        System.out.println("type = " + sf.getFolderType( ));

        // show the icon
        JLabel label = new JLabel(icon);
        JFrame frame = new JFrame( );
        frame.getContentPane( ).add(label);
        frame.pack( );
        frame.show( );

    }
}
```

ShellFolder is a wrapper for metadata of the selected file. With this object, you can retrieve both the icon and a text description of the file's type. A normal MP3 icon would be only 16×16 pixels (Figure 12-15), but if you ran the MP3 file through LargeIconText, it would print the string *type = MPEG Layer 3 Audio* and show a much nicer 32×32 pixel media icon (Figure 12-16).

Figure 12-15. Normal MP3 icon

Figure 12-16. Large MP3 icon

Make Frames Resize Dynamically

Make your application feel more responsive by turning on dynamic layout.

By default, JFrames don't resize dynamically. This means that the frame will not redraw itself as the user is resizing it. A repaint will only occur after the user lets go of the mouse and the window is refreshed. This behavior often results in extra gray areas and an unresponsive-feeling application. However, you can fix this with just one method call!

Just call one method on the default Toolkit:

```
Toolkit.getDefaultToolkit( ).setDynamicLayout(true);
```

You can query the dynamic layout property like this:

```
if(Toolkit.getDefaultToolkit().isDynamicLayoutActive( )) {
    // do something
}
```

or like this:

```
if(Toolkit.getDefaultToolkit().isDynamicLayoutSet( )) {
    // do something
}
```

isDynamicLayoutSet( ) will tell you if dynamic layout was set programmatically, while isDynamicLayoutActive( ) will tell you if dynamic layout is supported. You need to use both methods because some platforms don't support dynamic layout, and others don't let you turn it off.

A Word About Speed

When you have dynamic layout turned on, the window will repaint each time the user moves the mouse. This will make the application feel responsive because there is always information on the screen being updated. If your frame contains an animated component, it will continue to play while the user resizes the window.

The disadvantage of dynamic layout is that a resize will generate a whole lot of repaint requests in a very short time. Even if the user moves the window just one pixel, it will trigger a repaint on the entire frame (unlike scrolling, which usually requires just repainting a strip at the bottom). If your painting code is slow (or you have a lot of components on screen), then the dynamic layout could actually make your program feel *slower*. Be sure you make your painting as fast as possible, perhaps skipping some of the more complicated effects during the resize. You may also want to use dynamic layout only in a program with a small streamlined window, such as a media player or utility app.

Index

Symbols

& (AND) operator, 159
% (mod) operator, 445

Numbers

3D components, 316–321
  changing background, 320
  faking transparency, 319

A

absolute layouts, 3
AbstractBorder class, 14, 50
AbstractListModel class, 60
AbstractTableModel class, 113
  getColumnCount( ), 123
  getRowCount( ), 123
  getValueAt( ), 123
acceptDrop( ), 339
Action class, 65
ActionListener interface, 64, 243, 258
  updateProgressBar( ), 471
actionPerformed( ), 45, 65, 98, 100, 151
  animated sheet dialog, 237
  cursor animation, 445
  earthquake dialog component, 201
  mini application frame, 210
addAWTEventListener( )
  (Toolkit), 448, 489
addDirtyRegion( )
  (RepaintManager), 280
addItem( ), 60
addMovieAndStart( ), 374

AffineTransform class, 254, 256
  mirror image text, 273
AIFF audio files, playing, 390
alpha levels
  fade-in and fade-out
    animations, 255, 256
  shadow for vector-based button, 312
AlphaComposite class, 222
  getInstance( ), 54
AND (&) operator, 159
animations
  busy cursor, displaying, 443–446
  earthquake dialog, 197–202
  frame dissolves, 219–224
  glass pane as indefinite progress
    indicator, 251–256
  JList selections, 87–92
  JTree drops, 139–147
  mouse animation, 450–454
  picture as indefinite progress bar
    indicator, 249–251
  sheet dialog, 233–239
  slide-in window, 241–245
  spotlights, 325
  transitions between tabs, 32–39
    drawing the animation, 35
    scheduling animation, 33
    venetian blinds effect, 37
Ant, 433
anti-aliased text
  global anti-aliased fonts, 278–282
  with custom Look and Feel, 285
  without code, 283–285

We'd like to hear your suggestions for improving our indexes. Send email to *index@oreilly.com*.

Apple Events, 419
Apple System Properties, 414
AppleScript, 419
applets, playing sound, 359–364
    restrictive applet security, 363
applications
    Mac OS X, names of, 416
    mirroring, 486–492
Aqua Look and Feel, 414
Area, 328
ArrayList class, 60
Arrays class, sort( ), 114
arrow for drop-down menu button, 43
ascent (fonts), 11
audio
    controls for JavaSound
        playback, 401–407
    factory to generate, 402–407
    MP3 support, adding to
        JMF, 376–378
    playing a sound with
        JavaSound, 364–368
    playing non-trivial with
        JavaSound, 386–391
    uncompressed PCM files of
        arbitrary length, 387–390
    uncompressed WAV or AIFF files
        of arbitrary length, 390–391
    playing sound in an applet, 359–364
    playing sound with QTJ, 371–376
    playing sounds with JMF, 368–371
    showing information while
        playing, 392–401
    audio format information, 393
    level information
        calculations, 397–401
    waveform displays, 378–386
        basic audio term definitions, 379
        container, creating, 384
        converting raw data to samples
            and channels, 380–382
        creating single display, 382
        loading raw data, 380
        running the simulator, 385
AudioClip class, 359–364
    playing in an applet, 359–361
    supported audio formats, 364
AudioFormat class, 392
AudioInputStream class, 366, 380
AudioSystem class, 366
    getAudioInputStream( ), 433

auto-completing text fields, 265–272
AWT, 317
AWTEventListener interface, 448, 486,
    489

B

Background class, 320
background property (List), 69
BackgroundLoader class (example), 30
backgrounds
    default, turning off for TextField, 24
    drawing for custom tool tip, 225
    image-themed component, 2
    label, 4
    text area, putting NASA photo
        in, 29–32
backward text, writing, 272–275
BasicMenuItemUI class, 53
BasicPopupMenuUI class, 50, 55
big-endian, 392
binding to a port, 425
bit shifting, 160, 382
bitmaps, blurring pixel-by-pixel, 39
blocking a window, 296–299
blocking Load buttons, 464
blurring
    disabled components, 39–42
    spotlight borders, 325
BooleanControl class, 401
BorderLayout class, 189
borders
    drawing for custom tool tip, 225
    image-based, creating, 14–19
    insets, 15
    removing from transparent
        window, 217
    setting for button, 5
    shadow border, creating, 50
    text components and menu
        items, 437
    vector-based button, 313
BoxLayout class, 204
brightness of a picture as indefinite
        progress indicator, 249–251
brushed metal Look and Feel, 418
BufferedImage class, 15, 40
    3D scenes, using in, 320
    file icons, 332
    getSubimage( ), 233, 239, 244

buffers, rendering to
  intermediate, 40–42
buildIndex( ), 100
build.xml file (Ant), 433
buttons
  building colorful
    vector-based, 309–315
  creating image-based, 5
  custom tool tip, 227
  HTML, using, 275
bytes, endianness, 392
bytes2short( ), 160

C

calendar, custom, 19–22
Canvas3D class, 318
  faking transparency, 319
Caps Lock, Num Lock, and Scroll Lock
    keys, flashing light
    on, 446–449
cell renderers
  animated list cells, 91
  animating potential drops on
    reorderable list, 84
  for checkbox list, 69
  header cells, table columns, 106
  JFileChooser, 154
  JList with multiple layouts, 71–76
  PolyRenderer class (example), 78–79
  table cells, 113
    figuring cell size, 103
    renderer for colors, 119
  tree cell, 144
  turning methods into list
    renderers, 92–95
ChangeListener interface, 33
channel (audio), 379
checkboxes, 7
  making JLists checkable, 66–70
circular shape for indefinite progress
    indicator, 253
ClassLoader class, 429
classpaths
  loading image and sound as
    resources, 429–431
  resources on, 429
  running application from JAR
    file, 432
client, mirrored application, 487
Clip interface, 366, 386

close boxes, dialog, 229
code models, non-blocking, 465–471
collections
  creating List-based
    JComboBox, 95–99
  creating Map-based
    JComboBox, 99–101
Collections class, sort( ), 114
colorizeSelections( ), 90
colors
  eyedropper tool, 300–304
  list cell foreground and
    background, 69
  selection panel for drop-down
    component, 46–49
  system, using, 437
  vector-based button, 312
columnAtPoint( ) (JTableHeader), 109
columns, table
  adding column selection, 107–109
  sizing to suit content, 102–107
com4j package, downloading, 422
combo boxes
  collections-aware
    JComboBox, 95–101
  drop-down menu button, 43–49
    color selection panel, 46–49
  menus with drop shadows, 49–52
Comparable interface, 114
Comparator class, 113
  delegated sorting, 116
  resorting based on current
    comparator, 114
  sorting color values, 119
compare( ), 116
Component class
  createImage( ), 349
  dispatchEvent( ), 295
Component Object Model (COM), 422
  iTunes track information, 423
component references, 490
ComponentAdapter class, 176
ComponentListener interface, 176, 216
componentMoved( ), 177
components
  associating events via component
    name, 490
  debugging with custom glass
    pane, 481–486
  disabled, blurring, 39–42

components (*continued*)
  image-themed, creating, 1–8
  spin-open container, 203
Composite class, 222
CompoundControl class, 401
  Swing representation, 402
computeGrabRect( ), 292
ConcurrentModificationException, 475
connections, database (see database
  connections)
content-length header (HTTP), 471
context menus
  adding to JFileChooser, 149–153
  global right-click, 293–296
  (see also menus)
continueSearch( ), 259
Control class, 401
  Type subclass, 401
ControllerListener interface, 370
controls, JavaSound playback, 401–407
  factory to generate, 402–407
convertPoint( ) (SwingUtilities), 294
ConvolveOp class, 41
coordinates
  mouse, converting to screen
    coordinates, 179, 294
  status bar components, 191
createCompatibleImage( )
    (GraphicsConfiguration), 239
createDialog( ), 151
createFont( ) (Font), 307
createImage( ), 349
createScene( ), 318
createScreenCapture( ) (Robot), 214,
    287
createTempFile( ) (File), 331
createToolTip( ), 227
createUI( ), 54
CSS, enhancing text components, 277
cursors, displaying busy, 443–446
Cylon, 247

D

data flavors, 333
  image, 344
  java.net.URLs, 338
  native drag-and-drop, 336
data object, 494
data types, Control subclasses, 401

database connections, 122
  populating Swing TableModel
    from, 123–126
  testing JDBC-based table, 127
DatabaseMetaData objects, 126
DataLine interface, 366
  getLevel( ), 392
    bug in, 396
dates, displaying in custom
    calendar, 19–22
debugging
  components with custom glass
    pane, 481–486
  GUIs, 478–481
    redirecting output streams to
      Swing windows, 478–481
decorator (wrapper),
    TableModel, 133–139
DefaultListCellRenderer class, 93
DefaultListModel class, 60
DefaultMetalTheme class, 439
DefaultMutableTableModel class, 110
DefaultTableModel class, 110, 132
DeleteAction class, 151
deltas from drag events, 180
desktop Java applications, 408
  constructing single-launch
    applications, 424–428
  launching external programs on Mac
    OS X, 411–413
    controlling iTunes, 418–421
    making them behave
      normally, 413–418
  launching external programs on
    Windows, 408–411
    controlling iTunes, 421–424
    opening a directory, 411
    opening a text file, 409
    opening a URL, 410
    Runtime.exec( ), 409
detail pane, spin-open, 202–207
  dialog using (example), 206
  inner class spin triangle, 204
  invisible component, 203
  layout of components, 203
dialogs
  earthquake, 197–202
  modal, blocking window
    without, 296–299
  sheet, animating, 233–239

spin-open detail pane, 202–207
turning into frame-anchored
    sheets, 228–233
directories
  linked
    * displaying Windows
      shortcuts, 154–157
    Windows shortcut
      support, 158–163
  opening on Mac OS X, 412
  opening on Windows, 411
DirectoryItem class, 76
dirty region, components, 280
disabled components, blurring, 39–42
dispatchEvent( ) (Component), 295
dispose( ), 16
dissolving frames, 219–224
  basic steps, 219
  doing the drawing, 222
  genie effect, 223
  preparing the dissolve, 220
  running the animation, 221
Document class
  blocking, while loading a URL, 466
  insertString( ), 262, 263, 467
  non-blocking, on URL loading, 467
DocumentEvent class, 270
DocumentListener interface, 258, 269
documents
  constraining, 262–263
  regex-constrained, testing in text
    field, 263–265
drag gesture, 331
drag images, 333
drag-and-drop
  draggable window, 178–181
  droped Picts on Mac OS X, 345–349
  files, 330–335
  handling dropped images, 340–345
  handling dropped URLs, 336–339
  reordering JTrees, 139–147
  reordering lists, 80–86
  translucent, 350–357
DragGestureListener class, 140, 331
dragGestureRecognized( ), 143
DragGestureRecognizer class, 82
dragOver( ), 83, 143
DragSource class, 333
DragSourceAdapter class, 331
  dragEnter( ) and dragExit( ), 333

DragSourceListener class, 140
drawing
  animation, 35
  paintComponent( ) method, 39
  tool tip background and border, 225
drawing code, overriding in standard
    component, 25
  watermark, adding to text
    component, 23
  watermarking scroll panes, 26
drawRoundRect( ), 314
drawTextAntialiased( ), 283
drop( ), 143, 339
drop, handling on reorderable list, 85
drop shadows
  and embossing effects, 8–13
  on menus, 49–52
  text on vector-based button, 313
dropComplete( ), 339
drop-down menu button, 43–49
  color selection panel, adding, 46–49
DropTargetDragEvent class, 83
DropTargetDropEvent class, 339
DropTargetListener interface, 83, 339
dynamic HTML, 492–498

E

Ellipse2D, representing a spotlight, 325
email
  checking with Swing, 454–459
  opening application on Windows
    with start, 410
embossing effect, text labels, 8–13
endianness, 392
EndOfMediaEvent object, 370
EnumControl class, 401, 405
event-dispatch thread, moving
        complicated processing out
        of, 459–465
eventDispatched( ), 449
EventListenerList class, 477
events
  Apple, 419
  capturing all and mirroring
        application, 486–492
  collection, 97
  Java Media Framework, 370
  keystroke, application-wide, 448
  list selection, 67

events (*continued*)
ListDataEvent class, 60
mouse (see mouse events)
order of firing, 472–478
property change, 232
UI components, 176
window (operating system), 178
Excel spreadsheet, exporting table data
to, 130–133
exec( ) (Runtime), 409
calling open program, 412
launching email program, 456
Explorer (Windows)
icon, 182–185
status bar, 188–193
extension hook (JFileChooser), 164

F

fading to nothing, 222
file choosers
adding right-click context
menu, 149–153
displaying shortcuts, 154–157
image previewer, 164–167
previewing ZIP and JAR
files, 167–174
Windows shortcut support, 158–163
File class
createTempFile( ), 331
proxies, 168–172
FileItem class, 76
files
drag-and-drop, 330–335
linked, 154
opening on Mac OS X, 412
FileSystemView class, 161, 168
custom (ZipFileSystemView), 172
file icons, 499
getSystemIcon( ), 332
fileToString( ), 28
FileView class, 154, 161
fillRoundRect( ), 314
filter box, 58
FilterField class, 59
FilterModel class, 59
filters, adding history, 63–66
find( ), 260
fireUpdate( ), 98, 100
firing events in proper order, 472–478

flavor of data (see data flavors)
FloatControl class, 401
Swing widget for, 403–405
focus events, pop-up windows and, 45
Font class, createFont( ), 307
font metrics, 10
fonts
changing style or size in text
components, 436
changing throughout an
application, 304–307
email icons, 458
global anti-aliased, 278–282
HTML effects, 276
loading new at runtime, 307–309
foreground property (List), 69
FormLayout class, 190
frame-anchored sheets, turning dialogs
into, 228–233
frames
dissolving, 219–224
basic steps, 219
doing the drawing, 222
genie effect, 223
preparing the dissolve, 220
running the animation, 221
finding parent frame of drop-down
component, 45
minimizing to mini frame, 207–212
resizing dynamically, 500
sheet dialog, animated, 233–237
frames (audio), 380

G

genie effect, 223
getAudioInputStream( ), 433
getColumnClass( ), 113, 123, 134
getColumnCount( ), 123, 134
getColumnName( ), 123, 134
getComponent( ), 490
getControls( ) (Line), 401
getDeepestComponentAt( ), 295
getElementAt( ), 60
getFiles( ), 162
getFrame( ), 45
getIcon( ) (FileView), 154, 156
getIconHeight( ), 182
getIconWidth( ), 182
getInstance( ) (AlphaComposite), 54

getLevel( ) (DataLine), 392
  bug in, 396
getListCellRendererComponent( ), 71,
  93
getLocation( )
  (DropTargetDragEvent), 83
getLocationOnScreen( ), 290
getMaximumWindowBounds( ), 240
getNullDelimitedString( ), 160
getPathForLocation( ) (JTree), 143
getPixelColor( ) (Robot), 300
getPreferredSize( ), 9
  tool tip, custom, 226
  vector-based button, 311
getResource( ), 429
  loading image and sound as resources
    on classpath, 429–431
getResources( ), 429
getRowCount( ), 123
getScaledInstance( ), 290
getSize( ), 60
getSubimage( ) (BufferedImage), 233,
  239, 244
getSystemIcon( ), 332
getTreeCellRendererComponent( ), 145
getType( ), 401
getValueAt( )
  AbstractTableModel class, 123
  TableModel class, 131
ghosting, glass pane for, 353–355
GhostPictureAdapter class, 355
ghosts, 353
  handling component ghosts, 355
glass pane, 229–233
  blocking a window, 296
  capturing right-click events and
    triggering pop up, 293–296
  debugging components with
    custom, 481–486
  ghosting, 353–355, 357
  indicator for indefinite progress
    bar, 251–256
  sheet dialog, animating, 233–239
  spotlights, 324, 328
grab rectangle for magnifier
    component, 289, 292
Graphics object, 39
Graphics2D class
  round rectangle methods, 314
  transform( ), 273

GraphicsConfiguration class, 239
GraphicsEnvironment class, 240
GraphicsImporterDrawer class, 347,
  349
GridBagLayout class, 405
grouping in regular expression pattern
  matching, 31
grow box (Mac), 417
GUI (graphical user interface)
  debugging, 478–481
  threading complicated processing to
    free event-dispatch
    thread, 459–465

H

Hashtable class, 304
header cells (table columns), 106
headers
  content-length (HTTP), 471
  LNK files, parsing, 159
heavyweight components, 317
heavyweight menus, 57
hidePopup( ), 46
highlight, vector-based button, 313
HighlightedTextColor class, 442
history, filter, 63–66
HSQLDB, 127
HTML
  customizing labels, 8
  displaying AppletSound applet, 361
  dynamic, 492–498
  enhancing text
    components, 275–277
HTTP content-length header, 471
Hypersonic, 127

I

Icon interface, 181
icons
  Explorer, 182–185
  file, 332
  large file icons, getting, 499
  linked directory, 154, 156, 162
  MS Office, 185
  window resize (Windows), 181–186
  windows resize icons, 189
IITTrack object, 423
ImageFileItem class, 76
ImageIO interface, 165

ImageProducer class, 347
images
    3D scene, 321
    creating image-based borders, 14–19
    creation of, 7
    drag image, 333
    dropped, handling, 340–345
    dropped Picts on Mac OS
        X, 345–349
    loading as resource along the
        classpath, 429–431
    previewer, JFileChooser, 164–167
    using for cursor, 446
image-themed components,
        creating, 1–8
    buttons, 5
    checkboxes, 7
    custom calendar, 19–22
    labels, 3
    painting and testing the image, 3
    panel, 2
incremental searching, 257–261
indefinite progress bar, 247–256
    glass pane as indicator, 251–256
    picture as indicator, 249–251
index (table model), getting results
        from, 136
indexing, table model, 135
InputStream class, 433
InputStreamReader class, 30
insertString( ) (Document), 262, 263,
        467
insertUpdate( ), 61
insets
    border, 15
    shadow border, 51
    text components, 436
installUI( ), 55
instanceof operator, 76
invisible component, 203
invokeAndWait( ) (SwingUtilities), 464
invokeLater( ) (SwingUtilities), 298,
        456, 464
isControlSupported( ) (Line), 401
isDirLink( ), 155
isDragImageSupported( ), 333
isDynamicLayoutActive( ), 500
isDynamicLayoutSet( ), 500
isTraversable( )
    FileView class, 154
    JFileChooser class, 162

isValueAdjusting( )
        (ListSelectionEvent), 68
iTunes
    controlling on Mac OS X, 418–421
        AppleScript API, 421
    controlling on Windows, 421–424

J

JAR (Java ARchive) files, 428–433
    double-clicking, 432
    packaging application and resources
        in, 432
    previewing with file
        chooser, 167–174
Java Media Framework (JMF), 368–371
    MP3 suppport, adding, 376–378
    playing audio with, 369
Java Native Interface (JNI), 213, 409
Java2D
    Paint interface, 23
    special effects, tab transitions, 39
Java3D, 316
    AWT component, Canvas3D, 318
    BranchGroup, 320
JavaMail API, 454
JavaSound, 364–368
    controls for playback, 401–407
        factory to generate, 402–407
    playing audio with, 364–366
    playing non-trivial audio, 386–391
    showing audio information while
        playing, 392–401
JButton component, 40
JCheckBox component
    audio control value, 403
    HTML, using, 276
JComboBox component, 43
    collections-aware, 95–101
    HTML, using, 276
JComponent class, 44
    subclassing for ListCellRenderer, 71
JDBC table model, creating, 122–130
JDesktop Integration Components
        (JDIC), 408
JFileChooser component
    adding right-click context
        menu, 149–153
    displaying shortcuts, 154–157
    image previewer, 164–167
    opening in an applet, 363

previewing ZIP and JAR
files, 167–174
Windows shortcut support, 158–163
JFrame component (see frames)
JGoodies, FormLayout, 190
JLabel component (see labels)
JList
animating selections, 87–92
checkable, 66–70
filtering, 58–62
with multiple cell-rendering
layouts, 71–76
reordering with
drag-and-drop, 80–86
turning methods into list
renderers, 92–95
JMenu component, 53
adding custom, 54
(see also menus; pop ups)
JMF (see Java Media Framework)
JNI (Java Native Interface), 213
JNI (see Java Native Interface)
JOptionPane component, 197
creating dialogs, 231
earthquake dialog, 201
JPanel component (see panels)
JPopupMenu class, 53
filter text saved to, 64
translucence, handling, 54
JProgressBar component, 248, 466
JRadioButton component, using
HTML, 276
JScrollPane component, 26
JSlider component, 403
JTabbedPane component, 32
JTable component
column selection, adding, 107–109
searching easily, 133–139
sizing columns to suit
content, 102–107
sorting column contents, 110–121
JTableHeader component, 108
JTextArea component, 26
search, adding, 260
(see also text; text areas)
JTextComponent class, 258
JTextField component, 23
constrained text fields, 263–265
rendered as mirror image, 274
JToolTip class, 225

JTree component, reorganizing with
drag-and-drop, 139–147
JViewport component, 26
JVM property, swing.aatext, 284
JWindow class, 43
pop-up window, 45
(see also pop ups; windows)

K

kernel, 41
keyboard lights, flashing on and
off, 446–449

L

labels, 3
HTML, using, 276
mirror image text, 273–275
sprucing up, 8–13
LayeredPane class, 229
LayoutManager class, 290
layouts
absolute, 3
applet, 361
BorderLayout, 189
dynamic, 500
FormLayout, 190
spin-open detail pane
components, 203
letters in a word, spacing of, 8
level of audio being played, 392
calculating yourself, 397–401
DataLine.getLevel( ), problems
with, 395
lightweight components, 317
lightweight menus, 57
Line interface, 366
getControls( ), 401
isControlSupported( ), 401
line-break tags (HTML), 276
.link file extension, 155
linked directories
displaying Windows
shortcuts, 154–157
real support for Windows
shortcuts, 158–163
ListCellRenderer class, 66, 69
as subclass of JComponent, 71
ListComboBoxModel class, 97
ListDataEvent class, 60

ListDataListener class, 97
ListModel class, 60
lists
    checkable, 66–70
    creating List-based
        JComboBox, 95–99
    filter history, adding, 63–66
    filtering, 58–62
    making different items look
        different, 70–80
    reordering with
        drag-and-drop, 80–86
    turning methods into
        renderers, 92–95
ListSelectionEvent class, 68
    self-completing text field, 269
ListSelectionListener class, 66, 67
little-endian, 392
.lnk file extension, 158
LNK files, 158–163
    header parsing, 159
    parser, 158
    shell settings, 160
loading a URL into Text Area, blocking
        and non-blocking event
        dispatch, 464–465
local sockets, 424–428
locationToIndex( ) (JList), 83
locked variable, 177
Look and Feel (L&F), 1
    Aqua, native on Mac, 414
    brushed metal, 418
    creating inverse black-and-white
        theme, 439–442
    custom, enabling anti-aliasing, 285
    JComboBox components,
        customization, 43
    making quick changes, 434–438
        L&F properties, 434–435
        system colors, using, 437
        text components, 436
    Metal L&F, 152
Lucene (document indexing and search
        tool), 135
    table model and list decorators, 139

M

Mac OS X
    controlling iTunes, 418–421
    dropped Picts, handling, 345–349
    launching external
        programs, 411–413
    making external programs behave
        normally, 413–418
    sheets, 228
    slide-in window above the
        dock, 240–247
magnifying glass component, 287–292
mailto: URL protocol, 410
makeOffscreenImage( ), 239
Manager class, 370
Map-based combo box, 99–101
margins, setting for a button, 5
master gain, 404
Matcher class, 31, 259, 263
    self-completing text field, 269
MediaLocator class, 370, 377
menu bar (Mac), 415
MenuItemUI class, 53
menus
    borders for items, 437
    drop shadows on, 49–52
    drop-down button, building, 43–49
        color selection panel, 46–49
    heavyweight and lightweight, 57
    Mac and, 416
    translucence, adding, 52–57
    (see also context menus)
metadata
    DatabaseMetaData objects, 126
    shortcut, stored in .lnk file, 158
Metal Look and Feel, 152, 439
    black-and-white theme, 440–442
MetalFileChooserUI$5, 152
MetalTheme interface, 439
MIME type
    getting for data flavors, 336
    Java file list, 344
mini-mode for frames, 207–212
mirror image text, 272–275
mirroring an application, 486–492
mixed fonts with HTML, 276
mod operator (%), 445

modal dialogs, 202, 296
models
    filtered list, 58, 59
    ListModel class, 60
    non-blocking, 465–471
Model-View-Controller (MVC)
    architecture, 1
    use by JComboBox, 95
MoreInfo component, 202–207
motion, simple harmonic, 200
mouse coordinates, converting to screen
    coordinates, 179, 294
mouse cursor
    animation using Robot
        class, 450–454
    displaying busy, 443–446
mouse events
    blocking, 296
    global right-click component, 294
    press and release, 315
    receiving, 489
    sending, 488
    updating selected color, 302
mouseDragged( ), 179
MouseEvent class, translate( ), 290
MouseInputListener interface, 297
MouseListener class, 64, 108, 179
MouseMotionListener class, 179
    magnifying glass component, 288,
        289, 290
mouseMove( ) (Robot), 450
movies, QTJ, 373
MP3 player interface, 218
MP3 support, adding to JMF, 376–378
MS Office icon, 185
multi-lined text with HTML, 276
mutability of lists, 60, 80
MVC (Model-View-Controller)
    architecture, 1
    use by JComboBox, 95

N

names
    component, associating events
        with, 490
    Mac OS X applications, 416
native integration
    constructing single-launch
        applications, 424–428

iTunes on Mac OS X ,
    controlling, 418–421
iTunes on Windows,
    controlling, 421–424
launching external programs on
    Windows, 408–411
    opening a text file, 409
    opening a URL, 410
    Runtime.exec( ), 409
Look and Feel changes, 434–438
    inverse black-and-white
        theme, 439–442
    L&F properties, using, 434–435
    system colors, using, 437
    text components, 436
    making Mac OS X applications
        behave normally, 413–418
    opening a directory on
        Windows, 411
    opening files, directories, and URLs
        on Mac OS X, 411–413
    packaging in JAR files, 428–433
NeXTSTEP operating system, 411
non-blocking code models, 465–471
non-blocking Load buttons, 464
notes, sliding out from
    taskbar, 240–247
null returns, methods of FileView and
    subclasses, 155
Num Lock key, flashing light
    on, 446–449

O

ObjectOutputStream class, 488
Office icon, 185
offscreen BufferedImage, drawing, 239
open program (Mac OS X), 411–413
    spaces in filepaths, 412
openReceiver( ), 488, 492
openSender( ), 488, 491
openStream( ) (URL), 433
operating systems
    difficulties of using Swing with, 408
    drawing AWT widgets, 318
    linked files support, 154
    NeXTSTEP, 411
    system color, 438
    window events, 178
osascript, 419
outline effect (text), 12

P

packaging (JAR files), 428–433
double-clicking JARs, 432
putting application and resources in, 432
paint( ), called by its parent's paintChildren( ), 279–281
Paint interface, 23
paintBackground( ), 280
paintBorder( ), 16
paintChildren( ), 27, 280
paintComponent( ), 3, 165, 280
drawing in Swing components, 39
indefinite progress indicator, 254
overriding for status bar component, 188
paintIcon( ), 182, 186
painting, self, 237
paintTransition( ), 35
pan, 404
panels
handling translucence, 54
image-themed component, 2
separator panel for status bar, 191
panes (see glass pane)
paths
relative paths, resources in JAR files, 429
spaces in, handling with open, 412
Pattern class, 263
self-completing text field, 266, 269
Pattern objects, 31
PCM (Pulse Code Modulation) files, playing with JavaSound, 387–390
performance, dynamic layout and, 501
photos, putting in background of text area, 29–32
Photoshop slices, 7
using in image-based borders, 18
Picts, 345–349
pixels, blurring disabled components, 39–42
pop ups
drop-down menu button, 43–46
file chooser context menu, 149–153
forcing creation as heavyweight components, 319
global right-click, 293–296
menu with drop shadows, 50

menu with previous searches, 64
mini application window, 210
translucent menu, 55
PopupFactory class, 55
ports, binding to, 425
pressed state, button, 315
previewer (image), JFileChooser, 164–167
PrevSearchAction class, 65
progress bars
loading URL, 466
task of unknown length, 247–256
glass pane as indicator, 251–256
picture as indicator, 249–251
properties
Apple system properties, 414
JDBC connection strings, 127
L&F, visual changes with, 434–435
propertyChange( ), 165
PropertyChangeEvent class, 232
PropertyChangeListener class, 164
proxies
File class, 168–172
file proxy, creating, 331

Q

QTImageProducer class, 347
QuickDraw, 346
QuickTime for Java (QTJ), 346–349
handling Picts with, 345–349
playing sounds with, 371–376
compiling QuickTime code, 374
running the code, 376

R

read( ) (ImageIO), 165
recursion, window refreshing and, 217
references to components, 490
refilter( ), 60
reflection, using for list cell renderers, 92–95
refresh( ), 216
regular expressions, 257
creating Pattern object, 31
enforcing rules on typed input, 261–265
constrained document, 262–263
constrained text fields, 263–265
Matcher class, 259
self-completing text field, 266–269

renderers (see cell renderers)
rendering
   3D components for Swing
      applications, 316–321
   blocking window without modal
      dialog, 296–299
   changing fonts throughout an
      application, 304–307
   color eyedropper, 300–304
   colorful vector-based
      button, 309–315
   creating magnifying glass
      component, 287–292
   global right-click context
      menu, 293–296
   to intermediate buffer, 40–42
   loading new fonts at
      runtime, 307–309
   turning spotlight on Swing, 321–329
repaint( ), 165
repaint manager, 56
RepaintManager class, 280
resetBottomVisibility( ), 204
resizing frames dynamically, 500
resolution independent, 309
resort( ), 115
revalidate( ), 104
RightClickGlassPane class, 150
Robot class, 214, 289, 450–454
   createScreenCapture( ), 287
   getPixelColor( ), 300
   mouse animation, creating, 450–454
   problems with using for
      magnifier, 292
RootPaneContainer classes, 229
rounded rectangles
   highlight for vector-based
      button, 313
   shadow for vector-based button, 312
rows, TableModel methods for, 113
run( ), 30, 34
Runnable interface, 33, 216
   worker threads, 464
runNewSearch( ), 258, 259
Runtime class
   exec( ), 409
      calling open program, 412
      launching email program, 456
Runtime System Properties, Apple's Java
      1.4.1 release, 414

S

Safari web browser, sheet in, 228
sample, 379
sample size, 379
sampling rate, 379, 404
scaling
   vector-based button, 309–315
   waveform display of audio, 383
screen coordinates, 179, 294
screenshots
   color chooser component, 300, 302
   using for transparent
      windows, 213–216
   using in frame dissolves, 219
Scroll Lock key, flashing light
      on, 446–449
scroll panes, watermarking, 26–28
searches
   clearing search results for blank
      search, 138
   history, 63–66
   incremental searches, text
      components, 257–261
   JTables, 133–139
   table model, using Lucene, 136
searching tool (Lucene), 135
security, applet, 363
selectable lists, 66–70
selections
   animating for JList, 87–92
   column selection, adding to
      JTables, 107–109
separator panel (status bar), 191
serialization, 486
server, mirrored application, 487
server-side web technologies, mimicking
      in Swing application, 492–498
setAccessory( ), 164, 166
setAnimatingHeight( ), 239, 244
setBackground( ), 300
setBorder( ), 5
setCursor( ), 445, 446
setFont( ), 304
setIndeterminate( ) (JProgressBar), 248
setLocation( ), 177
sctLockingKeyState( ), 446, 449
setMargin( ), 5
setModel( ), 97
setOpaque( ), 24, 218
   watermarked scroll pane, 27

setPatternByString( ), 263
setPreferredSize( ), 2
setPreferredWidth( ), 103, 104
setSelectColor( ), 303
setSize( ), 2, 208
setSource( ), 239
setText( ), 298
setUndecorated( ), 217, 302
setView( ), 27
shadowing
    text labels, 8–13
    text on vector-based button, 313
    vector-based button, 312
shaped windows, 213
sheets, 228–233
    animating sheet dialog, 233–239
    differences from regular dialogs, 228
    mimicking in Swing with glass
      pane, 229–233
shell settings (LNK files), 160
ShellFolder class, 499
shortcut.lnk file, 155
shortcuts
    displaying in JFileChooser, 154–157
    Windows system, support
      for, 158–163
shorts, converting bytes to, 160
show( ), 302
showAt( ), 243
showDialog( ), 151
simple harmonic motion, 200
sine function for simple harmonic
    motion, 200
size and position of components, 3
    size, getPreferredSize( ), 9
Skin L&F, 285
slices, Photoshop (see Photoshop slices)
slide-in windows, 240–247
SmoothMetal Look and Feel, 285
snapping, window, 175–178
sockets, 424–428
    sharing resources over, 488
sort( )
    Arrays class, 114
    Collections class, 114
sorting JTable columns, 110–121
sounds
    loading as resource along the
      classpath, 429–431
    playing in an applet, 359–364

playing with Java Media
    Framework, 368–371
playing with JavaSound, 364–368
playing with QTJ, 371–376
(see also audio)
spaces in filepaths, handling with
    open, 412
spacing between letters (tracking), 8
spinning, shrinking window, 223
spin-open detail pane, 202–207
    dialog using (example), 206
    inner class spin triangle, 204
    invisible component, 203
    layout of components, 203
spotlight, turning on Swing, 321–329
spreadsheet (Excel), exporting table data
    to, 130–133
standard output and error streams,
    redirecting to Swing
    windows, 478–481
start program (Windows), 409
    opening a directory, 411
    opening an email application, 410
startAnimation( ), 236
stateChanged( ), 33
states, button, 6
status bars
    adding to windows, 187–193
    corner (resize) icon, 189
    left component, 189
    painting panel details, 188
    separator panel, 191
    standard MS Windows
      setup, 187
stopAnimation( ), 237
StringBuffer class, 467
strings, null-delimited, 160
Swing, 317
swing.aatext property, 284
SwingUtilities class
    convertPoint( ), 294
    getDeepestComponentAt( ), 295
    invokeAndWait( ), 464
    invokeLater( ), 298, 456, 464
SwingUtilities2 class, 283
    anti-aliased text variables, 284
    perils of using, 285
System Properties (Apple), 414
SystemTextColor class, 442

T

tab-delimited text file, 131
TableCellRenderer class, 113
TableModel interface, 110, 131
  decorator (wrapper) for JTable
    searches, 133–139
  exporting tab-delimited data, 131
  methods working with rows, 113
  populating from database
    connection, 123–126
TableModelListener class, 113
  listening to inner table updates, 138
tables
  column selection, adding, 107–109
  exporting data to Excel
    spreadsheet, 130–133
  JDBC table model,
    creating, 122–130
  searching JTables easily, 133–139
  sizing JTable columns to suit
    content, 102–107
  sorting column contents, 110–121
tabs, animating transitions
    between, 32–39
  venetian blinds effect, 37
TaskAllMovies class,
    addMovieAndStart( ), 374
taskbar, sliding out notes
    from, 240–247
templates, Velocity, 493
  filling with values, 497
text
  anti-aliased, with custom Look and
    Feel, 285
  anti-aliased, without code, 283–285
  auto-completing text fields, 265–272
  enhancing text components with
    HTML and CSS, 275–278
  global anti-aliased fonts, 278–282
  searchable text
    components, 257–261
  validating user input, 261–265
    constrained text fields, 263–265
  vector-based button, 313
  writing backward text, 272–275
text areas
  drawing watermark image in
    background, 26–28
  filter box, 58
  NASA photo in background, 29–32

text components
  adding watermark to, 23–25
  Look and Feel changes, 436
  (see also text)
text fields
  list filtering component with history
    button, 63
  with mirror image text, 274
  refiltering model on each
    keystroke, 60
text file, opening on Windows, 409
text labels (see labels)
TextFileItem class, 76
TextFileTransferable class, 333
TextHighlightColor class, 442
texture
  3D scene background, 320
  watermark scroll pane, 27
TexturePaint class, 15
  creating object for text
    watermark, 24
threads
  animation thread for indefinite
    progress indicator, 255
  animation, using Runnable, 33
  loader for background image, 30
  moving complicated processing out
    of event dispatch, 459–465
  non-blocking, 465–469
  worker thread, 464
Timer class, 200
  animated sheet dialog, use in, 237
  periodically checking on
    non-blocking load, 470
  slide-window animation, use in, 243
tool tips, custom, 225–228
  installing, 227
Toolkit class
  addAWTEventListener( ), 448
  createImage( ), 349
  querying dynamic layout
    property, 500
  setLockingKeyState( ), 446
toString( ), 92
  cell renderer using, 94
  Control class, 401
track information, iTunes on
    Windows, 423
tracking, 8
Transferable class, 143, 333
  supported image data flavors, 344

transform( ) (Graphics2D), 273
transformations, mirror-image, 273
transient component references, 490
transitions between tabs,
    animating, 32–39
    venetian blinds effect, 37
translate( ) (MouseEvent), 290
translucence, adding to menus, 52–57
translucent drag-and-drop, 350–357
transparency
    custom tool tip, 226
    drawing frame dissolves, 222
    faking in 3D components, 319
    implementing in icons, 181
    windows, 213–218
        transparent background
            component, 214
trees, drag-and-drop for
    JTrees, 139–147
TriangleSquareWindowsCorner-
    Icon, 189
trigonometry, use in earthquake
    dialog, 200
.ttf file (TrueType font), 308
Type class, 401
Types class, 126

U

UI classes, 50, 53
    events, 176
    translucence, handling for JPanels
        and JPopupMenus, 54
UIDefaults class, 304
    changing default fonts, 304
UIManager class, 51
    color changs in applications, 437
    put( ), 55
underlined text, using HTML, 276
updateBackground( ), 214
updateImage( ), 165
updateProgressBar( )
    (ActionListener), 471
URI lists, 344
URLs
    AudioClip, 361
    dropped, handling, 336–339
    getting from resources in JAR, 433
    opening on Mac OS X, 412
    opening on Windows, 410

V

validating input, 261–265
valueChanged( ), 67, 68
vector-based button, 309–315
Velocity template engine, 492–498
VelocityContext, creating, 497
venetian blinds effect, 37
View component, 26
viewports, 26
volume level of audio (see level of audio
    being played)
VTL (Velocity Template Language), 493

W

watermarking
    scroll panes, 26–28
    text component, 23–25
WAV audio files, playing, 390
waveform displays (audio), 378–386
    basic audio term definitions, 379
    container, creating, 384
    converting raw data to samples and
        channels, 380–382
    creating single display, 382
    loading raw data, 380
    running the simulator, 385
web browsers, opening URL on
    Windows, 410
web pages, opening on Mac OS X, 412
WebDings and WingDings fonts, 458
widths, resetting for table
    columns, 103–105
Window class, 43
WindowFocusListener class, 216
windows
    blocking with sheets, 229
    blocking without modal
        dialog, 296–299
    draggable, 178–181
    mini application window, 207–212
        clock with mini version, 208
        minimizing, 210
        restoring to normal, 211
    resize icons (Windows), 181–186
    resizing on Mac, 417
    saving settings, 193–197
    sliding in above taskbar, 240–247
    snapping, 175–178
    status bar, adding, 187–193

transparent, 213–218
   transparent background
      component, 214
Windows operating systems
   controlling iTunes, 421–424
   file chooser, displaying
      shortcuts, 154–157
   getting large file icons, 499
   launching external
      programs, 408–411
   opening a directory, 411
   opening a text file, 409
   opening a URL, 410
   Runtime.exec( ), 409

real shortcut support, 158–163
resize window icons, 181–186
status bars, adding to
   windows, 187–193
worker threads, 464
Wrap Look and Feel, 285
Wrapit class, 286

Z

ZIP files
   packaged in JARs, 433
   previewing with file
      chooser, 168–174
zoom level, 289

Colophon

Our look is the result of reader comments, our own experimentation, and feedback from distribution channels. Distinctive covers complement our distinctive approach to technical topics, breathing personality and life into potentially dry subjects.

The tool on the cover of *Swing Hacks* is a reflex mallet. Doctors most commonly use reflex mallets to test a patient's "knee-jerk" reaction, which indicates the integrity of the spinal cord in the lower back region. A reflex is a simple nerve circuit, and when tapped by a reflex mallet, sensory neurons send signals to the spinal cord. Reflex tests are part of a neurological exam, and they can be helpful in testing the presence and location of spinal cord injuries or neuromuscular disease.

Marlowe Shaeffer was the production editor and proofreader for *Swing Hacks*. Derek Di Matteo was the copyeditor. Sarah Sherman and Claire Cloutier provided quality control. Ellen Troutman-Zaig wrote the index.

Ellie Volckhausen designed the cover of this book, based on a series design by Edie Freedman. The cover image is a photograph from photos.com. Karen Montgomery produced the cover layout with Adobe InDesign CS using Adobe's Helvetica Neue and ITC Garamond fonts.

David Futato designed the interior layout. This book was converted by Keith Fahlgren to FrameMaker 5.5.6 with a format conversion tool created by Erik Ray, Jason McIntosh, Neil Walls, and Mike Sierra that uses Perl and XML technologies. The text font is Linotype Birka; the heading font is Adobe Helvetica Neue Condensed; and the code font is LucasFont's TheSans Mono Condensed. The illustrations that appear in the book were produced by Robert Romano, Jessamyn Read, and Lesley Borash using Macromedia FreeHand MX and Adobe Photoshop CS. This colophon was written by Marlowe Shaeffer.

Keep in touch with O'Reilly

1. Download examples from our books

To find example files for a book, go to:

www.oreilly.com/catalog

select the book, and follow the "Examples" link.

2. Register your O'Reilly books

Register your book at *register.oreilly.com*

Why register your books? Once you've registered your O'Reilly books you can:

- Win O'Reilly books, T-shirts or discount coupons in our monthly drawing.
- Get special offers available only to registered O'Reilly customers.
- Get catalogs announcing new books (US and UK only).
- Get email notification of new editions of the O'Reilly books you own.

3. Join our email lists

Sign up to get topic-specific email announcements of new books and conferences, special offers, and O'Reilly Network technology newsletters at:

elists.oreilly.com

It's easy to customize your free elists subscription so you'll get exactly the O'Reilly news you want.

4. Get the latest news, tips, and tools

http://www.oreilly.com

- "Top 100 Sites on the Web"—PC Magazine
- CIO Magazine's Web Business 50 Awards

Our web site contains a library of comprehensive product information (including book excerpts and tables of contents), downloadable software, background articles, interviews with technology leaders, links to relevant sites, book cover art, and more.

5. Work for O'Reilly

Check out our web site for current employment opportunities:

jobs.oreilly.com

6. Contact us

O'Reilly & Associates
1005 Gravenstein Hwy North
Sebastopol, CA 95472 USA

TEL: 707-827-7000 or 800-998-9938
(6am to 5pm PST)

FAX: 707-829-0104

order@oreilly.com
For answers to problems regarding your order or our products.
To place a book order online, visit:

www.oreilly.com/order_new

catalog@oreilly.com
To request a copy of our latest catalog.

booktech@oreilly.com
For book content technical questions or corrections.

corporate@oreilly.com
For educational, library, government, and corporate sales.

proposals@oreilly.com
To submit new book proposals to our editors and product managers.

international@oreilly.com
For information about our international distributors or translation queries. For a list of our distributors outside of North America check out:

international.oreilly.com/distributors.html

adoption@oreilly.com
For information about academic use of O'Reilly books, visit:

academic.oreilly.com

O'REILLY®

Our books are available at most retail and online bookstores.
To order direct: 1-800-998-9938 • *order@oreilly.com* • *www.oreilly.com*
Online editions of most O'Reilly titles are available by subscription at *safari.oreilly.com*